the complete cookery year

Gary

Rhodes

the complete cookery year

This gentleman has taken full advantage of his home-grown produce,
as well as incorporating a medley of characters from foreign soils.
The balanced result continues to sustain a 'Theatre of Dreams',
with each season providing a new platter of fulfilment.
Thank you for undivided inspiration.

I dedicate my *Complete Cookery Year* to the man for all seasons,

Sir Alex Ferguson

Published by BBC Books,
BBC Worldwide Ltd,
Woodlands, 80 Wood Lane,
London W12 0TT

First published 2003
Text © Gary Rhodes 2003
The moral right of the author
has been asserted.

Some of the recipes contained
in this book first appeared in
Spring into Summer
(BBC Worldwide 2002) and
Autumn into Winter
(BBC Worldwide 2002).

Photographs by Sîan Irvine
© BBC Worldwide 2003

Table linen on page 258
supplied by Frette.

ISBN 0 563 48867 0

Commissioning Editors:
Rachel Copus and Nicky Ross
Project Editor: Sarah Miles
Copy-editor: Deborah Savage
Art Director: Sarah Ponder
Designer: Andrew Barron @
Thextension
Production Controller:
Christopher Tinker
Food prepared for
photography by
Gary Rhodes
Food Economists:
Jo Pratt and
Wayne Tapsfield
Stylist: Bo Chapman

Typeset in Century ITC and
Gothic 720
Colour separations by
Radstock Reproductions Ltd,
Midsomer Norton
Printed and bound in China
by Toppan Printing Co Ltd

Acknowledgements

This book shares a collection
of fresh flavours that all work
together to produce the best
results. In the same way, the
following collection of friends,
new and old alike, have
provided inspiration and
support as I compiled the
recipes within these pages.
Thank you to Wayne Tapsfield,
Lissanne Kenyon, all Rhodes'
restaurant teams, Sue
Fleming, Sîan Irvine, Jo Pratt,
Bo Chapman, Nicky Ross,
Rachel Copus, Sarah Miles,
Andrew Barron, Nick
Vaughan-Barratt, Siobhan
Mulholland, Claire Popplewell,
the BBC filming team, Borra
Garson, Lynda Seaton (*Fresh
Produce Journal*) and not
forgetting, of course, my wife
Jennie and my sons, Samuel
and George, for still putting up
with me.

Writing my *Complete Cookery Year* was the natural culmination of *Spring into Summer* and *Autumn into Winter*. Individually each book encouraged a closer look at seasonal cooking, to help find the maximum flavours. But together, and with a host of new recipes and features, they give us a complete and richly detailed picture of our culinary year.

Fresh produce of all kinds has ceased to be governed by seasonal availability; there are almost unlimited choices of fresh foods over the full 365 days of a year. Greengrocers' shelves have become longer and wider to allow for this. 'Surely this is nothing but positive,' say the retailers. 'If we can offer our customers fresh strawberries throughout the year, then why not? After all, they appear in superb form, a bright red that contrasts with the paler white tops and frilly green finish. They feel firm, fresh and have a good shelf life.' The story is one of good intentions, a desire not to let anyone down, no matter what they are searching for. This, in many respects, I have nothing but admiration for. We should thank buyers and suppliers for presenting all sorts of new goodies to us on an educational trip all year round – pineapples, lychees, kumquats, apricots, nectarines, peaches and crisp Kenyan green beans all add new dimensions to our cooking habits. It's been sexy, it's been appealing and we've wanted more. But this culinary stepladder seems to be heading towards infinity with any seasonal thoughts left by the wayside. Basically, the addition of choice has ignored the quite blatant subtraction of flavour and quality – there's more to go round but so often the new 'treats' turn out to have very little to offer in return for their prominence.

The purpose of my *Complete Cookery Year* is to restore home-grown produce to the centre of attention. Each monthly chapter provides a guide, not just for your eating habits, but also for what should be on the shopping list throughout each month. This includes fish, meat, fruit and vegetables alike, of which Britain provides its public with some of the finest, if not *the* finest, in the world. Take English summer strawberries: the sweet, juicy, delicious red berries conjure up images of fine times and days filled with sunshine, as they just beg to be picked. These beauties put their imported neighbours to shame, and are never equalled for flavour and juiciness, as overfull brown paper bags of the hand-picked fruits, with their moistness bleeding through, testify.

And think of green asparagus spears – it's become quite common to find these beautiful sticks taking pole position on a Christmas menu. But why? We can be lucky, bunches of good Spanish may turn up a month or two after our classic season in May and June; these are hard to ignore and quite right too. In this book the message is certainly not to deprive ourselves of imported extras – you'll find avocados, sweet potatoes, Chinese artichokes, pak choi, mangetout and Brazilian mangoes all becoming part of this seasonal chart. At the same time, however, British asparagus only shows its face when it feels proud enough to do so and there is no pleasure to be compared with eating it at its peerless best.

I look upon cooking as a form of entertainment, each finished dish playing a part in the success of the whole occasion. Eating draws people together; the kitchen usually becomes the meeting place as people gather in anticipation of, and in preparation for, the main event. But mistakes can be made – we can be too adventurous with our ambitions and desire to impress, being led far too strongly by over-strict recipes that demand to be followed word for word. If instead you enlist the seasons as your escort, you will find yourself liberated rather than enslaved by your cookery books.

Foods chosen at their best need little help – quickly steaming the asparagus spears, before offering in abundance on a large platter with a pot of home-made hollandaise ready to dollop on the side is pure heaven. Follow with roast organic chicken, Jersey Royals and tossed salad leaves, with those red strawberries, screaming for lashings of cream, to finish. A meal like this will suit every occasion from an *al fresco* lunch to a serious dinner party, simply because of its immense flavours.

Buying eatables in season can also have an effect on the food budget. Most produce in its prime, when it is plentiful, will also be at its cheapest, so you can enjoy it to the maximum before its days are done. This also provides spare change to invest in organic-reared chicken or Gloucester Old Spot pork, for example, which will reward with pleasure while cooking and eating.

I look forward to each season with great anticipation, just as in the days when I was a child, being told on an autumn morning that the day was to be spent at Grandma's, which meant one thing – Grandma's home-made apple pie. The fruits were picked from the garden and embedded between thick sheets of the crumbliest of sweet shortcrust pastry. Had this been a flavour to enjoy throughout the year, complacency would have set in and the magic been lost. This applies to so many of the best recipes. The clue to summer pudding is in its title; the Glorious Twelfth of August makes headline news – with rival restaurants aspiring to be first with roast grouse; and late-summer simmering pans with sweet aromas signal the time for preserves.

My *Complete Cookery Year* sets about supplying you with lists of ingredients suited to finding their way into recipes in each month. None of these assemblies is trying to dictate to you; so many ingredients can be swapped and blended to suit your individual tastes. Some of the lists of ingredients may look long at first glance, but on closer inspection many are identifiable as basic storecupboard or fridge products. And the methods are not difficult – take a second glance and read through slowly to see how the ingredients are respected and how the techniques allow the flavours to enhance the finished dish.

As you pass through the culinary year, trends and styles change, with each season showing off its own array of colourful ingredients, with a range of cooking techniques to suit them. No month is too strict, each sharing ingredients, so there is a smooth and gradual progression through the seasons. The purpose of these pages is to investigate a cornucopia of culinary thoughts and flavours, which I'm certain you will enjoy.

I leave you with these lines from *Cuisine of the Sun* by Roger Verge (translated by Caroline Conran), which, I feel, reflect the message to be found in the four seasons:

My father was a blacksmith…the tender bouquets of vegetables he brought were so full of flavour and aroma that all that was needed was the addition of a few of the big rosy strips of pork fat which sizzled in the big cast-iron pot.

This was the 'cuisine heureuse', which consisted of marrying natural products with one another, of finding simple harmonies and enhancing the flavour of each ingredient by contact with another complementary flavour…It is the antithesis of cooking to impress.

Gary Rhodes

Here are a few tips and guidelines that will help you achieve the best possible results with the recipes that follow.

Ingredients

Butter Unsalted butter is mostly used, giving greater control over the seasoning of a dish.

Cooking oil Vegetable or groundnut oil can be used. Groundnut oil is a product sourced from peanuts.

Egg sizes All eggs used are large, unless otherwise stated. Try to find eggs with the Lion Quality mark, which means that the eggs have been produced to the highest quality standards of food safety in the world.

Herbs All herbs are fresh, unless otherwise stated. All soft herbs, such as tarragon, flatleaf parsley and basil, are best torn by hand to prevent them bruising and to avoid breaking the texture. If you substitute fresh herbs with dried, remember to use only half the amount specified.

Instant sauces and stocks There are a number of sauce and stock recipes included in the book (with a quick *Instant stock* recipe on page 416), but there are also many good bought alternatives (tinned consommé, carton, fresh, dried or cubed) available in supermarkets.

Gelatine Use 2 leaves of gelatine or half a sachet of powdered gelatine to set 300ml (½ pint) liquid, 4 leaves of gelatine or one sachet of powdered gelatine to set 500ml (1 pint) liquid. If using powdered gelatine, follow packet instructions for preparation.

Seasoning Or 'season' simply means seasoning with salt and pepper – preferably freshly ground white peppercorns, unless otherwise stated.

Vinegars I use a selection of vinegars in this book. Many red wine vinegars are available, some quite shallow in flavour. I suggest selecting a vinegar that bears the hallmark of a good red wine – a Bordeaux or a Cabernet Sauvignon. If balsamic vinegar is to be used, an aged bottle will have a thicker and fuller flavour.

Techniques and guidelines

Measurements Follow one of the measurements only; do not mix metric and imperial. All spoon measurements are level unless otherwise stated.
- a tablespoon is 15g (½oz) for solids and 15ml (½fl oz) for liquids
- a dessertspoon is 10g for solids and 10ml for liquids
- a teaspoon is 5g for solids and 5ml for liquids

Oven temperatures Be aware that if you are using a fan-assisted oven the temperatures may need to be adjusted and lowered to your oven manufacturer's recommendations.

Removing pin bones from fish Fine pin bones are found in round fish fillets, for example red mullet, trout, salmon and cod. The bones run down the centre of most of these fillets and are easily removed with fine pliers or tweezers. It's worth spending the time needed to remove them, as the fish then becomes more comfortable to eat.

Sterilizing jars It is important to ensure that any jars to be used for jams, etc., are sterilized. First wash the jars in soapy water and rinse well. Place in a large saucepan, cover with water and bring to the boil. Cover with a lid and continue to boil for 15 minutes. Remove from the heat, leaving the lid on the pan, and allow to cool slightly. Remove the jars and stand upside down on a clean tea towel to drain. The jars must still be hot when you fill them with the jam. (Alternatively, heat the sterilized jars in a moderate oven for 5–10 minutes before use.)

Once the jars are filled, cover the preserve or chutney with waxed paper before closing and placing in a cool dark place, making sure the jars are not touching. Most jams and marmalades will have a 12-month shelf life if left unopened, providing the right quantity of sugar has been used. Once opened, keep refrigerated and use within 3–4 weeks.

Using a gas gun Powerful blow torches fuelled by butane gas canisters can be used in the kitchen to give a crispy glaze to many dishes. They are available from almost any hardware store and can also be found in the kitchen sections of department stores. Follow the instructions and use carefully and, of course, keep them away from children.

1 sprin

*'Move suddenly upwards or forwards in a single
motion, jump. Cause to happen unexpectedly.
Develop unexpectedly. Originate (from). Season
between winter and summer.'*

It is the last of these definitions that constitutes
the three-month spell of March, April and May, which
sits comfortably between its cold and warm seasonal
friends. The comfort that spring brings, however, is
accompanied by unpredictable seasonal fidgets that also
bring to mind some of the other senses of the word
'spring'.

The look of the days changes in spring. With the
clocks moving forward a new light glistens over the
morning dew, leading into a longer day, with the
promise of a touch of warmth to come. But no cook
should be fooled by this; spring is a difficult time,
difficult for the variety of what it offers, yet it rewards

g

your care with the distinctiveness of its flavours. A quiet few weeks may follow the first burst of springtime light and warmth, but there is no mistaking the promise of a new culinary season beginning.

The first month we encounter is March, still with very sharp, cool mornings and days. These four and a bit weeks can find themselves caught, 'piggy-in-the-middle'; winter offerings are still hanging around with many past their best and spring produce may not yet be on the scene. It's generally the root vegetables whose quality is depreciating. Parsnips, swedes and turnips are beginning to take on a spongy-textured finish, which may still suit if they find their way into a soup recipe, but they are rarely fit to be seen garnishing a roast.

Spring begins with shades of off-white, leading on to pale greens, running through still deeper tones until the deep rich colour of March spring greens appears. Fruit offers quite a colour selection too, with blood oranges, kumquats and pineapples flying in to join us, each confident in its own identity with flavour to match. For home-grown fruit we rely heavily on the delicate pink to ruby red of 'champagne' rhubarb, a fruity vegetable that shouts much louder than its imported friends, making sure we take notice of exactly what these beautiful stems have to offer. The affinity between forced rhubarb and the more aggressive, sharp, piquant flavour of deep red and green outdoor rhubarb, appearing towards late spring and running through the summer, is recognizable. But instead of your taste buds being a little shocked by the intensity of the sharpness of outdoor rhubarb, they are gently 'fizzed' by champagne stalks, which need only a little sugar to counter their sharp bite. Still, you will find that garden rhubarb wins a place in our repertoire a little later on, with the more robust flavour suiting a more robust partner.

A quite rare home-grown vegetable that first makes an appearance in mid- to late February, just about holding on into the warmth of April, is sea kale. Celery-like in its appearance, with a touch of white asparagus once sampled, sea kale is more often imported these days, being offered from our own soils only during its short season.

Spring cabbages and greens move us through the tints, the more open-leaved being the best to look out for. You'll also notice that late cabbages, in particular the Savoy, have not been forgotten (*Bacon-fried scallops with late cabbage or early greens*, page 28). The large, outer, deeper green leaves, right now usually an off-green, are purely for discarding, with the paler crisp hearts still good enough to shred and serve.

The medley of green leaves is adopted by all three of our spring months, with young spinach leaves and sorrel also coming in now and spring onions joining them in the forthcoming brighter spells.

Mauves, some with slightly blue/black tinges, also join us. One of the stars of March for me is purple sprouting broccoli. Some time ago this was the only broccoli we recognized and knew. This was before the Italian, much neater and bigger calabrese that appears a little later in the year began to push aside the richer and more flavoured purple sprouting variety. Blue/black truffle potatoes also clamour for notice, very wealthy in colour and appearance, impressing *Pan-roasted mackerel and truffle potato salad with a goat's cheese fondue dressing*, two seasonal musts they accompany on page 24.

A professional chef's favourite is the morel mushroom. These have quite a short seasonal life span, and carry an expensive price tag, but offer a flavour worth every penny. These very distinctive mushrooms, featured on page 20, with a photograph for recognition, can be hand-picked, which is a lot cheaper but can be quite costly in time. They are found in moist open areas, usually around old elm, sycamore and ash trees. They stand upright, with a more bulbous, honeycomb look than any other mushroom. They also have a flavour like no other, with only ceps having a chance against them. Morel mushrooms have a great ability to spread and infuse their flavours, without losing their own natural strength. Dried morels are available throughout the year, but do need to be pre-soaked in water before use.

A March component lasting throughout the spring months is ramson, probably better known as wild garlic. These onion-like leaves thrive on damp soil and are consequently usually found in open woodland areas, often close to streams. Once torn the leaves exude garlic, though still offering a milder finish than their cultivated bulbous friends. They are used in one or two recipes here, corresponding very well with the mushrooms in *Morel mushroom and wild garlic omelette* (page 51).

From our native waters, wild salmon and winter scallops are a good price to buy and try right now. Other seafoods are oysters, best eaten through all months containing the letter 'r' in their names. Mussels are also still plump and juicy before summer brings us smaller offerings. Flounder is a flat fish often ignored, not only by us – the buyer – but also by the fisherman. Being labelled 'the poor man's plaice' doesn't help but, to a certain extent, the label is true; if not caught at its plumpest, flounder quickly finds its way back into the sea. They'll be found mostly between March and November and, if super-fresh, will eat as well as their counterparts, such as dab,

Dover and lemon soles, halibut and plaice. March and April catches will bring best results, with a sweeter taste, unlike the not-so-good, muddy and earthy autumn net.

So, March is not the month to over-fill; instead it's a time to take advantage of what is available, and to look forward to the unpredictable month of April. Regardless of the weather on any day, April has quite a lot to recommend it. A late Easter brings good news for family parties, with so much more on offer for the table. Chocolate, in particular, does dessert duty to supplement the few home-grown fruits available, so rich chocolate cakes, flans and mousses are a must. Imported fruits, such as bananas and pineapples, are available and both have a liking for Easter chocolate as a co-ingredient.

The succulent sweet meat of spring lamb appears at this time, usually originating from the West Country, which tends to be the warmest part of Britain now. As spring turns to summer, lamb from more northerly Scottish lands comes into season.

The fishmonger's marble slab becomes laden with good things, with soles still in good order, red mullet showing its face and meaty monkfish, the twelve-monthly beauty, seeming to achieve prize-winning standards during this month and the next. Now the winter has definitely passed, shellfish reappears after its break of a few months. The most regular crustacean on offer is the common brown crab, eaten fresh from the shell. The alternative is the great shellfish luxury, spider crab. They are not the easiest to find, but pre-ordering from your fishmonger will certainly help. There's a recipe for these (and common brown crab), rolling the sweet flakes through pasta, binding with a sauce that takes full advantage of every flavour, even the shells – *Warm spider crab linguine with orange and tarragon sauce* (page 53).

So, with April, the sun is rising higher and the weather is getting warmer. The first fresh green shoots appear on trees. Purple sprouting broccoli, cabbages, spring greens and spring onions are still part of the collection. Cauliflowers and fresh herbs – mint, chives, rosemary, thyme and sage – take part in this culinary change of pace, with lighter and often quicker dishes replacing the warming casseroles of former months. Daffodils, crocuses and pansies have all started to bloom and

the end of this month reveals the first Jersey Royal potatoes and, with extra sunshine, asparagus.

It's May and spring is really here. They say May is one of the sunniest months of the year; with summer just round the corner we're teased with hot days in between cool spells, with flavours to match. Asparagus steals the limelight with the British variety becoming the star of the show, running through this last month of spring until the end of June. It's so important to take advantage of these home-grown green sticks; in a good year they show in abundance, affordable to all pockets. They need little help: a good splash of melted butter with maybe a bowl of steaming Jersey Royals will make a meal in itself. White asparagus, mostly imported, also hits the scene about now, offering a different texture and flavour.

Our early brassicas Primo and Hispi join the vegetable shelves, and are not to be ignored after previous over-reliance on cabbage for 'greens'. The matt green Primo leaves, holding tinges of purple sprouting broccoli colours, marry well with sweet red peppers and a hint of garlic on page 97.

Apricots and peaches appear at this time of year. Many will be under-ripe and pale, far too firm to the touch. These are the ones to ignore; under-developed, they are consequently under-flavoured. With careful prodding and searching, though, you may well find the first of the season's perfectly ripened sweet treasures.

The short spell of the St George's mushroom is at its height, after it appears first around 23 April, hence the name. Tiny young broad beans begin to excite the eye and palate. We often have to wait for these until the official summer months, so these sweet nuggets held in their pods are a must to add to your basket if spotted.

Samphire is an unusual vegetable that can sometimes be found in late spring. This has an aromatic seasoned flavour with a definite salt bite, and I have utilized its quite unique saltiness in several recipes to enhance other flavours in each dish.

By the end of spring, Jersey Royal potatoes are becoming cheaper and more plentiful and, like first radishes, strawberries and imported cherries are arriving, much fuller and richer, brightening up the end of this season and heralding the advent of summer.

vegetables

Simple sea kale 17

Blood orange and chive sea kale 17

Steamed purple sprouting broccoli with melting wild garlic
and orange butter 18

Celeriac soup with wild garlic 18

Mushroom and spring spinach Bourguignonne with
poached eggs 19

Fried egg and spinach with morel mushrooms 20

fish

Roast monkfish with spring cabbage and clam casserole 23

Pan-roasted mackerel and truffle potato salad with a goat's
cheese fondue dressing 24

Mustard-brushed flounder with steamed leek greens 25

Crispy cod with candied orange spring green hearts 26

Warm scallops and prawns hollandaise 27

Bacon-fried scallops with late cabbage or early greens 28

Mussel 'champ' stew with caper croûtons 29

meat

Casseroled shoulder of pork on Brussels tops with spring onion
and carrot butterbean broth 31

Softly roasted pork belly with warmed curly kale 32

Grilled goat's cheese on cider apples and black pudding with
a cider and mustard cream 33

Steak au poivre with buttered spring greens and shallots 35

fruit and puddings

Steamed kumquat marmalade roly-poly 37

Vanilla white chocolate mousse with warm syruped kumquats 38

Rhubarb and almond jalousie with rhubarb pulp and cream 38

Softened rhubarb with orange mascarpone cream 41

Pineapple carpaccio with rum and raisin syrup and
lemon sour cream 41

Black grape Beaujolais jelly 42

simple sea kale

Sea kale is a vegetable that has become quite a rarity on our plates. Often found in abundance during its short season between late February and late April, it grows wild on the coasts of the United Kingdom. However, it is also commercially grown inland on a small scale, from where it will be sold bunched in local greengrocers and now and again in large supermarkets. Sea kale resembles individual young celery sticks, usually 23–25cm (9–10in) in length, with a small white, yellow to green leaf sitting around the top. The flavour resembles that of white asparagus, with a mild, crisp finish and an almost soft sweetness. Sea kale makes a nice alternative starter served, as you would asparagus, with hollandaise sauce or just melted butter. This simple recipe is along the lines of the latter, with just a squeeze of citrus juice to sharpen the finish.

Sea kale suits just one basic cooking method, which is simply to boil it for a few minutes in salted water. After this, other cooking methods, such as frying or grilling can be effective. Steaming is an alternative to boiling, but this does need a longer cooking time.

SERVES 4 AS A STARTER OR ACCOMPANIMENT
2 bunches of sea kale
salt and pepper
50–75g (2–3oz) butter
juice of 1 lime or ½ lemon

Trim away the base from each stalk of sea kale and wash well to remove any soil or sandy grit. To cook, drop the stalks in boiling salted water and cook for a few minutes. This cooking time will leave them tender although still very crisp. If you prefer a softer finish, simply continue to cook for a few minutes more, 10 being the maximum. Lift from the pan with a slotted spoon and transfer to a large clean pan. Add the butter, which will emulsify with the residual moisture as it is shaken into the pan. Season with salt and pepper, and add the lime or lemon juice. Divide the sea kale between plates and spoon the butter over each.

Once seasoned with pepper, each portion can be lightly sprinkled with coarse sea salt for a crunchier finish. Lots of freshly chopped parsley or a selection of herbs can also be added to the liquor.

OPPOSITE: BLOOD ORANGE AND CHIVE SEA KALE

blood orange and chive sea kale

Blood oranges are imported and with us through the late winter and early spring months. This quite stunning fruit can be used in so many sweet or savoury dishes. It is probably most famous used in *Sauce maltaise* (page 418), a buttery hollandaise sauce finished with a strong reduction of blood orange juice and finely grated zest.

Here the juice is used to flavour a simple butter sauce, garnished with diced segments of the fruit and lots of chopped chives to add their oniony bite.

SERVES 4 AS A STARTER OR ACCOMPANIMENT
2–3 blood oranges (1–2 of these segmented,
saving all juices)
1 sugar cube or a pinch of caster sugar (optional)
6 tablespoons *Vegetable stock* (page 417) or water
2 bunches of sea kale
salt and pepper
75g (3oz) butter
squeeze of lemon juice
1 heaped tablespoon finely chopped chives

To make the sauce, finely grate the zest from a quarter of the unsegmented oranges, then halve and juice. Pour the juice into a small saucepan along with the grated zest and juices saved from segmenting. Bring to the boil and reduce in volume by two-thirds. It is not essential to segment two oranges; one will probably be enough. However, I do love the fruit and two will provide extra flavour. Cut each segment into two or three pieces and keep to one side. Taste the reduced orange liquor; if too sharp and bitter, add the sugar cube or sugar to taste, and stir until dissolved. Add the vegetable stock or water to loosen the syrupy orange, and strain off the orange zest. (This reduction stage can be done well in advance, just to be reheated and finished with the butter when needed.)

To prepare the sea kale, remove the base from each kale stem, washing and rinsing away all soil and sandy grit. Plunge into boiling salted water and cook until tender. Drain well once cooked and divide between four plates.

While the kale is cooking, bring the blood orange reduction to a simmer and whisk or stir in the butter, a knob at a time, until completely emulsified. Season with salt, pepper and a squeeze of lemon juice. Add the orange segment pieces and warm through, then add the chopped chives. Serve the sauce with the sea kale.

steamed purple sprouting broccoli with melting wild garlic and orange butter

The rich green broccoli – calabrese – is a fairly recent addition to our culinary repertoire, having become readily available here only in the late 1960s and early 1970s. Before being blessed with such an outstanding vegetable from Calabria, the Italian region in which it was developed, purple sprouting was the variety more likely to be available.

This springtime variety, best eaten in March and April (although it can be found as early as January), can be treated like asparagus with which it is often compared. Although mainly coloured purple, pale green and white varieties can also be found, all with much the same flavour.

This dish, using the large or smaller sprouts, makes a good starter or vegetable accompaniment, which works well with most types of fish and seared scallops, all white meats, chicken, pork, veal, etc., as well as roast lamb.

Most Italian recipes suggest garlic, herbs, anchovies and olives as garnishes for broccoli, or a simple lemon butter is another classic. Taking a little from both of those ideas, I'm using wild garlic as a strong herb flavouring, accompanied by the citrus touch of orange.

The early spring months, March in particular, are perfect for wild garlic. If it still cannot be found, substitute 1–2 crushed garlic cloves cooked with the shallots.

SERVES 4 AS A LIGHT STARTER OR ACCOMPANIMENT
450–675g (1–1½lb) purple sprouting broccoli spears
1 tablespoon very finely chopped shallot or onion
juice of 2 large oranges
1 teaspoon finely grated orange zest
2–4 wild garlic leaves
100g (4oz) butter
salt and pepper

If small trimmed broccoli sprouts can be found, 450g (1lb) will be plenty. If larger, then simply break the spears from the thicker central stalk. If very fresh and young, the actual stalks need not be peeled. This is best tested by taking a raw bite: if good and tender to eat, then leave them unpeeled; if slightly chewy, the skin is best peeled by hand or carefully with a small knife or peeler. Steam the broccoli when needed, above boiling water for just a few minutes until just tender but still with a bite.

To make the butter (which when made in this quantity can be frozen, keeping for several months), rinse the shallot or onion in a sieve under cold running water as this helps wash away the very raw oniony bite. Drain and place in a saucepan with the orange juice. Bring to a rapid simmer and allow to boil to reduce until almost dry. Remove from the heat, add the orange zest, then leave to cool.

The quantity of wild garlic is really down to personal taste. Both quantities work for me, the four leaves offering the right flavour when I'm in a real garlicky mood. Wild garlic leaves are powerful to eat and don't quite betray their strength by nose alone. Chop the leaves carefully and mix two into the butter along with the orange shallot or onion. Season with salt and pepper. Taste for wild garlic flavour and add more chopped leaves if needed. Roll the flavoured butter and wrap in cling film, then refrigerate or freeze until needed.

To serve, stack or lay the warm steamed broccoli spears on plates and top with a generous knob of the garlicky orange butter to melt and flavour the vegetables.

Olive oil or Lemon oil (page 421) can be drizzled around the plate to finish.
For a wild garlic and orange butter sauce, heat 3 tablespoons of water and, once bubbling, remove from the stove and whisk small knobs of the flavoured butter in until a buttery sauce consistency is achieved.

celeriac soup with wild garlic

Celeriac is predominantly an autumn–winter vegetable, and despite being at the end of its season now, I wanted to remind you that it is during the first months of spring that you will still find the last of the British-grown on the shelves. Celeriac marries well with the wild garlic leaves which are just arriving.

SERVES 4 AS A STARTER
2 small or 1 large head of celeriac
juice of ½ lemon
50g (2oz) butter
5–8 wild garlic leaves
750ml (1¼ pints) milk
150ml (¼ pint) whipping or single cream
salt and pepper
freshly grated nutmeg

Cut away the root and skin of the celeriac and chop into rough 2cm (¾in) dice. Toss the celeriac in a bowl with the lemon juice to help retain its white colour.

Melt the butter in a saucepan and, once bubbling, add the celeriac and cook on a low heat, covered with a lid and stirring from time to time. After 8–10 minutes, add five of the wild garlic leaves. Add the milk and bring to a soft simmer. Cook at this temperature for 20–25 minutes until the celeriac is completely tender.

At this point the wild garlic leaves can either be left in to be puréed with the celeriac, or removed for a slightly milder finish.

Purée to a smooth consistency in a blender or liquidizer, add the cream and season with salt, pepper and a touch of nutmeg. The soup should now have a creamy but not over-thick consistency. If necessary add a little more milk to loosen. For the silkiest smooth of finishes, strain through a sieve. The remaining wild garlic leaves, if using, can now be finely shredded and sprinkled across each portion.

A trickle of walnut oil to finish adds a rich nutty flavour that brings out all the others.

mushroom and spring spinach bourguignonne with poached eggs

Flat mushrooms have such a meaty texture they can replace actual meats quite easily. Basically comprised of red wine, baby onions, fried bacon pieces and mushrooms, the Bourguignonne label is normally associated with braised beef, steaks or chicken dishes.

The mushrooms in this version have become the main feature with bacon and red onions, which are also in season during these spring months, helped along by the addition of wilted young spinach and red wine. For a vegetarian option, the bacon can be omitted.

This dish eats very well as a starter, lunch or supper dish, but can also make a substantial main course by using the quantities below to serve two. Flat mushrooms come in many sizes; if large are the only ones available, two per portion will be plenty; for medium mushrooms (6–7.5cm/2½–3in in diameter), three or four each are ideal.

SERVES 4

6 rashers of streaky bacon
12–16 medium flat mushrooms, wiped
and stalks trimmed
salt and pepper
1 red onion, finely chopped
1 garlic clove, finely chopped
1 tablespoon olive oil
200ml (7fl oz) red wine
1 sugar cube
25g (1oz) butter, diced
1–2 handfuls of young spinach leaves
(or torn large ones), washed
4 *Poached eggs* (page 423)
1 dessertspoon chopped curly parsley
squeeze of lemon juice (optional)

Cut the bacon rashers into thin strips. Heat a large frying pan and add the bacon. The strips will now release their own fat content and fry to a crispy finish. Spoon the bacon from the pan, leaving the fat in which to fry the mushrooms. Place the mushrooms in the pan and cook over a high heat for 3–4 minutes on each side until well coloured, seasoning with salt and pepper. Remove from the pan and keep warm.

Mix together the chopped red onion and garlic. Add the olive oil to the pan and fry the onion mixture for a few minutes until softened. Pour over the red wine, which will begin to sizzle, lifting all residue in the pan.

Add the mushrooms, along with any juices. Increase the heat and allow the red wine to boil until reduced in volume by half. Add the sugar cube and the butter, gently shaking the pan until both have dissolved and mixed in. Add the spinach and bacon pieces and warm for just a minute until the spinach has wilted. Check for seasoning.

Reheat the pre-made poached eggs by plunging them into rapidly simmering water for 1 minute. Divide the mushrooms and spinach between plates and top each with a warm poached egg. Add the chopped parsley to the Bourguignonne sauce, along with a squeeze of lemon juice, if using, and spoon a little over each dish.

fried egg and spinach with morel mushrooms

This serves either as a starter or a lunch/supper dish, perhaps accompanied by a few new potatoes. For an even more seasonal feel, the spinach can be replaced with spring greens.

The addition of the morel mushrooms makes it a spring recipe, but these can be replaced with almost any other mushroom, wild or cultivated, for an all-year-round recipe. Morel mushrooms need to be carefully washed and rinsed, not steeping them in the water as, if left submerged, they will absorb too much and become spongy. Cleaning them becomes a lot simpler, quicker and thorough if the mushrooms are halved; leaving them whole obviously maintains their unique shape, although they will take a little longer to cook.

SERVES 4 AS A STARTER OR LUNCH

350g (12oz) young spinach, washed and stalks removed
salt, plus coarse sea salt
iced water
100g (4oz) fresh morel mushrooms
25–50g (1–2oz) butter
50–75ml (3–5 tablespoons) whipping cream or crème fraîche
twist of black pepper
freshly grated nutmeg
4 eggs
dash of balsamic vinegar or sherry vinegar

The spinach can be cooked in advance by blanching in rapidly boiling salted water for just a minute, until tender, before refreshing in iced water, then draining. Gently squeeze to remove excess water. The cooked leaves can now be refrigerated until needed, ready to reheat in butter or quickly microwave.

Trim away the base of the morel stalks (keeping them for later use when making stock). Split the large mushrooms in half lengthwise. Gently brush and then lightly wash and rinse them to make sure they are completely clean and free of grit.

To assemble the dish, the spinach can be reheated if pre-blanched or, if cooking to order, melt a knob of butter in a large saucepan and, once this is bubbling, add the spinach leaves. Cook on a fairly high heat and stir. Any moisture within the leaves will help steam them, speeding up the cooking time. After a minute or two the spinach will be ready. If sitting in too much natural water, quickly drain away the excess. Add 3 tablespoons of the cream or crème fraîche and stir in. Season with salt, pepper and nutmeg; keep warm to one side.

Fry the eggs for a few minutes in a good knob of sizzling butter, seasoning with coarse sea salt and black pepper when cooked.

Serve the spinach on plates or in bowls. If it's slightly too thick, loosen with the remaining cream or crème fraîche. Place a fried egg on top of each portion. Quickly return the pan to a high heat and add a knob of butter. Add the morels and quickly fry to warm through and tenderize. Sprinkle with a dash of vinegar – this will quickly evaporate, just gently adding a piquancy to the mushrooms. Season with salt and pepper and add the remaining butter. When bubbling, spoon it over the eggs and spinach before serving.

If using spring greens these should always be pre-cooked in boiling water. The torn leaves take about 3 minutes to become completely tender. Refresh in cold water and drain well. Season and reheat when needed before stirring in the warmed cream.
If you have truffle oil just a few drops will take this dish even further. Dried morel mushrooms can also be used. Soak 50g (2oz) in cold water for 30 minutes, then rinse, squeeze dry and use as above.

OPPOSITE: FRIED EGG AND SPINACH WITH MOREL MUSHROOMS

roast monkfish with spring cabbage and clam casserole

Monkfish and clams are available all year round, but it is during mid-spring that monkfish is at its best. At the same time we also have young spring cabbages, which need no more than softening and buttering. It is important that clams are well washed before use, discarding any that will not close when lightly tapped.

SERVES 4 AS A MAIN COURSE

1kg (2¼lb) monkfish (weight on the bone)
1 spring cabbage
50g (2oz) butter, plus 3 knobs
salt and pepper
iced water (optional)
freshly grated nutmeg
40 clams, well washed
2 shallots or ½ onion, finely chopped
1 garlic clove, finely crushed (optional)
pinch of caster sugar
150ml (¼ pint) white wine
flour, for dusting
2 tablespoons olive oil
1 tablespoon chopped flatleaf parsley
1 teaspoon chopped tarragon

The monkfish must first have its dark skin removed. This will come away quite simply, if you pull it sharply from the thick end to the thin end of the tail. Two fillets can now be cut away from the central bone. The fillets will still have a thin membrane coating, so trim it away with a sharp knife. Try to get your local fishmonger to do all this for you.

Each fillet can now be cut into two portions providing four pieces in total, each approximately 175g (6oz). These can be refrigerated until needed.

Quarter the cabbage and remove the stalks from the leaves. Tear the leaves into bite-sized pieces. While the fish is frying, the cabbage can be cooked in a knob of butter and 5 tablespoons of water, until tender. The alternative is to pre-cook it (to reheat later), by plunging it into boiling salted water and cooking for a few minutes until tender, then refreshing it in iced water and draining well in a colander.

If reheating later in the microwave, at this point the leaves can be buttered, adding the salt, pepper and nutmeg.

Pour 300ml (½ pint) of water into a large saucepan and heat until bubbling. Add the clams, cover with a lid and cook on a high heat, shaking the pan. After 2–3 minutes, the clams should all be open (discard any that aren't). Drain, saving the cooking liquor. All of the clams can be removed from their shells or leave 4–5 per portion still in shell for a more rustic finish. Keep to one side.

While the clams are cooking, melt a knob of butter in another pan and add the shallots or onion and garlic, if using. Cook for a few minutes until beginning to soften. Add the caster sugar and white wine, bring to the boil and reduce in volume by two-thirds. The drained clam liquor can now be poured in through a fine sieve or muslin cloth, before bringing back to the boil. Reduce in volume by a third to half for a good intense flavour, then keep to one side.

Lightly flour the monkfish fillet portions and season with salt and pepper. Heat the oil in a large frying pan or roasting tray. Fry the fish fillets in the hot pan for 6–7 minutes, colouring on all sides, and then remove the pan from the heat. The fish will now continue to cook while the remaining flavours are put together.

Reheat the cabbage in a pan with a knob of butter and season with salt, pepper and nutmeg (or microwave).

Return the sauce to the stove and bring to a simmer. Add the 50g (2oz) butter and whisk in well. The clams, in and out of shell, can now be added to warm through, but not allowed to boil. Add the fresh herbs.

This dish is best served in a bowl, placing the cabbage in the centre, spooning the clams and sauce around, and presenting the monkfish fillets on top of the cabbage. It is also quite nice simply to plate the cabbage and fish, offering a bowl of clam casserole on the table.

A squeeze of lemon or lime juice can be added to the finished sauce, or a drizzle of Lemon oil *(page 421).*

OPPOSITE: ROAST MONKFISH WITH SPRING CABBAGE AND CLAM CASSEROLE

pan-roasted mackerel and truffle potato salad with a goat's cheese fondue dressing

Mackerel is a fish that links well with so many of our foods during the months of spring, leading through to and including the ones of autumn. It's during these times that they will be in abundance, providing easy fishing for many a boat. Although still available in the winter, mackerel are much harder to find: most are hibernating, waiting for the spring months to return.

Translated into French, mackerel is *maquereau*, this name also standing for 'pimp'. I'm not quite sure which came first, but perhaps it was the over-lingering taste and brightly coloured dress code of this fish that gave it this title.

Mackerel also has the honour of being a cousin to tuna. This is confirmed when studying the fish, its firm tail leading down to an almost pointed finish, before ending with its quite sharp 'v' shape.

Here the fish are to be roasted in the frying pan, leaving an oven-roast bite and flavour. Fillets can also be used, but then larger fish need to be chosen to provide the right portions.

The title 'truffle potato salad' is slightly misleading: there are no truffles to be found within the salad at all. This title purely represents the potato variety I've chosen to use, truffle potato (*truffe de Chine*). Still available in spring, this unusual tuber can be dug from our own soils, but most are delivered from France. To identify, they are smallish long purple/black fingers, their colour and slightly nutty flavour not fading during cooking. Similar varieties that can also be used in this dish are the Blue Congo (found here in the UK and Australia), and Maori Chief from New Zealand. The Maori Chief carries the same colours, offering a more sweet potato flavour. The Blue Congo slightly lacks the depth of the others, but does carry a beautiful purple-blue tinge. Should any of these not be found, the recipe lends itself well to a basic new potato.

Finishing with the dressing, goat's cheese joins us this time of the year; a soft, creamy texture is preferred for this recipe. Once blended with a little yoghurt, lime and other characters, it binds and finds itself holding a smooth velvety fondue consistency.

SERVES 4 AS A STARTER OR LIGHT LUNCH
4 whole small mackerel, gutted and trimmed
2 tablespoons groundnut or vegetable oil
flour, for dusting
knob of butter
coarse sea salt and pepper

FOR THE SALAD
750g (1½lb) truffle potatoes, unpeeled
1 small red onion, finely chopped

FOR THE DRESSING
100g (4oz) rich soft goat's cheese
1 tablespoon lime juice
3 tablespoons natural yoghurt
1 large garlic clove, crushed (optional)
salt
pinch of Cayenne pepper

In salted water, boil the potatoes in their skins for approximately 20 minutes until tender. Drain the water from the potatoes, peeling away the skins. The rich truffle potatoes can now be cut into thick slices, or simply broken with a fork into pieces, mixing them with the chopped red onion. Season with salt and pepper and keep warm to one side.

To cook the mackerel, first score the skin and flesh in three diagonal lines on each side. Heat a large frying pan with the oil. Once hot, lightly dust the fish with plain flour on each side. Place the fish in the pan, shallow-frying on a medium-hot heat for 4–5 minutes on each side. During this time the mackerel will have taken on a rich golden-brown crispy finish.

While cooking the fish, place all of the dressing ingredients, including the garlic, if using, in a small food processor or liquidizer, blending until smooth. Should the dressing be too thick, milk can be added to loosen, leaving a single-cream consistency. This can now be spooned over the potatoes, mixing it in well, or simply drizzle over once plated.

To finish the mackerel, add the butter to the pan, basting its sizzling nutty flavours over the fish. Season with a sprinkling of coarse sea salt and a twist of pepper.

To present, place the mackerel on warm plates, spooning a little butter over each, finishing with the potato salad beside.

A mixture of fresh herbs added to the dressing – parsley, chervil, tarragon and chives – works very well. A pinch of ground cumin, coriander and/or cardamom can also be added for a spicier finish, all working well with yoghurt and soft cheeses.

mustard-brushed flounder with steamed leek greens

Flounder – 'poor man's plaice' – is available from March to early winter. This flat fish, much the same shape as plaice, dab or lemon sole, is best eaten within the first two months of its season. Being a fairly well-travelled fish, its quality can deteriorate after too many exhausting journeys. If you do manage to find this fish during March and April, though, do take advantage of its availability. When very fresh, it will eat as well as any plaice during this short spell. Used mainly as bait by fishermen, this will give you an indication of its more than competitive price.

To enhance and set off what flounder has to offer, this recipe, which I first came across in the USA, works very well. It simply involves a combination of mayonnaise and mustard brushed over the fillets before grilling. The leeks lift the fish with their oniony bite, and in the month of March are just ending a more than successful season.

An optional extra is the *Chive and tarragon oil*. Both flavours also match well with mustard and leeks. If you're not too sure about the blanching and blitzing, both herbs chopped and added to olive oil will work almost as well.

SERVES 4 AS A MAIN COURSE
1½lb (675g) leeks
knob of butter, plus more for greasing
salt and pepper
4 × 350–450g (12oz–1lb) flounders, filleted and skinned
2 teaspoons English or Dijon mustard (wholegrain
  mustard can also be used)
2 tablespoons *Mayonnaise* (page 419, or bought)
squeeze of lemon juice
4–6 tablespoons *Chive and tarragon oil* (page 421,
  optional)

Remove the bases of the leeks and split each leek in two lengthwise. Remove the tough outside layer, then shred the leeks finely, including the maximum quantity possible of the green tops. Wash well and leave to drain in a colander.

To cook the leeks, melt the knob of butter in a large saucepan. Add the leeks and cook on a fairly high heat. The moistness of the leeks will create steam; in just 2–3 minutes they'll be tender. Once cooked, season with salt and pepper.

While the leeks are cooking, season the flounder fillets with salt and pepper. Butter a large baking tray (you may need two) and place the fillets on it. Mix the mustard into the mayonnaise and finish with a squeeze or two of lemon juice. Brush this liberally over each of the fillets. Place the fillets under a preheated grill and cook for just 2–3 minutes, until golden brown and cooked through. The fillets can now be arranged on plates, followed by the leeks. To finish, drizzle with the chive and tarragon oil, if using.

A teaspoon of extra chives and tarragon can be added to the flavoured oil just before serving.

MUSTARD-BRUSHED FLOUNDER WITH STEAMED LEEK GREENS

crispy cod with candied orange spring green hearts

Cod is one of Britain's most popular fish, its flaky texture taking many a 'battering' during its time. However, its flavour comes more alive when it is fried or grilled. Straightforward poaching or steaming, unless the fish comes almost direct from the boat, can often leave you searching for something to happen. Having said that, the steaming process the fish experiences when battered and fried is quite a different kettle of fish altogether.

For the spring greens, I'm choosing the central heart cores, cutting each into halves or quarters. The fresh flavour of the spring greens is lifted, picking up a bitter-sweet bite from the oranges.

SERVES 4 AS A MAIN COURSE

4 × 175g (6oz) portions of cod fillet, pin-boned
　(page 9), with skin on
150–175g (5–6oz) coarse sea salt
3 small young spring greens
salt and pepper
iced water (optional)
knob of butter
flour, for dusting
2 tablespoons vegetable oil

FOR THE ORANGE SAUCE

2 shallots, finely chopped (or 1 heaped tablespoon
　finely chopped onion)
100ml (3½fl oz) white wine
juice of 1 orange
2 tablespoons single cream
50g (2oz) butter, diced

FOR THE RED WINE DRESSING

150ml (¼ pint) red wine
1–2 sugar cubes
1 tablespoon olive oil

FOR THE CANDIED ORANGE PEEL

3 oranges
50g (2oz) caster sugar

To make the candied orange peel, remove the zest from all three oranges with a vegetable peeler. Slice the pieces of zest lengthwise into very thin strips. Cover with cold water and bring to a simmer. Drain and refresh in cold water. Repeat the same process twice more.

Squeeze and strain the juice from all three oranges. Pour into a saucepan with the sugar and blanched orange strips. Slowly bring to a simmer and cook on a low heat for 30 minutes, reducing it to a syrup. As the syrup cooks, the orange zest becomes tender. Remove from the heat and leave to cool. This quantity gives more than is needed here, but if refrigerated will last almost indefinitely.

Score the cod skins with a sharp knife in strips 5mm (¼in) apart. Sprinkle the coarse sea salt on a suitable platter and place the fish, skin-side down, on top. Leave for 30 minutes to draw excess moisture from the skin. When cooking the fish, the skin then very quickly becomes crispy.

Remove the outside leaves from the spring greens, splitting the central hearts and cutting them into quarters. These can now be cooked to order, or pre-blanched. Whichever option you wish to take, simply plunge them into rapidly boiling salted water and cook for just 2–4 minutes until tender. If pre-cooking, refresh in iced water. The spring greens can now be microwaved or heated with a knob of butter and a little water, then seasoned with salt and pepper.

CRISPY COD WITH CANDIED ORANGE SPRING GREEN HEARTS

To make the orange sauce, place the shallots or onion in a saucepan with the white wine. Bring to the boil and reduce until almost dry. Add the orange juice, return to the boil and reduce in volume by half. Add the cream and, once warm, stir in the diced butter. Season to taste.

To cook the cod, remove the fillets from the salt, rinse and wipe dry, then dust with flour and season with a twist of pepper. Heat the oil in a frying pan and, once hot, carefully place the fillets in, skin-side down. Cook for 6–7 minutes, until golden brown and crispy. Turn the fish in the pan and cook for just another minute. Remove the fish and keep warm.

Drain any excess oil from the pan, then pour in the red wine. Boil and reduce in volume by two-thirds, then stir one sugar cube in, tasting for sweetness. If still too harsh, add the other sugar cube, then add the olive oil. Strain through a tea strainer.

Arrange the cod fillets and 3–4 pieces of spring greens per portion, side by side, on plates. Sprinkle 6–7 strands of candied orange over each portion of spring greens and spoon the orange sauce over. The red wine dressing can now be spooned around the fish.

warm scallops and prawns hollandaise

Potted prawns and shrimps are the ones set in butter and served accompanied by brown bread or warm toast. It is from this concept that this dish was born.

Scallops are reaching the end of their British season at the beginning of the spring. This is often a good time to buy, with the prices lower than during the winter months. Their texture softens the finished dish, with the firmness of the prawns preventing an over-milky finish.

The butter connection with the two seafoods is to be found with a sauce hollandaise, offering its creamy consistency as their binder. An extra flavouring touch is the *Prawn dressing*, its lemon/bisque bite cutting into the overall taste. It's not essential to add the dressing – a sauce hollandaise with scallops and prawns is a pretty sound dish alone – but an alternative finish that maximizes the prawn flavour really shouldn't be ignored.

The quantities given here are measured so as to not offer too much of an over-rich start to your meal. These portions can of course be increased, with plenty of hollandaise and dressing to share.

SERVES 4 AS A STARTER
225g (8oz) whole North Atlantic prawns, preferably raw
175g (6oz) (approx 8–10) cleaned scallops
knob of butter
salt and pepper
1 quantity *Simple hollandaise sauce* (page 418)
10 green peppercorns in brine, cut in halves (optional)
1 quantity *Prawn dressing* (page 117)
handful of rocket leaves or watercress (optional)
drizzle of olive oil (optional)

If raw, the prawns first need to be plunged into boiling salted water for 30 seconds, then removed and left to cool. Shell the prawns, saving 50g (2oz) of the shells for the dressing. Refrigerate the prawns until needed, using the shells to follow the dressing method on page 117.

If the scallops are bought in the shell, prise them open with a knife and detach the scallop from the lower shell. The surrounding membrane can now be pulled away and discarded (unless using to flavour a stock or sauce). Rinse the scallops and dry on kitchen paper or a cloth. The coral can now be separated from the 'meat', utilizing it as noted below. The scallops can now be cut into quarters if small or eighths if larger. Also refrigerate until needed.

Melt the knob of butter in a small saucepan with 2 tablespoons of water over a low heat. Once melted, add the scallops and prawns. Heat gently until just warmed.

It is important not to boil the seafood, as this will toughen and dry their texture. Once warmed, season with salt and pepper and transfer to a bowl. Any juices left in the pan should be quickly boiled and reduced to just a tablespoon, then poured over the shellfish. Add 4–6 tablespoons of the hollandaise sauce, just enough to bind without over-masking (any excess can be offered separately).

Spoon the seafood between plates or bowls. If using, place five green peppercorn halves around each portion (these provide a perfumed bite to the complete dish) and drizzle the prawn dressing around the portions. Season the rocket or watercress with salt, pepper and a drop of olive oil, if using, and then arrange 4–5 leaves on top of each.

The scallop corals can be kept frozen, to be used in future scallop salads or other dishes. If blitzed and blended with an equal quantity of butter before freezing, the butter can then be used as a fish sauce thickener and enhancer. Only very little of this particular butter needs to be added to a fish sauce and once it is whisked into a hot sauce it must not be reboiled, or this will result in a grainy consistency.

bacon-fried scallops with late cabbage or early greens

'Home-grown' plump scallops have been showing their faces since autumn, reaching their peak during the months of winter, and holding their own to the beginning of spring. It's this particular mollusc that bears its sweet flavour so predominantly once cooked. Serving it with the heart of a late Savoy cabbage or early spring greens counterbalances the bitterness on offer.

The choice of 'greens' is up to you, with either variety usually available. If using Savoy cabbage, it's best this time of year to benefit purely from the heart, the outer leaves being tough and not in prize-winning condition. As for spring greens, young gentle leaves (removing the stalks), will cook almost like spinach.

The bacon is to be fried (here a smoky aroma offered, although unsmoked can also be used), until crispy, leaving its fat content in the pan, ready to sear the scallops. The slightly sharp creamy dressing will help cater for a softer finish.

SERVES 4 AS A STARTER OR
2 AS A VERY GENEROUS MAIN COURSE

4 rashers of smoked streaky bacon (unsmoked can also be used)
1 large Savoy cabbage (or 2 small) or 450g (1lb) spring greens
10 scallops (8 if particularly large), cleaned (page 27)
25g (1oz) butter
coarse sea salt

FOR THE DRESSING
6 tablespoons loose natural yoghurt
generous squeeze of lemon juice
1 teaspoon chopped chives (optional)
salt and pepper

Chop the rashers of bacon into small dice. Heat a frying pan and, once hot, add the chopped bacon. Cook over a medium heat, allowing the fat content of the bacon to melt into the pan. Fry the chopped pieces until they have a crispy finish. Spoon the crispy bacon into a sieve, saving the fat in a bowl beneath. Place to one side.

If using Savoy cabbage, remove all the outside leaves and discard. Cut the remaining cabbage into quarters, also cutting away the central core from each. The rest can now be finely shredded. Spring greens will simply need to be torn into individual leaves (discarding any damaged ones), before removing any tough stalks, washing and also finely shredding.

Each of the white scallop muscles can now be halved, leaving 20 discs. If particularly large, each of the eight can be sliced into three, leaving 24 discs.

To make the dressing, whisk together the yoghurt and lemon juice, seasoning with salt and pepper. The chives, if using, are best added just before serving. This will prevent then from discolouring due to the citric acid. The cabbage/greens and scallops are to be cooked more or less at the same time, which preserves their flavours at their most prominent.

In a large saucepan, melt the butter. Once bubbling, add the shredded cabbage/greens, cooking only on a medium heat. Season with salt and pepper before placing a lid on top. This will create a steam that helps speed up the cooking. Stir the cabbage from time to time, adding a tablespoon of water should the cabbage begin to stick. The total cooking time for finely shredded cabbage will only be 4–5 minutes, adding an extra minute or two if it was coarsely cut.

The moment the cabbage has been dropped in the pan, heat a large frying pan on the stove. With just 2–3 minutes left of cabbage cooking time, pour the saved bacon fat into the pan. Once hot, the scallop slices can be placed in the pan, cooking on a high heat. Literally sear on one side for just a minute or two, leaving a golden brown edge on each.

Season with a twist of pepper only. Remove the scallops from the pan, placing them on a warm plate, fried-side up. Stir the cooked bacon pieces into the cabbage, dividing it between four warm plates, moulding into a rectangular shape on which to place the scallops.

Arrange the five (or six) scallop slices per person, slightly overlapping, on top of the greens. To finish, simply spoon the dressing around, sprinkling a little coarse sea salt over the scallops.

A level teaspoon of English or Dijon mustard can be added to the dressing, providing a warm bite.
A very finely chopped, heaped tablespoon of onion can be cooked in the butter before adding the cabbage. This gives the bacon and greens a slightly different edge to their finished flavour.
If using green (unsmoked) bacon, a few tablespoons of diced smoked salmon can also be added, offering a new blend of flavours.

mussel 'champ' stew with caper croûtons

March is considered to be the last official month of the mussel, as it's still quite plump – the summer tends to offer large shells with tiny fillings. This recipe is almost a soup, loose and creamy with a chunky finish.

Champ is the classic Irish potato dish, put together with buttery mash and lots of spring onions. It's not mash we're going to be using here but, instead, cooked and broken Maris Pipers, good at this time of the year, with creamy white flesh to help thicken the mussel liquor.

Croûtons are usually butter-fried crispy cubes of bread; these are here replaced with oil-fried capers, crisping as they sizzle in the pan. These can be just dried on kitchen paper before frying, but I prefer to rinse them first, calming their strong acidic bite.

These quantities will offer a generous starter or supper dish feeding four. For two or three people this becomes a hearty stew, needing just crusty bread to dip.

SERVES 4 AS A STARTER
1kg (2¼lb) live mussels
2 large Maris Piper potatoes, unpeeled
salt and pepper
600ml (1 pint) *Fish stock* (page 417), *Instant stock* (page 416) or water
1 bunch of spring onions
25g (1oz) butter
100ml (3½fl oz) crème fraîche or whipping cream
squeeze of lemon juice
vegetable oil, for frying
1 heaped tablespoon capers, rinsed and dried

Wash the mussels well, discarding any that remain open when lightly tapped. Scrape off any barnacles from the mussels, also pulling away the fibrous beards. Rinse once more, or leave in cold water until ready to cook.

Simmer the whole Maris Pipers in salted water until tender, piercing with a knife to check they are cooked.

While waiting for the potatoes, the mussels can be cooked. Bring the stock or water to the boil before adding the drained mussels. Cover with a lid and cook for just 3–4 minutes, stirring occasionally, until the mussels have opened. Strain the liquor and reserve; this will have taken on the mussel flavour. Remove the mussels from their shells,

checking for and removing any beards still remaining. Discard any that have not opened. The cooking liquor can now be checked for strength of flavour. If slightly shallow, return to a saucepan along with the mussel shells. Simmer gently for 10 minutes, allowing the stock to infuse, before straining through a fine sieve.

To prepare the spring onions, peel away the tough outside skins, trimming the stalk base and tops and slicing them into small rounds no more than 5mm (¼in) thick.

With the potatoes cooked and removed from the water, peel away the skin, cutting them into rough cubes and saving all the crumbly bits.

Melt half the butter in a saucepan. Once bubbling, add the sliced spring onions, cooking over a moderate heat for a few minutes until tender. Add the diced potatoes and bits, stirring them into the onions. Pour over the mussel stock and bring to a simmer. A stir or whisk will begin to break the potatoes into the stock, thickening to a soup consistency.

Add the crème fraîche or cream with a squeeze of lemon juice, checking for seasoning with a twist of pepper and pinch of salt if needed.

Heat 5mm (¼in) of vegetable oil in a small frying pan. Once hot, add the dried capers, frying for about 2 minutes until they have become crispy. Using a slotted spoon, lift them from the oil and place on kitchen paper.

Spoon the mussels into the soup with the remaining butter, creating a stew, and bring to a soft simmer. It's important not to over-simmer or boil, as this will toughen the mussels. Divide between bowls and serve, offering the crispy capers to sprinkle over.

A sprinkling of chopped flatleaf parsley or tarragon (or both) can be added to this recipe.
The crème fraîche/whipping cream can be omitted, leaving a very natural finish, relying on the potato bits for that creamy finish.

casseroled shoulder of pork on brussels tops with spring onion and carrot butterbean broth

The seasonal flavours to be found here are the welcome and farewell of the spring onions and sprout tops. The spring onions are very young, just joining us, with the tops in the last month of their season. Brussels sprouts grow on quite tall plants, with the small deep green sprouts attached tightly to the stem. It's the floral leafy arrangement, similar to spring greens, sitting on top, which I'll be using here. They come in various sizes, many more generous in leaves than others. Four to six are listed below, the maximum quantity providing more than enough for the already generous recipe.

The shoulder of pork is the cheapest of 'roast' joints. One of the fattiest of cuts, which keeps it succulent, it has a sweeter flavour than the leg. This cut is normally found boned, rolled and tied, which is exactly what I want, but with the pork rind previously removed. This is not difficult to do, but even easier when your butcher prepares it for you. The rind now becomes an optional extra with the best option roasting it to a crispy crackling to serve with the succulent shoulder.

SERVES 6 AS A GENEROUS MAIN COURSE

1.5–1.8kg (3¼–4¼lb) boned and rolled rindless shoulder of pork (saving the rind, if wished)
salt and pepper
2 tablespoons cooking oil, plus extra for brushing
1 onion, chopped
3 carrots, cut into 1cm (½in) slices
1 sprig of rosemary (optional)
600ml (1 pint) *Chicken stock* (page 416) or *Instant stock* (page 416) or water
1 bunch of spring onions
1 × 400g tin of butterbeans, drained
knob of butter
4–6 Brussels tops, coarse stems removed and leaves rinsed
1 tablespoon picked and chopped flatleaf parsley leaves (optional)

Preheat the oven to 160°C/325°F/Gas 3. Season the rolled pork with salt and pepper. Heat the cooking oil in an ovenproof braising pot and brown the joint well on all sides over a medium heat.

Once browned, remove the pork from the pot, pouring away most of the excess fat, leaving approximately 2 tablespoons remaining. The onion, carrots and rosemary, if using, can now be added to the pot, cooking for just a few minutes. Place the shoulder on top, pouring the stock around and bringing to a simmer. Cover with a lid and place in the preheated oven, braising for 3 hours, basting from time to time.

While the pork is cooking, the rind, if using, can be scored with a sharp knife and brushed lightly with cooking oil. Sprinkle well with salt, placing it on a wire rack sitting over a baking tray. Place in the oven and cook to a golden brown crispy finish. This will take a minimum of 1 hour, depending on the strength of the oven. Once crispy, simply remove and keep warm to one side, ready to snap into crunchy pieces, offering them with the pork.

The spring onions simply need the stalk base to be trimmed, peeling and discarding the outside tough layer before cutting into 5mm (¼in) slices.

Once the pork is cooked, remove it from the pot, keeping it warm to one side. Strain the cooking juices through a sieve, skimming away excess fat. Check the liquor for seasoning, adding the butterbeans, spring onions and strained carrots and onions and returning it to a gentle simmer.

Bring 1cm (½in) of water to the boil in a large frying pan or wok. Add a pinch of salt along with the Brussels tops. Return to the boil, cooking for just a few minutes until tender. Drain the water well, adding the knob of butter and seasoning with salt and pepper. Gently stir-fry for a further minute and the tops are ready.

To serve, spoon the Brussels tops into the centre of large bowls. Remove the string from the pork, carving into thick slices, or breaking into pieces and placing them with the Brussels. Add the chopped parsley, if using, to the broth, spooning it around the casseroled shoulder. Break the crackling into pieces, if using, and put a few pieces on each serving.

OPPOSITE: CASSEROLED SHOULDER OF PORK ON BRUSSELS TOPS WITH SPRING ONION AND CARROT BUTTERBEAN BROTH

softly roasted pork belly with warmed curly kale

Pork belly is a very versatile cut of meat. With this recipe, several hours of slow cooking gives the fat content time to melt through the meat, producing a very tender and moist finish. If the rind is left on the pork it will provide a crisp crackling topping to finish.

Curly kale is one of our greens that is so often at its best during the spring month of March. Although similar to spring greens, curly kale has its own texture and taste, loving lots of butter and seasoning.

For this recipe, I'm suggesting a butter sauce finished with wholegrain mustard for a silky warmth to the dish.

SERVES 4 AS A MAIN COURSE
1kg (2¼lb) piece of pork belly, boned, with rind left on
2 large onions
1 tablespoon cooking oil
coarse sea salt and pepper, plus salt for the kale
300ml (½ pint) *Chicken stock* (page 416) or *Instant stock* (page 416) or water
675–900g (1½–2lb) curly kale
iced water (optional)
knob of butter
1–2 tablespoons wholegrain mustard (optional)
1 quantity *Basic butter sauce* (page 418, optional)
squeeze of lemon juice (optional)

Preheat the oven to 160°C/325°F/Gas 3. Score the pork belly rind with a sharp knife at intervals of 1cm (½in). Peel the onions, cut them in halves and place in a roasting tray. These will act as a trivet, preventing the pork meat from touching the hot tray. As the belly roasts, its fat content and juices will be absorbed by the onions, almost caramelizing them towards the end of the cooking time. These can then be served with the meat.

Lightly oil the pork rind and sprinkle with coarse sea salt. The meat side can also be seasoned with the salt and a good twist of pepper. Place the meat on top of the onions, and into the preheated oven and roast for 3 hours. During this cooking time the fat content of the meat will provide a self-basting service. After 1½–2 hours it's best to check the onions are not becoming too dry and beginning to stick and burn on the tray. If they are, add a few tablespoons of water to moisten.

Once cooked, remove the pork and onions from the oven and tray and keep warm to one side, while the meat rests. Heat the tray on the stove and add the stock or water. This will instantly bubble up with the heat in the pan, lifting all residue and juices from the onions. Bring to a simmer and cook for a few minutes. If too shallow in flavour, continue to cook the stock until reduced in volume by a third. The stock gravy can now be strained through a fine sieve before serving.

While the pork is roasting, prepare and cook the curly kale. Remove the stalks and wash the leaves well. If cooking the kale in advance, it can be blanched in boiling salted water for 3–4 minutes until tender. Plunge into iced water to stop the cooking process and maintain its colour, and strain. It can be either microwaved or heated with a knob of butter and a few tablespoons of water. This creates an instant liquor, heating the kale through in just a minute or two. Season with salt and pepper. If simply cooking before serving, cook as above and finish with a knob of butter and seasoning.

Add a tablespoon of the mustard, if using, to the butter sauce. This will provide an extra warmth to the sauce; for a hotter finish add the remaining mustard. Finish the sauce with a squeeze of lemon juice, if using.

The pork crackling can now be broken and snapped into pieces, then cut chunky portions of the belly and divide both between plates.

Moisten the curly kale with half of the mustard sauce and serve with the pork, trickling the rest of the sauce over and around the leaves. The softly roasted pork is now ready to serve, offering the stock gravy separately.

grilled goat's cheese on cider apples and black pudding with a cider and mustard cream

Cheese has a double value. It can be eaten as a course on its own, but is also the perfect enhancer for savoury dishes. Here I've created a combination of the two – goat's cheese with apples and, for an extra bite, some spicy black pudding. This dish will eat well as a simple lunch or supper dish or as an alternative to a dessert.

Goat's cheese can have quite a dry and crumbly texture, which works well broken into salads or creamed into dressings. This recipe, however, grills the cheese, softening its finish. The slices are melted on top of thickly cut apples that have been poached in cider, then placed on black pudding. The dressing utilizes the cider cooking liquor, increasing the finished flavour.

SERVES 4

2 apples, peeled and cored
300ml (½ pint) dry cider
4 thick slices of black pudding (each 1–2cm/
½–¾in thick)
butter, for brushing
4 thick slices of goat's cheese log (each 50–60g/2–2¼oz)

FOR THE DRESSING
2 teaspoons wholegrain mustard
pinch of caster sugar
6 tablespoons single cream
salt and pepper
squeeze of lime juice (optional)
1 teaspoon snipped flatleaf parsley
1 teaspoon snipped chives

Halve the apples to provide four thick apple rings. Place these in a saucepan and cover with the cider. Bring to a simmer and cook for 2 minutes. Remove the pan from the heat, leaving the apples in the cider to continue cooking, without losing their texture.

To make the dressing, drain two-thirds of the cider into another pan and simmer and reduce in volume by three-quarters. Whisk 3 tablespoons of the reduced cider into the mustard along with the caster sugar and single cream. Season with salt and pepper and a squeeze of lime juice, if using. If the cider flavour has become masked by the strength of the mustard, simply add a few more drops of the reduction to increase its flavour. The herbs are best added to the dressing just before serving. If added too early, the acidic bite of the cider and lime juice will discolour their rich green colour and diminish their flavour.

Preheat the grill to hot. Brush the black pudding slices with butter and cook under the grill for 2–3 minutes, then turn the slices and repeat the cooking time. Meanwhile, warm the apple rings in the remaining cider. Place the slices of grilled black pudding on a baking sheet and top with the apples, followed by the slices of goat's cheese.

Place the stacked savouries under the hot grill until the cheese is golden brown and beginning to melt. The dish is now ready to serve; mix the herbs into the dressing and spoon it over. The three different textures of cheese, apple and black pudding eat so well together, each offering their individual flavour and complementing one another.

A tossed salad of leaves and fresh herbs (chives, parsley, tarragon, chervil) can be served with this dish, as a simple garnish or side salad. A quick mix of 4 tablespoons of olive or hazelnut oil, whisked with 1–2 tablespoons of reduced cider and 1 teaspoon of lime juice, provides a dressing for the leaves.

The humble cabbage has a rich history, and has spawned any number of offshoots. The original wild *Brassica oleracea* was a plant that grew in temperate regions, usually beside the sea. It did not have a heart or head and its long leaves were very bitter. Over the centuries, the plant was intensively cultivated and encouraged to develop different forms. One cultivar formed a head of tight leaves, which gave us Savoy, maturing with its quite robust character along with the familiar white and green cabbages; another had a head of loose leaves, thus curly kale, one of the most attractive members of the family, having an almost curly-parsley-leaf look. One tight-headed cabbage was made to change colour and the red cabbage was born. It didn't stop there: another was persuaded to grow numerous small budding heads on long stalks, and Brussels sprouts were created.

Cabbages encouraged to flower introduced to us some distant relatives, with their fully pronounced floral glory: cauliflower and broccoli.

Cabbage is now available most of the year round, as there are winter, spring and summer varieties. The loose-headed spring cabbage, if plucked a month or so early, in March, is what we know as spring greens – although genuinely unhearted varieties can share this name, as can Brussels sprouts tops, cauliflower tops, turnip or rape tops (the latter the lately fashionable, Italian *cime di rapa*). Other spring greens – which our forefathers would have greeted enthusiastically in March – include sorrel, spinach, wild garlic, dandelions and young nettle tops.

One of the cabbage relations that I most value in March is purple sprouting broccoli. This is a cabbage cultivar that, although created in Italy (*broccoli* means 'little arms' or 'little shoots' in Italian), became a main feature of our eating habits, before the longer, more shapely and attractive calabrese broccoli followed. Another March passion is sea kale which, despite the 'kale' suffix, is not a cabbage offshoot, although it belongs to the same extended family (the *Cruciferae*). If allowed to grow naturally, the stalks develop large, tough, unpleasant-tasting leaves, but if blanched – when the whole plant is kept from the light – the leaves are tiny, at the top of fat, succulent, white stalks. If boiled until tender, these can be eaten like asparagus.

steak au poivre with buttered spring greens and shallots

The skirt steak, although one of the cheaper cuts of meat, is one you'll probably have to order in advance. It is one of the most popular steaks served in brasseries all over France, where the cut is known as *bavette*.

This steak requires only a very quick few minutes of cooking in a hot pan. Once rested, it will be tender, and packed with flavour. To help make it even more tender, the skirt steak can be gently batted before cooking, using a meat-tenderizing hammer, which will break up its fibres and give a softer finish once cooked.

The seasonal feature of this dish is our home-grown spring greens. Sautéed with sliced shallots in nutty butter, they are guaranteed a good relationship with the steak.

OPPOSITE: STEAK AU POIVRE WITH BUTTERED SPRING GREENS AND SHALLOTS

SERVES 4 AS A MAIN COURSE
4 tablespoons black peppercorns
salt and pepper
75g (3oz) butter
4 shallots, sliced
2 tablespoons olive oil
4 × 225g (8oz) skirt steaks, preferably batted (see above)
5 tablespoons cognac
450g (1lb) spring greens, torn into 5–7.5cm (2–3in) pieces
freshly grated nutmeg

Crush the black peppercorns before sieving to shake off any excess powder. The peppercorns will now offer a perfumed aroma and warmth; pepper powder only provides excessive heat. Press the peppercorns on both sides of the steaks and sprinkle with salt.

In a large saucepan, melt 15g (½oz) of the butter. Once hot and bubbling, add the shallots. Cook on a high heat for a few minutes until golden brown and tender. Remove from the pan and keep to one side.

Wipe the pan with kitchen paper, return to the stove and add the olive oil. Once this is very hot and at the point of almost smoking, place the steaks in the pan (this may have to be done in two batches). Cook the steaks for 2–3 minutes, then turn over. Continue to cook for a further 2–3 minutes for a medium-rare to medium finish. Remove the steaks from the pan and keep to one side.

Now add the cognac to the frying pan, lifting all the sediment and juices. Allow to reduce in volume by half, then pour in any juices collected from the resting steaks. Add 50g (2oz) of the butter. This cooking liquor is not a sauce, but a moistener to pour over the steaks when serving.

While the steaks are frying, cook the spring greens. Plunge them into boiling water and cook for a few minutes until tender. Pour into a colander and allow to drain. In a large saucepan or wok, melt half the remaining butter and, once bubbling, add the sliced shallots. Cook on a fairly high heat until golden brown. Add the rest of the butter; once it's melted, add the spring greens. Cook for a few minutes, seasoning with salt, pepper and nutmeg.

The steaks can be left whole or sliced before presenting on plates with the greens, and pouring the cognac butter liquor over.

steamed kumquat marmalade roly-poly

Classically, roly-poly is made with jam, but marmalades are close relatives, so find their way into this recipe very easily. Almost any sweet preserve can be rolled in the suet paste and steamed, orange in particular offering a contrasting, but at the same time complementing, combination of sharp tang and bitterness with the sweet syrupy finish.

Imported kumquats, around at this time, are a perfect substitute for the traditional Seville orange, combining all of the assets just mentioned. This is a very simple marmalade recipe, making more than enough for this dessert – the rest will store in sterilized jars (page 9) – and the ice-cream is purely an optional extra.

SERVES 4–6
FOR THE MARMALADE
(MAKES ABOUT 550–600ML/1 PINT)

450g (1lb) kumquats, quartered, with seeds removed
600ml (1 pint) orange juice (preferably carton for
    increased flavour)
275g (10oz) granulated, preserving or jam sugar
generous squeeze of lemon juice (optional)

FOR THE ICE-CREAM

225g (8oz) kumquats, halved, with seeds removed
600ml (1 pint) single cream
4 egg yolks (6 for a richer custard finish)
100g (4oz) caster sugar
3 tablespoons Grand Marnier

FOR THE ROLY-POLY

225g (8oz) self-raising flour
1 teaspoon baking powder
pinch of salt
finely grated zest of 1 lemon or orange
150g (5oz) vegetarian or beef suet
100–150ml (3½fl oz–¼ pint) milk
150–175g (5–6oz) kumquat marmalade

To make the marmalade, place the kumquat quarters in a saucepan, along with the orange juice, sugar and lemon juice, if using. Bring to a very gentle simmer and cook for 1 hour. The fruits should now be tender but still with a slight bite in the zest. To check the setting point, spoon a little marmalade onto a saucer and chill. It should lightly jellify and wrinkle when moved. If still slightly chewy and loose in consistency, continue to cook for a further 10–15 minutes and recheck. Remove from the heat, skim away any impurities and allow to cool for 15 minutes, then spoon into sterilized jars.

To make the ice-cream, place the kumquats in a food processor or liquidizer and purée. For a smooth finish, push the purée through a sieve. Bring the cream to the boil. While heating the cream, whisk together the egg yolks and sugar to a light fluffy ribbon stage. Pour the boiling cream over the eggs, stirring well. Return the custard to the saucepan and cook over a gentle heat until thick enough to coat the back of a spoon. Remove from the heat and add to the kumquat purée. Leave to cool. Once cold, add the Grand Marnier and pour into an ice-cream machine. It will take approximately 20–25 minutes to thicken. At this point, remove the ice-cream mix from the machine and freeze to set.

To make the roly-poly, sift together the self-raising flour, baking powder and pinch of salt. Add the grated lemon or orange zest, along with the suet, and work to a breadcrumb consistency. Add the milk a little at a time, until a soft texture is formed. Wrap in cling film and allow to rest for 20–30 minutes.

Roll the suet dough into a rectangle approximately 35 × 25cm (14 × 10in). Spread the marmalade on the dough, leaving a border of 1cm (½in) clear. Brush the border with extra milk or water, then roll the dough from the wider edge and pinch at either end to retain all of the marmalade. Wrap the roly-poly loosely in greaseproof paper, followed by loose aluminium foil, and tie with string at either end.

Steam the pudding in a steamer for 2 hours, topping up with hot water, if necessary, during the cooking time. Once cooked, unwrap, slice and serve, offering the kumquat ice-cream separately.

A large steamer is needed for this recipe. If unavailable, two smaller roly-polys can be made.
Late in the spring and early summer season many kumquats can be tougher in texture, often needing between 1½ and 2 hours' cooking time.

OPPOSITE: STEAMED KUMQUAT MARMALADE ROLY-POLY

vanilla white chocolate mousse with warm syruped kumquats

Although not grown in the UK, the kumquat, a small oval orange citrus fruit, finds itself in season during winter and spring months. This fruit, like the orange, is not native to the Mediterranean. China is its original home, with the name derived from the Cantonese *kam kwat*, meaning 'gold orange'. The difference between the orange and kumquat is that the tiny kumquat can be eaten peel and all. The zest and pith are quite sweet, with a bitter, sour centre to counter this flavour. These fruits will eat very well with meats, fish and desserts, whether pickled, preserved or poached.

Here, we will poach them in an orange juice and water syrup, serving them warm to go with the rich cold chocolate mousse. They can be poached as whole fruits, or halved and the pips removed before cooking. With young small kumquats it is fine to leave the pips in, but once May approaches, when the fruits become much larger, I would suggest removing them.

As for the white chocolate mousse, it's a very simple recipe that can be set in individual 150ml (¼ pint) moulds or simply set in one dish and spooned into portions. One of the ingredients of the mousse is *Pastry cream*. This obviously means tackling that recipe before even thinking about this one. Pastry cream, however, is simple to make and forms a base to many other dessert recipes, too.

SERVES 4–6
225g (8oz) white chocolate, chopped
150ml (¼ pint) *Pastry cream* (page 427)
seeds from 1 vanilla pod (optional)
200ml (7fl oz) double cream

FOR THE KUMQUATS
350g (12oz) kumquats
300ml (½ pint) orange juice
225g (8oz) caster sugar

Melt the chocolate in a bowl over gently simmering water, making sure the base of the bowl is not in contact with the water. Once melted, whisk it into the pastry cream with the vanilla seeds, if using. Whip the double cream to soft peak stage, then fold it into the chocolate custard mix. The mousse can now be spooned into individual ramekins or one large serving dish. Refrigerate until chilled.

Prepare the kumquats. If young and small fruits are available, simply pierce each skin with a cocktail stick; for larger ones, it is best to split the fruits in half and remove the seeds before cooking. Place the orange juice and sugar in a saucepan with 150ml (¼ pint) of water and bring to the boil. Reduce the temperature to a simmer and cook for 5–6 minutes. Add the kumquats and bring the syrup back to a gentle simmer.

If halved and young, the fruits may only take 30 minutes of stewing before becoming tender. For whole, or larger, 'tougher' fruits, the cooking can take between 50 minutes and an hour, with a maximum cooking time that may be needed of 1½ hours. The kumquats can now be left to cool slightly to a warm serving temperature. As with a lot of fruits cooked in syrup, in particular citrus fruits, storing them in an airtight jar and refrigerating them will give them a fairly long shelf life.

To serve, present spoonfuls of mousse, or each small ramekin, on plates with a spoonful or two of the syruped kumquats. The two flavours and colours of white and orange can stand alone without garnish, just offering their distinctive tastes to one another.

If you prefer to garnish your desserts, here are a few suggestions. Dark *Chocolate shavings or pencils* (page 427) can be presented on top or beside the mousse. Finely shredded mint can be sprinkled over the kumquats, or the Melba toasts, used for the *Grilled raspberry Melba stack* (page 196) will give a crisp biscuit bite.

rhubarb and almond jalousie with rhubarb pulp and cream

Rhubarb, regarded as a fruit, is in fact a vegetable. The fruity label has become established probably due to the acidic tartness of the vegetable needing the sweetness of sugar to balance it. The late-autumn to mid-spring forced rhubarb, or the outdoor thicker garden variety, can be used for this recipe. The forced kind becomes very pink, holding minimal leaves due to lack of sunlight, and has a very tender finish. Our garden stalks grow more robust, redder in colour, but with that need more attention because of their slightly tougher texture. Moving into the summer, they may even need to be peeled before use.

OPPOSITE: RHUBARB AND ALMOND JALOUSIE WITH RHUBARB PULP AND CREAM

Jalousie is a classic French pastry, usually made with an almond paste, as here, and jam. *Jalousie* means 'slatted blind'; the connection between the two comes with the slatted finish of the pastry, snipped in lines across the top to expose the fruit filling. This is a very attractive dish, with many textures, from the crispy pastry and succulent rhubarb, to the sponge-like almond paste. It can be prepared hours in advance, cooking just 60 minutes before eating. The extra pulp adds more of a fruity finish, making sure that the rhubarb is not lost amongst its rich friends.

SERVES 6 GENEROUSLY

350g (12oz) *Puff pastry* **(page 426, or bought)**
flour, for dusting
knob of butter, plus more for greasing
550g (1¼lb) rhubarb, washed
2 tablespoons caster sugar
1 egg, beaten
icing sugar, for dusting
150ml (¼ pint) cream, for whipping or pouring

FOR THE ALMOND PASTE

60g (2¼oz) butter
60g (2¼oz) caster sugar
60g (2¼oz) ground almonds
1 teaspoon plain flour
1 egg

Roll out a third of the puff pastry into a 30 × 10–12cm (12 × 4–4½in) strip on a lightly floured surface. This can now be placed on a buttered baking tray. At this stage it's not important to trim the strip to a perfect rectangle. Prick with a fork and refrigerate.

Preheat the oven to 190°C/375°F/Gas 5. Cut the rhubarb into approximately twenty 6.5–7cm (2½–3in) sticks, starting from the top of each stick and working down. This will probably use about 400g (14oz) of the total. Roughly chop any remaining rhubarb and trimmings.

Lay the twenty sticks on a baking tray and sprinkle them with 1 tablespoon of the caster sugar. These can now be only just softened in the preheated oven for 6–8 minutes, taking away their absolute rawness. If the sticks are particularly thick, this may well take up to 10 minutes. It is important not to overcook, so test by gently prodding the rhubarb, which should respond with a slight give. Some of the sugar will now have dissolved through the sticks, possibly creating a syrup. Remove the tray from the oven, transferring the sticks to a separate plate and leaving to cool. Any juices

can be kept to cook with the pulp trimmings.

To make the almond paste, cream together the butter and sugar, adding the ground almonds and flour (this can be done in a food processor). Now beat the egg into the mix. If the paste is very soft, refrigerate to cool and firm.

Spread the almond paste on the pastry strip, leaving a 1½cm (⅝in) border all round. Now place the rhubarb sticks lengthwise on top in rows of five. Roll the remaining two-thirds of the pastry into a 32 × 14–15cm (13 × 5½–6in) rectangle, allowing extra width to cover the filling. Fold the strip in half from the long side. At the fold, using scissors or a sharp knife, cut strips approximately 1cm (½in) apart, leaving a 2cm (¾in) border at either end and on the opposite side of the pastry. Brush the egg wash around the almond paste and rhubarb filling on the pastry base. Carefully place the folded pastry piece along one side of the base before opening it out across the rhubarb and sealing around the edges. Now trim the rectangle to a neat straight-edge finish, leaving as large a border as possible. The edges can now be decorated by marking with a fork, or left plain. Brush the jalousie with egg wash and refrigerate to rest for 20 minutes.

Increase the oven temperature to 220°C/425°F/Gas 7. Before baking, brush the jalousie again with the egg wash and sprinkle a teaspoon of water onto each side of the baking tray to create a steam that will help the pastry rise. Bake for 40–45 minutes. During this time the puff pastry will become well risen, very crispy and cooked through, leaving a light pastry edge to surround the soft moist centre.

To finish with a glossy glaze, dust the cooked jalousie liberally with icing sugar and place under a preheated grill – keep a watchful eye at this stage, as the sugar caramelizes very quickly. This stage can be repeated once or twice more for an even crisper golden glaze finish. The dessert is now best left to cool until warm as, if piping hot, the fruit and almond paste will have had no time to relax and change texture.

While the jalousie is cooking, melt a small knob of butter in a saucepan. Once bubbling, add the smaller rhubarb pieces along with the remaining caster sugar and any rhubarb juices. It's also best to add 3 tablespoons of cold water to help create a soft finished consistency. Cook on a low heat, allowing the rhubarb to soften and break down to a pulp. This will usually take just 8–10 minutes. Offer the pulp with the jalousie either hot, warm or cold along with whipped or pouring cream.

softened rhubarb with orange mascarpone cream

The simmered, sweetened and cooked rhubarb pieces, almost softening to a pulp, are finished with an orange sabayon, enriched with mascarpone cheese and whipped cream. It's a sort of cold variation of rhubarb and custard, with a few touches here and there. Orange and rhubarb are a lovely combination and, if Grand Marnier is available, the two are lifted even higher.

SERVES 4–6
350g (12oz) rhubarb, cut into 1½cm (¾in) pieces
2 tablespoons caster sugar

FOR THE MASCARPONE CREAM
3 egg yolks
75g (3oz) caster sugar
5 tablespoons orange juice
1 heaped tablespoon orange marmalade
175g (6oz) mascarpone cheese
3 tablespoons Grand Marnier (optional)
150ml (¼ pint) double or whipping cream

Place the rhubarb and sugar in a large saucepan with 3 tablespoons of water. Cook on a low heat, allowing to simmer gently for 6–8 minutes until tender, and approaching a pulp. The maximum cooking time is usually about 10 minutes. If the rhubarb is too syrupy once cooked, drain in a sieve and reboil the juices until reduced in volume and thickened. The syrup juices can now be mixed with the fruits again. Leave to cool. Once cooled the softened rhubarb can be spooned into glasses (cocktail glasses are very attractive for this dessert).

To make the mascarpone cream, place the egg yolks, sugar and 3 tablespoons of the orange juice in a bowl. Sit this over a pan of simmering water and whisk vigorously (an electric hand whisk will make life a lot easier) until at least double in volume, the whisk leaving a ribboned trail across the sabayon's surface. Remove from the heat and continuously whisk until cold (an electric mixing bowl and whisk attachment can help here).

Warm the remaining 2 tablespoons of orange juice with the marmalade, then strain through a sieve or tea strainer. A microwave oven will obviously warm the two together very quickly. If a fine-cut or smooth marmalade has been used, it needn't be strained.

Beat the mascarpone until smooth, mixing in the softened marmalade and Grand Marnier, if using. This can now be folded into the cold egg sabayon. Whip the cream until thickened but not firm (more of a soft peak stage). Fold into the mascarpone and sabayon mix, and spoon on top of the softened rhubarb.

The dessert can be served immediately or chilled for several hours. If chilled, the consistency of the cream changes, producing a more dense finish, which is equally good to eat.

Small almond or pistachio Tuile biscuits *(page 429), 2–3 per portion, will eat very well, offering another texture and flavour to the dish.*

pineapple carpaccio with rum and raisin syrup and lemon sour cream

Pineapples in early spring are particularly good, with those from Madagascar beginning their season in February, leading through to September. Most others are available throughout the year, reaching a richer and fruitier prime throughout winter and early spring.

Carpaccio has been adopted into our culinary glossary, the original beef classic having lent its title to numerous versions using other ingredients. Beef carpaccio is quite a young dish, which first found its way onto a plate at Harry's Bar in Venice. The dish was named after the Venetian Renaissance painter, Vittore Carpaccio, known for his amazing use of reds and whites on canvas. Hence, it comprises raw red beef with a mayonnaise and Worcestershire sauce-style dressing strewn from side to side on top. Here, I've changed this great artist's colour scheme, opting for bright yellow finished with a mixture of white and deep brown rum and raisin syrup.

This dessert needs very little work, offering a visually impressive, as well as flavoursome, finish.

SERVES 4
1 medium pineapple
caster or icing sugar, for dusting (optional)
3 tablespoons soured cream
squeeze of lemon juice

FOR THE RUM AND RAISIN SYRUP
75g (3oz) caster sugar
2 tablespoons dark rum
75g (3oz) raisins

Top and tail the pineapple, before cutting away the skin, maintaining the round shape of the fruit. The fruit can now be sliced thinly into 2–3mm (about ⅛in) rounds. This is very easily achieved on an electric slicer, but if a slicer is not available a long, sharp knife will do the trick. This preparation can be done well in advance, refrigerating the slices until needed. To create a good, slightly overlapping circle or square on a plate, 7–9 thin slices will be needed per portion.

The central core of the pineapple is to be left in; when sliced so thin, this is very tender to eat, offering a slight contrast in texture.

To make the syrup, measure out 150ml (¼ pint) of water. Place the sugar and 2 tablespoons of the water in a large shallow pan over a gentle heat. As the water warms the sugar will dissolve. Stir once or twice until it becomes a clear syrup. At this point, raise the temperature, cooking to a light caramel colour, before removing the pan from the heat. Allow to cool for a few minutes before carefully adding the remaining water and the rum, as the caramel will begin to spit. Add the raisins before liquidizing to a smooth purée. Strain through a fine sieve and the rum and raisin syrup is ready. If too thin once cooled, reboil and allow to reduce to a thicker consistency.

The soured cream can now be mixed with the lemon juice, adding a sprinkling of icing sugar for a slightly sweeter finish if preferred.

To decorate the pineapple to best effect, put the syrup and soured cream in small squeezy bottles or simply use teaspoons.

To finish, place the pineapple slices slightly overlapping in a circle or square onto a plate. The syrup and sour cream can now be drizzled in a rustic style over the top, leaving the dessert ready to serve. *Chantilly cream* (page 427) can be offered with this dessert.

The soured cream can be mixed in equal quantities with natural yoghurt for a lighter finish.

black grape beaujolais jelly

Throughout the year we have black grapes, but there are many, in particular the Australian and South African varieties, which have definite seasons, this month included.

Beaujolais tends to have a young fruity flavour that blends with the grape very well, offering an extra red-fruit edge. With the finished jelly, I am also serving peeled black grape halves, steeped with icing sugar and vanilla seeds. This little salad is not essential, purely optional, but it does present a new bite to the dish. Thick fresh cream helps the jelly along or perhaps *Chantilly cream* (page 427).

SERVES 6
FOR THE JELLY
450g (1lb) black grapes, picked and quartered
450ml (¾ pint) Beaujolais
150ml (¼ pint) fresh orange juice
225g (8oz) caster sugar
6 leaves of gelatine, soaked in cold water

FOR THE GRAPES (OPTIONAL)
6–8 grapes per portion, picked and halved (removing seeds if necessary)
1–2 tablespoons icing sugar
1 vanilla pod, split and scraped of seeds
few mint leaves, finely shredded (optional)

Put the grapes, wine, orange juice and caster sugar in a saucepan and bring to the boil. Once at this point reduce the heat to a very gentle simmer, stirring and cooking for 15 minutes. Remove the pan from the heat and leave to stand for a further 15 minutes before draining through a muslin cloth into a clean pan. The grapes can be gently squeezed, releasing any remaining juices, but if they are over-squeezed, the liquor will become cloudy.

Squeeze excess water from the gelatine leaves and stir them into the grape liquor. This should still be warm enough to melt the leaves. If not, then simply return to the heat for a minute or two.

The sweet grape wine jelly can now be poured into individual glasses or a suitable glass bowl, refrigerating for several hours, or overnight to set.

If serving with the grapes, simply mix the prepared fruits in a bowl with 1 tablespoon of icing sugar and the vanilla. These can now be kept refrigerated; they will create their own syrup and sweet flavour. For an even sweeter finish, add another tablespoon of icing sugar.

To serve, if presented in individual glasses, spoon the grapes and juices on top. If in a large bowl, spoon the jelly onto plates, decorating with a pile of the salad grapes, sprinkling with the shredded mint leaves, if using.

This jelly is quite soft in texture, not firm enough to turn out of the dishes or moulds. If a firmer finish is preferred, an extra 2 or 3 gelatine leaves will need to be added.

OPPOSITE: BLACK GRAPE BEAUJOLAIS JELLY

vegetables

Warm leeks with vegetable vinaigrette 47

St George's mushrooms with garlic, lemon and parsley 47

Celeriac and Parma ham on toast 48

Watercress and spinach pesto salad or sauté 50

Morel mushroom and wild garlic omelette 51

fish

Warm spider crab linguine with orange and tarragon sauce 53

Red mullet with a rosemary cream sauce on broken new
potatoes 54

Flounder fillets with boiled chips and sorrel mayonnaise 55

Pan-fried turbot with nutty Béarnaise sprouting broccoli 56

Wild salmon slices with sorrel crème fraîche 57

Potted crab 59

meat

Roast lemon peppered lamb with baked potato cake 61

Grilled lamb chops with mint-rolled Jerseys and
apricot onions 62

Grilled beef fillet with baby turnips, marinated mushrooms
and a beetroot dressing 63

Braised beef brisket with tarragon carrots and cauliflower
champ 64

Beef steak pie plate with a casserole of oysters and
white mushrooms 66

Sautéed chicken steeped in vinaigrette with St George's
mushrooms 68

Duck boulangère with hazelnut-rosemary spinach 69

fruit and puddings

Cocoa sorbet with orange biscuits 71

Banana white chocolate marquise with strawberries 71

Toasted honey bananas with fresh goat's cheese 72

Soft chocolate pudding 72

Open rhubarb pie 73

Oeufs à la neige on baked rhubarb with brioche and
custard 75

warm leeks with vegetable vinaigrette

Leeks are often called 'poor man's asparagus' just as marsh samphire often is. For me, though, the leek stands alone, quite proud, with its texture and flavour (and price) lending itself to many dishes.

Here leeks are served as a simple starter or side dish. They are generally with us from the autumn to mid-to-late spring. Although they are coming to the end of their season, don't ignore them at this time, as spring leeks tend not to carry the sometimes woody centres found in summer ones. For this recipe it's best to choose thinnish leeks as these offer a softer and more gentle finish to the dish. It's best to cook the leeks until almost overdone. If too *al dente*, the leek will have a leathery texture and over-peppery flavour.

A little more extravagant, but adding such flavour, the variation recipe offered here, with morel mushrooms and Parmesan shavings, is a quite outstanding combination to accompany leeks. The morels join us between the months of March and April – perfect timing for this recipe.

SERVES 4 AS A STARTER OR ACCOMPANIMENT
8–10 young leeks
salt and twist of pepper
8 tablespoons *Vegetable vinaigrette* (page 420)

FOR THE VARIATION WITH MORELS AND PARMESAN
175–225g (6–8oz) fresh morel mushrooms
8–10 tablespoons *Vegetable vinaigrette* (page 420), featuring extra diced fennel only, or *Sweet port red wine dressing* (page 420)
1 heaped tablespoon chopped mixed herbs (such as chervil, parsley, tarragon, etc.)
1–2 knobs of butter
leeks, prepared and cooked as below
Parmesan cheese shavings, made using a vegetable peeler

Trim away the tough dark green tops of the leeks. Split the leeks lengthwise and wash and rinse thoroughly, removing the outside layer if it feels too tough. Cook in boiling salted water, uncovered, for 6–7 minutes, then check for tenderness. If too firm, continue to boil for a further 3–4 minutes. Remove the leeks from the pan directly onto a kitchen cloth to collect excess water. Season with salt and pepper and arrange on plates, then spoon over the vinaigrette.

Fresh herbs can be added to the dressing, along with quartered black olives.
Mascarpone cheese can be added to this recipe: its soft creamy texture melts across the warmed leeks.

For the variation prepare the morels as described on page 20. Mix the vinaigrette or dressing with the chopped herbs and set aside.

Melt a knob of the butter in a frying pan. Once bubbling well, add the mushrooms and fry for a minute or two until tender. Season with salt and pepper. Remove from the heat and add a touch more butter to emulsify all the flavours in the pan.

Spoon and scatter the morels over and around the cooked plated leeks. Parmesan shavings can now be strewn across the dish, before finishing with the butter and dressing.

St George's mushrooms with garlic, lemon and parsley

Garlic mushrooms, finished with chopped parsley and a squeeze of lemon juice, are better known in France as *champignons à la Bordelaise*. I absolutely love to eat them – and lots too – just sitting in a bowl with good crusty bread to mop up the juices. This particular recipe you'll only be able to make from 23 April (St George's Day, hence the mushrooms' name) through to June. However, don't forget there are so many other tasty mushrooms, cultivated and wild, available throughout the year – chestnut mushrooms, for instance, are not so distinctive, but can be used as an alternative.

SERVES 4 AS A STARTER OR ACCOMPANIMENT
675g (1½lb) St George's mushrooms, preferably small
2 tablespoons olive oil
2 garlic cloves, thinly sliced or finely crushed (more can be added for a stronger garlic finish)
juice of ½ small lemon
large knob of butter
salt and pepper (coarse sea salt can also be used)
1 tablespoon chopped curly or torn flatleaf parsley

Trim the stalks from the mushrooms and rinse them quickly under running water. They are best washed well in advance

OPPOSITE: WARM LEEKS WITH VEGETABLE VINAIGRETTE

and then placed on several layers of kitchen paper to drain. The dryer the mushrooms, the better the finished flavour will be, as they will fry and not stew in the pan.

Heat the olive oil in a large frying pan or wok. Add the mushrooms. (They may have to be cooked in two pans or two batches, as too large a quantity will cool the pan, causing stewing rather than frying.)

Fry the mushrooms, not turning them too often as this tends to cool the pan, for a few minutes until well coloured and tender. Add the garlic and continue to fry for a further minute. Add the lemon juice, stirring it quickly in amongst the mushrooms. Add the butter, season with salt and pepper, and finish with the chopped parsley before serving.

The garlic mushrooms will also eat well on thick slices of buttered toast. An attractive finish is to flavour the mushrooms with a splash of sherry and finish with cream. To do so, once the garlic has been added also add 2–3 tablespoons of medium sherry. Simmer for a few minutes, then add 100–150ml (3½fl oz–¼ pint) double cream. This will begin to thicken very quickly. Stir and season, before finishing with the lemon juice and chopped parsley.

celeriac and parma ham on toast

Here we are in mid-spring with all kinds of new flavours joining us, and 'old' is celeriac being featured – and why not? Once its initial month passes – with celeriac that's September, with the season sometimes leading on to May – full advantage of this ingredient should be taken and it should not forgotten. This is very much an Italian-style dish, often bound in quite a thick sauce strewn across crusty toasts.

Celeriac is not the most attractive of root vegetables, having a knobbly, patchy brown skin that does have a habit of collecting mud in every crevice. Placing all of its negatives to one side, however, there are plenty of positives to be found once it is peeled. A sort of magnolia interior is found, which comfortably suits so many styles of eating and cooking. Celeriac is delicious grated raw, bound with a dressing, or in its most famous of raw roles, *à la rémoulade*. Try *Kohlrabi rémoulade with warm salmon fillets* (page 321), simply replacing the kohlrabi with celeriac. It is perfect as an hors d'oeuvre, offering its services to many a fish, meat or vegetarian alternative.

In this recipe the celeriac is par-boiled and sautéed in

butter, mixing with the Parma ham and a spoonful or two of crème fraîche. Walnut dressing is also included as an option. The nutty flavour lends itself so well to the equally nutty bite celeriac oozes once pan-fried.

Chervil also hits the seasonal scene in April, home-grown lasting until October. An extra tang that can be added to this plate is crumbled goat's cheese, with so many different strengths to choose from.

SERVES 4 AS A STARTER
**2 small–medium celeriacs, approx 350g (12oz) each
salt and pepper
4 slices of Parma ham (6–8 for Parma enthusiasts)
2 tablespoons olive oil
knob of butter, plus more for spreading
3–4 tablespoons crème fraîche
4 thick slices of granary bread**

FOR THE WALNUT DRESSING (OPTIONAL)
**3 tablespoons walnut oil
1 teaspoon Dijon mustard
1 teaspoon white wine vinegar or lemon juice
½ teaspoon caster sugar
1 garlic clove, finely crushed
1 heaped teaspoon picked chervil leaves**

Cut away the top and bottom of the celeriacs. Trim away the remaining skin, before cutting the flesh into 1cm (½in) rough dice. Place the pieces in a saucepan, covering with water and adding a pinch of salt. Bring to a simmer, cooking for 2–3 minutes, before draining in a sieve.

Cut the Parma ham across into 1cm (½in) thick strips. Heat the olive oil in a wok or frying pan. Once hot, add the Parma strips. These will fry reasonably quickly, becoming golden brown and crispy. Remove the Parma from the pan with a slotted spoon, placing them on kitchen paper to dry. The remaining olive oil in the pan will now have taken on a Parma flavour.

Add the celeriac to the pan with a knob of butter. Fry over a moderate heat, for 5–6 minutes – the celeriac will take on a golden brown edge while becoming tender. Season with salt and pepper.

While the celeriac is cooking, the dressing can be made, if using: place all of the ingredients into a small screw-top jar and shake, or whisk all together in a bowl. Spread the granary bread slices on both sides with butter, placing them

OPPOSITE: CELERIAC AND PARMA HAM ON TOAST

under a preheated grill and toasting to a golden brown on each side.

Add the Parma ham to the celeriac, also spooning in the crème fraîche – 4 tablespoons will give a creamier finish. Present the toasts on plates, topped with the celeriac and Parma ham. Drizzle over and around with the walnut dressing, if using.

Prepared raw celeriac, unless used immediately, will slightly discolour. To prevent this, place the vegetable pieces in water acidulated with a squeeze of lemon juice.

watercress and spinach pesto salad or sauté

The 'sauté' and 'salad' are cooking and preparation methods each having their own identity, but sharing the same concept. Basically, here are two dishes within one recipe.

The pesto is not added as a pre-made sauce, instead I simply use pesto ingredients to flavour the spinach and watercress: olive oil, a hint of garlic, toasted pine nuts, Parmesan and a few leaves of basil all find their way into this dish.

The quantities for each version, in terms of spinach and watercress, are quite different. The ones listed below are for the sautéed version, which needs much more because the greens break down and reduce in volume once cooked. For a salad version, literally a good couple of handfuls of spinach and one large bunch of watercress will be plenty, acting as a starter or side salad. The pesto flavours stay the same, finishing the salad with a squeeze of lime, for extra bite.

As a cooked vegetable, this dish can eat well as a starter served with a poached egg. It also lends its services very comfortably to a grilled chicken breast, lamb or pork chops, or steak, as well as many a fillet of fish.

From a seasonal point of view, fresh spinach is entering its last month of home-grown glasshouse production, mingling with the initial 30 days of young outdoor spinach. Watercress tends to be found and produced all year round, classically holding a March to November official season. Not forgetting basil, always available on the shelves, from our own soils usually between May and September, with many a young leaf appearing right now.

350g (12oz) young spinach (for salad quantity, see above)
2 bunches of watercress (for salad quantity, see above)
2 garlic cloves
2 tablespoons olive oil
knob of butter
salt and pepper
2 heaped tablespoons pine nuts
1–2 tablespoons freshly grated Parmesan cheese
8 basil leaves, torn into smaller pieces

Wash the young spinach leaves, removing any excess stalks. If only coarser leaves are to be found, each can be torn into small pieces. The watercress should also be rinsed, trimming away excessive stalks, leaving a fair quantity of stalk still attached to leaves. These are not tough, but very nutritious and flavoursome.

Place the garlic cloves in a small saucepan and cover with water. Bring to a simmer, before draining and refreshing under cold water. Repeat this process twice more, simmering for a couple of minutes on the third blanching process. This releases the rawness of the garlic, removing the pungent bite, and at the same time leaving it tender. The cloves can now be cut into very thin slices, or roughly chopped ready to add to the sautéed vegetables.

The pine nuts can be left whole or halved, before toasting or dry-frying to a golden brown, adding a roasted bite.

If choosing the sauté option, heat a wok or large frying pan with 1 tablespoon of the olive oil. Once hot, add both the spinach and watercress, along with the knob of butter. Cook on a medium–high heat, stirring for even cooking. Season with salt and pepper, adding the sliced garlic and pine nuts. Cook for just 1–2 minutes until softened. Tougher spinach may need an extra minute. The first tablespoon of grated Parmesan can now be added, sprinkling with the second if a cheesier finish is preferred. The dish is now ready to serve, sprinkling with the torn basil leaves and drizzling with the last spoonful of olive oil.

If choosing the raw salad option, all of the ingredients can be tossed lightly in a large bowl, adding a squeeze of lime juice to finish.

morel mushroom and
wild garlic omelette

Two of the ingredients featured here are not the easiest to find, although the wild garlic can be picked in abundance while on a spring walk in Britain's damp woods and lanes. Two small or one large leaf per omelette should be enough. True garlic lovers will get to know their depth and can add as they wish. The youngest of leaves will be at their best between the months of March and April, which leads us on to the morel mushrooms with their season occupying the same two months and more. Here I'm offering a recipe for two 3-large-egg omelettes to be cooked in a 15–18cm (6–7in) omelette pan. The morels create their own stock and sauce to spoon over the wild soft eggy 'soufflé' beneath.

SERVES 2

50–75g (2–3oz) fresh morel mushrooms
4 tablespoons dry vermouth or white wine (optional)
2–3 tablespoons single cream
25g (1oz) butter, plus 2 knobs to cook the omelettes
salt and pepper
squeeze of lemon juice
trickle of olive oil
few wild garlic leaves
6 large eggs

Prepare the morel mushrooms as described on page 20 and split them in half lengthwise, saving the stalk bases for the sauce stock. Once the mushrooms have been brushed and washed, dry on a cloth or kitchen paper. To make the sauce, take a few of the mushrooms, maybe one or two that are not so perfect, and chop finely. Place these in a small pan with the saved stalk bases. Top with the vermouth or white wine, if using, boiling and reducing in volume by three-quarters. Now pour in 8 tablespoons of water (beginning at this stage if no alcohol is to be used) and bring to a soft simmer. This will infuse the morel flavour into the loose 'stock'. Cook for a few minutes until reduced in volume by half. Now add the single cream and, once simmering, stir in the butter. Check for seasoning with salt, pepper and a squeeze of lemon juice if needed to sharpen the finish. Now strain through a tea strainer into a clean pan.

The remaining morels can now be pan-fried in the olive oil for a minute or two until tender. Once cooked, drain and dry on kitchen paper before adding them to the sauce. This stage should obviously be carried out before starting the omelette. The wild garlic leaves can now be finely chopped or shredded.

Crack three of the eggs into a bowl and beat with a fork to combine the white and yolk. Add a twist of pepper, adding salt just before pouring the mix into the pan. Salt added too early will break down the consistency of the eggs, also discolouring them to a deeper orange-yellow.

Melt a knob of butter in the omelette pan over a medium heat. Once the butter begins to bubble, but not brown, pour in the egg, sprinkling with half of the shredded garlic leaves. The pan can now be gently shaken over the heat, using a spatula or fork to keep the eggs on the move. This will prevent the base from becoming over-set and golden. For me, a perfect omelette is when the eggs are only just set, maintaining the gentlest of finishes. A golden-brown version will leave you with a tough, almost leathery, dry outside.

Once beginning to set but still moist on top, the omelette can be folded or left flat, the advantage of a folded omelette being that the soft, scrambled-egg-like centre retains its warmth and moistness.

To fold, hold the pan at a slight angle and tap it so the omelette slides towards the front of the pan. Fold a third of the egg over towards the handle, folding the other third away. Turn the omelette onto a plate, repeating the process to make the other omelette.

The oval shape can be made neater by covering with kitchen paper and shaping by hand.

Once both omelettes are made, reheat the morel sauce and spoon over.

If making a simpler, flat omelette, omitting the sauce, the morels can be quickly sautéed in the knob of butter, leaving them in the pan while pouring in the eggs and sprinkling with the wild garlic. Continue to stir until set before sliding onto a plate.

warm spider crab linguine with orange and tarragon sauce

Mid-to-late spring, and the spider crab becomes available. Sadly this wonderfully sweet and tender shellfish is not so commonly found and available as the brown crab. It would seem most of this almost spider-shaped culinary treat is exported to Europe, to be enjoyed in France and Spain.

Cooking and picking the meat from crabs does seem to become laborious, the spider crab probably the most fiddly, and perhaps this is why we send them on to our European friends. Whatever the case, should you manage to stumble upon these richly flavoured creatures, treat yourself and cook and clean them, even if just to add them to a salad. You won't be disappointed.

This recipe makes starter portions, the crab and pasta served back in the shell topped with a home-made bisque-like cream sauce. For a light finish, the sauce is blitzed with an electric hand blender, leaving you with a frothy foam to spoon over the crabs, hiding a very tasty surprise underneath. The crabs for this recipe are best between 675 and 1kg (1½ and 2¼lb) each. The larger ones probably provide enough for main courses, the smaller ones suiting generous starter/supper portions. The crabs can be cooked in salted water or court-bouillon (the latter will obviously lend more flavour to the crabs, enhancing their natural sweetness).

SERVES 4 AS A GENEROUS STARTER

3.5 litres /6 pints *Court-bouillon* (page 417, optional)
salt and pepper
4 × 675g–1kg (1½–2¼lb) spider crabs
knob of butter
225g (8oz) cooked linguine pasta or noodles
**1 large orange, segmented and each segment cut into
   3–4 pieces**
1 heaped teaspoon chopped tarragon

FOR THE SAUCE

1 tablespoon olive oil
1 small fennel, cut into roughly 5mm (¼in) dice
1 small carrot, cut into roughly 5mm (¼in) dice
1 small onion, cut into roughly 5mm (¼in) dice
1 garlic clove, crushed

OPPOSITE: WARM SPIDER CRAB LINGUINE WITH ORANGE AND TARRAGON SAUCE

**350g (12oz) crab claw and leg shells from the spider
   crabs, finely chopped**
juice of 2 oranges and 3 strips of peel
4 tomatoes, roughly chopped
2 sprigs of tarragon
glass of white wine
pinch of saffron (optional)
**300ml (½ pint) water or fish-flavoured *Instant stock*
   (page 416)**
2–3 tablespoons whipping cream
squeeze of lemon juice
25g (1oz) butter

Bring to the boil the court-bouillon, if using, or 3.5 litres (6 pints) of water with 2 heaped tablespoons of salt. Place the crabs in the pot, making sure they are well covered. Bring back to the boil, lower the temperature slightly and simmer for approximately 8, maximum 10, minutes. Remove the pot from the stove and allow the crabs to cool in the stock for a further 8, maximum 10, minutes. There is a particular flavoursome bonus if court-bouillon is used, as when the shellfish relaxes, the meat absorbs the rich fragrant spicy flavours. Once cooled, the crabs can be cracked from their shells.

First remove the claws and legs and break them open with a nutcracker or with a sharp tap from the back of a knife. Many small spider crabs will not have much, if any, meat in their thin legs. However, it's best to crack them open anyway, as you don't want to waste or lose any of the meat. Once all the claw and leg meat has been removed, the flesh can be torn into strands, checking carefully for any shell splinters. The next stage is to detach the body of the crab from the back shell. Once turned onto its back, the bony pointed flap can be pulled away. Insert a strong knife between the shell and body and twist firmly to release the meat. Any grey-looking gills, or dead man's fingers as they are also known, should be detached and discarded. Before spooning the brown meat from the shell remove the stomach sac (intestines) and discard. This can easily be achieved by applying pressure to the small piece of shell situated just behind the eyes. Press, discarding both the bone and intestines. Pour away any excess water from the shell. The brown meat can now be spooned from the central body, rinsing under cold water quickly on removal. This brown meat can be pushed through a sieve to help remove any crushed shell and provide a smoother finish. Keep it separate from the white meat.

The central body can now be quartered, carefully removing all of the white meat with a pick, skewer or cocktail stick. (This stage does take some patience, but it's worth every minute.) Each quarter can be halved to check for any extra strands of meat. Check the meat for any broken shell, before adding it to the white claw meat. The claws, legs and central body shell can be chopped and used to make the sauce. The round crab shells can now be well rinsed, ready to present the finished dish. The shell edge can be trimmed, if needed, with scissors to remove any thin 'beard'.

To make the sauce, warm the olive oil in a saucepan and add the chopped fennel, carrot and onion along with the crushed garlic. Cover with a lid and cook on a gentle heat for 8–10 minutes, stirring from time to time, until soft. Add the finely chopped crab claws and legs along with the orange peel and cook for a further 5 minutes. Add the chopped tomatoes and tarragon and, after a few more minutes, the white wine. Bring to the boil and reduce in volume by two-thirds. Add the orange juice, bring back to the boil again and reduce in volume by two-thirds. Add the saffron, if using, and then the water or fish-flavoured instant stock. Bring to a simmer and cook for 10 minutes. At this point, the sauce can be passed through a sieve or liquidized for a smoother result. For the smoothest of finishes, push through a fine sieve.

Add the whipping cream and return the sauce to a simmer. Season with salt and pepper and a squeeze of lemon juice, then stir in the 25g (1oz) of butter to finish. The sauce needs to be of a glossy loose consistency. If too thick, it will not blitz to a light frothy finish.

To finish the dish, warm the brown crab meat in 1–2 tablespoons of the cream sauce. Melt the knob of butter in a large pan. Add the cooked pasta or noodles and season with salt and pepper. Warm gently, adding the orange pieces, the chopped tarragon and the white crab meat, along with a few tablespoons of cream sauce. This will now loosen the pasta, warming the complete dish. Check the seasoning again.

Spoon the brown meat into the base of each washed shell. Divide the crab, orange and tarragon noodles between each shell, then blitz the finished sauce and liberally spoon over each. The finished shells are best presented on a folded napkin on a plate or in a soup plate, the cloth preventing the shell from sliding. The shells have a 'pillow' presentation of creamy sauce sitting on top of the creamy crab noodles.

A splash of brandy or Grand Marnier can be added to the finished sauce for an even livelier flavour.
It is not essential to blitz the sauce to a frothy consistency. Simply loosen the noodles with a few extra spoonfuls and this will provide equally good finished flavours.

red mullet with a rosemary cream sauce on broken new potatoes

The combination of the red mullet and rosemary was made famous by a Swiss chef – Frédy Girardet. During the 1980s this man was reputed to be the number-one chef in the world, and a true master he was too. The beauty of this concept lies in its simplicity, utilizing the maximum flavour from the fish itself, which is at its best in early spring and peaks again in August.

The potatoes are a nice added extra, just cooked, then lightly forked with the mildest of garlic hints coming through. Here the quantities are for a starter. For a main course, simply double everything.

SERVES 4 AS A STARTER
2 × 350–400g (12–14oz) red mullet, pin-boned (page 9), scaled and filleted, with all the trimmings saved
3 knobs of butter
2 shallots or ½ small onion, finely chopped
good sprig of rosemary, plus more sprigs to garnish
150ml (¼ pint) white wine
100ml (3½fl oz) whipping cream
salt and pepper
lemon juice, to taste
flour, for dusting
2 tablespoons olive oil

FOR THE POTATOES
275–350g (10–12oz) new potatoes, well scrubbed
2 garlic cloves
2–3 tablespoons olive oil
squeeze of lemon juice

If your fishmonger is filleting the red mullets for you, ask for the central pin bones of each fillet also to be removed. Melt a knob of butter in a saucepan, and add the shallots or onion. Cook for a few minutes, until softened. Chop the red mullet head, bones and trimmings and add along with the rosemary. Continue to cook, without allowing to colour, for a further few minutes.

Add the white wine and, once boiling, reduce in volume by three-quarters. Add 150ml (¼ pint) of water and bring back to a simmer. Cook for 10–15 minutes, then increase the heat and reduce in volume by half. Strain the fish stock through a sieve, squeezing all flavour and juices from the bones. Add the cream and return to a simmer, then cook for a few minutes until slightly thickened. Remove from the heat and season with salt, pepper and a squeeze of lemon juice to taste – just to lift the other flavours, not to overpower them and make it a lemon sauce. The sauce can now be rewarmed when needed, not allowing it to overthicken, and finished with a knob of butter.

To prepare the potatoes, cook them in boiling salted water with the addition of one garlic clove, split in two. This will only give a slight garlic perfume to the potatoes. Once cooked, drain and, if not well scrubbed, it's best to peel them. Cut each potato into quarters. Split the remaining garlic clove and rub it around the inside of a bowl, leaving the halves in it. Add the potatoes, olive oil and a good squeeze of lemon juice, then season with salt and pepper. The potatoes can be left at this stage; simply toss all the flavours together and keep warm until needed.

To cook the fish, lightly season the mullet fillets with salt and lightly flour the skin sides. Warm the olive oil in a frying pan over a medium heat. Once hot, place the fish in the pan, skin-side down, and fry for 4 minutes, seasoning with salt and pepper. Turn the fillets in the pan, add a knob of butter to melt it and then remove from the heat. The residual pan-heat will finish the cooking without toughening the flesh, relaxing and softening it instead.

While the mullets are cooking and resting, the sauce can be warmed and the potatoes finished. Remove the two garlic halves from the bowl of potatoes and break down the potatoes with a fork. These can be as crumbly or smooth as you wish. However, with many new potato varieties, trying to oversmooth will create too much stickiness. The potatoes can now be either laid under the fish fillets or shaped/spooned at the top of the plates. Arrange the mullet fillets on the plates and pour the sauce around. Garnish each with a sprig of rosemary.

If serving as a main course, the best accompaniment is fresh peas or a green salad.

flounder fillets with boiled chips and sorrel mayonnaise

Flounder is a small flat fish similar in shape and look to plaice, dab and even lemon sole. Most fish is best when absolutely fresh but sadly this particular fish really suffers if it is not. Flounder is around to use during this time and marries well with the sorrel, which is plentiful in late spring through to summer. If flounder is unavailable, any of the similar fish mentioned can be used to replace it in this recipe.

The 'boiled chips' in the title is purely a description of the blanching method used before frying, to crisp and finish them. Classically, chips have always been pre-blanched in a lower-temperature fat, gently frying until tender before cooking, and then finished in hotter fat when required. The method does work well, but quite often the potato is greasy. Introducing the boiled method counters this problem, and instead the chips become tender and are ready to fry, with a clean, crisper finish.

Mayonnaise and chips are everyone's favourites. The addition of fresh lemony sorrel offers an extra complement to the fish itself. Making the mayonnaise with equal parts of vegetable and olive oil reduces the sometimes over-powerful olive flavour, which with this particular recipe would tend to mask the fresh sorrel. Individual fillets of flounder will generally weigh 50–75g (2–3oz), so it is best to serve three fillets per portion, meaning you need three flounders for four portions.

SERVES 4 AS A MAIN COURSE

12 × 50–75g (2–3oz) flounder fillets, skinned
salt and pepper
flour, for dusting
2–3 tablespoons olive oil
large knob of butter
½ quantity *Mayonnaise* (page 419, made with half
   vegetable oil and half olive oil)
1 heaped tablespoon chopped sorrel leaves
squeeze of lemon juice (optional)

FOR THE CHIPS

4–6 large floury potatoes, preferably Maris Piper,
   King Edward or Desirée, peeled
cooking oil, for deep-frying (vegetable, groundnut or
   olive for luxury chips)

To prepare the chips, trim the potatoes to a rectangular shape. Cut these into 1cm (½in) thick long slices, then cut each slice into sticks the same width. Blanch in boiling salted water for 4–6 minutes or until just tender. Carefully drain and leave to cool naturally, laid on a kitchen cloth. This will absorb any excess water, with the steam also removing any unwanted moisture as it rises.

Heat the oil to 180°C/350°F. While cooking the fish (see below), finish the boiled chips in the hot fat for just a few minutes, until golden brown and crispy. Shake off any excess fat and sprinkle with salt before serving.

Season the flounder fillets with salt and pepper and dust with flour. Heat a tablespoon or two of olive oil in a frying pan and, once hot, fry the fillets for 1–1½ minutes on each side until golden brown. Just before removing from the pan, add a little of the butter to finish. Remove the fish and keep warm while repeating the same process with the remaining fillets.

To finish the mayonnaise, add the chopped sorrel, along with a squeeze of lemon juice to enhance further if needed.

Present the flounder fillets on plates, drizzling with a little of their cooking oil and butter, together with the chips and sorrel mayonnaise.

Lemon or lime wedges can also be offered or presented on the plate.
It is not essential to add sorrel to the mayonnaise; it will also work very well plain.

pan-fried turbot with nutty béarnaise sprouting broccoli

Turbot begins its British season in April, going through to February. This flat fish carries the reputation of being the king of all fish. Its own distinctive flavour needs little help; just drizzling it with butter and a sprinkling of salt can be more than enough. In France the fish was traditionally cooked in a *turbotière*, a large diamond-shaped piece of equipment, used to steam or poach the fish. The simple accompaniment would be a sauce hollandaise. I'm not moving too far from this elegant simplicity; a green vegetable with the buttered fish creates an instant friendship. With purple sprouting broccoli really flourishing at this time of the year, the combination of the two seemed more than logical.

The *Nutty Béarnaise sauce* (page 418) holds flavours with which both are familiar. The turbot has always enjoyed a sauce in the style of a hollandaise, and the nutbrown butter flavour of this particular variety is one that this fish (and many others) is often paired with when shallow-fried.

The concept of this dish will work with almost all flat white fish (lemon sole, plaice, halibut, flounder, etc.), as well as with cod, salmon and skate. It's also not essential to serve the nutbrown variety of the sauce; a plain *Béarnaise* (page 418) or *Simple hollandaise sauce* (page 418) works well, or even just melted butter.

SERVES 4 AS A MAIN COURSE
1 quantity *Nutty Béarnaise* sauce (page 418)
450–675g (1lb–1½lb) purple sprouting broccoli spears
iced water (optional)
4 × 175–225 (6–8oz) portions of turbot fillet, skinned
flour, for dusting
1 tablespoon olive oil
salt and pepper, plus coarse sea salt
knob of butter
1 teaspoon chopped flatleaf parsley
1 lemon, quartered

Make the nutty Béarnaise sauce in advance, as instructed in the recipe, adding the chopped tarragon and the parsley just before serving.

To prepare the broccoli, cut the large spears from the tops and continue to cut away the smaller surrounding spears, leaving any small tender leaves attached. If the spears are young and tender, their stalks need not be peeled (this is best tested by taking a raw bite; if crisp and tender, then simply leave). If slightly chewy, it is best to peel away the outer skin by hand or with a peeler. The broccoli will now just take a few minutes to cook in rapidly boiling salted water, and will change in colour from purple to two-tone (purple top and green spear), finishing with rich green spears. If cooking the broccoli in advance, once tender quickly plunge into iced water, then drain and refrigerate until needed. To reheat, either microwave or plunge into boiling water for just a minute or two.

Lightly dust the skinned sides of the fish with flour. Heat the olive oil in a frying pan. Once hot, place the fillets in, floured-sides down, and season the exposed sides with salt and pepper. Fry the fish over a moderate heat for 5–6 minutes until a light golden brown. Add the knob of butter, then turn the fish over in the pan and remove from the heat. The fish will now finish cooking, needing just another minute or two in the pan, without becoming overcooked or leathery. Sprinkle each fillet with a little coarse sea salt.

Meanwhile, the warmed broccoli spears can be presented on plates and topped with the finished nutbrown Béarnaise sauce.

Arrange the turbot next to the broccoli, spooning a little of the cooking butter over each and garnishing with the parsley and lemon quarters.

wild salmon slices with sorrel crème fraîche

This combination of flavours, salmon and sorrel, was brought to us in the late 1970s by the Troisgros brothers, based at 'Les Frères Troisgros' restaurant in Roanne, France. The three Michelin-starred chefs produced a simple dish of gently pan-fried, thinly sliced salmon sitting on a herbed sorrel cream sauce, and a new classic was born. The beauty of this dish is that it will see you through the spring and summer months as both ingredients are readily available.

Wild salmon is with us from early spring to late summer and early autumn. It is during the summer months of June and July that you'll find it in more abundance, at a better price, but to get the first in spring is a real treat. If you find the wild salmon hard to come by, then simply replace it with farmed salmon, a product improving with every 'season'.

Young sorrel leaves are at their best from early March, the herb itself carrying a natural lemon flavour which can be helped along with a squeeze of the fruit itself. Instead of frying this fish, the thin slices will be plated cold, ready to be lightly oiled or buttered and then quickly warmed under a hot grill. As the top warms, it cooks but leaves a moist medium-rare finish underneath. The plates can be dressed with the fish well in advance, ready to finish when needed.

It is often best to purchase the whole salmon and enjoy its flavour in many different recipes over a two- or three-day period. This will also provide you with the salmon carcass from which to make your stock. The tail pieces can then be sliced for this particular dish, leaving the prime fillet for main-course portions.

SERVES 4 AS A STARTER
450g (1lb) wild salmon fillet, pin-boned (page 9)
knob of butter
1 dessertspoon groundnut oil
coarse sea salt
twist of black pepper

FOR THE SAUCE
100ml (3½fl oz) dry vermouth
150ml (¼ pint) *Salmon stock* (page 417) or *Fish stock* (page 417)
2 tablespoons double cream
100ml (3½fl oz) crème fraîche
25g (1oz) sorrel leaves
salt and pepper
25–50g (1–2oz) butter, diced (optional)
squeeze of lemon juice

Slice the salmon thinly, approximately 3–4mm (⅛–⅙in) thick. Place an open 15–18cm (6–7in) flan ring on the centre of each heatproof serving plate and carefully arrange the fillet slices to cover the space, creating a circle inside the rings. Remove the rings, cover the fish lightly with cling film and refrigerate until needed.

To make the sauce, boil together the vermouth and stock until reduced in volume by half to two-thirds. Add the cream and return to a simmer. Add the crème fraîche and whisk to emulsify with the stock. The sauce can be left at this stage until needed. It will be reasonably loose, not over-creamy and coating, resulting in a lighter finish.

Preheat the oven and grill. Gently wash and pick the stalks from the sorrel leaves. Shred these, just before serving.

Melt the knob of butter in a frying pan with the groundnut oil. Remove the cling film from the fish plates and brush each portion with the buttery oil. The plates can now be placed in turn under the preheated grill for just a minute or two to warm the tops of the slices. To continue this process, place the warmed plates on a lower shelf of the oven to retain the heat. While warming the wild salmon, reheat the sauce, season with salt and pepper and whisk in the butter, if using. Just 30 seconds before serving, add the shredded sorrel leaves and squeeze of lemon juice to enhance the rich lemon herb flavour.

To serve, brush the salmon again lightly with the buttery oil if needed, to leave a shiny finish. Sprinkle with coarse sea salt and a twist of black pepper, and then spoon the sauce around the salmon.

This dish also works very well with sea trout.

Crab meat is, to my mind, as delicious as lobster meat – and it is very much less expensive. Both lobsters and crabs are crustaceans, having a protective outer layer of shell, or exoskeleton; crabs are decapod crustaceans, which means they are ten-legged (although many have eight legs and two pincers or claws). Thousands of varieties of crabs exist throughout the world, in both icy and tropical waters, and range in size from pea crabs that can fit inside an oyster to the giant Alaskan king crab which can weigh up to 10kg (22lb).

In Britain the main culinary crab is the common, brown, edible or European crab (*Cancer pagurus*), which can grow up to 25cm (10in) across, and up to 5kg (11lb) in weight. Generally speaking, the meat from a crab will be about one-third of its whole weight, and most of that, about two-thirds, will be brown rather than white meat. Hen crabs are sweeter in flavour, but smaller, and cocks will have larger claws, therefore more white meat. For the maximum and most

memorable of results, try to buy crabs alive, and lively, and cook them at home yourself.

Also available at this time is the spider crab (*Maia squinado*). This wonderfully sweet and tender shellfish is not so commonly seen in fish shops as the brown crab. Although it is quite plentiful around British coasts, it would seem that most of this literally spider-shaped culinary treat is exported to Europe, to be enjoyed in France and Spain (as are many other home-grown delicacies such as langoustines, oysters and scallops).

All crabs shed their shells at certain stages throughout their life – to allow for growth – and it is then that they can be eaten as 'soft-shell' crabs (an American speciality, usually using the famous blue crab of the eastern US seaboard). To help you get a crab to 'shed' its shell after cooking – a fiddly business – see *Common brown crab*, page 425.

potted crab

The two crabs commercially available to us in this country are the brown crab and spider crab. April sees them returning from their winter break, with a lovely sweet meat flavour appealing to the appetite.

The traditional potted crab uses white crab meat only, occasionally layered with the brown. I prefer to mix the two together for a complete crab flavour. Brown crab meat doesn't carry quite the same shelf life as the white, so it's important to eat this starter/lunch dish within 24 hours. If using only white meat, an extra day or two can be added to its refrigerated lifespan.

All you need to accompany this dish are thick slices of a good crusty brown bread, toasted, with no butter required, and a wedge of lemon. It's also quite nice to garnish each pot with a small handful of rocket leaves bound in a little loose crème fraîche and olive oil. To prepare and cook your crab, you'll find a full explanation on page 425.

SERVES 4–6 AS A STARTER

350g (12oz) fresh crab meat, a combination of white and brown, taken from a 1kg (2¼lb) crab (page 425)
¼ teaspoon Cayenne pepper
generous pinch each of ground mace and freshly grated nutmeg
pinch of salt, if necessary
squeeze of lemon juice (optional)
50–75g (2–3oz) butter
4–6 lemon wedges

Mix together the white and brown crab meat (white meat only if using bought fresh pasteurised). Season with the Cayenne pepper, mace and nutmeg, adding a pinch of salt, if necessary. The crab meat can now be tasted for strength of seasoning. For more warmth and bite, add an extra generous pinch of Cayenne pepper. If using the lemon juice, stir into the seasoned meat.

Warm the butter in a saucepan and, once it's melted, skim away any impurities from the surface, pouring the butter into a bowl and leaving any milky curd-like scum in the pan. Leave the clarified butter to cool and thicken slightly, but not set.

The prepared crab can now be spooned and pressed into a bowl or round pot, or individual small ramekins. Cover the surface with the clarified butter and refrigerate. These will now need just an hour or two to set or can be left overnight.

To serve, the potted crab should be removed from the fridge and allowed to reach room temperature. This leaves a soft texture to spread onto warm toasts.

A quick alternative is to sit the pot or ramekins in a warm oven. Once the butter begins to melt leaving the edge of the pots, they're ready to serve, garnishing with the lemon wedges.

A teaspoon of chopped chives or flatleaf parsley can be added to the crab, giving an extra herby touch with spots of greenery.
For a slightly creamier finish, 1–2 tablespoons of Mayonnaise (page 419, or bought) can be mixed with the crab meat.

OPPOSITE: POTTED CRAB

roast lemon peppered lamb with baked potato cake

The new season's lamb is with us now, offering a sweet tender finish that really needs no help at all. However, the lemon and pepper do add a slightly fiery, piquant bite, only complementing, and not fighting with, the sweet succulent slices.

The baked potato cake is a French classic, usually known as *pommes Anna*, and consists of lots of potato slices layered in a tin and baked with the roasting lamb.

I'm also including young purple sprouting broccoli in this recipe. It is at its best in the months of March and April, so I thought we'd take advantage and include it. Should the broccoli be unavailable, freshly buttered spring greens (page 34) are the perfect substitute.

SERVES 4–6 AS A MAIN COURSE

1 lemon
1 × 1.5–1.75kg (3½–4lb) new season's leg of lamb, trimmed of excess fat
1 tablespoon finely cracked black pepper (mignonette)
1 tablespoon picked thyme leaves
cooking oil, for greasing
1 tablespoon clear honey
glass of white wine (approximately 150ml/¼ pint)
300ml (½ pint) *Instant stock* (page 416) or water
⅛ stock cube (optional)
150ml (¼ pint) double cream (optional)

FOR THE POTATOES

900g–1.25kg (2–2½lb) large potatoes, preferably Maris Piper, King Edward or Desirée, peeled
50–100g (2–4oz) melted butter, plus more for brushing (optional)
salt and pepper

FOR THE SPROUTING BROCCOLI

1kg (2¼lb) purple sprouting broccoli spears
knob of butter

To cook the potatoes, preheat the oven to 220°C/425°F/Gas 7. For a neater finish, it's best to peel three or four of the larger potatoes, leaving them a smooth, almost cylindrical, shape. Slicing these lengthwise, before drying on kitchen paper, provides the right length of slice to line the cake tin. It is

OPPOSITE: ROAST LEMON PEPPERED LAMB WITH BAKED POTATO CAKE

also best to cut two of these potatoes 2mm (⅟₁₆in) thick. A mandolin slicer will obviously make this a lot easier. All remaining potatoes are best sliced lengthwise very thinly. This will make them more pliable and easier to use.

Use a 18 × 8–10cm (7 × 3–4in) cake tin and brush well with some of the melted butter, saving the remainder to work through the potatoes. (100g/4oz is listed as an optional total quantity to use, which does look and sound extravagant – and that it is too. It is not essential but will leave you with a very rich and memorable flavour.) For the most attractive of finishes a disc of 5cm (2in) can be cut from one of the slices and placed in the centre of the base of the tin. Arrange the thicker potato slices overlapping neatly around this to cover the base of the tin. Place the thinner slices, also overlapping and standing upright, around the edge of the tin, making sure 1cm (½in) is folded and pressed onto the base. This helps the whole cake turn out with a gâteau-like presentation.

To finish, place all the remaining potato slices in a bowl, season with salt and pepper and mix with the remaining melted butter. Pack and press these into the tin until all are used. Any overhanging side slices can now be folded back in and pressed onto the 'cake'. Cover with foil, pressing it down firmly against the potatoes and place in the oven. The potatoes will take approximately 1 hour 20 minutes–1½ hours. This will be perfect timing, considering the lamb's roasting and relaxing time (see overleaf). After 30 minutes, remove the foil from the cake tin and continue to cook until tender and golden brown. To check the potatoes are completely tender, pierce with a knife.

It's always best to allow a resting time of 5–10 minutes before turning out the cake. To do so, gently loosen the edge from the tin with a small knife, then place a large flat baking tray over the cake tin and turn over. The cake will now fall from the tin onto the tray. The top of the cake may well still be a little opaque and not completely coloured. If so, lightly brush with butter, place under a preheated grill and finish to a rich crispy golden brown.

To prepare the lamb, finely grate the zest from the lemon before cutting the fruit in two. Rub one of the lemon halves over the leg of lamb, squeezing the juice. Now sprinkle the leg with the lemon zest, salt, cracked black pepper and thyme leaves. Put on a lightly oiled roasting tray and then place in the oven. Roasting from cold, without preliminary frying, will always take longer. (For medium-rare meat, cook for up to 1 hour and 15 minutes, for medium up to 1 hour 30 minutes, for medium-to-well-done 1 hour 40 minutes, and for completely well done 1 hour 50 minutes–2 hours.) After the first 30 minutes of cooking, the lamb should be basted every 20 minutes. For extra flavour and finish to the lamb, 20 minutes before its cooking time is complete remove the leg from the oven and tray and pour away any excess lamb fat. Return the leg to the tray and spoon over the honey. Return to the oven and baste frequently. As the honey cooks it will reduce in volume, leaving a slightly caramelized finish.

Remove the leg from the oven and roasting tray and allow to rest for a minimum of 15–20 minutes. Pour away any extra excess fat from the tray, leaving all residue behind. A very sticky finish can be achieved by heating the tray on the stove. Doing this will boil, reduce in volume and thicken the residue for an even stronger caramelized flavour. Pour in the white wine, which will instantly boil and sizzle, lifting the flavours from the pan. Once the wine is reduced in volume by half, add the stock or water. After just a few minutes of sizzling, the lamb-stock cooking liquor is formed. This should now be tasted and, if shallow in flavour, add the piece of stock cube. The liquor can be strained and served as a loose gravy.

For a lemon cream sauce finish, allow the stock to reduce in volume by a third, then add the double cream and cook for a few minutes to thicken. Add just enough of the juice from the remaining lemon half to enhance the flavour, and strain as for the loose gravy above.

The broccoli needs little preparation and cooking time. The finer spears can be picked from the large central stalk, leaving any small leaves attached to them. The large flower on top can now be cut off, leaving a good 5cm (2in) of stalk attached.

Place the large pieces in rapidly boiling salted water and cook for just 2–3 minutes before adding the smaller pieces. Cook for a further 1 minute, drain, season and finish with the knob of butter.

The complete presentation of a whole potato cake and bowl of sprouting broccoli with the roast leg of lamb and gravy is quite spectacular. To carve the lamb, it is best to cut it at a 45° angle, starting at the thin shank end. As you carve, the slices grow and the meat becomes pinker. The potato cake will slice into 6–8 wedges.

The purple sprouting broccoli can be cooked in advance, refreshing it in iced water once tender. To reheat, simply plunge back into boiling water for a minute or microwave. It is not essential to surround the edge of the cake tin with the upright potato slices; once the base is laid the rest can simply be packed on top for speed.

grilled lamb chops with mint-rolled Jerseys and apricot onions

Lamb with Jerseys – a definite spring meal. Both are quite young and, with that, very lively in flavour. The chops I've chosen are chump chops. These are the cut from the chump rear end, attached to the leg. At the other end of this joint is the loin, from which loin chops are cut, leading on to the best end, offering racks and cutlets.

For quality chops it's important to ask your butcher for good-sized chops at least 4cm (1½in) thick. Pre-cut chops are usually so thin and inadequate, needing two per portion, rather than just one if thickly cut.

Early Jerseys are wonderful; these are boiled, rolled in butter with lots of freshly chopped mint and offered with a lime-flavoured yoghurt to dollop on top. This works in the same way as Indian raita – mint and yoghurt are the base of that traditional sauce. As for the onions, these are pan-fried with garlic and sweetened with strips of ready-to-eat dried apricots.

For an extra vegetable, buttered spinach or *Watercress and spinach pesto salad or sauté* (page 50, omitting the pesto flavours) are the best accompaniments.

SERVES 4 AS A MAIN COURSE
675g (1½lb) Jersey Royal new potatoes
salt and pepper, plus coarse sea salt
4 thick lamb chump chops
cooking oil
25g (1oz) butter, plus 1 large knob
4 English onions, halved and sliced
2 garlic cloves, finely crushed
8 ready-to-eat dried apricots, cut into thin strips
1 heaped tablespoon cut mint leaves
juice of 1 lime
150ml (¼ pint) natural yoghurt

Preheat the grill. Bring a large pot of well salted water to the boil. Wash the Jerseys well, lightly scrubbing if necessary, leaving most of the skin on. Plunge the potatoes into the boiling water and simmer for 15–20 minutes, or until tender.

While cooking the Jerseys, season the chumps with salt and pepper. Heat a roasting pan on the stove top, with a small trickle of cooking oil. The fatty edge of the chops can now be placed in the pan, frying over a moderate heat. This will release excess fat, cooking and tenderizing this part of the chop (uncooked fat is chewy and inedible). Continue to cook for at least 5–6 minutes, before sealing both sides of the chop in the released lamb fat. When the potatoes are at least half cooked, place the roasting pan with the chops under the preheated grill. Grill the chops to your liking: for a pink finish, 3–5 minutes before turning will be plenty. Once turned, sprinkle with a little coarse sea salt and continue to grill for your preferred cooking time. Allow the chops to rest for a few minutes before serving.

During the pan-frying and grilling of the chops, heat a wok or large frying pan, adding the large knob of butter. Put the sliced onions in the pan and fry over a fairly high heat. Once beginning to soften in the pan, add the crushed garlic, seasoning with salt and pepper. Continue to fry the onions until they are tender and golden brown. Add the sliced apricots, cooking for a further minute or two.

Drain the potatoes, adding and rolling them in the 25g (1oz) of butter. Season with salt and pepper, sprinkling with the chopped mint leaves. Stir the lime juice into the yoghurt.

To serve, arrange the chops, Jerseys and apricot onions on plates, offering the lime yoghurt seperately.

For the last 2 minutes of grilling the chops, apricot jam can be brushed over each one. This will begin to sizzle, almost caramelizing for a bitter-sweet finish. An alternative is to add a teaspoon or two of apricot jam to the onions once cooked.

The mint can be replaced with a dessertspoon of finely chopped rosemary.

grilled beef fillet with baby turnips, marinated mushrooms and a beetroot dressing

A great mid-to-late spring dish as beetroots and turnips are just coming into season, this offers an alternative starter with the hot and cold combination of grilled (or seared) beef fillet, garnished with raw sliced mushrooms and turnips bound with a herby lemon and olive oil. The dressing is quite sweet, with the double act of beetroot and balsamic vinegar working together.

SERVES 4 AS A STARTER
10–12 baby turnips
10–12 button mushrooms, preferably same size as the turnips
juice of ½ lemon
3 tablespoons olive oil, plus more for brushing
salt and pepper
4 × 75–100g (3–4oz) beef fillet slices
1 heaped tablespoon chopped herbs (such as chives, chervil, dill, tarragon and parsley)

FOR THE DRESSING
1 cooked medium beetroot, peeled and finely chopped
1 tablespoon balsamic vinegar or red wine vinegar
2–3 tablespoons olive oil

Trim the turnip tops to just a short stem. The mushrooms are best wiped clean with a damp cloth rather than washed. Trim the stalks flush with the bases of the mushrooms. Now cut the turnips and mushrooms into thin slices. Mix the lemon juice with the olive oil, and season with salt and pepper. Spoon this marinade over the sliced turnips and mushrooms and gently mix. It's best to prepare to this stage 15–20 minutes before eating, turning every few minutes or so to help impregnate the marinade's flavour.

To make the dressing, place the chopped beetroot, vinegar, 2 tablespoons of the olive oil and 2 tablespoons of water in a liquidizer. Blitz to a smooth purée, then add the remaining tablespoon of olive oil if necessary, to loosen the consistency. Season with salt and pepper, then push through a sieve if necessary for a smoother finish.

Brush the beef fillets with olive oil and season with salt and pepper, then place on a preheated very hot griddle plate or frying pan. Cook for just 45 seconds–1 minute, then, if using a griddle, turn the fillets 90° to create a grilled criss-cross pattern. After a further 45 seconds, turn the fillets over and cook for just a further minute for a rare pink finish.

While cooking the beef, add the chopped herbs to the marinated vegetables and divide between four plates, placing them towards the top of the plate. Present the beef fillets in front of the mushrooms and turnips, then spoon the beetroot dressing around. Excess marinade can also be drizzled around the beef, mingling it with the beetroot dressing if wished.

braised beef brisket with tarragon carrots and cauliflower champ

This sounds like a very wintry dish, but we all know mid-spring has never offered summery conditions. So this dish will suit our April days perfectly.

Lincolnshire spring cauliflower seems to offer the best of flavours around this time. However, the champ recipe will work well with almost all cauliflowers, from all countries, all year round. It's basically taken from the Irish potato champ – creamy, buttery and finished with spring onion. The carrots are cooked in the pot with the beef, becoming overcooked and very tender, and offering their sweetness to the cooking liquor.

Beef brisket, a cut taken from the breast, is perfect for slow braising or stewing, but does have quite a high fat content. Usually this cut is sold pre-rolled, which is fine, but do ask for a lean piece and, if necessary, for it to be unrolled and the fat removed. The meat will cook equally well in its natural shape. It can be sold salted or plain, and either will work here. To help reduce the salt content, a salted joint can be blanched in water as described below. The dish is best planned a day in advance, allowing for the pre-soaking of the meat for 24 hours in cold water before rinsing and blanching the following day.

SERVE 4–6 AS A MAIN COURSE

1 × **1.5kg (3–3½lb) lean brisket of beef, soaked if salted (see above)**
***Chicken stock* (page 416) or beef- or chicken-flavoured *Instant stock* (page 416) or water, to cover the beef**
2 small onions
1 bay leaf
sprig of thyme
1kg (2¼lb) carrots, peeled and cut into 2cm (¾in) thick pieces
2 teaspoons snipped tarragon leaves
25g (1oz) butter (optional), plus a knob for the carrots

FOR THE CAULIFLOWER CHAMP

25g (1oz) butter, plus a knob for the spring onions
1 large or 2 small cauliflowers, cut into florets
300ml (½ pint) milk
salt and pepper
squeeze of lemon juice
6 spring onions, thinly sliced

To blanch the brisket if using salted beef, rinse it under cold water, place in a large saucepan and cover with fresh water. Bring to the boil and simmer for 2 minutes, then remove from the stove and rinse under cold water. This will help remove any excess salt content.

Place in a suitable large pot and cover with stock or water. Add the onions, bay leaf and thyme and bring to a simmer. Skim away any impurities floating on the surface before covering with a lid and cooking gently for 3 hours. The beef can also be cooked in an oven preheated to 160°C/325°F/Gas 3. After 3 hours, skim away any excess fat or impurities, adding the carrots and continuing to cook for a further hour. During this cooking time, the carrots will overcook. It is like this that they will eat at their best for this dish.

During this last cooking hour, make the cauliflower champ. Melt the 25g (1oz) of butter in a saucepan until bubbling. Add the cauliflower florets and cook, covered, on a low heat until they begin to soften without colouring. Add the milk and bring to a simmer.

Re-cover and cook until the cauliflower is at a purée stage. Transfer the florets, without the milk, to a liquidizer and blitz to a smooth purée, adding any of the remaining milk to loosen, if needed. Season with salt, pepper and a squeeze of lemon juice.

The spring onions can be quickly softened in the knob of butter and added to the purée just before serving, to ensure they don't discolour.

Once the meat is cooked, remove from the heat and allow to rest for 20–30 minutes. During this time, the meat will relax and become tender. While it's resting, the carrots can be removed with some of the stock, ready to reheat and season before serving the beef, finishing them with the tarragon and the knob of butter.

Strain 600ml (1 pint) of beef cooking liquor into a clean saucepan. If you like, add the optional butter for a softer buttery finish. Slice the brisket (it could almost be carved with a spoon, it is so tender), presenting it with the beef cooking liquor, tarragon carrots and cauliflower champ.

OPPOSITE: BRAISED BEEF BRISKET WITH TARRAGON CARROTS AND CAULIFLOWER CHAMP

beef steak pie plate with a casserole of oysters and white mushrooms

Oysters were a favourite with the Victorians. The plump molluscs could be found in abundance at the time, and were consequently looked upon as quite a cheap food, only for the poor man's diet. Their purpose was often purely to help bulk other dishes; steak, kidney and oyster pie became a classic.

There are two varieties of oysters available in the UK, the native and Pacific (rock). The native is the wild variety. This is the more expensive of the two, at least double, sometimes three times the price of the Pacific. The price is generally determined by the five years it takes to grow. The Pacific, however, will be 'grown up' after just three years, so it's more popular with growers.

The natural season of the native is between September and April. In the late spring and summer months they can still be found, but are best left alone during the spawning period, saving plenty for the season ahead and avoiding the over-milky consistency they have at that time of year.

The Pacific oyster is available throughout the year. These are the farmed variety, without the exclusivity of their friends but still offering a good rich flavour and having a smaller impact on the culinary budget.

This version of the old classic takes on a more family-friendly approach, the beef pie plate standing quite proud, ready to introduce its seafood partner. The choice is yours: you have a steak pie that can be enjoyed as it is, or finished with a spoonful of creamy oysters and mushrooms. The beef pie mix can be made the day before, ready to top with pastry and bake on the day.

SERVES 6 AS A MAIN COURSE
900g (2lb) braising steak, e.g. chuck, brisket, neck, trimmed of fat
vegetable oil or lard, for frying
2 large onions, chopped
2 celery sticks, cut into 1cm (½in) pieces
salt and pepper
450ml (¾ pint) *Instant stock* (page 416) or 1 × 415g tin beef consommé, topped up to 450ml (¾ pint) with water
25g (1oz) plain flour, plus more for dusting
sprig of fresh thyme
dash of Worcestershire sauce
cornflour, loosened with water (optional)
450g (1lb) *Shortcrust pastry* (page 425)
1 small egg, beaten (optional)

FOR THE CASSEROLE
2 shallots, finely chopped
175g (6oz) button mushrooms, sliced
1 tablespoon white wine vinegar
100ml (3½fl oz) white wine
150ml (¼ pint) double cream
12 oysters, opened, saving their juices (page 424)
1 heaped teaspoon picked chervil leaves

Cut the beef into 2.5cm (1in) cubes. Heat 1 tablespoon of vegetable oil or lard in a large frying pan, adding the chopped onions and celery. Fry for 6–8 minutes until beginning to soften and taking on a little colour. Transfer the vegetables to a large saucepan, adding a further tablespoon of oil or lard to the frying pan. Season the diced beef with salt and pepper and fry half the pieces, allowing to colour well. Repeat the same process with the remaining meat. As each batch is complete, transfer to the large saucepan with the vegetables. Return the frying pan to the stove and, once hot, pour in the tinned consommé or stock. This will lift any residue left in the pan, adding extra flavour.

Sprinkle the 25g (1oz) plain flour over the beef and vegetables, stirring it in well and cooking for a few minutes over a moderate heat. Add the stock from the frying pan, the thyme and a dash of Worcestershire sauce, bringing it to a gentle simmer.

Partially cover the saucepan with a lid and continue to cook for 1½–2 hours, until tender. Check for seasoning with salt and pepper. Should the gravy be too thin, simply strain into a fresh saucepan, bringing it to the boil, before whisking in a little water-loosened cornflour. Once at a coating consistency, pour over the meat and leave to cool.

Preheat the oven to 200°C/400°F/Gas 6 and place a baking tray in the centre of the oven to preheat. This will help create an even cooking of the pastry base, preventing it from becoming soggy. Butter a 1.2 litre (2 pint) pie dish or a 23cm (9in), deep pie plate. Roll half to two-thirds of the pastry, on a lightly floured surface, into a circle large enough to line the base of the buttered pie dish or plate. Spoon the pie mixture over the pastry, leaving a clean border. Brush the rim of the pie dish pastry with the beaten egg.

OPPOSITE: BEEF STEAK PIE PLATE WITH A CASSEROLE OF OYSTERS AND WHITE MUSHROOMS

Roll the remaining pastry and place on top, pressing together around the edge and trimming away any excess. Classically, steak pies are garnished with pastry leaves on top. The trimmings can be rerolled and cut if wished, using them to finish the presentation of the pie.

Make a small criss-cross incision in the centre of the pie, garnishing with the pastry leaves, if using, and brushing over completely with the beaten egg.

Place the pie on the well heated baking tray and bake for 45–50 minutes, until golden brown. Should the pastry be colouring too quickly in the oven, the temperature can be slightly reduced, covering the pastry with foil. To check the pie is ready to serve, pierce the centre with a skewer to see whether the meat is completely heated through.

While baking the pie, the oyster and mushroom casserole can be prepared. Place the shallots and button mushrooms in a small saucepan. Add the white wine vinegar and bring to the boil. This will now reduce in volume and evaporate quickly, leaving a tangy bite to the mushrooms. Once completely reduced in volume, add the white wine and return to boiling point. This now only needs to cook and reduce in volume by three-quarters. Add the double cream, bringing it to a simmer and cooking to a loose coating consistency. This stage can be achieved a little in advance.

When you want to serve the dish, return the sauce to a simmer, adding the oysters and their juice. Simmer very gently for just a minute (too much heat will toughen the oysters), checking for seasoning with salt and pepper and adding the picked chervil leaves.

The casserole is now ready to serve with the crispy beef steak pie.

Should the pie mix have been cooked well in advance and refrigerated, the baking time may need to be extended to about 1¼ hours. Top the pie with foil once well coloured to prevent the pastry getting a burnt bitter edge.

If only cooking the beef steak pie, two carrots, thickly sliced or diced, can be added, offering a sweeter finish.

A teaspoon of freshly picked thyme leaves can be added to the shortcrust pastry recipe, using just the stalks to cook with the beef. This leaves a more predominant herby edge to the finished dish.

The pastry can be made with just lard, omitting the butter. This would be a classic pie pastry, bound just with water.

sautéed chicken steeped in vinaigrette with st george's mushrooms

The chicken pieces are pure simplicity, literally just sautéed until tender before steeping in vinaigrette.

St George's mushrooms begin to appear on St George's Day, 23 April; one of the few mushrooms of spring. They tend to stay with us through to the end of May, offering their services to many a dish, and eating particularly well sautéed in butter with a touch of garlic and parsley (page 47).

SERVES 4 AS A MAIN COURSE
1 × 1.5–1.75kg (3½–4lb) free-range chicken, cut into 8 pieces (2 drumsticks, 2 thighs, 4 breast halves)
salt and pepper
flour, for dusting
2 tablespoons olive oil
1 tablespoon chopped chives

FOR THE VINAIGRETTE
3 tablespoons white or red wine vinegar (tarragon vinegar also works well)
2 teaspoons Dijon mustard
100ml (3½fl oz) olive oil
coarse sea salt
squeeze of lemon juice

FOR THE MUSHROOMS
450g (1lb) St George's or chestnut mushrooms
25g (1oz) butter

Preheat the oven to 220°C/425°F/Gas 7. Season the chicken pieces with salt and pepper and lightly dust with flour. Heat the olive oil in a frying pan or flameproof braising pan. Once hot, sauté the chicken pieces for approximately 8–10 minutes until well coloured. The pan can now be placed in the preheated oven for a further 10–15 minutes to complete the cooking.

Make the vinaigrette by whisking together the vinegar, mustard and olive oil, and seasoning with coarse sea salt and pepper and a squeeze of lemon juice. Spoon the dressing over the cooked chicken, cover with a lid and keep warm.

While the chicken is steeping, prepare the mushrooms. Trim off the stalks and, if necessary, rinse the mushrooms very briefly, making sure not to leave them soaking as they absorb water very easily. Melt the butter in a large hot frying pan and add the cleaned mushrooms. Sauté on a high heat for a good few minutes until tender. Season with salt and pepper. The sautéed mushrooms can now be added to the chicken pieces, finishing with the chopped chives.

The richness of the dressing, the vinegar and mustard in particular, lifts the flavour of the mushroom garnish. A good tossed salad, with lots of watercress and rocket leaves, provides a simple finish; or perhaps just a spoonful or two of very soft and creamy *Mashed potatoes* (page 422).

duck boulangère with hazelnut-rosemary spinach

Boulangère means 'in the style of the baker's wife' and is used for dishes braised or baked with potatoes and onions. The potatoes absorb the stock, leaving a crisply topped but very moist, almost creamy centre. In this recipe, the duck legs will simply be roasted on top of the potatoes, all juices and duck fat becoming absorbed by the layers beneath them. One other added flavour is a thinly sliced large Bramley cooking apple. Its sharpness helps the potatoes along and combines well with the rich duck juices.

During our spring months young spinach appears, very young and tender during the first eight weeks, with coarser leaves arriving in May. Either of these can be used for this recipe.

The hazelnuts for this recipe will need to be skinned (they can be bought pre-skinned). To do so, toast the nuts under the grill or in a moderate oven until the skins darken and become loose. At this point, place the nuts in a cloth and rub together well. This will release the skins. The rosemary flavour is lent to the dish via the butter working into the spinach.

SERVES 4 AS A MAIN COURSE

2 knobs of butter, plus more for greasing
2 large or 3 small onions, sliced
salt and pepper, plus coarse sea salt
6 large potatoes (approximately 675g/1½lb), peeled
1 large Bramley cooking apple, peeled and cored
2 tablespoons cooking oil
4 large duck legs
150–200ml (¼ pint–7fl oz) chicken-flavoured *Instant stock* (page 416) or *Chicken stock* (page 416)

FOR THE SPINACH

900g (2lb) young English spinach, washed and stalks removed
25g (1oz) butter
1 teaspoon chopped rosemary
freshly grated nutmeg
50g (2oz) hazelnuts, skinned (see above) and roughly chopped

Preheat the oven to 190°C/375°F/Gas 5. Melt a knob of butter in a frying pan and, once bubbling, add the sliced onions. These need only to be cooked for a few minutes until just beginning to soften. Season with salt and pepper and leave to cool.

Slice the potatoes very thinly. For a neater presentation, although certainly not essential, shape one or two into cylinders. When sliced, these can be used for the top layer. Cut the apple in half, then cut each half into thin slices.

Heat the cooking oil in a frying pan. Season the duck legs with coarse sea salt and pepper, and place them in the pan, skin-side down. Fry on a moderate heat until golden brown and just becoming crispy. This will take approximately 15 minutes.

Butter a suitably large ovenproof baking dish or braising pot, then sprinkle in a spoonful or two of the cooked onions. Now add a layer of potato slices and season with salt and pepper. Repeat with another layer of onion, then add some of the apple slices. Top with more potatoes, season and repeat the onion, apple and potato layers until all are used. If using cylindrical potatoes for the top layer, it's best to overlap each slice: start from the outside and work in to the centre. Heat the stock and pour over the potatoes, filling to about 1cm (½in) from the top layer. Break a knob of butter into pieces and dot over the top.

Place the golden-brown duck legs, skin-side up, on top of the potatoes. Place in the preheated oven, and cook for 1½–2 hours. After 1½ hours, check the legs: they should be cooked through, with the potatoes very moist and tender. For extra well-done legs, continue to cook for the further 30 minutes. More stock may well have to be added at this point (if all has previously been used, no more should be needed).

Cook the spinach once the duck *boulangère* is completely cooked and resting. Melt the butter in a large saucepan with the rosemary. Once bubbling, add the well-drained spinach leaves. Cook on a medium-to-high heat, stirring, for a minute or two. Season with salt, pepper and nutmeg, before adding the chopped hazelnuts. The nutty spinach is now ready to offer along with the duck legs *boulangère*.

cocoa sorbet with orange biscuits

The Easter extravagance of chocolate couldn't be overlooked in this seasonal book. This sorbet's bitter chocolate flavour is provided entirely by cocoa powder. The powder can be very bitter but, when balanced with the sugar and water and then frozen, does give a good rich chocolaty flavour. The sorbet can be infused with other flavours by simply omitting 100ml (3½fl oz) of water and replacing it with the same volume of a liqueur. Grand Marnier works very well, offering its orange flavour to work with the biscuits. Other alternatives include amaretto, kirsch or perhaps the coffee-flavoured Kahlúa.

SERVES 4–6

250g (9oz) caster sugar
150g (5oz) cocoa powder, sifted
1 tablespoon vanilla essence (if a particularly strong thick essence, add just 1 teaspoon)

FOR THE ORANGE BISCUITS (MAKES 16)

juice and finely grated zest of 1 orange
100g (4oz) caster sugar
100g (4oz) plain flour
50g (2oz) softened butter, plus more for greasing

Add the sugar to 900ml (1½ pints) of water in a pan and bring to the boil. Add the cocoa powder and mix well. Cook on a low heat for 20 minutes, keeping the mix moving during this cooking time. After 20 minutes, the mix will have become rich and thicker in consistency. Leave to cool.

When cool, add the vanilla essence, along with a flavoured liqueur, if using, as mentioned in the introduction. The sorbet can now be churned in an ice-cream machine for approximately 20 minutes until smooth and at setting point. Transfer to a suitable container and freeze until needed.

To make the biscuits, boil the orange juice until reduced to 2 tablespoons. Allow to cool. Now mix this well with all of the other ingredients. Cover and refrigerate for 2–3 hours to set.

Preheat the oven to 180°C/350°F/Gas 4. Roll the biscuit mix into 16 balls, then press each onto buttered baking trays and flatten them into 6–7.5cm (2½–3in) rounds. It is important to leave plenty of space between each, to allow room for spreading. Cooking 4–6 on each tray should give enough space for the biscuits.

OPPOSITE: COCOA SORBET WITH ORANGE BISCUITS

Bake in the preheated oven for 12–14 minutes until golden brown. Allow the biscuits to rest on the tray for 1 minute, then carefully lift them with a palette knife or fish slice onto a cooling rack. Should the biscuits begin to stick to the tray, return them to the oven to rewarm. Once cooled and crisp, the biscuits are ready to serve with the sorbet.

Lemon biscuits can also be made using the grated zest and juice from 2 lemons.

banana white chocolate marquise with strawberries

Bananas and chocolate are real old buddies, having met so many times in so many sweet guises. Most of those arranged dates have been with a dark bitter chocolate; here it's going to be with white. White chocolate is not really chocolate at all, because it doesn't contain any cocoa solids. It is a combination of fat, milk, sugar and cocoa butter, leaving a tinge of chocolate flavour. In *The A–Z of French Food* (Scribo Editions), *marquise* is explained as a term applied to various particularly refined desserts. In reference to chocolate, it reads 'a chilled dessert of creamy chocolate mousse'.

To finish the dessert I've chosen young strawberries to accompany this rich sweet pud. This can be served in individual Martini glasses or one large bowl.

SERVES 6 GENEROUSLY

1 tablespoon liquid glucose
1 leaf of gelatine, soaked in cold water
175g (6oz) white chocolate, finely chopped
3 large or 4 medium bananas
squeeze of lemon juice
300ml (½ pint) double cream
350–450g (12oz–1lb) strawberries, hulled and washed
icing sugar, for dusting (optional)

To make the mousse, pour 50ml (2fl oz) of water and the liquid glucose into a small saucepan and bring to the boil. Remove from the heat, adding the gelatine along with the chopped white chocolate. Beat until the chocolate is melted and completely smooth.

Peel the bananas and chop into pieces. These can now be mashed by hand to a coarse or smooth purée, adding a squeeze of lemon juice to prevent them from discolouring. The alternative is to blitz to a smooth purée in a food processor.

Whip the cream to a soft peak. Pour the melted chocolate into a large bowl, stirring in the mashed banana. Gently fold in the whipped cream and the mousse is complete. Spoon into individual glasses or one large bowl, refrigerating for several hours to set.

To serve, halve the strawberries, dusting with icing sugar, if using, for a sweeter finish. If individual glasses have been used, the strawberries can be piled on top, or serve a scoop of mousse from the large bowl, offering the strawberries separately.

A couple of tablespoons of the strawberries can be mashed with a teaspoon or two of icing sugar and then pushed through a sieve, providing a fresh strawberry coulis to bind with the halved fruits.
Madeleines (page 429) are a perfect accompaniment for this dish.

toasted honey bananas with fresh goat's cheese

It's said bananas are at their best in mid-to-late spring, holding a richer, fuller character. Many right now will be imported from the Caribbean and should be taken full advantage of.

We have a double bonus here – the sweet flavour of bubbling hot honey bananas countered with the sharp tangy, often zesty bite of fresh, in-season British goat's cheese, beginning to melt as it blends with the banana. Goat's cheeses come in many shapes and sizes – wrapped in leaves, dusted with charcoal-ash, with a crinkly magnolia tinge, or simply pure, smooth white. Four small individual-portion cheeses make serving very easy, or break two larger ones so they begin to crumble on the plate.

SERVES 4

6 medium bananas
4 tablespoons clear honey
goat's cheese for 4 people (50–75g/2–3oz per portion)

Preheat the grill to very hot. Peel the bananas, splitting each lengthwise in half. Place the banana halves, flat-side up, on a baking tray. Divide the honey over each, using a teaspoon. Place the honey bananas under the grill, as close to the heat as possible, cooking for a few minutes until the honey begins to bubble. If very close to the heat, the bananas will begin to caramelize lightly.

Remove the tray from the grill, placing three halves on each plate, drizzling each with the hot honey from the tray. Present the goat's cheese next to the bananas, either cutting into wedges, or breaking, allowing the cheese to crumble next to or over the hot fruits.

A bowl of strawberries will eat very well with this dish.

soft chocolate pudding

Although chocolate is not a seasonal ingredient, Easter Sunday wouldn't be the same without some form of chocolate dessert. This dessert has become a modern classic, which is very popular today and will remain so for many years to come. The mix can be made several hours in advance, poured into the prepared moulds and refrigerated until needed. One important detail is to make sure it is back to room temperature before baking. Once cooked and cut into, it won't be quite cooked through, revealing a thick, soft chocolate centre. I've included a recipe for chocolate sauce to go with the dessert, for real chocoholics. Extra-thick or pouring cream or vanilla ice-cream also work very well. For an orangey accompaniment, the perfect partner is the *Warm syruped kumquats* (page 38).

SERVES 5–6

125g (4½oz) butter, plus more for greasing
2 teaspoons flour, plus more for the ramekins
125g (4½oz) dark chocolate, chopped
2 eggs, plus 2 extra yolks
4 tablespoons caster sugar

FOR THE CHOCOLATE SAUCE (OPTIONAL)

100g (4oz) bitter dark chocolate (milk or white chocolate can also be used), chopped
150ml (¼ pint) single cream
25g (1oz) butter

For the pudding, preheat the oven to 220°C/425°F/Gas 7 and liberally butter and flour five or six 150ml (¼ pint) ramekins. In a bowl set over a pan of simmering water, melt the chocolate and butter together. It is important that the bowl is not in contact with the simmering water as this will separate the solids and fats from the chocolate. Once warm and melted, remove the bowl from the pan.

While the chocolate is melting, with an electric whisk mix together the eggs, extra yolks and caster sugar to a thick but light consistency. This mix will have taken on a cold sabayon stage, almost a combination of soft peak meringue and cream. Pour into the warm chocolate, and dust the 2 teaspoons of flour in through a sieve. Fold the three components together gently, then spoon into the prepared moulds. (If not cooking immediately, these can now be refrigerated for several hours, if wished, until needed, returning them to room temperature before baking.) Place in the preheated oven for 9 minutes.

Meanwhile, make the sauce, if using. Place all the ingredients together in a bowl set over simmering water until the chocolate has melted.

Remove the puddings from the oven and leave to rest for 1 minute before serving in the ramekins or turning out onto plates. The sides will be set but the middle soft. Serve with the warm chocolate sauce or your chosen accompaniment.

The Cocoa sorbet *(page 71) also eats very well with the warm pudding.*

SOFT CHOCOLATE PUDDING

open rhubarb pie

Pink forced rhubarb is the one to use here: encased in the pastry, but not totally covered, it shows off its attractive colour and appetizing richness.

This is an old method of making pies that's never lost its appeal; once the pastry is made, it's just a matter of stacking with the chopped rhubarb and baking.

To finish the experience, it has to be a jug of cream or warm fresh *Crème Anglaise* (page 426).

SERVES 6–8
350g (12oz) *Sweet shortcrust pastry* (page 425)
1 egg yolk, beaten
675g (1½lb) forced rhubarb, cut into 2.5cm (1in) sticks
finely grated zest of 1 orange (optional)
50g (2oz) caster sugar
25g (1oz) semolina
caster or demerara sugar, for sprinkling
icing sugar, for dusting (optional)
knob of butter (optional)

Preheat the oven to 200°C/400°F/Gas 6. Roll the pastry on a lightly floured surface into a circle, approximately 35cm (14in) in diameter. Lifting the pastry with the rolling pin, transfer the disc to a non-stick baking tray. Brush the egg yolk over the pastry. Sprinkle a central 23cm (9in) circle, leaving a clear border, with the semolina. This will help absorb some of the rhubarb juices as it bakes.

In a large bowl, mix the rhubarb pieces with the orange zest, if using, and caster sugar. Pile the fruit into the centre of the pastry, folding the rim over in a rustic fashion. A lot of the fruit will still be exposed, hence the 'open'.

Brush the folded border with the remaining egg yolk, sprinkling over the caster or demerara sugar.

Bake for 35–40 minutes until the pastry is golden brown. Serve warm, dusting with icing sugar and finishing with a knob of butter, if preferred.

25g (1oz) of chopped hazelnuts, walnuts or almonds can be sprinkled over the pastry with the caster or demerara sugar before baking.

oeufs à la neige on baked rhubarb with brioche and custard

Also known as 'floating islands', *oeufs à la neige* are basically egg whites that have been mixed with sugar, then whisked and poached in milk and water. The young rhubarb is cooked in the oven until tender, and any liquor released poured over the finished dish. The brioche slices are toasted and buttered and, as the rhubarb begins to bleed, its juices are absorbed into the brioche, giving a moist finish. The *Crème Anglaise* custard is an optional extra, but for me is just essential for poached meringues; it also adds a creaminess to the finished dish.

SERVES 4

3 egg whites
175g (6oz) caster sugar
300ml (½ pint) milk
icing sugar, for dusting
6–8 rhubarb stalks (forced rhubarb will not need peeling)
1–2 tablespoons caster sugar
4 slices of brioche, approximately 1.5cm (⅝in) thick, crusts removed
butter, for spreading
300ml (½ pint) *Crème Anglaise* (page 426, optional)

To make the meringue, whisk the egg whites to soft peaks in a spotlessly clean bowl. Continue to whisk, adding two-thirds of the sugar. When that has been whisked in, add the remaining sugar and whisk in to give a smooth firm finished texture.

Heat the milk and an equal amount of water in a large wide saucepan, not allowing it quite to reach a simmer. Shape the meringue mixture between two tablespoons, making 12–16 meringues. It is best to cook just six at a time, shaping and spooning them carefully into the milk. Turn the meringues over after 5–6 minutes and poach them for a further 5–6 minutes. Carefully remove them from the milk and place them on greaseproof paper lightly dusted with icing sugar. It is not essential to serve the meringues hot or even warm; room temperature will be enough, helped along by the warm rhubarb.

To prepare the rhubarb, preheat the oven to 190°C/375°F/Gas 5. Cut the rhubarb into 6–7.5cm (2½–3in) pieces, making approximately 4–5 pieces per stalk. Lay on a baking tray, sprinkle with 2 tablespoons of water and the caster sugar. Place in the preheated oven and cook for approximately 10 minutes until tender (thicker rhubarb may need an extra minute or two). Remove from the oven and keep warm while the brioche is toasted.

Spread the brioche slices with the butter, then dust fairly generously with icing sugar and colour under a preheated grill to give a slightly burnt bitter-sweet edge. For a crisper finish it is best not to toast them too quickly. Turn the slices, and repeat this process.

To serve, place the brioche toasts on plates and top each one with 6–8 pieces of rhubarb, saving any syrup left on the tray. Three to four meringues can now be arranged on and around the rhubarb, drizzling with any saved rhubarb syrup. Warm or cold *Crème Anglaise* can be offered separately.

OPPOSITE: OEUFS À LA NEIGE ON BAKED RHUBARB WITH BRIOCHE AND CUSTARD

vegetables

Hot tomato, courgette and cheese bake with fresh basil oil 79

Champ potato gnocchi with broad beans and blue cheese 79

Blue cheese fondue with spring dips 80

Flat asparagus salad with new potatoes and radishes 82

Asparagus on buttery toast with melting Parmesan cheese 83

White asparagus with a warm casserole salad of mushrooms and spring onions 85

fish

Fillet of sea trout on cauliflower cream with a fresh herb-pea dressing 87

Parsleyed plaice fillets with roast bananas and sweet mustard onions 88

Grilled plaice or lemon sole fillets with champagne-glazed spinach 88

Lemon sole and spinach with vanilla-rosemary carrots 90

Monkfish steaks with court-bouillon and mushrooms 90

Grilled mackerel fillets with a fennel, Parmesan and green olive salad 91

Prawn and crème fraîche tart with samphire and tomato salad 92

meat

Warm gammon with sticky pineapple 95

Boiled ham hock with braised lentils and wild girolles 95

Pot-roasted lamb with sorrel and samphire 96

Roast chicken with primo pipérade 97

Guinea fowl with spring greens and carrots and a mustard and marjoram sauce 99

fruit and puddings

Apricot tart with home-made almond ice-cream 101

Upside-down peach and blood orange cake 102

Poached peach and strawberry custard creams 102

Soft lemon pudding with young strawberries 103

hot tomato, courgette and cheese bake with fresh basil oil

This recipe is wonderful to enjoy in late spring – a foretaste of the flavours to come in the warmer months ahead. And that is the beauty of this dish – goat's cheese is perfect right now, with the tomatoes and courgettes just getting better as the weeks go on. The goat's cheese can be replaced with slices of mozzarella.

SERVES 4 AS A MAIN COURSE OR 6 AS A STARTER

2 large or 3 medium onions (red if available), sliced
3 tablespoons olive oil
salt and pepper, plus coarse sea salt
½ garlic clove (optional)
butter, for brushing
2–3 large courgettes, cut into 5mm (¼in) slices
**225g (8oz) goat's cheese, skinned (if applicable) and
    sliced**
5–6 tomatoes, preferably plum, cut into 5mm (¼in) slices
**3 heaped tablespoons grated Parmesan cheese or
    75g (3oz) diced Italian fontina cheese (rind removed)**

FOR THE BASIL OIL
**large bunch of loose basil (if in plastic packets,
    3 bunches will be needed)**
salt
100ml (3½fl oz) olive oil
3 tablespoons groundnut oil

To make the basil oil, pick all of the leaves and place in a liquidizer with a pinch of salt. Warm the olive and groundnut oils gently together in a small saucepan, bringing them to just above room temperature. Remove from the heat, pour over the basil leaves and liquidize until smooth. The flavour and colour of the leaves will now have joined company with the oils. Strain through a sieve and leave to cool. Refrigerated, this oil will keep for up to 2 weeks.

Preheat the oven to 200°C/400°F/Gas 6. To make the bake, fry the onions in a tablespoon of the olive oil for 5–6 minutes until golden brown and softened. Season with salt and pepper. Rub an ovenproof, preferably earthenware, dish with the garlic, if using, then brush with butter. Place the onions in the dish.

Heat another tablespoon of olive oil in a large frying pan. Sear the courgette slices quickly on one side only,

OPPOSITE: HOT TOMATO, COURGETTE AND CHEESE BAKE WITH FRESH BASIL OIL

allowing them to colour lightly but not cook. It is important that the pan is very hot and not too many slices are placed in the pan at the same time. Repeat with the remaining slices, heating another tablespoon of oil if necessary. Once all are coloured, leave to cool.

Cover the onions with the slices of goat's cheese and season with salt and pepper. Arrange the tomato slices and courgettes either overlapping or in alternate lines on top of the cheese. Season with coarse sea salt and pepper.

Bake in the preheated oven for 20 minutes. Sprinkle over the Parmesan or fontina cheese and return to the oven for a further 10 minutes until rich golden brown. If the colour is a little light, the bake can be coloured further under a preheated grill. Serve each portion drizzled with the basil oil.

A tossed salad eats well with this dish, along with crusty bread or toast, or just buttered new potatoes.

champ potato gnocchi with broad beans and blue cheese

Gnocchi are Italian dumplings, made either from semolina, choux pastry or, as with this recipe, potatoes. Champ is an Irish potato dish, consisting of mashed potatoes, spring onions and lots of butter. The oniony flavour, as we know, works well with almost any cheese, biting into its rich flavour.

Blue cheese is suggested here – Stilton, Roquefort or Irish Cashel Blue all work well. Other cheeses to use, although not blue, are Parmesan shavings or slices of Gruyère, just melted over the gnocchi to a golden brown.

The new season's young broad beans are merely boiled and buttered with the gnocchi just before serving. This dish is a good vegetarian option, as a starter or main course (with a salad), supper dish or savoury dessert.

SERVES 4

675g (1½lb) large potatoes
salt and pepper
25g (1oz) butter, plus 2 knobs
bunch of spring onions, finely chopped
125–150g (4½–5oz) plain flour, plus more for dusting
1 egg, plus 1 extra yolk
freshly grated nutmeg
iced water
225g (8oz) podded broad beans
1–2 tablespoons olive oil, plus more for drizzling

100–150ml (3½fl oz–¼ pint) single cream (optional)
100–175g (4–6oz) crumbled blue cheese (see above) or
Parmesan cheese shavings or Gruyère slices
squeeze of lime juice (optional)

Cook the potatoes whole in boiling salted water. While they are boiling, melt half of the 25g (1oz) butter in a frying pan. Once bubbling, add the spring onions and cook for just a minute barely to soften.

Once the potatoes are tender, peel while still warm and mash to a smooth consistency. Mix in 125g (4oz) of the flour, along with the spring onions, remaining measured butter, whole egg and egg yolk. Season with salt, pepper and nutmeg.

The gnocchi mix should now feel moist, but if too sticky add a little more flour. The dumplings can now be moulded and this is best achieved while the mix is still warm, shaping them by hand into 2cm (¾in) balls. The gnocchi are now ready to pre-cook in batches in salted simmering water. As they are placed in the water, they will sink and then rise to the surface when cooked. They cook in 3–4 minutes, maximum 5 minutes. Once cooked, it's important the balls are firm to the touch. Refresh in iced water. When cold, dry on a kitchen cloth or paper. The gnocchi can now be refrigerated until needed.

The broad beans can also be pre-cooked, blanching them in boiling salted water until tender. If making the dish during this month, the broad beans will be quite small, taking just a minute or two to cook. Later in their season, the beans may well need up to 5 minutes. Refresh in iced water, then peel the rich green beans from their shells. To reheat, the beans can be warmed for a minute or two in a few tablespoons of water with a small knob of butter. Season with salt and pepper.

To fry the gnocchi, melt a knob of butter with a little olive oil in a frying pan. Once bubbling, add the dumplings. (These can be cooked in batches so as not to overcrowd the pan. If so, place them in a moderate oven to keep warm while the rest are cooked.) Fry on a moderate heat until golden brown and completely warmed through.

Mix the warmed broad beans with the gnocchi, then spoon into one large or four individual ovenproof dishes. If using the single cream, warm 100ml (3½fl oz) of it with half of the cheese, adding the remaining cream if too thick. Spoon the cream over the gnocchi and broad beans and top with the remaining cheese before grilling. If not using the cream, just sprinkle with the crumbled blue cheese, Parmesan shavings or Gruyère slices and place under a hot grill, until the cheese melts.

A drizzle of olive oil, mixed with a squeeze or two of lime juice to finish, if using, offers a shiny glaze.

blue cheese fondue with spring dips

From the French, for 'melted', *fondue* is a term used in many recipe titles. This recipe is based on the Swiss classic cheese fondue – Swiss cheese melted in wine – but uses blue cheese instead. One particular blue cheese I enjoy is Beenleigh Blue, which is not the easiest to find, particularly at this time of the year, but if you do it will prove to be worthwhile. It's basically a ewe's milk cheese, quite full-flavoured without too dense a texture.

Another blue ewe's milk cheese is Lanark Blue, which resembles Roquefort in strength, needing to be calmed with another milder cheese for this recipe. There's also the more well-known Wensleydale, which is made from a combination of ewe's and cow's milk. Another favourite is the heavenly cow's milk Cashel Blue from Ireland.

To balance the richness of these strong-flavoured cheeses the quantity can be halved and the difference made up with Swiss Gruyère, the soft texture of which gives a smoother finish.

The spring garnishes are baby carrots, new potatoes and asparagus, along with radishes, spring onions and lots of crusty bread. The carrots, potatoes and asparagus can be served warm or cold; warm they do create a nice contrast with the other garnishes.

If you're not a fan of blue cheese at all, simply use all Gruyère. The spring vegetables then become the main feature.

SERVES 4 AS A MAIN COURSE OR SUPPER DISH
FOR THE GARNISHES
12 asparagus spears, trimmed of spiky ears and
 stalk base
salt and pepper
iced water
450g (1lb) baby carrots, peeled or scraped, leaving
 1–2cm (½–¾in) of stalk intact
450g (1lb) new potatoes
olive oil (optional)
bunch of radishes, trimmed
bunch of spring onions, trimmed
lots of crusty bread

OPPOSITE: BLUE CHEESE FONDUE WITH SPRING DIPS

FOR THE FONDUE
1 garlic clove, split in two (optional)
300ml (½ pint) white wine
450g (1lb) cheese (see above), grated or crumbled
1 level teaspoon cornflour or arrowroot
freshly grated nutmeg
juice of ½ lemon

The vegetable garnishes can all be cooked ahead, ready to reheat when needed. Cook the asparagus in boiling salted water for 2–4 minutes until tender but crisp. Refresh immediately in iced water. Cook the carrots in boiling salted water for 3–10 minutes, depending on their thickness. Refresh as above. Cook the new potatoes in boiling salted water for approximately 20 minutes. Drain and allow to cool naturally. If refreshed in cold water they do tend to become very soggy.

These can all be reheated in boiling water or in a steamer when needed, then drizzled with olive oil, if using, and seasoned with salt and pepper.

To make the fondue, rub the inside of a flameproof casserole or fondue pot with the garlic halves, if using. Add the white wine and bring to a gentle simmer over a medium-to-low heat. Gradually add the cheese, stirring as you do until melted. Loosen the cornflour or arrowroot with a little water and mix into the melted cheese, adding just enough to reach a fondue consistency. It's important to stir the fondue continuously during this process, to prevent the cheese from sticking to the base of the pan. Season with pepper, nutmeg and enough lemon juice to cut into the cheesy flavour.

Once the fondue is at a very gentle bubble, the right consistency will have been reached, and it will be ready to transfer to a spirit lamp on the table. The vegetables and the salad radishes and spring onions can be presented with the fondue, also offering crusty bread, all to be dipped into the fondue.

The baby carrots and asparagus can be left raw, giving your fondue experience a crunchy, crispy finish.
A tossed side salad eats very well with a fondue, its freshness cleansing the palate between dips.
If you decide on a pure Swiss fondue, using just Gruyère, the lemon juice should be replaced with 2–3 tablespoons of kirsch for the classic flavour.

flat asparagus salad with new potatoes and radishes

All the main components here are fortunate enough to share the same seasons, spring and summer. The 'flat' in the recipe title is purely a description of a very simple scattering of these ingredients flavoured with the dressings. Any of the new potatoes that are finding their way to us by the end of spring will work here, such as Jersey Royals, Pink Fir Apple, etc., along with the choice of salad leaves on offer. Once the salad leaves have been picked and washed it's important they are left to drain well.

SERVES 4 AS A STARTER
8 medium or 12 small new potatoes, cooked
salt and pepper
1 shallot, finely chopped
12–16 asparagus spears
iced water
225–350g (8–12oz) mixed salad leaves (such as
 dandelion, baby chard, lamb's lettuce, curly endive,
 spinach, lollo rosso, oak leaf, watercress, etc.)
8–10 radishes, washed and cut into thin wedges

FOR THE LEMON OIL DRESSING
3 tablespoons olive oil
3 teaspoons lemon juice

FOR THE SOURED CREAM DRESSING
2 tablespoons soured cream or crème fraîche
1 level teaspoon Dijon mustard
½ level teaspoon caster sugar
1–2 teaspoons lime juice or white wine vinegar

Quarter the hot cooked new potatoes, or halve if small, place in a bowl and season with salt and pepper. Make the lemon oil dressing by mixing the olive oil, lemon juice, salt and pepper and spoon half over the still-warm potatoes, with the chopped shallot. If the potatoes have been well cooked to a soft tender stage and are still warm, the dressing flavours will be absorbed.

For the soured cream dressing, whisk all of the ingredients together and season with salt and pepper. If too thick, loosen to a coating consistency with a drop or two of water.

Trim the pointy ears from the asparagus spears and snap or cut away the tough base of the stalks. Cut each spear in half and cook in boiling salted water for 2–3 minutes. When tender, refresh in iced water and pat dry. All of the previous preparation can be done several hours in advance, keeping the potatoes at room temperature.

To serve, mix the asparagus, salad leaves and radishes together, adding the remaining lemon oil dressing, gently spreading the flavour evenly. Spoon a little soured cream dressing onto the plates and scatter the asparagus salad and potatoes over it. Finish with trickles of the remaining soured cream dressing.

asparagus on buttery toast with melting parmesan cheese

There are very few ingredients in this dish – thick toast, fresh English spears and lots of Parmesan – but an awful lot of flavour. Asparagus crosses over the seasons, so you'll find it in both late spring and early summer.

SERVES 2 AS A STARTER
12–16 asparagus spears
salt and black pepper
2 thick oval slices of French stick
knob of butter, plus more for spreading and finishing
25–50g (1–2oz) fresh Parmesan cheese shavings or
**   grated Parmesan**

Trim the pointy ears away from the asparagus spears and snap or cut away 2–4cm (¾–1½in) of the tough stalk base. Cook the spears in boiling salted water for just 2 3 minutes (4 minutes maximum), until tender but still with a bite.

While the asparagus is cooking, spread both sides of the bread slices with butter and toast beneath a hot grill. Once golden, turn the slices and toast the other sides. Place the buttery toasts on plates.

Remove the asparagus from the water immediately when cooked and place in a separate pan with a knob of butter. Season with salt and pepper and lay on top of the toasts. Scatter the Parmesan shavings or grated Parmesan over the spears just before serving. For a softer finish place under the grill and warm to a melting stage.

The French bread can be rubbed with garlic before buttering and toasting.

May heralds a truly exciting season of British vegetables, with the English asparagus and new potatoes starting, and the first taste of the broad beans and peas to come (see page 128).

Asparagus is one of my favourite vegetables, and I probably appreciate it so much because its local season is short, no more than a couple of months. Asparagus is a member of the lily family, surprisingly enough, and is one of the rare edible plants that form shoots or stalks rather than fruits or leaves. Like sea kale, asparagus can be blanched while growing to make it white. White spears are popular on the continent, but we prefer them unblanched and green here, varying from the very thin spears called sprue, to fatter 'jumbo' specimens. (Rumour has it growers are experimenting with purple asparagus as well.)

Locally grown new potatoes are best at this time of year as well. Planted some fourteen or so weeks before, these 'first earlies' are small, firm, waxy in texture, with a tender, damp skin that can be scraped off. There are many different

varieties on the market, with sturdily British or exotically foreign names, but my favourite is one which still counts as British although it only grows on an island nearer to France than Britain. The Jersey Royal potato has a thin skin, matchless flavour and cooks very easily. Despite efforts from growers, the potato has not taken anywhere else other than Jersey, a 'fluke' (as it was once known) which has adapted itself to the volcanic soil of the island. Discovered in about 1880, it is now planted all over the island, fertilized by seaweed, and hand-planted and hand-picked – a very special May treat indeed. With just some butter drizzling on top, I could eat a plateful of Jerseys, with asparagus offering a welcome helping hand – as a meal in itself.

white asparagus with a warm casserole salad of mushrooms and spring onions

English spears of white asparagus can be found in mid-to-late spring and, although rare, are worth looking out for, but the Dutch variety is the more common during this season. The spears themselves can often be particularly thick, and will need to be peeled, trimming away the stalk ends. If you are lucky enough to find the thinner stalks, then perhaps they will still require a very light peeling and trimming for guaranteed tenderness.

Three to four thick spears per person will be plenty as a starter, or six to seven if smaller. The 'casserole salad' is purely a description of the loose stock-style of dressing that binds the thick chestnut mushrooms with the asparagus.

SERVES 4 AS A STARTER

12–16 or 24–28 (depending on size) white asparagus spears, prepared (see above)
salt and pepper
iced water
knob of butter
12 chestnut mushrooms (small white mushrooms can also be used)
5 tablespoons hazelnut, walnut or olive oil (nut oils will enhance the naturally nutty chestnut mushrooms)

2 tablespoons sherry vinegar
100ml (3½fl oz) *Vegetable stock* (page 417) or *Instant stock* (page 416)
squeeze of lemon juice
2–3 spring onions, outside layer of skin removed
1 tablespoon roughly chopped flatleaf or curly parsley

Blanch the asparagus spears in boiling salted water, allowing 4–5 minutes for the thin and 5–6 for the thicker. (It's best to cook them in batches – too many spears will reduce the temperature of the water, leading to stewing rather than boiling.) Remove from the water and plunge into iced water, which will instantly stop the cooking process. Once cold (the time in iced water need only be equal to the cooking time), remove and dry lightly on kitchen paper. The asparagus can now be refrigerated until needed. However, for this particular dish I'd suggest serving the spears at room temperature or lightly warmed with a brushing of butter under the grill or gently in a frying pan. Another warming method is to heat the spears in a tablespoon or two of water with a knob of butter.

Quarter each of the mushrooms. Heat 2 tablespoons of the oil in a large frying pan and season the mushrooms with salt and pepper. These can now be fried for a few minutes until golden brown and tender. Remove the mushrooms from the pan and keep warm.

On a medium heat, add the sherry vinegar to the pan. This will almost instantly reduce in volume and, at the same time, release all the flavours from the pan. Add the stock and bring to the boil. Add the remaining oil and a squeeze of lemon juice to taste. Season with salt and pepper. The 'casserole' liquor will now be in a loose vinaigrette form, with enough piquancy to enhance the dish. Split the spring onions lengthwise and, at quite an acute angle, cut the halves into long, very thin slices.

Divide the spears between plates or bowls and sit the mixed mushrooms and spring onions on top of each portion. Add the chopped parsley to the dressing and spoon over each serving.

The nut oils are more expensive and not essential to the dish, but can add a touch of luxury to the finished flavour. If sherry vinegar is unavailable, sherry itself can be used, or red wine vinegar. Pure lemon juice can also stand as the only acidity in the liquor.

OPPOSITE: WHITE ASPARAGUS WITH A WARM CASSEROLE SALAD OF MUSHROOMS AND SPRING ONIONS

fillet of sea trout on cauliflower cream with a fresh herb-pea dressing

This recipe will serve four as a starter, but it does also eat very well as a main course, simply multiplying the ingredients 1½–2 times. The herb oil certainly will not need to be increased, as quantities given make 150ml (¼ pint). The oil keeps very well refrigerated for up to a week or more, retaining its rich herb flavour and green colour. The fresh peas will be beginning to show their faces during this last spring month; if unavailable, frozen peas can also be used or simply carry the recipe through to their prime time of summer. The main feature of this recipe, the sea trout, is as good as salmon, and also with us through the months of spring into summer – well worth catching.

SERVES 4 AS A STARTER
75g (3oz) podded peas
iced water
450g (1lb) fillet of sea trout, pin-boned (page 9)
flour, for dusting
1–2 tablespoons olive oil
knob of butter
½ lime

FOR THE CAULIFLOWER CREAM
25g (1oz) butter
½ medium or 1 small cauliflower, cut into small florets
200ml (7fl oz) milk
salt and pepper
squeeze of lemon juice (optional)

FOR THE HERB OIL
1 tablespoon chopped curly or torn flatleaf parsley
1 tablespoon torn chervil leaves
1 tablespoon chopped dill
1 tablespoon chopped chives
1 tablespoon chopped tarragon
100ml (3½fl oz) olive oil
3 tablespoons groundnut oil

To make the cauliflower cream, melt the butter in a heavy-based saucepan. Add the florets, cover with a lid and cook on a very low heat, without colouring, for 10–15 minutes, until beginning to soften. Add the milk and, once gently simmering, return the lid and cook for a further 15 minutes until the cauliflower is cooked and collapsing. Season with salt and pepper. If the cauliflower has taken on a greyish muddy pink colour, don't worry: once liquidized the purée will whiten.

Blitz the cauliflower in a liquidizer, adding a spoonful at a time and loosening with the milk in which it was cooked. With continual liquidizing, a very soft smooth finish will be achieved. If using a food processor, the purée may well need to be pushed through a sieve for a completely smooth finish. Seasoning can now be added, and a squeeze of lemon juice as an optional extra, for a gentle citrus bite. This purée will eat at its best if served warm.

To make the herb oil, reserve a level teaspoon of each herb to garnish the peas. Place all of the remaining chopped herbs in a liquidizer. Heat the olive and groundnut oils together in a small saucepan until just warm. Pour on top of the herbs and liquidize to a smooth purée. Strain the oil through a sieve. Kept refrigerated, the oil will last for up to two weeks.

To cook the fresh peas in advance, plunge them into boiling salted water and cook until tender. Drain and refresh in iced water before redraining. To reheat, the peas can either be microwaved or plunged back into boiling water for a minute.

Cut the sea trout fillet into four equal portions, checking the flesh has been pin-boned. Now score the skin side with a sharp knife, cutting just two or three lengths. Season the flesh side of the fillets with salt and pepper, and the skin side with salt only. Lightly dust the skin side with flour. Heat a frying pan and add the olive oil. Once bubbling, place the fillets in, skin-side down, making sure the fish is left alone and not moved. Cook for 4–5 minutes (6 minutes maximum), then add the knob of butter. Turn the fish and remove the pan from the heat. The residual heat of the pan will finish the cooking process without overcooking the fish.

Warm the peas, then add them to just 4–6 tablespoons of the fresh herb oil. Add the reserved chopped herbs and juice from the half lime. Adjust the seasoning with salt and pepper. Spoon the warm cauliflower purée into the centre of plates or bowls. Spoon the peas and dressing around, creating a border. Sit the sea trout on top of the cauliflower cream and serve.

OPPOSITE: FILLET OF SEA TROUT ON CAULIFLOWER CREAM WITH A FRESH HERB-PEA DRESSING

parsleyed plaice fillets with roast bananas and sweet mustard onions

The title may give the impression of an overcrowded plate of fighting flavours, but this dish really does eat in quite the opposite way.

The recipe is a fresh and simpler look at a French classic known as *filet de plie caprice*. More familiarly associated with sole, the dish consists of grilled breadcrumbed fillets with pan-fried banana and a *sauce Robert* (a gravy-based sauce flavoured with onions, sugar, vinegar, pepper and mustard).

All of those flavours, bar the gravy, have some form of inclusion here, still complementing one another beautifully. Warm buttered new potatoes and/or a tossed salad make this dish a full meal.

SERVES 4 AS A MAIN COURSE
4 plaice fillets, taken from an 800–900g (1¾–2lb) fish, skinned and trimmed
salt and pepper
cooking oil
2 small bananas, split lengthwise
flour, for dusting
knob of butter

FOR THE CRUMBS
5–6 slices of thick white bread, crusts removed
generous handful of picked curly parsley
25g (1oz) butter, melted

FOR THE SWEET MUSTARD ONIONS
knob of butter
4 English onions, halved and thinly sliced
3 tablespoons white wine vinegar
2 level teaspoons demerara sugar
1 teaspoon ready-made English mustard
Cayenne or black pepper

To make the sweet onions, melt the knob of butter. Once bubbling, add the sliced onions and fry until well coloured and softened. Add the vinegar and sugar, stirring, and reduce until almost dry. Add the English mustard to taste and season with salt and your chosen pepper. The onions will now have taken on a thick relish consistency. Extra vinegar and sugar can be added and reduced in volume for a more sweet-and-sour finish.

To make the crumbs, cut the bread slices into rough dice and place in a food processor with the picked parsley. Blitz to fine crumbs, with the parsley turning the crumbs green. Season with salt and pepper. Place the crumbs in a bowl, folding in the melted butter. Either preheat the grill or preheat the oven to 200°C/400°F/Gas 6. Butter and season one large or two smaller baking trays. Season the fish fillets with salt and pepper and place on the baking trays. Each can now be topped with the crumbs, covering the fish completely. The plaice fillets can either be cooked under the preheated grill for 6–8 minutes or baked in the preheated oven for 8–10 minutes.

While the fish is cooking, heat a frying pan with a drop of cooking oil. Dust the banana halves in flour before pan-frying quickly in the hot pan, adding the knob of butter, until golden brown on both sides.

The dish can now be presented with the banana sitting on top of or beside the plaice, offering the sweet mustard onions separately.

The Lemon butter *on page 329 (omitting the tarragon) eats very well drizzled over or around the fish.*

grilled plaice or lemon sole fillets with champagne-glazed spinach

Either of these two flat fish can be used in this recipe, both available to us during this spring month.

It's not essential to use extravagant champagne; white wine will also blend with the other flavours. However, champagne or sparkling white wine does seem to add a little extra fizz to the end result, working well alongside the Noilly Prat vermouth.

SERVES 4 AS A MAIN COURSE
2 × 675g–800g (1½–1¾lb) plaice or lemon soles, filleted and skinned
flour, for dusting
knob of butter, plus more for greasing and buttering
salt and pepper
900g (2lb) fresh young spinach, washed and stalks removed

FOR THE CHAMPAGNE CREAM SAUCE
knob of butter
3 shallots, finely chopped
175g (6oz) button or chestnut mushrooms, sliced
200ml (7fl oz) champagne or sparkling white wine

100ml (3½fl oz) Noilly Prat dry vermouth
200ml (7fl oz) double cream
100ml (3½fl oz) crème fraîche
1–2 teaspoons lemon juice
salt
Cayenne pepper
2 egg yolks

To create an extra grilling effect with the plaice or lemon soles, they can first be marked with a hot skewer. Although not essential, it helps the finished presentation and imparts a slight bitter grilled flavour. To achieve this, simply heat thin metal skewers on a naked flame or under a hot grill.

Lightly flour the filleted presentation side of each fish fillet (you'll have two smaller fillets from each of the large ones, giving two pieces per serving) and mark at an angle by laying the hot skewer across it to form the deep lines, reheating the skewer as needed. Once all are marked, lay on a buttered and seasoned tray, then lightly butter and salt the fillets.

For the sauce, melt the knob of butter in a frying pan and add the chopped shallots. Cook for a few minutes until softened but not coloured, then add the mushrooms. Continue to cook until these are also softened. Add the champagne or sparkling wine and vermouth and bring to a simmer. Cook on a high heat to reduce in volume by three-quarters. Add half of the double cream along with the crème fraîche, and bring back to a simmer. Cook for 2–3 minutes, then add the lemon juice with salt and Cayenne pepper to taste. Strain the sauce into a clean pan, keeping the mushrooms and shallots to one side.

While making the sauce, melt a knob of butter in a small saucepan. Add the spinach leaves and cook for a few minutes until wilted and tender. Season with salt and a twist of pepper, squeezing away any excess water.

Add the reserved mushrooms and shallots from the sauce to the spinach and divide either between individual ovenproof dishes big enough to carry two pieces of fish each, or two large dishes that will hold four fish pieces each when served.

Preheat the grill. Lightly whip the remaining double cream to soft peaks, then mix with the egg yolks. Fold this into the champagne cream sauce and pour over the spinach. Glaze to a golden brown under a preheated very hot grill.

The fish will now take just 3–4 minutes to cook under the preheated grill. The grilled fillets can now be presented on plates or sitting on top of the glazed spinach and mushrooms.

The fish can also be plainly steamed, presenting the natural white fillets on top of the glazed spinach and mushrooms.

GRILLED PLAICE OR LEMON SOLE FILLETS WITH CHAMPAGNE-GLAZED SPINACH

lemon sole and spinach with vanilla-rosemary carrots

Vanilla is a spice that will work with many vegetables, and the baby carrots and young spinach available to us in late spring both accept its quite aromatic touch. Rosemary is a herb that can be so overpowering, but here lends just enough to complement all the other flavours. With this recipe the baby carrots are going to be well cooked, taking on a gentle softness so as not to fight the tenderness of the delicate sole fillets.

SERVES 4 AS A MAIN COURSE

**4 × 550g (1¼lb) lemon soles, each divided into
  4 skinned fillets**
**15–25g (½–1oz) butter, to finish the sauce, plus a knob
  for the spinach and more for greasing**
salt and pepper
**450g (1lb) baby carrots, peeled or scraped, leaving
  1–1½cm (½–¾in) of stalk on top**
1 vanilla pod, split and seeds scraped out
**sprig of rosemary, plus ½ teaspoon picked leaves, cut
  into shorter sticks**
1 teaspoon caster sugar
2–3 tablespoons double cream
squeeze of lemon juice
**675g (1½lb) baby spinach, washed and stalks removed
  if necessary**

Preheat the oven to 190°C/375°F/Gas 5. Fold each sole fillet into a looped cravat shape. Place on a large roasting tray lined with buttered and seasoned parchment paper and refrigerate.

Place the carrots in a large saucepan and barely cover with water. Add the vanilla pod and seeds, along with the sprig of rosemary, caster sugar and a pinch of salt. Bring to a simmer and cook for 8–10 minutes, or longer if the carrots are not so thin, until cooked through. Remove the carrots from the pan and keep to one side.

Boil the cooking liquor to reduce in volume by three-quarters. Remove the vanilla pod and rosemary. Add the double cream and bring to a simmer. When needed, the sauce can now be finished, adding just 15g (½oz) of the measured butter. For a thicker and richer finish add the remaining measured butter. Finally, add a squeeze of lemon juice, along with the cut rosemary leaves.

Season the fish with salt and pour a little water into the roasting tray to barely cover the base. Bring to a simmer on the hob, cover with foil and finish in the preheated oven for just a few minutes, 5 maximum. Once cooked, remove the fillets from the oven.

While the fish is cooking, melt the knob of butter in a large saucepan and, once bubbling, add the spinach leaves. These will cook in literally just a minute or two, becoming tender almost immediately. Season with salt and pepper, then drain off any excess water.

The carrots can now be reheated in a tablespoon or two of water or in a microwave for a few seconds. Arrange the sole fillets on plates, with the carrots and spinach sitting either side. Spoon the sauce over the carrots or simply around the plates to complete the dish.

If baby spinach is unavailable, a few extra minutes will need to be added to the larger spinach leaves' cooking time.

monkfish steaks with court-bouillon and mushrooms

Court-bouillon is the acidic stock usually made for cooking fish and seafoods, but which also works very well with vegetables and some meats. The one used here is much milder, omitting the vinegar and replacing it with the sweet acidic bite of fresh orange and lemon juices, and the white wine, so now all of the flavours work with the mushrooms. Having joined us during that last week of April, St George's mushrooms reach their healthy plump prime in May, and the monkfish is also at its prime through both of these spring months.

A 750g (1¾lb) fish, will be needed for this recipe. Once filleted from its central bone and trimmed (see method, page 23), the fillets are best cut at an angle, starting from the point of the tail, to provide good portions throughout, cutting each fillet into 4–6 slices, to create 2–3 steaks per portion.

SERVES 4 AS A MAIN COURSE

550g (1¼lb) St George's mushrooms
2 tablespoons olive oil
**1 × 750g (1¾lb) monkfish, filleted and portioned
  (see above)**
salt and pepper
flour, for dusting
50g (2oz) butter, plus an extra knob
1 tablespoon torn flatleaf parsley
1 heaped teaspoon chopped chives

FOR THE COURT-BOUILLON
3 small carrots
4 button onions, sliced
100ml (3½fl oz) white wine
juice of 1 orange
juice of ½ lemon
½ teaspoon light brown or demerara sugar

To clean the mushrooms, trim away the stalk base and rinse the mushrooms in cold water. Leave them to dry on kitchen paper, while the court-bouillon and fish are being prepared and cooked.

To prepare the court-bouillon, cut the carrots into very thin round slices. (Before slicing, the carrots can be shaped with a cannelle cutter knife which, when pulled along the carrots, will create grooves. About 3–5 grooves give a floral shape to the finished slices.) Place the carrot and onion slices, white wine, 50ml (2fl oz) of water, the juice of the orange and lemon and sugar in a saucepan. Bring to a simmer and cook for 1–2 minutes, then remove from the heat and leave to cool.

Heat the olive oil in a large frying pan (or two). Season the monkfish steaks with salt and pepper and lightly dust with the flour. Once the pan is hot the fish can be carefully placed in it, taking care not to overfill the pan as this will reduce the temperature, boiling the fish rather than frying it.

Fry the fish for 2–3 minutes until golden brown, then turn and fry the other sides for a further 2–3 minutes. Once cooked, remove the fish from the pan and place in a suitable ovenproof dish. The steaks can now be kept warm in a low oven while the mushrooms are frying.

Rinse the frying pan and place it back on the heat. Once hot, add the knob of butter and the mushrooms. Fry on a high temperature for a few minutes until beginning to soften.

Return the court-bouillon to a simmer while the mushrooms are cooking. Add the 50g (2oz) of butter, shaking it into the court-bouillon until blended to a silky finish. Add the chopped herbs and season with salt and pepper.

Divide the mushrooms between four large bowls. Remove the monkfish steaks from the oven and arrange on top of the mushrooms. Any juices released from the fish can be added to the court-bouillon, before spooning it around the fish and mushrooms.

Cultivated or other wild mushrooms (ceps, chanterelles, etc.) can be used in place of the St George's variety featured here.

grilled mackerel fillets with a fennel, parmesan and green olive salad

This recipe is portioned into four starters. However, this lively, hot and cold crisp salad will also eat well as a main course (simply double the ingredients), or as an accompaniment at your summer *al fresco* table.

The mackerel fillets are cooked on a ridged grill plate, but do eat well taken straight from a hot barbecue. If a grill plate is unavailable, pan-fry, following the same cooking times.

SERVES 4 AS A STARTER
12 juicy green olives, pitted
4 mackerel fillets, pin-boned (page 9) and skinned
coarse sea salt and twist of pepper
flour, for dusting
olive oil and softened butter, for brushing
1 quantity *Crisp fennel salad* (page 174), replacing
    1 teaspoon of lemon juice with 1 teaspoon of
    champagne vinegar or white wine vinegar
2 spring onions, very finely shredded
1 tablespoon chopped mixed herbs (basil, chives,
    chervil, etc.)
50g (2oz) fresh Parmesan cheese shavings (or coarse
    gratings)

Preheat a ridged grill plate or barbecue. Split the green olives in half lengthwise before cutting them into thin wedges.

Season the mackerel fillets with sea salt and pepper. Lightly flour the skinned sides, before brushing with olive oil.

Place the fillets on the preheated grill plate, floured-side down, cooking for 2 minutes before turning and continuing to cook for a further 2 minutes. While the mackerel are grilling, mix together the fennel salad, sliced olives, spring onions, herbs and Parmesan shavings or gratings.

Divide the finished salad between four plates. Brush each mackerel fillet with softened butter, sprinkling with a few sea salt flakes, before presenting with the salad.

If pan-frying, heat a tablespoon or two of olive oil in a pan. Once hot, lay the fillets in, floured-side down, cooking for 2 minutes on each side and finishing as above.

prawn and crème fraîche tart with samphire and tomato salad

The prawns used in this recipe are the North Atlantic variety, and are fairly easy to obtain cooked but unpeeled. Some of the shells will be used to make the dressing for the samphire salad. Samphire usually comes on the culinary scene during the last month of spring and goes on into summer. It is certainly not the easiest of ingredients to hunt down, mostly found growing on the salt marshes along the north coast of Norfolk. If unavailable, the prawn tart will survive on its own or with blanched French beans making a good substitute.

SERVES 6–8 AS A STARTER OR 4 AS A MAIN COURSE

175g (6oz) *Shortcrust pastry* (page 425) or *Puff pastry* (page 426)
flour, for dusting
4 tomatoes
iced water
350g (12oz) cooked unpeeled North Atlantic prawns
knob of butter
6 spring onions, finely shredded
2 eggs, plus 1 extra yolk
150ml (¼ pint) crème fraîche
salt and pepper
75g (3oz) Gruyère or Cheddar cheese, grated
1 tablespoon chopped chives (about 1cm/½in long)
***Prawn dressing* (page 117), using shells from the prawns**
350g (12oz) samphire

Roll out the pastry on a lightly floured surface and use to line an 18cm (7in) flan tin or ring set on a baking tray. Any overhanging pastry can be left (once cooked, this can be carefully cut away to give an even finish). Refrigerate and allow to rest for 30 minutes.

Preheat the oven to 190ºC/375ºF/Gas 5. Line the base of the pastry with greaseproof paper and fill with baking beans or rice. Bake blind for 20 minutes. Remove the beans and paper and return to the oven for a further 6 minutes. Then trim off excess pastry and leave to cool. Reduce the oven temperature to 160ºC/325ºF/Gas 3.

Blanch the tomatoes (this can be done up to 24 hours in advance). Using the point of a small, sharp knife cut around the edges of the tomato eyes until they become completely free and cut a small cross at the base of each. Plunge the tomatoes into rapidly boiling water, leaving firm tomatoes in the water for 8–10 seconds, very ripe ones for 6–8 seconds, then transfer to iced water. The tomatoes are now ready to peel, with the skin pulling away easily. To prepare the tomatoes for the salad, quarter them, remove the seeds and discard, and place the flesh on kitchen paper. This will absorb the excess water, leaving a firmer texture. The flesh can then be diced into 1cm (½in) pieces.

Peel the prawns, saving 50g (2oz) of the shells for the prawn dressing. Melt the butter and, when bubbling, add the spring onions. Turn in the pan just once or twice to remove their rawness, but retain their texture. Remove from the pan and leave to cool.

Beat together the eggs and egg yolk, then whisk in the crème fraîche and season with salt and pepper. Stir in the grated cheese, along with the chives.

Mix together the peeled prawns and spring onions, season lightly and sprinkle into the tart case. Pour the crème fraîche mixture over the prawns and bake for 40–45 minutes until the flan has just set. The flan is now best left to rest for 15–20 minutes before removing from the tin and serving. This not only allows the flan to cool slightly to a warm temperature, eating at its best, but also allows the cream filling to relax, giving a softer finish.

While the flan is cooking, prepare the dressing and salad. For the dressing, use the reserved prawn shells and follow the recipe on page 117.

For the salad, cut the woody roots from the samphire and wash well, then blanch in rapidly boiling salted water for 30–60 seconds. This will still leave it with a crisp texture. Refresh in iced water and drain. Add the tomato dice and season with a twist of pepper (salt is not really necessary due to the saltiness of the samphire).

Add enough prawn dressing to bind the salad before serving with the tart.

OPPOSITE: PRAWN AND CRÈME FRAÎCHE TART WITH SAMPHIRE AND TOMATO SALAD

warm gammon with sticky pineapple

This recipe is a lunch or supper plate, with slices of warm carved gammon, spoonfuls of sticky caramelized pineapple, maybe a bowl of salad leaves and hot Jersey Royals. The real essence of this combination is the pineapple, plentiful now and with a rich, fruity taste.

The cooked gammon component is optional. There are so many quality hams produced across the country, all with their own character and flavour, and readily available. So if you haven't got time for cooking the gammon, choose some good thick slices of ham, finishing with a spoonful of the warm sticky pineapple. If cooking the gammon, the middle cut is the leanest prime joint, taken from the middle part of the whole leg.

The difference between ham and gammon is quite simple. Ham is the hind leg of the pig, removed before salting and curing. The gammon is left attached to the carcass while being soaked in brine. Consequently, gammon is a lot less salty than ham, not really needing to be soaked in cold water for 24 hours (it's still best to check with your butcher, and take their advice).

SERVES 4–6 AS A LUNCH OR SUPPER DISH
1 × 1.5kg (3½lb) middle-cut boneless gammon joint
few black peppercorns
2 carrots, peeled and roughly chopped (optional)
2 onions, roughly chopped (optional)
3 celery sticks, trimmed and roughly chopped
(optional)

FOR THE STICKY PINEAPPLE
1 small–medium ripe pineapple
2 tablespoons light soft brown or caster sugar
coarse sea salt and black pepper
100–150ml (3½fl oz–¼ pint) apple juice
finely grated zest of 1 lime (optional)

Put the gammon joint in a large saucepan, covering with cold water. Bring to the boil. Once at this point, pour the water away; this also disposes of any scum collected on the surface. This blanching method will also have released any excess salt content. Refill with fresh cold water. Add the black pepper-corns and vegetables, if using, returning the pot to the boil.

OPPOSITE: WARM GAMMON WITH STICKY PINEAPPLE

Continue to simmer, allowing 20–25 minutes per 450g (1lb). Once the total cooking time is reached, remove the pan from the heat. This joint is to be served warm, more or less at room temperature, after leaving the meat to relax in the cooking liquor.

To prepare the fruit, cut off the top and bottom, trimming away the outer skin. Chop the pineapple into 1cm (½in) dice, discarding the central core. Heat a large non-stick frying pan over a fairly high heat. Once hot, add the diced pineapple, sprinkling with the sugar. Fry quickly, tossing or stirring the fruit cubes for a minute or two before adding 100ml (3½fl oz) of apple juice carefully, as this will often spit on hitting the pan. Once simmering, the juice will begin to thicken, forming a syrupy consistency. The extra 50ml (2fl oz) of juice can be added for a looser finish. Season with a sprinkling of coarse sea salt and a generous twist of black pepper, adding a hot spicy edge to the sweet fruits. For an extra sharp acidic bite, add the lime zest, if using. Transfer the pineapple to a suitable dish and keep warm. I prefer to eat the sticky pineapple warm. However, any left over will eat equally well cold.

Remove the warm gammon from the pot, cutting away the outside skin. The joint is ready to carve on to plates, spooning the sticky pineapple chunks alongside.

Any remaining sticky pineapple can be stored in an airtight jar for several days.
The gammon cooking liquor and vegetables can be reboiled, chopping and adding any gammon left over, to create a pot of broth.
Pan-fried gammon steaks will also eat well with the warm pineapple.

boiled ham hock with braised lentils and wild girolles

The ham hock is the same cut of the meat as the knuckle of pork. However, the ham hock has been salted and matured, while the knuckle will be taken from the untreated leg of pork. Either can be used for this recipe, but the ham finish does lend a different taste and texture.

Girolles are also known as chanterelles, and are quite often mistaken as exactly the same. Yes, they are related, but are actually different strains of the same species of mushroom. The girolle is found between the months of May and June, sometimes lasting into July. The chanterelle is available between midsummer and autumn. Another distinctive difference is in size: girolles do tend to be on the smaller side, lovely to use for both their flavour and garnishing qualities. Apart from these few pointers, the two mushrooms both hold a yellow orange or apricot colour and scent and are a delight to eat. To clean a girolle, it's best to scrape the stalk and trim its base and then rinse the mushroom under cold water to remove any grit. Leave to drain and dry. Another method is to blanch the cleaned mushrooms quickly in boiling water, plunging them in and out in seconds. The heat of the water seals the mushrooms, preventing them from becoming waterlogged or bleeding their juices.

SERVES 4–6 AS A MAIN COURSE

3 ham hocks (or pork knuckles)

2 onions

2 carrots

1 bay leaf

few peppercorns

few parsley stalks

175g (6oz) Puy lentils

1 large carrot, cut into 5mm (¼in) dice

1 large onion, cut into 5mm (¼in) dice

2 celery sticks, cut into 5mm (¼in) dice

salt and pepper

2 tablespoons chopped flatleaf parsley

2 knobs of butter

225–350g (8–12oz) girolles, cleaned (see above)

150ml (¼ pint) crème fraîche (optional)

squeeze of lemon juice (optional)

1 heaped teaspoon chopped chives (optional)

Cover the hocks with cold water and bring to a simmer. Cook for a few minutes, then drain and rinse under cold water. Return the hocks to the stove, adding the onions, carrots, bay leaf, peppercorns and parsley stalks. Cover with water (no salt; the ham already has enough) and bring to a simmer. Cook over a gentle heat for approximately 2½–3 hours, until very tender and the small bone within the ham hock becomes loose. Remove the pan from the heat.

To cook the lentils (this is best started 15 minutes before the hocks have finished their cooking time, with the lentils' total stewing time giving the hocks a reasonable resting period), quickly blanch them in boiling water and then drain and refresh under cold water. Place the lentils in a pan with 600ml (1 pint) of the ham cooking liquor, straining it over them. Bring to a simmer and cook for 25–30 minutes, topping up the pan with extra liquor if needed. It is best to keep the lentils soft and loose within the finished liquor.

While the lentils are cooking, place the diced carrot, onion and celery in a separate small pan, cover with strained hock-cooking liquor, bring to a simmer and cook for 10–12 minutes. Once tender, keep to one side, adding them to the lentils once they are softened. Remove the skin from the hocks, breaking chunks of tender meat from the bone. Add the ham pieces to the lentils, checking for seasoning, before adding the chopped parsley and a knob of butter.

Now fry the girolles very quickly in the remaining butter in a hot pan, for just a minute or two until tender.

To present the dish, spoon the ham lentils onto a large serving plate or bowl, then sprinkle with the sautéed girolles and serve.

If using the crème fraîche, once the girolles have been removed from the frying pan, add the squeeze of lemon juice to the pan, along with the crème fraîche, and bring to a simmer before seasoning with salt and pepper. Add the chopped chives and drizzle over and around dish.

pot-roasted lamb with sorrel and samphire

This dish has quite a combination of flavours, but all work with, and for, one another. There is also a honey-and-mustard glaze as an extra with which to finish the lamb, providing a sticky, hot sweetness to the meat. The fresh sorrel lends a lemony touch, that works well with honey and mustard, and finishes the light cream sauce.

Marsh samphire, a salty vegetable, grows by seashore rocks and is often found in the East Anglian marshes. It is most usually served with seafood; however, young marshland lamb is often served with samphire as a salty garnish, too. This shoulder may not be of the marshland variety but it does eat well with this well-seasoned vegetable and the creamy sorrel sauce. If you can't find samphire, extra-fine French beans or flat runner beans sliced thinly could act as a substitute, but they are best seasoned with rock salt to get the abundance of flavour required.

SERVES 4 AS A MAIN COURSE

1 shoulder of lamb, boned and rolled (about 675g/1½lb)

salt and pepper

2 tablespoons cooking oil

1 lemon

300ml (½ pint) white wine

900ml (1½ pints) *Chicken stock (page 416)* or *Instant stock (page 416)*
20 sorrel leaves
1 dessertspoon clear honey
1 tablespoon ready-made English mustard
1 heaped teaspoon butter, plus a knob for the samphire
1 heaped teaspoon plain flour
90ml (3fl oz) whipping or single cream
675g (1½lb) samphire

Preheat the oven to 160°C/325°F/Gas 3. Season the rolled shoulder with salt and pepper. Heat the cooking oil in a roasting tray, placing in the lamb. Cook over a moderate heat until the joint is well coloured all over.

Place the lamb in an ovenproof braising pot and rub with the juice from half the lemon. Add half of the white wine with the chicken or instant stock, bring to a gentle simmer and cover with a lid. The lamb can now be pot-roasted in the preheated oven for 2½ hours. After the first 2 hours, add 14 of the sorrel leaves to the pot. As the lamb continues to cook, the sorrel flavour will influence the stock. The joint will now be very tender. Remove the meat from the pot and place on a roasting tray.

Strain the cooking liquor through a sieve, and skim away excess fat. In a saucepan, boil the remaining white wine and the juice from the other half of the lemon, and reduce in volume by three-quarters, then add 200ml (7fl oz) of the cooking liquor. Whisk in the honey and mustard, then spoon this over the lamb and place the tray on top of the stove. On a medium heat, boil and reduce the liquor, turning the lamb as it glazes. This can be a little untidy, due to spitting, but does help the lamb accept the glaze very quickly. Once the liquor is completely reduced in volume and sticky, remove the lamb from the heat and leave to rest for 15–20 minutes.

In a clean saucepan, the remaining cooking liquor can now be boiled and reduced, if necessary, leaving you with approximately 300ml (½ pint). Mix together the teaspoon of butter with the flour, then whisk this in bit by bit. The butter and flour combination is a thickening agent known as *beurre manié* (kneaded butter). This small quantity will just start to thicken the sauce. Simmer gently for a few minutes, then add the cream. Any remaining last few drops of lemon juice from the two halves can also be added. Season with salt and pepper. Finely shred the remaining 6 sorrel leaves and add them to the sauce.

The samphire can be prepared in advance, washing it well and snipping away any woody stems. Plunge the samphire pieces into boiling unsalted water (the samphire is very salty).

Once reboiling, drain and season with a twist of pepper and add the knob of butter.

To serve, carve the shoulder into thick slices and offer them with the samphire and sorrel cream sauce.

Mashed potatoes (page 422) or new potatoes will eat well with this dish.

roast chicken with primo pipérade

Primo, along with Hispi, are our early brassicas, each expressing its own identity and flavour. These two are the first summer cabbages to arrive in our shops, best eaten straight from the ground, not allowing their crisp leaves to wilt.

Primo, the one featured here, has a British season stretching between May and July (the Hispi finishes in June). The advantage of these varieties is their ability to be eaten as you would a white cabbage – cooked or raw.

To bind with the butter-steamed Primo we have pipérade. This is a fondue of sweet peppers – home-grown begin in May, stretching comfortably through to October – flavoured with onions, garlic and tomatoes. A classic from the Basque region, pipérade is often cooked with scrambled eggs, sometimes with cured bacon to finish. Here, we're borrowing the sweet pepper, onion and garlic from the classic recipe and working them into the cabbage, accompanying the roast bird.

This is a meal in itself but a bowl of piping-hot new potatoes with a drizzling of butter is a good accompaniment. *Mashed potatoes* (page 422) are also a great choice.

SERVES 4 AS A MAIN COURSE
1 × 1.75kg (4lb) free-range chicken
75g (3oz) butter
salt and pepper
3 tablespoons olive oil
2 English onions, finely sliced
2 red peppers, seeded and cut into 5mm (¼in) strips
1 yellow pepper, seeded and cut into 5mm (¼in) strips
2 garlic cloves, finely crushed
Cayenne pepper
450g (1lb) Primo cabbage, washed, quartered lengthwise, with central stalk removed, and cut into 5mm (¼in) strips
3 plum tomatoes, blanched (page 92), skinned, quartered and cut into 5mm (¼in) strips (optional)

Preheat the oven to 200ºC/400ºF/Gas 6. Put the bird in a roasting tray, brushing it with two-thirds of the butter and seasoning with salt and pepper. Place the tray in the preheated oven, roasting for 1 hour and basting the melted butter over the bird from time to time. The chicken will now be a rich golden brown and tender. To check it is cooked through, the leg can be pierced with a skewer. If clear juices are released, the cooking of the chicken is complete. If still slightly pink, continue to roast for a further 10–15 minutes.

Once roasted, remove the tray from the oven, covering the chicken with foil and keeping warm to one side for 15 minutes, allowing the bird to rest.

While roasting the chicken the pipérade can be prepared. Heat the olive oil in a large saucepan, adding the sliced onions. Fry the onions for a few minutes until just beginning to soften. Add the red and yellow peppers and garlic, stirring them in well, before covering and simmering for approximately 7–8 minutes until tender. Season with salt and Cayenne pepper. This stage can be achieved a little in advance, ready to reheat with the cabbage.

For the cabbage, melt the remaining butter in a large pan. Once bubbling, add the shredded leaves, simmering over a moderate heat. Should the cabbage begin to stick, add a tablespoon or two of water. Continue to simmer, seasoning with salt and pepper, for a minute or two until tender. Add the pipérade and tomatoes, if using, stirring them together.

To carve the chicken, remove the legs, splitting each between the thigh and drumstick. The breasts can now be carved from the bird or totally removed, splitting each in two, for a chunkier finish. A piece of leg and breast can now be presented on each plate, spooning a generous helping of the primo pipérade to accompany.

Any chicken juices and butter remaining in the roasting pan can be quickly heated on the stove, spooning the bubbling flavours over each portion of the bird.

Slices of Parma or Bayonne ham (these can be left whole or cut into strips) can be pan-fried in a little olive oil until crispy, presenting them on top of the finished primo pipérade.

GUINEA FOWL WITH SPRING GREENS AND CARROTS AND A MUSTARD AND MARJORAM SAUCE

guinea fowl with spring greens and carrots and a mustard and marjoram sauce

Guinea fowl, available all year but especially plump at this time, are the slightly gamey alternative to chicken. Smaller in size and a little drier in texture, the bird needs to be 'buttered up' to guarantee moist results.

Compared to a basic domestic chicken, the guinea fowl wins hands down on flavour. For four portions one bird is not quite enough, unless you've found a particularly large bird. It's best to pick two smaller ones, offering half per portion. More fresh herbs are beginning to join us, with marjoram not being too difficult to find.

SERVES 4 AS A MAIN COURSE

75g (3oz) butter, at room temperature
2 teaspoons picked marjoram, stalks removed and
  saved
salt and pepper
2 guinea fowl
cooking oil
450–675g (1–1½lb) spring greens, stalks removed
iced water
freshly grated nutmeg
450g (1lb) baby carrots
generous pinch of sugar
300ml (½ pint) *Instant stock* (page 416 and see method)
  or *Chicken stock* (page 416)
150ml (¼ pint) double cream
1–2 teaspoons Dijon or ready-made English mustard

Preheat the oven to 200°C/400°F/Gas 6. Mix one-third of the butter with 1 teaspoon of the marjoram and season with salt and pepper. Push the butter under the skin of the breasts, folding the skin beneath the neck ends of the birds. Brush each bird with another third of the butter and season with salt and pepper. Heat a roasting tray with a tablespoon or two of cooking oil. Once hot, lay the birds on one side in the pan. Fry on a medium heat for a few minutes until approaching golden brown. Turn the birds onto the other breast and repeat the process. Sit the birds breast-side up in the pan and roast in the preheated oven for 40–45 minutes, basting every 10 minutes to guarantee a richer finish. Remove the birds from the oven and lightly cover with foil to keep warm. Rest for 15 minutes.

While the birds are roasting, prepare the spring greens. Gently tear the leaves into bite-size pieces and blanch in boiling salted water for approximately 3 minutes until tender. Refresh in iced water before draining and squeezing gently to remove excess water. Season with salt, pepper and nutmeg, then fold half the remaining butter through the leaves. These can now be microwaved when needed or heated in a saucepan.

The baby carrots can also be cooked earlier for microwaving or just at the end of the roasting time, while the birds are resting. Peel or scrape the carrots, leaving 1–2cm (½–¾in) of stalk attached. Place in a saucepan and barely cover with boiling water. Add a pinch each of salt and sugar, along with the rest of the butter. Return to the boil and simmer rapidly for 3–10 minutes until just tender. (The liquor the carrots have cooked in can be used as the base for the instant stock. If so, drain off 300ml (½ pint) and keep to one side, leaving the carrots in the pan with the remaining liquor.)

Remove the birds from the roasting tray, pouring away any excess fat. Place the tray on a medium heat and, when beginning to sizzle, add 300ml (½ pint) of chicken stock or stock made with the reserved carrot liquor. Add the saved marjoram stalks. As the water boils it will lift all of the flavours from the pan. Allow the stock to reduce in volume by a third, then pour in the double cream. Bring to a simmer and cook to a loose sauce consistency. Season with salt and pepper, adding any juices collected from the resting guinea fowl. Strain through a sieve. Now add the mustard along with the remaining marjoram leaves. Return the carrots and heat through quickly, along with the spring greens (microwaving or in a saucepan).

Cut the legs and breasts from the birds and present on plates, offering half a guinea fowl on each with the vegetables to the side. Spoon the sauce around or offer separately.

apricot tart with home-made almond ice-cream

Spanish apricots begin their welcome summer visit during the last month of spring. This recipe needs the firmer, earlier apricots to get the best result as the fruits hold their shape during cooking.

Most of the world's round golden fruits are cooked into preserves. Here, the rich fruits are placed raw in a cooked pastry case and baked until tender. The softness of the fruit provides the tender touch to accompany the crispy pastry, with no sponge or cream base necessary.

The almond ice-cream is also not really necessary, but is a pleasure to eat with this particular fruit. Almonds and apricots are a classic combination – perhaps it is the apricot's almondy central kernel that brings the two together, and that's why they've been paired for so long. If you haven't the time to make the ice-cream, then simply offer pouring or whipped cream.

SERVES 6

225g (8oz) *Sweet shortcrust pastry* **(page 425) or**
 ***Puff pastry* (page 426), or bought variety**
flour, for dusting
butter, for greasing
1 egg yolk
1 tablespoon semolina
750g–1kg (1¾–2¼lb) fresh apricots (depending on size
 of fruits)
50–100g (2–4oz) caster sugar

FOR THE ALMOND ICE-CREAM

300ml (½ pint) whipping or single cream
300ml (½ pint) milk
100g (4oz) ground almonds
1 vanilla pod, split
4 egg yolks
100g (4oz) caster sugar
3 tablespoons amaretto (almond liqueur) or water
few drops of almond essence (optional)

To make the ice-cream, heat together the cream, milk, ground almonds and split vanilla pod. While this is heating, whisk the egg yolks, sugar and amaretto or water together until light and fluffy. When just below the boil, pour the hot milky cream and almonds over the eggs, whisking well. Return the almond custard mix to the saucepan and cook over a low heat, stirring continuously, until thick enough to coat the back of a spoon. Remove from the heat, pour the custard into a bowl and leave to cool. Once cold, strain through a sieve, scraping out any vanilla seeds left in the pod halves and adding them to the strained mix along with the almond essence, if using. Now churn the flavoured custard in an ice-cream machine for 20–25 minutes, until thickened and increased in volume. Transfer the ice-cream to a suitable container and freeze for an hour or two to set.

For the tart, roll out the pastry on a lightly floured surface and use to line a buttered 20cm (8in) loose-bottomed tart tin. Any excess pastry can be left hanging over the edge. Prick the base of the case with a fork and refrigerate for 30 minutes.

Preheat the oven to 200°C/400°F/Gas 6. Line the pastry case with greaseproof paper and fill with baking beans or rice. Bake the tart case blind in the preheated oven for 20 minutes. Remove the beans and paper and return to the oven for a further 5 minutes.

Once cooked, any excess pastry can be trimmed off, leaving a neat finish. Now brush the case with egg yolk to seal, and sprinkle the base with the semolina. This will absorb some of the juices as the fruits cook, preventing the pastry from becoming soggy. Leave the oven on, increasing the setting to 230°C/450°F/Gas 8.

Cut the apricots in half and remove the stones. Place the apricot halves in the tart case, standing them upright and squeezing them closely together. Sprinkle with the caster sugar. Late spring (May) fruits will need 100g (4oz) to help soften and sweeten their firmer, slightly under-ripe texture. Once into the summer season, just 50g (2oz) will be enough. Bake the tart for 30–40 minutes, until golden brown and crispy. Cooking at such a high temperature will tinge the fruits, almost burning the tops, adding an extra bitter-sweetness to the finished dish.

Remove the tart from the oven and leave to cool slightly before removing from the tart tin. The apricot tart is now ready to serve and will eat at its best warm, offering the almond ice-cream separately.

OPPOSITE: APRICOT TART WITH
HOME-MADE ALMOND ICE-CREAM

upside-down peach and blood orange cake

Blood oranges from Spain are in their final run, possibly lasting another 4 weeks. Peaches from the same country are normally flying in during the last week of this month, with the Italians already holding prime spot on the continental peach shelf.

The softer of the two fruits featured here, the peach, is not that soft at all right now, needing another few weeks to reach full potential. But, for this recipe, firmer ones will be better, having plenty of time to soften under the sponge, sweetened with the drizzle of clear honey or golden syrup.

The sponge base is quite an old recipe, which includes Greek yoghurt in its collection of flavours, with the zest of blood orange having quite an influence.

SERVES 6–8

3–4 firm peaches
2 tablespoons clear honey or golden syrup
175g (6oz) butter, diced and softened
175g (6oz) caster sugar, plus 2 tablespoons
grated zest and juice of 4 blood oranges
3 large eggs, separated
50g (2oz) self-raising flour
½ teaspoon baking powder
200ml (7fl oz) Greek yoghurt

Preheat the oven to 160°C/300°F/Gas 2. Grease a 20cm (8in) cake tin (not one with a loose base) and base-line it with parchment paper. Halve each of the peaches, removing the stone. Slice each half into four wedges, arranging them in the base of the cake tin, drizzling the honey or golden syrup over.

In an electric mixer bowl (or use an electric hand whisk), place the butter, the 175g (6oz) caster sugar and the blood orange zest, whisking until pale, soft and creamy. Whisk in the egg yolks one at a time. Sift together the self-raising flour and baking powder, then whisk a spoonful into the cake mix. Follow this with a heaped tablespoon of yoghurt. Repeat the flour and yoghurt process until all is combined. Whisk the egg whites in a clean bowl to firm peaks. Mix a third in with the cake batter. The remaining whites can now be gently folded in. Spoon the blood orange cake mix on top of the peaches, and bake in the preheated oven for 1 hour–1 hour 10 minutes, until golden brown.

To check the cake, insert a small knife or skewer into the centre of the sponge. Once it can be removed clean, the cake is ready. Remove the cake from the oven and leave to stand for 10 minutes before turning out onto a large plate. The cake is best served warm, to make the most of the peach and blood orange flavours.

While baking the cake, strain the blood orange juice into a saucepan, adding the 2 tablespoons of caster sugar. Bring the juice to the boil, cooking and allowing to reduce and thicken by at least half, to a syrup consistency. This can now be kept to brush over the finished cake, or serve by trickling a little over each wedge. The cake will eat well on its own or as a dessert, perhaps offering pouring cream or *Crème Anglaise* (page 426) alongside.

poached peach and strawberry custard creams

Late spring, and the shops are becoming more colourful with imports galore brightening our shelves. Apricots, nectarines and peaches in particular catch the culinary eye. So early, not all are at their best, so do check that they're not too firm with a quick squeeze.

Early English strawberries are now looking bigger and redder than ever. Already delicious to eat, they go well with nicely poached peaches, particularly if set amid glazed custard.

SERVES 4

4 ripe medium peaches
iced water
12, 16 or 20 fresh strawberries (depending on size)
1 quantity *Vanilla whipped pastry cream* (page 427) at
    room temperature
icing sugar, for dusting

FOR THE POACHING SYRUP
200ml (7fl oz) white wine
150g (5oz) caster sugar

To make the syrup, pour the white wine and an equal volume of water into a saucepan, along with the caster sugar. Bring to a simmer and cook for just a few minutes.

To skin the peaches, first plunge them into boiling water for just 20–30 seconds, then refresh in iced water. The skins will now have become loose and easy to peel. Halve the peaches and remove the stones.

Place the peaches in the syrup and cover with greaseproof paper. Bring to a simmer and cook for a few minutes, then leave to cool. The peach halves can now be cut again into quarters. The sweet stock syrup is best kept refrigerated, to be used for poaching other fruits or sweetening fruit salads.

Hull and rinse the strawberries, if necessary, cutting the larger of the fruits in half, leaving smaller berries whole.

Divide the vanilla whipped pastry cream between four soup plates or flat bowls. Press the peach quarters and strawberries into the custard in no particular fashion, then dust with icing sugar through a very fine sieve or tea strainer. Place each under a preheated grill until the custard has a golden-brown glaze.

The finely grated zest of 1 lemon or orange, poached to soften in a few tablespoons of the syrup, can be added to the custard for a gentle citrus bite.

soft lemon pudding with young strawberries

This pudding reminds me of 'afters' following the family's Sunday roast in my childhood, which would be presented in the centre of the table for us to help ourselves, cutting through the sponge top to reveal the curd-like sauce beneath. Offering young fresh strawberries creates the perfect pudding partnership.

To bake the dessert you will need a 1 litre (1¾ pint) soufflé or pudding dish, made from ovenproof glass, if possible, to show off the various textures.

SERVES 4–6
75g (3oz) butter, softened, plus more for greasing
150g (5oz) caster sugar
finely grated zest and juice of 3 lemons
4 eggs, separated
50g (2oz) self-raising flour
½ teaspoon baking powder
150ml (¼ pint) milk
icing sugar, for dusting (optional)
450g (1lb) fresh strawberries, hulled and washed

Preheat the oven to 180°C/350°F/Gas 4. In an electric mixer (or by hand) beat together the softened butter, caster sugar and lemon zest until pale and creamy. Stir in the egg yolks, one at a time. Sift the self-raising flour and baking powder together over the mix, beating in well.

The lemon juice and milk can now both be stirred into the mix. This usually takes on a curdled consistency at this stage, but don't worry: it's normal with this recipe. Whisk the egg whites to a soft peak stage before gently folding them into the mix.

Grease the pudding dish well with butter before pouring in the mix. Place the dish in a deep baking tray that has been half-filled with boiling water. Place in the middle of the preheated oven and bake for 40–50 minutes, to a rich golden brown. The pudding should have taken on a spongy texture. If still too soft, return to the oven for a further 10–15 minutes.

Remove the pudding from the oven and baking tray, leaving it to rest for 5–10 minutes, before serving with a bowl of the young strawberries.

SOFT LEMON PUDDING
WITH YOUNG STRAWBERRIES

2   sum

They have arrived: the most colourful months of the year are with us and it is summer. The forthcoming weeks will produce a selection of culinary goodies, with reds, yellows, oranges and greens showing off their variety of tones and tangs, whetting our appetites.

These twelve or so weeks we have in front of us offer cooks time off from sweating and stewing. In return, we're presented with the long summer days, enjoying evenings in the garden; for once we're waiting for the sun to come down.

British foods, without doubt, will have exclusive rights to our plates, their case becoming stronger as time moves on. There's no room for second thoughts here, as this season shows off how strongly Britain can stand in the culinary world. We all become bounty hunters, happy and excited with the treasures we've picked, particularly when the catch is so easy. It's time

mer

for the simplest of combinations, whether for garden, picnic or table eating, with no effort needed to take most of what we eat from home-grown sources, but not ignoring the imported apricots, nectarines and peaches, so exquisitely ripe at this time.

The first summer month is June, with bundles and bundles of green asparagus spears waiting to be steamed and served bathed in trickles of butter, perhaps with wild salmon, and followed by bowls of the reddest of strawberries and lashings of fresh cream.

Other greens beginning to mature in strength are the broad beans and peas, with the English courgette chasing close behind. All of these vegetables have their own distinctive flavours, sweet tastes and slightly bitter edges, which help balance one another, adding bite to all sorts of vegetarian, fish and meat dishes.

There's not just wild salmon to share with summer flavours, but sea trout as well. This fish has similar eating habits to that of the salmon, living mostly off crustaceans, which results in a firm pink-red flesh. It is as good to eat as wild salmon, marrying well with hot Jersey Royals, finished with a sprinkling of sea salt flakes.

Reminders of childhood come to the fore, with the lettuce probably the most predominant, bringing back the Webbs, butterheads, Little Gems and Icebergs to our wooden salad bowls.

Cherries can be picked right now, becoming fatter and plumper as the weeks move on. Gooseberries too, boxes and boxes of them; as they mature their colour changes from its original deep green with an acidic bite, reaching a sweeter yellowy lusciousness. But the real stars must be the red and black soft fruits. All the signs of midsummer arrive on the scene. Raspberries and blackberries reveal a glimpse of what is to come next month, along with the scent of freshly cut grass and the ripening of many a fresh fruit.

July: warm weather, children finishing school, village fêtes, summer balls, sultry nights – all to be accompanied by intense aromas to savour – that's July. It's the time for cooking and eating *al fresco*, the barbecue an option for cooking so many different (and sometimes unusual) varieties of vegetables, fish and meat.

Anglo-Italian can be found in the following pages, with the conjunction of fresh tomatoes, courgettes and our own sweet red peppers re-establishing the classic ratatouille. There's also the *Crisp courgette tart with a tomato and basil salad* (page 147), the latter part of the dish relying heavily on the extra sunshine of long July days to fully ripen and maximize the individual bites of tomatoes and basil.

There are other herbs, too. Wild marjoram (fresh oregano) blooms between July and October. Coriander is also just waiting to be picked. And the salad leaves keep coming, with broad beans, peas, runner beans, beetroots, radishes, cauliflowers and juicy cucumbers wanting to garnish them.

Baby summer turnips and artichokes also make an appearance and it's during the summer months that our culinary imaginations can run riot in making unusual and individual combinations for salads and vegetable dishes. For midsummer fruits, to join imported peaches and others, we add to the list fresh plums and so many red and black berries.

Many of these thoughts are turned into reality in the coming pages, as in the *Summer fruit family slice* (page 163), with colourful fruits between crisp pastry biscuits and dollops of thick custard.

We now know we're into the final month – August. We Brits tend to look upon these 31 days as the beach season. It's the most popular time for holidays, with packed lunches, picnics and barbecues making up our diary dates. And so they should. The sun still shines brightly, most of the June and all of the July produce is with us – and there's more beginning to arrive.

Fresh aubergines, many from our own soils, arrive to join the never-ending supply of tomatoes, courgettes and fresh herbs. Fresh herrings and sardines look very plump, juicy and exciting to eat as they sit amongst the light smoke lifting from the open grill.

August justifies its juicy reputation year after year, with plums reaching their best, and the greengage a must for all its short two-month life – whether it be pickled, stewed or sweet preserved. Presented either as savoury or dessert, this versatile fruit deserves more recognition than it often receives.

This part of our summer season is also quite cheeky. Signs of autumn show quite early, the 'Glorious Twelfth' marking the start of the game season, with the race to be the first restaurant to serve grouse making headline news. The evenings become slightly shorter with a cooler finish, and harvesting begins.

We've now enjoyed the primest of foodie times, and made lots of great memories: the best of strawberries, the fattest of tomatoes, the juiciest of cucumbers, the most flavoursome of leaves – the list goes on. This is a time of year when culinary rules are to be broken – fruits can take on savouries, perhaps accompanying many ingredients they just wouldn't at any other time of the year. Salads become complete meals and fresh sardines become a household favourite. This season is not just a time for us to imagine this sweet picture, but for us actually to experience it.

OPPOSITE: BROKEN SALMON, CUCUMBER AND LETTUCE SALAD WITH FRESH DILL CREAM DRESSING (PAGE 141)

vegetables

fish

meat

fruit and puddings

pea soup with toasted sesame cod fillet

This must be one of the quickest and simplest of soups to make. The cod gives this starter just enough depth to warrant it being served as a simple lunch or supper dish. The sesame seeds provide a lovely nutty bite to the overall flavour, and you can also trickle the soup with a drop or two of sesame oil if you like. The most natural of pea soups can be made with just water. For a deeper flavour, a stock can be used in its place as listed below.

SERVES 4 AS A GENEROUS STARTER OR MAIN COURSE

600ml (1 pint) water, *Vegetable stock* (page 417),
   Chicken stock (page 416) or *Instant stock* (page 416)
450g (1lb) podded peas (frozen can also be used)
salt and pepper
pinch of sugar
100ml (3½fl oz) whipping or single cream

FOR THE FISH

4 × 100g (4oz) portions of cod fillet, skinned and
   pin-boned (page 9)
flour, for dusting
1 tablespoon cooking oil
knob of butter
1 heaped teaspoon sesame seeds
1 tablespoon sesame oil (optional)

Bring the water or stock to the boil in a saucepan and add the peas. Bring back to the boil and cook for 5 minutes until tender (longer if necessary). Remove from the heat, season with salt, pepper and a pinch of sugar, and liquidize to a smooth creamy soup. For the smoothest of finishes, strain through a sieve.

The soup at this stage can be cooled over ice (to help maintain its colour), then simply reheated when needed.

If serving immediately, add the cream and return to a gentle simmer, seasoning once again with salt and pepper.

While the soup is simmering, lightly dust the skinned sides of the cod fillets with flour and season with salt. Heat the cooking oil in a frying pan and add the fillets, floured-sides down. Cook for 4 minutes until golden brown, add the knob of butter, then turn and continue to fry for a further 2 minutes.

OPPOSITE: PEA SOUP WITH TOASTED SESAME COD FILLET

The sesame seeds can be used natural, as they are, or toasted to a golden brown under a hot grill for a richer and nuttier finish.

Place the cod fillets in soup plates and ladle the pea soup around. Sprinkle the fillets with sesame seeds and a drop of sesame oil, if using.

warm goat's cheese, potato and fresh pea salad with sweet mint dressing

The best type of goat's cheese for this dish is a rindless soft creamy variety which will soften quickly when warmed under the grill. The potatoes can be chosen from any of the new varieties available, cooking them until overdone for a softer texture. The dressing is flavoured with fresh mint but to provide the sweetness in place of sugar, and to augment the mint flavour, clear mint jelly is also added.

This salad works very well as a starter, or, when topped with sea trout or wild salmon gently fried in butter, as a main course. An extra 'dressing', that is not essential but does help draw everything together, is soured cream or crème fraîche. Just a drizzle or two is enough to finish the dish.

SERVES 4 AS A STARTER

100g (4oz) fresh peas (podded weight)
iced water
225g (8oz) new potatoes (Jersey Royals,
   Pink Fir Apple, etc.), overcooked
1 banana shallot or 2 small shallots, sliced into very
   thin rings
coarse sea salt
2 tablespoons olive oil
juice of ½ lime
225g (8oz) soft goat's cheese, cut into rough 1cm
   (½in) dice
1–2 handfuls of rocket leaves
4 tablespoons soured cream or crème fraîche, for
   drizzling (optional)

FOR THE DRESSING

1 teaspoon mint jelly
2 dessertspoons white wine vinegar
3 tablespoons olive oil
3 tablespoons groundnut, grapeseed or vegetable oil
salt and pepper
4 mint leaves, chopped

To make the dressing, warm the mint jelly through in the microwave for a few seconds to soften and moisten or heat very gently in a pan with the vinegar. Mix the jelly and vinegar with the remaining ingredients (except the fresh mint) and season with salt and pepper (this can be easily achieved in a screw-top jar with lots of shaking). If a sweeter or more piquant finish is preferred, add a touch more softened jelly or vinegar. The fresh mint should be added just before serving.

To cook the fresh peas in advance, plunge them into boiling salted water and cook until tender. Drain and refresh in iced water before redraining. To reheat, the peas can either be microwaved or plunged back into boiling water for a minute.

Peel the cooked potatoes if the skins are tough, or leave the skins on if they were well scrubbed. Roughly halve or quarter the potatoes, depending on their size, and place in a bowl along with the shallot rings. Season with coarse sea salt and pepper. Mix the olive oil with the lime juice, pour over the potato pieces and gently spoon around the bowl. Cover and keep warm for 10 minutes. The lime oil flavour will be absorbed by the warm potatoes and shallots, the gentle lime bite working well with the mint dressing.

Scatter the marinated potatoes over the plates along with the goat's cheese. Warm under a preheated grill or in a hot oven, allowing the cheese only to gently soften. While warming the plates, reheat the peas.

To serve, spoon the peas over the potatoes and goat's cheese. Add the chopped mint to the dressing and sprinkle a teaspoon or two over the rocket leaves. Drizzle the remaining mint dressing across all the plates, top with rocket leaves and drizzle with soured cream or crème fraîche, if using.

grilled asparagus with soft hard-boiled eggs and toasted sesame dressing

This delicious starter is a slight variation on the classic asparagus dish of hard-boiled eggs and nutty brown butter strewn across the rich green spears. Here the tips are grilled not boiled, with the nutty flavour provided by the toasted sesame seeds. Cooked for only 7–8 minutes, the hard-boiled eggs will be left with a moist centre.

SERVES 2 AS A STARTER
2–3 eggs
1 generous teaspoon sesame seeds
12–16 medium asparagus spears
groundnut, vegetable or olive oil, for brushing
squeeze of lemon juice
50g (2oz) butter
salt and pepper, plus coarse sea salt
1 teaspoon chopped chives (optional)
drizzle of sesame or olive oil

Place the eggs in boiling water and bring back to a rapid simmer. Cook for 7–8 minutes. Remove and place under cold running water for just 2–3 minutes to stop the cooking. Now remove from the water and leave to cool a little further before shelling.

Sprinkle the sesame seeds in a pan and toast under the grill or place over a medium heat and colour to a golden brown. This takes very little time and, once coloured, the seeds must be removed immediately from the pan to prevent any burnt bitter edge.

Preheat a griddle plate. Trim the spiky ears from the asparagus spears, and snap or cut away 2–4cm (¾–1½in) of the grey/white base. Brush each spear with the groundnut, vegetable or olive oil, place on the preheated griddle plate and cook until tender, allowing them to take on bold dark grill lines. Turn the spears when necessary.

While the asparagus is cooking, in a small saucepan bring 3 tablespoons of water and a good squeeze of lemon juice to the boil. Quickly whisk in the butter to create an emulsion of the two, providing an instant butter sauce. Remove from the heat (never reboil a sauce once butter has been added as this will separate the oils from the solids), season with salt and pepper and add a squeeze more lemon juice if needed. Add the sesame seeds and chopped chives, if using.

Cut the eggs in halves or quarters lengthwise and present with the asparagus spears divided between two plates. Season with a twist of pepper and coarse sea salt before spooning the sesame seed butter over and drizzling with the sesame or olive oil.

If a griddle plate is unavailable, the asparagus can be blanched and quickly pan-fried to a light golden edge, or simply boiled for a few minutes.

OPPOSITE: MELON AND CUCUMBER SALAD
WITH GORGONZOLA AND WATERCRESS

melon and cucumber salad with gorgonzola and watercress

Melons often start their quite extended season in mid-spring and carry on until Christmas. Most melon varieties – Charantais, Cantaloupe, Galia, honeydew and Ogen – first appear from France and Italy in April. The Spanish alternatives keep us waiting another four weeks. It's during these summer months, however, that melons are at their best, more fragrant and juicy.

When choosing a melon, its weight will obviously indicate how ripe it is, so compare two of more or less the same size, buying the heavier. A good, ripe melon will also be slightly soft around its stem, exuding a sweet fragrance, but still firm around the bulbous body.

Charantais or Cantaloupe are first choice here, both showing off a rich orangey flesh, with colourful flavour to match. This also helps distinguish the melon from the peeled cucumber cubes – the two presenting a refreshing starter or lunch snack.

Gorgonzola is an Italian blue cow's milk cheese, its greenish-blue streaks discharging a spicy bite, surrounded by a delicate rich creamy cheese, ready to melt in the mouth.

An even softer version of this prize-winning cheese is Dolcelatte ('sweet milk' in Italian). A mass-produced style of Gorgonzola, Dolcelatte is creamier and softer, with a sweet finish, melting in the mouth like ice-cream.

To finish this salad, I've chosen watercress sprigs, lightly tossed in natural yoghurt and black pepper, with a citrus dressing to drizzle.

SERVES 4 AS A STARTER
1 cucumber
salt and black pepper
1 Charantais or Cantaloupe melon
juice of 2 oranges
½ teaspoon caster sugar
1 tablespoon lemon juice
1 teaspoon lime juice
3 tablespoons olive oil (preferably with a fruity flavour)
175g (6oz) Gorgonzola cheese, thin rind removed
2–3 tablespoons natural yoghurt
1 large or 2 small bunches of watercress, picked into sprigs and rinsed

Peel the cucumber, splitting it in half lengthwise. Scoop out the seeds with a teaspoon. Cut each half into three long strips,

before cutting into approximately 1cm (½in) cubes. Place the cubes in a colander, sprinkling with a teaspoon of salt and stirring it in well. Leave the cucumber pieces to drain for 20–30 minutes. This releases excess water, leaving a more complete cucumber flavour. The cubes may well need to be lightly rinsed if slightly too salty.

Top and bottom the melon, cutting it into eight wedges. Remove the seeds, slicing away the skin beneath the flesh. You may need to split each wedge in two lengthwise, before cutting the melon into cubes. Once cut, refrigerate for a chilled crispy refreshing bite, but do not allow them to become too icy, as this blands, rather than enhances, their finished flavour.

Boil the orange juice in a small saucepan, allowing it to reduce in volume to approximately 2 tablespoons, taking on a more concentrated flavour. Remove from the heat and add the caster sugar. Once cooled, mix in a small bowl with the lemon and lime juice, whisking in the olive oil. Season with salt and pepper.

Mix together the cucumber and melon, drizzling with a few drops of the citrus dressing. Scatter the cubes over four plates, crumbling the Gorgonzola over each.

Spoon 2 tablespoons of the yoghurt into the watercress sprigs (adding the extra spoonful if preferred), tossing it through the leaves with a good twist of black pepper. Present the leaves on top of the fruits, finishing with a few extra drops of the citrus dressing.

Rocket leaves blend well with the watercress.
Broken walnuts or peeled pistachios could be an added extra.

green vegetable 'casserole' with buttered sea trout

During the month of June, English asparagus has only a few weeks to run, while broad beans and fresh peas are just beginning to enjoy their season. It's with all of this in mind that we should take advantage of their flavours during this first official summer month.

Also added are the fresh herbs that are available, not missing the lemony bite of sorrel and piquant touch of tarragon. The sea trout (salmon can also be used) is so softly cooked in butter, it is almost like poaching it so that it takes on the faintest of golden finishes.

SERVES 4 AS A STARTER

8 asparagus spears
salt and pepper
iced water
50–75g (2–3oz) podded peas
50–75g (2–3oz) podded broad beans
150ml (¼ pint) white wine
200ml (7fl oz) *Vegetable stock* (page 417), *Instant stock* (page 416) or water
2 sprigs of tarragon
2 sprigs of chervil
few flatleaf parsley leaves
2 sorrel leaves
4 × 100g (4oz) portions of sea trout fillet, pin-boned (page 9) and skinned
50g (2oz) butter, plus more for the sea trout
1 teaspoon flour (optional)
4 spring onions, cut into 4mm (⅛in) slices

Each of the vegetables can be prepared and cooked in advance. Most asparagus spears don't need to be peeled. For this dish, however, I suggest they are. This will then leave a paler green spear to counter the colour of the deep green beans and peas. Simply peel, leaving about 4cm (1½in) of the tips as they are. The woody base can now be broken or cut away. Cook the spears in boiling salted water for just a minute or two, 3–4 minutes maximum, until tender, then refresh in iced water.

Bring the salted water back to the boil and add the peas, cooking for just 3 minutes before refreshing in iced water. Bring the water back to the boil again and cook the broad beans for just 2 minutes, up to a maximum of 5 minutes if large. Also refresh these in iced water, then peel away the protective skin to reveal the green beans.

Once all the vegetables are drained, cut the cooked asparagus into 3cm (1¼in) sticks and refrigerate all of the vegetables until needed.

Bring the white wine to the boil and reduce in volume by three-quarters. Add 200ml (7fl oz) of your chosen stock or water, bring to the boil and reduce in volume by half. Leave to one side.

Gently chop all the herbs, finely shredding the sorrel.

To cook the sea trout, first season with salt and then place, skinned-side down, in a frying pan of gently bubbling melted butter. Cook on a low heat for 4 minutes, allowing the fish to colour just a little. Season with pepper, then turn the fish in the pan. Remove from the heat and allow the fish to finish cooking in the pan while the casserole is completed.

Heat the reserved, reduced wine mixture. To finish the

sauce, if a slightly thicker finish is preferred, first add the flour to the measured butter. As this is whisked in the liquor will begin to thicken, but stay loose enough not to become a sauce. If finishing in this way, simply simmer for a few minutes once the flour is added, to cook out its flavour. For a looser consistency, simply whisk the butter into the wine mixture.

Add the vegetables and spring onions to the liquor. Simmer for 1–2 minutes to heat them through, then add the herbs and season with salt and pepper. Spoon the casserole into suitable bowls, then place the buttered sea trout fillets in the bowls.

GREEN VEGETABLE 'CASSEROLE' WITH BUTTERED SEA TROUT

buttered prawns with a warm potato and fresh pea salad

It's best to buy large raw prawns for this dish. You are then in total control of their cooking time. If unavailable, cooked prawns still in the shell should be your next choice.

The prawn dressing is really quite unique, almost creating its own prawn bisque flavour to lift the taste of the shellfish. The other dressing, with a single-cream base, gives the salad a buttery feel without any being added.

I've suggested new potatoes in the salad as there are so many good varieties in season, including the classic Jersey Royals, Pink Fir Apple and Charlotte.

SERVES 4 AS A GENEROUS STARTER

20 large raw prawns (or 350g/12oz cooked unpeeled North Atlantic prawns)
salt and pepper
12–16 small new potatoes, scrubbed
175g (6oz) podded peas
25g (1oz) butter
2 handfuls of green salad leaves
8–10 picked tarragon leaves

FOR THE PRAWN DRESSING

100–150ml (3½fl oz–¼ pint) olive oil
2 strips of lemon peel
4 black peppercorns
1 bay leaf
juice of 1 lemon
cube of brown or white sugar

FOR THE CREAM DRESSING

2 dessertspoons sherry vinegar
1 teaspoon soft brown sugar
4 tablespoons single cream
2 tablespoons walnut oil
squeeze of lemon juice
1 tablespoon chopped chives

If using raw prawns, first plunge them into boiling salted water for 30 seconds. Remove and leave to cool. These can now be carefully peeled, removing the heads along with all of the tail shells, reserving 50g (2oz) of the shells for the prawn dressing. Make a fine cut along the back of each prawn and remove the black intestine. The prawns can now be kept refrigerated until needed.

To make the prawn dressing, heat 2 tablespoons of the olive oil with the reserved shells, lemon peel, peppercorns and bay leaf. Cook gently for a few minutes but don't fry. This will draw the flavour and colour from the shells. Add the lemon juice and sugar cube and continue to cook until the cube has dissolved. Add 100ml (3½fl oz) of the remaining oil, bring to a simmer, remove from the heat and leave to infuse for 8–10 minutes.

Remove the bay leaf and blitz the dressing in a liquidizer until almost completely blended. Check for seasoning at this point. Add a pinch of salt, and more olive oil if needed to calm the lemon flavour. Strain through a fine sieve or tea strainer and the dressing is ready. This can now be kept in a jar or squeezy bottle for up to 24 hours. However, this dressing eats at its best as soon as possible after making.

To make the cream dressing, whisk together the sherry vinegar, sugar and cream, then add the walnut oil. Add a squeeze of lemon juice and season with salt and pepper. This can also be kept refrigerated, adding the chives just before serving.

To cook the new potatoes, plunge them into boiling salted water and boil until almost overcooked – this will create a soft creamy finish. New potatoes do come in all shapes and sizes, consequently the cooking time will vary from 15–25 minutes. Once cooked, drain and, when cool enough to handle, cut into rounds 5mm–1cm (¼–½in) thick or simply quarter lengthwise. Season with salt and pepper and keep warm.

While cutting the potatoes, the peas can be cooked in boiling salted water. Good fresh young peas should literally take only as long as their frozen friends, about 3 minutes. However, it is best to check continually after the 3 minutes until they are completely tender. Once cooked, drain and add to the potatoes.

Heat the butter in a frying pan. Once melted and bubbling, add the peeled prawns. Simmer gently for just 2–3 minutes until the prawns have cooked through.

While frying the prawns, add the chopped chives to the cream dressing and spoon it over the potatoes and peas. Add the salad leaves and torn tarragon, and fold them in along with the prawns. Divide between four plates, drizzle liberally with the prawn dressing and serve.

OPPOSITE: BUTTERED PRAWNS WITH
A WARM POTATO AND FRESH PEA SALAD

quick-fried squid with provençal salad

squeeze of lemon juice
pinch of caster sugar
coarse sea salt and pepper
1 teaspoon chopped flatleaf parsley
1 teaspoon chopped fresh oregano

Squid can be quite frightening to some people, but is in fact, a very easy 'fish' to prepare and cook. With the texture squid holds, it lends itself well to two cooking methods – quick and slow. Try cooking it in between and you will produce a rubbery finish. *À la provençale* is described in *The A–Z of French Food* (Scribo Editions) as 'garnishes inspired by provençal cooking, usually including tomatoes, garlic and olive oil'.

The key to the salad side of this dish is choosing a small selection of green leaves, although one variety alone would be enough. Rocket and watercress, with their peppery bite, are to be calmed with the addition of young spinach leaves and corn salad. Spinach offers quite a rustic mixed finish, wilting and melting under the warmth of the hot squid.

A vegetable that appears from British soils in June is the courgette. These will be quite small – just two or three are needed to be sliced and sautéed with the squid. This green vegetable is not essential, but reminds us how well it deserves a good Provençal finish.

As for herbs, fresh oregano should be available along with parsley. If oregano is unavailable, tarragon will happily stand in.

To begin the method, I've included how to clean fresh squid, but this preparation can, of course, be arranged with your fishmonger. For this recipe, small squid are best, and you need at least 450g (1lb) for sensible portions.

SERVES 4 AS A STARTER OR LUNCH DISH
approximately 450–600g (1lb–1lb 5oz) fresh squid, prepared and cut into rings (see below)
2 tablespoons olive oil
squeeze of lemon juice

FOR THE SALAD
6 plum tomatoes, blanched (page 92)
200g (7oz) mixed green leaves, or one variety (see above)
4 tablespoons natural yoghurt or soured cream

FOR THE DRESSING
150ml (¼ pint) olive oil
2 tablespoons champagne vinegar or white wine vinegar
2 garlic cloves, very finely crushed
2 teaspoons finely chopped shallot or onion

To prepare fresh squid, hold the body with one hand and the tentacles at their base with the other, and gently pull the tentacles away. This will also remove the milky intestines from the body attached to them. From inside the body, pull away the clear quill. Remove the thin, purple membrane-like skin, which pulls away very easily. Also remove the two fins, pulling away the skin too. These can be kept for quick frying with the body and tentacles. To prepare the tentacles, cut them away just in front of the eyes, discarding the head. Squeeze out the small beak or mouth from the centre of the tentacles and discard. Should the tentacles be quite large, these can be cut and separated into individual fingers.

Wash all of the saved pieces, in particular the inside of the squid pouch. The pouch can now be sliced into thin rings. Should you wish to keep the ink sac, this is a small silvery pouch, found amongst the innards. Cut it away gently, being careful not to pierce it. To use in risottos or sauces, pierce in a small bowl, mixing the contents with a little water to loosen, before passing through a tea-strainer or fine sieve. The ink is now ready to use, and freezes very well.

Slice the blanched plum tomatoes into rounds approximately 4–5mm (¼in) thick. Arrange the slices in a circle on four separate plates, leaving an empty centre. Season with coarse sea salt and pepper.

To make the dressing, place all of the ingredients, except for the fresh herbs, in a small screw-top jar and shake well. Any not used in this salad will keep for a few days, refrigerated. A teaspoon or two of the finished dressing can now be spooned over the tomatoes, marinating them and strengthening their flavour.

Lightly rinse your chosen leaves under cold water, shaking off the excess in a wire salad basket or colander.

Spoon a tablespoon of yoghurt or soured cream into the empty centre of each tomato circle.

Heat a tablespoon of olive oil in a frying pan or wok. Once very hot, add half the squid pieces (including tentacles and fins), seasoning with salt and pepper. Fry for just a minute or two until beginning to colour. Spoon the squid into a bowl. Add the remaining olive oil and squid to the hot pan and repeating the same cooking process. Once all have been cooked and transferred to the bowl, add a squeeze of lemon juice, along with the salad leaves. Spoon the dressing over quite liberally before sprinkling with the chopped herbs. Divide the salad between the tomato plates and serve.

The salad leaves can be arranged in the centre of the tomato circles, drizzling liberally with the dressing. Once the squid has been fried, sprinkle with the fresh herbs, spooning them on top of the leaves.
The tomatoes can be each cut into eight wedges, removing their seeds. The wedges can now be mixed with the salad leaves, dressing and herbs, scattering them over the plates, finishing with the quick-fried squid pieces.

caesar sardines on toasts

A definite inclusion in the home summer-eats repertoire should be fresh sardines; these are at their plumpest now. There's also sardine's big brother, the pilchard, on offer: the very same fish, just bigger and older, and munching very nicely at this time of the year.

The fish are to be filleted (see below) and left to stand in a marinade for 30 minutes. The double edge to marinating the sardine is calming its quite strong fish taste, adding an extra bite, while softening, almost dissolving, the fine bones left in the flesh.

The 'Caesar' in the title refers to the accompanying salad. The dressing is bound with torn or shredded Cos lettuce or baby Little Gems, both at their prime right now. The salad can be served apart or arranged on the plate with the sardines. Another option is to shred the lettuce finely, mixing with some of the Caesar dressing and spooning it over the toast, before arranging the grilled fillets on top.

SERVES 4 AS A SNACK OR STARTER
8 sardines
***Caesar dressing* (page 179, treating the Parmesan as optional)**
2 Little Gem lettuces or 1 Cos lettuce
4 thick slices of country, Granary or olive bread
softened butter, for spreading and brushing
2 tablespoons olive oil (optional)

FOR THE MARINADE
125ml (4fl oz) dry white wine
1 tablespoon white wine vinegar
juice of ½ orange
juice of ½ lemon
1 teaspoon demerara sugar
½ teaspoon cumin seeds
coarse sea salt and pepper
2 tablespoons olive oil

To clean the sardines, scrape off the scales with your thumbnail, while gently rinsing under a cold tap. Cut off the heads. Cut open the belly, preferably with scissors, not tearing the skin and flesh. Remove the guts, carefully lifting out the backbone. This can be made easy by pushing your thumbnail under the tail end, releasing the spine before pulling it away. Alternatively, twist and pull the head away, bringing the guts and spine with it The fish are now ready to cook, needing very little trimming to tidy them up. The two fillets can be totally separated by cutting between them.

To make the marinade, place all of the ingredients in a small saucepan, bringing it to the boil. Remove from the heat and allow to cool. Put the sardine fillets in a tray, flesh-side down, pouring the cooled marinade over. Leave to stand for at least 30 minutes, allowing the fish to take on the many flavours.

While marinating the fish, the Caesar dressing can be made, following the recipe on page 179.

To prepare the lettuces, trim away the base stalk separating the leaves of the Cos, before rinsing and tearing into bite-size pieces, or finely shredding (just before serving). If using Little Gems, simply remove any damaged outside leaves, before shredding the whole lettuce. For torn leaves, prepare as for the Cos.

The bread slices can each be trimmed into a large square on which to present the four fillets of sardine. Spread each side of the bread with butter. These can be toasted when needed to a golden brown, the butter melting into the slices.

Preheat the grill. Remove the sardine fillets from the marinade, placing them on a baking tray skin-side up. Brush each fillet lightly with butter, seasoning with a small sprinkling of coarse sea salt and a twist of pepper. Place the tray under the grill, cooking the sardines for just a few minutes.

If shredded lettuce is to be used, mix the leaves with enough Caesar dressing just to bind, spooning the flavoured lettuce onto the four slices of toast.

For torn leaves, bind with the dressing as above, arranging a small pile on each plate.

Arrange the grilled sardine fillets on top of the toasts, placing top to tail in a neat square.

Mix the further 2 tablespoons of olive oil, if using, with the marinade, drizzling a teaspoon or two over each topped toast.

Any remaining Caesar dressing can be drizzled around the toasts, or kept refrigerated for a few days, for use as a salad dressing.

grilled fillets of gurnard with puréed white beans, samphire and a nutty red wine vinaigrette

Gurnard is a highly underrated fish, offering its services at a more than reasonable price. On the continent it is highly respected and enjoyed by many. Samphire, also referred to as 'poor man's asparagus' or 'sea asparagus', takes the shape of wrinkly extra-fine 'beans', mostly found around the salt marshes of Norfolk or other seaside marshes. Despite the 'poor man's' label, after quick boiling in unsalted water (the samphire already contains its own salt content), finished with just melted butter, or a more extravagant *Simple hollandaise sauce* (page 418), samphire is a culinary treat.

SERVES 4

knob of butter, plus more for brushing
4 × 450g (1lb) gurnard, or 2 large fish, filleted
 and trimmed
salt and pepper
350–450g (12oz–1lb) samphire
iced water (optional)
2 garlic cloves and milk, for poaching (optional)
1 × 410g tin of cannellini beans (Italian white haricots)
2–3 tablespoons olive oil
2 tablespoons double cream

FOR THE VINAIGRETTE

50g (2oz) butter
4 tablespoons walnut oil
1–2 tablespoons red wine vinegar, preferably a strong
 Cabernet Sauvignon

Butter a baking tray and season with salt and pepper. Butter the skin side of each gurnard fillet, seasoning with salt.

The samphire can be picked and washed well in advance, snipping away any woody base to each 'sprig'. For a crispy finish, blanch in boiling unsalted water for 30 seconds–1 minute, refreshing in iced water if not using immediately. For a softer finish, the samphire can be cooked for 1–5 minutes. Drain and refrigerate until needed.

If adding the garlic to the bean purée, poach the cloves in a little milk for 10–15 minutes until cooked through.

Warm through the cannellini beans in their liquor and, once simmering, drain, saving the liquor. Blitz the beans in a liquidizer with the garlic, if using, pouring in the olive oil as they blend. Season with salt and pepper. If too thick, the purée can be loosened with 3–4 tablespoons of the saved liquor. For the smoothest of finishes, push through a sieve.

To make the dressing, melt the butter until it's a deep golden and bubbly. This takes its natural flavour to a nutty brown. Remove from the heat and strain through a muslin cloth or tea strainer. Add the walnut oil, red wine vinegar, salt and pepper, whisking vigorously to emulsify all flavours and consistencies.

Place the gurnard fillets under a preheated grill and cook for 4–5 minutes. Turn off the heat and, while you are dressing the plates, the fish will complete its cooking while retaining its heat.

While the fish is grilling, warm the bean purée, adding the cream to soften. The samphire can be reheated quickly in a knob of butter with 2–3 tablespoons of water; this creates a soft steam to help warm through.

To serve, arrange all three components separately onto each plate, spooning the nutty red wine vinaigrette over the warm samphire and gurnard.

The gurnard can also be pan-fried, following the same cooking time.
A squeeze of lemon or lime juice or a dash of sherry vinegar can be added to the bean purée for a slightly piquant finish. Chopped fresh chives also work very well in the purée.
Walnut halves (1–1½ per portion) can be blanched, peeled and broken into small pieces before adding to the dressing for a nuttier finish.

seared mackerel with gooseberry and mustard seed sauce

The combination of mackerel and gooseberries goes back a long way, surviving many changes of fashion and culinary style with the tartness of the fruit cutting into the oily flesh of the fish.

Many recipes tend to opt for the puréed finish to the sauce. With this recipe, however, the fruits are only taken to the 'popping' stage, when they are just beginning to break down, the juices sweetened with a touch of sugar. The bite of mustard seed provides warmth, giving the finished sauce a loose chutney-like appeal.

This dish can be served as a starter or main course, either working very well with the *Creamy new potatoes with goat's cheese* (page 142).

SERVES 4

4 mackerel fillets, taken from 2 × 350–400g (12–14oz) fish, pin-boned (page 9) and skinned
flour, for dusting
1–2 tablespoons cooking oil
knob of butter

FOR THE GOOSEBERRY AND MUSTARD SEED SAUCE
2 teaspoons white (yellow) or black mustard seeds
finely grated zest and juice of ½ lime
225g (8oz) gooseberries, topped and tailed
1 tablespoon caster sugar
25g (1oz) butter
salt and pepper

To make the sauce, first soak the mustard seeds in the lime juice, adding a drop or two of water if needed. This will cause the seeds to swell, releasing their warmth and flavour. Place the gooseberries, sugar, lime zest and 5 tablespoons of water in a saucepan and bring to a simmer. As the gooseberries are cooking, they will begin to soften and pop, after approximately 7–8 minutes depending on the size of the fruits. At this point remove the pan from the heat. Allow the sauce to relax for 10–15 minutes, then stir and check the consistency and sweetness. If too thin, return to the stove and continue to simmer to a softer and slightly thicker consistency.

It is best not to make the sauce too sweet, but if over-tart, add sugar to taste. Once finished, add the mustard seeds with the lime juice and butter, stirring both in thoroughly, and season with a pinch of salt and a twist of pepper.

Season the mackerel fillets with salt and pepper, then dust the skinned sides with a little flour. Heat the oil in a large frying pan, and place the fillets in, floured-side down. Fry for up to 4 minutes, then add the knob of butter. Turn the fillets in the pan and remove the pan from the heat. Leave to bubble in the warm pan for a minute or two, during which time the fish will finish cooking and its texture will relax. The fillets can now be offered with the gooseberry sauce.

A light, green salad will eat very well with this dish, along with hot new potatoes.

SEARED MACKEREL WITH GOOSEBERRY AND
MUSTARD SEED SAUCE

crispy wild salmon with warm lemon and tarragon mayonnaise

It has been with us for a few months now, but the wild salmon is at its best during these summer months, with a richer flavour and at its most competitive price. The crispy edge is provided by the skin, which, when not cooked too rapidly, becomes a crackling to top the moist flakes.

The marriage of salmon and asparagus is one that is so outstanding. To finish this combination, I have borrowed a warm, creamy sauce recipe from a very good friend, a Mr Rick Stein. The base to this is a hollandaise sauce, using the oils from a mayonnaise to finish.

SERVES 4 AS A MAIN COURSE

24–28 medium asparagus spears
4 × 175g (6oz) portions of wild salmon fillet,
  pin-boned (page 9) with skin on (scaled)
salt and pepper
flour, for dusting
2 tablespoons cooking oil
knob of butter, plus more for brushing
coarse sea salt (optional)

FOR THE MAYONNAISE

125ml (4fl oz) sunflower or groundnut oil
3 tablespoons extra virgin olive oil
2 egg yolks
juice of ½ lemon
Cayenne pepper
1 heaped teaspoon chopped tarragon

First make the mayonnaise, which can then be kept warm while completing the dish. Put the sunflower or groundnut oil and the olive oil in a small saucepan and place on a very low heat just to warm through. Mix the egg yolks and lemon juice with 2 tablespoons of water in a bowl, and place over a pan of simmering water, making sure the water is not touching the base of the bowl. Whisk the yolk mixture vigorously until thick and frothy, then continue to whisk until the frothy consistency becomes almost creamy. Remove the bowl from the heat and gradually whisk in the warmed oils. Once all the oil has been added, whisk in 2–3 tablespoons of warm water to loosen the thick sauce. This addition of extra water will prevent the oils and eggs from separating. If the sauce continues to thicken as

it sets, simply add a little more water. Season with salt and Cayenne pepper, adding the tarragon and setting aside to keep warm while cooking the salmon and asparagus.

Trim the spiky ears from along the asparagus stalks and break or cut the grey-white stalk base away, keeping the spears a uniform length. Season the salmon fillets with salt and pepper and lightly flour the skin sides only. Put a large pan of salted water on to boil.

Heat the cooking oil in a large frying pan and place the fillets in, skin-side down. Fry on a medium-hot heat for 6–7 minutes, not shaking or moving the fish, just allowing the skins to fry and crisp. Turn the fillets, add the knob of butter and remove the pan from the heat. The remaining residual heat will continue to cook the fish for a further few minutes, keeping the flesh moist and buttery.

After turning the salmon, plunge the asparagus tips into the large saucepan of rapidly boiling salted water. Cook for just 2–3 minutes, until tender; 4 minutes should be the maximum. Lift the spears from the pan, drain well and brush with butter to add more flavour and create a shine.

Place the spears side by side on plates and season with a sprinkle of coarse sea salt, if using. Sit the crispy salmon on top, offering the warm lemon and tarragon mayonnaise separately.

This recipe works well with almost any fish.

OPPOSITE: CRISPY WILD SALMON WITH
WARM LEMON AND TARRAGON MAYONNAISE

jellied knuckle of pork with gooseberry relish

This makes a wonderful *al fresco* summer dish. It does take several hours of cooking, but needs very little preparation time, and can be made several days in advance.

Gooseberries often join us in late spring and stay with us until midsummer. This relish recipe is not quite a chutney, but pretty close. I prefer to cook the fruits until very tender, but not classic chutney style to a complete pulp. The touch of mustard seed does lift the flavour, providing a warm fragrant bite, with lime juice to finish.

The relish quantities will produce approximately 1kg (2¼lb) of finished relish and, if stored in sterilized jars (page 9), will keep for several weeks. The pig's trotter, as you can see, is purely an optional extra, simply adding a firmer jelly to the finished dish.

SERVES 4–6 AS A MAIN COURSE, 8–10 AS A STARTER

4 pork knuckles (hocks)
100g (4oz) streaky bacon
1 pig's trotter, split in two (optional)
1 carrot, peeled
2 celery sticks
1 onion
sprig of thyme, plus a sprig to garnish (optional)
sprig of sage
1 bay leaf, plus a leaf to garnish (optional)
6 black peppercorns
1.2 litres (2 pints) *Chicken stock* (page 416) or water
bowl of ice
½ packet powdered gelatine or 2 leaves of gelatine
 (optional)

FOR THE GOOSEBERRY RELISH

1 onion, finely chopped
3 strips of lime zest and juice of 1 lime
1 tablespoon white (yellow) mustard seeds,
 lightly crushed
1 teaspoon ground mixed spice
200ml (7fl oz) white wine vinegar
175g (6oz) caster sugar
900g (2lb) gooseberries, topped and tailed
pinch of salt

OPPOSITE: JELLIED KNUCKLE OF PORK
WITH GOOSEBERRY RELISH

Place the pork knuckles, bacon and split pig's trotter, if using, in a large saucepan along with the carrot, celery, onion, thyme, sage, bay leaf and peppercorns and add the chicken stock. (This stock is not essential, but does lift and enhance the overall flavour and jelly finish of the dish.) Now just top up to cover with water. If not using the stock, simply cover completely with water. Place on the heat and bring to a gentle simmer, skimming away any impurities. Partially cover with a lid and continue to cook at this soft simmer for 3 hours.

Once cooked, remove from the heat and allow to stand for 20 minutes, then remove the knuckles and bacon. Strain the stock through a fine sieve, preferably lined with a muslin cloth. Skim away any excess floating fat. This stock can now be reboiled and reduced to approximately 900ml (1½ pints). Check a few spoonfuls in a bowl over ice for setting point. If it does not set, gelatine can be added following the packet instructions.

While the stock is reducing and the pork is still warm, remove and discard the skin. The meat can now be broken into chunky flakes, removing any sinews. The bacon pieces can be broken and added to the pork, but this is purely a matter of personal taste. The bacon can also be eaten separately, broken into a salad to accompany the pork or discarded. Place the meat in a suitable deep dish. Pour over the stock and leave to cool, then cover with cling film and refrigerate until needed. This will now keep well for up to 1 week.

To make the relish, place the chopped onion and 6 tablespoons of water in a saucepan and bring to a simmer. Cook gently for 10 minutes until the onion has softened. Add the lime peel and juice, the mustard seeds, mixed spice, vinegar and sugar and return to a simmer. Cook for a further 5 minutes, then add the gooseberries. Stir the fruits to take on all of the flavours and simmer for 15 minutes until they have become well softened but not totally puréed. Strain the gooseberries, remove and discard the lime peel. Reboil the liquor and reduce in volume by at least three-quarters to a thick syrupy consistency. Lightly press the gooseberries and add any collected juices to the strained liquor pan as it reduces in volume.

Once reduced, add the gooseberries, seasoning with a pinch of salt. The relish can now be served warm or cold, to accompany the jellied knuckles, or many other cold meats and poultry.

A sprig of thyme can be set on top of the jellied knuckles with a fresh bay leaf, as garnish, to serve.

pork loin in milk with soft sage onions, broad beans and peas

The two green vegetables, both available from late spring to late summer, go together so well. Whether it be a hot dish like this or in a good tossed green salad, the soft delicate sweetness of the pea and the meatiness of the broad bean working as one are irresistible.

The pork loin cooked in milk does leave the meat with a softer finish. Preliminary gentle frying in butter before adding the pork to the warm milk helps give it a tender touch in contrast to the quickly hot-seared, golden-brown edge we're used to.

The 'sauce' to accompany this dish is a combination of fried onions and some of the cooking milk blitzed to a loose purée. The peas and beans are finished with a lemon mustard dressing.

SERVES 4 AS A MAIN COURSE
**4 × 175–225g (6–8oz) pork loin fillets, free of all fat
and sinew
salt and pepper
25g (1oz) butter, plus a knob for the vegetables
600ml (1 pint) milk
2 sprigs of sage
2 large onions, sliced
225g (8oz) podded broad beans
225g (8oz) podded peas
iced water**

FOR THE DRESSING
**6 tablespoons olive oil
2 tablespoons lemon juice
finely grated zest of ½ lemon
2 teaspoons English mustard powder (heaped
teaspoons for a stronger finish)
pinch of caster sugar**

Season the pork loin fillets with salt and pepper. Melt the measured butter in a frying pan and, once bubbling, add the pork pieces. Cook on a low-to-medium heat, only allowing the pork to take on a little colour. The fillets will almost be poaching. Continue until sealed on all sides, saving the butter in the pan.

While the pork is frying, warm the milk to just below simmering point. Tear four sage leaves from the sprigs and keep to one side. Place the remaining sage, including the stalks, in the milk.

Put the pork loin fillets in the milk, maintaining the same temperature. After 6 minutes, check the pork. If too 'soft' in texture, continue to poach for a further 2–4 minutes for a medium finish. If you prefer pork well done, simply poach for 15–20 minutes.

While the pork is cooking, fry the onions in the fried pork butter. Cook on a medium heat for 6–8 minutes until completely softened and golden brown. Season with salt and pepper.

Once cooked, remove the pork from the milk and keep warm, allowing it to rest for 4–5 minutes. Add 3 tablespoons of the milk to the onions and liquidize to a soft purée. If too thick, add a further 2 tablespoons of milk to soften. This should now be a thick purée sauce consistency. Chop the reserved sage leaves and add to the onions, checking for seasoning with salt and pepper.

The broad beans and peas, if both young and small, can be cooked together in boiling salted water for just 2–3 minutes, then refreshed in iced water, before peeling the broad beans. Should you not be so lucky, I suggest cooking them separately: the beans will take 2–5 minutes, depending on size, and the peas also 2–5 minutes but, if late in their season, they can take up to 12–15 minutes before they are completely tender. To reheat, the two can either be microwaved with a knob of butter, or warmed in a few tablespoons of water, also with a knob of butter, seasoning just before serving.

To make the dressing, mix all of the ingredients together with a pinch of salt. Once all the components are ready, spoon 2–3 tablespoons of the onion purée onto each plate. The pork loins can now be cut into five or six slices and laid beside or on top of the purée. Spoon the beans and peas onto the plates, drizzling with the lemon and mustard dressing. This dish is now ready to serve.

barbecued lamb steaks with caper mint sauce and asparagus spears

These lamb steaks will have been cut from a leg of lamb, and are now quite a common alternative to beef rump for sizzling over the charcoal fire. Make sure your butcher cuts these steaks from a slightly aged lamb, ready for marinating, guaranteeing tenderness.

Most basic lamb-steak marinades include lemon juice and olive oil. Here, I'm substituting orange zest for the lemon. This alternative citrus bite leaves a slightly fruitier, sweeter finish, matching well with the sharply flavoured sauce. In this are capers, mint and parsley: all three, in particular capers and mint, having had quite a long-term relationship with lamb.

The asparagus needs little preparation and can simply be scattered onto the barbecue, or steamed in a pot. These prize-winning green sticks love to be dipped in the same caper and mint sauce, flavours that often find themselves in alliance in Italy.

I've added an extra dressing at the end of this recipe. This one I use to bind broken overcooked new potatoes, with cut sticks of asparagus. This almost creates a full meal, perhaps just needing a *Lettuce leaf salad* (page 142) as an accompaniment.

SERVES 4 AS A MAIN COURSE

4 leg of lamb steaks, 2.5cm (1in) thick
8 black peppercorns, crushed
grated zest and juice of 1 orange
squeeze of lemon juice
2 tablespoons olive oil
salt and pepper, plus coarse sea salt
24–32 asparagus spears
knob of butter

FOR THE SAUCE

4 tablespoons capers preserved in vinegar, drained
1 garlic clove, crushed
100ml (3½fl oz) olive oil
½ bunch flatleaf parsley, picked
good handful of mint leaves

Place the lamb steaks in a shallow dish. Mix the crushed black peppercorns, orange zest and juice and olive oil. Season the lamb with coarse sea salt, pouring the orangey marinade over. Cover and leave in a cool place for at least 4 hours, preferably 6–8, turning the meat occasionally.

Preheat the barbecue ready to grill the lamb. Just before cooking the lamb, the asparagus can be prepared and the sauce made. Trim the pointy ears away from the asparagus spears and cut away 2.5–4cm (1–1½in) of the tough stalk base.

To make the sauce, put the drained capers, crushed garlic and olive oil in a small food processor or liquidizer, season with a pinch of salt and pepper, and blitz to a smooth purée. The herbs should be added at the very last moment. This will prevent them discolouring, as a result of the vinegar base in the capers.

Once finished, spoon the sauce into a bowl ready for dipping. Grill the steaks on the barbecue, spooning a little marinade over them as they cook. This particular cut of meat is best served medium. Steaks of this thickness will need just 7–8 minutes on each side, allowing them to colour well. Once cooked, remove the steaks from the barbecue, keeping them warm and resting for 2–3 minutes before serving. Should a barbecue not be available, a ridged grill plate or large frying pan can be used.

While grilling the steaks, the asparagus can be cooked. To barbecue, brush the spears with butter, placing them on the hot grill. These will now take just a few minutes to colour and cook; then turn and continue to grill for a further couple of minutes. Once cooked, remove the spears from the grill, seasoning them with salt and pepper. The alternative is to plunge the spears in boiling salted water and cook for just a few minutes (4–5 maximum) until tender but still maintaining a bite. These can now be strained and rolled in the knob of butter.

Just before serving, add the picked herbs to the sauce, blitzing until smooth and green. The three components are ready to serve: the bitter-sweet barbecued lamb steaks, fresh asparagus spears and the caper mint sauce.

The asparagus spears can be cut into 5cm (2in) sticks and quickly boiled for a few minutes before straining. These can now be spooned into warm, cooked and broken new potatoes (allowing 100–175g (4–6oz) per portion) and mixed with the following dressing. Put 2 finely chopped shallots in a small saucepan and cover with 1 glass of sweet white wine. Cook on a medium heat and simmer until the wine has almost completely evaporated. Leave to cool. Spoon 1 heaped teaspoon of wholegrain mustard into a bowl, with 1 tablespoon of mayonnaise (bought variety) and the juice of 1 lime. Whisk slowly, adding 4 tablespoons of walnut oil and 1 tablespoon of olive oil. Once completely whisked in, add the cooked shallots, seasoning with salt and pepper. The dressing is now ready to stir into the warm asparagus and potatoes.
You can make a quicker version of this salad dressing by whisking together 75ml (3fl oz) natural yoghurt, 50ml (2fl oz) soured cream, 1 heaped teaspoon of wholegrain mustard, the juice of ½ lime, and salt and pepper.

Count yourself lucky if you have access to a vegetable garden in June, for home-grown broad beans are one of life's delights. You can harvest the pods when small and eat them whole, rather as you would French or runner beans. You can also eat the tops, cooking them like spinach. The seeds of course can be eaten raw or cooked, then, as they grow larger, cooked and skinned to reveal the emerald-green kernel inside.

The broad bean is the bean of the western world, and we have been eating it for millennia. In the Middle Ages the broad bean might have been eaten fresh, but it was more likely to have been grown on until large and then dried for winter food. After the discovery of the New World by the Old in the late fifteenth century, the broad bean was introduced to the Americas. More significantly, green beans (French, haricot, kidney, runner, etc.) were brought back. Because we were familiar with beans – the concept of edible pods and inner seeds – we took to them much more readily than to other introductions (the suspicious tuber that was the

potato and the oddly coloured fruit-vegetable that was the tomato, for instance).

If you also have access to home-grown peas, you are doubly fortunate, for many of the same criteria apply. The fresher the pea, the sweeter it is; the longer it is eaten after picking, the poorer the quality. The pea is as ancient a vegetable as the broad bean. The variety of pea cooked in the pottages of the Middle Ages was the field pea, a coarse vegetable which was dried and used as fodder. It was these peas that were made into traditional British foods such as pease pudding, and bacon and peas. It wasn't until the sixteenth century that Italian gardeners developed tender varieties – garden peas – that could be eaten fresh. Other pea varieties, the completely edible pods sugar snaps and mangetout, have since joined us, each one maintaining its own identity and individual flavour.

grilled chicken with a warm bacon and broad bean salad

This salad of broad beans and bacon is a perfect summer accompaniment to chicken. There are many salad leaves available throughout the late spring and summer months; one in particular I do like to include in this recipe is dandelion. Known as *pissenlit* in France, its long thin leaves, ranging in colour from white to yellow and green, have a similar flavour to rocket, and do seem to work and eat so well with bacon.

SERVES 4 AS A MAIN COURSE

4 × 175g (6oz) skinless chicken breast fillets
175g (6oz) podded broad beans
salt and pepper
iced water
100g (4oz) piece of streaky bacon or diced pancetta
2 tablespoons olive oil, plus more for brushing
2–3 tablespoons red wine vinegar
knob of butter
100–175g (4–6oz) mixed salad leaves, preferably
  including a bunch of dandelion leaves, washed
1 tablespoon chopped chives (optional)

Place the chicken breasts between sheets of cling film and flatten a little. These will now hold their shape while cooking. Refrigerate until needed.

To cook the broad beans, plunge them into a pan of rapidly boiling salted water and cook for 1–2 minutes if small or up to 5 minutes for larger ones. Once tender, lift them from the pan and drop into iced water. When cold, drain and remove their shells. The beans can be prepared to this stage a few hours in advance and refrigerated until needed.

If using bacon, cut it into 5mm (¼in) strips and then again into slices. Heat a dry frying pan or wok and add the bacon or cubes of pancetta. Cook, tossing from time to time, until light golden brown, crispy and rendered of all fat. Strain through a colander, saving the fat. Add the 2 tablespoons of olive oil, and red wine vinegar to taste, to the fat. Season this dressing with a twist of pepper.

Brush the chicken breasts with olive oil and season with salt and pepper. These can now be cooked either under a hot grill or on a barbecue, or in a hot frying pan, for just a few minutes on each side. Grilling will obviously produce grill lines, adding an extra bite to the flavour.

While the chicken is cooking, warm the broad beans in a saucepan with the knob of butter and 2 tablespoons of water. Once warm, season with salt and pepper. Mix the broad beans and bacon or pancetta with the salad leaves, adding 2 tablespoons of the dressing. Then either place the chicken breasts on plates and top with the leaves or vice versa. Finish by adding the chopped chives, if using, to the dressing and drizzling it over and around the salad.

It's not essential to serve the broad beans rewarmed. They will eat very well just at room temperature. Soured cream can also be drizzled into and around the salad for a creamier and more piquant finish. The chicken breasts can be flattened into very thin escalopes for an even quicker cooking time.

OPPOSITE: GRILLED CHICKEN WITH A WARM BACON AND BROAD BEAN SALAD

fricassee of chicken with summer vegetables and fresh almonds

A fricassee is a stew, usually of chicken pieces, cooked in stock with the sauce finished with a touch of cream or butter. This sounds quite rich, and that it can be, but only if the sauce is so intense and creamy that it becomes sticky and coating, rather than a loose soft consistency. The cooking liquor can be a chicken stock, but with this recipe it's simply water we shall be using, cooking the chicken carcass with the pieces to create the flavour.

Summer vegetables are so sweet, and here asparagus, broad beans, peas, baby carrots and onions are featured, although it's not essential to include them all. All of these can be cooked well in advance and added to the finished dish. The fresh almonds are a luxury extra, not essential to this dish, but if available do treat yourself to their quite amazing soft sweet bite, so different from the hard dried variety we're used to. The ingredients list may look extensive, but read on and you'll see it is all quite simple.

To prepare the chicken for the fricassee is quite a simple operation. The first step is to remove the legs, then separate the drumsticks from the thighs. The breasts can now be removed from the carcass and each split into two pieces. The carcass can now be cut into four pieces, ready to cook with the meat to create the stock. Pre-cut chicken pieces can also be used.

SERVES 4 AS A MAIN COURSE
1 × 1.75kg (4lb) free-range chicken, cut into pieces (see above)
salt and pepper, plus a few peppercorns
2 tablespoons olive oil
1 onion, chopped (optional)
1 carrot, chopped (optional)
300ml (½ pint) white wine
sprig of thyme (optional)
150ml (¼ pint) double or whipping cream
12 fresh almonds, shelled and split in half (page 424)
1 heaped tablespoon chopped mixed herbs (such as chives, parsley, marjoram, tarragon)
squeeze of lemon juice

FOR THE SUMMER VEGETABLES AND HERBS
100g (4oz) podded peas
100g (4oz) podded broad beans
iced water
8 asparagus spears, trimmed of spiky ears and stalk base
12 baby onions, peeled
pinch of sugar
12 baby carrots, peeled, leaving 1–2cm (½–¾in) of stalk attached
2 knobs of butter

Season the chicken pieces with salt and pepper. Heat the olive oil in a large flameproof braising pot and fry the chicken pieces on all sides until golden brown. Remove them from the pot and add the chopped carcass, trimmings, onion and carrot, if using. Fry on a medium heat until golden, then add the white wine, thyme, if using, and peppercorns. Bring to the boil and reduce in volume by half. Return the chicken pieces and their juices to the pan, then add 300ml (½ pint) of water. Bring to a simmer and cover with a lid. Cook gently on top of the stove, or in an oven preheated to 190°C/375°F/Gas 5 for 20 minutes.

Remove the chicken and carcass pieces from the pot, discarding the carcass bones and keeping the chicken pieces warm to one side. Bring the liquor to a simmer, then add the cream and cook for 5–6 minutes before straining through a fine sieve. Check the sauce for seasoning.

The summer vegetables can all be cooked well before cooking the chicken, or while it is braising. Each will be cooked individually to ensure their even tenderness. The peas and beans can simply be cooked separately in boiling salted water, both needing just a few minutes until tender. When cooking either of these vegetables it is best to check as they cook. If not absolutely 'just picked fresh', they may need a little longer in the pan. It is also important to make sure no lid is placed on the pan as they cook, to maintain their rich green colour. Once tender, refresh in iced water. Cut the asparagus spears in half and cook for 2–3 minutes, with 4–5 minutes the absolute maximum, then refresh in iced water.

Place the onions in a saucepan of cold water, bring to the simmer and cook for 10–12 minutes until tender. Strain and keep to one side. Place the baby carrots in a saucepan only just covered with water. Add a pinch each of salt and sugar and a knob of butter. Bring to a simmer and cook until tender. Depending on the size of the carrots, this can take 3–10 minutes. When cooked, lift the carrots from the pan and keep to one side. Boil and reduce the cooking liquor in volume by half. This can be kept and used to reheat the vegetables.

Once the chicken sauce has been finished and the pieces of bird are being kept warm in the oven – pouring any juices collected into the sauce – the vegetables can be warmed. The quickest route is to place all of them in a glass or china dish, season them with salt and pepper, add a knob of butter and then microwave them. The alternative is first to warm the baby onions and carrots in a large pan with the reduced carrot liquor. Place a lid on the pan to create a steam. Once warmed, add the peas, beans and the cut asparagus spears. After a few minutes all will be ready, then add the seasoning and a knob of butter.

Arrange the chicken pieces, vegetables and almonds on a large plate or bowl and sprinkle with the chopped herbs. Add a squeeze of lemon juice to the sauce, then spoon it over the chicken to complete the dish.

caramelized lemon-shredded chicory with roast pigeon and cherry dressing

Slowly caramelized chicory is so good – the finished bitter-sweet, tender flavour eating well with many fish and meats. This caramelizing method is going to be a lot quicker, the chicory first being finely shredded. I've introduced spinach leaves and, although they are not essential, they do go well with the chicory.

Cherries begin their season in June and have quite a classic relationship with duck dishes, working equally well with smaller birds, such as the pigeons featured here.

SERVES 4 AS A STARTER OR SUPPER DISH
4 wood pigeons
salt and pepper
25g (1oz) butter, plus a knob for frying
4 heads of chicory
2 teaspoons caster sugar
100g (4oz) spinach leaves, torn into bite-size pieces
juice of ½ lemon
20 cherries, halved and pitted
2 tablespoons walnut oil (optional)

FOR THE CHERRY DRESSING
knob of butter
3 juniper berries, lightly crushed
2 strips of orange zest
12 cherries, halved and pitted
few black peppercorns
1 bottle of red wine, preferably claret

4 sugar cubes (white or brown)
splash of red wine vinegar

Preheat the oven to 200°C/400°F/Gas 6. Remove the legs from the pigeons. The back carcasses beneath the breasts can now be cut away. Trim off the wings. The breasts now sit proudly on the bone ready to be roasted. Refrigerate until needed.

To make the cherry dressing, roughly chop the pigeon legs, back carcasses and wings (it's from these that the dressing will capture its gamey flavour). Melt the knob of butter in a saucepan and add the chopped pigeon pieces. Fry on a fairly rapid heat until well coloured. Add the juniper berries, orange zest, cherry halves and black peppercorns. Continue to cook for 5–6 minutes, then add the red wine. Bring to a simmer and allow to reduce in volume to just 300ml (½ pint). Strain the wine liquor through a fine sieve or muslin cloth, squeezing all juice from the bones and cherries. Return to the boil, cooking until reduced in volume by half. Add the sugar cubes and, once dissolved, the gamey wine liquor will have a syrupy consistency. Now add a little splash of red wine vinegar to give piquancy to the sweet sauce.

To cook the pigeons, season the breasts with salt and pepper. Melt a knob of butter in a frying or roasting pan. Once bubbling, place the pigeons in, breast-side down, and cook for a few minutes until golden brown. Turn and colour the breasts on the other sides, then finish in the preheated oven, breast-sides up, for 10–12 minutes. This will keep the pigeons pink. Remove from the oven and allow to rest for 5–6 minutes.

While the pigeons are cooking, prepare the chicory. Remove any bruised outside leaves and split the heads lengthwise, cutting away any base stalk. Shred the halves very finely. Melt the measured butter in a frying pan. Once bubbling, add the shredded chicory. Cook on a fast heat for a minute, then add the caster sugar. Continue to cook for a further 2–3 minutes until the sugar has dissolved and the chicory is beginning to caramelize gently. Add the spinach leaves. These will be tender within 30 seconds–1 minute. Squeeze over the lemon juice and season with salt and pepper.

Just before serving, lightly warm the cherries in a saucepan with 2 tablespoons of the dressing.

Remove the pigeon breasts from the bone, also removing the skins to reveal the moist meat. Divide the chicory between four plates or bowls. The pigeon breasts can now each be cut into two or three slices or left whole before placing on top of the chicory. Spoon the softened cherry halves over and around, finishing with the warm cherry dressing. If using, drizzle with a little walnut oil.

gooseberry and lime pastry plate

This is simply a sweet shortcrust pastry disc baked until crispy, spread with fresh lime curd and sweet, softened gooseberries. The pastry base is the plate in the recipe title. It can be cut to a perfect 30cm (12in) circle or left as rolled, in a more rustic fashion. The lime curd can quite easily be omitted from the recipe, leaving just the cooked base and fruits. This would then become a sort of upside-down 'Old English' gooseberry pie.

The lime curd can also be mixed with whipped cream (100–150ml/3½fl oz–¼ pint) and offered as an accompaniment.

SERVES 6–8

50g (2oz) butter, plus more for greasing and an extra knob
350g (12oz) *Sweet shortcrust pastry* (page 425)
flour, for dusting
50g (2oz) caster sugar, plus 3 tablespoons
finely grated zest and juice of 2 limes
2 eggs
675g (1½lb) gooseberries, topped and tailed
icing sugar, for dusting
whipped or pouring cream (optional)

Very lightly butter a baking tray or line it with greaseproof paper. Roll out the pastry on a lightly floured surface to a 30cm (12in) circle. Roll the pastry around the rolling pin and transfer it to the prepared baking tray. Prick with a fork and refrigerate for 30 minutes.

Preheat the oven to 180°C/350°F/Gas 4. Bake the pastry for 20–25 minutes, until golden brown. Remove from the oven and allow to cool on a wire rack.

In a small saucepan, warm the measured butter until softened. Add the 50g (2oz) of caster sugar, lime zest, lime juice and eggs and mix all together well. Place on a moderate heat and whisk continuously until approaching a soft simmer and thickened to a lime curd. Remove the pan from the heat and pour the curd into a chilled bowl. Cover and leave to cool.

Melt the knob of butter in a large saucepan, add the gooseberries and the remaining 3 tablespoons of caster sugar, warming and stirring gently so as to not break the fruits. Cook for a few minutes, then add a tablespoon of water and

continue to cook for a further minute or two, until the gooseberries are becoming tender but not breaking down. Remove from the heat and leave to cool.

Carefully spoon the soft fruits into a colander and allow the syrup juices to drain. Once drained, the syrup can be boiled for a few minutes and reduced in volume to a thicker coating consistency.

Spread the lime curd on the pastry plate base, leaving a 1–2cm (½–¾in) border all round. Place the gooseberries on top of the curd, keeping them close together. Before brushing with the syrup, a few burnt baked tinges can be made on the fruits. To achieve this, dust the gooseberries with icing sugar and glaze and colour with a gas gun (page 9). Once coloured, brush with the sweet syrup to glaze, and dust the exposed pastry border with icing sugar.

Whipped or pouring cream makes a lovely optional extra to this sharp sweet plate.

A teaspoon of elderflower cordial can be added to the gooseberries once they are softened. When boiled with the natural syrup and reduced in volume, the elderflower lifts the total gooseberry flavour wonderfully.
To guarantee the lime curd will not curdle, place all the ingredients – butter, sugar, zest and juice of the limes, and the eggs – in a bowl over simmering water. Stir and cook for 20–30 minutes until thickened, then cool.

OPPOSITE: GOOSEBERRY AND LIME PASTRY PLATE

soft gooseberry and roquefort salad

This recipe is literally a tossed salad consisting of the two main ingredients – gooseberries and Roquefort – sprinkled amongst mixed leaves and finished with a creamy dressing. As an accompaniment to a summer salad table or as a sweet-and-savoury dessert, these distinctive flavours blend very well. Freshly carved ham welcomes this recipe to its plate, or perhaps mix tender Parma ham or crisply grilled strips of bacon into the salad as an alternative.

SERVES 4

225g (8oz) gooseberries, topped and tailed
1 dessertspoon caster sugar, or more if required
approximately 150g (5oz) mixed salad leaves
4 teaspoons olive oil

FOR THE DRESSING

50g (2oz) Roquefort cheese
4 tablespoons single cream
2 tablespoons lemon juice
twist of pepper

Place the gooseberries in a saucepan with 3 tablespoons of water and the dessertspoon of sugar. Cook gently over a low heat until the fruits have become tender but not puréed. Taste for sweetness. One dessertspoon of sugar may well have been enough; if the fruits are still too tart, add a little more, stirring it in to dissolve until the preferred flavour is obtained. Leave to cool. The gooseberries are best served at room temperature.

To make the dressing, mash or blitz the Roquefort in a small food processor, adding the cream, lemon juice and a good twist of pepper. Salt will not be needed in this recipe; the salty Roquefort provides this part of the seasoning.

To finish the salad, mix the leaves with some of the softened berries, binding all of the flavours with the Roquefort cream. Divide between plates or bowls and serve, drizzling each with a teaspoon of olive oil.

Alternatively, spoon the softened gooseberries between the plates or bowls, mix the salad leaves with the Roquefort cream and sit them on top of the fruit. The olive oil can now be drizzled around each serving.

orange and strawberry salad with sorrel syrup

In summer, fresh oranges have joined us from abroad and British strawberries are in abundance.

Fresh sorrel syrup is an optional extra: the lemony herb can be omitted from the syrup recipe, perhaps even replaced with a few mint leaves – another herb that will complement the fruit. Fresh sorrel can be used in a lot of dessert recipes, however. The herb's lemony flavour makes strawberries a perfect combination with orange and chocolate. It's not really important to include the *Cocoa sorbet* here; it's purely an extra idea to try. The fruit salad itself is clean, crisp and refreshing on its own.

SERVES 4

4 large oranges
450g (1lb) fresh strawberries, hulled and rinsed
1 quantity *Cocoa sorbet* (page 71, optional)

FOR THE SORREL SYRUP

300ml (½ pint) orange juice
100g (4oz) caster sugar
10 sorrel leaves

With a sharp knife, top and tail the oranges, and peel, cutting away all the surrounding zest and pith to leave you with a clean fruit, ready to segment. Cut away the individual segments.

Halve, quarter or slice the strawberries, according to their size.

To make the syrup, pour the orange juice and caster sugar into a saucepan, along with 50–75g (2–3oz) of the strawberries and 6 shredded sorrel leaves. Bring to a simmer and cook for 15 minutes, until the strawberries are puréeing and the syrup is reduced in volume by a third. The syrup will now have reached a coating consistency. Push through a sieve for a smooth orangey-pink glossy finish.

The remaining strawberries and the orange segments can now be arranged in bowls casually, or overlapping in a circle, before spooning over the syrup. If serving the cocoa sorbet, or any other ice-cream, scroll it with a warm tablespoon or scoop it into balls and place these in the centres of the bowls. The last remaining sorrel leaves can now also be finely shredded and the strands sprinkled around the salad.

strawberry summer puddings

At their sweetest, a large bowl of glistening red English berries, just as they come, provides us with a simple, delicious pudding. Summer pudding, however, is a classic British favourite, with an assortment of colourful berries all held together with the juice-soaked bread slices. In this month not all of the berries have quite reached their best, so let's start with the fruits in their prime – pure strawberries.

This recipe can be made using six 150ml (¼ pint) plastic pudding bowls or deep rings or size-1 ramekins. For one large pudding, a 1.2 litre (2 pint) basin will be needed.

SERVES 6

1kg (2¼lb) strawberries, hulled and rinsed, leaving
  6 with stalks to decorate
50g (2oz) caster sugar
2 tablespoons *crème de framboise* (raspberry liqueur,
  optional)
8–12 slices of medium-cut white bread, crusts removed
strawberry syrup (see below, optional)
mint sprigs, to decorate(optional)
icing sugar, for dusting (optional)
extra-thick pouring or whipping cream

Cut the larger berries in half. Place all of the strawberries in a saucepan with the caster sugar. Cook gently for 4–5 minutes until the juices begin to seep out. At this point the raspberry liqueur can be added (if using), with 2 tablespoons of water. If not using the liqueur, add 4 tablespoons of water. Stir it into the strawberries and leave to cool. Carefully strain the strawberries, saving the strawberry syrup in a bowl.

Cut discs from the bread slices to fit the base and tops of each basin or ramekin (if using a large basin, the tops can be achieved with several strips). If using rings as moulds, stretch cling film over the base of each before placing on a tray. Dip the bread in the cooled syrup, and place in the base of each mould. The remaining slices can now be cut into strips for the sides of the moulds. These can now also be dipped in the syrup, placing them slightly overlapping around the sides, leaving any excess hanging over the top. Dip the remaining discs for lids in the syrup, keeping them to one side.

Pack the moulds with the softened strawberries, right up above the rim, folding over the excess bread and trimming if necessary. Top each with the saved lids before covering with cling film. Press with a plate and weight – two or three tins of baked beans for a large basin is usually enough. For individual moulds it's best to cover them all with a flat baking tray, then apply the weight from several tins. These are best left weighted and refrigerated for 6–8 hours, or preferably overnight.

To turn out, place a plate on top of the large pudding, before turning and gently squeezing the basin. This will release the pudding very easily. Smaller individual basins are just as easy to remove, turning out the ring moulds or ramekins onto plates.

If making the strawberry syrup below, spoon over each, leaving a quite shiny red finish. Garnish each with the saved strawberry and a mint sprig, if using, and dusting with icing sugar, if you like.

Extra-thick pouring or whipped cream is the best accompaniment for this dish.

To make the strawberry syrup, it's best to buy over-ripe strawberries. Alternatively, frozen strawberries or mixed berries can be used. Place 350g (12oz) strawberries (or other berries), hulled, rinsed and halved, in a saucepan with 100g (4oz) caster sugar and 100ml (3½fl oz) water. Bring to a simmer. Cook for 5–6 minutes before cooling slightly, and straining through a fine sieve, pressing the fruit flesh through. The strawberry syrup is now ready to use.

sweet cherry shortcakes

In abundance now are these little round rubies, with contrasting shades from tomato-red to deep aubergine-purple. From May to the first month of autumn you'll find cherries on every street trader's cart. They basically grow all over the world, coming in many varieties and flavours. An easy guideline to follow is that bright reds are sweeter than the more acidic and slightly sour aubergine-coloured. Then there's the morello cherry, too sour and tart to eat raw, but beautiful once steeped in brandy or syrup.

SERVES 6

450–675g (1–1½lb) cherries, stalks removed
iced water
75g (3oz) caster sugar
150ml (¼ pint) sweet white wine or water (sweet port can also be used)
150ml (¼ pint) double cream
1 vanilla pod, split and seeds scraped out (optional)
icing sugar or caster sugar, for dusting or sprinkling

FOR THE SHORTCAKE BISCUITS

100g (4oz) butter
50g (2oz) caster sugar
100g (4oz) plain flour, plus more for dusting
50g (2oz) semolina
pinch of salt

Using a cherry stoner, pit the cherries before immersing them in a bowl of iced water. This helps them plump up, offering a fuller and rounder appearance. This is not essential, but should you do this, leave the cherries in the water for just 20–30 minutes. Before cooking, remove the cherries from the water and drain thoroughly.

Warm a non-stick frying pan, adding the cherries and sugar. Cook over a medium heat, turning the cherries from time to time, for 1–2 minutes. Add the sweet white wine or water, bringing it to a gentle simmer. Cook for a further 2 minutes before spooning out the majority of the cherries and keeping to one side, leaving a few in the pan for extra flavour. Simmer the syrup, mashing the fruits to help release extra strength to the liquor. Once at a thick coating consistency, strain the syrup through a sieve and leave to cool, along with the cherries.

To make the shortcake biscuits, beat together the butter and caster sugar, until pale and creamy (an electric hand whisk or food processor will help). Sift together the plain flour, semolina and pinch of salt. Gradually add the dry ingredients to the creamed butter and sugar and work them in until they reach a dough consistency. Refrigerate for 30–40 minutes to firm.

Roll the dough on a lightly flour-dusted surface until it's approximately 3mm (⅛in) thick. Prick over the dough with a fork before cutting into twelve discs, each with a diameter of 6–7cm (2½–3in), with a pastry cutter (either a plain round or fluted cutter can be used). You may find that to achieve the quantity of biscuits required, the dough trimmings will need to be rerolled and cut. With a palette knife, transfer the discs to a non-stick baking tray, and chill for 30–40 minutes.

SWEET CHERRY SHORTCAKES

Preheat the oven to 180°C/350°F/Gas 4. Bake the biscuits for 10–12 minutes until lightly golden brown. Transfer the biscuits to a wire rack and allow to cool.

To flavour the double cream, add the vanilla seeds, if using, and a few tablespoons of the cooled cherry syrup. Whip the cream to a soft peak stage. Spoon or pipe the cream onto six of the biscuits, placing them on plates. Arrange the cherries on top of each. Any syrup not used in the cream can be spooned over or around the cherries, before topping with the remaining biscuits. Dust or sprinkle with icing or caster sugar to finish.

For an alternative, the same quantity of mixed summer berries can be used.

To make the vanilla cream (*crème chantilly*), whisk together the cream, icing sugar and vanilla seeds to a thick soft-peak stage. Spoon the cream on top of the cherries or serve separately.

A lemon syrup can be made, offering an extra kick to the finished dish. Put the finely grated zest of 2 lemons, the juice of 4 lemons and 75g (3oz) caster sugar into a saucepan. Bring to a rapid simmer and cook to a syrupy consistency. Strain through a sieve or tea strainer and the syrup is ready.

stewed kirsch cherries with vanilla cream

Fresh cherries – or almost any summer fruit for that matter – simmered in syrup until tender and served with thick vanilla cream, are a pure summer delight.

SERVES 4–6
100g (4oz) caster sugar
550g (1¼lb) dark red cherries, pitted
100ml (3½fl oz) kirsch

FOR THE VANILLA CREAM
150ml (¼ pint) double cream
25g (1oz) icing sugar
1 vanilla pod, split and seeds scraped out

Boil 150ml (¼ pint) of water with the caster sugar for 5 minutes. Add the pitted cherries and bring the syrup back to the boil and remove from the heat. If the cherries are under-ripe and over-firm, simmer for a minute or two before removing from the heat. Add the kirsch and leave to cool.

Once cold, the cherry syrup can be thickened with some of the fruits. This is not essential, but does add more depth to the overall taste. To do this, strain the cherries through a sieve and pour the syrup into a liquidizer. Add 2–3 tablespoons of the fruits and blend to a purée. For the smoothest of finishes, strain through a fine sieve, before trickling over the fruits. Divide the sweetened cherries between glasses and serve at room temperature or chilled.

vegetables

fish

meat

fruit and puddings

broken salmon, cucumber and lettuce salad with fresh dill cream dressing

Although prepared indoors, this is most certainly a dish for the garden. Few of our home-grown delights need playing with or garnishing during these three peak summer months. Fresh salmon can be poached and served cold, or lightly steamed – as here. And during these summer months, cucumber finds a new identity, its watery flesh offering a more pronounced flavour.

This dish is simply a combination of the two main ingredients tossed amongst gentle leaves, which are sweet, not too bitter and overpowering, finished with a creamy dill dressing. To bulk up the salad, broken steamed or boiled potatoes can be added, or served just rolled in butter and sitting in a bowl alongside.

SERVES 4 AS A LUNCH OR SUPPER DISH

1 small butterhead or loosehead lettuce
1 small Cos lettuce
1 Little Gem lettuce
handful of baby spinach leaves or purslane sprigs
½ cucumber
knob of butter, plus more for greasing
coarse sea salt and pepper
450g (1lb) salmon fillet, skinned and pin-boned
   (page 9)

FOR THE DRESSING

2 tablespoons natural yoghurt
3 tablespoons single cream
juice of 1 lime (or 1–2 tablespoons white wine vinegar)
2 tablespoons olive oil
1 tablespoon chopped dill

Remove any damaged leaves from the lettuces, before tearing the leaves from the base stalk. These can now all be gently rinsed under cold water along with the spinach or sprigs of purslane. Leave to drain in a large colander or whizz in a wire salad basket.

Split the cucumber in half lengthwise, dividing each half into three or four long wedges. These can now be sliced into 5mm (¼in) thick pieces.

OPPOSITE: BROKEN SALMON, CUCUMBER AND LETTUCE SALAD WITH FRESH DILL CREAM DRESSING

To steam the salmon, butter a sheet of greaseproof paper, seasoning with the coarse sea salt and pepper. Place the salmon on one half of the paper, skinned-side down, topping with a knob of butter and sprinkling with a little sea salt. Fold the paper over the fish, and place in a steamer basket or colander over a saucepan of rapidly simmering water. Cover with a lid and steam for 8–10 minutes. This will leave a pink centre with a succulent bite. To check, lift the folded greaseproof paper. The salmon should be slightly opaque, still showing signs of its natural pink. If too soft to the touch, continue to steam for a few minutes more until just beginning to firm. Once at this stage remove the basket from the pan and leave to one side.

While steaming the fish, spoon the yoghurt, single cream and lime juice or vinegar together, whisking in the olive oil. Season with salt and pepper and add the chopped dill.

In a large bowl tear the salad leaves and mix with the cucumber. Using a fish slice, transfer the steamed salmon onto a plate, whisking any juice left on the greaseproof paper into the dressing, and break it into bite-size pieces with a fork. Add the salmon to the leaves, pouring the dressing over. Gently spoon all of the flavours together in a rustic fashion, serving as it is or in individual portions.

A thin fillet of salmon may take only 6 minutes to steam, leaving moist pink flakes.

creamy new potatoes with goat's cheese

Melting goat's cheese rolled around new potatoes enhances their already rich summery flavour. It's important that a soft goat's cheese is used as this will then melt easily with the cream or milk and butter.

This dish works as a good accompaniment to many meat, fish and vegetarian courses.

SERVES 6 AS A STARTER OR 4 AS A LIGHT LUNCH

675g (1½lb) new potatoes, scrubbed
salt and pepper
50–100g (2–4oz) soft goat's cheese, skin removed
5–7 tablespoons single cream or milk
25–40g (1–1½oz) butter

Cook the new potatoes in boiling salted water for 20 minutes or until soft and tender. While the potatoes are cooking, chop the goat's cheese and melt it gently with the cream or milk and butter: 50g (2oz) of cheese along with 5 tablespoons of cream or milk and 25g (1oz) of butter will provide just enough to bind the potatoes. The extra quantities will make the mixture sauce-like.

Once the potatoes are cooked, drain and halve while still hot. Season with salt and pepper, then stir in the soft creamy cheese.

Chopped chives or shallots can be added to this recipe, finishing the creamy flavour with an oniony bite.

lettuce leaf salad

The lettuce leaf salad of today, probably of the last 20 years, is the *mesclun* (mixed). *Mesclun* is simply a mixture of various leaves, so often to be found in the chilled cabinets of supermarkets. There's nothing actually wrong with a good mixed combination, as long as their flavours are blending and not fighting, but so often a bag will hold a devil of a leaf that's so bitter as it's being eaten, that its soft, gentle friends have no chance to express their characters.

Hence this lettuce leaf salad, choosing from British originals – Cos, butterhead, Iceberg and Webbs. All of these, when crispy, torn and tossed in a basic dressing, can stand proudly alone.

At the same time, it would be foolish to ignore our continental friends. Rocket (*roquette*), watercress and mizuna are all crisp but gentle peppery leaves, sometimes needing a softer young spinach to counter their bite. Bitter amongst these heads, we find chicory, curly endive and escarole, which have a less bitter finish if you use young and pale leaves, rather than the slightly toughened dark ones. Lamb's lettuce (corn salad, or *mâche* in French), with baby spinach and summer purslane, are sweeter; the purslane is the most robust amongst the three, providing a sharp kick.

With these lettuces in mind, dressings should really follow suit, with contrasting strengths to enhance. I'm treating this recipe as a starter for four, with a quantity of leaves listed, a basic dressing to drizzle, and a few alternative dressings to choose from. You can find other dressings on pages 419–21.

SERVES 4 AS A STARTER
225g (8oz) chosen lettuce leaves (see above), separated and lightly washed

FOR THE DRESSING
1 teaspoon Dijon mustard
2 tablespoons red or white wine vinegar (tarragon vinegar can also be used)
2 teaspoons lemon juice
pinch of caster sugar
125ml (4fl oz) olive oil
coarse sea salt and pepper

Gently tear any large leaves into easier bite-sized pieces. Place all the leaves in a large bowl.

To make the dressing, whisk together the mustard, chosen vinegar, lemon juice and sugar, slowly pouring and whisking in the olive oil. Season with salt and pepper. Alternatively, the dressing can be made by simply shaking all of the ingredients together in a screw-top jar.

Drizzle enough of the dressing over just to coat the leaves, toss them all together and serve immediately or simply offer the dressing separately. It's important that any form of salad is served at once if the dressing has been added. Any remaining dressing can be refrigerated, lasting two to three weeks.

For a sherry and mustard seed dressing, put 1 tablespoon wholegrain mustard, 2 tablespoons sherry vinegar, 75ml (3fl oz) olive oil, 75ml (3fl oz) groundnut oil, and some salt and pepper in a screw-top jar and shake to bind.
For a lemon dressing (this recipe can be multiplied if necessary), put 3 tablespoons olive oil, 1 tablespoon fresh lemon juice, a pinch of caster sugar and some salt and pepper in a screw-top jar and shake to bind.
For a fresh raspberry and walnut dressing, place 75g (3oz) fresh raspberries, 100ml (3½fl oz) walnut oil, 50ml (2fl oz) groundnut oil, 2 tablespoons cider vinegar (white wine vinegar, lemon or lime juice can also be used), ½ teaspoon caster sugar, 1 heaped teaspoon Dijon mustard and some salt and pepper in a small food processor and blitz to a purée. Strain through a sieve and the dressing is ready.
For a creamy red wine dressing, whisk together 1 teaspoon Dijon or English mustard, 1 tablespoon red wine vinegar, 150ml (¼ pint) double cream and some salt and pepper to a light, loose, soft-ribbon stage.

OPPOSITE: LETTUCE LEAF SALAD

jellied tomato cake with ricotta herb cream

Summer is peaking and tomatoes are in abundance, with the added advantage of being at quite a low price. It is at this time of year that this recipe should be tried. The jelly is made from pure tomato water – just a question of liquidizing the tomatoes and draining them of all their juices. The result is quite an intense flavour.

The ricotta herb cream involves a last-minute blitzing of the cheese, creamed with a bite of garlic, red wine vinegar, olive oil and lots of herbs. To finish, a handful or two of salad leaves and herbs can be arranged as a garnish.

SERVES 4 AS A STARTER
675g (1½lb) fresh, ripe tomatoes, quartered
3–4 leaves of gelatine, soaked in cold water (these quantities are for 225–300ml/8fl oz–½ pint tomato water)
8 large tomatoes
iced water
salt and pepper

FOR THE CREAM
175g (6oz) ricotta cheese
1 small garlic clove, crushed
1 teaspoon red wine vinegar
1 tablespoon olive oil
1 teaspoon chopped chives
1 teaspoon chopped flatleaf parsley
1 teaspoon chopped tarragon

FOR THE GARNISH (OPTIONAL)
1 tablespoon olive oil
½–1 tablespoon balsamic vinegar
1–2 handfuls of mixed salad leaves
12–16 × 2cm (¾in) pieces of chive
12–16 flatleaf parsley leaves
12–16 tarragon leaves

Liquidize the quartered tomatoes first, enough to break down the texture. Drain through a muslin cloth or fine sieve. To maximize the full flavour and allow the tomatoes to drain completely, it is best to carry out this procedure 24 hours in advance. The minimum time required will be at least 5–6 hours. It is also important not to push the purée through the cloth as this will result in a tomato coulis, too thick and cloudy for this

dish. Once drained, a very gentle squeeze will help release the last few drops, resulting in approximately 225–300ml (8fl oz–½ pint) of liquor.

Remove the gelatine leaves from the water and squeeze to extract excess water, then place them in a small saucepan with a few tablespoons of the tomato water. Warm gently to melt the gelatine, then stir into the remaining tomato water.

To peel the large tomatoes, remove the eyes with a sharp knife and then blanch in boiling water for 10 seconds. Plunge into iced water and, once cold, peel them. Cut away the domed tops of four of the peeled tomatoes (opposite the stalk end). Try to make these domes neat and round and approximately 1cm (½in) thick as they will form the tops of the jellied cakes. Quarter and seed the remaining parts of the tomatoes, as well as the other four whole ones. This stage can also be prepared in advance.

To build the cakes, stretch cling film over four 8 × 5cm (3 × 2in) metal cooking rings and turn them over. Season the tomato quarters with salt and pepper, only salting the dome tops. Place the pieces in the moulds, layering with the jelly, not overpressing or squashing the tomatoes too tightly. Once all the quarters have been used, place the four domes on top. Spoon extra jelly over the tomatoes, leaving a few millimetres of top exposed. Refrigerate until set.

To turn out the cakes, remove the cling film. If left to stand for a few minutes the cakes should, with a gentle push from the domed top, be quite easy to turn out. Another method is holding the metal rings tightly, to lightly warm them with your hands. The fastest method is to warm quickly with a gas gun (page 9).

To make the cream, blend the ricotta cheese to a smooth paste with the crushed garlic, red wine vinegar and olive oil. Season with salt and pepper and fold in the chopped herbs.

To finish the dish, if using the garnish, mix the olive oil and balsamic vinegar together and season. Mix the salad leaves with the chive pieces, parsley and tarragon leaves, and add the vinegar dressing. The three components – tomato cake, ricotta cream, salad leaves – can be placed individually on each plate, forming a trio of flavours and colours.

red pepper mousse with crispy onion strips

This is a recipe that can be made all year round, with imported red peppers permanently on offer. However, during this summer month, the ripe English red peppers join us, and they should certainly be tried and taken advantage of during these warm sunny days.

The onion strips are very quick and easy to make. For a completely vegetarian dish, the anchovy fillets can be omitted. The strips are made from puff pastry and for this particular recipe I recommend a fresh or frozen bought variety.

This recipe eats very well as a starter or can become part of a summer barbecue buffet or picnic. The quantities listed for the onion strips may seem quite high, but they give generous portions. The recipe can be halved, providing just enough for a light starter.

SERVES 4–6 AS A STARTER
knob of butter
1 shallot, finely diced (or ½ small onion)
1 garlic clove, chopped
1 bay leaf
675g (1½lb) red peppers, seeded and chopped into
    rough 1cm (½in) dice
½ teaspoon caster sugar
3 tablespoons red wine vinegar
3 tablespoons white wine
2 leaves of gelatine, soaked in cold water
150ml (¼ pint) double cream
squeeze of lemon juice
salt and pepper

FOR THE CRISPY ONION STRIPS
225g (8oz) *Puff pastry* (page 426)
flour, for dusting
oil, for greasing
4 large onions, finely sliced
knob of butter
2 teaspoons demerara sugar
½ teaspoon picked thyme leaves (optional)
1 tin of anchovy fillets (optional)

Melt the butter in a large saucepan and, once bubbling, add the shallot or onion, garlic and bay leaf. Cover with a lid and cook for a few minutes until the shallots are beginning to soften. Add the red peppers, replace the lid and cook for a further 10–15 minutes, stirring from time to time, until tender.

Add the sugar, red wine vinegar and white wine, increase the heat and allow to boil and reduce until almost dry.

Remove the bay leaf and liquidize the mixture to a purée, straining through a sieve for a smooth finish. While still warm, add the soaked gelatine leaves, squeezing them first to release excess water, and stir in well. Leave to cool. Once cold but not approaching a setting point, lightly whip the double cream to soft peaks. Spoon and fold the cream into the pepper purée, adding a squeeze of lemon juice and seasoning with salt and pepper. Now spoon the mousse mix into a suitable bowl, cover with cling film and refrigerate for 1–2 hours until set.

To prepare the crispy onion strips, cut the pastry into four rectangular pieces. On a lightly floured surface roll each piece individually into a long thin strip, approximately 2mm (½in) thick and 4cm (1½in) wide. These can be trimmed to achieve a straighter edge or simply left quite rustic. Place all four on a greased baking sheet and prick along the centres . with a fork. Refrigerate.

Fry the onions in the butter (this may need to be done in stages) almost until approaching burnt, then add the demerara sugar. Continue to cook for a few minutes until the sugar is beginning to caramelize. Season with salt and pepper and add the thyme, if using. Remove from the heat and leave to cool.

Once cold, preheat the oven to 200°C/400°F/Gas 6. Spoon the onions along the pastry strips, leaving a 5mm (¼in) border on either side. Cut the anchovy fillets lengthwise into two or three slices, and lay these top to tail along the middle of the onions (cutting the anchovies thinly will balance their strong flavour with that of the onions and pastry).

Bake in the preheated oven for 10–15 minutes until crispy. These will eat at their best warm, but not too hot. The mousse can now be presented on the table along with the strips, cut into 2cm (¾in) slices – just nice bite-size pieces on which to spoon the mousse.

crisp courgette tart with a tomato and basil salad

This recipe makes the most of two main favourites of the English summer – courgettes and tomatoes, both in abundance throughout this season. The salad also benefits from the experience of the fresh basil leaves accompanied by a few shavings of Parmesan cheese. In all, a classic combination.

SERVES 6 AS A GENEROUS STARTER OR
4 AS A MAIN COURSE

175g (6oz) *Puff pastry* (page 426, or bought)
flour, for dusting
½ tablespoon olive oil, plus more for brushing
1 red onion, thinly sliced
½ teaspoon caster sugar
salt, plus coarse sea salt
twist of black pepper
4–5 large courgettes, topped and tailed and cut into
**   3–4mm (⅛–⅙in) slices**
1 egg yolk, loosened with a drop of milk (optional)
1 teaspoon picked thyme leaves
squeeze of lemon juice

FOR THE SALAD
7–8 plum or salad tomatoes
iced water
3 tablespoons olive oil
1 teaspoon aged balsamic vinegar (for a vinegar
**   of lesser strength add ½–1 teaspoon more)**
5–6 basil leaves
25–50g (1–2oz) Parmesan cheese shavings

Preheat the oven to 230°C/450°F/Gas 8. Roll out the puff pastry on a lightly floured surface to a thickness of about 2mm (½in) and cut into a 25cm (10in) disc. Use a large round cake tin or plate as a guide. Place on a lightly greased baking sheet and refrigerate.

Heat the ½ tablespoon of olive oil in a frying pan and, once hot but not smoking, add the red onion. Cook on a medium heat for a few minutes until softening and with a little colour. Add the sugar and stir to dissolve. Season with salt and pepper and remove from the pan. Leave to cool.

Plunge the courgettes into a large pot of rapidly boiling salted water for just 30 seconds. (This begins the cooking process, and enhances the green colour of the skins.) Drain immediately and leave to cool and dry on a clean cloth or kitchen paper.

Prick the base of the rolled chilled pastry with a fork, then spoon the cooked onions over, leaving a 5mm (¼in) border. The onions will spread very loosely, not actually covering the complete base (too many onions will create a steaming effect rather than allowing the courgettes to bake). Arrange the courgette slices overlapping around the pastry, from the outside into the centre, finishing with one central slice. Brush lightly with a little olive oil, season with salt and pepper and brush the pastry border with egg yolk to glaze, if using. Refrigerate until needed or bake the tart in the preheated oven for 20–25 minutes. Remove from the oven after 15–20 minutes and sprinkle with the thyme leaves. Return to the oven and continue baking for the remaining 5–10 minutes.

To serve, brush with just a touch more olive oil for a shiny finish, transfer to a large plate and sprinkle with a little coarse sea salt and a squeeze of lemon juice.

To make the salad, while the tart is baking, remove the eyes from the tomatoes, cut a cross at each base and then blanch in boiling water for just 10 seconds. Plunge into iced water. Once cold, the skin will peel away easily. Cut the tomatoes into rings about 5mm (¼in) thick, slicing horizontally across the tomatoes.

Arrange the slices on a large plate in the same fashion as the courgettes. Season with a twist of pepper and sea salt. Whisk together the olive oil and balsamic vinegar and season, then spoon over the tomatoes. Tear the basil leaves and sprinkle over the tomatoes along with the Parmesan shavings. The salad and tart are now ready to serve.

The dressing, basil leaves and Parmesan should not be sprinkled over the tomato plate until just before serving. For a richer golden brown, the courgette slices can be very quickly seared, on one side only, in a hot pan drizzled with olive oil. Leave to cool before placing them on the onions.

OPPOSITE: CRISP COURGETTE TART WITH A
TOMATO AND BASIL SALAD

crackling cod on stewed onions with bacon and a fresh pea sauce

For this recipe, the cod will need to be prepared at least 1 hour before cooking and serving. To create the crispy crackling, the skin is pre-salted, drawing out excess moisture, so that once fried, it will crisp in the pan.

While the fish is being salted, the onions can be stewed, cooking them to a very soft consistency. With peas probably at their sweetest this time of the year, the sauce shows them off at their best. The bacon completes this garnish, creating an almost *petits pois à la française* touch alongside the onions and peas.

SERVES 4 AS A MAIN COURSE

4 × 175–200g (6–7oz) portions of cod fillet, pin-boned (page 9), with skin on (scaled)
175g (6oz) coarse sea salt
4 tablespoons olive oil
550g (1¼lb) onions, sliced
sprig of thyme
salt and pepper
8 rashers of streaky bacon
knob of butter

FOR THE PEA SAUCE

125ml (4fl oz) *Fish stock* (page 417) or *Instant stock* (page 416)
100g (4oz) podded peas
bowl of ice
knob of butter

Score four or five short lines in the cod skin across the length of each fillet, leaving at least 1cm (½in) unscored around the edge. Sprinkle the sea salt on a tray, place the fillets skin-side down on it and leave to sit for at least 45 minutes–1 hour.

While the cod is salting, heat 2 tablespoons of the olive oil in a flameproof casserole or large saucepan. Add the onions and thyme, and cook for 2 minutes, then cover with a lid and stew, stirring from time to time, for 30 minutes over a low heat. Season with salt and pepper. The onions can be cooked in advance, ready just to reheat when needed.

The bacon can be cooked in either of the following ways. The rashers can be placed in an oven, preheated to 200°C/400°F/Gas 6, between two baking sheets for 30 minutes to guarantee a flat and crisp finish. Alternatively, slowly fry or grill, releasing all the fats, for a more rustic finish.

All stages of this dish can be cooked in advance, the sauce included. Boil the stock, add the peas and cook rapidly for 2 minutes, then liquidize to a smooth finish. Strain through a sieve and cool over a bowl of ice. This will maintain the rich green colour of the vegetables, ready to reheat.

To cook the fish, wipe all salt from the skin. Heat the remaining olive oil in a large frying pan. When very hot, lay the fillets skin-sides down in the pan, season the flesh sides with a twist of pepper and cook for 5–6 minutes until the skins are crispy. Add a knob of butter to the pan, turn the fillets and turn off the heat. The residual warmth of the pan will finish the cooking process, the fillets needing just another minute or two.

The pea sauce can now be reheated, adding a knob of butter and checking for seasoning. Spoon the onions onto plates, top them with the crisp bacon rashers and finish with the cod fillets. Pour the pea sauce around.

When making the pea sauce, 2–3 mint leaves can be added.

steamed halibut and soft fennel tarts with rhubarb and pernod dressing

Although this dish has quite an elaborate title, it is filled with reasonably simple but robust flavours. The tart is made of just four very thin, crisp puff pastry discs, topped with softened fennel and enhanced with the help of onion and snipped fennel tops. The unforced garden rhubarb, abundant in summer, carries an acidic sharp bite that does blend well with the aniseed touch of Pernod. All of this is topped with the almost pure white of lightly steamed halibut.

SERVES 4 AS A STARTER OR A LUNCH OR SUPPER DISH

175–225g (6–8oz) *Puff pastry* (page 426 or bought)
flour, for dusting
oil, for greasing
2 bulbs of Florence fennel
juice of 1 lemon
large knob of butter
1 onion, thinly sliced
½ teaspoon caster sugar
salt and pepper
4 × 100g (4oz) slices of halibut fillet, skinned

225g (8oz) rhubarb, washed
1 teaspoon caster sugar, plus an extra pinch
large knob of butter
¼ teaspoon coarse sea salt
1 tablespoon Pernod
2 tablespoons groundnut oil (optional)
2 tablespoons hazelnut oil (optional)

Roll out the puff pastry very thinly on a lightly floured surface, refrigerate and allow to rest for 10 minutes, then cut out four 9–10cm (3½–4in) discs. Place these on a lightly greased baking tray (or one topped with parchment paper), prick with a fork and leave to rest in the refrigerator for 30 minutes.

Preheat the oven to 200°C/400°F/Gas 6. Once the pastry has rested, bake in the preheated oven for 10–15 minutes until crisp. For a completely flat finish, it's best to cover the pastries with parchment paper and top them with another baking tray while baking. This will keep the discs completely flat.

To make the dressing, cut 50g (2oz) of the rhubarb into 3mm (⅛in) dice. Place in a sieve and sprinkle with the pinch of caster sugar. As I prefer to leave these pieces of rhubarb raw, the sugar will help to calm their tartness. Cut the remaining rhubarb into rough 1cm (½in) dice. Melt the knob of butter in a saucepan and add this rhubarb, the sea salt and the teaspoon of sugar. Cook for 5–6 minutes until beginning to soften. Add 4 tablespoons of water and the Pernod. Cook for a further 5 minutes, then liquidize to a purée. Strain through a sieve. To finish, whisk in the two oils (using 4 tablespoons of groundnut if hazelnut is unavailable). The oiled finish is an optional extra, creating more of a dressing than a sauce. It's not essential and can be left to personal choice. This dressing is best served warm, adding the uncooked diced rhubarb just before serving.

To prepare the fennel, remove any green tops, cutting enough of the fronds to make about 1 teaspoon when snipped, for adding to the fennel just before serving. Split the fennel bulbs through the centre and remove the base stalks. Thinly slice the cut fennel and place in a bowl, adding a little of the lemon juice to prevent the slices from discolouring.

Melt the large knob of butter in a saucepan and, once bubbling, add the sliced onion. Cook for 5–6 minutes until beginning to soften. Add the fennel, with the remaining lemon juice and caster sugar. Continue to cook for 10–12 minutes until the fennel has also softened. Season with salt and pepper.

Place the halibut slices on buttered and seasoned pieces of greaseproof paper. Lightly salt the fish and place in a steamer over a pan of simmering water. Cover with a lid and steam for just a few minutes, 4–5 maximum, until only just firm, and tender to the touch.

While the fish is cooking, place the warm pastry discs on plates. Add the snipped fennel fronds to the cooked shredded bulbs. Divide the soft fennel between the four tarts and spoon the rhubarb dressing or sauce around. Remove the halibut fillets from the steamer and greaseproof paper and present the slices over the fennel tarts.

grilled grey mullet with frothy butter courgettes

There's more than one variety of grey mullet, although here at home we class them all as the same fish. On foreign soils, the individual varieties are more widely recognized, with the common grey mullet (thick-lipped), the thin-lipped and the golden grey mullet (very popular in France). All have the advantage of thick scales that are very easy to scrape away without any danger of damaging the fish.

Baby courgettes have been chosen. If unavailable, approximately 450g (1lb) large courgettes can be cut into thick slices, finishing as below.

butter, for brushing
coarse sea salt and pepper
2 × 800g (1¾lb) grey mullet, cleaned, scaled and
  filleted
12–16 baby courgettes
2 tablespoons olive oil
50g (2oz) butter
1 heaped teaspoon chopped curly parsley
1 heaped teaspoon chopped chives
½ lemon

Preheat the grill. Grease a baking tray with butter, seasoning it with a few sea salt flakes and a twist of pepper. Score the grey mullet skin with four lines at an angle on each fillet. Place the fillets on the greased tray, skin-side-up, brushing each with butter and sprinkling with sea salt.

Halve each of the courgettes lengthwise. Heat the olive oil in a large non-stick frying pan (two may be needed). Once hot, place the courgette halves in the pan cut-sides down. Fry on a fairly high heat for 3–4 minutes until beginning to colour, with tinges of deep gold at the edges. Turn the courgettes in

the pan and continue to fry for a further few minutes, seasoning with salt and pepper.

Once the vegetables are turned, the mullet can be placed under the preheated grill. The fillets will only take between 3 and 4 minutes, 5 minutes maximum, depending on the thickness of the fish.

Add the butter to the courgettes. Once melted and bubbling, sprinkle with the chopped parsley and chives. Squeeze the lemon juice over the courgettes; this will lift the butter, creating a frothy consistency. Arrange the grilled grey mullet on plates, garnishing with the frothy butter courgettes.

A few thin shallot rings can be thrown in with the courgettes during their last 2–3 minutes of cooking.

steamed skate with runner beans, chanterelles and sweet red pepper dressing

The chanterelle wild mushrooms arrive in this month and go through to the frosty winter days. With an appealing egg-yolk-yellow colour, when very fresh they give off an aroma almost like that of fresh apricots.

The dressing made with the *Red pepper oil* will give you the maximum flavour, but a basic olive oil and balsamic dressing can replace it: simply add 1 teaspoon of the vinegar to 2 tablespoons of olive oil (or multiply these quantities to your required quantity).

SERVES 4 AS A STARTER
2 small red peppers
225g (8oz) runner beans
salt and pepper
4 × 100g (4oz) skate wing fillets, skinned
knob of butter, plus more for greasing
175–225g (6–8oz) chanterelles, cleaned (page 423),
    or chestnut mushrooms
3 teaspoons balsamic vinegar
6 tablespoons *Red pepper oil* (page 421)
1 tablespoon chopped chives

OPPOSITE: STEAMED SKATE WITH RUNNER BEANS, CHANTERELLES AND SWEET RED PEPPER DRESSING

FOR THE BEURRE BLANC SAUCE (OPTIONAL)
1 tablespoon white wine vinegar
2 tablespoons white wine
2 tablespoons single cream
50g (2oz) butter
squeeze of lemon juice

If you are using the beurre blanc sauce, boil the white wine vinegar and white wine together until reduced in volume by two-thirds. Add 3 tablespoons of water and the single cream. Bring to a simmer, then whisk in the butter, adding a squeeze of lemon juice and seasoning with salt and pepper. If making the sauce in advance, follow the method only to the cream stage, adding the remaining ingredients when needed.

The red peppers will eat at their best when skinned. To achieve this, place under a preheated grill, keeping the peppers as close to the heat as possible and cooking until almost burnt. This will ensure the peppers become tender and their skins will pull away readily. As the peppers colour, turn until completely coloured and tender. Remove from the heat and leave to one side until just warm enough to handle. The skins can now be easily removed, then split the peppers in half lengthwise. Remove the stalk and seeds, then cut into 1cm (½in) dice. Save any pepper juices to add them to the finished dressing.

Top and tail the runner beans, pulling away any side strings attached. Cut the beans at an angle into 7–8cm (3in) long thin strips. Pre-cook in boiling salted water. Once brought back to the boil, the beans will take just a minute to cook. If they are coarser runner beans rather than the flat variety, however, they may well take 2–3 minutes. Strain and leave to one side. For this particular dish it's best to serve them just warm.

Place the skate fillets on buttered and seasoned greaseproof paper. Season the fillets with a pinch of salt, then place in a steamer over rapidly simmering water. Cover with a lid and cook for 6–8 minutes until tender to the touch.

While the fish is cooking, melt the knob of butter in a large frying pan. Once bubbling, add the chanterelles. These will now just take a few minutes to fry. Season with salt and pepper.

Place the warm runner beans and chanterelles in a bowl with the sweet peppers. Mix the balsamic vinegar and red pepper oil and add 2–3 tablespoons to the beans. Stir together carefully, then spoon onto plates and drizzle the remaining dressing around. Place the skate on top. Sprinkle the chopped chives over or add to the warmed beurre blanc sauce and spoon over the fish to serve.

pan-fried monkfish medallions with fennel and thyme marmalade

The marmalade is not quite the consistency of the jellied orange variety with which we are all so familiar. This particular marmalade holds a soft sweet-and-sour flavour, with the aniseed of the fennel, and the thyme, both noticeable. The recipe can be doubled and, once made, it will keep in sterilized airtight jars (page 9) for up to one week. I've also included an optional accompanying salad of sorrel and baby spinach with a lime crème-fraîche dressing. It is not essential, but does lend a fresh crisp bite to the complete dish.

SERVES 4 AS A MAIN COURSE

12 × 50–65g (2–2½oz) medallions (mini round steaks) of monkfish fillet taken from 1kg (2¼lb) fish (for preparing the whole fish, see page 23)
flour, for dusting
salt and pepper
2 tablespoons olive or groundnut oil
knob of butter

FOR THE FENNEL AND THYME MARMALADE

4 shallots, thinly sliced
6 tablespoons cider vinegar or white wine vinegar
sprig of thyme
1 star anise
2–3 bulbs of Florence fennel
½ teaspoon finely grated lemon zest
large knob of butter
2 heaped tablespoons caster sugar
twist of cracked white pepper
good pinch of coarse sea salt
½ teaspoon picked thyme leaves

FOR THE SALAD (OPTIONAL)

juice of 1 lime
pinch of caster sugar
4 tablespoons crème fraîche or single cream
2 tablespoons walnut oil
175–225g (6–8oz) baby spinach leaves
50g (2oz) sorrel leaves

To make the marmalade, place the shallots, vinegar, thyme and star anise in a saucepan. Bring to a simmer on a low heat and cook for several minutes, until the liquid is almost completely reduced in volume and the shallots are just moist. Place to one side. Trim the tops and base from the fennel, split the bulbs in half and cut the stalk from each half. Finely shred the fennel pieces and mix with the lemon zest.

Melt the knob of butter over a moderate heat and add the sliced fennel along with the caster sugar and 2 tablespoons of water. Cook gently for 15–20 minutes until tender. Add the shallots and bring back to a simmer, stirring all of the ingredients together well, and seasoning with the cracked pepper and sea salt. The sprig of thyme and star anise can now be removed. The picked thyme leaves are best added just before you serve it, to introduce a fresh flavour to the marmalade. The marmalade can be kept (see above) or allowed to cool until just warm before adding the fresh thyme and serving. The marmalade can be served chilled, or rewarmed when needed. If made 24 hours in advance all of the ingredients get a chance to blend and mature, for a more distinctive flavour.

To make the dressing for the salad, if using, whisk together the lime juice and sugar, then add the crème fraîche or cream followed by the walnut oil. Season with salt and pepper. This can be kept refrigerated in a screw-top jar or squeezy bottle, ready to drizzle over the mixed spinach and sorrel leaves.

To finish the dish, lightly flour the monkfish medallions and season with salt and pepper. Heat the oil in a large frying pan and, when very hot, place the medallions in the pan. Cook for 2 minutes, then add a knob of butter, turning the fish pieces and continuing to cook for a further 2 minutes.

The monkfish is now ready to serve, offering three medallions per portion, along with the salad, if using, and the fennel marmalade.

pan-roasted sea trout with cucumber and cornichon salad

English cucumbers will be with us from late spring to mid-autumn, the sea trout more or less sharing the same season. *Cornichon* is French for gherkin – they are the small tart pickles made from tiny gherkin cucumbers. The acidity they hold creates an almost instant dressing with which to bind the salted cucumber. To accompany both the fish and cucumber, there's a warm English mustard and crème-fraîche cream to drizzle around the plate, adding a soft warmth to the complete flavour. The experience of warm crispy fish and the cold cucumber salad with a bite leaves a very fresh and lively finish on the palate.

SERVES 4 AS A MAIN COURSE

1 small cucumber
salt and pepper
4 × 175–225g (6–8oz) portions of sea trout fillet,
   pin-boned (page 9), with skin on
flour, for dusting
4 tablespoons olive oil
4 tablespoons crème fraîche
½ teaspoon ready-made English mustard
squeeze of lime juice
2–3 cornichons (gherkins) cut into small dice,
   plus 1 tablespoon cornichon vinegar
1 teaspoon caster sugar
1 large shallot, sliced into thin rings
1 teaspoon chopped tarragon

Peel the cucumber and slice into approximately 3mm (⅛in) slices. Add 1 teaspoon of salt and mix in well. Place in a colander over a bowl and leave for 20–30 minutes. During this salting period, a quantity of liquid will be drawn from the flesh. This will remove the rawness from the cucumber, leaving a more pliable texture but still preserving its bite.

After this time the cucumber can be rinsed of any excess salt; however I'm not so keen on this practice as water can then be reabsorbed by the cucumber. Taste the slices and, if not over-salty, just pat dry with a cloth. The salad may then not need any more salt.

Lightly dust the skin side of the sea trout fillets with the flour. Warm 2 tablespoons of the olive oil in a large frying pan to medium hot. Place the fillets in, skin-sides down, leaving them undisturbed to fry, and not shaking the pan, for 4–5 minutes. (If portions are taken from a particularly thick fillet, 6 minutes may be needed.) Season the flesh side of the fish with salt and pepper and turn over in the pan, then turn the heat off. The residual warmth of the pan will be enough to continue the frying without drying the flesh. This will leave you with a few minutes to complete the garnishes, it being almost impossible to overcook the fish.

Warm together the crème fraîche, mustard and lime juice, whisking to a smooth emulsion. Season with salt and pepper, adding a touch more mustard if preferred.

In a bowl, whisk together the remaining olive oil with the cornichon vinegar and caster sugar. Season with salt and pepper, then mix in the cucumber slices, shallot rings, chopped cornichons and tarragon. Divide between the top ends of four plates, then place the sea trout in front and drizzle the warm crème-fraîche mustard cream around each.

Hot buttered new potatoes are the perfect accompaniment to this dish.
The cucumber and cornichon salad also eats well with pan-fried or barbecue-grilled chicken breasts.

barbecued rump steak with a bourguignonne salad

Rump steak is one of the most flavoursome cuts of beef. On the animal it sits next to the sirloin and, with its daily workout, picks up additional beefy flavour. The disadvantage is the firmer texture it also takes on, needing careful thought when purchasing. A good 'eat like butter' rump will have been given a long maturing (hanging) period of up to 3 weeks. The meat colour will be quite a deep red, with a full flavour and tender finish. Steaks, of any kind, are best at least 2.5cm (1in) thick, so you can really enjoy their full texture.

Bourguignonne in the title refers to the style of garnish, born in the Burgundy region of France – red wine and mushrooms with bacon and onions. The red wine is in the dressing with a choice of two styles. The more usual button onions are replaced with spring onions.

The mixed leaves can afford to have a bitter, peppery bite, as the garnishes will cope very well. The *Boiled chips* on page 55 are a great accompaniment.

SERVES 4

225g (8oz) mushrooms, button, chestnut or chanterelles
6 thick rashers of streaky bacon
1 bunch of spring onions
4 × 225–275g (8–10oz) thick rump steaks
salt and pepper (sea salt flakes can be used)
cooking oil
knob of butter
225g (8oz) mixed salad leaves, prepared and rinsed
***Red-wine dressing* (page 420, optional)**

FOR THE VINAIGRETTE DRESSING (OPTIONAL)

1 tablespoon red wine vinegar, preferably Cabernet Sauvignon
1 tablespoon sherry vinegar
5 tablespoons extra virgin olive oil
sea salt and black pepper

Preheat a barbecue or ridged grill plate. Wipe clean the button or chestnut mushrooms, before halving or quartering, depending on size. If using chanterelles, follow the preparation method on page 423.

OPPOSITE: BARBECUED RUMP STEAK WITH A BOURGUIGNONNE SALAD

Cut the bacon rashers into 1cm (½in) thick strips. These can now be fried in a dry hot pan, allowing their fat to melt, until crispy. Strain and keep to one side, saving the bacon fat for frying the mushrooms.

Remove the coarse outside layer of the spring onions, trimming the stalk, and cutting a 5cm (2in) piece from the base. The remaining tops can be sliced thinly.

To make the vinaigrette dressing, if using, simply shake all the ingredients together in a screw-top jar.

Season the steaks with salt and pepper. Brush the barbecue grill or ridged grill plate with oil, and place on the steaks. To which stage you grill the steak is up to you. For rare steaks give them just a few minutes on each side, adding 2–3 minutes as you need to go on.

While barbecuing, heat the frying pan with the saved bacon fat. Once hot, add the mushrooms, quickly frying for about 2 minutes, before adding the base-cut spring onion pieces with the knob of butter. Season with salt and pepper, continuing to fry for a further 2 minutes. Add the bacon to reheat quickly, before spooning into a bowl with the mixed leaves and the sliced spring onion tops. Drizzle the chosen dressing over.

Serve the rump steaks on plates. The salad can remain in the bowl or be presented on the plates with the steaks.

roast saddle of lamb with creamed runner beans and bacon

Although we tend to associate lamb with spring, it's equally good in summer, too. The saddle of lamb, along with the best-end racks, is among the prime cuts. The two fillets sitting along the backbone cook beautifully and are so tender they almost melt in the mouth. Short-cut saddles can be bought from the butcher, trimmed and oven-ready. 'Short-cut' means that it is minus the chump end.

The summer's runner beans are cooked and bound in cream with sautéed onion and bacon pieces.

SERVES 4 AS A GENEROUS MAIN COURSE

1 short-cut saddle of lamb, weighing approximately 2kg (4½lb)
salt and pepper
2 tablespoons cooking oil

157

duckling with gooseberry and marjoram onions and beetroot salad

This recipe produces two courses. The first consists of the roast duck breasts with gooseberries, accompanied by duck-fried new potatoes. The second course is a beetroot salad, topped with the twice-roasted duck legs.

This way of serving duck is quite classic in France, the breasts cooked beautifully pink with the legs returned to the oven for a well-done finish. Here the duck breasts are more well done, with the moist fresh gooseberry and marjoram onions to accompany them. You'll notice that two ducks are needed for four portions, but these are the smaller ducklings rather than the usual 'six-pounders'.

SERVES 4

2 oven-ready ducklings, each approximately
   1.5kg (3¼lb)
salt and pepper, plus coarse sea salt
450g–675g (1–1½lb) new potatoes
1 tablespoon roughly chopped parsley

FOR THE GOOSEBERRY AND MARJORAM ONIONS

knob of butter
225g (8oz) onions, finely chopped
225g (8oz) gooseberries, topped and tailed
finely grated zest and juice of 1 lime
1 tablespoon caster sugar
1 heaped teaspoon marjoram

FOR THE SALAD

2–3 medium beetroots (or 6 baby beetroots),
   cooked and peeled (page 149)
4 tablespoons olive oil
2 tablespoons red wine vinegar
1 teaspoon clear honey
1 tablespoon finely chopped shallot
100–175g (4–6oz) mixed salad leaves
2 tablespoons soured cream (optional)

OPPOSITE: DUCKLING WITH GOOSEBERRY AND
MARJORAM ONIONS AND BEETROOT SALAD

For the first course, preheat the oven to 220°C/425°F/Gas 7. To help release the excess fat from the ducks, score each breast five or six times with a sharp knife. Season with coarse sea salt and pepper. If possible, place a roasting rack in a large roasting tray and sit the ducks on top. Place in the preheated oven and roast for 30 minutes. Reduce the oven temperature to 180°C/350°F/Gas 4 and continue to roast for 2 hours. During the cooking time, a lot of duck fat will collect in the pan.

Every 45 minutes, remove the ducks from the oven, lift off the rack and pour the excess fat into a bowl. This will be used to fry the potatoes.

To cook the gooseberries, melt the knob of butter and add the chopped onions. Cook for 7–8 minutes until beginning to soften. Add the gooseberries along with the lime zest, juice and sugar. Cook for 10–15 minutes, until the fruits begin to soften. The fruits can now be stirred and broken. Remove from the heat, add the marjoram and season with salt and pepper. The gooseberries are best served warm and can be reheated when needed.

Once the ducks are cooked, remove them from the oven and leave to rest for 15–20 minutes. The last of the fat from the duck roasting tray can be strained.

To cook the new potatoes, place them in a pan of boiling salted water and simmer for 20 minutes until tender, then drain. (These can be cooked in advance, while the duck is roasting, allowing them to cool naturally out of the cooking water.) Peel the potatoes, cutting any of the larger ones in half. Shallow-fry in 2–3 tablespoons of the saved duck fat until light golden brown. Season with salt and pepper and finish with the chopped parsley.

Remove the duck breasts from the carcasses and return the legs, still attached, to the oven. (During the first course, the legs will reheat and continue to roast, ready for the salad.) The breasts can now be presented with the warm gooseberries and duck-fried new potatoes.

For the second-course salad, the beetroots can be cut into wedges, diced or coarsely grated.

To make the dressing, whisk together the olive oil, red wine vinegar and honey. Raw shallot, when added to dressings, is best first rinsed under cold water to release its acidity. Now add it to the dressing and season with salt and pepper. Spoon some of the dressing over the beetroots and mixed salad leaves.

Present the leaves and beetroots on plates and, if using, drizzle with a drop or two of soured cream before finishing with the remaining honey dressing. Remove the duck legs from the carcasses and place one on top of each salad.

summer fruit family slice

This summer dessert is simply a combination of baked pastry slices, with lots of our traditional summer berries, sandwiched together with a soft vanilla spread. The quantities of fruit and pastry cream spread are quite generous, more than will be needed to fill this sweet crispy sandwich, with any extra being offered separately.

The basic *Pastry cream* recipe will make a larger quantity than required here. The remainder can be kept refrigerated for a few days, finding its way into many more puddings.

The puff pastry used here can be either the *Puff pastry* or *Quick puff pastry* featured on page 426. Bought, frozen puff pastry can also be used.

SERVES 6 GENEROUSLY
butter, for greasing
175–225g (6–8oz) *Puff pastry* (page 426), or *Quick puff pastry* (page 426, or bought)
flour, for dusting
1 egg, beaten
1 heaped teaspoon icing sugar, plus more for dusting
450g (1lb) mixed soft summer fruits (such as strawberries, raspberries, blackberries, blackcurrants, blueberries, redcurrants)
2 heaped tablespoons caster sugar
200ml (7fl oz) *Pastry cream* (page 427)
100–150ml (3½fl oz–¼ pint) double cream
seeds from 1 vanilla pod (optional)

Lightly butter a large baking tray or line it with parchment paper. Roll out the pastry on a lightly floured surface into a 30 × 24cm (12 × 9½in) rectangle. Carefully roll the pastry around the rolling pin and then unroll it onto the prepared baking tray. Refrigerate, to allow to rest, for 20–30 minutes.

Preheat the oven to 220°C/425°F/Gas 7. Prick the rested pastry with a fork and brush with the beaten egg. Place towards the top of the preheated oven and bake for 20–25 minutes, until lightly risen and golden brown. If still too pale, brush again with egg and bake for an extra minute or two.

Remove the pastry from the oven and carefully cut it lengthwise into two rectangles. For a rich glazed finish, dust each liberally with icing sugar and, very quickly and carefully, lightly caramelize and glaze under a preheated grill. Once coloured, turn the rectangles over and repeat the process. The crispy pastry strips can now be transferred to a cooling rack.

Place 75g (3oz) of the fruits in a small saucepan with the caster sugar and 3 tablespoons of water. Bring to a simmer and cook for a few minutes, then gently mash with a fork to help release the juices. Strain through a sieve, squeezing all flavours from the fruits. (Discard the fruit pulp.) If the juices are too thin, return to a rapid simmer and cook to a syrupy consistency. Keep to one side.

Beat the pastry cream to a smooth consistency, then whip the double cream with the vanilla seeds, if using, and the heaped teaspoon of icing sugar to a soft-peak consistency. Fold the cream into the softened pastry cream, to taste.

To assemble the slice, place a pastry rectangle on a suitable serving plate or board. Spoon half of the pastry cream or pipe it (using a 1cm/½in plain tube and piping bag) onto the slice. Spoon the remaining fruits on top, without being over-generous and overspreading the cream. Now drizzle a tablespoon or two of syrup over the fruits and top with a little more cream. Place the remaining slice of glazed pastry on top. The summer fruit family slice is now ready to serve. As mentioned above, any fruits and pastry cream left over can be offered separately.

An extra dusting of icing sugar can be sprinkled over the top before serving.

sabayon-glazed gooseberries

Sweet white wine has been chosen here to flavour the sabayon. However, calvados also blends very well, offering its appley bite to the small green gooseberries.

SERVES 6
knob of butter
900g (2lb) gooseberries, topped and tailed
3 heaped tablespoons caster or demerara sugar

FOR THE SABAYON
3 large egg yolks
100ml (3½fl oz) sweet white wine or calvados
75g (3oz) caster sugar
150ml (¼ pint) double cream, lightly whipped

To prepare the gooseberries, melt the knob of butter in a large saucepan and add the gooseberries and the sugar. Add 2 tablespoons of water and cook for a few minutes until the gooseberries have become tender, but are not totally breaking

cream in a saucepan, warming slowly on top of the stove. The slow warming helps release the rich vanilla flavour from the seeds.

Place the whole egg, egg yolks, caster sugar and cornflour in a bowl, whisking to a foamy, almost thick sabayon consistency. Bring the cream to the boil, pouring and stirring it (this will thicken very quickly) into the egg mix. Return the custard to the pan and cook gently for a few minutes until completely thickened, not allowing it to boil. Pour the custard into four size-1 ramekin dishes and leave to cool, before refrigerating for several hours until completely chilled.

Preheat the oven to 180°C/350°F/Gas 4. To prepare the nectarines, slice through the seam line of the fruit towards the stone all around the fruit. Twist the two halves in opposite directions to separate. The stone will be left in one of the halves – this can be levered out with the point of a knife. Rub each of the halves with lemon juice to prevent discoloration. Butter a baking dish and place the nectarines in cut-side down. Put the fruits in the preheated oven, baking for 10 minutes. At this point the honey can be spooned over each one. Continue to bake the fruits until tender; this will take a further 8–10 minutes. Preheat the grill, sprinkling each of the fruit tops with caster or demerara sugar. The nectarine dome tops can now be caramelized, allowing a slightly burnt finish.

Place the warm fruits on top of the custards, spooning a little of the warm honey over each before serving.

A dollop of crème fraîche is a nice accompaniment. Fresh peaches can be used in the same way as nectarines.

roast figs on toast with triple-cream cheese

All of the cheeses suggested for this dish, which serves as a starter or a pudding, are rich French cheeses, each with a fat content of at least 75 per cent. Mostly found all year round, many are available from delicatessens and supermarkets. Brillat-Savarin has a buttery texture with a milky, slightly sour flavour. Explorateur, although soft, has quite a firm texture with a mild but very creamy taste. Boursin can be found plain or with a variety of savoury flavourings. Soft Brie can also be used in this recipe.

OPPOSITE: ROAST FIGS ON TOAST WITH TRIPLE-CREAM CHEESE

SERVES 4

- 8–10 fresh figs
- 40g (1½oz) butter
- 1 vanilla pod, split in two
- ½ teaspoon freshly grated nutmeg
- 2 tablespoons caster sugar
- 4 small sprigs of rosemary (optional)
- 2–3 tablespoons olive oil
- 4 thick oval slices of French stick (approximately 10cm/4in long)
- 175–225g (6–8oz) triple-cream cheese (either Brillat-Savarin, Explorateur or Boursin), cut into 8 slices and at room temperature

Preheat the oven to 200°C/400°F/Gas 6. Trim the stalks from the figs and split each fig in two. Grease an ovenproof dish with half the butter. Place the figs in the dish, cut-sides up. Scrape the vanilla seeds from the split vanilla pod and mix them with the remaining butter. Dot the spiced butter over the figs and sprinkle with the grated nutmeg, followed by the sugar. Split each of the empty vanilla pod halves into two strips, lengthwise, and keep to one side.

If including the rosemary, place the sprigs in a small pan with the olive oil and bring to a simmer. Remove from the heat and leave to infuse.

Bake the figs in the preheated oven for 15–20 minutes, until softened and syrupy. Remove from the oven.

Brush the French bread slices with some of the rosemary-infused or natural olive oil on both sides. These can now be baked in the oven along with the figs until golden brown, or can be simply toasted.

To serve, the warm figs can be presented on the toasts, offering 4–5 halves per portion. Drizzle each portion with any remaining fig syrup juices. Place the cheese slices on top of the figs. These can be served as they are, the warmth of the fruits softening the cheese even more. Alternatively, very lightly melt the cheese over the figs under a preheated grill.

To finish, decorate each serving with a strip of vanilla pod and an infused rosemary sprig, if using, and a trickle of olive oil.

You can also grill this dish, placing the sliced figs on top of oil-brushed toasts, topping with the sugar and nutmeg and adding the cheese when the sugar is bubbling and the figs have taken on a little colour. Melt the cheese, as above, and drizzle with olive oil.

back and snapped off, discarding as you do so. Continue until left with just the central cone of yellow leaves, still with a green top. Cut away the green top, also trimming any green from the base with a small knife or peeler. Halve the artichoke lengthwise, revealing the hairy choke set in each side. This can be removed with a teaspoon. Rub the halves all over with the cut lemon. Follow the same process with the remaining 2 artichokes.

Once all are cleaned and prepared, the halves can be cut into wafer-thin slices lenthwise, or into almost equally thin wedges. In a large bowl, mix the remaining 4 tablespoons of olive oil with the juice from the remaining lemon half. Add the artichoke slices and season with salt and pepper, mixing them well. These can be prepared to this stage a few hours in advance, while the tomatoes are 'drying'.

To cook the artichokes, preheat the grill and lay them on a non-stick baking tray, making sure they don't overlap. Pour over the lemon oil. These can now be placed under the preheated grill, toasting for a few minutes until beginning to sizzle and colour. If a few begin to burn slightly, this adds another flavour to the dish, with a more rustic finish.

To serve, arrange the warm tomatoes, 3 per portion, onto plates or in bowls, scattering the grilled artichokes over, with the basil leaves. Drizzle with the tomato dressing and the dish is complete.

ratatouille feuilleté with fresh tomato confit and basil sauce

Feuilleté literally means 'leaved', the title representing the layers in cooked puff pastry. Here, squares of the pastry, baked like vol-au-vents, are to be filled with a ratatouille selection of summer vegetables, including baby sweet peppers, courgettes, aubergines and red onions. Should the baby variants not be available, the larger standard version of each can be used, cutting them into wedges, slices or dice. Whichever is used, the vegetables can be grilled, cooked on a ridged grill plate or pan-fried until tender, before spooning into the pastry shell. To finish, they are topped with a warm poached egg and coated with a basil and crème fraîche butter sauce.

SERVES 4 AS A MAIN COURSE
450g (1lb) *Puff pastry* (page 426, or bought)
flour, for dusting
1 egg, beaten

450g (1lb) tomatoes
iced water
1 tablespoon olive oil, plus more for the vegetables
salt and pepper
¼ teaspoon caster sugar (optional)
1 baby aubergine
6 baby courgettes
3–4 baby red peppers
3–4 baby yellow peppers
2 small red onions
4 *Poached eggs* (page 423)

FOR THE BASIL SAUCE
2 tablespoons white wine vinegar
4 tablespoons white wine
4 tablespoons crème fraîche
50g (2oz) butter
8 basil leaves, snipped or shredded

Preheat the oven to 220°C/425°F/Gas 7. Roll out the puff pastry on a lightly floured surface, to a thick square approximately 18–20cm (6–8in). Quarter this into four 9–10cm (3½–4in) squares. Place these on a baking tray lined with greaseproof paper. Refrigerate for 15 minutes to allow to rest.

Now gently cut a border into each pastry square about 5mm (¼in) in from each side. This will make lids that will be removed once the pastry is cooked. Brush carefully with the beaten egg, preferably not allowing it to drip down the sides as this can prevent the pastry from rising when baking. Bake in the preheated oven for 30–40 minutes until risen, golden brown and crispy. If not quite crisp or coloured, brush once more with the beaten egg and continue to bake for a further 5–6 minutes. Remove from the oven and leave to cool.

The central lids can now be cut out, also cutting and trimming away any excess undercooked central layers. This will leave you with crisp empty pastry cases ready to be filled with the ratatouille.

To make the tomato confit, remove the eyes from the tomatoes with a sharp knife, cut a small cross at the base and then blanch in boiling water for 10 seconds. Plunge into iced water and, once cold, peel the tomatoes. Halve them and scoop the seeds and juices into a sieve over a bowl. Gently press any excess liquid from the seeds and discard the seeds. The tomato liquid will be used in the cooking of the tomatoes as they reduce in volume, making an even more intense flavour. Cut the tomato halves into rough 1 cm (½in) dice. Warm the

OPPOSITE: RATATOUILLE FEUILLETÉ WITH
FRESH TOMATO CONFIT AND BASIL SAUCE

1 small red pepper, cut into 8–10mm (⅓in) dice
1 small yellow pepper, cut into 8–10mm (⅓in) dice
1 courgette, cut into 8–10mm (⅓in) dice
1 teaspoon wild marjoram (oregano) leaves
4 basil leaves, torn

FOR THE SAUCE
knob of butter
225g (8oz) tomatoes, quartered
1 teaspoon caster sugar
2 tablespoons double cream
salt and pepper
1 tablespoon port

Score the skin of the salmon fillets with a sharp knife (four or five cuts will be plenty), leaving a 1cm (½in) border around the edge of each. Refrigerate until needed.

To make the sauce, melt the knob of butter in a saucepan, add the tomatoes and sugar and cook for 10–15 minutes until most of the tomato liquid has evaporated. Liquidize to a purée and then push through a fine sieve. Return to the pan and add the cream. Cook for a minute or two and then season with salt and pepper.

For the gazpacho salad, lightly salt the diced cucumber, then leave it for 15–20 minutes in a sieve to drain off the excess liquid. Heat the olive oil with a knob of butter in a saucepan. Once bubbling, add the diced fennel and garlic halves, cover with a lid and cook for 6–7 minutes on a low-to-medium heat, until just tender. Add the red and yellow peppers along with the courgette and cook for a further 2 minutes. The rawness will now just come off the vegetables, leaving a slight bite. Place to one side.

To cook the salmon, season the skin with salt and lightly dust with flour. Heat the olive oil (a little extra may be needed). Place the fillets skin-side down in the pan and season with salt and pepper. Cook on a moderate heat for 6–7 minutes without shaking the pan or moving the fish (this will only take heat from the pan). Add a knob of butter and, once bubbling, turn the salmon and switch off the heat. The residual heat of the pan will finish the cooking process, the fish needing just a minute or two more.

While the fish finishes, add the drained cucumber and herbs to the gazpacho salad vegetables. When ready to serve, add the port to the sauce and stir well. The dish can now be presented on plates, either placing the salmon on top of the gazpacho and spooning the sauce around, or setting these two main ingredients side by side and drizzling with the sauce.

crispy red mullet and shrimps with tomatoes and herbs

The flavour of red mullet, with lots of our summer tomatoes and fresh mixed herbs is a very seasonal combination, helped along by the addition of warm shrimps.

This recipe offers supper or main course portions if the fillets are from large 675g (1½lb) mullets. Smaller starter portions from 400g (14oz) fish can also be used, slightly reducing the quantity of the other ingredients.

It is not essential to chop the herbs; all bar the chives can be torn. This prevents any bruising, discoloration and change of flavour. However, a good sharp knife can be used to cut carefully and neatly.

SERVES 4
4 red mullet fillets (see above)
1 kg (2¼lb) ripe tomatoes
iced water
Creamy caesar salad (page 179, optional)
salt and pepper, plus coarse sea salt
6–8 tablespoons olive oil
flour, for dusting
butter, for greasing
175g (6oz) peeled cooked shrimps or prawns (250g/9oz
    if only available in shell)
1 large garlic clove, finely chopped (optional)
4 tablespoons chopped mixed herbs (such as tarragon,
    basil, chervil, chives, flatleaf parsley)
juice of 1 lemon

There are several stages to this recipe that can be made well in advance. The mullet fillets should have all pin bones removed with tweezers (page 9) and their scales scraped and rinsed away.

Using the point of a small, sharp knife, cut around the tomato eyes to free them and cut a small cross at the base of each. Plunge the tomatoes into rapidly boiling water, leaving firm ones in the water for 8–10 seconds, very ripe ones for 6–8. Transfer to iced water, then peel and quarter and discard the seeds. Place the flesh on kitchen paper to absorb all excess juice and refrigerate until needed. When ready to use, cut each quarter into neatish 1cm (½in) dice, not wasting any trimmings.

If serving the Caesar salad with this dish, the dressing can be made well in advance and the Cos lettuce leaves rinsed, ready to tear or cut.

Preheat the oven to 190°C/375°F/Gas 5. Season the mullet fillets, flesh-sides up, with salt and pepper, only salting the presentation skin sides to keep them clean of pepper dots. Using one large (or two smaller) frying pans, heat 2–3 tablespoons of the olive oil. Once hot but certainly not smoking, lightly flour the skin sides of the fillets and place floured-sides down in the pan. Cook on a medium heat for 5–6 minutes. During this time the skin will have crisped, but the fillets will be a few minutes short of being cooked. At this stage, remove each from the pan and place skin-side up on a buttered baking tray. Finish the cooking in the preheated oven for a further 2–3 minutes. This will keep the fish very moist and only just cooked through.

While the fish is in the oven, add the shrimps or prawns and tomatoes to the oil in the pan along with the garlic, if using. Bring to a soft simmer. Add a further 3 tablespoons of olive oil, all the chopped herbs and lemon juice to taste, and season with coarse sea salt and pepper. If a looser finish is preferred, add the remaining oil. The tomatoes and shrimps can now be spooned onto a serving dish or plates before placing the red mullet fillets on top, and offering with the Caesar salad, if using.

CRISPY RED MULLET AND SHRIMPS WITH
TOMATOES AND HERBS

sage and lemon veal escalopes with roasted nectarines

Veal escalopes are a cut of meat taken from the cushion (topside) of the leg, with silverside and thick flank also found in this section of the calf. Once cut, the escalopes are then pounded flat, tenderizing them. Germany and Austria helped make veal escalopes world-renowned, showing off their classic breadcrumbed *Wienerschnitzels*. These escalopes borrow this idea, adding freshly chopped sage and finely grated lemon zest to the crumbs, frying in butter to a golden brown.

Nectarines may sound an odd combination with veal, but August sees them in full glory, absolutely oozing juice and packed with flavour. When baked in the oven to an over-cooked stage, with the soft flesh beginning to collapse, they become an almost instant fruity relish, similar to offering apple sauce with pork.

The escalopes need quite a lot of frying-pan space, so if you have two large pans, all the better. Failing that, keep the first two warm in the oven while frying the remainder.

Chicken breasts can also be pressed into escalopes, replacing the veal in this recipe.

SERVES 4

2 large or 4 small nectarines
finely grated zest and juice of 1 large lemon
50g (2oz) butter, plus more for brushing
sprinkling of caster sugar
10 sage leaves, chopped
175g (6oz) fresh white breadcrumbs
4 × 175g (6oz) veal escalopes
salt and pepper
2 heaped tablespoons plain flour
1 large egg, beaten
4 tablespoons olive oil

Preheat the oven to 180°C/350°F/Gas 4. To remove the stones from the nectarines, cut with a small knife around the natural line towards the centre of the fruit. Twist the two halves in opposite directions, releasing one from the other. The stone can be easily pulled away or levered with the point of the knife to loosen.

Brush the cut faces with lemon juice and butter, sprinkling with a little caster sugar. Arrange on a greased baking tray, cut-sides up, and place in the preheated oven. These will now slowly roast, softening after 20–25 minutes.

If still slightly too firm, and not beginning to break down, continue to bake for a further 5–10 minutes.

While baking the nectarines, mix the chopped sage and lemon zest into the breadcrumbs. Season the escalopes with salt and pepper, lightly dusting both sides in the flour before dipping in the beaten egg and, finally, pressing into the crumbs, coating both sides.

With the nectarines almost ready, heat 2 tablespoons of oil in each of two large frying pans. Once hot, place the escalopes in the pans, frying for just 2–3 minutes on each side until golden brown. Split the measured butter between the two and, once sizzling, add half the juice from the lemon to each pan.

The escalopes are now ready to serve, spooning the sizzling butter over and garnishing with the soft roasted nectarines.

Freshly chopped curly parsley or extra chopped sage can be sprinkled into the sizzling lemon butter, adding a tablespoon of capers for a tangy finish.
To flatten your own escalopes, lay the cut meat between sheets of cling film and lightly pound with a cleaver or rolling pin, not spreading them too thinly, but just enough to tenderize.

OPPOSITE: SAGE AND LEMON VEAL ESCALOPES WITH ROASTED NECTARINES

coarse pork pâté with sweet-and-sour cherries and beetroot

This recipe requires some forward planning. It's best to order the meats from your butcher ready minced, and if you prefer a smoother finish to your pâté ask for fine-cut mince. Although the ingredients list does look quite long, most of the other items are dry and only need measuring, with no preparation involved. This is a perfect dish for a summer picnic or family gathering, offering at least twelve generous portions. For a completely full flavour, it is best if allowed to mature, once cooked, for a minimum of two days, preferably three, in advance.

The sweet-and-sour cherries are a separate recipe, with cooked beetroots added when ready to serve.

SERVES 12 AS A STARTER

900g (2lb) pork belly, coarsely minced
100g (4oz) pork kidney, coarsely minced
175g (6oz) pork fat, coarsely minced
12 juniper berries
12 black peppercorns
1 teaspoon salt
¼ teaspoon ground cinnamon
¼ teaspoon allspice
¼ teaspoon ground mace
1¼ teaspoons ground ginger
1 teaspoon chopped sage
1 teaspoon chopped thyme
finely grated zest of 1 orange
2 garlic cloves, crushed
50g (2oz) chopped pistachio nuts (optional)
5 tablespoons brandy
5 tablespoons whisky
lard, for greasing, and sealing (optional)

FOR THE CHERRIES AND BEETROOTS

75g (3oz) dark soft brown sugar
2 tablespoons honey
175ml (6fl oz) red wine vinegar
150ml (¼ pint) port or water
8 juniper berries (optional)
8 black peppercorns (optional)
½ stick of cinnamon (optional)
450g (1lb) cherries, pitted
350g (12oz) fresh uncooked beetroots

If ready-minced meat isn't available, either mince the meats and fat through a medium blade or pass in stages through a food processor until roughly chopped. Place all the meats and pork fat in a large bowl. Crush the juniper berries and peppercorns reasonably finely, then add to the meats along with the salt. Mix all together well, then add all of the spices, chopped herbs, orange zest, garlic and the pistachios, if using. Mix well again throughout the meats, then add the brandy and whisky. Turn a few times more, then cover and leave to stand for 2–3 hours. This will help the flavours to develop.

Preheat the oven to 160ºC/325ºF/Gas 3. Grease a 450g (1lb) loaf tin or terrine, or a 25 × 8 × 8cm (10 × 3 × 3in) earthenware terrine with lard, then spoon and press in the pâté mix. Cover with a lid and place in a roasting tray. Fill with enough hot water to reach at least halfway to three-quarters of the way up the sides of the container. Bake in the preheated oven for 1½–1¾ hours. Check after 1½ hours, piercing with a skewer; it should come out hot, not just warm. If done, remove from the oven or return for the extra 15 minutes if needed. Remove the terrine from the roasting tray and leave to cool – don't pour away any of the juices. At this point, lay a foil- or cling-film-wrapped piece of wood or cardboard on the pâté and sit a suitable weight on top. This will press the mixture together, preventing too crumbly a finish.

After 1 hour of pressing, pour any escaped juices over the pâté and replace the weight. If possible, it is best to leave the pressed pâté to refrigerate for several hours or overnight. Once completely set, remove the weight and replace the lid or cover the terrine with cling film until ready to use. To ensure a longer shelf life, lard can be melted and poured across the pâté. Once set, this prevents any air from entering. Chilled, the fat will pull away easily.

The cherries can be cooked a few days in advance or simply cooked on the day. To prepare them, place the soft brown sugar, honey, red wine vinegar and port or water (the port is not essential but will leave a richer flavour) into a saucepan. If using the juniper berries and peppercorns, lightly crush both and tie in a muslin cloth. Add to the pan along with the cinnamon, if using. Bring to a simmer and allow to cook gently for 15 minutes. Bring to the boil and add the cherries. After 2 minutes remove from the heat. Strain the cherries from the liquor along with the cinnamon and muslin bag (which can now be discarded). The juices can now be returned to the boil and reduced to a syrup consistency, then poured over the cherries. Leave to cool. The cherries can be served cold, but are best at room temperature, or just warmed with the beetroots before serving.

Boil the beetroots until tender. This can take up to an hour, depending on their size. To check, lift a beet from the pan: the skin should pull away easily with the thumb when the beetroots are ready; if not, return to the pan until tender. It's best not to test with a knife as this will only encourage the vegetable to bleed its rich juices. Once cooked, remove the beetroots from the pan and leave to cool before peeling. They can now be cut into 1cm (½in) dice and added to the cherries.

To turn out the terrine, submerge the tin or container in hot water. This will slightly melt the setting jellies and the pâté should now fall easily onto a chopping board or serving dish. Cut into portions, offering the sweet-and-sour cherries and beetroot apart.

The pâté will also eat very well just with pickled gherkins, onions and crusty bread.

sautéed chicken livers with garlic chanterelles and spinach

These wild mushrooms are just very quickly fried in butter with garlic, then served on toast with the pan-fried chicken livers.

An optional extra to this dish is a spoonful or two of *Sweet port red wine dressing* (page 420). This adds a robust red wine punch, sweetened by the addition of port: two flavours that will certainly eat well with both the livers and the chanterelles.

SERVES 4 AS A STARTER OR SUPPER DISH

8 chicken livers

milk, to cover

2 garlic cloves, thinly sliced

4 thick slices of granary, brown or white bread

2 knobs of butter, plus more for spreading

1 tablespoon groundnut or cooking oil

salt and pepper

225g (8oz) chanterelles, cleaned as described on page 423

100g (4oz) spinach leaves, torn

1 quantity *Basic butter sauce* (page 418, optional)

4–6 tablespoons *Sweet port red wine dressing* (page 420, optional)

This dish is best planned 1–2 days in advance, to provide time in which to soak the livers in milk. I would always suggest a minimum of 24 hours, but 48 hours will help remove more blood from the livers, taking away any bitter flavour and leaving a sweeter and more *foie-gras*-like texture and taste. Once soaked, drain and rinse the livers under cold water and dry well before cooking.

The sliced garlic cloves can be used in their completely raw state, but to make their flavour a little more mellow, place the slices in cold water and bring to a simmer, then refresh under cold water and repeat the process twice more. Drain and dry on kitchen paper. The garlic flavour will now not overpower the dish or make you unsociable.

Spread the slices of your chosen bread with butter on both sides, then fry them over a moderate heat until golden brown and crisp on each side. Keep warm to one side.

Add the oil to the same pan. Once very hot, add the chicken livers and sauté for 1–2 minutes on each side, keeping them slightly pink. It is important that the pan is very hot for this stage; the livers will then colour and sauté well, and not just poach and stew. When almost cooked, add a small knob of butter and season with salt and pepper. Remove from the pan and keep warm.

After quickly wiping the pan clean, reheat it again, adding another knob of butter. Quickly fry the chanterelles for 1–2 minutes, adding the garlic slices and torn spinach leaves. Season with salt and pepper.

Slice the livers and place on the toasts. Spoon over and around the garlic chanterelles and the spinach. If including the butter sauce, spoon this over the livers. If using the sweet port red wine dressing, spoon a trickle over and around each portion.

If you are not using the dressing or butter sauce, add extra butter to the mushrooms before spooning over the livers. Wild ceps and chestnut mushrooms can be used instead of the chanterelles.

soaked lemon semolina wedge with warm blueberries

The soaking process is achieved by spooning a warm lemon syrup over the cake. The dense, soft texture happily absorbs the flavour and moistness, producing a very rich result.

Blueberries tend to be with us from July into mid-autumn, so they're perfect right now. Cooked in sugar, lemon juice and water, they soften, becoming very tender partners to this dessert (the cake also eats very well on its own). To finish, extra-thick cream could be offered as a first-choice accompaniment with whipped or pouring cream close behind.

SERVES 8

butter, for greasing
flour, for dusting
100g (4oz) caster sugar
3 tablespoons vegetable oil
finely grated zest of 2 lemons
4 eggs
225g (8oz) semolina
2 teaspoons baking powder
100g (4oz) ground almonds
7 tablespoons milk

FOR THE LEMON SYRUP

100g (4oz) caster sugar
juice of 3 lemons

FOR THE BLUEBERRIES

225g (8oz) blueberries
50–75g (2–3oz) icing sugar

Preheat the oven to 160°C/325°F/Gas 3 and butter and flour a 20 × 2.5–4cm (8 × 1–1½in) cake tin. Mix together the sugar, oil and lemon zest. Beat the eggs together and then pour and whisk into the sugar mixture. Add the semolina and baking powder, mix in well and then add the ground almonds and milk. Pour into the prepared cake tin and bake in the preheated oven for 30–35 minutes, until just set. Remove from the oven and leave to rest.

While the cake is baking, make the lemon syrup. Boil together the sugar and 200ml (7fl oz) of water for 8–10 minutes. At this point a syrupy consistency should have been reached.

OPPOSITE: SOAKED LEMON SEMOLINA WEDGE
WITH WARM BLUEBERRIES

Add the lemon juice, return to a rapid simmer and cook for a further few minutes.

Once the warm cake has been allowed to rest for 15 minutes, prick with a knife or fork and spoon the warm syrup over, a little at a time, until all of the syrup has been absorbed. This cake is best served at warm to room temperature.

To prepare the blueberries, place them in a pan with 50g (2oz) of the icing sugar and 3 tablespoons of water. Warm until the sugar dissolves and the blueberries begin to soften. At this point, if the berries are too tart, add more icing sugar until the right flavour is achieved. If the syrup is too thin, remove the blueberries, return the syrup to the stove and simmer rapidly until reduced to a thicker consistency. Pour back over the blueberries and they are ready to serve with the warm cake.

Almost any soft summer fruit or a summer pudding mixture can be used in this recipe.
If available, a splash or two of blueberry liqueur, crème de myrtilles, or crème de cassis (blackcurrant), can be added to the warm fruits or simply used in place of the water for a richer finish.

iced summer fruit soufflés

This soufflé cannot fail. It is almost like eating an ice-cream set in soufflé ramekin moulds, but with a much lighter texture. July and August are the best months for this dessert, particularly August, with every soft summer fruit available.

This recipe will fill six 150ml (¼ pint) ramekins. To create the risen soufflé effect, cut six strips of parchment paper, long enough to completely wrap around the ramekin moulds with a slight overlap and wide enough to stand 2.5–3cm (1–1¼in) above the rim. The strips can be secured in place with elastic bands or sticky tape. Place the moulds in the freezer, to chill, ready for filling.

SERVES 6

450g (1lb) mixed soft summer fruits (such as strawberries, raspberries, blackberries, loganberries, redcurrants, blackcurrants, etc.)
1 tablespoon icing sugar, plus more for dusting
225g (8oz) caster sugar
4 egg whites
pinch of salt
300g (10½oz) crème fraîche

**fruits, to garnish – say, a mixture of 1 or 2 strawberry
halves, whole raspberries, blackberries, blueberries,
plus sprigs of redcurrants and blackcurrants
(optional)**
few mint leaves (optional)

Wash the 450g (1lb) of fruit and pick over the currants and
hull the strawberries. In a liquidizer, blend the fruits to a
purée with the tablespoon of icing sugar. For a smooth
seedless purée, pass the fruits through a fine sieve. Refrigerate
the strained fruit purée.

Place the caster sugar in a saucepan with 8 tablespoons
of water and cook over a fairly high heat. The sugar will
dissolve, creating a syrup with the water, and this needs to
be cooked to 120°C/250°F. The easiest way to check the
temperature is with a sugar thermometer. If unavailable, once
the syrup is producing large bubbles, take a teaspoon and
spoon a little of the syrup into a bowl of iced water. If the iced
syrup can easily be formed into a small soft ball, the syrup is
ready.

While the syrup is boiling, place the egg whites and
a pinch of salt in a very clean electric-mixer bowl. Begin to
whisk (making sure the whisk is also spotless) at a reasonable
speed, increasing the speed when the whites begin to foam.
At a firm-peak stage, and when the syrup has just reached
the required temperature, begin to pour the syrup into the
whisking egg whites very steadily and slowly. Once all the
syrup is added, continue to whisk until this meringue mixture
has cooled.

Mix the fruit purée into the crème fraîche, then fold in
the meringue. Spoon the soufflé mix into the frozen moulds,
levelling the tops if possible. The soufflés will now need to be
frozen for at least 2–3 hours to freeze completely and set. The
frozen soufflés are best eaten within 24–48 hours. After this,
the fruit flavour will become less pronounced. It is always best
to transfer frozen desserts to the fridge for 1–1½ hours before
serving. This allows the deep-frozen texture to soften slightly,
making the dessert more pleasant to eat.

Before serving, carefully remove the paper and dust
each soufflé with icing sugar through a tea strainer. The
garnishing fruits can now be arranged on top, along with a
small mint leaf or two (whole or finely shredded), if using,
dusting once again with just a little more icing sugar. The
soufflés are ready to serve.

Almond or pistachio Tuile biscuits *(page 429) make nice
accompaniments to offer with the soufflés.*

grilled raspberry melba stack

This dish is a variation on the French classic, *millefeuilles*
('thousand leaves'), using very thin Melba toasts rather than
puff pastry. Melba toast was created by one of the greatest
culinary artists known, Auguste Escoffier, who was for many
years Executive Chef at the Savoy Hotel, London. A regular
visitor to the hotel's restaurant was the great Australian opera
singer Dame Nellie Melba. She requested thin toast and the
classic Melba toast was born.

The Melba toast featured here takes on a new identity,
not being allowed to curl (one of the distinctive features of
Melba toast). Instead it is caramelized and crisped between
icing sugar and baking trays.

Virtually all summer fruits can be used here, but the
beauty of raspberries with this particular dish is not only their
wonderful texture and flavour, but also that they are so uniform
in size the stack stands upright. Raspberries are at their best
from July to early September, particularly during August when
the Scottish raspberry is probably the best you'll ever taste.

SERVES 4
6 slices of thin-cut white bread (preferably 2–3 days old)
icing sugar, for dusting
20–24 raspberries per portion
1 quantity *White chocolate mousse* (page 38)

FOR THE RASPBERRY COULIS (OPTIONAL)
100g (4oz) raspberries
50g (2oz) icing sugar
1–2 teaspoons raspberry jam (optional)

Preheat the oven to 180°C/350°F/Gas 4 and line a baking tray
with greaseproof paper. Toast the slices of bread, remove the
crusts and cut through the width, splitting each into two very
thin squares. Scrape away any excess crumbs from the untoasted
sides, then cut each slice into a 7.5–8.5cm (3–3½in) disc. Place
untoasted-side up on the baking tray, each spot on the tray first
being dusted well with icing sugar. Now dust the top of the discs
generously with more icing sugar. Cover with another sheet of
paper and top with a second baking tray. This will prevent the
natural curl of the Melba toasts when exposed to heat.

Place in the oven and bake for approximately
12 minutes, until dried and with a crisp golden finish. Remove
from the oven and transfer the toasts to a cooling rack. These
can be made several hours in advance and kept in an airtight
container to maintain their crispness. Dust four of the Melba

toasts with icing sugar and grill-mark with a heated skewer to create four or five lines, before doing this again at a different angle for a criss-cross finish.

To make the raspberry coulis, if using, chop the raspberries and place in a saucepan with the icing sugar and 4 tablespoons of water. Bring to a simmer and cook for 2–3 minutes before liquidizing and pushing through a sieve. A teaspoon or two of raspberry jam can also be added while simmering. This will give the sauce a richer flavour.

Now place the raspberries on the remaining eight Melba toasts, all around the edges, leaving the centres to be generously filled with the chocolate mousse. For this recipe the mousse does not need to be refrigerated until set. Once the double cream has been whipped in, it will be just the right consistency. Spoon a tablespoon or two into each raspberry-surrounded toast. If using the raspberry coulis, this can be spooned into pools on plates, 2 tablespoons per portion, before building the stacks on top, or just offer the sauce separately. If you're not saucing the plates, spoon a teaspoon of the white chocolate mousse onto the centre of each plate. (This creamy base will prevent the stacked dessert from sliding on the plates and quickly becoming the leaning tower of Pisa!) Now place the base layer on top and finish with the remaining layer and marked top.

Sweet whipped cream is an option to the mousse.

pannacotta with stewed black fruits

Pannacotta is Italian for 'cooked cream'. Such a light dessert, pannacotta has a silky polish in its structure, and is smooth, creamy and moreish. The reward is how genially this dessert introduces itself to many other characters. On the Italian table fresh fruits, chocolate and caramel are fairly regular partnerships; for home, fruits are the most obvious choice. August begins to wave goodbye to blackcurrants, but blackberries and blueberries are still showing off their wares, with a couple of months of full bloom to look forward to.

Many pannacotta recipes suggest turning the cream from the mould. For me this is far too jelly-like, whereas helping yourself to a scoop straight from a large bowl is pure pleasure. This particular recipe includes natural yoghurt, a fresh-flavoured addition to the standard recipe. Having experienced the pleasure of this delightful pudding with a friend, Peter Barratt (my tutor of old), it seemed the most natural of things to share it more widely.

Peter makes pannacotta purely with yoghurt, for the lightest possible result, but here the yoghurt is halved with mascarpone, which is needed to cope with, rather than be lost behind, the rich black fruits. This dessert requires some thinking ahead, needing a minimum 8 hours, preferably 12–24 hours, to set completely.

SERVES 6–8
250ml (8fl oz) double cream
1 vanilla pod
75g (3 oz) caster sugar
2 leaves of gelatine, soaked in cold water
250ml (8fl oz) natural set yoghurt
250ml (8fl oz) mascarpone

FOR THE FRUIT
175g (6oz) blackberries, rinsed
175g (6oz) blackcurrants, picked and rinsed
175g (6oz) blueberries, rinsed
100–175g (4–6oz) icing sugar

PANNACOTTA WITH STEWED BLACK FRUITS

Pour the double cream into a saucepan. Split the vanilla pod lengthwise, scraping each half of its seeds. Add the seeds and pod to the cream, heating gently, not allowing it to boil. Once at a gentle simmering point, add the sugar, stirring it in to dissolve. Remove the pan from the heat and leave to stand for a few minutes, giving the vanilla flavour time to infuse, before removing the scraped pods.

Squeeze the gelatine leaves of excess water, also stirring them in to dissolve. Beat together the yoghurt and mascarpone before straining and stirring in the cream. The pannacotta is now ready to be poured into a suitable pudding dish or dishes, and left to chill and set.

Place the fruits in a large saucepan or frying pan. Add 4 tablespoons of water, sprinkling over 100g (4oz) of the icing sugar. Warm on a moderate heat, dissolving the sugar while gently stirring the fruits. Once the fruits begin to soften, if too tart add more of the remaining sugar until the right flavour is achieved. Should the syrup be too loose, drain the fruits, boiling the syrup until it thickens to a better consistency. Pour it back over the fruits. The softened black berries are now ready to serve warm or cold, to accompany the set pannacotta.

The set pannacotta can be removed from the fridge 20–30 minutes before serving, to loosen the texture slightly and to serve at room temperature.
A thick-cream-consistency pannacotta, rather than the set one above, can be made by simply omitting one of the gelatine leaves.

roast plums and greengages with set honey triple cream

The plum holds a lot more identity and character than it perhaps is given credit for. Across the world there are apparently over 2000 varieties, though the number in our stores only just breaks into double figures. However, amongst this reduced offering, the varieties are very individual, with shades of reds, purples, oranges and yellows (and greens from their greengage partners) on their silky-smooth skins. The main choice lies between the sweet eating plums and the more acidic, tart cooking fruit.

The tart plums, as with slightly under-ripe greengages, are superb for cooking, the new sharp edge governed by a sugar sprinkling. Sweet plums do carry the double bonus of eating beautifully as a natural fruit (as with fully ripe

greengages), or lending themselves just as well to a crumble, flan or pie, or being roasted, as here.

A brief story of the greengage is told on page 200. As for its season, it runs with the plum between August and September; plums extend their season either side. The most common plums to choose are the Santa Rosa, Burbank, Marjorie's Seedling and English Victoria.

The set honey triple cream is a sort of cheesecake mix, amalgamating cream cheese, mascarpone and crème fraîche, with the addition of honey to sweeten and vanilla to spice.

Two other spices I haven't yet mentioned are nutmeg and cinnamon. This pair eat very well with plums, particularly when sprinkling and roasting with sugar to leave a spicy syrup, enhanced here with grenadine (a pomegranate syrup), which adds a rich colour and flavour.

SERVES 4–6
6 plums
6 greengages
2 heaped tablespoons demerara or light soft
** brown sugar**
½ teaspoon ground cinnamon
½ teaspoon freshly grated nutmeg
2 tablespoons grenadine (pomegranate syrup)

FOR THE TRIPLE CREAM
1 vanilla pod
100g (4oz) cream cheese
100g (4oz) mascarpone
2 tablespoons clear honey
100g (4oz) crème fraîche

To make the triple cream, split the vanilla pod lengthwise, scraping each half of its seeds with the point of a small knife. Put the cream cheese, mascarpone and honey in a bowl, and add the vanilla seeds. Beat together until smooth. In a separate bowl, whisk the crème fraîche to a soft-peak stage, then fold it into the cream-cheese mix. Spoon the triple cream into a suitable pudding dish, refrigerating to set for several hours, leaving overnight for a firmer touch.

To cook the fruits, preheat the oven to 190ºC/375ºF/ Gas 5. Halve each of the plums and greengages, cutting around their natural line, before twisting to reveal the stone. This can now be removed, levering with the point of a small knife.

Place the fruits, cut-sides up, on a small, preferably non-stick baking tray. Mix together the sugar and cinnamon, sprinkling it over each of the halves. Spoon 3 tablespoons of water and the grenadine syrup, if using, onto the tray (or just use 5 tablespoons of water). Place it in the preheated oven and roast until tender. Depending on the ripeness and softness of the fruits, this can take 8–15 minutes. Once softened, with the sugar lightly caramelizing, remove the plums from the oven.

For a more caramelized, slightly bitter, burnt edge, the fruits can be placed under a hot grill for just a minute or two. Sprinkle with the fresh nutmeg before transferring to plates, offering 3 pieces of each fruit for 4 portions, or a smaller portion of 2 pieces of each for 6 portions. A syrup will have formed on the tray; spoon this over the soft red and green halves. The set honey triple cream can be served separately or divided between each plate.

The quantity of honey used in the triple cream can be halved, leaving a more tart bite.

greengage biscuit tart with wine and vanilla cream

The greengages featured here are baked in a pastry case sprinkled with broken digestive biscuits (ginger snaps can also be used for a spicier finish), hence the recipe title. As the fruits bake gently, caramelizing with the sugar, any juices are collected by the biscuits, preventing the pastry from becoming soggy.

Sabayon is very much like Italian *zabaglione*, but once whisked to its fluffy thick stage it is then continuously whisked until cold. It is at this point that whipped cream is to be added, allowing you then to keep this light 'custard' refrigerated (for 24–48 hours) without collapsing.

SERVES 8–10 GENEROUSLY
50g (2oz) butter, melted, plus more for greasing
350g (12oz) *Sweet shortcrust pastry* (page 425)
flour, for dusting
100g (4oz) digestive biscuits, crushed to crumbs
1kg (2¼lb) greengages
100g (4oz) light soft brown sugar

FOR THE SABAYON CREAM
3 egg yolks
60g (2¼oz) caster sugar
seeds from 1 vanilla pod
125ml (4fl oz) sweet white wine
125ml (4fl oz) double cream

Preheat the oven to 200°C/400°F/Gas 6 and lightly butter a 25cm (10in) flan ring set on a baking sheet. Roll out the pastry to approximately 3mm (⅛in) thick on a lightly floured surface and line the flan ring with it, leaving any excess hanging over the edge. Prick the base of the tart case with a fork and refrigerate for 30 minutes.

Before baking, line the chilled pastry case with greaseproof paper and fill with baking beans or rice. Cook in the preheated oven for 20–25 minutes. Remove the paper and beans, return the pastry case to the oven and bake for a further 6–8 minutes. Remove from the oven, leaving the oven switched on. Allow the pastry to cool. Carefully trim off any overhanging edges, before sprinkling with the biscuit crumbs to cover the base.

Halve and stone the greengages. Place the halves, skin-side up and overlapping, in the tart case, starting with an outside border and continuing, circle by circle, until the centre is reached. Trickle the melted butter over the fruits and then sprinkle with the soft brown sugar. Bake towards the top of the preheated oven for 55–60 minutes. At this point the fruits should be beginning to caramelize slightly, with the pastry also becoming a rich golden brown. Remove from the oven and leave to cool to just a warm stage before removing the ring.

While the tart is baking, make the sabayon cream. Place all the ingredients, except the double cream, in a bowl sitting over a pan of simmering water. Whisk vigorously (this can be made very simple using an electric hand whisk) until at least doubled in volume and holding thick ribbons. This sabayon can now be used as it is, but to turn it into a sabayon cream, and for speed, transfer it to an electric mixer bowl and continue to whisk until cold.

The double cream can now be quickly whisked by hand to a soft peak stage, and folded into the cold sabayon. The cream is now ready to serve as an accompaniment to the tart.

The biscuit quantity can be halved and replaced with toasted, nibbed almonds for a rich nutty finish. The sweet white wine can also be halved, or completely replaced with amaretto. If using almonds in the tart, this becomes the perfect accompaniment.

Plums are considered second only to apples and pears in temperate regions. *Prunus* is a large family, thought to have originated in the east, and includes plums, greengages, damsons, sloes and bullaces (and the cherry).

Imported plums are available throughout the year, both for eating in the hand and for cooking. As far as home-grown are concerned, the Victoria joins us in mid-to-late summer, reaching its best in early autumn. This particular dessert plum has a sweet juicy flavour and can be easily recognized by its red-yellow colour. Another around now is Marjorie's Seedling, a large blue-black variety which again has a rich flavour. Many plums are used on the continent for liqueurs (the *mirabelle*, for instance), and for drying as prunes (the *prune d'Agen* prime among them).

The greengage has a shorter season, between late July and September. In France it is known as *reine Claude*, after the wife of François I. This rich green, tender fruit became known as the greengage in this country purely by chance. In the early eighteenth century Sir Thomas Gage received a collection of

plants from his brother in France. When the gardener lost the name tag for this particular fruit, he decided to baptize it with a simple combination of its colour and his employer's name.

Damsons are smaller, blue-black in colour, and have quite a sexy name – *Prunus damascena* – meaning 'plum of Damascus' (where they originated). They are usually cooked, particularly in jams and fruit cheeses.

The sloe, the fruit of the blackthorn, is a wild plum native to Britain. It is found in hedges and scrubby woodland, and now grows wild throughout Europe (as does the larger bullace). The small berries very much resemble blue-black plums in miniature. The greenish juicy flesh is so tart and sour that it is inedible raw – but makes a wonderful liqueur if steeped in gin (see page 237).

baked blue cheesecake with warm lemon-and-thyme greengage compote

The blue cheese featured here is the British classic Stilton. There are many others available on the market – Beenleigh Blue, Blue Vinney, Wensleydale and Cashel Blue to name just a few. All of these will work well in this recipe. The greengages become available from late summer, with a good season taking us through to mid-autumn. This particular fruit is part of the plum family, regarded by many as the finest of all gages. The touch of lemon and savoury thyme blends with the flavour of the rich fruit, as a perfect accompaniment to the blue cheese. The cheesecake can be served as an alternative dessert.

SERVES 8–10

100g (4oz) butter, melted, plus more for greasing
225g (8oz) digestive biscuits (preferably savoury or wholemeal), crushed to crumbs

FOR THE FILLING

3 tablespoons cornflour
50–100g (2–4oz) caster sugar (less for a more savoury finish)
450g (1lb) full-fat soft cream cheese, softened
225g (8oz) Stilton or other blue cheese, rind removed and crumbled
2 eggs
150ml (¼ pint) crème fraîche
150ml (¼ pint) whipping cream

FOR THE COMPOTE

1kg (2¼lb) greengages, halved and stoned
finely grated zest of ½ lemon
4 tablespoons icing sugar
juice of 1 lemon
1 heaped teaspoon picked thyme leaves

Preheat the oven to 180°C/350°F/Gas 4. Butter a 25cm (10in) loose-bottomed cake tin, then line the base with parchment paper. Mix the crushed digestive biscuits and melted butter. Spoon and press the base-mix into the prepared cake tin.

To make the filling, mix together the cornflour and caster sugar, then beat in the cream cheese and Stilton. Add and stir in the eggs, followed by the crème fraîche and whipping cream, beating constantly to produce a thick almost softly-whipped-cream consistency. This process will take a little while, even with an electric mixer (leave it on maximum speed).

Spoon and spread the mix into the biscuit-lined cake tin. Cover the outside base of the tin with foil and place in a baking tray, filled with 3mm (⅛in) of warm water to help create steam during cooking. Place in the preheated oven and bake for 50 minutes–1 hour, until the top is just firm to the touch and golden brown. If not quite ready, continue to bake for a further 10–15 minutes until firm (the cooked cheesecake can be finished under the grill for a deeper colour).

Remove from the oven and leave to cool until just warm before lifting from the tin. It is at this, or room temperature, that the cheesecake will eat at its best. It can be refrigerated, but then does take on a more solid 'cakey' texture, rather than a warm creamy finish. Increase the oven temperature to 190°C/375°F/Gas 5.

While the cheesecake is cooling, make the compote. Place the greengages in a large ovenproof dish or tray, cut-side up. Sprinkle with the lemon zest and icing sugar. Bake in the preheated oven for 10–12 minutes. During this time the fruits will become tender (if not very ripe, they may take 12–15 or even 20 minutes), releasing their juices, which will combine with the sugar to create a greengage syrup. The greengage halves will be soft and tender, still holding their shape.

Remove the fruits from the pan, pouring any syrup into another saucepan. Add the lemon juice to the syrup and bring to a simmer. This acidity will counter the sweetness of the fruits. Add the thyme leaves to the greengages, stirring well, then pour the lemony syrup over the fruits. Mix well and the warm compote is ready to serve with the cheesecake.

OPPOSITE: BAKED BLUE CHEESECAKE WITH WARM LEMON-AND-THYME GREENGAGE COMPOTE

3 autu

mn

With summer passed, although leaving many bright thoughts with us, autumn is here. Sun-filled early mornings still exist, exuding a slightly cooler touch with a sharp finish to follow. This may appear to some a rather negative turn, but in fact it's quite the opposite: often the sun will save its best for September, creating a contrast of colours, textures and tones in the gold and bronze of autumn. A picture emerges, developing as the weeks pass, as fresh aromas, essences and piquancy all contribute finishing touches to a culinary masterpiece – just ready to savour.

This is the time of the year to reacquaint ourselves with the English apple, the fruit that has so many faces, each with a quite distinctive personality that can enhance such a range of different desserts and savoury dishes. Another tree-bred fruit to accompany the apple, similar in texture but with such contrast in flavour, is the pear.

The Conference arrives first, with a host of good friends to follow, like the apples, in shades of green, some taking on red or yellow sides.

September has some secrets it just loves to share with us that no other month is quite capable of matching. Two of these are almost forgotten and too long ignored – the damson and the sloe. The damson is in its prime between September and October, but can still be with us in late autumn too – depending on weather conditions. The sloe is native to Britain, but this fruit of the blackthorn has, over the years, spread its wares much further afield. Over the pages to follow you'll find these wild plum-style fruits infusing in gin with a helping of sweet crystals ready for winter drinking (page 237).

The arrival of the Pink Fir Apple, the potato taken from our main crop between September and May, knobbly in shape and nutty in flavour, shows definite signs that autumn is with us. Other culinary characters to look out for include Swiss chard, an all-year-round vegetable that is at its prime right now, and home-grown sweetcorn, plenty of it too, with its

bright yellow kernels that adapt so easily to poultry, game and many a fish or vegetarian dish.

Game, which has been with us since August, grows into a tempting selection, with partridge, wild duck, woodcock and wood pigeons joining the pack.

Another cast of characters that appear are the wild mushrooms, each with their own individual structure, flavour and texture, and with a pick'n'mix assortment of colours to please and tempt the eye. This medley of tasty morsels reminds us of the vast selection of 'home-growns' we produce on this island. Our reluctance to let go of summer tones is catered for by tomatoes still shouting loudly, with summer cabbages, peas, courgettes and spinach equally noisy, rich in colour and freshness too. Summer-born cauliflowers are brilliant white, and a favourite of mine, runner beans, are still crispy at their peak. Following all of these in sweet harmony are the Scottish raspberries, the finest of them all, with blackberries still strong, perfect to simmer with apples beneath a crisp pastry or crumble topping, and strawberries

still not quite at the end of their hand-picked run.

Shorter days and early dark evenings are married with a mellow warmth as October arrives and autumn is truly with us. The first two weeks will provide us with a last-chance list. A last chance to enjoy those late-summer specials, many of the colourful fruits included.

As we move through each month within each season, cooking techniques change, and the closer to winter, the more stews and casseroles adorn the table. October doesn't quite need those; these four weeks have more in common with late August and September. Roasts certainly feature, with perhaps a different fashion of garnish, maintaining the individual character of all the ingredients.

Pumpkins, butternuts and more of the orange-fleshed vegetables are making an appearance, with their richer-flavoured structure adapting to many recipes. The wild cep mushroom, without doubt wearing the crown for this time of year, is plumper, fuller and firmer than ever, and will maintain this quality for quite a few more weeks to come. *Green garden soup*, featured on page 248, brings together the last of summer's tastes, simmering them with young curly kale, leeks and new Brussels sprouts. Fresh eels (page 252) are complemented by a stew, with lots of herbs and a sharp caper bite, whilst dabs work well in a warm green horseradish dip (page 252).

A fruit that begins to make an understudy appearance, before taking central stage in months to come, is the quince. This is a fruit that seems to have lost favour with Britons many, many years ago. Mrs Beeton, in the nineteenth century, was one of the last food writers still believing in its virtues, with jams, jellies and many more dishes using quince featuring in her works. When seen, this fruit immediately captures your interest. The golden yellow colour of its skin has such a smooth, almost silk-like finish and the shape is reminiscent of an apple or pear. But the quince surprises as it changes from an inedible raw state into a lusciously different colour, look and feel once simmered or baked slowly and sweetly.

With November very close, fresh figs and the versatile celeriac tubers start to appear. The last thoughts in October are of preparations for Hallowe'en parties, with a dazzling array of foods to choose from.

A very definite change in cooking styles and methods tells us we are in November. Perhaps it's the soft murmur of bubbling soups, stews and casseroles that relate this story, helped along by the sharp frosts of late autumn; trees are stark and bare, the 'fall' has completed its natural course. Comfort foods become a daily feature on our kitchen table, with a hot mug of *Pumpkin soup* (page 281) or a bowl of goulash (page 282), both waiting patiently for 5 November, as well as baked potatoes and toffee apples.

Our root vegetables – carrots, swedes, turnips and parsnips – will soon become daily features. Brussels sprouts are a firmer and a richer green than ever, perfect to be rolling in a buttery pan and slightly jumping from a peppery bite. We now find ourselves having to think and plan ahead a little more carefully. Late-autumn foods so often need extra care and attention.

During this season the clocks go back and, in the same spirit, our classic cooking methods and combinations of old come to the fore. You'll find examples of these featured in this month, with a simple *Conference salad* – a dish that draws together the crisp flavours of pears, chicory and walnuts – finished with crumbled Roquefort cheese and a light creamy dressing (page 280). *Rabbit and pork pot with rhubarb and mustard soured cream* (page 297), *Roast loin of venison with savoury fig tarts* (page 300) and *Slow-roast shoulder of pork with a celery, Bramley apple and potato pot* (page 296) are all late-autumn classics and home-made *Crab apple jelly* (page 305) is a perfect seasonal accompaniment.

The essence of this whole season, with its tones of oranges and browns amongst its scenery of fallen leaves, is new, completely changed from what has gone before. The purpose of this chapter is to excite your thoughts and tastes through the next three months of this year. Autumn is a season of give and take, with elements from summer giving their last brave performances before retirement and some from winter eagerly taking centre stage. The weather begins with sunny warm days and reasonably late evenings, but changes to short light spells with almost bitter cold nights. The colour range of foods also reaches both extremes, with early light pinks, reds, oranges and yellows, but darker tones coming in as the season leaves us. Cooking techniques and eating habits take new directions to remain well balanced.

Autumn daylight may well be disappearing, but new tastes are just beginning. These recipes make us aware of this, and of the ever-increasing range of great British flavours.

OPPOSITE: BAKED CIDER, CINNAMON AND HONEY QUINCES WITH RASPBERRIES AND SWEET VANILLA CREAM (PAGE 274)

vegetables

Beenleigh Blue and courgette egg cake 209

Early autumn Provençal bake 209

Swiss chard and sweet red pepper mascarpone crumble 210

Swiss chard cheese pie 211

Mushroom and leek egg baked pots 212

fish

Fresh haddock and smoked bacon with celeriac sage fries 215

Fried cod with a Florence fennel and red onion Parmesan bake 216

Pan-fried and roasted skate wings with a sweetcorn, caper and lemon parsley butter 216

Steamed courgette-scaled brill with a cherry tomato, black olive and tarragon compote 217

Brill on the bone with celery, cider and apples 218

Dover sole meunière with garlic mousseron mushrooms and courgettes 220

Natural steamed mussels with a piquant spread 221

meat

Roast walnut chicken with cider, apples, onions and thyme courgettes 223

Chicken sauté with sweetcorn à la française 224

Grilled quail salad with a warm muscat grape and lentil dressing 225

Roast wild duck over parsnips and potatoes with a damson sauce 225

Fricassee of rabbit with a creamed lentil sauce and wild mushrooms 229

Foil-baked rabbit and garlic with sea salt and lemon Pink Fir Apples 230

Pot-roast hand of pork with Cumberland broccoli 231

fruit and puddings

Raspberry rice pudding flan 233

Peach tart and bellini sabayon 234

Baked plum pudding 235

Stewed damson Yorkies with lashings of sweet cream 236

Greengage lime cake 236

Sloe gin 237

Blackberry Eton mess with cider apples 238

beenleigh blue and courgette egg cake

Beenleigh Blue is a blue Devonshire unpasteurized ewe's-milk cheese. It has quite a rich robust flavour and is normally available from September to February. The British courgettes are with us from midsummer to mid-autumn. This recipe, however, can be put together throughout the year, with plenty of alternative blue cheeses, like Stilton and Roquefort, available and with imported courgettes to match.

SERVES 4 AS A STARTER OR 2 AS A MAIN COURSE
450g (1lb) courgettes
4 tablespoons olive oil
salt and pepper
6 eggs
1 tablespoon chopped chives
large knob of butter
75g (3oz) Beenleigh Blue cheese, crumbled

Cut the courgettes into thin slices – if possible, cut them into thin julienne strips (spaghetti-style) using a mandolin slicer. Alternatively, simply shred/grate in a food processor.

Heat 2 tablespoons of the olive oil in a 28cm (11in) diameter frying pan, preferably non-stick. Once hot, fry the courgettes for a minute or two, until beginning to soften and taking on a little colour. Season with salt and pepper and remove the pan from the heat.

Fork the eggs together in a large bowl, adding the chopped chives and knob of butter. Now add the courgettes, spooning the mix in well, to spread the vegetables and warmth evenly.

Preheat a grill to hot. Spoon the remaining olive oil into the frying pan, swirling to cover the whole pan, and return to the heat. Pour the courgette egg mix into the frying pan and cook on a medium heat, moving the mixture with a fork or spatula to ensure an even cooking. As the egg warms it will begin to thicken.

After a few minutes, lower the temperature, allowing the mix to set on the base, leaving a thickened but still soft centre and top.

Crumble the cheese across the top and finish under the preheated grill until melted and golden brown. The courgette egg cake is now ready to serve hot or just warm. It is nice to

OPPOSITE: BEENLEIGH BLUE AND COURGETTE EGG CAKE

present the cake on the table while still in the pan. This provides a rustic homely feel to the dish.

If you are serving this as a starter or vegetarian main course, a salad of mixed leaves and soft red peppers offers a refreshing finish.

early autumn provençal bake

From September until about mid-October you can find the home-grown ingredients required here. The combination is very much along the lines of ratatouille, utilizing these flavours during their last weeks. The list of vegetables is purely a guideline and any of them can stand alone within the Parmesan cream. Basically, it is a quiche-style recipe without the pastry case, a 25cm (10in) ovenproof ceramic fluted flan dish taking its place. I prefer to serve the warm bake as a vegetarian starter or main course dish. It also works very well as an accompaniment to other foods, in particular grilled chicken breasts or gammon steaks.

SERVES 4–6
1 small aubergine
salt and pepper
2 medium courgettes
1 large red pepper
1 large green pepper
2 small red onions
olive oil and butter, for frying and brushing
1 garlic clove
2 plum tomatoes, quartered and seeded

FOR THE PARMESAN CREAM
2 eggs, plus 1 extra yolk (optional)
300ml (½ pint) milk
150ml (¼ pint) double cream
4 tablespoons finely grated Parmesan cheese

Cut the aubergine into 2.5cm (1in) dice and place the pieces in a colander. Sprinkle with a level teaspoon of salt, mix it in well and leave to stand for 30 minutes. This will draw the bitter juices from the vegetable. After the 30 minutes, the aubergine should not need to be rinsed as the salt will purely have seasoned it; if you are a little unsure, quickly rinse and dry on a kitchen cloth.

While salting the aubergine, preheat the oven to 160°C/325°F/Gas 3 and cut the remaining vegetables. Slice the courgettes into 2.5cm (1in) pieces, preferably at an angle to provide a neat oval pointed shape. Split the red and green peppers, then cut each half into four or five strips and trim away the seeds and stalk, maintaining their curved edge (the stalk can be left on for a more rustic finish). Cut each red onion into eight wedges.

Heat a little olive oil in a large frying pan. Once it is hot, fry the aubergine pieces for just 2 minutes, allowing them to take on a fried edge. Remove and return to the colander or place on a tray lined with kitchen paper. Sauté the courgette pieces in a similar fashion, cooking for an extra 2–3 minutes, until they have just a light golden-brown finish. Season with salt and pepper, and transfer to the tray.

Fry the peppers in olive oil, or brush with butter and placed under a preheated grill. These strips need only be gently softened, so cook for just a few minutes. Lastly, grill, fry or bake the onions, seasoning with salt and pepper and brushing with butter. The onions will take a little longer to soften, so cook them for 8–10 minutes.

While the onions are cooking, make the Parmesan cream. Whisk together the eggs and egg yolk, if using (this will enrich the finished flavour), adding the milk and cream. The Parmesan cheese can all be added or just add 3 tablespoons, reserving the remainder to sprinkle on top during the last 5 minutes of cooking. Season with salt and pepper.

Split the garlic clove and rub the flan dish liberally with both halves. Brush the dish with butter, then spoon in the softened vegetables and tomatoes. Pour the Parmesan cream over and bake in the preheated oven for 35–40 minutes until just set, sprinkling with the reserved Parmesan at the end, if wished. Once cooked, remove from the oven and allow to rest for 5–10 minutes before serving.

The garlic halves can be crushed and added to the cream for a stronger Provençal finish.
Chopped fresh herbs can also be added to the filling.

swiss chard and sweet red pepper mascarpone crumble

Swiss chard can be found most of the year, but does particularly well during the months of August and September. Within the recipe for *Swiss chard cheese pie* (page 211), only the vegetable's leaves are used. Here we use purely the celery-like stalks, mixed with sweet red pepper and a smooth mascarpone cream, enhanced with the addition of Parmesan cheese. The loose Swiss chard leaves can be put to use and cooked in butter, as you would spinach, to accompany another meal. The crumble topping offers a garlic and fresh herb finish, and all of these flavours together will suit the first of our autumn months, September.

If serving as a vegetarian main course, all the dish needs is a mixed leaf salad with a red wine vinegar dressing to finish it off. The crumble also eats particularly well with roast chicken or grilled chicken breasts.

SERVES 4 AS AN ACCOMPANIMENT OR
2–3 AS A MAIN COURSE
12 Swiss chard stalks
juice of ½ lemon
salt and pepper
3 sweet red peppers
olive oil, for frying
2 knobs of butter, plus more for greasing
2 red onions, sliced
175g (6oz) mascarpone cheese
50g (2oz) Parmesan cheese, finely grated
1 egg, plus 1 extra yolk

FOR THE CRUMBLE TOPPING
3 slices of thick-cut white or granary bread, preferably 24–48 hours old
8 basil leaves, torn into small pieces
1 teaspoon torn tarragon leaves
1 teaspoon chopped parsley
1 teaspoon chopped chives
25g (1oz) butter
1 small garlic clove, crushed

Preheat the oven to 200°C/400°F/Gas 6. Should the chard stalks be large and quite tough, it's best to peel away the fine membrane on each side. Cut the stalks into 5cm (2in) pieces and place them in a bowl of water acidulated with the lemon juice to prevent any discoloration. To cook the chard, plunge the pieces into rapidly boiling salted water and simmer for 10 minutes, until just tender. Drain in a colander and allow to cool.

To prepare the peppers, halve and quarter each one, removing the stalk and seeds, then cut each quarter into two or three thick strips. Heat 2 tablespoons of olive oil in a large frying pan. Once hot, add the pepper strips and fry on a medium heat for 6–7 minutes, until becoming tender. Transfer to a large bowl.

Return the pan to the heat and warm another tablespoon of olive oil. Add the pieces of chard and fry for a few minutes, until approaching golden brown. Add a knob of butter, increase the heat and allow the butter to reach a nutbrown stage. Add the chard to the peppers and repeat the frying process with the red onion slices.

Once all these vegetables are together in the bowl, season with salt and pepper. Mix the mascarpone, Parmesan, egg and egg yolk, then season with salt and pepper. Stir this into the vegetables and spoon into a greased 1.5 litre (2½ pint) ovenproof dish.

To make the crumble topping, remove the crusts from the bread slices, then blitz the slices in a food processor to a rough crumb consistency. Transfer the crumbs to a bowl and stir in the herbs. Melt the butter in a saucepan with the crushed garlic, until beginning to bubble. Season the crumbs with salt and pepper and pour the butter over. Stir the butter into the crumbs, keeping them quite loose.

Sprinkle the crumbs over the chard and sweet pepper mascarpone. Bake in the preheated oven for 15–20 minutes, until golden brown and bubbling. If white crumbs have been used and are not well coloured in the oven, simply finish under a preheated grill. The crumble is ready to serve.

swiss chard cheese pie

Swiss chard is a green-leaved vegetable of the beet family that is rather similar to spinach. The advantage it has over similar greens is that the stalks of the young vegetable can also be cooked, offering a celery-like finish, or shredded raw for a salad.

With this recipe it is purely the leaves we shall be using, flavouring them with shallots for an extra bite, and Parmesan cheese for enrichment. The pastry has a texture similar to that of shortcrust with the addition of olive oil to lend a stronger finished flavour that is welcomed by both the chard and the cheese.

SERVES 6–8 AS A STARTER OR 4–6 AS A MAIN COURSE

1kg (2¼lb) unpicked Swiss chard (450g/1lb picked leaves are needed for a full pie filling; if the leaves are too small 1.5kg/3lb unpicked chard will be needed)

salt and pepper

iced water

knob of butter

2 tablespoons finely chopped shallots

2 eggs

50g (2oz) Parmesan cheese, finely grated

freshly grated nutmeg

6–8 thin slices of Gruyère cheese, about 75–100g (3–4oz)

150ml (¼ pint) crème fraîche (optional)

1 tablespoon chopped chives (optional)

1 teaspoon Dijon or wholegrain mustard (optional)

FOR THE OLIVE OIL PASTRY

225g (8oz) plain flour, plus more for dusting

1 egg

3 tablespoons lukewarm water or milk

3 tablespoons olive oil, plus more for brushing

To make the pastry, sift the flour and a pinch of salt into a bowl. Add the egg, water or milk and olive oil, and spoon the ingredients together. Once they are beginning to amalgamate, work the mix well by hand to a soft dough. Mixing the dough to this stage can also be achieved by simply placing all of the ingredients in a food processor. After just 30–60 seconds the mix is ready to finish by hand to a smooth texture. It is now best to cover and chill the pastry for at least 1 hour to let it rest well.

While the pastry is resting, pick the chard leaves for the filling from the stalks (as mentioned above these can be cooked separately, using them as you would sea kale or celery). Wash the leaves, tear them into smaller pieces and blanch them in rapidly boiling salted water for a few minutes until tender. Drain the chard and refresh in iced water. This will instantly stop the cooking and also retain the rich green colour.

Once chilled, remove the leaves from the iced water and squeeze to release excess water. Melt the knob of butter in a small saucepan and, once bubbling, add the shallots. Cook gently for 5 minutes, without allowing them to colour, until tender. Leave to cool.

Roll just over half of the pastry on a floured surface into a 25cm (10in) diameter circle. Roll this onto the rolling pin, place on a very lightly oiled baking tray and chill once more, letting it rest for 10–15 minutes. Preheat the oven to 190ºC/375ºF/Gas 5.

While the pastry is resting, fork the eggs together and add them to the chard, along with the shallots and Parmesan. Season to taste with salt, pepper and nutmeg. Spoon the chard mixture onto the pastry base, packing it fairly firmly and leaving a 1cm (½in) clear border around the edge. Roll the remaining pastry into a slightly larger disc to cover the pie. Once placed on top, the edges can be trimmed for a neater finish or left untrimmed for a more rustic touch. Lightly flouring your fingers, crimp the border together, press with a fork or twist over to give a rope-effect finish. Brush the pie with olive oil and bake in the preheated oven for 25–30 minutes, until crispy and golden brown.

For the cheesy finish, preheat a hot grill and lay the Gruyère slices on top to cover. Place under the preheated grill until bubbling and melted. The pie is ready to serve. If using the crème fraîche, mix with the chives and mustard, then season with salt and pepper and offer as an accompaniment to the pie.

The Swiss cheese can also be included in the filling, dividing the chard into two layers, sandwiching the cheese slices in between.

mushroom and leek egg baked pots

It is autumn and the wild mushrooms and leeks have arrived. The choice of wild mushrooms is quite extravagant, with ceps, chanterelles, black trompettes, shiitake and mousserons all on offer.

The egg baked pots can work equally well with chestnut mushrooms, a mushroom that offers a much fuller flavour and firmer texture than basic buttons, or perhaps with oyster mushrooms, which were once naturally wild but are now cultivated 'wild', available throughout the year. The quantity of mushrooms listed below will suit all of these fungi, and, if deciding on wild, mixed bags are available, or you can buy them loose as a selection, or feature just one variety.

SERVES 6 AS A STARTER OR SNACK
225g (8oz) wild or cultivated mushrooms (see page 423)
1 leek
25g (1oz) butter
1 garlic clove, crushed to a paste
salt and pepper
200ml (7fl oz) double cream
75g (3oz) Gruyère cheese, grated
6 eggs

Preheat the oven to 200ºC/400ºF/Gas 6. If using wild mushrooms, simply clean and trim them as explained on page 423. For cultivated mushrooms, simply wipe or rinse and trim the stalks, then slice.

Split the leek in half lengthwise, removing the outside layer. The halves can now be rinsed, releasing any grit caught between the layers. Trim the stalk and green tops, then slice thinly.

Heat half of the butter in a large frying pan. Once hot and bubbling, add the mushrooms and crushed garlic, and fry over a high heat for just a minute or two, to tenderize rather than completely cook through. Season with salt and pepper and drain in a sieve or colander.

Wipe the pan clean and melt the remaining butter. Once bubbling, add the sliced leek and cook, again on a fairly high heat, for a few minutes, until it is approaching a tender stage. Season with salt and pepper and drain in a colander.

OPPOSITE: MUSHROOM AND LEEK EGG BAKED POTS

While the mushrooms and leeks are cooling, place a baking tray in the oven to warm through. Divide half of the cream between six size-1 (150ml/¼ pint) ramekins. Mix together the mushrooms and leeks and divide these between the pots. Sprinkle each with the grated cheese, then crack an egg on top. Season the remaining cream with salt and pepper, and pour over each of the eggs.

Place the pots on the warmed baking tray in the preheated oven and cook for 15 minutes, until golden brown. At this stage the eggs will still be soft, continuing to cook once removed from the oven. For a firmer finish, cook for a further

3–5 minutes. The pots are now ready to serve, eating very well with crusty bread or thick toast.

The finished presentation is very rustic and homely looking; this is certainly not a 'designer' dish. The true focus is purely in the overall finished flavour.
A little olive oil can be drizzled on top before serving; mix this with some chopped mixed herbs for extra taste.

fresh haddock and smoked bacon with celeriac sage fries

Fresh haddock is a member of the cod family. Although not as popular as cod worldwide and quite often ignored, it still remains a favourite on home ground. Right now it's in the middle of its official season, although often found at many other times of the year.

Smoked haddock is very popular, more common on restaurant menus than its fresh counterpart. The bacon is the smoky element here, wrapped around the fish to influence the fresh fish flavour. Streaky smoked is being used; *pancetta* (Italian cured and spiced pork belly) or *prosciutto crudo* (raw cured ham from Parma or San Danielle) can also be used, without the smoky edge, but each offering its own identity.

Celeriac runs through autumn and winter and is usually still around in the spring. Also known as 'turnip-rooted celery', these large knobbly brown tubers do hold a celery flavour but, once cooked, this becomes more akin to the taste of potatoes. When purchasing, it's best to look for the smoothest of skins, providing the minimum of wastage once peeled. For guidance, a 450g (1lb) celeriac will leave approximately 350g (12oz) of peeled vegetable.

SERVES 4

4 × 175g (6oz) fillets of fresh haddock, skinned
salt and pepper
12 rashers of smoked streaky rindless bacon
2 small–medium celeriac
4 tablespoons olive oil
25–50g (1–2oz) butter, plus an extra knob
squeeze of lemon juice
6 sage leaves, neatly chopped

If the haddock fillets are thin and include the tails, these can be folded, placing the pointed tail under the main fillet. Season each with a twist of pepper only.

Bacon rashers can be quite thick; if so, place them between two sheets of cling film and press with a rolling pin to thin them. Place the rashers on a board, overlapping very slightly in threes to form each portion. The haddock fillets can now be placed on top horizontally or vertically, whichever will cover the maximum area of the fish. Fold the rashers over,

pinning them together with one or two cocktail sticks. Refrigerate until needed.

Top and tail the celeriac, cutting away the skin. Cut the vegetables into sticks approximately 1cm (½in) thick, not worrying too much about neatness. These can now be plunged into boiling salted water. Once returned to the boil, cook for a minute or two before draining in a colander and allowing to cool slightly. Dry on a clean cloth. This blanching method cuts into their rawness, which will leave these fries with a softer interior. Heat 2 tablespoons of the olive oil in a large frying pan. Once hot, add the celeriac sticks, frying until golden brown and approaching crispy on all sides. This will take 8–10 minutes.

With the celeriac fries cooking, heat another large frying pan with the remaining olive oil. Once hot, place the wrapped haddock fillets in the pan, presentation-side down, and fry for 5–6 minutes, until the bacon is well coloured and golden. Add a knob of butter, turning the fish, and continue to fry for a further 4–5 minutes; turn off the heat at this point and leave the fish in the pan.

Add a generous squeeze of lemon juice to the celeriac, along with 25g (1oz) butter, shaking it into the juice and cooking oil. This will emulsify quite smoothly; add the extra 25g (1oz) butter for a smoother, richer finish, if preferred. Season with salt and pepper, sprinkling over the chopped sage. Twist the cocktail stick(s) from the haddock, presenting on plates along with the celeriac sage fries.

An alternative finish for the celeriac is to add the butter once they are completely fried, increasing the heat to create a bubbly, nutbrown finish. Squeeze over the lemon juice and sprinkle on the sage, spooning the foaming butter over the fries.

An extra sweet warm twist can be added to this dish by mixing together a dessertspoon each of Dijon mustard and clear honey. This can now be brushed on the presentation side of the haddock fillet, before wrapping in the bacon.

OPPOSITE: FRESH HADDOCK AND SMOKED BACON WITH CELERIAC SAGE FRIES

fried cod with a florence fennel and red onion parmesan bake

Florence fennel is a vegetable that should be taken full advantage of. It has been with us through the summer and continues to hold its own during these slightly colder months of autumn. Its aniseed flavour can be appreciated in two totally different forms – raw, just lifted with a lemon juice (or balsamic vinegar) and olive oil dressing, or cooked until tender, with a more subtle finish that stands alone and works well with both fish and meat. The fish, fennel and red onions are finished here with a baked Parmesan topping – few ingredients, lots of flavour.

SERVES 4

4 (not too big) bulbs of Florence fennel
salt and pepper
4 red onions
25g (1oz) butter, plus more for frying and greasing
6 tablespoons olive oil
1 tablespoon red wine vinegar
75–100g (3–4oz) Parmesan cheese, finely grated
4 × 175g (6oz) portions of cod fillet, pin-boned
(page 9), with skin on
flour, for dusting

Preheat the oven to 200°C/400°F/Gas 6. Cut away the top stalks from the fennel, and trim the base. Any damaged outside layers should also be removed, leaving very attractive, round bulbs. Now quarter each from top to bottom. Cook the fennel in rapidly simmering, salted water, covering with greaseproof paper to ensure each piece stays submerged. Simmer for 12–15 minutes, before removing the fennel pieces and draining in a colander.

Cut each red onion into six wedges, then gently fry in a large knob of butter for a few minutes, until beginning to soften.

In a small bowl, mix together 4 tablespoons of the olive oil and the red wine vinegar. Place the red onions in a separate bowl, season well with salt and pepper, and add the dressing. Leave to stand for 15 minutes, stirring from time to time. Arrange the red onions and fennel (squeezing these gently to release unwanted water), rustic-style, in a greased ovenproof dish, and pour over any remaining dressing. Dot with the measured butter and sprinkle with the Parmesan (the more you use, the richer the finish).

Bake in the preheated oven for 20 minutes until the Parmesan is golden brown. During the baking, fry the cod fillets. Heat the remaining olive oil in a frying pan. Season the cod fillets with salt and pepper, and lightly dust the skin side with flour. Place the fish, skin-side down, in the pan and cook on a medium heat for 8 minutes. At this point, turn the fish, adding a knob of butter, and continue to cook for a further 2 minutes. Remove the pan from the heat and leave the fish to continue cooking for a further 2–3 minutes.

The fish can now be presented on plates, each drizzled with any butter from the pan. Offer the Parmesan-baked fennel and red onion at the table with the fish.

Almost any other fish, including sea bass, turbot, skate or salmon, will eat well with the fennel and red onions. A wedge of lemon is a simple and perfect accompaniment for this dish.

pan-fried and roasted skate wings with a sweetcorn, caper and lemon parsley butter

Skate is more or less available throughout the year, but always seems to be in abundance during our autumn and winter months. This is a fish that needs to be fresh, before the renowned ammonia odour sets in, spoiling its flavour. However, if you try to eat skate fresh from the boat, its flesh will still have quite a tough texture. It needs 24–48 hours to relax and be ready for cooking, but the maximum age out of the water you should ever consider cooking this fish is 5–6 days. It is purely the wings that are sold, and these are mostly to be found ready-skinned. If purchased with the skin left on, I'd suggest cooking the fish in this way, as the skin becomes easily removable once cooked.

Sweetcorn appears on grocers' shelves in late summer and early autumn. August and September are its biggest months, with home-grown lasting into October. This very popular vegetable can work with so many flavours, such as those included here. The sweet yellow kernels help along the classic combination of capers, lemon and parsley with the skate.

4 skate wings, approximately 275g (10oz), skinned
salt and pepper
flour, for dusting
2 tablespoons olive oil
50g (2oz) butter, chopped, plus a large knob and more
  for greasing
2 sweetcorn cobs, husks removed
juice of 1 lemon
1 tablespoon small capers, roughly chopped if large
1 tablespoon torn flatleaf parsley

Preheat the oven to 200°C/400°F/Gas 6. Season the skate wings with salt and pepper and then lightly flour them, tapping away any excess.

Heat 1 tablespoon of the olive oil in a large frying pan. Once hot, place 2 of the skate wings in the pan and fry for 5 minutes until golden brown. Turn the wings and cook for a further minute, then transfer to a large greased roasting tray. Repeat the same process with the remaining fish. You may find the wings will need to be fried one at a time, depending on size. Brush each wing with a little butter and roast in the hot oven for 12 minutes.

While the fish roasts, prepare the sweetcorn. Hold the corn upright on a chopping board and, using a sharp knife, slice down against the cob, to release the kernels. Turn the cob and repeat this process until all the kernels have been removed.

Cook the corn kernels in boiling water (without salt as this tends to toughen the corn) for 5–6 minutes until tender. Drain and keep to one side.

To finish the dish, remove the skate wings from the roasting tray and transfer them to hot plates. Place the tray on top of the stove and heat to lift all of the juices. Add 4 tablespoons of water and the lemon juice. Bring quickly to the boil, stirring in the 50g (2oz) of butter. Strain these pan juices through a sieve or leave as they are for rustic style. Add the capers, parsley and a couple of handfuls of the sweetcorn (any extra can be offered separately). Season with salt and pepper, spooning this collection of flavours over the wings. The skate is now ready to serve.

The sweetcorn can be cooked in advance still on the cob.
Boil in water for 15 minutes, then remove and leave to cool.
The kernels can then be released by just easing them out
with a fork.

steamed courgette-scaled brill with a cherry tomato, black olive and tarragon compote

This is a dish of clearly very seasonal ingredients. The flat brill is now ready to eat, with the courgettes, cherry tomatoes and tarragon following suit. Its whole appearance supplies you with provincial French and Italian thoughts, totally unembellished, yet with distinctive home-grown flavours.

The preparation is also unfussy, another reason to appreciate the value of this dish.

4 medium courgettes
salt and pepper
butter, for greasing
4 × 175g (6oz) brill fillets, skinned
2 tablespoons olive oil
450g (1lb) cherry tomatoes, halved
½ teaspoon light soft brown sugar
2 tablespoons extra virgin olive oil
2 teaspoons red wine vinegar
2 teaspoons sherry vinegar
12 quality black olives, stoned and quartered
16–20 tarragon leaves
sea salt (optional)

Wash the courgettes well, wiping to remove any soft bristles. Top and tail, slicing them into very thin rounds about 1–2mm (1⁄16in) thick. This can be made easy using a mandolin slicer.

Put the courgettes in a colander and lightly toss in a good sprinkling of salt. These can now be left to drain of their excess water for 30 minutes, leaving the slices more pliable. Once drained, dry the slices on kitchen paper.

Preheat the oven to 200°C/400°F/Gas 6. Grease a reasonably deep baking tray. Season the brill fillets with salt and pepper, placing them on the tray. Arrange the courgette slices over each fillet, to resemble overlapping scales. Pour 6 tablespoons of water in the tray and bring to a simmer on top of the stove. Cover with foil (this will trap the steam), not allowing the foil to touch the courgettes, and place in the preheated oven, steaming for 5–7 minutes until just cooked.

Once the fish is in the oven, heat the 2 tablespoons of olive oil in a large frying pan. Once hot, place the tomatoes in the pan, cut-side down, sprinkling over the sugar and frying for a minute before turning each with a palette knife.

Continue to cook for a further minute.

In a bowl, mix the extra virgin olive oil and two vinegars, adding the cut black olives. This can now be poured over the tomatoes, allowing the olives to just warm through. Season with salt and pepper. Tear the tarragon leaves, sprinkling them over the warm compote.

Divide the tomatoes between four plates, placing a courgette-topped brill fillet on top or next to them.

Any remaining olive oil and juices left in the pan can be spooned over the tomatoes or fish. A small sprinkling of sea salt flakes over the courgettes can also be added, but this is purely an optional extra touch.

brill on the bone with celery, cider and apples

Brill is the understudy to 'the king of all flat fish', turbot. Less expensive to buy, it is no less exciting to eat. This is a fish that will adapt to all cooking methods, whether on or off the bone. It is rare to find one bigger than perhaps 3.5kg (8lb) in weight; for four good-sized portions a 1.5kg (3¼–3½lb) fish will be perfect. This weight takes into account the head and fins still to be removed, and the weight of the bone to be left in the fish.

Celery and apples are readily available during the earliest of the autumn months (having been around throughout summer too). October will offer a wider range of apples, with the early Windsor (quite juicy with a honeyed edge), Egremont Russet (with its famous nutty flavour) and Cox's Orange Pippin (Britain's most popular, also nutty with extra sweetness) all filling the greengrocers' shelves.

The brill is cooked in two stages. Stage one is frying it on one side only; stage two is poach-baking on top of the celery and cider in the oven. The fish takes on the cider flavour, releasing some of its juices into the alcohol, to create a stock with which to finish the lightly creamed liquor.

SERVES 4 AS A MAIN COURSE
6 celery sticks
25g (1oz) butter
2 tablespoons groundnut oil
**1 × 1.5kg (3¼–3½lb) brill, dark side skinned,
  head removed, trimmed of fins and tail and
  cut into 4 portions**
flour, for dusting
salt and pepper

200ml (7fl oz) cider
3 apples, peeled (red apples need not be peeled)
sprinkling of caster sugar
1–2 tablespoons calvados (optional)
2–3 tablespoons crème fraîche
**1 heaped teaspoon torn flatleaf parsley or tarragon
  (optional)**

Preheat the oven to 190°C/375°F/Gas 5. Wash the celery sticks, pulling away the stringy fibres attached (or simply peeling) for a more tender finish. Cut the sticks into 5mm–1cm (¼–½in) dice. Melt half of the butter in a large shallow ovenproof pan and add the celery. Cook over a gentle heat for a few minutes until the pieces are just beginning to soften.

In a separate frying pan, heat the groundnut oil. Lightly dust the skin side of the brill steaks with flour and season with salt. Place the fish in the hot oil, skin-side down, and fry over a moderate heat for about 5 minutes, until golden brown. Season the skinned side of the fish with salt and pepper while still in the pan, then place the steaks on top of the celery, fried-side up.

Pour the cider into the pan around the celery and bring to a simmer, then place in the preheated oven, and bake for 8–10 minutes, until the fish is cooked through.

While the fish is cooking, cut each of the apples into eight wedges, removing the central core from each piece. Melt the remaining butter in a non-stick frying pan. Once bubbling, fry the pieces of apple quickly to a golden brown, turning each and repeating the same process on the other side. This will take just a minute or two, as Russet apples in particular soften very quickly. Once coloured on both sides, sprinkle with a little caster sugar and baste with the butter to give a slightly caramelized finish. If using, the calvados can now be added, and reduced until dry. Keep warm to one side.

Remove the brill steaks from the pan and keep warm. Bring the cider and celery to the boil, allowing the cider to reduce in volume by half to two-thirds. Stir in 2 tablespoons of the crème fraîche – for a silkier, creamier finish add the remaining tablespoon. Season with salt and pepper. The torn parsley or tarragon leaves can now also be added, if using.

Divide the baked brill between four plates, fried-side up, along with the creamy cider celery. Garnish each with five or six apple wedges and the dish is complete.

OPPOSITE: BRILL ON THE BONE WITH
CELERY, CIDER AND APPLES

dover sole meunière with garlic mousseron mushrooms and courgettes

Dover sole has a texture that is unique amongst flat fish. At times I've even found it to be too tough, if caught and cooked on the same day. The flesh needs a relaxing period, making way for a quite heavenly flavour and feel. Two to three days since the fish last swam is about perfect.

During early autumn all the three main ingredients of this dish are around, home-grown courgettes slowly coming to the end of their season, with the small mousseron mushrooms in the same situation.

The mousseron has quite a rich, strong flavour for such a small mushroom. Should you find it unavailable, a straightforward button mushroom can be used, or towards October you could try many more of the wild mushroom varieties, with chanterelles, *trompettes-de-la-mort* and ceps in abundance.

This must be one of the simplest recipes in the book – pan-fried sole with quickly sautéed courgettes, garlic, wild mushrooms and a squeeze of lemon.

SERVES 2

2 × 450–675g (1–1½lb) Dover soles, heads and dark skin removed
100g (4oz) mousseron mushrooms
1 large or 2 small courgettes, cut into 5mm (¼in) dice
salt and pepper
flour, for dusting
2 tablespoons olive oil
40g (1½oz) butter, plus a large knob and more for greasing
1 lemon
1 large garlic clove, finely crushed (2 cloves for garlic lovers)

With any flat fish, I like to keep on the white skin. This can become almost crispy, and it also protects the flesh, keeping it moist during cooking. To remove the dark skin, simply make a cut at the tail and scrape a little of the skin away. Once enough is free to get a grip on, pull it towards the head. This skin will come away cleanly. The white skin must be scraped clean of all scales. Cut away the side fins and trim the tail. The head can now also be cut away if it hasn't already been removed. Any roe sitting in the fish can easily be pushed towards the head and pulled away. Now just wash away any blood lying along the main bone and the fish is ready to cook.

The mousseron mushrooms are sometimes found without stalks; if so, simply wipe clean with a damp cloth or rinse quickly in cold water, then dry on a kitchen cloth.

The courgettes can be fried from raw, but to speed up their cooking process it is best to blanch the diced vegetables quickly in boiling salted water. As soon as the water returns to the boil, drain in a colander and allow to cool naturally. This enriches their green skin colour, leaving a deeper finish.

To fry the soles, lightly flour the white skin side of the fish and season with salt only. Heat the olive oil in a large frying pan (or two smaller pans). Place the fish in the pan, floured-side down, and fry for 5–6 minutes, until golden brown. Add the knob of butter, season the flesh side of the fish with salt and pepper and turn them over in the pan. Continue to fry for a further 5 minutes, basting the fish with butter from the pan. Finish with a squeeze of lemon juice from half of the lemon.

To grill, butter a baking tray and season with salt and pepper. Lay the soles, skin-side up, on the tray, buttering their presentation side and seasoning with salt only. Place under a preheated grill and cook for 8–10 minutes until golden brown. Finish with lemon juice as above.

When there is just a minute or two left of cooking time for the fish, fry the mushrooms and courgettes. Melt the measured butter in a frying pan. Once bubbling, add the courgettes and fry on a reasonably high heat, allowing them to take on a little colour. Add the mushrooms and garlic and continue to fry for a further 30–60 seconds.

At this point the cooked soles should be presented on hot plates. Season the mushrooms and courgettes with salt and pepper. When just approaching the nutbrown stage, sizzling vigorously, squeeze the remaining lemon juice into the butter and spoon over the Dover soles.

Chopped parsley and tarragon, a mixed teaspoon of the two, can be added to the butter with the lemon juice at the last moment.
I've kept the recipe for just two portions, but it can be doubled, though I would then suggest grilling rather than trying to fry four fish.

natural steamed mussels
with a piquant spread

September is the month to dream of small blue-black shells opening to reveal yellowy-orange, plump, steaming mussels. It's now that they'll begin to land on the fishmonger's marble, each year presenting themselves cleaner, and more barnacle-and beard-free, as the purification techniques of production move on. However cleanly they're presented, though, it's still best to give them a complete recheck, scraping off the barnacles and pulling the beards, with at least two good rinses.

Nothing's going to be added to this potful, just a drop of water and their naturally released juices to cook them.

The piquant spread is really a salsa. *Salsa* is Mexican for sauce (the same word is used in other Spanish dialects); in Italian it is *salse*. The combinations for salsas are almost unlimited, with red, yellow and green salsas all finding their way into a cookery book somewhere. With the recipe below, changes can easily be made. The red wine vinegar can be replaced with white wine vinegar, or omitted, doubling the lemon juice. Half the capers (or all) can be exchanged for chopped gherkins. Breadcrumbs are not essential, but make a thicker spread. A generous handful of basil leaves can join the parsley and mint. Once made, the piquant spread can be kept refrigerated for a few days.

SERVES 4

1kg (2¼lb) fresh mussels

FOR THE SPREAD

50g (2oz) stale white breadcrumbs
generous bunch of flatleaf parsley, picked
handful of mint leaves
1 large garlic clove, crushed
5 tinned anchovy fillets, roughly chopped
1 heaped teaspoon Dijon mustard
1 teaspoon caster sugar
1 tablespoon red wine vinegar
2 heaped tablespoons capers, drained and rinsed
**125–150ml (4fl oz–¼ pint) olive oil (preferably with a
   fruity flavour)**
1 tablespoon lemon juice
salt and pepper

To make the piquant spread, moisten the breadcrumbs with a few tablespoons of water and allow to stand for 2–3 minutes. Squeeze the moisture from the crumbs, putting them into a food processor. Add all of the remaining ingredients, except for the olive oil, lemon juice and seasoning. Blitz to a smooth purée, scraping down the sides from time to time. Once smooth, continue to blitz, slowly adding the first 125ml (4fl oz) olive oil. If too thick, the remaining 25ml (1fl oz) can be added. Finish with the lemon juice, a twist of pepper and a pinch of salt, if needed.

Scrape and pick the mussels of any barnacles and beards, washing at least twice to remove any grit. Discard any that do not close when tapped.

Heat 150ml (¼ pint) of water in a large saucepan. Once boiling, add the drained mussels, covering with a lid. Cook on a fairly high heat, shaking the pan now and again, or spooning around to ensure an even cooking. The mussels will take just 3–4 minutes, 5 minutes maximum, until opened and ready to spoon into a large suitable dish, pouring over the liquor left in the pan. Discard any that refuse to open after this time. The steaming hot mussels are now ready to be served, eating each with a touch of the piquant spread to enhance their natural flavour.

roast walnut chicken with cider, apples, onions and thyme courgettes

The title of this recipe has a real wintry feel. This dish is quite simple, however, without over-rich gravies, roast potatoes and lots of veg. In early autumn, courgettes are still sublime, and should be totally taken advantage of. Here they're just sautéed and then rolled in thyme with a knob of butter. You may also be lucky with early British walnuts and apples in September.

SERVES 4

65g (2½oz) walnut halves, preferably skinned
75g (3oz) butter, plus 3 extra knobs for the onions,
  apples and courgettes
2 teaspoons brandy (optional)
salt and pepper
pinch of freshly grated nutmeg
1 × 1.75kg (4lb) free-range chicken
vegetable or groundnut oil, for brushing
3 onions, sliced
450g (1lb) apples
300ml (½ pint) dry cider
550g (1¼lb) courgettes
1 tablespoon oil, preferably walnut
1 teaspoon picked thyme
1 tablespoon chopped flatleaf parsley (optional)

Chop the walnuts reasonably finely, leaving just a slight rustic edge. Mix the nuts with the butter and brandy, if using, and season with salt, pepper and a pinch of nutmeg.

Carefully lift and release the skin from the chicken breasts at the neck end of the bird, by pushing your fingers between the skin and the breasts, creating enough space to cover the breasts entirely with the butter. Spoon and spread the walnut butter over the breasts under the skin, saving 25g (1oz) for later. Fold the skin back under the neck and secure with a cocktail stick. The chicken can now be refrigerated for 20–30 minutes, allowing the butter to firm.

Preheat the oven to 200°C/400°F/Gas 6. Place the chicken in a roasting tray, brush with oil and season with salt and pepper. Put the tray in the preheated oven and roast the chicken for 1 hour–1 hour 10 minutes, until golden brown.

During the roasting, butter will be released from the bird; this can be used for basting every 15 minutes, helping to colour the chicken. Once cooked, remove from the oven and leave to rest for 10–15 minutes.

During the last 15–20 minutes of roasting time, fry the onions in a knob of butter. While the onions are frying, peel, quarter and core the apples. When the onions are well coloured, remove them from the pan. Add another knob of butter to the pan and fry the apple quarters on a fairly high heat for just a few minutes, allowing them to colour. At this point, return the onions to the pan, adding the cider and 150ml (¼ pint) of water. Bring to the boil and reduce in volume by half. Reduce the heat to a simmer, cover with a lid or foil, and cook for 15 minutes.

Meanwhile, cook the courgettes. If using young and small courgettes, just wash and cut into 1cm (½in) thick slices at a slight angle. If large, split lengthwise into halves or quarters, then cut in the same way. These can now be blanched for 30 seconds in boiling salted water, and then drained in a colander. Warm the walnut or other oil in a large frying pan. Add the courgettes and fry well for 5–6 minutes, until tender and with a golden edge. Add a knob of butter and the thyme, and season with salt and pepper.

When the apples are tender, carefully strain the onions and apples from the cider stock, keeping them to one side. Boil the liquor to reduce it in volume, if necessary, for a stronger flavour. Add the remaining walnut butter, whisking it in well, and add the chopped parsley, if using.

Carve the chicken, offering a thigh or drumstick and half a breast per portion. Divide the soft onions and apples between the plates, top with the chicken pieces and spoon the sauce around. Serve the courgettes separately.

If skinning the walnuts, simply boil in water for 3 minutes. Remove the pan from the stove, leave them in the water and, taking one out at a time, scrape them while still warm. This leaves you with a less bitter and more tender component to the dish.
When pre-blanching the courgettes, it is best simply to drain and not refresh in iced water. Any extra moisture will steam off, leaving them dry to fry.

OPPOSITE: ROAST WALNUT CHICKEN WITH CIDER, APPLES, ONIONS AND THYME COURGETTES

It's in this month that the first home-grown parsnips will be pulled from our soil. These should not be too big, allowing them to be roasted whole. If only large are available, however, just split them lengthwise. As for the potatoes, I suggest Desirée, part of the main crop so also available right now.

Damsons should need little introduction – they are one of our wild hedge-grown berries that are also commercially available. The deep blue-black skins cover quite a strong and tart fruit that eats better cooked than raw, leaving a sweet spicy finish, ideal for wild duck.

SERVES 4

4 Desirée potatoes, washed but unpeeled
8 small–medium parsnips (12 if particularly small)
3 tablespoons olive oil
salt and pepper, plus sea salt flakes
freshly grated nutmeg
2 wild duck
large knob of butter, softened
1 tablespoon chopped curly parsley (optional)

FOR THE DAMSON SAUCE

300g (10½oz) damsons, washed
knob of butter
2 shallots, finely chopped
150ml (¼ pint) sweet sherry
1 tablespoon redcurrant jelly

Preheat the oven 200°C/400°F/Gas 6. Halve the potatoes lengthways, dividing each half into three wedges. Peel the parsnips; these can be left whole or split in two, depending on their size. Dry the potatoes and parsnips before putting them in a large roasting tray. Add the olive oil, shaking the pan so they are all well coated. Season with a teaspoon of scattered sea salt flakes and a generous grating of fresh nutmeg. The pan can now be placed towards the bottom of the oven, leaving plenty of space for the wild duck rack. Roast for 30 minutes.

While roasting the potatoes and parsnips, score the wild duck breasts with the point of a sharp knife, just slitting the skin. This can be done in long strips lengthwise, approximately 1cm (½in) apart or in thinner strips, scoring from the breast bone on both sides in downward strokes. Brush the birds with the softened butter. Season the cavity with salt and pepper, followed by the breasts.

To make the sauce, cut the damsons in half, removing the stones. This job is a bit of a chore but is worth it. Now roughly chop the fruits. Melt the butter in a saucepan, adding the chopped shallots. Cover and cook over a low heat for 6–7 minutes until tender but without colour. Add the damsons, sherry and redcurrant jelly. Once gently simmering, cook for 15 minutes until the damsons have become tender. This can be left as a rustic chunky sauce or liquidized before pushing through a sieve for a smooth finish. If too thin, bring back to a simmer and allow to cook to a more light syrup consistency. Season with salt and pepper.

When the potatoes and parsnips have roasted for 30 minutes, put the wild ducks on the oven rack and place in the oven above the roasting tray. Increase the oven temperature to 230°C/450°F/Gas 8, roasting the birds for 20 minutes for rare, towards 30 minutes for a definite medium; overcooked wild duck, unless braised, can become tough, so do not cook for longer than this.

During the cooking time, fat and juices will have collected in the pan below, flavouring the vegetables. Remove the ducks and vegetables from the oven and leave to rest for 10 minutes before carving, serving a leg and breast per portion.

Spoon the parsnips and potatoes around in the pan, absorbing all the juices, before presenting in a serving dish, finished with the chopped parsley, if using.

The damson sauce can be offered separately, in a sauceboat.

The damson sauce can be made several hours in advance, rewarming when ready to serve the complete dish.
When roasting wild duck (or domestic), flavourings can be placed in the cavity, such as orange or lemon wedges, sprigs of herbs (rosemary, thyme), onions or juniper berries. These flavours add their own strength to the ducks. The damson sauce can also take on one or two influences, adding a small nugget of ginger (removing it once the sauce is cooked), strips of orange or lemon rind or even a small, finely chopped chilli.

OPPOSITE: ROAST WILD DUCK OVER PARSNIPS AND POTATOES WITH A DAMSON SAUCE

September is a great month for avid collectors, avid eaters – and avid chefs! This is when wild mushrooms are seriously hitting the scene. It is on the continent that the enthusiasm for these fungal wonders of nature is most apparent, while in this country we seem always to have been afraid of picking and collecting ('maybe they're all toadstools?').

The cep (*Boletus edulis*) is the prime wild mushroom – *cèpe* to the French and *porcino* ('little pig') to the Italians. Its round shiny cap looks like the Victorian penny bun, but it will now cost rather more than that (unless you find it for free, of course). They form near trees, in clearings in the woods, and around the edges of woods. They eat like a dream, also drying very well for later use.

Available now too is the chanterelle, which is also known as girolle (*Cantharellus cibarius*). They are quite often thought to be exactly the same, but are actually different strains of the same species. The girolle is found between the

months of May and June, sometimes lasting into July. The chanterelle is available between midsummer and autumn. And of course in the autumn you also find (although, sadly, not in Britain) the black Périgord and the white Alba truffle.

But we must not forget about the other season, which follows on from the prime one of autumn. The morel (*Morchella esculenta*) appears in spring, although it is fairly uncommon in Britain. I love cooking with this, and it also dries very well. And we can also find the St George's mushroom (*Tricholoma gambosum*), named because it appears traditionally on the English patron saint's day, 23 April (although it is actually better a week or so later). This small white mushroom grows on road verges and the edges of woods and pastureland, sometimes in 'fairy rings', and has a particularly good texture when cooked.

fricassee of rabbit with a creamed lentil sauce and wild mushrooms

A fricassee is a stew that begins its cooking process by sautéing the main ingredient in butter, before casseroling it gently in stock. Here lentils are also added to give another flavour, as well as to act as the thickening agent to help produce the finished creamy consistency.

Wild or farmed rabbit can be used in this dish. Wild rabbits, available in the early autumn, have a stronger, more gamey flavour than the farmed. However, they are also tougher, and need a longer stewing time. The farmed rabbits have less depth of flavour, but do tend to cook far more easily, with more of an appealing and recognizable flavour. It is best to buy two small rabbits, offering three pieces per portion. With this, everybody is served a leg, shoulder and piece of saddle.

The obvious seasonal touch is to be found in the wild mushrooms. Here a selection has been listed, but not all are essential; just one variety will be more than enough.

SERVES 4

225g (8oz) mixed wild mushrooms, e.g. chanterelles, *trompettes-de-la mort*, ceps, oyster mushrooms, cleaned (page 423)
2 small rabbits, each cut into 6 pieces
salt and pepper
2 tablespoons groundnut oil
large knob of butter, plus an extra knob

2 shallots, or 1 onion, finely chopped
300ml (½ pint) white wine
generous sprigs of thyme, rosemary and sage, plus a few extra sage leaves for chopping or shredding
450ml (¾ pint) *Chicken stock* (page 416) or *Instant stock* (page 416)
50g (2oz) Puy lentils, rinsed
100–150ml (3½fl oz–¼ pint) double or whipping cream (optional)
squeeze of lemon juice (optional)

Once all the mushrooms have been cleaned, cut or tear into similar-sized pieces.

Season the rabbit pieces with salt and pepper. Heat the groundnut oil and a large knob of butter in a large, preferably thick-bottomed saucepan. Once bubbling, add the rabbit pieces, just a few at a time if short of saucepan space, and fry on a fairly gentle heat until golden brown. Remove the rabbit pieces from the pan as they are cooked and keep to one side.

Add the chopped shallots or onion to the pan and cook on a medium heat until softening. Return the rabbit to the pan, add half of the white wine and bring it to a simmer. Baste the rabbit with the wine from time to time, until the wine has reduced in volume by three-quarters. Add the remaining wine and repeat the process.

Add the herbs along with the chosen stock and lentils. Bring the stew to a very gentle simmer, cover with a lid and cook for 50 minutes–1 hour. The rabbit will now be very tender and can be removed from the liquor, along with the herb sprigs, which can be discarded. The sauce can now be liquidized to a purée, straining through a sieve for the smoothest of finishes, if preferred. Return the sauce to the pan, add the cream, if using, and bring back to a simmer. Season with salt and pepper if needed, along with a squeeze of lemon juice to lift its flavour. Return the rabbit to the sauce.

Pan-fry the mushrooms in a knob of butter for just a few minutes until tender and season with salt and pepper. If presenting the rabbit in the cooking pot, add the mushrooms along with the chopped, shredded sage leaves, or spoon each rabbit portion into bowls before sprinkling each with the mushrooms and sage.

Two or three extra sage leaves per portion can be very lightly dusted with plain flour before quickly deep-frying in 2.5cm (1in) of hot vegetable oil to crisp them up.

OPPOSITE: FRICASSEE OF RABBIT WITH A CREAMED LENTIL SAUCE AND WILD MUSHROOMS

foil-baked rabbit and garlic with sea salt and lemon pink fir apples

Here, rabbit legs are baked in foil, absorbing the flavour of the garlic. During this roast and self-steaming process, natural juices are bled, waiting to be dribbled across the tender meats.

Pink Fir Apple potatoes are the long knobbly blushing-pink tubers hiding light yellow flesh that holds a waxy firm texture and nutty flavour. These are impossible to peel, needing just a good scrub. Boiling, roasting, sautéing and serving in salads covers their cooking range – a pretty good repertoire for one that is usually thought of as a boiler only.

Britain's potato seasons are often broken into harvesting categories: first earlies (new), May–July; second earlies (new), August–March; main crop, September–May. Using the Pink Fir Apple here, in its first month of picking, shows it falls into the main-crop bracket.

While the rabbit is baking, the potatoes are going to be sautéed and roasted, finishing with sea salt flakes and lemon zest, splashing with soured cream and chives before serving.

SERVES 4

675g (1½lb) Pink Fir Apple potatoes, well washed
salt and pepper
12 garlic cloves, unpeeled
7–8 tablespoons olive oil, plus more for the garlic
4 large rabbit legs
25g (1oz) butter, plus 1 large knob
4 sprigs of thyme
1 teaspoon sea salt
finely grated zest of 1 lemon
juice of ½ lemon
150ml (¼ pint) soured cream
1 tablespoon finely chopped chives

Preheat the oven to 200°C/400°F/Gas 6. Bring the potatoes to the boil in a large pot of salted water, simmering for 15–20 minutes until just tender. Drain and leave to one side.

Place the garlic in a small ovenproof dish with a drizzle of the olive oil. These can be placed in the oven to begin their cooking while you colour the rabbit legs. Heat a roasting tray on the stove with 2 tablespoons of the oil. Season the legs with salt and pepper, putting them in the tray. Shallow-fry for a few minutes on each side until golden brown.

Lay out a large double sheet of foil, big enough to hold the legs without overcrowding. Grease a central round area with some of the butter. Put the legs top to tail on the greased spot. Remove the garlic cloves from the oven and scatter over and around the legs, topping each leg with a sprig of thyme. Carefully pull up the foil around the edges, forming a border. Drizzle 3–4 tablespoons of water over the legs, along with another 2 tablespoons of olive oil and the remaining measured butter.

Two sides of the foil can now be brought together above the legs, being careful not to pierce the foil. Twist the foil from one side to the other, as if folding and sealing a Cornish pasty.

Place the foil bag in the roasting tray, heating on top of the stove. As the heat conducts, the steam begins inside the bag, creating a 'soufflé' effect, puffing up the bag (this cooking method in buttered foil or paper is known as *en papillote* in French). After a minute or two, the roasting tray can be placed in the oven, baking for 20–25 minutes (it's not essential to preheat on top of the stove; the roasting tray can be placed directly in the oven).

While baking the rabbit, cut the Pink Firs in half, preferably at an angle. Heat the remaining 3–4 tablespoons of olive oil in a roasting tray and, once hot, add the potatoes, coating them well in the oil. Fry over a fairly high heat, colouring well on all sides. Scatter with sea salt flakes and the grated lemon zest. These can now be finished in the oven with the rabbit, needing just 15 or so minutes to help crisp their finish.

Once the rabbit is cooked, remove the tray from the oven, placing to one side to allow the rabbit legs to rest for a few minutes.

Mix half of the lemon juice with the soured cream, along with the chopped chives. Finish the Pink Fir Apples with the knob of butter. Transfer the foil bag onto a large warm serving plate. This can now be cut at the table, releasing the flavours enclosed. The potatoes and the lemon chive soured cream can be offered separately.

Home-grown mangetout peas will still be around; these can be quickly steamed for a couple of minutes and offered as a perfect sweet, crisp vegetable for this dish.

pot-roast hand of pork with cumberland broccoli

Hand of pork is taken from the shoulder and trotter, usually boned and rolled, often found stuffed with a savoury filling. This is an inexpensive cut, with a weight between 2.25 and 3.15kg (5–7lb). I'd suggest angling towards the 2.25kg (5lb), which will feed 6–8 people very comfortably. To achieve the maximum moist tenderness, a long, slow 5 hours of cooking, needing little or no attention, offers best results.

For a finishing touch, there's an optional charcuterie sauce recipe included here. This is a French mustard and gherkin sauce, normally bound with a gravy; this one is purely a creaming of the stock created during the pot-roasting of the pork.

The seasonal touch is from the broccoli; home-grown is still ripe and green, lending this autumn dish a late-summer feel. The Cumberland comes from slices of Cumberland sausage (now sold in 450g/1lb packs), which are first poached with the pork and then shallow-fried in butter with the broccoli. This is an Italian touch, though without the garlic, olives and chilli that's from a favourite dish in that beautiful country.

SERVES 6–8

1 × boned and rolled hand of pork, weighing approximately 2.25kg (5lb)
salt and pepper
450g (1lb) Cumberland sausage
2 tablespoons olive oil
1kg (2¼lb) broccoli, divided into florets
2 shallots or 1 small onion, finely chopped
25g (1oz) butter

FOR THE CHARCUTERIE SAUCE (OPTIONAL)

1 onion, finely chopped
½ teaspoon caster sugar
125ml (4fl oz) white wine vinegar
1–2 teaspoons ready-made English mustard
150ml (¼ pint) double cream
4–5 cocktail gherkins, thinly sliced

Preheat the oven to 160°C/325°F/Gas 3. Season the pork generously with salt. Put the joint skin-side up in a large, deep ovenproof braising dish. Pour 600ml (1 pint) of water into the dish; this will form the base of the stock. Cover and place in the oven, cooking unattended for 2 hours. At this point,

remove the lid and check the quantity of water in the pot. Should it have reduced, top it up to its original volume with more water. The Cumberland sausage can now also be added, poaching it in the stock before shallow-frying later. Its spicy edge also infuses the stock. Return the pot to the oven without a lid, cooking for a further 30 minutes, before removing the sausage and allowing it to cool naturally. Once cold, cut the sausage into 1cm (½in) thick slices.

Continue to pot-roast the joint, increasing the oven temperature to 180°C/350°F/Gas 4. Leave to roast for a further 2½ hours, checking the water level does not reduce in volume by more than half (this is unlikely at this temperature). The pork will continuously supply juices to the pot.

While pot-roasting the pork, if making the charcuterie sauce, put the chopped onion and sugar in a saucepan with the vinegar. Bring to a simmer, cooking until almost dry. Leave to one side.

With the 5 hours complete, remove the pork from the pot and keep warm to one side, allowing to rest for at least 15 minutes. Strain the stock, skimming away excess fat. This liquor can be used as it is to moisten the carved pork.

To make the sauce, add 300ml (½ pint) of the pork stock to the cooked onion. Boil and cook until reduced in volume by a third to a half. Add the mustard and double cream, returning it to a simmer. Sprinkle in the gherkin slices and the sharp, warm sauce is complete.

Heat the olive oil in a large frying pan, adding the sliced sausage. Shallow-fry over a medium heat until golden brown.

While frying the sausage, plunge the broccoli florets in boiling, salted water, cooking for 4–5 minutes until just tender. These can now be strained, adding them to the sausages with the chopped shallots or onion and the butter. Season with salt and pepper.

Once all has been tossed in the pan, the vegetables and rested pork are ready to serve. Remove the string from the pork, slicing it thickly and presenting it with the spicy-flavoured, seasoned broccoli. The sauce or saved meat juices can be spooned over the succulent pork.

A heaped teaspoon of chopped parsley can be added to the sauce.

raspberry rice pudding flan

Fresh raspberries are still with us, the Scottish variety at its absolute best, the soft red berries packed with flavour. This particular fruit should be with us until October, depending on reasonable weather, so this dish has a good two-month autumn life span.

The rice pudding is slightly different from the traditional, as it uses Arborio rice in place of the usual short-grain pudding rice. This does offer a slightly different texture and flavour, the rice being very absorbent, but each little grain maintains its consistency and texture, leaving us with a sweet risotto finish.

This recipe can be made without the tart case, purely offering the fresh raspberries to accompany the warm creamy pudding. However, the pastry case does offer an extra crisp biscuity bite.

SERVES 6–8

large knob of butter, melted, and more for greasing
350g (12oz) *Sweet shortcrust pastry* (page 425)
flour, for dusting
600ml (1 pint) milk
300ml (½ pint) double or whipping cream
1 vanilla pod, split
1 tablespoon finely grated lemon or orange zest
50g (2oz) caster sugar
freshly grated nutmeg
100g (4oz) Arborio rice
225g (8oz) raspberries
icing sugar, for dusting (optional)

Butter a 25cm (10in) flan ring, 4cm (1½in) deep, and place it on a greased baking tray. Roll out the sweet pastry on a lightly floured surface and use to line the flan ring. It is best to leave any excess pastry hanging over the edge; once the tart is cooked, this can be trimmed away, leaving a neat finish. Prick the base of the pastry and chill for 30 minutes. Preheat the oven to 200°C/400°F/Gas 6.

Line the pastry case with greaseproof paper and baking beans or rice, place in the preheated oven and cook for 25 minutes. After this time, remove the beans and paper and return the pastry case to the oven for a further 10–15 minutes to seal the base. Remove from the oven, trim away the excess pastry and leave to cool.

OPPOSITE: RASPBERRY RICE PUDDING FLAN

While the pastry case is baking, make the rice pudding. Pour the milk and cream into a suitably sized saucepan, add the split vanilla pod and bring to the boil. Remove the pan from the stove, add the grated lemon or orange zest, the caster sugar and a generous sprinkling of freshly grated nutmeg. Leave to stand and infuse for 10 minutes.

Add the rice to the flavoured milk, return the pan to the heat and bring to a gentle simmer. Stir the rice and cook for 30–35 minutes, until very tender and creamy. Remove the pan from the heat and take out the vanilla pod from the rice.

Arrange the raspberries in the cooked pastry case and spoon over the rice pudding. Leave to relax for 5–6 minutes, then drizzle with the melted butter, and sprinkle with grated nutmeg. Alternatively, dust liberally with icing sugar and glaze quickly (to a light golden brown) under a preheated hot grill or with a gas gun (page 9), or heat long trussing needles or skewers and press these in lines across the icing-sugar-topped tart. All of these finishes are optional extras, none essential, but all presenting and eating very well. The raspberry rice pudding flan is now ready to serve.

For a lighter finish, the cream can be totally omitted, replacing it with an equal quantity of milk. For a richer alternative, the cream can be increased to 450ml (¾ pint), and the milk reduced to the same quantity.
A tablespoon or two of raspberry jam can be spread across the tart case before the fresh fruits are added.

peach tart and bellini sabayon

In the autumn peaches are just about to leave us, having had a wonderful summer adorning many a plate. At this time of year many of them come from Portugal or France. This recipe follows the principles of a tarte Tatin, a classic French dish made with apples that was created by two French sisters (the Mademoiselles Tatin) from the Loire valley who earned their living making and selling the tarts. It has, in recent years, become fashionable and comes in various fruity forms, many of which work very well – this being one of them. Usually a thick-bottomed Tatin flan dish or copper-based pan is used in which to caramelize the apples. Here I am simply using a 23cm (9in) ovenproof frying pan.

Bellini is a champagne and white peach cocktail. Here, I am using tinned peaches to provide the flavour. This doesn't take long to make and will be ready in plenty of time if started once the tart is in the oven.

SERVES 6–8

6 large peaches
cooking oil
25g (1oz) butter, plus more for brushing
50g (2oz) caster sugar
225g (8oz) *Puff pastry* (page 426, or bought)
flour, for dusting
pouring or whipped double cream, for serving

FOR THE BELLINI SABAYON

1 small tin of peach halves or segments
2 egg yolks
100ml (3½fl oz) champagne (or sparkling wine)
50g (2oz) caster sugar

Halve and stone the peaches, then cut each half into three wedges. Dry these on a cloth or kitchen paper. Heat a little cooking oil in the frying pan (see above). Once hot, quickly colour the peach wedges to a light golden, just searing, then turning and colouring the other sides in the same way. It is best to colour only a few at a time, to maintain the heat and avoid stewing the peaches. Once all are coloured, remove them from the pan and leave to cool.

Place the butter in the frying pan and, once melted, add the caster sugar. Cook on a medium heat until the syrup takes on a rich golden caramel colour. Leave to cool.

On a lightly floured surface, roll the pastry into a circle 2.5cm (1in) larger in diameter than the frying pan. Place on a plate lined with a sheet of greaseproof paper and chill for 20 minutes. Preheat the oven to 220ºC/425ºF/Gas 7.

Place the peaches around the edge of the caramel-filled frying pan, positioning them on their seared sides and slightly overlapping. Once the initial border is complete, the centre can be packed in a more rustic fashion, or continuing in a circular shape. Place the pastry on top of the peaches, pushing any excess inside the pan to enclose the fruits. Prick the pastry with a sharp knife in several places to help release excess steam while baking. Place the tart in the hot oven and cook for 25–30 minutes until crisp.

To make the sabayon, remove the tinned peaches from the syrup and purée in a liquidizer until smooth. Place the egg yolks, champagne or sparkling wine and sugar in a bowl over a pan of rapidly simmering water, making sure the bowl and water are not in contact (this tends to scramble the yolks). Whisk vigorously (an electric hand-whisk can be used) until the sabayon is thick and creamy and almost quadrupled in quantity. At this stage, whisk in the peach purée and the sabayon is ready to serve.

Remove the pan from the oven and leave to rest for 5 minutes. Place a plate slightly bigger than the tart on top of the pan. Hold either side of the plate and pan firmly and turn the two over. Lift the pan from the plate to reveal the caramelized peaches. You may find one or two peaches have moved, or even decided to stay in the pan. If so, don't be concerned: this often happens and all that is needed is a helping hand to rearrange them.

The peach tart and bellini sabayon are now ready to serve, offering pouring or whipped double cream to finish.

Very ripe peaches will release a lot of juices during the baking, so be careful when turning out the tart.
The bellini sabayon also eats well spooned over a bowl of autumn strawberries.

baked plum pudding

Most imported plums are available throughout the year. As far as home-grown are concerned, we have the Victoria, which joins us in mid-to-late summer, reaching its best in early autumn. This particular plum has a sweet, juicy flavour, and can be easily recognized by its red/yellow colour. Another with us at this time is Marjorie's Seedling, a large, blue-black variety, which again has a rich flavour.

This dessert is very simple to make, the plums lightly warmed with the butter and sugar, before being topped with the citrus sponge mix. Once cooked, the plums have softened amongst their own sweet juices, with the baked sponge topping enhancing the lemon and orange flavours. This pudding is best cooked in a 1 litre (1¾ pint) ovenproof clear glass dish, which shows off the bubbling plums sizzling in their own juices.

SERVES 4–6

12 plums, halved and stoned
75g (3oz) caster sugar
knob of butter

FOR THE SPONGE TOPPING
100g (4oz) butter, plus more for brushing
100g (4oz) caster sugar
finely grated zest of 1 small lemon
finely grated zest of 1 small orange
generous pinch of ground cinnamon (optional)
2 eggs, beaten
225g (8oz) self-raising flour, sifted
2 tablespoons milk
1 tablespoon demerara sugar, for sprinkling
pouring cream or *Crème Anglaise* (page 426), to serve

Preheat the oven to 180°C/350°F/Gas 4. The plum halves can be mixed with the sugar and a little water, and baked from raw. I prefer, however, to begin their cooking process gently. I find this helps release their juices and produce maximum flavour. To do so, melt the knob of butter in a large saucepan. Once bubbling, add the plum halves, cut-sides down, and cook on a medium heat for just a few minutes, then add the caster sugar. Continue to cook for just a further minute or two, before adding 4 tablespoons of water. Transfer the plums and juices to the pudding dish and leave to cool.

To make the sponge, beat together the butter and caster sugar until pale and creamy. Add the grated lemon and orange zest, along with the cinnamon, if using. Pour the beaten eggs into the bowl and mix slowly until all are added. Fold in the flour gently, followed by the milk. Alternatively, this mix can be made by placing all the ingredients in a food processor and blitzing to a smooth consistency. Lightly butter the rim of the plum dish, then spoon and spread the sponge mixture on top of the plums and sprinkle with the demerara sugar.

Place the dish on a baking tray and cook in the preheated oven for 55 minutes–1 hour, until the sponge top has become golden brown and crispy. To check the sponge is completely cooked through, pierce with a skewer and leave for 10 seconds before removing. The skewer should come away clean without any uncooked pudding mix attached. If not quite ready, return to the oven and continue to bake for a further 10–15 minutes.

The baked plum pudding is now ready to serve, accompanied by pouring cream or crème Anglaise.

Should the plums be slightly under-ripe, the caster sugar quantity can be increased to 100g (4oz) to compensate. Many other fruits can be cooked beneath the sponge, such as rhubarb, blackberries and apples or pears.

stewed damson yorkies with lashings of sweet cream

Damsons are the small blue-black plums in season from late summer to, in a good year, late autumn. This dessert is a fresh alternative to a classic damson tart – the tender, sweet fruits eat very well with the savoury Yorkshire puddings, with thick cream to finish.

The damsons can be halved, and their large stone cut away with the point of a small knife (alternatively, use an olive stoner, which works providing the fruits are not rock-hard).

The batter is best made in advance, needing a minimum of 1–2 hours to rest before baking, preferably 24 hours.

SERVES 6

150g (5oz) plain flour, sifted
2 eggs, plus 1 extra white
200–300ml (7fl oz–½ pint) milk
vegetable oil, for greasing

FOR THE DAMSONS

1kg (2¼lb) damsons, stoned (see above)
275g (10oz) caster sugar
pinch of ground cinnamon
150–300ml (¼–½ pint) double cream (extra-thick
   is even better)
1–2 heaped tablespoons icing sugar, plus more for
   dusting

Whisk together in a bowl the flour, eggs, egg white and 200ml (7fl oz) of the milk. The consistency should be one that coats the back of a spoon. If too thick, add the remaining milk. The batter can now be left to rest for a minimum of 1 hour (preferably chilled for 24 hours). If only 200ml (7fl oz) of the milk has been added, you may find that, after resting, the batter has congealed and needs the last 100ml (3½fl oz).

Preheat the oven to 220°C/425°F/Gas 7. Oil six individual 10cm (4in) flan tins generously and place them on a baking tray. Preheat in the oven to very hot. Fill each mould with the batter until almost full and bake for 25–30 minutes (if using one large flan tin, 45 minutes–1 hour will be needed). The puddings will have risen, ready for filling with the fruits and serving.

While the Yorkshire puddings are baking, place the stoned damsons, sugar, cinnamon and 4 tablespoons of water in a large saucepan. Cover with a lid and poach over a gentle heat, stirring carefully from time to time, for 12–15 minutes,

until the fruits are tender. If particularly under-ripe, an extra 5–10 minutes may be needed. Should a lot of water and juices have been released, so there is too much syrup and it is too watery, strain the fruits in a colander sitting above a clean saucepan. The syrup can now be simmered rapidly, to reduce it to a coating consistency. Return the fruits to the pan, spooning the syrup over them.

In a bowl, whisk together the preferred quantity of cream and icing sugar and whip until the cream has thickened but is still pourable. Extra-thick cream will not need to be whisked; just spoon sugar through it. Present the Yorkshire puddings in bowls or plates, filling each with the poached damsons and offering the sweet cream to spoon over.

greengage lime cake

The greengage is a member of the plum family, with virtually all of the family – Victoria, Marjorie's Seedling, Excalibur, damsons and more – in season between late July and September.

The greengage lime cake can be enjoyed simply as a nice wedge of cake or, if warmed in the microwave and served with vanilla ice-cream, it stands well as a dessert. Included in the recipe is an optional addition of ginger-syruped crème fraîche, using syrup taken from a jar of stem ginger.

SERVES 8 (MINIMUM)

350g (12oz) self-raising flour
1 teaspoon baking powder
1–2 vanilla pods, split (optional)
4 eggs
225g (8oz) caster sugar
100g (4oz) butter
finely grated zest and juice of 3 limes
8 greengages
icing or caster sugar, for dusting
4 tablespoons ginger syrup, from a jar of
   stem ginger (optional)
300ml (½ pint) crème fraîche (optional)

Preheat the oven to 180°C/350°F/Gas 4. Line the base and sides of a 23cm (9in) loose-bottomed cake tin with buttered parchment paper. Sift together the self-raising flour and baking powder, then scrape the vanilla seeds out of the pods, if using, and add them to the flour, spreading them evenly throughout. Using an electric mixer or electric hand whisk, beat together the eggs and caster sugar until reaching a thick and creamy sabayon stage. Lift the whisk from the mix and, if a thick trail is left, the sabayon is ready. While beating, melt the butter and then leave to cool. Add the lime zest to the flour, then fold it into the whipped eggs and sugar. Stir in the lime juice, along with the melted butter.

Halve and stone the greengages, then cut each half into six wedges. Add two-thirds of the greengages to the cake mix and pour it into the prepared cake tin. Sprinkle with the remainder of the fruits, which will slowly sink into the sponge. Place in the preheated oven and bake for between 1 hour 20 minutes and 1½ hours, until only just cooked through, leaving a slight hint of moistness in the centre.

Remove the cake from the oven and leave to cool for 10 minutes before turning out to stand on a wire rack, then dust it with icing or caster sugar. The cake can now be left to cool completely to enjoy as it is, or served warm as suggested above.

To make the ginger-syruped cream, whip the syrup into the crème fraîche, and offer separately or spoon over each slice of cake.

A very sticky topping can be achieved by mixing 3–4 heaped tablespoons of Greengage jam *(page 428) with 4–6 tablespoons of water. Warm the two together until a syrupy consistency is reached. This can now be brushed or rustically drizzled over the cake, allowing a little to trickle down the sides.*

sloe gin

Sloes are a type of wild plum, the fruit of the blackthorn, which is native to Britain, found in hedges and scrubby woodland, and now growing wild throughout Europe. The small berries, with their blue-black skins, very much resemble the plum in a tiny form. Beneath the skin lies a greenish juicy flesh, so tart and sour that, as a raw fruit, it is quite inedible. Picking them through autumn provides the perfect opportunity to prepare sloe gin, having it ready for the festive Christmas to follow. However, some do recommend that the fruits not be picked until after the first frost. This damages the skin, so the flesh is slightly bursting through to release a sweeter flavour. Having said that, many a purist believes the natural flavour is all that becomes damaged.

Gin itself is a fairly young alcohol, it being just a couple of hundred years since it first appeared on our shelves. Initially produced as quite a raw neat alcohol, 'distilled gin' developed later and is made by macerating juniper berries, citrus peels and other botanicals (bitter almonds are also sometimes added) in neutral spirit and distilling it in a pot still.

Sloe gin is a traditional English liqueur; its antiquity is not really known, but country folk over many centuries have used berries as flavourings for spirits. It is a deep, clear red, holding a rich, slightly bitter plum flavour, a pleasure to appreciate.

MAKES APPROXIMATELY 600ML (1 PINT)
600ml (1 pint) gin
225g (8oz) sloes
100g (4oz) caster sugar

Wash the sloes well, pricking them all over with a skewer if not pre-frosted (see above). Place the fruits in a clean bottle (preferably sterilized, see page 9), adding the sugar and gin. This can now be sealed and left to infuse and mature for a minimum of 3 months, shaking the bottle 3–4 times a week, to help to release more flavour.

As mentioned in the introduction, bitter almonds are sometimes added to distilled gin for an extra flavour. To imitate this, simply add a few drops of almond essence at the beginning of the infusing process.
For a slightly sweeter finish, an extra 50g (2oz) sugar can be added when making the sloe gin.

blackberry eton mess with cider apples

'Eton mess' obviously takes its name from the public school, where the dessert was created to celebrate King George III's birthday, the 'mess' simply describing how it is presented. Eton mess has assumed many guises over the years with ice-cream, soft cream cheese, lots of fruits and different styles of meringues all playing a part. I prefer using meringue, cream and fruit – this is probably the simplest variation, which can so often be the best.

The berries normally chosen are strawberries or raspberries; here it is a summer/autumn cousin of the two, the blackberry. Blackberries do not normally appear until August, running through to October. The apples to use for the most perfect of flavours are Discovery, Katy or Spartan. All three are red-skinned, with a touch of strawberry within their crisp, slightly acidic juiciness.

SERVES 4–6
FOR THE MERINGUES
2 egg whites
100g (4oz) caster sugar

FOR THE CIDER APPLES
150ml (¼ pint) sweet cider
50g (2oz) sugar
3 apples, preferably Discovery, Katy or Spartan

350g (12oz) blackberries (slightly over-ripe if possible)
50g (2oz) caster sugar
1 vanilla pod, split, or a few drops of vanilla extract
   (optional)
300ml (½ pint) double or whipping cream

Preheat the oven to 120°C/250°F/Gas ½. First make the meringues. Using a scrupulously clean bowl and whisk (an electric hand whisk or mixer will offer the best results), beat the egg whites until very stiff. Add half of the caster sugar and continue to beat until smooth and thickened. Add the remaining sugar and continue to whisk to stiff peaks. Spoon the meringue in small dollops onto a baking tray lined with parchment paper, not worrying about shape or quantity, as these will be broken to mix with the blackberry cream. Bake the meringues in the preheated oven for 2 hours, then switch the oven off and leave the meringues in it for 30 minutes while it cools.

While the meringues are baking, prepare the apples. First, bring the cider and sugar to the boil. Peel and quarter the apples, removing the core. Cut the quarters in half, providing eight wedges per apple. Place these in the cider and bring back to a simmer. Cook for 1–2 minutes, until the apples are tender. Remove from the cider and keep to one side. Boil the syrup until reduced in volume by a third to a half, giving a syrupy consistency. Leave to cool.

To make the blackberry cream, place the blackberries and caster sugar in a saucepan and lightly warm over a gentle heat to soften the berries. Should the sugar begin to caramelize, loosen it with a tablespoon or two of water. Once the blackberries are tender but not completely broken down, remove the pan from the heat. Lightly crush the fruits with a fork, keeping a rough texture throughout. Leave to cool.

Break the cooked meringues into pieces; if not completely dry throughout, this will provide a toffee-like cream. If using, scrape the inside of the vanilla pod into the cream, or add the vanilla extract, and whip to soft peaks. Three-quarters of the forked blackberries can now be spooned in, and the remainder saved to trickle around. Fold the broken meringues into the blackberry cream, also saving a spoonful or two for sprinkling over.

To serve, divide the apple wedges between the plates, and spoon the blackberry meringue cream on top. Sprinkle with the reserved meringue and trickle the reserved forked blackberries and the cider syrup over or around. The Eton mess is ready to serve.

A few of the softened blackberries can be left whole as a garnish.

OPPOSITE: BLACKBERRY ETON MESS
WITH CIDER APPLES

vegetables

fish

meat

fruit and puddings

roast carrot and parsnip salad with soured cream, beetroot and walnut vinaigrette

This salad is a wonderful mid-autumn and winter starter. Endless varieties of root vegetables can be added, with turnips, celeriac and swedes amongst them. Here, I'm sticking to just three – two root vegetables with beetroot to add its natural piquancy. The carrots and parsnips are just quartered lengthwise and roasted to a succulent finish with a slight caramelized edge. The creamy beetroot-rippled vinaigrette stands alongside to enhance the dish.

Between the months of September and October, walnuts are at their ripest and best. It is important that fresh walnuts are eaten as soon as possible after buying to prevent their natural oils from becoming rancid, and for them to offer the finest of nutty flavours.

At this time of the year a lot of imported lettuces fill the shelves, but the home-grown will still provide rocket, curly endive, lamb's lettuce (corn salad/mâche), mizuna and oakleaf.

SERVES 4 AS A STARTER
2 medium beetroots

salt and pepper

4 medium carrots

4 medium parsnips

2 tablespoons olive or cooking oil

6 fresh walnuts, shelled

100g (4oz) mixed salad leaves (see above)

FOR THE VINAIGRETTE
1 heaped teaspoon Dijon mustard

100ml (3½fl oz) soured cream

2 tablespoons sherry vinegar or red wine vinegar

100ml (3½fl oz) walnut oil, plus more for drizzling
  (optional)

Preheat the oven to 200°C/400°F/Gas 6. Trim the stalks from the beetroots, not cutting into the root, as this tends to release the natural juices. To cook, place the beetroots in a small saucepan, cover with cold water and add a pinch of salt. Bring to a rapid simmer and cook for 50 minutes–1 hour, until tender. Drain and leave to cool slightly, before peeling.

OPPOSITE: ROAST CARROT AND PARSNIP SALAD WITH SOURED CREAM, BEETROOT AND WALNUT VINAIGRETTE

While the beetroots are cooking, peel the carrots and parsnips, trim away the top stalk and quarter lengthwise, to produce sharp sticks. The central core of the parsnips can also be trimmed away, should they appear to be woody. The vegetables can be roasted from absolutely raw, but I often find a short blanching produces a creamier centre. To do so, plunge the carrots into boiling salted water. After 2 minutes add the parsnips and cook for a further 2 minutes. At this point, spoon the carrots and parsnips on to a cloth or kitchen paper, and leave to cool. The vegetables will still be very firm, but with their rawness removed.

Preheat a roasting tray on top of the stove, adding the olive or cooking oil. Add the carrots and parsnips and fry on all sides until well coloured. Season with salt and pepper. Place the roasting tray in the preheated oven and cook for 15–20 minutes, turning the vegetables from time to time, until they are becoming crispy. Remove the vegetables from the oven and season with salt and pepper. These are going to be best served very warm, rather than piping hot.

While the carrots and parsnips are roasting, cut the beetroots into 5mm (¼in) dice or grate coarsely.

To make the dressing, whisk together the mustard, soured cream and vinegar. The oil can now be trickled in as you whisk, allowing it to emulsify with the cream. Should the dressing be too thick, simply loosen with a little water. Season with salt and pepper. You may only need half to two-thirds of the dressing; any left over can be kept in the fridge for several days to be used with other salads.

Once the beetroot is diced, mix half with the dressing and this will create a pink, rippled effect. If the beetroot is grated, any juices can be added to the dressing, also providing a suitable rippled effect.

Arrange the carrots and parsnips in a rustic fashion on four serving plates, sprinkling with the remaining diced beetroots. If using grated beetroots, simply divide between the plates, spooning a base on which to place the vegetables. Break the walnut halves into pieces and mix them with the salad leaves, then drizzle with extra walnut oil, if liked. Season with salt and pepper and sprinkle on top of the carrots and parsnips. Spoon over and around with the beetroot and soured cream dressing to finish.

A teaspoon of dark soft brown sugar and a knob of butter can be added to the vegetables 10 minutes before they have finished cooking. This will leave a slight bitter-sweet edge to the roasted flavour.

savoury sweetcorn custard tarts with an apple and walnut dressing

Sweetcorn is with us between August and September, leading into this month of October.

This recipe is for six individual tartlets, but one 20cm (8in) flan ring can be used (it must be at least 2cm/⅞in deep). Virtually all the tart ingredients featured here can be placed in the tart case, together with one or two others, like the red onion and chives from the dressing, creating a seasonal sweetcorn quiche as an alternative.

SERVES 6

butter, for greasing
350g (12oz) *Quick puff pastry* (page 426) or *Shortcrust pastry* (page 425), or 225g (8oz) for one large flan
flour, for dusting
2 sweetcorn cobs, husks removed
2 eggs, plus 1 extra yolk
175ml (6fl oz) double or whipping cream
salt and black pepper

FOR THE DRESSING

2 apples, preferably Russets
squeeze of lemon juice
3 tablespoons olive oil
3 tablespoons walnut oil
1 small red onion, finely chopped
10 walnut halves, broken into smaller pieces
1 tablespoon cider vinegar
½ teaspoon caster sugar
1 tablespoon chopped chives

Lightly butter and flour six individual tartlet rings, about 9cm (3½in) in diameter. Roll out the pastry thinly on a floured surface and divide it into six pieces. Line each tartlet case, leaving any excess pastry hanging over the edge. Line each pastry case with a round of greaseproof paper and fill with baking beans or rice. Chill on a greased baking tray for 20–30 minutes to allow the pastry to rest.

Preheat the oven to 200°C/400°F/Gas 6. Bake the pastry in the oven for 20 minutes. Remove the greaseproof paper and beans, and return the tarts to the oven for a further 3 minutes. This helps to set the base of the pastry. Remove from the oven and allow to cool, then trim off the excess pastry. Reduce the oven temperature to 180°C/350°F/Gas 4.

Cook the sweetcorn cobs whole in boiling water (without salt as this tends to toughen the kernels) for 15 minutes, then remove from the pan and allow to cool. The kernels can be eased off with the help of a fork. Alternatively you can remove the kernels before cooking. Stand each cob upright on a chopping board and, with a sharp knife, slice against the cob to release the kernels. Turn the cob and continue until all the kernels have been removed. Now cook the kernels for just 5 minutes in boiling water, drain well and sprinkle into the tart cases.

To make the savoury custard, beat together the eggs and egg yolk, then beat in the cream. Season with a good pinch of salt and a very generous twist of black pepper for a spicy finish. Pour over the sweetcorn in each of the six pastry cases, then bake in the cooler, preheated oven for 15–20 minutes until only just set. Remove the tarts from the oven and leave to relax and cool slightly for about 10 minutes, then remove the tartlet rings.

While the tarts rest, make the dressing. Peel and quarter the apples, removing the cores. Cut the apples into 5mm (¼in) dice, adding a squeeze of lemon juice to prevent them discolouring.

To finish the dressing, warm the oils with the red onion. Remove from the heat and add the walnuts, apples, cider vinegar, sugar and chives. Season with salt and pepper and spoon the dressing around the tartlets.

A level teaspoon of Dijon or wholegrain mustard can be whisked into the oil for a more fiery finish to the dressing. A tablespoon or two of crème fraîche or soured cream can be added to the dressing or simply drizzled around the tarts.

mixed mushroom and bacon pie with melted blue cheese crème fraîche

The mixed mushrooms basically consist of simple button mushrooms, making more of a stuffing base, along with a variety of wild mushrooms that are at their most abundant during our autumn months.

There was a time when wild mushrooms were only to be found in restaurants, unless you happened to have time for a visit to Harrods. They were a luxury food, something that hadn't really changed since the pharaohs of Egypt became so intrigued with their delicious flavour that it was decided that wild mushrooms were fit only for royalty.

Fungi have been growing since prehistoric times and have been used by us for hundreds of years, often in the preparation of beverages and medicines. 'Mushroom' was first recorded as a word in the English language in the ninth century, coming from the French word *mousseron*, which nowadays applies only to one of the small wild mushrooms, in season mostly during the summer months leading into autumn.

This recipe is a 'flat' pie, not using any pie dish or flan case. It is simply a rectangle of puff pastry, topped with the button mushroom stuffing, followed by the sautéed wild mushrooms and bacon rashers. The juices from the bacon bleed into the mushrooms, giving them a very distinctive flavour. Smoked or green (unsmoked) bacon can be used; the smoked can, however, sometimes become a little too overpowering for the distinctive wild mushroom flavours.

Today packs of mixed wild mushrooms can be found in most supermarkets. As for the blue cheese, Stilton, Roquefort, Cashel Blue, Beenleigh Blue or blue Wensleydale can all be used. I've suggested 50–100g (2–4oz), allowing you to decide the strength that suits your palate.

This recipe will feed four very comfortably as a main course, with a large bowl of buttered curly kale served separately (which eats particularly well with the blue cheese crème fraîche). Omitting the bacon leaves you with a delicious vegetarian dish.

SERVES 4 AS A MAIN COURSE

large knob of butter, plus more for greasing
450g (1lb) *Quick puff pastry* (page 426, or bought – frozen or fresh can be purchased, usually in 450g/1lb blocks)
flour, for dusting
1 egg, beaten
450g (1lb) button mushrooms
2 onions, very finely chopped
1 teaspoon marjoram or thyme leaves
salt and pepper
450g (1lb) mixed wild mushrooms (see page 423 for different varieties)
2 garlic cloves, crushed
6 rindless rashers of streaky bacon
1 tablespoon roughly chopped curly parsley
50–100g (2–4oz) blue cheese, crumbled
150ml (¼ pint) crème fraîche

Grease a baking sheet. Cut a third of the puff pastry and on a floured surface roll this thinly into a rectangle, measuring about 30 × 25cm (12 × 10in). Lay this on the greased baking sheet, prick the base with a fork and brush with the beaten egg. Roll the remaining pastry into a rectangle slightly bigger than the first to provide the excess required to cover the mushroom topping. This piece of pastry will also be thicker, to give a lighter, more 'puffed' finish, while the thinner base will be crispier. Place on a tray and chill for 30 minutes with the base.

Quarter the button mushrooms, then place in a food processor and blitz to reasonably small pieces. Place in a large shallow saucepan with the chopped onions and marjoram or thyme and cook on a low-to-medium heat. As the mushrooms warm, their natural juices will be released, creating a stew. Increase the heat and continue to cook until the mushrooms and onions are virtually dry. Season with salt and pepper and leave to cool on a clean tea towel to absorb any remaining liquor.

The wild mushrooms will need to have their stalks trimmed and scraped, or perhaps just torn, before being rinsed and left to dry on a cloth or kitchen paper. If ceps are being used, just the stalks will need trimming, and if they are not too dirty, just wipe them before slicing.

Melt the knob of butter in a frying pan over a high heat. Once bubbling and almost at the nut-brown stage, add the mushrooms with the crushed garlic. Fry quickly for just a minute or two to take away their rawness. Season with salt and pepper, then drain in a colander and leave to cool on kitchen paper.

The bacon rashers are best rolled between sheets of cling film to extend their length to at least 25cm (10in), just the right size for this dish.

To build the pie, remove the two pastry rectangles from the fridge. Add the chopped parsley to the button mushrooms and spread these along the centre of the smaller rectangle, leaving a 2.5cm (1in) clean border all around. Spoon the wild mushrooms on top, then lay the six rashers of bacon lengthwise on top of them, slightly overlapping.

Now fold the remaining rectangle of puff pastry in half from the long side. At the fold, using scissors or a sharp knife, make cuts about 1cm (½in) apart, leaving a 2.5cm (1in) uncut border at either end and at the long outer edges. Brush around the border of the 'pie' base with egg, then place the folded sheet on one side and open up and seal to the other side. The central cuts will release any steam and also finish the dish with a French *jalousie* dessert presentation. The sealed edges can now be pressed together to produce a rustic finish, or pinched by hand or marked with a fork. It is also not essential to trim the pastry for a very neat edge as a ragged look often quite suits this home-made pie. Chill for 15–20 minutes.

Preheat the oven to 200ºC/400ºF/Gas 6. Brush the pastry with more of the egg and bake in the oven for 30–35 minutes, until crispy. For maximum colour, rebrush the pie with egg 15 minutes before the end of the cooking time.

While it is baking, mix the crumbled blue cheese with half of the crème fraîche and warm the two together, allowing the cheese to melt. Add the remaining crème fraîche and season with a twist of pepper. The baked pie and warm blue cheese crème fraîche are now ready to serve.

Half, or all, of the wild mushrooms can be replaced with sliced and sautéed chestnut mushrooms, which offer a nutty finish, also making this a year-round dish. A heaped teaspoon of chopped chives can be added to the crème fraîche.

waldorf salad

This is a classic salad that they say was devised at New York's Waldorf Astoria hotel back in the 1890s. The original version contained just apples, celery and mayonnaise, with the chopped walnuts being added at a later date.

Salad is a word that carries a very summery image – lots of mixed leaves with tomatoes, cucumbers, spring onions and more. But salads can adopt many guises, taking advantage of almost all ingredients. The Waldorf is without question an autumn speciality, particularly for the months of October and November, when all of its prime ingredients are home-grown.

This version is slightly different from the original. Celeriac takes the lead role, an alternative that has been used many a time, with the mayonnaise being replaced by crème fraîche for a lighter and fresher finish. The preferred apples are Russets, although more or less any variety can be used, but it was apparently the Russet that was chosen for the original. The beauty of this apple is its quite distinctive juicy sweetness and nutty edge.

For an extra dressing, diced celery is bound with oil, red wine vinegar and a touch of mustard to offer a contrasting finish.

SERVES 4 AS A STARTER OR SIDE DISH
1 medium celeriac
squeeze of lemon juice
2 Russet apples
salt and pepper
1 small shallot, very finely chopped
18 walnut halves, roughly chopped
100–150ml (3½fl oz–¼ pint) crème fraîche
1 heaped teaspoon Dijon mustard
1–2 tablespoons red wine vinegar
2 tablespoons olive oil
2 tablespoons walnut oil
2 celery sticks, cut into 5mm (¼in) dice
handful of washed rocket leaves or watercress sprigs
** (optional)**

Cut away the celeriac's tough skin, then chop the root into 5mm (¼in) dice or slice it into spaghetti-like strips. This can be made easy by simply halving the celeriac and cutting into thin strips on a mandolin slicer. Once cut, add a squeeze of lemon juice and mix it in well.

Quarter the apples, cutting away the core and seeds, then peel each quarter. This helps retain the natural shape of the apple. Once peeled, cut each piece into thin slices and add them to the celeriac. Season with salt and pepper.

Rinse the chopped shallot under cold water, shaking away any excess. This removes the raw bitterness, leaving a slightly more subtle finish. Add the shallot to the celeriac and apples along with the walnuts.

Stir in 100ml (3½fl oz) of the crème fraîche to bind the flavours. If a slightly looser consistency is preferred, add the remainder. Season with salt, pepper and lemon juice.

To make the dressing, whisk together the mustard and a tablespoon of red wine vinegar. Whisk in the two oils and season with salt and pepper. The remaining tablespoon of vinegar can be added for a sharper bite. Mix the diced celery into the dressing.

To serve, divide the Waldorf salad between the plates and spoon over the celery and red wine vinaigrette. A few rocket leaves (or watercress sprigs) can now be arranged on top, and drizzled with just a drop or two of the vinaigrette.

butternut mussel stew

When autumn arrives so do pumpkin and winter squash. Here, the pear-shaped butternut is combined with very meaty mussels, the two flavours complementing each other perfectly, in a loose soup-style brothy stew, suitable for a starter, lunch or full supper dish. As with all mussel dishes, crusty bread to mop up the juices is the perfect accompaniment.

SERVES 4–6 AS A STARTER OR 3 AS A MAIN COURSE
2kg (4½lb) fresh mussels
2 onions, finely chopped (saving all trimmings)
2 large garlic cloves
150ml (¼ pint) white wine
1 medium butternut squash
3 tablespoons olive oil
salt and pepper
50g (2oz) butter
1 tablespoon chopped curly parsley
1 tablespoon chopped chives
1 tablespoon chopped chervil

Although mussels can often be found pre-cleaned, it is imperative that they are all cleaned again to ensure they are totally free of any impurities.

Place them in a sinkful of cold water and scrape off any barnacles and hairy beards. If any mussels are slightly open,

a short sharp tap should make them close. Any that don't close should be discarded. You may also find one or two that are particularly heavy. If so, I recommend these also be discarded, as they are more than likely full of sand. Once cleaned and rinsed, the mussels are ready to cook.

Place the onion trimmings in a large saucepan. Roughly chop one of the garlic cloves and add it to the pan along with the white wine and 750ml (1¼ pints) water. Bring to a simmer and cook for 10–15 minutes.

Meanwhile, prepare the butternut squash. Cut it in half lengthwise, scoop out the seeds and threads and cut each half into thirds or quarters. Cut away the skin, then chop the flesh into 1cm (½in) pieces.

Bring the white wine liquor to the boil, add the mussels and cover tightly with a lid. The mussels will take just a few minutes to open. To ensure even cooking, shake the pan from time to time, or spoon the mussels around.

Once they have all opened, strain the mussels into a colander, collecting the liquor and juices in a saucepan or bowl below. Strain the cooking liquor through a fine sieve and return it to a simmer. Taste the mussel stock for strength. If it is a little shallow in flavour, continue to simmer and reduce in volume slightly to increase the total flavour strength, not allowing it to become over-powerful and mask the butternut.

Heat the olive oil in a large saucepan and add the onions and diced squash. Crush the remaining garlic clove and add it to the pan. Fry these vegetables on a fairly high heat, allowing them just to begin to soften and colour.

After a few minutes, add the stock and bring to a simmer, then cook for about 15 minutes, until the squash has become tender.

While this is cooking, remove the mussels from their shells, discarding any that haven't opened.

Add the mussels to the butternut squash stew, allowing it to simmer gently to warm them through. Season the stew very carefully with salt, if needed, and a generous twist of pepper. Stir in the butter and herbs and the stew is ready to serve.

green garden soup

During October, young curly kale, leeks and Brussels sprouts are only in their second month and still not quite at their prime. Home-grown courgettes, runner beans and celery are now in their final run. This soup is bringing them all together, but if some are not available, there are one or two others which could happily take their place – broccoli and spinach offer rich green flavours.

The only other vegetable ingredients are onion and garlic, adding bite to the finished flavour, with a couple of herbs for added essence. Included in the recipe, as an optional extra, is a combination of egg yolk and cream. This is a rich thickening agent usually referred to in culinary terms as a *liaison*. It can only be added just before serving, as reboiling will scramble it. Without this, the soup can be enjoyed purely as a broth.

Another optional extra is a slice of French bread placed in the bowl before ladling in the soup. The liquid-soaked bread offers an additional texture to enjoy.

SERVES 6–8

100g (4oz) small Brussels sprouts
100g (4oz) curly kale
100g (4oz) runner beans
100g (4oz) courgettes
3 tablespoons olive oil
1 onion, thinly sliced
2 celery sticks, thinly sliced
2 garlic cloves, thinly sliced or crushed
1.25 litres (2 pints) *Vegetable stock* (page 417),
   ***Instant stock* (page 416) or water**
1 small leek, thinly sliced
salt and pepper
knob of butter (optional)
2 egg yolks (optional)
4 tablespoons double or whipping cream (optional)
1 tablespoon chopped chives
1 tablespoon picked chervil leaves
6–8 slices of French bread about 2cm (¾in) thick
   (optional)

To prepare the vegetables, remove the bases of the stalks and outside leaves from the sprouts and halve each sprout. Pick the curly kale leaves from the stalks, washing the leaves and tearing into bite-sized pieces. Remove the outside strings from the runner beans and finely shred the beans. Halve the courgettes lengthwise and cut into thin slices. All this preparation can be completed well in advance of making the soup.

Warm the olive oil in a large saucepan. Add the sliced onion, celery and garlic and cook for 5–6 minutes, until beginning to soften. Add the stock or water and bring to a simmer.

After 5 minutes of simmering, increase the heat to bring the stock to the boil. Now it's time to add the vegetables – first add the sprouts and after a minute the curly kale. These will now both need 3 minutes before adding all the remaining vegetables – runner beans, courgettes and leek – and cooking for a further 3–4 minutes, until all are tender.

Season the soup with salt and a generous twist of pepper, and add the knob of butter, if using. If slightly thickening with the liaison, mix together the egg yolks and cream. Add a ladle of the soup liquor to this and mix well. Remove the soup from the heat and pour the liaison mix into the soup as you stir, slightly thickening and enriching the end result. Add the two herbs and the soup is ready to serve. Place a slice of bread, if using, into each bowl before ladling the soup over.

OPPOSITE: GREEN GARDEN SOUP

mussels bonne femme

Mussels are generally 'in season' between the months of September and March, but it is said that the months of October and November will offer the best. Mussels sold are virtually all cultured by a technique invented by the French well over 500 years ago. It was the Dutch, however, who introduced the bags of well scrubbed mussels. It's still a good idea to wash them in plenty of cold water, scraping away any barnacles and pulling away the beards (byssus). It's with these beards that the mussels attach themselves to rocks, poles, ropes, etc. If any mussels are slightly open, a short sharp tap should make them close. Any that don't close should be discarded, along with any that are particularly heavy. Once cleaned, they are ready to cook.

The term *bonne femme* is generally used of a fish dish, usually featuring sole. It basically consists of white wine cream sauce flavoured with mushrooms, shallots and parsley. All of these flavours are to be included here, with the addition of fresh tarragon.

Wild mushrooms are also in season right now and can be used in place of the buttons.

SERVES 4 AS A VERY GENEROUS STARTER OR
AS A MAIN COURSE

50g (2oz) butter, plus an extra knob
1 onion, sliced
2kg (4½lb) fresh mussels, cleaned (see above)
150ml (¼ pint) white wine
1 teaspoon plain flour
2 tablespoons finely chopped shallot or onion
225g (8oz) button mushrooms, sliced
2 egg yolks
100ml (3½fl oz) double cream
1 tablespoon roughly chopped parsley
1 heaped teaspoon torn tarragon leaves
salt and pepper
squeeze of lemon juice

Melt a third of the measured butter in a large saucepan and add the sliced onion. Cook for a minute or two, then add the mussels and white wine. Place a lid on top and cook over a fierce heat, turning the mussels from time to time, until they have all opened. This will literally take just a few minutes once the liquor is boiling. Any mussels that refuse to open should be discarded. Drain the mussels in a colander, saving all of the juices.

Strain the saved liquor through a fine sieve into a saucepan and bring to a simmer. Mix another third of the butter with the flour to make a *beurre manié*, before whisking it into the liquor. This will thicken the sauce to a coating consistency. If still too thin, mix the remaining third of butter with a little more flour and add to the liquor. Cook the sauce on a very low heat for 3–4 minutes to cook out the flour flavour.

The mussels can now be removed from their shells, and any remaining beards can be pulled away. Preheat the grill to hot.

Melt the knob of butter in a large frying pan and add the chopped shallot or onion. Cook on a fairly high heat for 2–3 minutes, then add the mushrooms, frying for a further few minutes.

Mix the mushrooms with the mussels and spoon them into a large ceramic flan dish or ovenproof bowl. Add the egg yolks to the double cream and lightly whip to soft peaks. Stir the parsley and tarragon into the mussel sauce, seasoning with salt, pepper and the lemon juice. Fold in the whipped egg cream.

Spoon the sauce over the mussels, and finish under the preheated grill until a light golden brown. The dish is now ready to serve.

OPPOSITE: MUSSELS BONNE FEMME

white eel stew with fresh herbs and capers

It is during our autumnal months that these silver-skinned fish eat at their best. They are now preparing themselves for a long swim back to the Sargasso Sea in the Atlantic and this guarantees the eel will be plump and meaty.

It is best to buy live eels, where possible, preferably asking your fishmonger to kill and skin them for you, perhaps even cutting into them pieces too.

Once bought ready-prepared, it's best to rub the eel with a cloth, removing the shine left on the flesh. They are rich in flavour; usually 175g (6oz) per portion is plenty. This is a pretty easy recipe, most of it happening in one pot.

There are still quite a lot of our own herbs available, and here they're taken advantage of, sharpening the bite with a few capers. Traditionally, eel stews are served with fried bread and I have followed this custom here, though this is entirely optional.

SERVES 4 AS A MAIN COURSE OR SUPPER DISH

800g (1¾lb) eels, cut into 4cm (1½in) pieces
salt and pepper
flour, for dusting
2 tablespoons olive oil
25g (1oz) butter
2 onions, sliced
1 garlic clove, crushed (optional)
2 bay leaves
300ml (½ pint) dry white wine
300ml (½ pint) *Chicken stock* (page 416), *Instant stock*
  (page 416) or tinned chicken consommé
4 slices of white bread, crusts removed (optional)
squeeze of lemon juice (optional)
6 sorrel leaves, chopped
1 tablespoon chopped flatleaf parsley
1 tablespoon chopped curly parsley
1 tablespoon chopped chervil
1 teaspoon chopped sage
10 tarragon leaves, chopped
1 tablespoon small capers, drained

Season the eel pieces with salt and pepper, lightly dusting each with flour. Heat the olive oil in a large frying pan, adding the eel once hot. Fry the pieces over a medium heat for a few minutes on each side until golden brown. These can now be transferred to a stewing pot.

Add a third of the butter and, once foaming, spoon in the onions, pan-frying for 7–8 minutes, until they soften and take on a slight colour. Add the garlic, if using, and cook for a further minute or two, before scooping into the eel pot with the bay leaves. Pour the white wine and stock or consommé over the eels and bring to a simmer, gently cooking for 15–20 minutes until tender.

While the eel stew is cooking, wipe the frying pan clean, returning it to the heat with the remaining butter. Cut each of the bread slices, if using, diagonally in half. These can now be shallow-fried until golden brown, keeping them warm once coloured on both sides.

To finish, correct the seasoning with salt and pepper, adding a squeeze of lemon juice if needed, and sprinkling the chopped herbs and capers over.

The fried bread can be offered separately, or placed in the base of large bowls, ladling the eel stew on top.

This loose cooking liquor can be slightly thickened, if preferred, with a liaison. *This is a mixture of 1 egg yolk and 2–3 tablespoons of double cream stirred together. If using, add a small ladle of the liquor to the* liaison, *whisking in well, then stir the mix into the stew. This must now be warmed through on a gentle heat, not allowing it to boil, until softly thickened.*

roast dabs with green horseradish dip

Dabs are a very similar fish to the flounder, alike in colour and shape, but there are more of them on general offer. As with the flounder, this fish will suit just about all plaice recipes, and likewise plaice would suit this one very well. To save a lot of preparation, it's best to ask your fishmonger to skin the dabs on the dark side (not essential, but it's not that attractive), and trim the fins and tails, with heads on or off as you like.

It wouldn't be easy to find enough grill space or, for that matter, enough frying pans to shallow-fry four whole dabs at once. Roasting requires just two greased baking trays and the oven preheated to full temperature.

Horseradish can be found throughout the year, although this hot root finds its official British season between September and January. The green is an emulsion of spinach and lots of herbs. Other flavours often added to this mixture are anchovy fillets and chopped hard-boiled egg but I've kept this one totally vegetarian.

SERVES 4

25g (1oz) softened butter, plus more for greasing
salt and pepper, plus sea salt flakes
4 × 450g (1lb) dabs, prepared (see above)
4 lemon wedges

FOR THE GREEN HORSERADISH DIP

100g (4oz) spinach, picked and washed
4 tablespoons olive oil
1 tablespoon chopped flatleaf parsley
1 tablespoon chopped chives
1 tablespoon chopped chervil
1 tablespoon chopped tarragon
2 heaped tablespoons finely grated fresh horseradish
1 heaped teaspoon chopped capers

Preheat the oven to its maximum temperature. Grease two baking trays, seasoning each with salt and pepper. Present the dabs with the white-skin side up on the trays, brushing with half the measured butter. Season with a pinch of salt or sprinkling of sea salt flakes.

To make the horseradish dip, put the spinach in a large saucepan, placing it over a medium heat. Cook for a few minutes, until the damp leaves are steaming and beginning to wilt. Drain in a colander and leave to cool. Squeeze of any excess water before chopping finely.

Put the chopped spinach in a small food processor or liquidizer with the olive oil and remaining dip ingredients. Season with salt and pepper and whizz to a chunky purée. Spoon the sauce into a suitable dish ready to serve with the dabs.

Place the fish in the preheated oven, roasting for 8–10 minutes, 12 minutes maximum, depending on the thickness of the fish. Before serving, brush each fish with the remaining butter, garnishing with a lemon wedge.

Offer the green horseradish dip separately, its herby warm flavour enhancing this simple fish.

Extra grated horseradish can be added for a sharper hotter flavour.
One or two tablespoons of creamed horseradish could be used in place of the fresh.
One or two tablespoons of mayonnaise can be whizzed with the dip ingredients for a creamier finish.
A spoonful of crème fraîche as well as the dip is a good optional extra.

smoked haddock cakes with poached eggs and curly kale

The crinkly leaves of curly kale offer a great strength of flavour, holding their own well when partnered with such a smoky fish. The horseradish crème fraîche sauce adds extra warmth, along with a piquant bite to complement the golden smoked haddock cakes.

SERVES 6 AS A STARTER OR 4 AS A MAIN COURSE

350g (12oz) potatoes (preferably Maris Piper), peeled and quartered
salt and pepper
1 tablespoon finely chopped shallot or onion
375g (12oz) natural smoked haddock fillet, pin bones removed (page 9)
150ml (¼ pint) white wine
squeeze of lemon juice
450–675g (1–1½lb) curly kale
large knob of butter
flour, for dusting
3 tablespoons olive oil, plus more for greasing
4 or 6 *Poached eggs* (page 423)

FOR THE SAUCE

1 heaped tablespoon very finely grated horseradish (or 1 heaped teaspoon horseradish cream)
200ml (7fl oz) crème fraîche
2 tablespoons chopped chives
knob of butter

Cook the potatoes in boiling salted water for approximately 20 minutes, until totally tender. Drain in a colander for a few minutes.

While the potatoes are cooking, sprinkle the chopped shallot or onion in a small greased roasting tray or frying pan and top with the smoked haddock. Season with a twist of pepper, then pour over the white wine, followed by 150ml (¼ pint) of water and a squeeze of lemon juice. Bring to a gentle simmer, cover with a lid and cook for just 2 minutes. Remove from the heat, keeping the lid on, and allow to cool.

Once the fish has cooled, remove it from the liquid and pull the skin from the flesh and discard. Break the haddock into flakes. Strain the shallot or onion pieces from the cooking liquor over a bowl, squeezing to release all their juices, before adding the shallot or onion to the haddock. Set the bowl of cooking liquor to one side.

Mash the warm potatoes, seasoning with salt and pepper. Beat half of the smoked haddock mix into the potatoes until quite smooth, then gently fold in the remainder. Cover the fish cake mix with cling film and chill for several hours. This allows the mix to rest, becoming far more compact and not as likely to break up during frying.

The curly kale can be prepared and cooked in advance or at the last minute. To do so, remove the stalks from the kale and wash the leaves, then tear them into bite-sized pieces. Plunge the leaves in lots of boiling salted water for 3–4 minutes, until tender. Drain in a colander, then plunge into iced water, if cooking in advance. Once cold, drain again, squeezing out all excess moisture, then season with salt and pepper, adding a knob of butter and covering with cling film, ready to microwave. If cooking at the last minute, drain, squeeze gently, add the butter, season with salt and pepper and serve.

To make the sauce, boil the reserved fish cooking liquor with the grated horseradish or horseradish cream, allowing it to reduce in volume by two-thirds, and keep to one side.

Preheat the oven to 180°C/350°F/Gas 4. To make the fish cakes, divide the haddock mix into four (six if serving as a starter) and roll into balls. Press these into round cakes and lightly dust and coat with flour. Heat the 3 tablespoons of olive oil in a frying pan. Place the fish cakes in the pan and fry over a medium heat until golden brown. Turn over carefully with a fish slice and colour the other sides. Transfer to a baking tray and finish in the preheated oven for 10–12 minutes.

To serve, reheat or cook the curly kale as mentioned above, also warming the poached eggs in simmering water for 1 minute. Rewarm the sauce, whisking in the crème fraîche, chopped chives and the knob of butter. Divide the kale between the plates, top with a smoked haddock cake, followed by a poached egg, and spoon the sauce over.

steamed halibut with leek tagliatelle and mussels

Halibut can sometimes be found as quite 'beautifully grotesque' large-sized beasts, with a weight exceeding 200kg (approximately 440lb). A flat fish, the halibut suits virtually all cooking techniques – baking, poaching, braising, frying – but steaming is the process used here, leaving the fillets with a very natural taste. Adding a different edge are two seasonal flavours, leeks and mussels.

The 'tagliatelle' is actually the leeks, cut into long, 1cm (½in) thick strips. Once tender, these are bound with the mussels and their lightly creamed liquor.

SERVES 4
2 medium leeks
900g (2lb) mussels
100ml (3½fl oz) white wine
1 teaspoon flour
**1 teaspoon butter, plus 2 large knobs and more
    for greasing and brushing**
salt and pepper, plus coarse sea salt
4 × 175g (6oz) portions of halibut fillet, skinned
4 tablespoons double cream
squeeze of lemon juice

Trim the coarse green top of the leeks (approximately 2.5cm/1in) and the stalks from the base of each one. Split lengthwise, discarding the first tough outer layer. The leeks can now be well rinsed, to remove any grit, before cutting each one lengthwise into 1cm (½in) thick strips.

Wash the mussels well in plenty of cold water, scraping away any barnacles and beards, and discarding any mussels that don't close on being tapped or are heavy. Drain. Heat the white wine in a large saucepan. Once boiling, add the mussels and cover with a lid. These will now take just 4–5 minutes to cook. During the cooking process, shake the pan, with the lid on, or stir from time to time, to ensure an even cooking. Drain in a colander, saving all of the juices. The mussels can now be picked from the shells, keeping them to one side.

Strain the cooking liquor through a fine sieve to remove any grit, then bring it to a simmer. Mix together the teaspoon of flour and the teaspoon of butter. This is *beurre manié*, or 'kneaded butter'. When added to warm sauces, the melting butter helps the flour find its way evenly into the liquor, thickening as it does so. Once the mussel liquor is simmering, whisk in the *beurre manié*, return to a simmer and cook for a few minutes.

Butter four small squares of greaseproof paper, season with salt and pepper and place a halibut fillet on top of each. Season the presentation side with coarse sea salt only and place the fish in a steamer above rapidly simmering water. The fillets will now take 8–10 minutes to cook.

While the fish steams, the mussel sauce and leeks can be finished. Add the cream to the sauce and check the seasoning, before adding a squeeze of lemon juice. Whisk in a large knob of butter to finish.

Melt another large knob of butter in a large pan and add 2 tablespoons of water. Once bubbling, add the leeks and cover, removing the lid and stirring from time to time. After 5 minutes the leeks will be tender. Season with salt and pepper.

To serve, warm the mussels gently in the cream sauce. Remove the halibut fillets from the steamer, place one on each warm plate and brush with butter. Spoon the mussels next to the halibut and top with a pile of the leek tagliatelle. Spoon any of the remaining sauce over and around the leeks. The dish is ready to serve.

The leeks can be added to the cream sauce with the mussels. Spoon between plates or bowls and finish with the steamed fish.

honey and lemon toasted mullet with roast carrots and fennel

Grey mullet is the fish being used here (a brief outline of this fish is given in a July recipe on page 151).

To accompany the mullet, fennel bulbs, the Florence fennel, are featured. Their natural aniseed flavour is lifted with a sprinkling of fennel seeds (these resemble caraway and dill seeds in shape). Fennel seeds are often used as a seasoning in Indian cooking, adapting well to fish, meat or vegetables. Within this hot culinary tradition, they are also toasted and served after meals as a digestive, leaving a sweeter breath.

In Italy the fennel vegetable is often par-boiled before roasting and finishing with Parmesan. That same cooking method is to be adopted here, omitting the Parmesan, roasting the fennel slices with sweet carrot.

The honey and lemon combination is drizzled over the mullet, which is then toasted, sizzling and slightly caramelizing

within minutes. That's basically the entirety of this dish, with perhaps a spoonful of crème fraîche to calm these strong flavours.

SERVES 4

2 bulbs of Florence fennel
juice of ½ lemon
4 small–medium carrots, peeled
salt and pepper, plus sea salt flakes
2 tablespoons olive oil
1 teaspoon fennel seeds
2 tablespoons clear honey
large knob of butter, plus more for greasing
2 × 800g (1¾lb) grey mullet, scaled, filleted and pin-boned (page 9), with skin on

Preheat the oven to 190°C/375°F/Gas 5. Trim the fennel tops, saving any sprigs of herb for later use. Split the fennel bulbs in half, removing any outside bruised layers, along with the central core. Slice the halves finely, cutting across the bulbs. Add ½ teaspoon of the lemon juice, mixing it in well with the fennel strips. This will prevent them from discolouring. Halve the carrots lengthwise, slicing each approximately 2–3mm (about ⅛in) thick. The carrots and fennel strips can now both be plunged into a saucepan of boiling salted water. Cook for 2 minutes before draining in a colander and allowing to cool.

Once cool enough to handle, put the vegetables in a small roasting tray, working the olive oil evenly amongst them. Season with salt, pepper and fennel seeds. Put the tray in the preheated oven and roast for 15–20 minutes until tender.

While roasting the vegetables, in a small bowl mix the honey with the remaining lemon juice.

The mullet fillets can be scored with the point of a small knife, making three parallel incisions on each. Butter a baking tray, seasoning it with salt and pepper. Place the fillets on the tray, drizzling each with the flavoured honey. Sprinkle each of the fillets with a few sea salt flakes and a twist of pepper.

With the vegetables almost cooked, preheat the grill. Place the fish under – the closer, the better – toasting for just 3–4 minutes, 5 minutes maximum. The honey will be sizzling, the skin beginning to crisp, ready to serve. Spoon the large knob of butter into the carrots and fennel, chopping and adding any saved fennel tops. The dish can now be presented on individual plates or a large platter.

wing of skate with creamed salsify and red wine mushrooms

Skate is available throughout the year, often reaching its best during our autumn months. This happily coincides with salsify and mushrooms, which are also with us.

Salsify is mostly an imported vegetable during mid-to-late autumn and through the months of winter. It comes in two forms – black and white. Both are similar in shape and size, with long, slightly knobbly roots and, although different in colour, they have more or less identical interiors. Peeling reveals beautiful white roots, which have a distinctive flavour not too dissimilar to that of asparagus.

The ribbed-textured skate wing is roasted, while the mushrooms are finished in a red wine liquor and the off-white sticks of salsify are flavoured with cream.

Here I don't specify any particular type of mushroom. There are plenty of wild or cultivated to choose from.

SERVES 4
10 salsify sticks
juice of 1½ lemons (or 2 tablespoons white wine vinegar)
4 × 275–350g (10–12oz) skate wings, skinned
   (as usually found in the fishmongers)
flour, for dusting
salt and pepper
2 tablespoons olive oil
large knob of butter, plus more for greasing
100–150ml (3½fl oz–¼ pint) crème fraîche
1 level teaspoon Dijon mustard (optional)
squeeze of lemon juice
1 tablespoon chopped parsley

FOR THE MUSHROOMS
450g (1lb) mushrooms (if using wild mushrooms refer
   to page 423 for cleaning)
40g (1½oz) butter

FOR THE RED WINE LIQUOR
2 tablespoons finely chopped shallots
1 garlic clove, crushed
1 bottle of red wine
2–3 sugar cubes

Preheat the oven to 200°C/400°F/Gas 6. It is best, whenever peeling salsify, to wear rubber gloves and use a swivel peeler. This prevents being covered in too much dirt and permits reasonably stress-free peeling. To peel, place the salsify on a chopping board, peeling in long strips as you would asparagus. Once each stick has been peeled, place it in a large bowl of cold water acidulated with a third of the lemon juice or 1 tablespoon of the vinegar. Once all are peeled, each stick can be cut in two or three. Rinse and place in a saucepan with fresh cold water and the remaining lemon juice or vinegar. Bring to a simmer and cook for 10–12 minutes, 15 minutes being the maximum time required. Once cooked, remove the salsify from the pan and leave to drain and cool in a colander.

To make the red wine liquor, place the chopped shallots and crushed garlic in a saucepan, and pour over the red wine. Bring to a rapid simmer, and allow the wine to reduce in volume by two-thirds to three-quarters, until slightly thickening. Add 2 sugar cubes and stir them into the wine. The sugar removes the wine's bitterness and slightly thickens the liquor. The last cube can also be added for a slightly sweeter finished flavour.

It is best to colour the skate wings one or two at a time. To do so, lightly flour the presentation side of the fish and season with salt only. Heat 1 tablespoon of the olive oil in a large frying pan. Place the fish in the pan, floured-side down. Fry for 5 minutes until golden brown, then season with salt and pepper. Remove the fish, transferring to a greased baking tray. Wipe the pan clean before repeating the same process with the remaining skate wings. Roast the fish in the preheated oven for 8 minutes until tender.

While the skate is roasting, heat the remaining olive oil in a non-stick frying pan. Gently fry the salsify, adding the knob of butter, until the sticks just begin to colour. Season with salt and pepper.

Mix together 100ml (3½fl oz) of the crème fraîche with the Dijon mustard, if using. For a creamier finish, add the remaining crème fraîche. Add a squeeze of lemon juice, and season with salt and pepper. This can now be spooned into the pan with the salsify, removing it from the heat, or simply spooned over the sticks once presented on the plate.

While the salsify are colouring, fry the mushrooms. Heat the butter in a frying pan. Once sizzling, add the mushrooms and sauté for 2–3 minutes, until golden brown and tender. Season with salt and pepper.

To serve, present the skate wings on large warm plates, placing piles of the creamy salsify alongside. Spoon the mushrooms around the skate, finishing with the shallot red wine liquor and chopped parsley.

OPPOSITE: WING OF SKATE WITH CREAMED SALSIFY AND
RED WINE MUSHROOMS

roast goose with stuffing, gravy and apple chutney

The goose is a farmed bird, but still only seems to present itself during the mid-autumn to mid-winter season. Quite heavily boned and with a large fat content, the best size to roast is around 4.5kg (10lb); this is when they're about 6–9 months old. As they get older, they tend to toughen, and are not as sweet and succulent.

During the roasting a lot of fat is released, which is perfect for the *Classic roast potatoes* on page 422. As far as vegetables are concerned, the *Sesame and ham sprouts* (page 317) or just *Buttered Brussels sprouts* (page 423), offer themselves as the perfect side dish, this complete meal then becoming a good forerunner of the big feast on 25 December.

There's stuffing and chutney within this recipe and having the two might make it look a bit too involved. The chutney, however, can be made well in advance, maturing for a deeper flavour, having about a 6-month lifespan before it begins to lose its character and quality. The stuffing is pretty basic really, just sage and onion, with a meaty pork and bacon edge. These two flavours are the usual garnish to be found with roast turkey – as pork chipolatas and rolled rashers of crispy bacon.

The chutney can be made from almost any apple but I prefer to use Egremont Russet. This apple is at its absolute prime right now, its lively personality speaking volumes, with a distinctive, nutty, pear-like flavour. The addition of apricot adds an even sweeter fruity edge. The chutney can be eaten almost immediately once cooled, but is best served at least a week after.

The stuffing can be made 24 hours in advance, giving it time to mature.

SERVES 6

1 × **4.5kg (10lb) oven-ready goose**
salt and pepper
butter, for greasing
450ml (¾ pint) *Chicken stock* (page 416) or *Instant stock* (page 416) or tinned chicken consommé
cornflour, for thickening the gravy (optional)

OPPOSITE: ROAST GOOSE WITH STUFFING, GRAVY AND APPLE CHUTNEY

FOR THE CHUTNEY (MAKES APPROXIMATELY 1 LITRE/1¾ PINTS)

900g (2lb) apples, preferably Egremont Russet
squeeze of lemon juice
175g (6oz) ready-to-eat dried apricots, roughly chopped into 5mm (¼in) pieces
225g (8oz) light soft brown or caster sugar
2 onions, finely chopped
175ml (6fl oz) white wine vinegar
finely grated zest and juice of 1 orange and 1 lemon
1 teaspoon salt
½ teaspoon Cayenne pepper
½ teaspoon ground cinnamon
½ teaspoon freshly grated nutmeg
50g (2oz) preserved ginger, finely grated (fresh ginger can also be used)

FOR THE STUFFING

2 onions, finely chopped
knob of butter
finely grated zest of 1 lemon
450g (1lb) lean pork sausagemeat
100g (4oz) unsmoked back bacon, roughly cut into 5mm (¼in) dice
2 heaped tablespoons chopped sage
2 heaped tablespoons chopped parsley
2 apples, peeled, grated and squeezed of excess juice (optional)
½ teaspoon ground mace
100g (4oz) white breadcrumbs
1 egg, beaten

To make the chutney, peel, core and chop the apples into a rough 1cm (½in) dice, rolling in a squeeze of lemon juice to prevent discoloration. Place all of the ingredients, except for the apples, in a saucepan, simmering for 40 minutes. Add the chopped apples and continue to simmer until the apples are tender and just beginning to break down. Should the chutney be very loose, strain and reboil the juice, allowing it to cook, reduce in volume and thicken, without becoming over-syrupy. Add the chutney liquor to the apple mix and spoon into sterilized jars (page 9), covering and sealing while still warm. This can now be stored in a cool dark place or refrigerated.

To make the stuffing, pan-fry the onions in the knob of butter for several minutes, until softening with a golden-brown edge. Leave to cool.

In a large bowl (or electric mixer), beat together the cooked onions, lemon zest, sausagemeat, diced bacon, chopped sage and parsley, along with the grated apple, if using, and the breadcrumbs. Season with salt and pepper, adding the ground mace. Once mixed, beat in the egg.

Preheat the oven to 200°C/400°F/Gas 6. To prepare the goose, lift the skin at the neck end of the bird. The wishbone can now be removed, cutting on either side of its natural line. Once both sticks of the bone are revealed, simply twist and pull away. This is not essential, but does create more space for the filling, and also makes carving easier, leaving a clean slice.

Turn the bird over onto its breast and loosen the skin, before filling the cavity with stuffing as generously as possible. Pull the skin back over the stuffing and secure with cocktail sticks in the base, or stitch up with a trussing needle and string. Should there be any remaining stuffing, this can be spooned into a suitable buttered dish ready for baking, or rolled in a sheet of greased foil, forming a sausage shape.

To roast, season the bird with salt, placing it on a wire rack set in a baking tray (this is not essential but does prevent the goose from baking in excess released fat). Place in the preheated oven for 30 minutes, before removing and pouring out the goose fat collecting in the pan into a bowl (this is superb to keep and use for general frying). Return the bird to the oven, reducing the temperature to 180°C/350°F/Gas 4 and roasting for a further 1½–1¾ hours, basting every 20 minutes and pouring away excess fat if need be. Any extra stuffing can be placed in the oven 45 minutes before the goose has completed its roasting time.

Once cooked, remove the bird from the oven (along with the extra stuffing) and keep warm to one side, resting for 15–20 minutes.

Pour away any fat from the tray, before placing it on the stove top. Once the pan is sizzling, add the stock or consommé, scraping all trimmings from the base. Simmer for a few minutes to draw the maximum flavour. Some goose juices may be sitting under the saved goose fat. If so, spoon the fat into a separate bowl, adding the juices to the loose gravy. If a thicker consistency is preferred, simply thicken with cornflour loosened in a little water. Strain through a fine sieve to remove any impurities.

To carve, remove the cocktail sticks or cut the string connecting the skin to the base of the bird. Cut off the legs, dividing the drumsticks and thighs, and carve the breast meat, offering on each plate with a slice or spoonful of the stuffing. Drizzle with gravy and the roast is ready to serve with the apple chutney to accompany.

150ml (¼ pint) of double cream can be added to the stuffing, leaving a softer texture to the meaty flavours. Cold goose and apple chutney makes a lovely supper plate.

pigeon with peppery orange fennel

I don't exactly class pigeons as seasonal game. There is the domestic squab, extremely tender and plump, superb to eat but quite expensive. Then there is the wood pigeon, the one I'm suggesting here. Wood pigeons are at least a third of the price of squabs, maybe not quite as plump, but having a gamey flavour nevertheless, tempting you to feature them during the autumn and winter seasons. They are just going to be plainly roasted here and served with peppery orange fennel, for which green peppercorns are simmered with fresh orange juice, a splash of white wine and chicken stock (game stock here would mask the natural fennel flavour).

As it is, the recipe could supply you with 4 generous starters or 4 small main courses, serving a pigeon per portion.

SERVES 4
4 oven-ready plump pigeons
salt and pepper
25g (1oz) butter

FOR THE FENNEL
2 large bulbs of fennel
1 teaspoon of butter, plus 1 large knob
1 teaspoon caster sugar
3 strips of orange zest
3 tablespoons cognac
1 glass of white wine
200ml (7fl oz) orange juice
150ml (¼ pint) *Chicken stock* (page 416), *Instant stock* (page 416) or tinned chicken consommé
1 teaspoon plain flour
1 teaspoon green peppercorns (dried or tinned in brine)
squeeze of lemon juice (optional)

Preheat the oven to 220°C/425°F/Gas 7. Trim the fennel stalks (saving any green herb tops), halve each bulb and cut out the hard central core before finely slicing. The herb tops can be picked and chopped, ready to be added to the finished dish.

Melt the knob of butter in a large saucepan. Once foaming, add the sliced fennel and stir on a fairly low heat, not allowing the fennel to colour. Add 2 tablespoons of water to the pan and cover with a lid, allowing to simmer and steam for 8–10 minutes until the slices are becoming tender. If still too firm, a few more drops of water can be added, continuing to simmer until tender.

Remove the lid and add the caster sugar, orange zest and cognac. Increase the heat slightly, allowing the liquor to simmer rapidly and reduce until almost dry. Add the white wine, simmering and reducing to the same stage.

The orange juice can now be poured in, returning to a simmer and cooking until reduced in volume by at least half, maximum two-thirds. Add the stock or consommé and simmer for 3 minutes until all the flavours have combined.

Mix together the teaspoon of butter with the flour. This is to be used as a thickening agent, known as a *beurre manié*. Small nuggets can be dropped and stirred into the pan, adding just enough to thicken to a coating consistency (not all of the *beurre manié* may be needed). It's at this point that the green peppercorns can be added. Simmer to release their flavour and cook out the floury thickener. Adding the peppercorns this late prevents them from becoming too strong and hot. If you prefer a pepper sauce with more bite, simply add the peppercorns earlier. Season with salt and pepper, removing the strips of orange zest and adding a squeeze of lemon juice, if using, to sharpen the finished flavour.

While the fennel is cooking, the wishbones can be removed from the pigeons. This is not essential, but will help release all of the meat usually left behind once cut from the carcass. Lift the skin to expose the wishbone. Scrape either side with a small knife to reveal the bones. Cut each side against the wishbones and then twist to release. The birds are now ready to cook, seasoning each with salt and pepper.

Heat an ovenproof frying pan and melt the 25g (1oz) butter. Once bubbling, place the birds on their sides in the pan, shallow-frying for 2–3 minutes until golden brown. Repeat the same process on the other side, finishing each breast-side down. Once completely golden brown, turn the birds onto their backs, roasting in the preheated oven for 6–8 minutes. At this point the birds will be pink. Remove from the oven and leave to rest for a further 6–8 minutes.

To serve, cut the legs and breasts from each, presenting them on plates. Add any saved herb tops to the fennel, spooning it next to the pigeon and drizzling with the peppery orange sauce.

The Sweet port red wine dressing *(page 420) can be sprinkled over the pigeon, adding another dimension of flavour.*

roast partridge with celeriac and blue cheese risotto

Most game bird recipes tend to stick to 'traditional' accompaniments – roasted vegetables, cabbage, chestnuts. This recipe takes a totally different approach.

The flavoured rice carries the autumnal flavours of the nutty knobbly celeriac tuber, enriched with a softening of blue cheese. Giving priority to British and Irish cheeses, the most obvious would be ewe's milk Beenleigh Blue – officially joining us between September and February – which leaves a bitter sweet edge, with a slight spicy finish. Other exciting cheeses with as much to share are Harbourne Blue goat's milk and Devon Blue cow's milk. These two are available throughout the year. There's also the cow's milk Blue Vinny, a Devonshire cheese with a more crumbly texture, creaming once added to the warm risotto. A sort of Roquefort-styled Scottish ewe's milk cheese, Lanark Blue, is another worth thinking about, with a pale sweetness to crumble in the rice, and, of course, don't forget Stilton.

SERVES 4

4 oven-ready partridges, preferably red-legged (see page 268), barded with a thin slice of back fat or rasher of bacon
salt and pepper
2 tablespoons groundnut oil
large knob of butter

FOR THE RISOTTO

75g (3oz) butter
1 celeriac, peeled and cut into approximately 5mm (¼in) dice
2 onions, finely chopped
225g (8oz) Carnaroli, Vialone Nano or Arborio rice
1 glass of white wine (optional)
1.2 litres (2 pints) *Vegetable stock* (page 417) or tinned chicken consommé
100–175g (4–6oz) blue cheese (see above), crumbled
1–2 tablespoons chopped chives (optional)
2 tablespoons olive or walnut oil (optional)

Preheat the oven to 220°C/425°F/Gas 7. To make the risotto, melt 25g (1oz) of the butter in a frying pan. Once bubbling, add the diced celeriac, cooking on a fairly high heat, allowing the vegetable to become golden brown. At this stage remove the celeriac from the pan.

Melt the remaining 50g (2oz) butter in a saucepan and add the chopped onion. Cook without colouring for 6–7 minutes until softening, before adding the rice. Raise the heat slightly, stir and allow the rice to take on a shallow golden-brown colour. Add the white wine, if using, allowing it to boil and reduce in volume by three-quarters. Add the pan-fried celeriac to the rice, along with a ladle or two of warm stock. Reduce the heat to a gentle simmer, stirring the rice until the stock is completely absorbed. Continue this, adding a ladle or two of stock at a time, stirring continuously to create an even cooking. The rice will take approximately 20 minutes until tender, leaving it with a slight bite.

After the first 5 minutes of making the risotto, season the partridges with salt and pepper. Heat a roasting tray with the groundnut oil, then place the seasoned birds in the tray on their side. Fry for 2–3 minutes until well coloured, before turning them over and repeating the same process. Now turn each bird breast-side down, sealing and colouring for a further 2–3 minutes.

Turn the birds on their backs and roast in the preheated oven for 6–7 minutes. If particularly plump, roast for an extra 2 minutes. Remove the birds from the oven and place upside-down on a plate, leaving to rest for 5–6 minutes, allowing all the juice to be absorbed into the breast.

This provides plenty of time to finish the risotto, adding 100g (4oz) of the crumbled blue cheese, with extra stock, if necessary, to loosen, creating a soft creamy finish. You may find that not all of the stock is needed. For a richer flavour, the remaining blue cheese can be added. Season with salt and pepper. If using, mix the chopped chives with the olive or walnut oil, spooning over the finished risotto.

The partridges can now be untied, and the back fat discarded before removing the legs and breasts. Present the breasts and legs in bowls, arranging to recreate the shape of the bird, offering the risotto separately.

roast grouse with celeriac potato rösti and calvados apple sauce

Although having quite a lengthy season, grouse are really at their best throughout the months of September and October. It's best to purchase young birds, as these have a more gentle flavour, not the sometimes over-bitter gaminess found in the older birds. They also need a little hanging – 2 or 3 days – to allow their flavour to develop.

Home-grown celeriac began to appear last month, with more and more available through to spring. Here they are just shredded, with the potatoes, into matchsticks.

Apples are in abundance right now, with so many varieties to choose from, with Russets, Cox's, Laxton's, Worcester Pearmain and Bramley all amongst the selection. Apple sauce is classically cooked almost to a purée, but this is a cream-enriched, calvados-flavoured game sauce, lifted in flavour and texture by a small dice of fresh apple gently poached in the sauce.

As an optional extra, diced cooked ham is added to the dish for succulence, replacing the bacon so often offered with game. There are also a few marjoram leaves added to the finished sauce. Marjoram has a sweet scented flavour that works well with poultry and game dishes.

SERVES 4

1 celeriac
2 potatoes (preferably Romano or Desirée)
salt and pepper
25g (1oz) butter, plus 1 large knob
2 tablespoons groundnut oil
4 young oven-ready grouse, preferably barded (breasts covered) with back fat or bacon
2 shallots, quartered

FOR THE SAUCE

2 apples (see above)
squeeze or two of lemon juice
150ml (¼ pint) apple juice
generous sprig of marjoram, plus ½ teaspoon picked marjoram leaves (optional)
100ml (3½fl oz) calvados (or ordinary brandy)
200ml (7fl oz) *Chicken stock* (page 416) or tinned game consommé
100–150ml (3½fl oz–¼ pint) double cream
1 × 5mm (¼n) thick slice of cooked ham (approximately 100g/4oz, optional)

Preheat the oven to 200°C/400°F/Gas 6. Trim away the tough skin of the celeriac and peel the potatoes. These can be sliced into matchsticks, using a mandolin slicer. If cutting by hand, sticks of 5–7.5cm × 3mm (2–3 × ⅛in) will be needed. Squeeze any excess moisture from the potatoes and dry the sticks on a cloth. Mix together the celeriac and potato sticks and season with salt and pepper.

Melt the measured butter, add three-quarters of it to the celeriac and potatoes and mix it in well. Brush a large baking tray with one of the knobs of butter. Divide the mix into four and shape into discs approximately 10–13cm (4–5in) in diameter on the baking tray. A large pastry cutter or small flan ring will help make this a lot easier, and give a rounder finish.

Place the tray in the preheated oven and bake for 10–15 minutes until golden on the base side. Carefully turn the discs over on the tray and continue to bake for a further 10–15 minutes, to give the crispy golden-brown finish to the other side.

Remove the rösti from the oven, leaving them on the tray, and keep to one side. Increase the oven temperature to 230°C/450°F/Gas 8.

To start the sauce, peel and core the apples. Cut each apple into 5mm (¼in) thick sticks, then neatly cut into small dice. Once cut, keep the small pieces in a little water acidulated with lemon juice, to prevent them from discolouring. Keep any trimmings for use in the sauce. Drain the water from the diced apples and place them in a small saucepan with the apple juice. Bring to a simmer and cook for 30 seconds, then drain again, saving the apple juice. This will have just tenderized the apples, leaving a slight bite.

To cook the grouse, heat the groundnut oil and remaining knob of butter in a roasting tray. Once bubbling, season the grouse with salt and pepper, and colour on all sides in the sizzling oil and butter. Add the quartered shallots. Turn each of the birds on to one leg, place the tray in the preheated oven and roast for 5 minutes. Turn the birds on their other leg and return to the oven for the same time. Now turn the grouse on their backs, breast-side up, and roast for a final 5 minutes. Once cooked, remove the tray from the oven, basting the birds well with the pan juices. Lift the grouse from the tray and keep to one side. (Should the grouse have been barded with back fat, this can be removed at this point, and the breast skin quickly fried in the roasting tray to colour it where it has been protected.) Reduce the oven temperature to 180°C/350°/Gas 4. Pour away most of the fat from the roasting pan, leaving the shallots in the tray. After 10 minutes of resting, remove the legs and breasts from the birds and keep them warm, covered with foil, to one side.

To finish the sauce, chop the grouse carcasses, adding them to the shallots in the roasting tray, and fry over a high heat for a few minutes to colour them well. Add any apple trimmings, along with a generous sprig of marjoram, if using. Add the calvados, bringing to the boil and reducing in volume by three-quarters. Add the apple juice and continue to boil until reduced in volume by half. Pour over the chicken stock or consommé, and simmer rapidly until also reduced in volume by half.

The grouse-flavoured stock can now be strained through a fine sieve, pressing all the juices from the carcasses. Return the stock to a simmer and skim off any impurities. Add 100ml (3½fl oz) of the double cream and taste for depth of flavour. For a creamier finish, add the remaining cream and continue to simmer for just a few minutes. Season with salt and pepper. A squeeze of lemon juice can also be added to enhance the finished flavour.

While finishing the sauce, reheat the celeriac and potato röstis in the oven (now at 180°C/350°F/Gas 4), along with the grouse. Cut the ham, if using, into small dice and add to the sauce, along with the diced apples. Add the picked marjoram, if using, and warm through for 1–2 minutes.

Place the röstis in the centre of four warm plates. Arrange the grouse on top, placing the legs onto the röstis and topping with the breasts, or simply arrange the legs criss-crossed at the top of the plate, leaving just the breasts on the röstis. Spoon the sauce around and the dish is complete.

The cooking times given will produce grouse that is pink. For medium, an extra 2 minutes will need to be added to each roasting stage; for well done, at least an extra 5 minutes to each stage.
The sauce can be made without adding the chopped carcasses. This will not be as grouse-flavoured as you might wish, but if using the tinned consommé a light flavour will be produced.

poached beef fillet with lots of vegetables

In mid-to-late autumn, there are plenty of home-grown root vegetables to choose from. With this recipe it's not what you actually choose, so much as taking advantage of as many flavours as possible.

As you can see, glancing at the ingredients list, there are lots of vegetables to warrant the title of this dish. It is, in fact, a reasonably quick recipe, with the meat, potatoes and abundance of vegetables simply poached and all appearing from the one pot. In France this style of dish is known as *à la ficelle*, which literally translates as 'on a string', as each beef fillet is tied with string to help retain its neat round shape. Enough string is usually left to tie the meat to the saucepan handle, making it a lot simpler when lifting the fillets from the pot, but a slotted spoon is more than adequate for the job.

SERVES 4–6

1 small swede, peeled
1–2 medium turnips, peeled
1 large or 2 medium carrots, peeled
2 celery sticks, peeled
1–2 parsnips, peeled and quartered, with the central core removed
2 medium potatoes, peeled
¼ Savoy cabbage
12 button onions, peeled
1.2 litres (2 pints) *Beef stock* (page 416), *Instant stock* (page 416) or tinned beef consommé
2 bay leaves
large sprig of thyme
salt and pepper
4–6 × 175g (6oz) beef fillet steaks (preferably taken from the central fillet to ensure equal portions), trimmed of all sinews
knob of butter (optional)
1 tablespoon chopped parsley

Cut the swede, turnips, carrots, celery and parsnips into rough 2cm (¾in) dice or into baton-shaped sticks about 5cm (2in) long and 5mm (¼in) thick. They don't need to be perfectly neat, or exactly that size, but making all of them similar in size helps ensure even cooking. Cut the potatoes into rough 2cm (¾in) chunks and shred the cabbage into strips of about 5mm (¼in).

Place the button onions in a small saucepan and cover with water. Bring to a simmer, then refresh in cold water. Repeat this process twice more to help remove the raw onion flavour and begin their cooking.

Place the potatoes, carrots, celery, swede and blanched onions in a large saucepan or braising pot, and cover them with the stock or consommé. Add the bay leaves and thyme and bring to a simmer. Once at simmering point, cook the vegetables gently for 10–15 minutes (10 minutes will be plenty if they are cut into sticks), adding the turnips and parsnips after the first 5 minutes when the other vegetables are becoming tender. Season with salt and pepper.

While the vegetables are simmering, tie the beef fillets loosely to help retain their round shape. Season each with salt and pepper. After the first 10–15 minutes of cooking the vegetables as above, lower the beef into the stock. It is now very important to allow the pot to be at a slight murmuring simmer only; any more and the beef will become toughened. About 8 minutes of poaching will cook the beef to a rare stage, 10 minutes for medium rare; for well done, at least 20–25 minutes of poaching will be needed, so in this case it is best to add the beef to the pot with the vegetables. Add the cabbage for the last 4–5 minutes of poaching. As the beef cooks, spoon away any impurities that may rise to the surface. By the time the beef is cooked, the vegetables will have reached an 'overcooked' stage, making them even more tender.

To serve, lift the beef fillets from the pot and remove the string. Add a knob of butter to the vegetables, if you wish, before spooning into bowls. Place the beef fillets in the centre of each bowl, ladling the cooking liquor over and sprinkling with chopped parsley.

Any remaining vegetables and stock can be served as a vegetable broth the following day, or liquidized into a puréed vegetable soup.

OPPOSITE: POACHED BEEF FILLET WITH LOTS OF VEGETABLES

calf's liver steak with red wine and port figs and celeriac purée

Imported figs join us at this time of the year – from the Mediterranean, in late summer into autumn, and from the USA, into early winter. This beautifully shaped fruit can be found in various colours, ranging from an opaque gold through green, to the renowned purple-black Mission fig. It is this last variety that I find the most satisfying; at their ripest, they have a flavour and texture that no other fig can match.

Celeriac is becoming increasingly popular as it has a great capacity to work alongside almost as many flavours as you wish. Here, the vegetable is puréed, adding just one potato to help maintain a starchy solidity. The potato is not essential, however, as the celeriac can be puréed to a very soft, almost sauce-like cream. Either consistency will work very well with the calf's liver, adding a smooth finish to its seared texture. If omitting the potato, simply increase the quantity of celeriac by 175g (6oz).

SERVES 4

4 × 175g (6oz) calf's liver steaks, each cut 1–1.5cm (½–⅝in) thick
8 figs
cooking oil
1–2 pinches of light soft brown sugar
100ml (3½fl oz) red wine
100ml (3½fl oz) port
flour, for dusting
knob of butter (optional)

FOR THE CELERIAC PURÉE

1 large potato
salt and pepper
450g (1lb) celeriac
25g (1oz) butter
150ml (¼ pint) milk

Preheat the oven to 200°C/400°F/Gas 6. The calf's liver has been cut thicker than normal to create a steak-like texture. This does give you a little more control when frying, allowing extra time to reach your perfect stage. Once cut, the steaks can be chilled until needed.

Peel the potato and dice into rough 2.5cm (1in) pieces. Put in a pan, cover with water, add a good pinch of salt and simmer until tender (10–15 minutes). Drain.

While the potato is cooking, peel the celeriac and cut into a slightly smaller dice than the potato. Melt the butter in a saucepan and add the celeriac pieces. Season with salt and pepper, cover with a lid and cook on a low heat, not allowing the pieces to colour, for 8–10 minutes until just approaching the tender stage. At this point, add the milk and bring to a simmer, then continue to cook for a further 5–6 minutes until very tender.

Remove the celeriac from the milk and push it through a large fine sieve with the potato. Loosen with the milk. Alternatively, spoon the celeriac and potato into a liquidizer with just a third of the milk and purée until smooth, adding more milk if necessary. Season with salt and pepper. The purée can be made in advance, reheating when needed.

Halve the figs lengthwise. Heat a dessertspoon of oil in an ovenproof frying pan or small roasting tray. Once hot, lay the figs in, cut-side down, and fry on a fairly high heat for just a minute or two until golden brown. Turn the figs over in the pan, season and sprinkle with a little sugar. Add the red wine and port, and bring to a simmer, then bake in the preheated oven for just 10–15 minutes, until softening. Remove all but four of the fig halves from the pan and keep warm to one side. Boil the red wine and port with the remaining four fig halves until reduced in volume by a quarter. As the liquor is reducing, mash the figs with a fork to spread the flavour. To finish, simply squeeze every bit of flavour through a sieve, or liquidize to help thicken before sieving. Adjust the seasoning and add another pinch of sugar if necessary.

While the figs are being finished, cook the calf's liver. Heat a tablespoon of cooking oil in a large frying pan. Lightly flour the liver steaks, carefully placing each in the pan. Fry on a fairly high heat for 3–4 minutes on each side, until well coloured, reaching a medium-rare to medium stage. Once cooked, season with salt and pepper. (Liver is one meat that should always be seasoned once cooked. If salted too early, the blood is drawn from the liver, leaving a drier texture and slightly burnt bitter flavour.) The calf's liver steaks can now be presented on a plate with a spoonful of the celeriac purée and three fig halves per portion. Finish the red wine and port fig liquor with a knob of butter, if using, and drizzle over the fruits.

A little fig liquor can be brushed over the liver steaks for a shinier finish.

grilled gammon steaks with butternut squash gnocchi and sage

Gnocchi is Italian for 'dumplings', and they can be made in different ways, from semolina, choux pastry or potato. Here the butternut squash is the most predominant flavour bound with potato. This particular squash is with us throughout the autumn, offering a quite densely packed texture and carrying a sweet and nutty, buttery flavour. For the gnocchi, it is best to bake the butternut in the oven, along with the potato. This will prevent the vegetable, which has a naturally high moisture content, from absorbing any more water.

To complement the gammon and gnocchi is a sage sauce.

SERVES 4

4 × 175–225g (6–8oz) gammon steaks
olive oil, for brushing

FOR THE GNOCCHI

1 medium butternut squash
1 large Maris Piper or Desirée potato, pierced
** with a knife**
knob of butter (optional), plus more for greasing
175g (6oz) plain flour, plus more for dusting
1 egg
salt and pepper
freshly grated nutmeg
50g (2oz) Parmesan cheese, grated (optional)
2–3 tablespoons olive oil (optional)

FOR THE SAGE SAUCE

juice of 1 orange
1 shallot, finely chopped
50g (2oz) butter
4 sage leaves, chopped

Preheat the oven to 200°C/400°F/Gas 6. To make the gnocchi, halve the squash lengthwise, seed and cut each half into three wedges. Loosely wrap these and the potato in buttered aluminium foil. Place on a baking tray and cook in the preheated oven for 1–1¼ hours, until tender. Remove both from the oven, leave for 10–15 minutes to rest and cool slightly, then scoop both from their skins. Mash the vegetables separately or pass them through a potato ricer. Once mashed, the butternut squash can be squeezed in a very fine sieve or muslin cloth, to get rid of as much excess moisture as possible.

Drain this into a saucepan. The quantity of purée remaining will be approximately 150g (5oz), with the juice measuring 300–450ml (½–¾ pint). Boil the juice to reduce in volume by three-quarters, leaving approximately 100ml (3½fl oz) of finished liquor with a richer flavour. This will be used to make the orange and sage butter sauce, spreading the butternut flavour further into the complete dish.

While both of the purées are still warm, mix them together, adding the flour and egg, then season with salt, pepper and nutmeg. The Parmesan can now also be added to the mix, if using, or saved to sprinkle over the gnocchi once cooked and ready to serve. Knead into a pliable dough on a floured surface. This can now be divided into two. Roll each into a long thin cylinder and cut each into 16–20 pieces, ready to roll into balls. This will provide 8–10 gnocchi per serving.

Bring a large pan of water to the boil. Add the gnocchi, just a handful or two at a time, and cook for 2–3 minutes, until the pieces all rise to the surface. Remove the dumplings with a slotted spoon, transfer them to a bowl of iced water and leave to refresh for just a few minutes, before removing and patting dry on kitchen paper. Repeat the same process until all are cooked.

Season the gammon steaks with pepper and brush with olive oil. Preheat a large griddle plate or a grill. Trim the rind of the gammons to prevent the steaks from curling as they cook. Grill the steaks for 6–7 minutes on each side.

While the gammon is cooking, make the sage sauce. Mix the orange juice with the shallot in a saucepan and bring to the boil. Cook for a few minutes until the juice has reduced in volume by half. Add the reduced butternut squash liquor and bring it to a simmer, then whisk in the butter just before serving. Season with salt and pepper, adding the chopped sage at the last moment. This provides enough liquor to help loosen the gnocchi.

Fry the gnocchi in the olive oil with a knob of butter, to warm them through and give them a golden finish, or just microwave them with the knob of butter until heated through. Either way, they can be sprinkled with the Parmesan, if using (if you have not added it to the mix) and gratinéed to a golden brown under a hot grill if a crisper edge is preferred.

Divide the finished gnocchi between four plates (or place them in one large serving bowl). Place the gammon steaks on the plates and trickle the sage sauce over and around the gnocchi.

For a creamy finish, a tablespoon of whipping cream can be added to the sauce before whisking in the butter.

game birds

By the time October arrives, the game season in Britain has already started, but October and November are the months when much feathered game is considered to be at its best.

The season starts with a bang – literally – on 12 August, the 'Glorious Twelfth'. This is when the red grouse can be shot (until 10 December, a very short season). The red grouse (*Lagopus lagopus scoticus*) is found only in Scotland, Ireland and northern parts of England and Wales. It is the sole British representative of the Arctic willow grouse. Other close relations are found here, among them the ptarmigan (white grouse), capercaillie (wood grouse) and black grouse (blackcock and greyhen). Although all native grouse can be shot and eaten, the red grouse is the aristocrat, possibly because of its unique flavour. It has a pure diet, composed almost entirely of the ling heather which clothes the northern moors on which it lives (a specialist habitat which has limited its spread elsewhere), plus blackberries and seeds.

The native grey-legged partridge comes into season later (the beginning of September), as does its imported French counterpart, the red-legged partridge. Connoisseurs swear that the grey, although smaller and, now, sadly less common than the red, is much the better in flavour.

The pheasant is the other prime game bird (in season from October to February). This can be truly wild, but is also bred for the hunt by gamekeepers. That such an exotic-looking bird as the pheasant – the cock in particular – should have naturalized here (it comes from the Caucasus) amazes me.

Wild duck and wild geese can be bought around now, as can woodcock – which some maintain is the king of game birds. Guinea fowl and quail are also with us, but are now farmed and available virtually all year round. And there's pigeon as well, wild or bred, each holding its own distinctive, wonderful flavour.

sautéed pheasant and spinach with almond sauce

Pheasant join us on 1 October, leading on to 1 February. During most of their season, particularly in the latter part, they'll need up to 10 days of hanging, to develop a real game-flavoured tenderness. October offers warmer days, so just now you'll find a short three-day hanging spell will be sufficient.

There are both cock and hen pheasants to choose from. The cock is quite a large bird, with enough meat for almost four portions. The hen is smaller, with a more delicate edge, and perfect for two portions.

English spinach is still rich, softening amongst the buttered game pieces. To drizzle over the two there's a modern French classic – almond cream sauce.

SERVES 4
2 hen pheasants
2 tablespoons groundnut or vegetable oil
flour, for dusting
25g (1oz) butter
salt and pepper
450g (1lb) spinach, picked and washed

FOR THE ALMOND SAUCE
knob of butter
2 shallots, finely chopped

OPPOSITE: SAUTÉED PHEASANT AND SPINACH
WITH ALMOND SAUCE

8 button mushrooms, sliced
150ml (¼ pint) white wine
100ml (3½fl oz) Noilly Prat (calvados can also be used)
300ml (½ pint) *Chicken stock* (page 416), *Game stock* (page 416) or tinned consommé
25g (1oz) flaked almonds, toasted
150ml (¼ pint) single cream
150ml (¼ pint) crème fraîche
squeeze of lemon juice (optional)

Preheat the oven to 220°C/425°/Gas 7. Cut the legs from the pheasants, splitting each between the thigh and drumstick. To remove the breasts, cut along the breast bone, following the line of the carcass. The carcass becomes more exposed, finishing at the base of the breast connected to the wings. Once completely removed, each breast can be cut in two. This now provides each portion with a drumstick, thigh and two pieces of breast. The carcasses can be frozen for making game stock at a later date.

To make the sauce, melt the knob of butter in a saucepan, adding the chopped shallots and sliced mushrooms. Cook, without colouring, for 6–7 minutes, until softening. Add the white wine and Noilly Prat or calvados, simmering and allowing to reduce until almost dry. Add the stock or consommé, simmering and reducing in volume by three-quarters. Add the toasted almonds to the sauce with the single cream and crème fraîche. Bring to the boil and simmer for a few minutes, seasoning with salt and pepper. Liquidize the sauce before straining through a sieve into a clean pan.

Heat a small roasting tray on top of the stove and add the oil. Season the pheasant pieces with salt and pepper, lightly dusting each with flour. Place the drumsticks and thighs in the roasting tray, frying over a medium heat until golden brown on all sides. Place the tray in the oven, roasting for 15 minutes until cooked through.

Halfway through the cooking time, heat a large frying pan with the butter. Once foaming, add the breast pieces, skin-side down. Cook over a moderate heat for 3–4 minutes, then turn the pieces and continue to fry for a few more minutes. Add the legs and thighs from the oven to the pan with the breasts.

The spinach leaves can now also be placed in the frying pan. The leaves will cook amongst the sautéed pheasant, becoming tender after just a minute or two. Warm the sauce, adding a squeeze of lemon juice, if using. The pheasant and spinach can now be transferred to a serving dish, pouring some of the sauce over, offering any extra separately.

An extra 25g (1oz) of flaked almonds can be toasted, sprinkling them over the pheasant before serving.

bramley and russet apple pie

The old English Bramley apple pie is normally cooked in a relatively deep pie dish and simply covered with the pastry before baking. This recipe has found great success, because of its pure simplicity. Another pie-making technique is one that, they say, was introduced to us from America. Basically it consists of the apples totally encased in pastry. There are many other combinations, with the French extra-fine apple tart and the upside-down-baked caramelized tarte Tatin amongst them. Here I have chosen a totally encased pie. This does take a little longer to prepare, but finishes with the best of results. The quantity of apple slices is balanced well with the quantity of crispy pastry within which it is cooked.

The autumn and winter months, particularly October, provide us with a wonderful selection of home-grown apples. Here we use the Bramley's Seedling, which has an established reputation for use in cooking; its piquant bite will never let you down, needing only a slight helping hand with a sprinkling of sugar to counter its sharp cut on the palate. The Egremont Russet is also eating at its absolute prime. The flesh is surrounded by a rusty-coloured skin and has a distinctive, nutty, pear-like taste. Texturally the two apples marry very well, and the finished flavour is the best of combinations.

I also like to add finely grated orange and lemon zest. Neither begins to take over, but instead each adds an extra essence. The sweet pastry used here will offer exactly the right quantity to line and top the pie mould, leaving a crisp finish. For a thicker finish, the quantities can be increased to 450g (1lb) flour, 225g (8oz) butter, 100g (4oz) icing sugar, 1 egg, 50–75ml (2–2½fl oz) milk and a pinch of salt.

SERVES 8–10
FOR THE PASTRY
350g (12oz) plain flour, plus more for dusting
pinch of salt
175g (6oz) butter, diced, plus more for greasing
75g (3oz) caster or icing sugar, sifted
1 egg, beaten, plus 1 egg for brushing
2–3 tablespoons milk

FOR THE FILLING
675g (1½lb) Egremont Russet apples
1.25kg (2½lb) Bramley's Seedling apples
large knob of butter

OPPOSITE: BRAMLEY AND RUSSET APPLE PIE

75g (3oz) caster sugar (or 100g/4oz for a slightly sweeter finish)
finely grated zest of 1 orange
finely grated zest of 1 lemon
1 heaped tablespoon semolina

First make the pastry. Sift together the flour and salt. Rub the diced butter into the flour until the mixture resembles breadcrumbs, before adding the caster or icing sugar. Work the beaten egg into the mix, then slowly add the milk until it just begins to form into a dough. It is always best not to overwork the pastry; if you do, the finished result will lose some of its shortness. Cover and leave to rest in the fridge for 30 minutes.

While the pastry is resting, prepare the apples. Keeping the varieties separate, halve each apple and cut each half into three wedges. Using a paring knife, cut away the skins and cores. The apples can be left as they are or cut once more into thinner wedges, or simply cut in half for a chunkier finish.

Melt the butter in a large saucepan and, once bubbling, add the Russet apples and cook them on a medium heat for 5–6 minutes, then add the Bramleys and the sugar, along with the orange and lemon zest. Continue to cook on a medium heat, turning from time to time, until the apples are beginning to soften. Strain the apples in a colander, collecting all juices in a bowl beneath. Leave to cool.

Preheat the oven to 200°C/400°F/Gas 6. Grease a baking tray and butter and flour a 25 × 4cm (10 × 1½in) flan ring. On a floured surface, roll two-thirds of the pastry into a circle large enough to line the prepared flan ring. Press the pastry well into the ring, leaving any excess pastry hanging over the edge. Allow to rest in the fridge for 20 minutes.

Line the rested pastry case with greaseproof paper and baking beans or rice. Bake the pastry case in the preheated oven for 25 minutes. Remove the beans and paper, return the case to the oven and continue to bake for a further 5–10 minutes to crisp the base. Remove the case from the oven and carefully cut away the excess pastry hanging over the edge of the ring. Leave to cool. Trimming the case while still warm will prevent the pastry from splitting as it cools and retracts within the ring. Should the pastry have split during its cooking process, simply fill with raw pastry pieces once cold.

Roll a long thin strip from a small piece of the remaining pastry. Beat the remaining egg, brush the edge of the cooked pastry case with a little of it and cover with the thin strip of pastry. This will ensure the pastry lid will stick to the sides and not shrink over the pie. Brush this new edge with egg and brush the base of the case itself. Sprinkle the semolina into the case. This will help absorb excess liquor from the apples, preventing the pastry from becoming too wet. Spoon the apples into the case (the reserved apple syrup can be offered to accompany the finished pie). Roll the remaining pastry into a disc slightly larger than the flan ring. Roll on to the rolling pin and place across the top. Press the edge gently, then trim away any excess. Cut a small cross in the centre of the pastry to release excess steam from the pie. Leave to rest for just 10 minutes. During this short rest period, increase the oven temperature to 230°C/450°F/Gas 8. Brush the pie with egg and bake for 25–30 minutes, until golden brown. Remove from the oven and leave to relax for 15–20 minutes before removing the ring.

The pie is ready to serve, along with any saved apple syrup. This pie will eat very well with fresh cream, or perhaps *Crème Anglaise* (page 426) or *Prune and Armagnac custard* (page 426).

When peeling and preparing the apples you can place them in acidulated lemon water to help prevent discoloration. It is, however, always best to remove them from the water as soon as possible, so as not to allow the apples to absorb too much. Ground cinnamon, nutmeg or vanilla seed can also be added to this recipe for a slightly spicy finish.
The sweet pastry can be made in a food processor, simply mixing to the dough stage.

walnut butter scones with warm blackberries, raspberries and orange double-cream custard

In the first month of autumn, blackberries and raspberries are at their best, with walnuts just arriving to join them. To add to this over-indulgence of good produce, topping the whole thing with an orange double-cream custard takes on a sort of very attractive obscenity.

This dessert can be planned several hours or days ahead, but the scones should be made and eaten when still just warm from the oven, while light and moist.

MAKES 10–12 SCONES
**75g (3oz) butter, slightly softened, plus more
  for greasing**
225g (8oz) self-raising flour, plus more for dusting
1 teaspoon baking powder

pinch of salt
50g (2oz) caster sugar
50g (2oz) chopped walnuts
approximately 125ml (4fl oz) milk
1 egg, beaten (optional)

FOR THE ORANGE DOUBLE-CREAM CUSTARD
3 egg yolks
50g (2oz) caster sugar
1 vanilla pod, split (optional)
300ml (½ pint) double cream
finely grated zest of 2 oranges

FOR THE FRUITS
knob of butter
225g (8oz) blackberries
225g (8oz) raspberries
2 heaped tablespoons icing sugar

Preheat the oven to 220°C/425°F/Gas 7 and grease a baking tray. Sift the flour, baking powder and pinch of salt together into a bowl. Stir in the sugar, add the softened butter and rub quickly into the flour to create a fine breadcrumb consistency. Add the chopped walnuts, along with the milk, a spoonful at a time, and mix to a smooth dough. Should the dough seem too dry, add a little more milk, but do not allow it to become sticky. Roll the dough on a lightly floured surface until approximately 2–2.5cm (¾–1in) thick. Using a 5cm (2in) pastry cutter, cut scone shapes from the dough with one sharp tap, not twisting the dough as you cut, as this results in uneven rising.

Brush the scones with the beaten egg for a shiny glaze, or lightly dust them with flour for a matt finish. Place the scones on the greased baking tray and bake towards the top of the preheated oven for 10–12 minutes until golden brown. These are best served just warm.

To make the custard, beat the egg yolks and sugar together in a bowl until well blended. Scrape the insides of the vanilla pod, if using, into the double cream, then add the pod, along with the orange zest. Bring the cream to the boil, then whisk it into the egg yolks and sugar. Place the bowl over a pan of simmering water, the bowl not making contact with the water as this will become too hot and begin to scramble the egg yolks. Keep stirring until the egg yolks have begun to thicken sufficiently to coat the back of a spoon. Remove the bowl from the heat, and take the vanilla pod from the custard. The custard is now ready to serve hot, or leave to cool slightly for a warm finish. The orange zest can be left in or strained before serving. This custard also eats very well cold.

To prepare the fruits, heat the knob of butter in a large frying pan. Once bubbling, add the blackberries and cook on a fairly high heat for 2–3 minutes, then add the raspberries. Continue to cook for a further minute, then add the icing sugar. Roll the fruits quickly in the syrup and loosen with a few tablespoons of water. The syrupy fruits are now ready to serve.

To serve, split the warm walnut scones in half, serving two, three or four halves per portion. Spoon the warmed fruits on top, pouring the custard over and around, or offering it separately.

softened blackberries with hazelnut, almond and chocolate cake

Home-grown blackberries are on their way out and hazelnuts are just joining us – this recipe offers the chance to indulge in both. The cake is a flourless chocolate slice with a quite rich, nutty finish, perfect with the warm, softened blackberries.

SERVES 8 GENEROUSLY
175g (6oz) softened butter (almost at melting point), plus more for greasing
150g (5oz) shelled hazelnuts
100g (4oz) ground almonds
4 eggs, separated
175g (6oz) caster sugar
225g (8oz) plain chocolate, grated or finely chopped in a food processor
2 tablespoons brandy or whisky
pinch of salt
350g (12oz) blackberries, lightly rinsed
50g (2oz) icing sugar (or to taste), plus more for dusting (optional)

Preheat the oven to 180°C/350°F/Gas 4. Butter a 20–23cm (8–9in) diameter, deep, loose-bottomed cake tin, base-line with parchment paper, and grease the base and sides once more.

Roast the hazelnuts for 8–10 minutes until the skins have become loosened. The nuts can now be easily skinned by rubbing them in a cloth. Once all are skinned and cooled, blitz the nuts in a food processor until finely crushed. They can now be mixed with the ground almonds.

Whisk together the egg yolks and caster sugar to a thick frothy stage. This can be quickly and easily achieved using an electric mixer. Spoon the grated chocolate, ground mixed nuts, softened butter and brandy or whisky into the mix, folding everything in well. Whisk the egg whites and pinch of salt together (it is important that a scrupulously clean bowl and whisk are used), to a thick soft-peak stage. Fold the whisked whites into the cake mix, spooning it into the lined cake tin. Bake in the preheated oven for 50 minutes–1 hour until firm to the touch. Remove from the oven and allow to cool until just warm, before turning out of the tin.

While the cake is cooling, place the blackberries in a large saucepan with the icing sugar. Warm over a low heat, allowing the fruit juices to blend with the sugar, creating a syrup. Once warmed and beginning to soften, should the berries still have a tart bite, dust with more icing sugar until you achieve the preferred sweetness. The hazelnut, almond and chocolate cake can be dusted with icing sugar before portioning and serving with the warm blackberries.

spicy syrup butternut tart

This recipe is a sort of classic in the USA, often finding its way onto the Thanksgiving menu. The usual main feature is pumpkin, but I have found our home-grown butternut squash offers an extra depth of flavour, with a sweet, nutty and almond buttery edge.

SERVES 8–10
1 tablespoon butter, plus more for greasing
flour, for dusting
225g (8oz) *Sweet shortcrust pastry* (page 425)
550g (1¼lb) butternut squash, peeled, seeded and diced
2 eggs, beaten, plus 1 extra yolk
75g (3oz) light soft brown sugar
1 dessertspoon golden syrup
1 dessertspoon treacle
1 heaped teaspoon ground mixed spice
300ml (½ pint) double cream

Butter and lightly flour a 20cm (8in) loose-bottomed flan case and place on a baking tray. Roll the pastry on a lightly floured surface into a large circle before lifting with a rolling pin and unwinding it across the case. Press to fit neatly, leaving any excess pastry hanging over the edge. This can be left attached while pre-baking the tart case, to ensure a neat even edge. Chill the tart case for 30 minutes to relax and set. Preheat the oven to 180°C/350°F/Gas 4.

To make the filling, melt the measured butter in a large saucepan or roasting tray. If using the saucepan, add the diced squash and cook on a low heat, cover with a lid and stir from time to time. Cook the squash for 20–30 minutes, until tender, then transfer to a colander and allow any excess juices to drain. If using a roasting tray, simply melt the butter in the tray, add the squash and cover with a double layer of foil. Then bake in the preheated oven for the same cooking time until tender, also draining in a colander.

While the squash is cooling, pre-cook the pastry case. Prick the base of the pastry case with a fork and line with greaseproof paper and baking beans or rice. Bake in the preheated oven for 20 minutes, then remove the beans and greaseproof paper. Return the tart case to the oven and bake for a further 5 minutes, then remove from the oven. Leave to rest for 10 minutes. Trim away the excess pastry and brush the pastry case with a little of the beaten egg. Reduce the oven temperature to 160°C/325°F/Gas 3.

Gently squeeze away any excess moisture left in the squash, before pushing it through a sieve into a clean bowl (if blitzed in a food processor, the consistency tends to become too wet and loose). Spoon the sugar, syrup and treacle into the purée, then add the mixed spice, eggs and extra yolk, and the cream. Pour the tart mix into the pre-baked tart case and cook for 35–40 minutes. It's best to check the tart every 15 minutes. If it seems to be over-colouring, cover lightly with foil. Once baked and just set, remove from the oven and leave to cool until just warm.

This eats very well with whipped or pouring cream.

Toasted chopped or flaked almonds or walnuts can be sprinkled over and dusted with icing sugar just before serving.

baked cider, cinnamon and honey quinces with raspberries and sweet vanilla cream

Home-grown quinces can be found, but are not produced on a commercial basis. This yellow-golden fruit, originally from western Asia, is closely related to apples and pears. Quinces are either pear- or apple-shaped, according to variety. First choice is the pear-shaped, as these tend to be richer and sweeter, turning a delightful shade of pink once cooked.

Ripe quinces have a wonderful flavour and a rich golden colour. With a high pectin content, the quince is perfect for marmalade and jellies, as well as various puddings and savouries; indeed sweetened quince is traditionally served with roasted pheasant and many more game dishes.

SERVES 4

4 small (approximately 175g/6oz each) or 2 large quinces
½ lemon
100g (4oz) clear honey
300ml (½ pint) sweet cider
4 strips of orange zest
5cm (2in) piece of cinnamon stick
1 vanilla pod
25g (1oz) icing sugar
150ml (¼ pint) double cream
225g (8oz) raspberries

Preheat the oven to 190°C/375°F/Gas 5. Peel the quinces and halve them. Remove the core and seeds using a teaspoon. This is not essential, as once cooked and served, cutting around the core is simple enough. Rub each of the quince halves with the lemon half to prevent any discoloration. Place the fruits, cored-side up, in a roasting tray. Whisk together the honey and sweet cider and, once totally combined, pour over the quince halves. Add the orange zest and cinnamon stick to the tray. Split the vanilla pod and scrape out the seeds, keeping them for flavouring the cream. You can also add the scraped pod to the tray for an extra spicy edge. Cover the tray with foil and bake in the preheated oven for 40 minutes.

At the end of this time, remove the foil, baste the fruits generously and return them to the oven uncovered. Continue cooking for another 40 minutes until tender. During this time, baste the quinces occasionally until golden brown, with the honey cider also becoming syrupy. Once cooked, remove the quinces from the oven and leave to cool until just warm.

In a bowl, mix the vanilla seeds and icing sugar with the double cream. Whip this to soft-peak stage, just creamy enough to hold its own shape. The warm quinces can now be served drizzled with the syrupy cider honey, finishing with the raspberries and sweet vanilla cream.

OPPOSITE: BAKED CIDER, CINNAMON AND HONEY QUINCES WITH RASPBERRIES AND SWEET VANILLA CREAM

vegetables

Sautéed cep mushrooms and Cox's apples on walnut toasts 279

Sweetened potatoes and chestnuts with chives 279

Cauliflower casserole 280

Conference salad 280

Pumpkin soup 281

Pumpkin goulash 282

Buttered curly kale with broken potatoes, onions and chestnuts 282

fish

Seared peppered tuna fish with sharp rhubarb sticks 285

Roast cod with braised celeriac, button onions and bacon 285

Sesame halibut with Brussels sprout choucroute 286

Fillet of hake with butter-fried mizuna and dauphinoise potatoes 287

Salt and vinegar sea bream with fennel chips 288

Grilled herring fillets with stir-fried parsnips and apples and a mustard nut dressing 290

Grilled sardine, fennel, onion and black olive tart 291

meat

Braised lamb shanks with pumpkin and Swiss cheese mash 293

Roast topside of beef with braised cranberry red cabbage 294

Roast loin of veal with Jerusalem artichokes Lyonnaise 295

Slow-roast shoulder of pork with a celery, Bramley apple and potato pot 296

Rabbit and pork pot with a rhubarb and mustard soured cream 297

Roast partridge with soft chestnut sauerkraut and cranberry turnips 298

Roast loin of venison with savoury fig tarts 300

fruit and puddings

Hot pear and chestnut sponge with roasted Conference halves 303

Pear and roast almond tarts 304

Crab apple jelly 305

Sweet whole crab apples 305

Poached apples and pears with a lemon and vanilla sabayon 307

Warm sticky orange damsons with damson sorbet 308

Almond mousse with poached rhubarb and pomegranate liquor 308

sautéed cep mushrooms and cox's apples on walnut toasts

This recipe is a very simple starter or snack dish using two very 'in season' ingredients. Cep mushrooms join us in the summer and carry through to the autumn and early winter very well. This particular mushroom is one of the finest, with a strong meaty texture and a flavour that more than matches it. Should ceps not be available, a good alternative is the chestnut mushroom, not a wild mushroom, but one that is available throughout the year.

The Cox's apple carries the title 'the king of English apples'. This is due to its rich flavour, creamy consistency, with a juicy, sweet, nutty edge and enough acidity to work through all three.

The balance between the mushrooms and apples is helped by the walnut bread toasts and the fromage frais and chive dressing. The toasts can be just toasted or buttered and pan-fried for a richer finish. Fromage frais is a soft, fresh, unripened cheese made from skimmed milk and beaten to a smooth consistency. Almost all fromage frais has zero fat content and is mostly packed and marketed like yoghurt. With the help of vinegar, mustard and chives, it blends well with the ceps and apples. Fresh salad leaves can also be added to the recipe, garnishing the finished dish.

SERVES 4
8 ceps (12 if small)
4 slices of walnut bread, about 2cm (¾in) thick
knob of butter, plus more for spreading (optional)
2 Cox's Orange Pippin apples
1–2 tablespoons walnut or groundnut oil

FOR THE DRESSING
4 tablespoons fromage frais
2 tablespoons vinegar (white wine, red wine or sherry)
1 teaspoon Dijon mustard
salt and pepper
1 tablespoon chopped chives

Wipe the ceps clean with a damp cloth and trim the bases of the stalks. Cut the mushrooms into 5mm (¼in) thick slices.

The walnut bread can be toasted at the last moment, while you sauté the mushrooms. If pan-frying, first butter both

OPPOSITE: SAUTÉED CEP MUSHROOMS AND
COX'S APPLES ON WALNUT TOASTS

sides of the bread. Warm a frying pan and sauté the slices of bread to a golden brown on both sides. Keep warm to one side.

Quarter the apples, then peel and cut away the core with a small paring knife. Cut each quarter into three, providing six slices per portion.

Heat the oil in the frying pan and, once hot, fry the mushrooms for a few minutes on each side, to a rich golden brown. While the mushrooms are sautéeing, make the dressing by mixing the fromage frais with the vinegar and mustard, and seasoning with salt and pepper. Add the chives just before serving.

Once the ceps are ready, season with salt and pepper, and add the sliced apples and the knob of butter, if using. Stir for just a minute to warm the apples through before spooning them over the toasts. The dish can now be finished by drizzling the dressing over and around.

sweetened potatoes and chestnuts with chives

New potatoes have two seasons – the first earlies between May and July and the second earlies from August through to March. For this dish, varieties such as Charlotte or Estima will fit the bill, first cooked in boiling water, then caramelized with chestnuts in butter and sugar. The flavours suit many different main courses, although eating with most game birds and meats would be the first choice. They also make a very good stand-in for roast potatoes, perhaps even to accompany the Christmas turkey.

SERVES 4
550g (1¼lb) new potatoes (see above)
salt and pepper
40g (1½oz) butter
1 tablespoon caster sugar
16 cooked chestnuts (page 424 – if braising,
  omit the glazed finish), cut into quarters
1 heaped tablespoon 1cm (½in) chive sticks

Cook the potatoes in boiling salted water for approximately 20 minutes, until tender. Drain in a colander.

Melt the butter in a frying pan and add the caster sugar. Cook on a low heat for 1–2 minutes, then add the cooked potatoes and chestnuts. Continue to cook on a medium heat for 5–6 minutes, turning the potatoes and chestnuts from time to time, to ensure an even caramelization.

Season with salt and pepper and sprinkle with the chive sticks. The rich golden potatoes and chestnuts are ready to serve.

Once boiled, the new potatoes can be peeled before caramelizing.
This recipe can be doubled (or more) in volume, providing plenty for larger numbers.

cauliflower casserole

Cauliflower is a member of the same brassica family as cabbage, kale, kohlrabi, broccoli and Brussels sprouts. The differences among them have come about from the thousands of years of cultivation and selective propagation. This particular vegetable was developed by the Arabs during the Middle Ages, but was not highly regarded in Europe until the eighteenth century. The cauliflower can be found today in three basic colours, white, green and purple.

The growers say the best time to enjoy cauliflower is during the autumn, and it is indeed exceptionally good at this time of the year, but there are also the Lincolnshire cauliflowers which join us in spring.

This casserole mixes tender cauliflower florets with carrots and onions, binding them all with a loose cooking liquor enhanced by a garlic butter and some chopped parsley. The dish goes well with many roast and braised meat dishes and fish. It also stands well on its own as a vegetarian stew, to be mopped up with crusty bread.

SERVES 4 AS AN ACCOMPANIMENT
OR 2 AS A MAIN COURSE
1 large or 2 small cauliflowers, divided into small florets
salt and pepper
2 medium carrots
1 onion
4 tablespoons olive oil
1 bay leaf
sprig of thyme
150ml (¼ pint) white wine
juice of ½ lemon
75g (3oz) butter
2 garlic cloves, finely crushed
pinch of caster sugar
1 heaped tablespoon roughly chopped parsley

Cook the cauliflower florets in boiling salted water for 5–6 minutes, until completely tender, with just the slightest of bites. Drain in a colander and leave to stand until all excess steam has lifted. This releases the water from the vegetable.

Cut the carrots into very thin slices. For a more attractive presentation, carrots can first be 'grooved' in five or six lines, using a canelle cutter, from top to bottom. This will produce slices with a floral face. Slice the onion into thin rings.

Heat the olive oil in a flameproof braising pot on top of the stove. Add the carrots, onion, bay leaf and thyme, and cook slowly until the vegetables are tender and beginning to take on a little colour.

At this point, add the white wine and bring to the boil. Simmer the wine to reduce it in volume by two-thirds, then add 150ml (¼ pint) of water. Season with salt, pepper and the lemon juice. Simmer gently for 5 minutes, allowing the water to take on the other flavours.

While these vegetables are cooking, melt 25g (1oz) of the butter in a frying pan. Add the cauliflower florets and cook on a fairly low heat, the butter bubbling and heating the florets, while they begin to take on a light golden brown colour. Season with salt and pepper.

Mix together the remaining butter with the crushed garlic. Add the coloured cauliflower to the carrot and onion liquor, along with the pinch of sugar and garlic butter, stirring to emulsify. Sprinkle with the chopped parsley and the dish is ready to be served straight from the pan.

conference salad

The title spotlights the Conference pear amongst many other flavours. This salad basically consists of a lot of old favourites – chicory, watercress, grapes, walnuts and Roquefort – most having previously met in some form of salad. The bonus of this particular collection is that many are fresh in season now, the pears having been with us since October, walnuts a month earlier, grapes coming towards the end of their generous stint, with the chicory (also known as Belgian endive or witloof) available throughout the year but hitting its prime between November and March.

The grapes serve a double purpose, some being tossed amongst the leaves, others puréed for the dressing. The dressing quantity is quite generous, but it will keep refrigerated for a couple of days to use for other dishes.

The walnuts, once shelled, can be left in their skins or blanched for a minute in boiling water, scraping clean while still warm. This is a bit fiddly and time-consuming and is not essential but will leave a cleaner, neater finish and flavour.

SERVES 4 AS A STARTER OR LUNCH/SUPPER DISH
FOR THE DRESSING
100–175g (4–6oz) seedless white grapes
1 tablespoon sherry vinegar
1 tablespoon light soft brown sugar
100ml (3½fl oz) single cream or crème fraîche
4 dessertspoons walnut oil
salt and pepper
squeeze of lemon juice (optional)

FOR THE SALAD
4 small chicory heads
2 Conference pears
**1 large bunch of watercress, picked in sprigs and
   rinsed**
8 walnuts, shelled and roughly chopped
75–100g (3–4oz) Roquefort cheese, crumbled

To make the dressing, pick and quarter 50g (2oz) of the seedless grapes, mixing and liquidizing (an electric blender is best) with the sherry vinegar and light soft brown sugar. Strain through a sieve, pushing through all of the flavours.

Whisk the single cream or crème fraîche with the walnut oil and 3–4 dessertspoons of the grape liquor. Season with a pinch of salt and a twist of pepper, adding a squeeze of lemon juice, if preferred, to sharpen the finished flavour. This dressing is best kept in a screw-top jar, shaking well before using, as the ingredients will separate.

To make the salad, cut away the chicory root base, separating all of the layers and discarding any bruised parts. Peel and quarter the pears, trimming them all of the core. Cut each quarter into three or four slices. The remaining grapes can be peeled or left with their skins on, halving or quartering each one.

In a large bowl, gently mix the chicory leaves, watercress sprigs, chopped walnuts, grapes, crumbled Roquefort – adding the extra 25g (1oz) if preferred – and pear slices. Season with a twist of pepper, binding all lightly with enough creamy grape dressing to coat, before serving.

The dressing can be mixed with just the chicory leaves, watercress and pears, sprinkling the remaining ingredients over the finished salad.

pumpkin soup

Pumpkins run for quite a season, finding their prime in the month of October. In November, however, a good thick soup is more than welcome at the family table, or perhaps even to keep our hands warm in large mugs on Guy Fawkes' Night. The orange zest here is not just relating to the colour of the pumpkin. Without taking over, its citrus fruit flavour tends to lift and enhance the overall taste of the soup.

SERVES 6
1kg (2¼lb) pumpkin
1 teaspoon finely grated orange zest
1 large onion, finely chopped
1 large carrot, cut into small rough dice
1 teaspoon caster sugar
**900ml (1½ pints) *Vegetable stock* (page 417), *Chicken
   stock* (page 416) or *Instant stock* (page 416)**
**150ml (¼ pint) crème fraîche or single cream (if
   preferred without cream, simply use more stock)**
50g (2oz) butter, to finish (optional)
salt and pepper

Cut away the skin and seeds from the pumpkin, cut the flesh into rough 2cm (¾in) dice, then place in a saucepan with the orange zest, chopped onion, carrot, sugar and stock. Bring to a simmer and cook fairly rapidly for 20 minutes.

The soup can now be blitzed in a liquidizer to a smooth consistency. If slightly grainy, strain through a sieve. Return the soup to a simmer, whisking in the cream, and butter, if using. Check for seasoning with salt and pepper to finish.

Large croûtons of bread cubes fried in butter eat very well with this soup.

pumpkin goulash

The home-grown pumpkins, encased within the thick orange crust that helps them store so well, have a slightly softer flesh, which purées superbly, with soups often the most obvious choice of recipe. Here, this concept is used, providing a smooth puréed sauce to accompany many tender pan-fried chunks.

Goulash is a meat stew of simmering beef (sometimes pork, lamb or veal) in a paprika-flavoured sauce, paprika being the national spice of Hungary. This bright red powder is created from many varieties of pepper, some similar in shape to chillies but not holding their pungency.

This recipe is a vegetarian variation, throwing in a handful of chopped red peppers and tomatoes to balance the dominance of the pumpkin. Plain-boiled rice or cooked noodles or spaghetti are ideal to complete the dish.

SERVES 4 AS A MAIN COURSE OR SUPPER DISH

1kg (2¼lb) pumpkin
25g (1oz) butter, plus an extra knob
1 onion, finely chopped
1 garlic clove, crushed
1 teaspoon paprika
1 × 400g tin of chopped tomatoes, drained
1 teaspoon tomato purée
450–600ml (15fl oz–1 pint) *Vegetable stock* (page 417)
   or *Instant stock* (page 416)
salt and pepper
2 tablespoons soured cream or 100ml (3½fl oz) single
   cream (optional)
1 large red pepper
2–3 tomatoes, blanched and skinned (page 92)
2 tablespoons olive oil
freshly grated nutmeg
1 tablespoon chopped flatleaf parsley (optional)

Remove the seeds from the pumpkin (see below) and cut away the skin from the vegetable. For the sauce, cut 300g (11oz) of the flesh into rough 2cm (¾in) dice. The remainder can be cut into neater 1cm (½in) dice ready for pan-frying.

Melt the measured butter in a large saucepan, adding the 300g (10oz) of roughly diced pumpkin, the onion and garlic. Cook on a moderate heat for a few minutes, not allowing to colour, before adding the paprika, tinned chopped tomatoes and tomato purée. Continue to cook for a further few minutes before pouring in 450ml (¾ pint) of the stock, bringing it to a simmer. Cook for 15–20 minutes until the pumpkin is tender and beginning to break down.

Season with salt and pepper before liquidizing to a purée, pushing through a sieve for the smoothest of finishes. The sauce needs to be of a coating consistency. If too thick, loosen with some of the remaining stock. Recheck for seasoning with salt and pepper, stirring in the soured or fresh cream, if using.

While cooking the sauce, quarter the red pepper, cutting away the stalk and seeds. Each quarter can now be cut into 5mm (¼in) dice. The tomatoes can also be quartered, removing the seeds and cutting each piece into similarly sized dice.

Warm the olive oil in a large frying pan and add the remaining diced pumpkin. Cook over a moderate heat until just tender and golden brown. Add the diced red pepper with the knob of butter, and continue to fry for a further 2–3 minutes, before sprinkling the chopped tomatoes into the pan. Season with salt and pepper.

To finish the dish, the pan-fried vegetables can be added to the warm goulash sauce, ready to spoon over your choice of pasta or rice, if using. Grate a little fresh nutmeg over each portion, along with the chopped parsley, if using.

The pumpkin seeds are edible and can be dried, spreading them on a baking sheet, before lightly salting and placing in a preheated oven (180ºC/350ºF/Gas 4) for 15–20 minutes. These make nice pre-dinner nibbles or can be sprinkled over the finished goulash.

buttered curly kale with broken potatoes, onions and chestnuts

Curly kale is a leafy green vegetable related to the cabbage family, available from late autumn until very early spring. This vegetable does have quite an impressive history, having been around for over 2000 years, with many varieties developed by the Romans.

Here the kale is paired with some simple boiled and broken potatoes, fried sliced onions and fresh chestnuts, which are in abundance during autumn and winter. This loose, rustic 'bubble and squeak' style of vegetable dish suits these colder months so well, and also offers an alternative accompaniment to many roast meats, in particular the classic turkey and trimmings. This side dish also eats very well with most late-autumn game recipes.

4 large floury potatoes, unpeeled (Maris Piper work
  well, as do Desirée)
salt and pepper
450g (1lb) curly kale
2 large onions, sliced
50g (2oz) butter
12 cooked chestnuts (baked, boiled or braised,
  see page 424)
freshly grated nutmeg

Place the potatoes in a large saucepan, cover with cold water and add a good pinch of salt. Bring the potatoes to the boil and simmer until slightly overcooked. Depending on the size of the potatoes, this will take 20–30 minutes. Once cooked and soft, drain the water from the pan and cover with a lid to retain the heat.

While the potatoes are cooking, trim the curly kale of its stalks and discard any bruised or yellowing leaves. Each leaf can now be torn into smaller pieces, making them far easier to eat once cooked, before rinsing and leaving to drain in a colander.

Fry the sliced onions for 5–6 minutes in a knob of the measured butter, until golden and tender. Keep to one side. Cut or break the peeled chestnuts into quarters.

To finish, bring a large saucepan of salted water to the boil and add the curly kale leaves. Cook for 3–4 minutes, until tender. Meanwhile, peel the potatoes and break them down into chunky bite-sized pieces with a fork. Melt the remaining butter in a separate pan and add the sliced onions and chestnuts. Once warm, add the potatoes and gently turn them in the pan to coat with the butter. Drain the tender kale in a colander, lightly pressing to remove excess moisture, then spoon into the potatoes. Season with salt, pepper and freshly grated nutmeg to serve.

BUTTERED CURLY KALE WITH
BROKEN POTATOES,
ONIONS AND CHESTNUTS

283

seared peppered tuna fish with sharp rhubarb sticks

The main seasonal item here is the first of the indoor-forced rhubarb. Growers have named it champagne rhubarb, and it lives up to that title too. Each of the pink stalks is tender and slim, and not in need of too much of a sweet helping hand. Cooking champagne rhubarb needs only a little time, tenderizing quite quickly.

Tuna fish can be found more or less throughout the year, but it's mostly the blue fin tuna, probably the best of all, that finds itself in our markets at this time of the year. It is not a cheap fish, but then nothing in the premier league is. For a main course, only 175g (6oz) portions are needed, bearing in mind that this will eat as tender and clean as a fillet steak.

The tuna and rhubarb both have rich flavours, and their partners – white peppercorns for the tuna and balsamic vinegar for the rhubarb – help to create an exciting combination as well as a balanced overall taste.

SERVES 4

2 teaspoons white peppercorns
4 × 175g (6oz) tuna fish steaks, ideally blue fin
   (see above)
15g (½oz) butter, plus an extra knob
8 sticks of forced rhubarb cut into 2.5cm (1in) chunks
   (saving any trimmings)
1–2 tablespoons caster sugar
½–1 teaspoon balsamic vinegar, preferably aged
cooking oil
sea salt

Crush the white peppercorns to a texture slightly larger than milled pepper, then pat this on to just one side of each tuna steak. These can now be chilled while the rhubarb is being prepared and cooked.

Melt the measured butter in a large saucepan and add the rhubarb pieces, 1 tablespoon of the sugar and 6 tablespoons of water. Cover and bring to a gentle simmer, then cook for just a few minutes until tender. Carefully spoon the rhubarb chunks from the liquor and keep to one side.

Chop any reserved trimmings into rough small dice and add to the liquor. Bring to a simmer and cook gently for a few

OPPOSITE: SEARED PEPPERED TUNA FISH WITH
SHARP RHUBARB STICKS

minutes, mashing the rhubarb to thicken the liquor. Purée the liquor to thicken (if it is still too loose, simply increase the heat and reduce in volume further). Strain through a sieve, then add ½ teaspoon of vinegar and taste for a sharp acidic bite. The remaining vinegar can be added if needed for a sharper bite and the extra tablespoon of sugar for a slightly sweeter finish.

While the syrup is simmering, heat a tablespoon of cooking oil in a frying pan and, once hot, place the tuna fish, peppered-side down, in the pan. Cook for 2 minutes, turn the fillets and add the knob of butter to the pan. Continue to cook for a further 2 minutes, basting frequently with the butter. Season with sea salt.

Spoon the warm rhubarb chunks onto warm plates, drizzle with the sharp syrup and place the tuna fish alongside.

Simple steamed new potatoes eat very well with this dish.

roast cod with braised celeriac, button onions and bacon

The celeriac season runs through autumn and winter, and they are often still with us in early spring. Closely related to celery, with a similar flavour but with more of a nutty edge, and not the most attractive of vegetables, this rugged round tuber root is slowly but surely becoming more popular. The texture suits roasting and puréeing well, also sautéeing like potatoes.

This recipe uses celeriac in place of potato in a classic French dish. *Pommes au lard* is basically quartered or diced potatoes with button onions and fried bacon pieces, baked in the oven with chicken stock to moisten the dish. The potatoes absorb the flavour of the stock, enhanced by the onions and bacon. This is exactly how the celeriac chunks react. The meaty, nutty, savoury flavour accompanies the cod fillet very well, the fish keeping its own 'meaty' texture, with enough flavour to hold its own.

SERVES 4

150g (5oz) button onions, peeled
2 medium celeriac
25g (1oz) butter, plus an extra knob for brushing
salt and pepper
2 tablespoons olive oil
100g (4oz) piece of streaky bacon or diced pancetta
200ml (7fl oz) *Chicken stock* (page 416) or *Instant stock*
   (page 416)

**4 × 175–225g (6–8oz) portions of cod fillet, pin-boned
(page 9), with skin on
flour, for dusting
2 tablespoons cooking oil
1 tablespoon roughly chopped curly parsley**

Preheat the oven to 220°C/425°F/Gas 7. Place the button onions in a small saucepan of cold water and bring to a simmer, then cook for a few minutes. Strain and leave to cool. This short cooking takes away the raw onion flavour and they begin to tenderize.

Cut away the outer skin from the celeriac and chop the flesh into 2.5cm (1in) dice. Melt the measured butter in a large frying pan and, once bubbling, add the celeriac. Fry gently for just 2 minutes, season with salt and pepper and transfer to a large bowl.

Add a drop of the olive oil to the pan and increase the heat. Cut the bacon or pancetta into 5mm–1cm (¼–½in) dice and fry in the hot oil for a few minutes, until golden brown. Add to the celeriac and wipe the frying pan clean.

Split the button onions in half and heat the remaining olive oil in the frying pan. Sear the onion halves to a rich golden brown, cut-side down, turn them and continue to fry for a further minute or two. Season with salt and pepper, and add to the celeriac.

Mix the celeriac, onion and bacon, and spoon into a suitable earthenware or ovenproof dish (approximately 25 × 18 × 4cm/10 × 7 × 1½in). Bring the stock to the boil and pour it over the vegetables. Place in the preheated oven and bake for 40–45 minutes until golden brown and tender. Turn the oven off, leaving the dish in it, so the celeriac can relax and keep warm while you are cooking the cod fillets.

Season both sides of each fillet with salt and only the flesh side with pepper, before dusting the skin side with flour. Heat the cooking oil in a frying pan and, once hot, place the fish in, skin-side down. Cook on a medium heat for 10 minutes, then turn the fish over in the pan and remove from the heat. Leave to stand for 2–3 minutes. The residual heat in the pan will continue the cooking process, without imparting a dry, leathery texture to the fish.

To finish, sprinkle the chopped parsley over the celeriac and divide between the plates, along with the cod fillets, brushing each fillet with a little butter.

Halibut, John Dory and salmon also eat well with the celeriac, onions and bacon.

sesame halibut with brussels sprout choucroute

Choucroute is the more appetizing French word to describe *sauerkraut*. Sauerkraut is usually made from shredded white cabbage, pickled in white wine vinegar, with juniper berries and more. The basic idea is adapted here for the much softer member of the brassica family, the Brussels sprout. Marinating a green vegetable in any acidic liquid would result in a total discoloration, making it quite unappealing. Instead, a more mellow acidic reduction is prepared and mixed with the sprouts at the last moment. To enhance the flavour, fresh tarragon is added, along with very thin slices of kumquat and orange juice. These two are designed to complement, working so nicely with the nutty sesame-topped halibut, while at the same time accompanying the softened sprouts. All the ingredients mentioned suit late-autumn-to-early-winter eating.

SERVES 4

**4 × 175g (6oz) portions of halibut fillet, skinned
salt and pepper
50g (2oz) sesame seeds
1 egg, beaten
675g (1½lb) Brussels sprouts, outside leaves removed
6–8 kumquats (optional)
50g (2oz) shallots or small onions, sliced
2 teaspoons white wine vinegar
150ml (¼ pint) white wine
100ml (3½fl oz) orange juice
50g (2oz) butter, plus an extra knob
2 tablespoons olive oil
2 teaspoons picked and torn (or chopped) tarragon
leaves**

Season the halibut with salt and pepper, and scatter the sesame seeds on a plate. Dip the filleted presentation side of each fish portion in the beaten egg, then lay in the sesame seeds to coat, patting them on generously. As the fillets are coated, place them, sesame-side up, on a large plate, and chill.

Halve the Brussels sprouts, cutting away the small stalk base. Finely shred the halves and blanch in a pan of rapidly boiling salted water for just 2–3 minutes, until tender. Drain in a colander and allow to cool.

If including the kumquats, each one can be sliced into very thin rings, removing any seeds. Place the shallots or onions and kumquat rings, if using, in a saucepan with the vinegar. Bring to a rapid boil and reduce until almost dry. Add the white wine and boil to reduce in volume by three-quarters. Add the orange juice, bring back to a simmer and cook for a few minutes more, until reduced in volume by just a third. Whisk the measured butter into the liquor and season with salt and pepper.

To cook the fish, heat the olive oil in a frying pan over a medium heat. Place the halibut fillets in the pan, sesame-side down. Cook for 2–3 minutes until golden brown. Should the seeds begin to colour earlier, then turn the fish at that point to maintain an attractive finish. Once turned, add the extra knob of butter and continue to cook for a further 8–10 minutes (thin fillets of the fish could take just 6 minutes).

For the last 4–5 minutes of the fish cooking time, add the shredded sprouts to the orange choucroute liquor to reheat (they can also be quickly microwaved). Season with salt and pepper and add the tarragon.

To present the dish, divide the sprout choucroute between the plates, spooning any liquor over and around. The sesame cod can now be placed on top.

One or two lightly crushed juniper berries can be added to the shallots, and left in the finished dish to offer an extra flavour.
Diced or strips of fried bacon can be added to the choucroute. Almost all flat fish can be used in this recipe – skate, turbot and brill are all favourites – with our round-shaped salmon very close behind.

fillet of hake with butter-fried mizuna and dauphinoise potatoes

Hake is a member of the cod and haddock family. In this country it's the one often left out and ignored but in Spain its definite flavour and milky-textured flakes are much appreciated. The biggest problem we have is usually the price, always quite high due to its popularity overseas.

Dauphinoise potatoes are a classic: thinly sliced raw potatoes baked with garlic-flavoured milk and cream (sometimes with grated Gruyère cheese although this is no longer strictly the classic recipe). As the potatoes bake they absorb and thicken the cream mix, finishing as a soft mass.

Serving this potato dish with the hake has a definite purpose – creating a form of fisherman's pie. Here, however,

hake has a far more definite say, not lost amongst so many other flavours as can happen with fish pie.

Mizuna originated in China, although it's been cultivated in Japan since antiquity. These rocket-style salad heads have been taken up by British growers in recent years, who are certainly not short of a culinary audience to try them. With a mild peppery bite and almost nutty edge, the leaves suit simple rinsing and salad mixing, or steaming, boiling or stir-frying as a vegetable. That's the way they are to be used here, the peppery bite leaving a soft mustard flavour, perfect for hake and potatoes alike. For seasonal notes mizuna are picked mainly between July and November, stretching to December.

Hake steaks can also be used in this recipe, any bones easy to spot and remove, as they are large like cod bones.

SERVES 4
FOR THE DAUPHINOISE POTATOES
5 medium–large potatoes (Desirée, Belle de Fontenay or Cara)
350ml (12fl oz) full-fat milk
150ml (¼ pint) double cream
salt and pepper
freshly grated nutmeg
1 garlic clove, halved
butter, for greasing

FOR THE HAKE
4 × 6–8oz (175–225g) portions of hake fillet, with skin on
large knob of butter

FOR THE MIZUNA
2 tablespoons olive oil
25g (1oz) butter
500g (1lb 2oz) mizuna, picked and washed

Preheat the oven to 150°C/300°F/Gas 2. Peel the potatoes, slicing them very thinly, preferably using a mandolin slicer for consistency and ease, before patting them dry with a clean kitchen cloth. It's important the potato slices are not washed, as the starch is the thickening agent for the milk and cream. Pour the milk and cream over the potatoes, seasoning with salt, pepper and grated nutmeg, mixing together without breaking the potato slices. Rub an ovenproof dish with the garlic-clove halves, squeezing each well to release the garlic juices. Smear the dish with butter before spooning in the potato mix, finishing with an even spread.

Bake the potatoes in the preheated oven for 1 hour until completely tender and golden brown. If colouring too

To make the batter, whisk the cider into the sifted flour. Lightly flour a handful of the fennel wedges, dip each into the batter and place in the preheated deep-fat fryer. Cook until golden brown, drain, season with salt and keep warm in the oven while continuing to fry the rest.

Once cooked, remove the sea bream from the oven and tray and keep the fillets warm to one side. Reduce the oven temperature to 140°C/275°F/Gas 1, using it purely as a 'hot cupboard' for the fish and fennel chips while making the sauce. Transfer the bream court-bouillon to a saucepan, bring it to the boil and reduce in volume by half. Whisk in the olive oil, remaining butter and torn tarragon leaves, then season with salt and pepper if necessary.

To serve, place the sea bream fillets on warmed plates, pouring any excess fish juices into the sauce. Sprinkle a few sea salt flakes over each fillet. Arrange stacks of fennel chips beside (or offer them separately) and spoon the sauce over the fish fillets.

The fennel chips are also nice to serve as a snack or starter, with Mayonnaise *(page 419, or bought).*

grilled herring fillets with stir-fried parsnips and apples and a mustard nut dressing

The herring, with its distinctive flavour and moist texture, is a totally underrated and often ignored fish. It is possibly the fiddly cleaning that is to blame; if bought scaled and filleted, however, they need very little extra preparation. If placed skin-side down on a chopping board, any remaining bones and 'sinews' connected to the belly flap can be scraped away, leaving the fillets totally clean. Any tiny bones still embedded in the flesh will virtually disintegrate during the cooking. An autumn catch will provide you with plump fish, with the parsnip and apple accompaniments also reaching their prime.

The nut dressing is a combination of hazelnut oil and chopped chestnuts, with the wholegrain mustard and chives adding a sweet, peppery, onion edge.

SERVES 4 AS A STARTER
1 large or 2 medium parsnips, quartered
2 apples (Cox's, James Grieve or Laxton's Superb
   all work well), peeled and cored
squeeze of lime juice

1 tablespoon hazelnut oil
15g (½oz) butter, plus more for greasing and brushing
4 × 275–350g (10–12oz) herrings, scaled, filleted and
   trimmed (see above)

FOR THE DRESSING
1 teaspoon wholegrain mustard
1 tablespoon white wine vinegar
pinch of caster sugar
1–2 tablespoons crème fraîche (optional)
3 tablespoons olive oil
3 tablespoons hazelnut oil
salt and pepper
4–6 cooked chestnuts (page 424), chopped
1 tablespoon chopped chives (or cut into 1cm/
   ½in lengths)

To make the dressing, mix together the mustard, vinegar, caster sugar and a tablespoon of crème fraîche, if using (the extra tablespoon will give a creamier finish). Pour the oils slowly into the mix, whisking continuously. Once all the oils are added, season with salt and pepper. The chopped chestnuts and chives can be stirred in just before serving.

Remove the woody central core from the parsnip quarters, then cut each quarter into rough 1cm (½in) dice. Plunge the diced parsnips into boiling salted water. When it has returned to the boil, drain the parsnips in a colander and leave to cool naturally. Dice the apples to a similar size and squeeze the lime juice over them. This maintains their natural colour while offering a citrus bite.

Preheat the grill to hot. Heat the hazelnut oil in a wok or frying pan. Once hot, add the blanched parsnips and fry them over a moderate heat for 4–5 minutes, until just tender. Increase the heat and add the measured butter and apples. Quickly fry for a further minute or two, then season with salt and pepper.

While the parsnips are cooking, grease a baking tray and season it with salt and pepper. Place the herring fillets on the tray, skin-side up. Brush each with butter and season with salt and pepper. Place under the preheated grill and cook for a few minutes (5–6 maximum), until just approaching a firm touch. Stir the chestnuts and chives into the dressing. Arrange the herring fillets on warm plates with the stir-fry and finish with the dressing.

Mackerel also eats very well with the parsnips and apples. A few grains of coarse sea salt can be used to season the skin side of the fillets.

grilled sardine, fennel, onion and black olive tart

Sardines have been with us since the summer (they are particularly good barbecued), continuing through the winter months. Fennel is now coming to an end in late autumn, hence our taking advantage of its flavour while it's still with us.

The tart is made in a rectangular form, very much like a sort of one-layered savoury *mille-feuilles*. This is a very simple starter to put together (it can also make a main course for two sardine fans), with just the fennel, onions and olives baked on the puff pastry strip, before topping with the sardine fillets.

SERVES 4 AS A STARTER OR 2 AS A MAIN COURSE

6–8 sardines (12–16 fillets), scaled and filleted
olive oil, for brushing
salt and pepper, plus coarse sea salt
flour, for dusting
175g (6oz) *Quick puff pastry* (page 426, or bought)
large knob of butter, plus more for greasing and
    brushing
2 large onions, thinly sliced
1 large or 2 small bulbs of fennel
good squeeze of lemon juice
8 black olives, stoned
milk, for brushing

FOR THE FENNEL BUTTER SAUCE (OPTIONAL)

1 tablespoon crème fraîche or whipping cream
50g (2oz) butter
squeeze of lemon juice
1 teaspoon chopped fennel tops or dill

Lay the sardine fillets on a greased and seasoned baking tray. Brush the fillets with olive oil and season with coarse sea salt and a twist of pepper. Chill until needed.

On a lightly floured surface, roll the puff pastry into a long thin rectangle, approximately 25–30 × 10cm (10–12 × 4in). Transfer the pastry to a buttered baking tray. This can now be left as it is for a rustic uneven finish, or trimmed for a neater shape. Prick the strip of pastry with a fork and chill.

Preheat the oven to 200°C/400°F/Gas 6. Heat the knob of butter in a large frying pan. Once bubbling, add the onions and fry them over a fairly high heat, until softened and a rich golden brown. Season with salt and pepper and leave to cool.

Trim the fennel tops, saving any sprigs for the sauce, if you are making it. Split the fennel bulbs in half, removing any bruised outside layers, along with the central core. Now shred the halves finely, cutting across the bulbs. Place the cut fennel in a saucepan and add a good squeeze of lemon juice. Top with 250ml (8fl oz) of water and bring to a simmer. Gently simmer for 10 minutes until just becoming tender. Strain the fennel, collecting all of the flavoured liquor if you are making the sauce.

Spoon the cooked and cooled onions onto the pastry, leaving a 1cm (½in) clear border on all sides.

Cut the olives into quarters and sprinkle these over the onions. Spoon the drained fennel on top of the onions and season with salt and pepper, then brush with a little butter. Brush the pastry with milk and bake in the preheated oven for 15 minutes.

If you are making the butter sauce, warm the fennel liquor and add the crème fraîche or cream and the butter. Whisk to a smooth consistency, seasoning with salt and pepper and a squeeze of lemon juice. Just before serving, add the chopped fennel tops or dill.

During the last few minutes of cooking the tart, place the sardines under a preheated grill and cook for just 3–5 minutes, until tender.

To serve, lay the sardine fillets on top of the tart, offering the fennel sauce, if using.

braised lamb shanks with pumpkin and swiss cheese mash

The shank of lamb is a cut taken from the leg that can be quite awesome in appearance, purely in terms of its sheer size. However, almost 50 per cent of it is bone and it is not such a hard task to cook it by very slow braising, producing a sublime melting eating experience.

In this recipe, oranges and red wine are added to the cooking liquor, both working very well with lamb, the meat already being quite sweet. The seasonal edge to this dish is to be found in the pumpkin. Although it is with us through quite a few months, it is during October and November that the pumpkin is at its best. Here it is cooked until just softened, then coarsely mashed and gratinéed with Swiss cheese.

SERVES 4

4 lamb shanks
salt and pepper
2–3 tablespoons cooking oil
large knob of butter
2 onions, each cut into 6 wedges
2 carrots, cut into 1cm (½in) slices
3 celery sticks, cut into 1cm (½in) slices
4 garlic cloves
generous sprig of thyme
2 bay leaves
juice of 2 oranges and peeled zest of 1 orange
1 bottle of full-bodied red wine
generous pinch of demerara sugar
cornflour or arrowroot, for thickening (optional)

FOR THE PUMPKIN

1kg (2¼lb) pumpkin, skinned and seeded
large knob of butter
1 heaped tablespoon finely chopped shallot
freshly grated nutmeg
100ml (3½fl oz) whipping or double cream (optional)
50–75g (2–3oz) Gruyère cheese, grated

Preheat the oven to 160ºC/325ºF/Gas 3. Season the lamb shanks with salt and pepper. Heat the cooking oil in a large

OPPOSITE: BRAISED LAMB SHANKS WITH PUMPKIN AND SWISS CHEESE MASH

frying or roasting pan. When at a medium heat, place the shanks in the pan and slowly fry until golden brown all over. This will take up to 15–20 minutes, and a good percentage of the lamb fat will have been released. Remove the joints from the pan and keep to one side, discarding the lamb fat once cooled.

Melt the knob of butter in a braising pot large enough to cook the shanks. Place the cut vegetables, garlic cloves, thyme and bay leaves in the pot. Cook over a moderate heat for 10–15 minutes, until the vegetables are beginning to soften. At this point, add the orange juice, peeled zest, red wine, 600ml (1 pint) of water and the sugar. Bring to a simmer. Add the lamb shanks to the pot, cover with a lid and place in the preheated oven. The secret to good shanks of lamb is to cook them very slowly for 2–3 hours, depending on their size. It's always best to check after every 30 minutes, turning and basting the joints, and checking their tenderness. This will quite easily be identified by applying slight pressure by hand or with a spoon – the meat should give, almost wanting to fall off the bone. During the cooking time, should the simmering process be too lively, simply reduce the temperature of the oven. After 2 hours have a good check. If still slightly firm, leave for a further 30 minutes–1 hour to achieve a perfect 'carve with a spoon' texture.

Once cooked, carefully lift the shanks from the pot and keep warm to one side. Strain the liquor through a sieve. If you wish to serve the vegetables, garlic and herbs, they can be kept warm with the lamb. Bring the liquor to a simmer, continually skimming away any fat content and impurities. The liquor can now be served as thin or thick as you wish. It is important to taste as it simmers and reduces in volume; if too strong, the lamb flavour can be lost behind the over-strong wine reduction. If you feel the flavour is right, but a thicker consistency would be preferred, mix a little water with a teaspoon or two of cornflour or arrowroot, and whisk this into the sauce a few drops at a time until the right consistency is achieved. Whichever you prefer, it's always a good idea to boil and reduce 100ml (3½fl oz) of the cooking liquor to a thicker syrupy stage. This can then be brushed over the warmed lamb just before serving to give a shiny finish. Return the shanks to the sauce (the vegetables can also be added to the sauce or microwaved) and warm through for 10–15 minutes.

While the shanks are braising in the oven, the pumpkin can be cooked. Cut it into rough 2.5cm (1in) dice. Melt the butter in a large saucepan and, once bubbling, add the pumpkin pieces and the shallot. Cook on a medium heat for a good few minutes to start the cooking process without colouring. Add 4 tablespoons of water and cover with a lid.

Cook very gently, stirring from time to time, for 15–20 minutes, until the pumpkin is tender. If a lot of liquid is created within the pot, drain the pumpkin in a colander before returning it to the pan to be mashed. This liquor can now be discarded, or boiled in a separate pan and reduced to a thick syrupy consistency. This will intensify its flavour, and it can be added to the finished mash. Remove the saucepan from the heat and mash the pumpkin, as coarsely or as fine as you wish. Season with salt, pepper and grated nutmeg. If using the cream, this can be mixed into the mash or spooned over the pumpkin once in a suitable serving dish.

To finish, preheat the grill to hot. Sprinkle the grated Gruyère cheese over the top of the pumpkin and gratinée under the preheated grill until golden brown. The lamb shanks can now be presented on plates or in bowls, with the vegetables, garlic and herbs, if serving them. Spoon some of the lamb sauce over, offering the pumpkin mash separately.

When simmering and reducing the lamb cooking liquor, it is best not to allow it to reduce in volume by more than half. At this point the flavour should be full enough, needing just a little arrowroot, cornflour or instant gravy granules or powder (using a gravy thickener will also add a depth of colour to the finished sauce) to thicken if preferred. Should the sauce be lacking its orange bite, 100–150ml (3½fl oz–¼ pint) of extra orange juice can be boiled and reduced to a syrup consistency, enlivening the finished result.

roast topside of beef with braised cranberry red cabbage

Topside of beef is a boneless joint from the top of the inside hind leg. A close-textured cut with little or no marbling of fat to moisten as it cooks, the topside, if roasting, is best served rare to medium rare. The natural meat juices are then maintained, providing a succulent bite.

Red cabbage is filling the greengrocery shelves at this time of year, waiting to be introduced to the stove. The beauty of braising red cabbage is how it improves if made 24–48 hours in advance. All of the flavours have time to be absorbed by one another, coming together when reheated.

The addition of fresh cranberries makes a wintry, almost Christmassy, change from the ubiquitous fresh apples (though these can still be added) and the raisins that are also sometimes seen. Red wine vinegar is another classic flavour associated with red cabbage. I find this overpowers the cranberries, so here raspberry vinegar takes its place, adding a sweeter fruit piquancy to the braising pot.

The quantity of topside for six people is generous but I find it's always eaten, whether sliced hot or served cold later.

SERVES 6
2kg (4½lb) topside of beef
2 tablespoons vegetable oil or beef fat
salt and pepper
1 × 400g tin of beef consommé

FOR THE CABBAGE
1 large red cabbage (approximately 1kg/2¼lb)
1 onion, finely chopped
3 tablespoons raspberry vinegar
225g (8oz) fresh cranberries
450ml (¾ pint) cranberry or apple juice
3 tablespoons demerara sugar

Preheat the oven to 160°C/325°F/Gas 3. Cut the cabbage into six wedges, trimming away the central stalk and discarding any tough outside leaves. Slice each wedge very thinly. This can be made easy using a food processor or mandolin slicer.

Mix the shredded cabbage with the remaining ingredients and ½ teaspoon of salt in a large braising dish, placing a tight-fitting lid on top. Cook slowly in the preheated oven for 2 hours before checking. The cabbage should be very soft and tender. If not, continue to braise for a further 30 minutes–1 hour. Once tender, there will still be a percentage of loose cooking liquor. This can be left with the cabbage, ready to be absorbed when reheating, simply warming on top of the stove. Leave to cool, refrigerating until needed.

To roast the topside, preheat the oven to 220°C/425°F/Gas 7. Season the joint liberally with salt and pepper. Heat the vegetable oil or fat in a large roasting tray, then place the topside in the tray. Fry and colour well on all sides, allowing the outer layer of fat to melt into the pan. To colour well, this stove-top frying will take 15–20 minutes. Place the joint in the oven, roasting for 1 hour for a rare/medium-rare finish, basting from time to time. Topside will generally take 10–12 minutes per 450g (1lb) for rare and up to 15 minutes for medium-rare approaching medium. Well-done beef will need at least 20–25 minutes per 450g (1lb). Once roasted, remove from the oven, transferring the beef to a separate tray, loosely covering with foil while the joint rests for 25–30 minutes (during this time the red cabbage can be reheated).

Pour away the excess fat from the roasting tray, leaving any juices and sediment in the pan. Heat the tray on top of the stove, adding the beef consommé. As the liquor simmers, stir to release all the flavours from the base of the tray. Season with salt and pepper, if needed, before straining through a fine sieve.

The topside is now ready for carving and serving along with the loose roast gravy and braised red cabbage.

The *Classic roast potatoes* (page 422) or *Mashed potatoes* (page 422) will make perfect accompaniments – *Dauphinoise potatoes* (page 287) are a good alternative.

Two tablespoons of cranberry or redcurrant jelly can be added to the red cabbage just before serving. This leaves a shiny, almost sticky finish. A generous sprinkling of ground cinnamon can be added or perhaps a mixture of cinnamon, ground nutmeg and cloves for a complete spicy finish.

roast loin of veal with jerusalem artichokes lyonnaise

The knobbly Jerusalem artichokes are at their best from late autumn into spring. It is always best to choose the smoothest as this makes for easier peeling and less wastage. These artichokes do purée and roast very well, and are also delicious sautéed, as here.

The Lyonnaise concept has been borrowed from the French potato repertoire, where it consists of sauté potatoes with fried onions and chopped parsley. Here the onions are replaced with raw chopped shallots.

Veal is the meat from young calves. The imported Dutch variety is mostly milk-fed, giving a pale pink colour to the meat. There is also grass-fed, which is what you'll normally find here with our home-reared veal (organic is also available), carrying a richer darker colour but never quite reaching red. The loin cut of veal is the equivalent to that of the beef sirloin. It is a very tender piece of meat that, when off the bone, needs no more than 15–20 minutes' roasting.

SERVES 4
900g (2lb) Jerusalem artichokes
1 lemon
drop of cooking oil (optional)
900g (2lb) loin of veal, net weight without bone
salt and pepper

4 tablespoons olive oil
400ml (14fl oz) *Chicken stock* (page 416) or *Instant stock* (page 416)
100ml (3½fl oz) double cream (optional)
25g (1oz) butter (optional), plus an extra knob for the artichokes
2 tablespoons finely chopped shallots, rinsed
1 tablespoon roughly chopped curly parsley

Preheat the oven to 200°C/400°F/Gas 6. Peel the artichokes using a small paring knife, placing them in a bowl of water acidulated with the juice from half of the lemon. This will maintain the white colour of their flesh.

ROAST LOIN OF VEAL WITH
JERUSALEM ARTICHOKES LYONNAISE

If it is possible to obtain the veal bone as well as the meat, ask your butcher for it to be chopped into relatively small pieces. To help add flavour to the sauce, these pieces of bone can now be fried in a drop of cooking oil to a golden brown and added to the veal once ready to place in the oven. Season the veal loin with salt and pepper. Heat 2 tablespoons of the olive oil in a roasting tray and place the veal in, fat-side down. Fry on a medium heat, turning, until a deep golden brown on all sides. Leave the joint fat-side up in the tray, place in the preheated oven and roast for 15–20 minutes for a rare-to-medium-rare stage. Add another 6–7 minutes to take on to each further stage.

Remove the joint from the oven and roasting tray and leave to rest for 10 minutes. Pour away any fat, then heat the juices in the pan on top of the stove. Once hot, add the stock and bring to a simmer (if using the veal bones, it is here they will help flavour the stock), until the liquor has reduced in volume by half. If using the cream, add it at this point and return to a simmer, then cook for just a few minutes and add the butter, if using. Whatever the choice, the thin cooking liquor will have taken on a good veal flavour, the cream and butter offering a softer finish. Squeeze the remaining lemon half into the liquor and strain the sauce through a fine sieve.

While the veal is roasting, pat the artichokes dry and slice into 5mm (¼in) thick slices. Heat a little of the remaining olive oil in a frying pan and add a handful or two of the artichoke slices. Fry over a medium heat to a golden brown, turning the chokes from time to time. Season with salt and pepper and transfer to an ovenproof dish to keep warm in the oven while the rest are fried in the remaining olive oil. Once all are done, return them to the frying pan and add the knob of butter, chopped shallots and parsley. Season with salt and pepper.

Once rested, carve the veal, offering two or three slices per portion, accompanied by the Jerusalem artichokes and lemon cooking liquor.

slow-roast shoulder of pork with a celery, bramley apple and potato pot

All three main features in this dish have a long affinity with one another – apples and pork, celery and apples, and now the three together. This is an autumn dish through and through, with the Bramleys and celery in abundance. These fruits and vegetables are cooked slowly together, sitting on the potato, absorbing each other's flavours, ready to accompany a 4-hour slow-roasting of pork.

The advantage of choosing a shoulder of pork when slow-roasting is that it tends to carry a reasonable quantity of fat, self-basting as it cooks and maintaining a moist finish. After 4 hours the meat is ready to be virtually carved with a spoon, eating well with the soft, overcooked celery, bound with what is almost a Bramley apple sauce. For slow cooking, a larger piece of pork than usual needs to be purchased. This will then provide plenty of meat to share between four.

SERVES 4

1.25kg (2½lb) boned and rolled shoulder of pork, rind scored
cooking oil, for brushing
salt and pepper
3 jacket potatoes
50g (2oz) butter, plus more for greasing
1 large onion, finely chopped
2 large Bramley apples, peeled and cored
2 teaspoons demerara sugar
1 head of celery, stringy fibres removed
300ml (½ pint) sweet cider
450ml (¾ pint) *Chicken stock* (page 416) or *Instant stock* (page 416)
6–8 sage leaves, chopped

Preheat the oven to 160°C/325°F/Gas 3. When purchasing the pork, ask the butcher if it's possible to have a few pork bones on which to place the meat. This will prevent the joint from becoming stuck and burnt to the base of a roasting tray, over such a long cooking time. If bones are unavailable, use a small wire rack. Oil the pork skin and sprinkle liberally with salt. Place the joint on the bones or wire rack in the roasting tray and begin the slow roast in the preheated oven. This can now be left to roast for 1 hour before basting with any pork fat collected under the meat. Continue to roast, basting once more after the second hour. From here, I prefer not to baste, just leaving the joint to self-baste with the fat layer between the skin and meat. This helps the skin to crisp well, becoming crunchy crackling.

While the pork is roasting, prepare the celery, Bramley apple and potato pot. This will also be baked at the low temperature with the pork, needing 1½ hours before the celery is as tender as butter to eat. Place the jacket potatoes in a large saucepan, cover with cold water and add a generous pinch of salt. Bring to a simmer and cook for just 5 minutes, then remove the potatoes from the pan. Once cool enough to handle, peel the potatoes and cut each into 1cm (½in) thick slices. Grease a large ovenproof dish with butter and season it with salt and pepper. Lay the potato slices in the dish, overlapping if necessary, topping with the chopped onion and seasoning with salt and pepper. Slice the Bramley apples into similar thick round slices, lay them across the top and sprinkle with the demerara sugar. Cut the celery into 7.5–10cm (3–4in) pieces and place across the top. Season with salt and pepper.

Stir together 150ml (¼ pint) of the cider with 150ml (¼ pint) of the stock and pour over the celery. Dot with 25g (1oz) of the butter, cover with a lid or foil and place in the oven 1½ hours before the pork is due to be finished. After the first hour the lid can be removed, allowing the celery to take on a little colour, or it can be left to serve as it is.

Once the pork is cooked, remove from the oven and leave to rest for 15 minutes. This provides a little extra cooking time for the celery, should it be needed, also relaxing the meat ready to be carved (or broken) with a spoon.

Pour away any excess fat from the roasting tray and heat the tray on the stove. Add the remaining cider and boil to reduce in volume by two-thirds. Add the remaining stock and boil to reduce in volume by half. This now leaves a well-flavoured liquor to support the moistness of the pork. The remaining butter can be whisked in for a slightly silky finish before checking for seasoning and straining through a fine sieve, and then adding the chopped sage.

Remove the crackling from the pork, breaking it into pieces to serve. The meat can now be divided into portions, offering the crackling pieces and sage and cider liquor along with the celery, Bramley apple and potato pot.

For a more golden finish to the cooked celery, Bramley apple and potato pot, brush it with butter and colour under a preheated grill.

rabbit and pork pot with a rhubarb and mustard soured cream

Domestic rabbits are available throughout the year, but do have a suggested season between the months of August and February. From September to November, the rabbit is said to be at its prime. Unlike wild rabbit, the domestic needs no hanging time to help develop flavour and tenderize, particularly when made oven-ready at the age of three months. The meat is usually cooked in very much the same way as many a chicken or pork dish. The legs and saddle suit a simple roast, with the shoulders (legs also) working well in a casserole or pâté.

In this recipe a whole rabbit is used, cooked slowly with pork belly. When completely tender, the two meats are shredded and flavoured. The result is a very coarse pâté-style dish, the pork fat content acting as the preservative, ready to eat with lots of toast.

As an accompaniment to help offset this rich flavour, we have a purée of forced rhubarb, which joins us in November. The sharp, slightly sweetened rhubarb flavour is warmed by either wholegrain or Dijon mustard and bound with thick soured cream.

SERVES 8–10

1 rabbit (domestic, approximately 1.5kg/3½lb)
450g (1lb) pork belly, boneless
2 tablespoons olive oil
salt and pepper
1 large onion, finely chopped
2 bay leaves
sprig of thyme
2–3 strips of lemon zest
300ml (½ pint) *Chicken stock* (page 416) or water

FOR THE RHUBARB AND MUSTARD SOURED CREAM
225g (8oz) forced rhubarb, cut into 1cm (½in) pieces
1 teaspoon caster sugar
1 tablespoon Dijon or wholegrain mustard
150ml (¼ pint) soured cream

Preheat the oven to 120°C/250°F/Gas ½. Divide the rabbit, separating the shoulders, saddle and legs (I'm sure your butcher will do this for you). Remove the rind from the pork belly, keeping it to one side, and cut the belly into 2.5cm (1in) dice.

Heat the olive oil in a suitable large ovenproof braising

pan, add the pork dice and cook on a low heat, allowing the fat to be released and the pork to colour slightly. This will take a good 15–20 minutes.

Using a slotted spoon, remove the pork pieces from the pan. Season the rabbit with salt and pepper, and lightly colour it in the pork fat left in the pan. Once it is sealed, return the pork to the pan, along with the chopped onion, bay leaves, thyme and lemon rind. Add the chicken stock or water and bring to a simmer. Arrange the pork rind on top of the meats (this prevents them from becoming dry, also releasing any remaining fat content) and cover the pan with a tight-fitting lid. Place in the preheated oven and cook slowly for 2½ hours.

Take the meats from the oven, leaving them in the pot to cool slightly until comfortable to handle. Remove the rabbit meat from the bone, shredding or tearing into thin strands. Shred the pork pieces with a knife or fork, and mix with the rabbit. Drain the cooking liquor through a sieve, removing the bay leaves, thyme and lemon zest. Add the onion to the meats, along with the strained liquor and fat. Season with salt and pepper, then spoon into a suitable 1.2 litre (2 pint) pot or terrine. The shredded meat pot can now be chilled for several hours until set.

While the meats are chilling, make the rhubarb and mustard soured cream. Place the rhubarb pieces in a saucepan with 2 tablespoons of water. Cover with a lid and cook on a moderate heat for 8–10 minutes, until the pieces have become tender. Add the caster sugar and cook uncovered, stirring from time to time, to a thick pulp. Leave to cool. Mix together the mustard and soured cream with the cooled rhubarb. Season with salt and pepper and the cream is ready.

The rabbit and pork pot will now eat at its best with lots of toast, helped along with the accompanying cream.

The meats, once shredded and chilled, will keep for several days. To extend their life span, melt 100g (4oz) of pork lard and, as it begins to cool and thicken, pour it over the meats and place in the fridge to set. Providing the pot is completely covered (more fat may be needed), this will now have at least a fortnight's shelf-life. The pork fat, when set, scrapes away quite easily.

Ramekins can also be used in which to set the meats for individual portions.

roast partridge with soft chestnut sauerkraut and cranberry turnips

The partridge was once, during the 1800s, our most common of game birds. It would seem that over the years, being highly susceptible to modern farming techniques, it has become much harder to find, particularly our own British grey variety. This is smaller than the French red-legged, first introduced to Britain in the seventeenth century, but does have a slightly fuller flavour. Both the grey and red-legged are available from 1 September to 1 February. The best time to enjoy their rich flavour is during the autumn and early winter months, when the birds are younger and their meat more tender. I'd suggest you opt for the red-legged partridge, as these are bigger – just one a portion is ideal – still with a very good flavour.

Cranberries have a similar season to the partridge, almost all coming from the USA between October and January, with turnips mostly available from September to February. The two together create a fruity vegetable accompaniment that eats well with almost all game dishes, often becoming a family favourite to be served alongside the Christmas turkey, grouse or duck.

Sauerkraut is normally shredded white cabbage marinated in white wine and vinegar for a few days before cooking. This breaks down the coarse cabbage texture, also giving it a distinctive sharp flavour. Here the cabbage is not to be pre-soaked; instead simply cooked on the day. It is important to shred the white cabbage very thinly – to achieve this easily, I recommend using a razor-sharp mandolin slicer.

The partridges are 'barded' with back fat. This is the process of tying a thin layer of fat across the breast to protect the meat from drying out during roasting – a self-basting technique. Most birds are purchased with this already in place, but if not, a rasher of bacon can be used in this way or the bird can be left unprotected and basted while it roasts.

SERVES 4

4 oven-ready partridges, preferably red-legged, barded with a thin slice of back fat or rasher of bacon (see above)
2 tablespoons vegetable or groundnut oil
knob of butter for the partridges, plus 25g (1oz) for the sauce
1 teaspoon picked thyme leaves

FOR THE SAUERKRAUT

½ white cabbage, quartered and cored
25g (1oz) butter
150ml (¼ pint) white wine
3 tablespoons white wine vinegar
1 star anise (optional)
4 juniper berries (optional)
1 level teaspoon pickling spice (optional)
10 cooked chestnuts (page 424), cut into chunky pieces
salt and pepper

FOR THE TURNIPS

4 medium turnips
225g (8oz) fresh cranberries
300ml (½ pint) cranberry juice
1 heaped tablespoon caster sugar
2 knobs of butter

To make the sauerkraut, slice the cabbage as thinly as possible, preferably using a mandolin slicer. Melt the 25g (1oz) butter and, once bubbling, add the cabbage. Cook on a medium heat for 8–10 minutes, without colouring, until the cabbage begins to soften. Add the white wine and white wine vinegar, along with the spices, if using, tied in a muslin bag. Turn the cabbage well in the liquor. Place a lid on top, reduce the temperature and cook very gently for 30 minutes, until the cabbage is tender, with only the very slightest of bites. During this cooking time, should the liquor be running dry, add a few tablespoons of water and continue to simmer. The cabbage can be cooked several hours in advance, just needing to be reheated, adding the chopped chestnuts and seasoning with salt and pepper before serving.

To prepare the turnips, cut each into five or six wedges, then peel each wedge. This helps maintain a more even and smooth round finish. Place the wedges in a saucepan and cover with water. Add some salt, bring to the boil and drain immediately. This helps release some of the bitterness that turnips tend to have. Leave to one side.

Place the cranberries in a saucepan along with the cranberry juice. Bring to a simmer and cook for 5 minutes, then strain through a sieve, squeezing all of the juice from the berries.

Return the turnips to an empty pan, top with the strained cranberry juice and add the sugar and a knob of butter. Bring to a simmer, cover with a lid and cook for 5 minutes. Now remove the lid and increase the heat, allowing the cranberry liquor to boil and reduce to a syrupy consistency. As the liquor reduces, spoon the turnips around to ensure an even flavour and colour. Season with salt and pepper, and leave to one side.

To roast the partridges, first preheat the oven to 200°C/400°F/Gas 6. Season the birds with salt and pepper, heat the oil in a roasting pan and fry the birds on one side over a moderate heat, until golden brown. Turn the birds to colour on the other side, then fry and colour breast-side down. Stand the birds on their backs in the pan, breast-side up, add the butter and, once bubbling, baste the birds and put them in the oven. Roast the birds for a minimum of 8 minutes for a rare finish, or 12–15 minutes for a more medium touch. Remove the partridges from the oven and tray, and leave them to rest for 5–10 minutes, breast-side down. (This enables any juices to soak back into the meat.)

Pour away any excess fat from the roasting tray, before heating on top of the stove. Add 300ml (½ pint) of water. This will lift all of the flavours from the pan. For the maximum flavour, reduce the water in volume by two-thirds. Whisk in the 25g (1oz) butter to give the liquor a silky finish, and season with salt and pepper.

The rested partridges can now be untied and the barding or bacon fat removed. The skin can be left on or removed, as you wish. Cut away the legs, then the breasts, following the natural breastbone line with a sharp knife. The cutting does take a few minutes so, if necessary, the legs and breasts can be quickly heated through in the oven, while the sauerkraut and turnips are warmed and presented on plates. Any partridge juices can be added to the buttered liquor before straining. This can also be flavoured with a few drops of the cooked sauerkraut juices, to give a slightly piquant finish.

To serve, rewarm the sauerkraut and cranberry turnips. A few tablespoons of water may need to be added to each; this will create a steam, heating them through a lot more quickly. The remaining knob of butter can be dropped into the turnips, shaking it in to melt.

Arrange the partridges in a rustic fashion towards the front of each of four plates. The sauerkraut and cranberry turnips can now also be divided between each one. Drizzle the partridge liquor over the birds and the plates are ready to serve.

An optional enhancer is to chop the carcasses of the birds roughly when removing them from the bone. These can then be added to the buttered liquor, allowing it to simmer softly while presenting the birds, sauerkraut and turnips on plates. This can then be strained quickly and poured around, holding a more distinctive partridge flavour. Tinned game or chicken consommé can be used in place of the water, leaving a stronger finish. If using, this will only need to be boiled and reduced in volume by a third to a half.

roast loin of venison with savoury fig tarts

Venison offers such a distinctive gamey flavour, its strength controlled by hanging, and it is also one of the healthiest and most nutritious foods available. It may well be a 'red' meat, but it is lower in fat, higher in protein, richer in vitamins and minerals, and contains fewer calories than most other red and white meats.

There are five or six species of deer available in the UK, but the finest to choose from are the roe or fallow deer. The beauty of these two types of venison is that they need very little hanging and maturing. If cooked particularly young with no hanging, the meat will still be very tender with a beefy flavour, enhanced with a gamey punch. After 7 days of hanging the gamey flavour improves, and after 14 days a more distinctive taste will be found. So, as mentioned, you can be in command of the gamey strength.

In France the roe (*chevreuil*) is considered the ultimate. This is the youngest and usually most tender, but I feel the fallow stands as its equal. The meat's title – venison – applies to all deer once killed, including the elk, moose and reindeer of America.

For roasting, the best cut is the saddle, the leanest of loins with a moist succulent finish. The haunch (leg) adapts well to most cooking methods, as does the boned and rolled shoulder (if roasting, the shoulder needs a long, slow cooking time). Other cheaper cuts are perfect for slow stewing and braising.

This recipe gently roasts the loin and serves it with a savoury fig tart. November is the perfect time for venison and figs to work together. Figs are at their prime, with young venison available from Scotland and the first of the English. The tarts are peppered and cooked until slightly caramelized, to enhance their crisp, savoury-sweet, pepper-fruit flavour. The venison itself will then sit happily alongside, on a spoonful of buttered curly kale and red wine game sauce.

SERVES 4

450–675g (1–1½lb) curly kale (or spinach)
salt and pepper
iced water (optional)
2 large knobs of butter
4 × 175–225g (6–8oz) pieces of venison loin, trimmed
1 tablespoon groundnut oil

FOR THE SAUCE

50g (2oz) shallots, sliced
8 black peppercorns, crushed
6 juniper berries, crushed
1 bay leaf
4 tablespoons red wine vinegar
300ml (½ pint) full-bodied red wine
300ml (½ pint) *Game stock* (page 416) or tinned game or beef consommé
1 teaspoon plain flour
1 teaspoon butter
1 level tablespoon redcurrant jelly

FOR THE FIG TARTS

flour, for dusting
225g (8oz) *Quick puff pastry* (page 426, or bought)
25g (1oz) butter, plus more for greasing
6 figs, halved lengthwise
2 tablespoons groundnut oil
1 egg, beaten
4 teaspoons demerara sugar
black pepper

The sauce and kale can be prepared well in advance of serving the dish. To make the sauce, place the shallots, peppercorns, juniper berries and bay leaf in a saucepan with the red wine vinegar. Bring to the boil and allow to reduce until almost dry. Add the red wine, return to the boil and reduce in volume by two-thirds. Add the game stock or tinned consommé, return to the boil and reduce in volume by a third. The depth of flavour will have increased, producing a loose broth consistency. Mix together the flour and butter, then whisk this into the broth, which will thicken as it regains its temperature. Simmer gently for a few minutes to cook away the raw flour taste. Whisk in the redcurrant jelly, allowing it to melt into the sauce. This adds an extra flavour to accompany the venison, also giving the sauce a glossy shine. Adjust the seasoning with a pinch of salt and strain through a fine sieve. Reheat before serving.

Remove the thick stalks from the curly kale leaves. Rinse them and tear into smaller pieces. To cook in advance, blanch the leaves in boiling salted water for 3–4 minutes until tender, refresh in iced water and drain in a colander. Lightly squeeze of excess water and season with salt and pepper, then melt a large knob of butter and pour it over the leaves. These can now be reheated in the microwave when needed. Alternatively, the kale can be cooked while the roasted venison is resting. Melt the butter in a large saucepan with a few tablespoons of water. Once it is bubbling, add the washed torn leaves, stir, season and cover with a lid to create steam. Cook for

5–6 minutes, stirring from time to time, until tender. The kale is now ready to serve. If offering spinach, halve the cooking times.

To prepare the tarts, preheat the oven to 200°C/400°F/Gas 6. On a floured surface roll the puff pastry very thinly into a rectangle large enough to provide four smaller rectangles, each approximately 13 × 7.5cm (5 × 3in). Place the pastries on a lightly greased baking tray, prick each lightly with a fork and chill. Lightly dust the cut side of each fig with a little flour. Heat the oil in a large frying pan and, once hot, quickly fry the fig halves, floured-side down, to a golden brown. This literally takes seconds to achieve. Remove the fruits from the pan and leave to cool. Brush the pastries well with the beaten egg and place three fig halves, cut-side up, top to tail on each rectangle. Dot with the butter, and sprinkle each tart with a teaspoon of demerara sugar and a good twist of black pepper. Bake the tarts in the preheated oven for 15–20 minutes, until the pastry is crisp and the figs tender.

While the tarts are baking, roast the venison. Heat the groundnut oil and remaining butter in a roasting tray on top of the stove. Once sizzling, season the pieces of meat with salt and pepper and place them in the tray. Fry for a few minutes, until well coloured on all sides. Place the venison in the preheated oven and roast for 8 minutes for a medium-rare finish or 10–12 minutes for medium (well done will need 15–20 minutes), turning each piece over halfway through the chosen cooking time. Remove the roasted loins from the oven and tray and leave to rest for 6–8 minutes.

To serve the venison dish, spoon the cooked kale in a rectangular shape on one side of the plate and place a fig tart by its side. Pour a spoonful or two of the warmed sauce over and around the curly kale. Carve the loins into round slices and present them overlapping on top of the kale.

Port, between 3 tablespoons and 100ml (3½fl oz) depending on strength preferred, can be boiled and reduced in volume by two-thirds, before adding to the sauce for a classic finish.

ROAST LOIN OF VENISON WITH SAVOURY FIG TARTS

hot pear and chestnut sponge with roasted conference halves

The freckled, Russet-apple-lookalike Conference pear usually arrives at the beginning of October, lasting through the winter. And during this month, chestnuts also begin to appear, particularly those from Spain and Portugal, which are in full flow. Here the sponge is also flavoured with orange zest, which helps the two seasonal tastes to come into their own. For maximum extravagance, a mixture of golden syrup and treacle is allowed to bleed its way into the sponge, leaving a sticky trail of flavour. This recipe makes a good alternative to Christmas pudding.

SERVES 4

5 Conference pears
large knob of butter, plus more for greasing and
**   brushing**
1 tablespoon demerara sugar
caster sugar, for coating
whipped or pouring cream, to serve

FOR THE SPONGE

100g (4oz) butter
100g (4oz) caster sugar
finely grated zest of 2 oranges
2 eggs
100g (4oz) self-raising flour, sifted
pinch of salt
1 teaspoon freshly grated nutmeg
75g (3oz) cooked and peeled chestnuts (page 424),
**   roughly chopped**
2 tablespoons golden syrup
1 teaspoon black treacle

Peel three of the pears, halve and core them, then cut into large, roughly 2cm (¾in) dice. Melt the large knob of butter in a frying pan and, once bubbling, add the demerara sugar. When the sugar begins to caramelize, add the pears and cook quickly until golden brown and beginning to soften. Remove the pears from the pan and leave to cool.

To make the sponge, beat the butter and caster sugar with the orange zest until light and fluffy. Add the eggs, one at a time, until well mixed in. Mix together the flour, salt and nutmeg and beat into the creamy butter, along with the chestnuts.

Work together the golden syrup and treacle, then spoon into a buttered and floured 900ml (1½ pint) pudding basin (preferably plastic). Add a third of the caramelized pears. Stir the remaining pears into the sponge mix and spoon into the pudding bowl.

Cover the bowl with buttered greaseproof paper and foil, then place in a hot steamer and cook for 1¼–1½ hours. If you don't have a steamer, simply place the bowl in a saucepan, fill with hot water halfway up the bowl, cover with a lid and steam for the same amount of time. Check the level of the water from time to time to make sure it doesn't run dry. If a plastic bowl has been used, it is best to place a small plate or a piece of cardboard in the pan, to prevent it making contact with the bottom of the hot pan.

About 30 minutes before the sponge is due to be ready, prepare the remaining two pears. Preheat the oven to 200°C/400°F/Gas 6. Peel the pears and halve lengthwise, cutting carefully through the stalk and leaving it on for presentation, if possible. Scoop out the core with a coffee spoon or melon baller. Alternatively, leave the pears in their natural shape with the cores left in. Dry the pear halves on kitchen paper, then brush all over with butter and dip in the caster sugar to coat. Place the pears, flat-side down, on a baking sheet.

Bake in the preheated oven for 15 minutes, turn the pears over and baste with any syrup juices. Return them to the oven and continue to roast for a further 5–10 minutes. The pears should now have taken on a rich golden colour. If slightly opaque, finish the colouring process under a preheated grill. Once the sponge is cooked, remove it from the steamer and leave it to stand for 5 minutes before turning it out on to a plate.

To serve, divide the pudding into four portions and serve each with a roasted pear half, trickling them with any juices. Serve with whipped or pouring cream.

OPPOSITE: HOT PEAR AND CHESTNUT SPONGE WITH
ROASTED CONFERENCE HALVES

pear and roast almond tarts

Pears enjoy a reasonably short season, some only from September to October, others from November leading into the winter months. The pear used here, the Comice, gives us a slightly longer run, arriving in November and, with the right weather conditions, carrying on through to March.

The almond flavour here is to be found in a sponge. The almonds to be used are the whole blanched and peeled variety, which are then to be dry-roasted until beginning to take on a golden edge, providing a stronger, more intense finish.

Fresh almonds can be found at this time of the year, still encased in their green velvety skin, not quite forming the firm shell that normally surrounds them. The ones you'll find will have been imported from Greece, Spain or Italy. If you do decide to buy them fresh, increase the weight required by at least a third, taking into account the 'shells' to be peeled away. The recipe for the almond sponge will fill a 20cm (8in) round or square flan case.

SERVES 4

2 Comice pears
juice of ½ lemon
***Stock syrup* (page 429), to cover**
225g (8oz) *Puff pastry* (page 426, or bought)
flour, for dusting
butter, for greasing
milk (or 1 egg yolk), for brushing
caster sugar, for sprinkling
***Crème Anglaise* (page 426), pouring cream or**
 ***Prune and Armagnac custard* (page 426),**
 to serve (optional)

FOR THE ALMOND SPONGE

100g (4oz) fresh whole peeled almonds (see above)
 or bought blanched almonds
100g (4oz) unsalted butter
100g (4oz) caster sugar
2 eggs
25g (1oz) plain flour

Peel and halve the pears. Remove the central cores of the pears with a round potato scoop (noisette cutter) or teaspoon. Roll the pears in the lemon juice, then place them in a small saucepan and cover with the stock syrup. Top with a circle of greaseproof paper, bring to a gentle simmer and poach in the liquor for 2–3 minutes. Remove the pan from the heat and

place a small side plate on top of the greaseproof paper to keep the pears submerged in the syrup, thus preventing them from discolouring while the cooking process continues as they cool.

The tarts are going to be individual. To help them match the shape of the pear, cut a tear-drop shape from a thin piece of card, large enough to leave a 1.5–2cm (⅝–¾in) border around the pear. Roll the pastry into a rectangle 2–3mm (½–⅛in) thick on a lightly floured surface. The card can now be placed over the pastry and cut around with a small sharp knife. Once four have been cut, place each onto a greased baking tray. Prick the pastries with a fork and leave to rest in the fridge.

Preheat the oven to 200°C/400°F/Gas 6. To make the almond sponge mix, place the whole almonds in a dry frying pan and roast on top of the stove to a golden brown. Alternatively, bake the almonds in the preheated oven until golden. Leave to cool, then blend in a food processor to a ground almond consistency. Add the remaining sponge ingredients to the food processor and blend until smooth and creamy. This can now be chilled until needed.

Remove the pears from the syrup (this will then keep for several weeks in a jar in the fridge) and dry on kitchen paper or a clean cloth.

Spoon the sponge mix into a buttered 20cm (8in) round or square cake tin and bake in the preheated oven for 25–30 minutes, until firm to the touch. Remove from the oven and leave to cool.

The cooled almond sponge can now be turned out of the tin. To cut for the tarts, place the pear halves on top, flat-side down, and cut around with a sharp knife, before placing them on top of the tear-drop pastries. Brush the pastry border with the milk or egg yolk, sprinkle each pear liberally with caster sugar and bake in the preheated oven for 25–30 minutes, 35 minutes maximum.

The tarts are best eaten warm, serving them with *Crème Anglaise*, pouring cream or *Prune and Armagnac custard*, if using.

A splash of amaretto can be added to the almond sponge mix for an even richer finish. Finely grated zest from a lemon can also be added for a citrus bite.
This recipe can be adapted for apples, cooking the apples as for the pears and simply cutting a circle of pastry and sponge.
Once four portions have been cut away from the cooked sponge, the excess trimmings will make excellent accompaniments to a cup of tea.

crab apple jelly

The wild crab apple and its jelly hold a sort of Women's Institute image, made purely for prize-giving and presents. There's obviously an element of truth in this thought – I just wish I were one of the receivers.

These small overweight-cherry-like fruits also tend to provoke the 'can't be bothered' line, in terms of 'first we have to pick them, followed by the cooking, overnight draining and then the jamming'. However, once tried, this jelly will become an annual kitchen necessity. Once set, it spreads well on buttered bread or toast, or does sterling service alongside roast pork or game.

These pearls of flavour can be found in a rainbow of colours – bright yellow, rich green, orange, from pinks to deep reds. Cooking the fruits to a pulp will release their natural colour, leaving the jelly with a rich glistening shade.

MAKES 1 LITRE (1¾ PINTS)

2.5kg (5½lb) crab apples, washed, stalks removed and halved
approximately 600g (1lb 6oz) granulated or preserving sugar

Put the apples into a large deep saucepan, covering them with water. Bring to the boil, before simmering to a pulp. Pour the entire contents of the pan into a jelly bag or folded muslin cloth (free-standing jelly bags are now available, which you clip to a bowl or saucepan beneath). Leave to drip for several hours, preferably overnight to ensure the maximum amount of juice is released.

The quantity of sugar required is 450g (1lb) to every 600ml (1 pint) of liquid. Bring the liquid and sugar to a simmer, stirring from time to time, until the sugar has dissolved. At this point, boil for 3–5 minutes, before testing the jelly liquor for setting point. It's best to keep a few saucers refrigerated whenever testing jam or jelly. Pour a spoonful or two onto a cold saucer – once cooled and wrinkling when pushed with a finger, the crab apple liquor is ready. Skim away any scum collecting on the surface, before pouring into sterilized jars (page 9), cooling, sealing and dating.

Peeled zest of a lemon or an orange (or both) can be added to the jelly while cooking, leaving a faint citrus bitter-sweet bite in the jelly.

sweet whole crab apples

Here, crab apples are to be cooked in a simple, sweet stock syrup. Many other flavours can be added, with a choice of cinnamon, vanilla and nutmeg, or perhaps thyme, sage or rosemary. These ingredients will leave these small fruits with a very welcoming sweet/savoury flavour, eating well with meats, game and pâtés.

600g (1lb 6oz) granulated or preserving sugar
1kg (2¼lb) crab apples (preferably red apples), washed

Pour the sugar and 450ml (¾ pint) of water into a saucepan and bring to a gentle simmer, cooking until the sugar has completely dissolved, leaving the syrup transparent.

Put the apples into the syrup and return to a gentle simmer, cooking the fruits until just tender, but not splitting; at this point they begin to take on a pulpy consistency. The cooking process may take up to 1 hour. Once just approaching tender, remove the pan from the heat and leave the apples to cool.

They can now be transferred to sterilized jars (page 9) and sealed, ready for future use.

Apples (*Malus*) and pears (*Pyrus*) are the most important tree fruits in the temperate regions of the world. Both are descended from wild stock (the apple from the crab apple), and are thought to have originated in Asia. The ancient Romans and Greeks cultivated both, and there are now said to be some 2000 varieties of apple in Britain alone, and some 20 species of pear. Both fruit can be eaten in the hand or cooked, and are used in alcoholic drinks (cider from special cider apples, for instance, and perry from pears).

The autumn and winter months provide us with a wonderful selection of home-grown apples. The Bramley's Seedling, for example, has an established reputation for use in cooking, needing only a slight helping hand with a sprinkling of sugar to counter its sharp cut on the palate. Egremont Russet is also good at this time, the distinctive, nutty, pear-like flesh surrounded by a rusty-coloured skin. And another favourite is the Laxton's Superb, which made its first appearance in this country in 1897, courtesy of the Laxton brothers of Bedford.

Pears vary as much in flavour and texture. I cook with Conference, Williams and Comice primarily. Williams Bon-Chrétien were introduced to this country in about 1770, via a Mr Stair at Aldermaston. (These pears are known as Bartlett in the USA after their importer.) Comice is actually short for Doyenné de Comice, which basically means 'top of the show', a sentiment with which I certainly agree. The taste of a Comice is quite sweet, and the texture lacks that slightly grainy consistency of many other pears.

Quinces are closely related to both apples and pears, and can be found on a domestic scale in Britain. This yellow orchard fruit, originally from Asia, is high in pectin, perfect for marmalade and jellies as well as various puddings and savouries. Indeed sweetened quince is traditionally served with many roasted game dishes.

poached apples and pears with a lemon and vanilla sabayon

In the last days of autumn, Cox's Orange Pippin apples are already with us and the sweet and succulent Comice pear is just perfect to enjoy. In this recipe, the fruits are poached in sweet white wine, enhanced with lemon zest. Served trickled with the syrup and whipped cream alone, they will eat beautifully, but, although a little more involved, whisking the syrup with egg yolks to a light frothy sabayon stage offers the perfect accompaniment for the simple fruits.

SERVES 4

100g (4oz) caster sugar
400ml (14fl oz) sweet white wine
finely grated zest and juice of 1 lemon
2 Cox's Orange Pippin apples
3 Comice pears

FOR THE SABAYON

3 large egg yolks
1 vanilla pod, split

First make the syrup for the apples and pears. Spoon the caster sugar into a saucepan and add the sweet white wine and the lemon zest. Bring the syrup to a simmer and cook gently for 5–10 minutes, until the sugar has dissolved, slightly thickening the liquor.

While the syrup is cooking, pour the lemon juice into a bowl. Peel and quarter the apples, cutting away the core carefully with a sharp knife. (When peeling apples and pears, it is always best to peel from 'top to tail', rather than around, as this helps maintain the natural shape of the fruits.) Halve the apple quarters into wedges and place them in the lemon juice to prevent discoloration. Peel and halve the pears, then halve each piece again to provide twelve wedges. If possible, the stalk can be left on, perhaps between two wedges, to give a very natural appearance to some of the quarters. The core can also be carefully removed with a sharp knife, before the fruits are added to the lemon juice.

Once all the fruit is prepared, place all of the wedges into the simmering sweet white wine syrup, along with the lemon juice. Cover the fruits with a small disc of greaseproof paper to ensure they are fully submerged in the syrup. Bring the liquor back to a simmer and cook for 3–5 minutes. Remove the pan from the heat and leave to cool until just warm. While cooling, the fruits will continue to cook, becoming very succulent and tender.

When the fruits are just warm, make the sabayon. Spoon 100ml (3½fl oz) of the syrup into a large bowl and add the egg yolks and seeds scraped from the vanilla pod. Whisk over a saucepan of simmering water (an electric whisk or hand blender with attachment will make life a lot easier). It is important that the water is not in contact with the bowl, as this tends to scramble the egg yolks – the steam created will provide enough warmth on its own. Continue to whisk the ingredients until at least doubled in volume and creating thick ribbons. Remove the bowl from the pan.

Divide the fruits between four bowls, offering four pieces of apples and three of the pears per portion. Drizzle with a spoonful or two of the syrup, finishing the dish with the sabayon.

Apple or pear juice (or a mixture of both) can be used in place of the sweet white wine. If so, increase the sugar content of the syrup by 50g (2oz).
The split vanilla pod, if stored in an airtight container with caster sugar, will provide a beautiful vanilla sugar with which to make other sweet dishes.
For a sweeter finish to the sabayon, add 25g (1oz) of caster sugar along with the egg yolks and vanilla seeds.

OPPOSITE: POACHED APPLES AND PEARS WITH
A LEMON AND VANILLA SABAYON

warm sticky orange damsons with damson sorbet

A healthy season of damsons will carry them through quite comfortably to November. These country-lane hedgerow fruits, small deep-mauve-, black- or blue-skinned, are so sharp, with a raw bite that almost cuts the back of your throat. Mostly associated with preserves, jellies and gins (these adapt perfectly to the *Sloe gin* recipe on page 237), here the fruits are served just warm and sticky, ready to be cooled by the sorbet.

Below I've included a recipe for mascarpone cream. This is very quick to beat up and scoop onto the plate, offering a creamy texture and flavour to contrast with the sharp fruits.

SERVES 6
FOR THE DAMSON SORBET
675g (1½lb) damsons
250ml (8fl oz) *Stock syrup* (page 429)
juice of ½ small lemon

FOR THE STICKY DAMSONS
675–900g (1½–2lb) damsons
175g (6oz) caster or demerara sugar
grated zest of ½ orange
juice of 1 large orange
icing sugar, to taste (optional)

To make the sorbet, wash and halve the fruits. Remove the large stone, loosening it with the point of a small knife. Alternatively an olive stoner can be used, providing the fruits are ripe enough.

Place the prepared damsons in a saucepan, covering them with the stock syrup. Bring to a simmer gently, cooking for 8–10 minutes until the fruits are completely tender. Remove the pan from the heat, liquidizing the contents to a purée. Stir in the lemon juice and strain through a sieve. Allow the purée to cool before churning in an ice-cream machine for 20–25 minutes until thickened. Pour into a suitable container and leave to complete its setting in the freezer. If you don't have an ice-cream maker, freeze the sorbet mix and whisk it occasionally until it reaches a firm setting point. This will take several hours. Now remove from the freezer and blend in a food processor to a smooth slush, before refreezing completely.

For the sticky damsons, prepare the fruit as above (they can be left whole if you prefer, removing the stones as you eat them). Place the damsons, sugar, orange zest and juice in a saucepan. Cover with a lid and gently poach, stirring from time to time, until the fruits are tender. This will take 6–12 minutes, depending on their ripeness. Should a lot of loose juice have been released, this can be strained from the damsons, boiling until thickened to a sticky syrup consistency and pouring back over the fruits. For a sweeter finish, dust and stir with icing sugar to your desired taste. The damsons are ready to serve warm in glasses or bowls with a scroll of their own sorbet.

Here's the recipe for mascarpone cream: beat 25g (1oz) caster sugar into 100g (4oz) mascarpone cheese until smooth. Add 150ml (¼ pint) double cream and lightly whip to soft peaks. This can now be refrigerated to set firmer, or served soft and creamy as it is. This recipe can be doubled in volume.
The juice of ½ lemon or scraped seeds from ½ vanilla pod can be added to the mascarpone before sweetening, offering extra flavour.

almond mousse with poached rhubarb and pomegranate liquor

This almond mousse is a variation on a basic *bavaroise* (a classic French velvety cream dessert), one that has been with us for some time, adapting its soft creamy qualities to many flavours.

The liquor is a simple fruit syrup, taking on the essence of both fruits – the young forced rhubarb mixed with the juice and seeds of the pomegranate.

Pomegranates are a beautiful fruit, their firm almost leathery skin showing off the deep yellowy orange with tinges of red. Once cut, the real fruit is exposed – small pearls of translucent pink jelly encasing the pine-nut-lookalike seeds. Each of these can be eaten as they are, seeds included, or nibbled to enjoy just the jelly.

Pomegranate juice can also be taken from the fruit halves, squeezing gently as you would a lemon or orange using a basic juicer (an electric juicer tends to break the seeds, giving the finished juice a slightly bitter edge). A splash of bottled pomegranate syrup can be added to the finished liquor, not allowing the rhubarb to become too predominant.

SERVES 6
FOR THE MOUSSE

300ml (½ pint) full-cream milk

100g (4oz) ground almonds

4 large egg yolks

75g (3oz) caster sugar

almond essence, to taste

4 leaves of gelatine, soaked in cold water

250ml (8fl oz) double cream

50g (2oz) flaked almonds

FOR THE LIQUOR

350g (12oz) rhubarb

6 pomegranates

125g (4½oz) caster sugar

½ cinnamon stick (optional)

pomegranate syrup, to taste (optional)

To make the mousse, pour the milk into a saucepan, adding the ground almonds and bringing to the boil. While heating the milk, whisk together the egg yolks and sugar to a pale thick creamy ribbon stage (this is best achieved in an electric mixer).

Whisk a third of the milk into the whipped egg mix, pouring it into the saucepan with the remaining milk. Stir and cook over a low heat until it's thickening and coating the back of a spoon. The mixture must not boil. Once thickened, remove the pan from the heat. Squeeze excess water from the pre-soaked gelatine leaves, stirring them into the hot custard. Leave to stand, stirring from time to time until cooled.

This can now be strained through a fine sieve, squeezing all of the flavoured custard from the ground almonds. A few splashes of almond essence can now be added, enriching the nutty flavour, so that it's not lost once the cream is added. Whip the double cream to a soft-peak stage, before gently folding in the custard when it has cooled close to setting point.

The mousse can now be spooned into a suitable bowl, or small individual glasses or moulds. Refrigerate for a few hours to set completely. The mousses can be turned out by first quickly dipping the glasses or moulds in hot water before inverting onto plates.

The flaked almonds can be toasted or roasted (at 180°C/350°F/Gas 4) until golden brown. Leave to cool before blitzing, using a small food processor or coffee grinder, to a ground almond stage. Sprinkle them over the finished mousse, providing a slightly bitter almond flavour that enriches the sweet almond mousse.

To make the liquor, roughly chop 200g (7oz) of the rhubarb, placing it into a saucepan with the sugar and 75ml (3fl oz) of water. Halve and gently squeeze the juice from five of the pomegranates, adding the juice to the rhubarb in the pan. Bring to a simmer, cooking for 8–10 minutes, or more if need be, until the rhubarb has become very pulpy.

Strain the liquid into a clean saucepan. Cut the remaining rhubarb into 1cm (½in) dice. If cut at an angle this creates small diamonds of rhubarb, leaving a more decorative finish.

Add the rhubarb pieces and ½ cinnamon stick, if using, to the strained liquor and bring to the boil, before pouring into a large bowl and allowing to cool. While cooling, the rhubarb will continue to soften. Once cooled, a tablespoon or two of pomegranate syrup, if using, can be stirred in to the liquor, lifting the pomegranate flavour.

Cut the base end from the remaining pomegranate, dividing the fruit into six wedges. Bending back each segment, push the seeds into a bowl. The pith and membrane can now be removed, leaving the seeds loose and free. The seeds can now be added to the sweet liquor, ready to spoon around the finished mousse.

All sorts and sizes of moulds can be used in which to set the mousse; loose rings can also be used, covering each with cling film at one end before filling. This quantity of mousse provides approximately 150ml (¼ pint) per portion. Plastic moulds are handy to use, squeezing each gently to help release once dipped in hot water.

Once topped with the ground toasted almonds, a light sprinkling of icing sugar can be dusted on top, leaving a contrast of finish.

Amaretto (almond-flavoured liqueur) can be added, to taste, to the thickening custard, just before folding in the whipped cream.

4   wint

er

Winter has arrived; the final season of the year is with us. December carries the reputation of frosty starts to each morning; it's quite dark when we leave home, and often the same prospect is repeated on our return. But freezing thoughts are soon forgotten once we are welcomed with the crackling sound of the fire as we pass through the front door.

Winter is often described as cold or unfriendly; the coldness brooks no argument, but unfriendly it is not. The first of this season's months draws the family together. Eleven months have passed with probably too few 'table' occasions; however, this month sees the grand finale of the year, holding a true spirit of festivity as our preparations and gatherings lead us to 25 December. Christmas itself is one of the most sociable occasions of them all, embracing families and friends, and more or less all the vegetables, fish and meats produced on and

311

around this small island, with fruits welcomed from further afield, are included in our Christmas recipes. It's with our vegetables above all that the 'unfriendly' case against winter is lost, going back to our roots, with carrots, parsnips, swedes and more showing off their full potential once they have been scrubbed and the gritty layers of leeks rinsed. Brussels sprouts adorn shelf after shelf, their greener, firmer and crisper touch testifying to their peak condition.

The 'borrowed' fruits add the colourful decoration that Christmas demands, with tangerines, clementines, pineapples, pomegranates and cranberries furnishing the shelves of every greengrocer.

During those well-wrapped-up shopping trips for such items, the nose may pick up the smoky trail of roasted chestnuts, to be enjoyed by the bagful. On the big day itself, however, they'll be chopped and spooned through the rich roast turkey stuffing. Among December's recipes you'll find new turkey dishes from which to choose. The *Roast turkey and cranberry Wellington* (page 336) borrows its style and standards from the

classic beef Wellington – the large turkey breast is wrapped in its own stuffing and bacon, before being rolled in puff pastry and baked. There's also the *Crown of roast turkey served with its own bacon and sherry raisin pâté* (page 334), perhaps an idea to save for another year, instead presenting your table of gathered friends and family with a *Roast leg of pork with sage roast parsnips, apples and prunes* (page 340).

With the main course and accompaniments served, we move to pudding time. No Christmas would be the same without the deep rich fruity pudding itself, but there are alternatives. *Tangerine curd ice-cream with marshmallow meringues and Grand Marnier syrup* (page 346) is one, with *Cranberry, orange and port jelly with tangerine biscuit fingers* (page 346) another – both truly in the spirit of this annual event.

A tradition not to be forgotten for the festive table is Stilton – sitting proudly on the table, waiting to be scooped onto plates, perhaps with wedges of crisp ripe pears and a fine glass of port. The alternative approach to this particular blue cheese capitalizes on how well it adapts to so many flavours. The *Roast*

fig and Stilton salad with Parma ham and a port vinaigrette (page 351) is a great example of this cheese's strengths.

The game season continues in December – venison and wild duck, both carrying a very seasonal feel, are plentiful. And many apples and pears are still ready for picking with others being kept in cold store. Make the most of this conjunction with *Roasted and braised wild duck with red wine juniper onions and buttered pears* (page 341).

Almonds, quinces and celeriac, along with plump scallops, turbot and salmon, are also playing a very strong part in our menu planning, all available at quite a good price considering they have such unpredictable weather to contend with.

The twelve days of Christmas continue with many more presents to be unwrapped. A lot of these are from home soils, in particular curly kale and Jerusalem artichokes, though kohlrabi and salsify both need support from elsewhere. A lovely little oval orange exotic – the kumquat – is still in evidence, with no shortage throughout all of the winter months.

Virtually all of the culinary characters mentioned here can be found, tried and tested, in the first month of this particular season and, as the Christmas festivities draw to a close, it's time for a new year and new month to open the door to plenty of new helpings. January is a time for real hearty winter foods. Braises, slow roasts and stews come into their own. This time of year demands these styles, with little or no chance of arguing – but then, who would want to? Few require major strengths in the kitchen, and with so much scope the variety of what you can do becomes almost unlimited.

There are many brassicas on show, in varying shades of deep reds and greens, all suited to accompanying the simmering pot of goodies waiting to be ladled out onto our plates.

The *Braised Seville orange beef with horseradish dumplings* (page 371) offers not only tender large chunks of beef and steaming-hot dumplings, but also introduces the Seville orange – one we hear a lot about but, with its short season, so rarely see in recipes. Virtually all of the crop of this Spanish orange crosses into English waters, as in Spain it is held in little respect. Not a fruit for eating raw, the Seville first found fame for its bitter strengths and citrus flavours in marmalades. It's with this sort of flavour in mind that it came to make quite a strong contribution to this beef casserole, blending in very comfortably with the other flavours but each still having its say in the bitter-sweet and tender finish.

So what else does this month bring us? Pilchards, whiting, hake, gurnard and turbot have all been included, some, with nostalgia, cooked in a classic style, while others explore flavours from further afield, with blood orange sauce and avocado and mango salad offering a sweet, sharp finish to hake and turbot respectively (pages 364 and 369). Cod stands us in good stead throughout these months, eating particularly well once topped with a walnut crust, served sitting alongside the smoothest of parsnip purées (page 366).

Parsnips are home-grown roots that just seem to thrive on frosty conditions. If you're lucky enough to be offered organic parsnips, buy as many as you can. They are quite sensational, not just in their eating, but in the pleasure of their preparation, as you simply ease away that usually coarse outer skin with just a push of the thumb.

All winter vegetables should be taken full advantage of, with Jerusalem artichokes, kohlrabi and celeriac still supporting the home-grown sign in most of our markets, while the sweet potato from the tropical world provides us with a supper omelette – tortilla-style (page 355).

And fruits? Well, apples and pears are still available, as well as citrus fruits – the small peelable varieties still plentiful and holding their own with their larger partners. And don't forget our attractive, soft, sweet friend from the southern hemisphere, the lychee. They're in total abundance and can be enjoyed in *Lychee lemon whip with shortbreads* (page 386).

As January reaches its close, we begin to approach a quieter spell. February is more of a follow-on from the previous month, certainly as far as home-produced goods are concerned. There are the Bramley apples, with a few eating varieties still around, and the pears and citrus fruits we've already mentioned, and don't forget forced tender 'champagne' rhubarb, which adds its slight touch of fizz to the close of winter. Purple sprouting broccoli is also hitting its peak.

Valentine's Day on 14 February leads to happy warm eating, with this month still having a few culinary secrets it's willing to share. There are Chinese artichokes, oysters, sprats, fresh mackerel, salsify, pak choi and shrimps with mangoes, pineapples and coconut flavours to finish.

In this, the coldest of our seasons, we wrap up in plenty of pullovers, thick coats, scarves and gloves, or huddle in front of a roaring fire. And that's just fine by me, for, if you're hibernating at home, you're closer than ever to the stove.

OPPOSITE: CHAMPAGNE RHUBARB CLAFOUTIS (PAGE 412)

vegetables

fish

meat

fruit and puddings

sesame and ham sprouts

Whenever choosing Brussels sprouts, it is important to buy them as small and tight-leaved as possible. These signs will indicate their freshness, and they will thus need less cooking time. The ones you should steer clear of are the loose-leafed ones, almost like small fully grown cabbages, or those that are yellowing around the edges.

Bacon and sprouts do eat well together, but for a change I'm introducing ham. This adds a more subtle bacony touch, with the roasted sesame seeds enhancing the already nutty flavour of the sprout.

This recipe is easily doubled/trebled in volume for larger numbers at Christmas.

SERVES 4

100g (4oz) cooked ham (1 × 5mm/¼in thick slice
   should be plenty)
450g (1lb) small Brussels sprouts
salt and pepper
1 dessertspoon sesame seeds
1 tablespoon sesame oil
knob of butter

Cut the slice of ham into 5mm (¼in) dice and chill until needed. To prepare the sprouts, remove any damaged outside leaves, then halve each sprout. Cook them in a large saucepan of rapidly boiling salted water for a few minutes until tender, but still with the slightest of bites. Drain in a colander.

While the sprouts are cooking, heat a non-stick frying pan and add the sesame seeds. Cook on a medium heat for just a minute or two to roast the seeds to a golden brown. Remove the seeds from the pan. Add the sesame oil to the pan, along with the knob of butter, and warm the ham in the bubbling butter and oil, then add the drained sprouts. Increase the heat and fry for just 1–2 minutes, then season with salt and pepper.

To finish, add the roasted sesame seeds, and spoon the sprouts into a vegetable dish.

If the sprouts are particularly small, it is best to leave them whole, rolling them in the oil, butter and seeds once cooked. The sprouts can be cooked in advance, refreshed in iced water, drained and chilled until required. To reheat, either microwave or plunge them back into boiling water and simmer for a minute before draining.
Chopped hazelnuts or walnuts, with their respective oils, can be used in place of the sesame seeds.

leek, sprouts and onion egg cake with hazelnut dressing

Cooked in a similar fashion to a Spanish omelette – cooked potato slices and fried onions set in egg – this winter supper dish takes shape in just the one pan. The leek and sprouts are the two main seasonal items, with hazelnuts adding a nutty finish to this filling omelette. Once golden brown and ready to serve, there's also the option of topping the cake with either grated Parmesan or Gruyère and finishing under a hot grill until bubbling.

SERVES 6 AS A STARTER OR 4 AS A MAIN COURSE

1 leek
225g (8oz) Brussels sprouts
1 tablespoon hazelnut oil
1 onion, sliced
2 large knobs of butter
black pepper
6 eggs
50–75g (2–3oz) Parmesan or Gruyère cheese, grated
   (optional)

FOR THE DRESSING

10 hazelnuts, shelled
1 teaspoon Dijon mustard
1 tablespoon sherry vinegar
100ml (3½fl oz) crème fraîche
3 tablespoons hazelnut oil
salt and pepper
1 heaped teaspoon finely chopped chives (optional)

First make the dressing. Preheat the oven to 200°C/400°F/ Gas 6. Roast the hazelnuts in the oven for 6–8 minutes, darkening the skins. Remove from the oven, turning the oven off, place the nuts in a cloth and rub them together to remove the skins. The nuts can now be roughly chopped.

Mix the Dijon mustard with the vinegar and half of the crème fraîche. Slowly whisk in the oil to emulsify. Add the rest of the crème fraîche and season with salt and pepper. The chopped hazelnuts and chives can be added just before serving.

To make the egg cake, split the leek lengthwise, removing the outer leaf layer. Finely shred the two halves, rinsing them in a colander under cold water to remove any

OPPOSITE: SESAME AND HAM SPROUTS

grit. Leave to drain. Prepare the sprouts by pulling away and discarding any yellowing outside leaves, trimming the stalk base and halving each sprout. Finely shred them and blanch in boiling salted water for 2 minutes, then drain and allow to cool naturally.

Heat the hazelnut oil in a 20cm (8in) frying pan. Add the sliced onion and cook for 5–6 minutes, until softening and lightly coloured. Season with salt and pepper. Add a knob of butter, along with the leek, and continue to cook for a few minutes more, stirring the onion and leek together. Now add the drained sprouts and season well with salt and freshly milled black pepper. After a few minutes all will be heated through.

Beat together the eggs, season and pour over the vegetables. Cook over a reasonably high heat, until a soft scrambled egg stage is reached. Reduce the heat and leave the cake to cook without stirring for a few minutes, until the base is golden brown. To check, slide a palette knife or spatula down the side and under the omelette. Once completely golden brown, release the cake gently around the edge, then place a large dinner plate on top. The pan can now be turned over, releasing the omelette onto the plate. Return the frying pan to the heat and add the remaining knob of butter. Once bubbling, place the cake back in the pan, to cook the other side for 4–5 minutes, then remove from the heat. If glazing with cheese, sprinkle with the Parmesan or Gruyère and bubble under a hot grill.

The egg cake is ready to serve. Finish the dressing with the chopped hazelnuts and chives, and offer it separately.

roast parsnip, sage, onion and cheese pie

This pie is assembled in a very French manner, resulting in a 'pithiviers' finish. *Pithiviers* is a French pastry cake, classically consisting of two rounds of puff pastry sandwiching and encasing frangipane (a sweet almond filling). It is purely the shape we're borrowing here, which does make it very simple indeed – you just have to arrange and cover it, without shaping it into moulds. A late-autumn/winter dish, this takes full advantage of the sweet parsnip, helped by a roasted edge.

As for the cheese, a British goat's or sheep's cheese, soft or semi-soft, would be just perfect. One that is suitable is the Innes Button, a small goat's cheese, weighing just 50g (2oz), from Staffordshire. With a very creamy texture it has an almond edge to its taste, with honey and a taste of tangerine also happening, all of which suit parsnips. For this recipe, at least

three, if not four, of these particular cheeses will be needed.

I've included a cream sauce here, which does go very well with the pie, but is certainly not essential.

SERVES 8 AS A STARTER OR 6 AS A MAIN COURSE
8 medium–large parsnips, peeled
4 tablespoons olive or groundnut oil
knob of butter
salt and pepper
flour, for dusting
675g (1½lb) *Quick puff pastry* **(page 426, or bought)**
3 large onions
6–8 sage leaves, chopped
175–225g (6–8oz) soft or semi-soft goat's or sheep's cheese (see above)
freshly grated nutmeg
1 egg, beaten

FOR THE CREAM SAUCE (OPTIONAL)
2 tablespoons sherry vinegar
200ml (7fl oz) *Vegetable stock* **(page 417) or** *Instant stock* **(page 416)**
3 tablespoons whipping cream
squeeze of lemon juice
3 tablespoons hazelnut or walnut oil

Preheat the oven to 200°C/400°F/Gas 6. Cut the parsnips into 13cm (5in) lengths, measuring from the points rather than the large tops. The measured pieces can now each be quartered lengthwise and the woody centre cores cut away. The remaining tops can also be quartered, cored and trimmed.

Heat half of the olive or groundnut oil in a roasting tray. Place all of the parsnips in the tray and fry over a moderate heat until golden brown on all sides. Add the knob of butter. Place the tray into the preheated oven and roast for 12–15 minutes, until the parsnips are tender. Remove the parsnips from the tray, season them with salt and pepper, and leave to cool. Increase the oven temperature to 220°C/425°F/Gas 7.

On a floured surface, roll a third of the pastry into a 28–30cm (11–12in) round. Place the round on a large baking tray lined with greaseproof or parchment paper and chill to rest.

Slice the onions into thin rings and separate them. Heat the remaining olive or groundnut oil in a large saucepan, fry the onion rings over a moderately high heat, until tender, and allow them to take on a light colour. Season and leave to cool. Once cold, add the chopped sage.

The cheese, if soft, may not need to have its outer skin removed first, but semi-soft cheeses often do. If necessary, trim away any such hard outer skin, being careful not to waste any of the soft centre.

Lay the measured parsnip pieces on the pastry round with the points all meeting in the centre, leaving a 2.5cm (1in) border clear. This naturally forms a neat circle. If they are packed tightly, all of the pieces can be used. Sprinkle with freshly grated nutmeg, spoon a third of the sage onions on top, with most placed towards the centre. Slice or crumble the cheese and scatter on top of the onions. The remaining small pieces of parsnip can now be packed into the centre. Finish these with a little nutmeg. Top and surround the central parsnips with the remaining onion, to produce a slightly domed finish.

Brush the border of exposed pastry with the beaten egg and roll the large piece of puff pastry on a floured surface into a circle slightly larger than the first. Roll this loosely on the rolling pin and unroll it over the parsnip base. Firmly press the edges of the pastry together and chill for 20 minutes to set. To give a neat finish, place a large flan ring or glass bowl over the pastry and trim, leaving a 2–2.5cm (¾–1in) border. Classically a *pithiviers* has the pastry top scored with the point of a small knife in curved lines from the centre to produce a spiral pattern. This is not essential, but is very effective once baked. Brush the top with the egg, not allowing the egg wash to drop around the sides as this will result in an uneven rising of the pastry.

Bake in the preheated oven for 30–35 minutes, until golden brown and ready to serve, the cheese having softened and melted all over the parsnips.

If serving the pie with the cream sauce, boil the sherry vinegar to reduce in volume by half, then add the stock. Return to the boil and allow to reduce in volume by half again. Add the cream and simmer for a few minutes. Flavour the sauce with the lemon juice and salt and pepper, then whisk in the nut oil. The sauce is ready to serve with the pie.

sharp roasted parsnips with creamed spinach and parmesan cheese risotto

Parsnips are with us, and at their best, throughout the autumn and winter months. The sharp edge is to be found not only on their pointed tips, but also through the extra kick these vegetables are given with a caramelization of honey and balsamic vinegar. The touch of vinegar balances the sweetness of the honey and the natural sweetness of the parsnip. The risotto is flavoured and coloured with a spinach cream purée. Parmesan, a cheese so often added to risottos, works well with both these vegetables, the complete dish holding a good variety of textures. This vegetarian dish suits winter perfectly.

SERVES 6 AS A STARTER OR 4 AS A MAIN COURSE

900g (2lb) parsnips, peeled
salt and pepper
2 tablespoons olive or cooking oil
2 tablespoons clear honey
1–2 tablespoons balsamic vinegar

FOR THE RISOTTO

50g (2oz) butter
1 large onion, finely chopped
1 large garlic clove, crushed (optional)
225g (8oz) Vialone Nano, Arborio or other risotto rice
1 litre (1¾ pints) *Vegetable stock* (page 417) or
  ***Instant stock* (page 416)**
225g (8oz) fresh spinach, picked
4 tablespoons whipping cream
50g (2oz) Parmesan cheese, finely grated

Preheat the oven to 220°C/425°F/Gas 7. Quarter the parsnips lengthwise and remove the central core from each piece. This woody part of the vegetable can spoil the tender 'meat'.

Blanch the parsnips in rapidly boiling salted water for just 2 minutes, quickly drain in a colander and allow any excess moisture to steam away. Heat the oil in a roasting tray on top of the stove. Fry the parsnips in this over a medium heat, until golden brown on all sides, allowing them to become slightly burnt on the edges. This will help create a slightly bitter flavour to counter the natural sweetness of the vegetable. Roast in the preheated oven for 20 minutes.

After the parsnips have been roasting for 10 minutes, start the risotto. Melt half of the butter in a large saucepan and add the chopped onion and garlic, if using. Cook on a low heat for 6–8 minutes, until the onion is beginning to soften. Add the rice and continue to cook for a further 2 minutes. Pour in a quarter of the hot stock and simmer very gently, stirring until virtually all of the stock has been absorbed. Just a ladleful at a time can now be added each time the stock has been absorbed, while you continue stirring. Repeat this stirring and adding process for approximately 20 minutes, until the rice is creamy and tender, with still the slightest of bites. Not all of the stock may be needed to reach this stage.

While the risotto is cooking, make the creamed spinach. Shred the spinach leaves quite finely. Pour 2 tablespoons of water into a large saucepan on top of the stove. Once bubbling, add the spinach, season with salt and pepper and cook for 6–7 minutes. The spinach will now be completely tender. Transfer the spinach and liquor from the pan into a liquidizer and add the cream. Blitz to a smooth purée and keep to one side.

Remove the parsnips from the oven and pour over the honey. Return the parsnips to the oven and continue roasting, turning them from time to time, for a further 10 minutes. Remove the parsnips from the oven and place on top of the stove. If the honey is only lightly caramelized, place on a medium heat, allowing the honey to colour as the vegetables are turned in the pan. Once approaching a rich deep golden brown, carefully add a tablespoon of the vinegar (this may well begin to spit once in the pan); for a sharper bite, add the remaining tablespoon. Turn the parsnips once or twice more before removing from the heat and seasoning with salt and pepper.

To finish the risotto, stir the creamed spinach, Parmesan and remaining butter into the rice, then check for seasoning with salt and pepper. The complete dish is now ready to serve – offer both components separately or spoon the risotto into large bowls and top with the sharp roasted parsnips.

An alternative finishing method for this dish is just to add the finely shredded raw spinach to the rice, about 6–7 minutes before the end of the risotto's cooking time. The cream can then be omitted or added at the very end. Thin Parmesan shavings can be sprinkled over the finished dish.

avocado pear guacamole

Avocados are fruits, often looked upon as vegetables, served with so many savoury accompaniments. This particular fruit is native to Mexico, where guacamole – a dip for vegetables or a snack with taco chips – comes from. The name 'avocado' derives from its original Aztec name *ahuacti*, which, translated, is the shortened word for 'testicle tree'.

The pear within the title for this particular recipe is in fact the Comice pear, adding an element of the home-grown. The Comice is to replace tomatoes, now out of season, which are usually very much part of a guacamole recipe. I find adding this second fruit to the dish leaves a very clean and refreshing flavour, cutting through the sometimes paste-like finish that mashed avocado offers. The rest of the ingredients are much as expected – a fine dice of spring onion and chillies, a squeeze of lime and chopped coriander.

This can be served with hot French bread toasts as a snack or starter. It also eats very well with the *Sweet potato tortilla* on page 355. I've included a few optional accompaniments below: lamb's lettuce (mâche/corn salad) is one. This comes in bunches of nutty-flavoured green leaves, and is very much a winter salad.

SERVES 4
2 ripe avocados
2 small red chillies, halved, seeded and finely diced
3 spring onions, finely diced
juice of 1 lime
1 garlic clove, finely crushed (optional)
salt and pepper
2 small or 1 large Comice pears
1 heaped tablespoon chopped coriander leaves

FOR THE SALAD (OPTIONAL)
2 tablespoons soured cream
2 bunches of lamb's lettuce, picked and washed
1 tablespoon olive oil

Halve the avocados, removing the stones, before cutting into quarters. The skin can now easily be pulled away, scraping any excess flesh left in the skins. Place the quarters in a food processor, or in a bowl if only mashing. Add the red chillies, spring onions, half the lime juice and the garlic, if using, seasoning with salt and pepper. Whizz to a purée, or mash roughly with a fork, leaving a chunky finish.

Peel and quarter the pears, cutting away the core from each. Cut the quarters into a small dice, drizzling with the remaining lime juice. The diced pear and chopped coriander can now be stirred into the avocado mix. Cover with cling film and refrigerate until needed. It's important not to make the guacamole more than 1 hour before eating. If made too far in advance the avocados and pears will discolour. The avocado pear guacamole is now ready.

If serving with the salad, the guacamole can be spooned and lightly pressed in a pastry cutter, forming a fishcake-style disc on the centre of four plates. Drizzle the soured cream around each, topping the guacamole cakes with a stack of lamb's lettuce leaves, drizzled with olive oil.

kohlrabi rémoulade with warm salmon fillets

Kohlrabi, a member of the cabbage family, is found in colours ranging from white to pale green and even purple. This vegetable is best eaten when it is at its most tender, basically when about the size of a medium-to-large turnip; any bigger and the texture seems to toughen, almost becoming spongy. The smaller types of this vegetable are delicious grated and eaten raw. The flavour of the kohlrabi can range from that of cabbage, moving on to that of celeriac, with a sort of radish bite. As with many other vegetables, braising, boiling, sautéeing or steaming all suit it well.

Rémoulade is a mayonnaise, a bit like tartare sauce, enhanced with mustard, capers, gherkins and anchovies. Normally the flavouring ingredients are just chopped and left in the sauce. Here I liquidize them into the mayonnaise base, before straining. The rémoulade will now contain all of the flavours, with a smooth finish ready to spoon together with the kohlrabi and chives.

SERVES 4 AS A STARTER
2 medium–large kohlrabi, peeled
1–2 tablespoons olive oil
flour, for dusting
4 × 100g (4oz) salmon fillets, pin-boned (page 9)
  and skinned
knob of butter
1 tablespoon chopped chives

FOR THE RÉMOULADE SAUCE
100ml (3½fl oz) *Mayonnaise* (page 419, or bought)
1 teaspoon Dijon mustard
1 teaspoon chopped capers
1 teaspoon chopped gherkins
2 tinned anchovy fillets, chopped
3 tablespoons double cream
salt and pepper

First make the rémoulade sauce. Blend together the mayonnaise, mustard, capers, gherkins and anchovy fillets until smooth. Add the double cream and season with a twist of pepper, adding more salt if necessary (taking into account the anchovies' salt content).

Coarsely grate the kohlrabi and dry on kitchen paper. Season with salt and pepper, then stir in enough rémoulade sauce to bind.

Heat the olive oil in a frying pan. Lightly flour the presentation side of the salmon fillets and place them in the oil, floured-side down. Cook on a gentle heat for 6–7 minutes, only allowing the fish to become a pale golden brown. Season the fish with salt and pepper and add the knob of butter to the pan just before turning the fish over. Once turned, remove the pan from the heat, also lightly seasoning the presentation side with a pinch of salt only. Left in the pan for a further 2–3 minutes, the fish will continue to cook in the residual heat, maintaining a moist pink finish.

Add the chopped chives to the kohlrabi and divide it between the plates. Present the salmon on top of, or beside, the kohlrabi, ready to serve.

A trickle of olive oil flavoured with a squeeze of lemon or lime juice can be drizzled over the salmon before serving. Small dice of smoked salmon (50–75g/2–3oz would be plenty) can also be added to the kohlrabi, offering an extra smoky edge to the finished dish.

KOHLRABI RÉMOULADE WITH WARM SALMON FILLETS

Root vegetables are virtually synonymous with the cuisines of colder climates – you won't find many parsnip recipes in the Mediterranean. They are temperate plants on the whole, preferring a defined cold period, often with frosts, for successful growth, which is why most are at their best in winter.

Our familiar root vegetables belong to a variety of families: turnips and swedes (and radishes) to the *Cruciferae* (*Brassicaceae*); scorzonera and salsify (and Jerusalem artichokes) to the *Compositae* (*Asteraceae*); and carrots, parsnips and celeriac to the *Umbelliferae* (*Apiaceae*). Beetroot stands by itself, as a member of the *Chenopodiaceae* family.

All grow underground, and although all are commonly called 'roots', some – like swedes and turnips – are actually the swollen stem bases of the plant. All have developed from wild origins: wild carrots, parsnips and celery can still be found, although they are too sharp in flavour to be pleasant to eat. They were all three once used as a flavouring rather than as a vegetable, until they were cultivated to form larger,

sweeter roots, and often to change colour (carrots were white and purple at first). Also, interestingly, many root vegetables have been – and still are – used as sweeteners and in sweet contexts. Parsnips and carrots were used to sweeten foods (think of the old, now fashionable, carrot cake).

Few root vegetables are very attractive to look at, having thick skins, knobs, wrinkles and crevices in which dirt can accumulate. Placing these negatives to one side, there are plenty of positives to be found once they are peeled. All have aromatic, colourful flesh, which can be cooked in a variety of ways: puréed as a vegetable accompaniment or soup, classically roasted or sautéed in butter.

parsnip fritters with blue cheese walnut whip

Deep-frying these fritters gives them the nutty caramel amber edges so recognizable when roasting the white roots. Not difficult to make, they are a lovely warm snack to offer at winter social gatherings and the blue cheese and walnut whip is the perfect dip for them. A selection of blue cheeses can be used, but my favourite is the Irish cow's-milk Cashel Blue, made in roughly the same way as Roquefort (a ewe's-milk cheese that whips just as well into this recipe), but with a slightly softer texture and less salty finish. The whip is put together with mayonnaise (for home-made, try the one featured on page 419, but a quality bought variety works just as well), lime juice, double cream and walnuts.

SERVES 4–6 AS A SNACK OR STARTER
(MAKES 30–35 FRITTERS)
1kg (2¼lb) parsnips, peeled
salt and pepper
½ onion, very finely chopped
2 eggs
25g (1oz) butter, softened
25g (1oz) plain flour
oil, for deep-frying

FOR THE BLUE CHEESE WALNUT WHIP
75g (3oz) blue cheese (see above), crumbled and at room temperature
150ml (¼ pint) *Mayonnaise* (page 419, or bought)
juice of 1 lime
8–10 walnut halves, chopped into small pieces
pinch of Cayenne pepper
100ml (3½fl oz) double cream

Quarter the parsnips lengthwise and remove the central woody core. Cook in boiling salted water until completely tender, then drain. Place the parsnips back in the saucepan and stir over a low heat, allowing them to dry. Then purée with a potato masher for a coarse finish or blitz until smooth in a food processor.

Rinse the chopped onion in a sieve (this helps remove its raw flavour), dry it well and add to the parsnips along with the eggs and butter. Add the flour, beating it in well. Season with salt and pepper.

While the parsnips are cooking, make the whip. Whisk the cheese into the mayonnaise, breaking it down until reasonably smooth. Add the lime juice and walnuts, and season with a pinch of Cayenne pepper. Lightly whip the cream into soft peaks, then gently fold it in to achieve the required whipped consistency. It can now be chilled for a firmer consistency or served at room temperature for the creamiest of finishes.

Preheat the oil for deep-frying to between 160°C/325°F and 180°C/350°F. The parsnip mix can literally just be spooned (using dessert or soup spoons) into the hot fat (oiling a spoon first helps create a non-stick effect). Turn the fritters from time to time, until a deep golden brown. Once they are cooked, remove them from the hot fat, drain on kitchen paper and lightly salt. The fritters and walnut whip are now ready to be enjoyed.

The walnuts can be blanched in boiling water for a minute, which will enable their skins to be scraped away. It's a bit of a fiddly job, but will remove the bitter edge that the skins carry.
If chilled, the blue cheese walnut whip can be piped into a bowl to emulate its chocolate predecessor.

OPPOSITE: PARSNIP FRITTERS
WITH BLUE CHEESE WALNUT WHIP

scallops with puréed shallots and black-peppered tangerines

Scallops are without doubt one of the culinary luxuries of the world. Although they are available throughout the year, winter is their prime time.

When buying scallops, it's only really worth taking them home if freshly opened by the fishmonger or still in the shell, ready to open and eat. It is only with this freshness that their full succulent sweetness will be appreciated. Tubs of open scallops have often been soaked in water to plump up their size and weight to command a better price. Unfortunately, the soaked scallop is washed of its flavours, and can become a quite tasteless muscle.

Attached to the scallop is the brightly coloured coral. These I find are best for sauce-making, or perhaps eating fried in salads. They're not to be used in this recipe, but do freeze well, or can be blitzed to a purée with an equal quantity of butter, for dropping a knob or two into a fish sauce to act as a thickening agent.

The sweet flavour of tangerines (also in season during the winter months), with a peppery bite, finishes the overall experience.

SERVES 4

12 scallops
drizzle of olive oil
knob of butter
coarse sea salt
2 tablespoons brandy (optional)
juice of 6 tangerines
1cm (½in) chive sticks (approximately 2 sticks
**   per scallop, optional)**

FOR THE SHALLOT PURÉE

2 tablespoons olive oil
knob of butter
325g (12oz) shallots, peeled and thinly sliced
4 tablespoons double cream
salt and pepper

FOR THE TANGERINES

24 fresh tangerine segments
oil, for greasing
butter, for brushing
black pepper

To make the shallot purée, warm the olive oil and the knob of butter in a saucepan. Once bubbling, add the sliced shallots, cover and cook over a gentle heat for 15 minutes, without allowing to colour, stirring from time to time. To guarantee the shallots do not stick and colour in the pan, 3–4 tablespoons of water can be added once the shallots begin to soften. Add the cream and continue to cook for a further 5 minutes, then remove from the heat, season with salt and white pepper, and liquidize to a smooth purée. The shallot cream is now ready. This stage can be made several hours in advance, chilled until needed, then simply reheated gently when required.

To prepare the tangerines, gently peel away the thin outer skin that surrounds each segment with the point of a small knife. This is a little time-consuming, but does produce a far more tender finish. Place the peeled segments on a lightly oiled baking tray, brushing each with melted butter and topping with a twist of black pepper. These are now ready to warm when needed.

To clean the scallops, begin to prise the shells open with a knife, scraping and loosening the scallop from the flat shell. The scallop can now also be detached from the lower shell by cutting beneath the white muscle with a knife. Pull away and discard the surrounding membrane (unless used to flavour a stock or sauce). The coral can now also be separated from the 'meat' (use as mentioned in the introduction). Rinse the scallops briefly and dry on kitchen paper or a cloth. The scallops are now ready to cook.

To cook the scallops, heat a drizzle of olive oil in a large frying pan. Once hot, place the scallops in the pan, adding the knob of butter. Cook for 1–1½ minutes, depending on the size of the scallops. Once coloured with deep tinges on their border, turn them over and continue to cook for a further 1–1½ minutes. This will leave the scallops at a medium-rare stage. For particularly large scallops, 2 minutes on each side will be the maximum cooking time needed to reach this stage. Season each with a few granules of coarse sea salt. Transfer the scallops from the pan to a plate and keep to one side. Preheat the grill to hot.

Pour away excess fat from the scallop pan and return it to the heat. Add the brandy, if using, to lift all residue from the pan, possibly flambéeing. Once the pan is almost dry, add the tangerine juice and boil quickly, allowing it to reduce in volume by at least half, to a syrupy consistency. Strain the syrup through a fine sieve or tea strainer into a small bowl.

While the tangerine juice is boiling, warm the peppered segments under the grill.

Lay 3 tablespoons of the warm shallot purée on each plate (offering any remaining separately). Place a scallop on top of each, then place two warm peppered tangerine segments on top of each scallop. The syrup can now be drizzled over, finishing with two chive sticks, if using, per scallop.

Any shallot purée not used can be kept and added to mashed potatoes for an oniony bite.

grilled herrings with a casserole of smoked bacon, onions, carrots, celery and grapes

All of the ingredients included here are in season now, with the main-crop onions seeing us through our coldest of months, and carrots, which rarely freeze due to their sugar content, enjoying this cold spell. As for celery, home-grown can hold out into December, providing the frost hasn't quite set in. Thompson seedless grapes, flown in from Spain, are probably the best to go for, with their natural sweet juiciness in full flow. Herrings are particularly plump at this time of year.

The bacon (smoked is not essential, but does work well with herrings), onions, carrots and celery are all braised in the oven until completely tender before stirring the grapes in for a sweet fruity finish.

Double cream is not essential but does help create a sort of creamy sauce consistency.

SERVES 4–6 AS A MAIN COURSE
4 × 275–350g (10–12oz) herrings, scaled and gutted
butter, for brushing
salt and pepper, plus sea salt flakes

FOR THE CASSEROLE
2 tablespoons olive oil
6 rashers of smoked streaky bacon, cut into thin strips
4 onions, sliced
450g (1lb) carrots, thinly sliced
½ head of celery, thinly sliced
1 tablespoon cider vinegar
175–225g (6–8oz) seedless white grapes, halved
25g (1oz) butter
2 tablespoons chopped flatleaf parsley
150ml (¼ pint) double cream (optional)

Preheat the oven to 160°C/325°F/Gas 3. To make the casserole, heat a large ovenproof casserole dish with the olive oil. Once hot, fry the strips of bacon over a high heat until golden brown. Reduce the temperature to a moderate heat and add the sliced onions, carrots and celery and continue to fry for 2–3 minutes. Season with a twist of pepper, placing the lid on top and braising in the oven for 40 minutes. Remove the lid and check for over-cooked tenderness. If still too firm, continue to braise for a further 10 minutes. Once completely tender, remove the pan from the oven, stirring in the vinegar and grapes. Replace the lid and keep warm to one side. Preheat the grill.

Make three to four incisions on each side of the herring fillets, cutting to the bone. Season inside the belly with salt and pepper. Butter the fish liberally, placing them on a baking tray. Sprinkle each with a few sea salt flakes. These can now be placed under the preheated grill, cooking for 4–5 minutes on each side.

Stir the butter and chopped parsley into the vegetables and grapes, checking for seasoning with salt and pepper – bearing in mind that smoked bacon is quite salty. If using the cream, this can now also be added, quickly bringing it to the simmer.

Arrange the whole grilled fish on plates, accompanied with a spoonful or two of the casserole.

Herring fillets can be used in place of the whole fish.

haddock champ cakes
with mâche

Champ needs little or no description, the Irish mashed potato and spring onion classic having featured on many a menu. Haddock, eaten fresh or smoked, is quite a delicious fish, flaking into these cakes with the spring onions very comfortably.

Mâche is a winter salad, also known as lamb's lettuce or corn salad, with a refreshing nutty flavour, and is here bound with sweet beetroot.

SERVES 8 AS A STARTER OR 4 AS A MAIN COURSE
FOR THE FISHCAKES
350g (12oz) floury potatoes, peeled and quartered
salt and pepper
600g (1lb) haddock fillet, pin-boned (page 9)
1 bunch of spring onions
25g (1oz) butter
flour, for dusting
2 tablespoons olive oil

FOR THE SALAD
1 large or 2 medium beetroots, cooked (page 398)
2 tablespoons groundnut or grapeseed oil
2 tablespoons walnut oil
squeeze of lemon juice
4 bunches or 2 bags of mâche (lamb's lettuce/corn salad), picked and washed

Boil the potatoes in salted water for 15–20 minutes until tender. Drain and mash until reasonably smooth. A slightly lumpy finish offers a more rustic texture. Keep warm to one side.

The haddock fillets can be steamed over simmering water for 6–8 minutes until just tender. This can also be achieved by microwaving with a trickle of water for just a few minutes. Once cooked and slightly cooled, the fish can be flaked from the skin. Leave to one side.

Peel away the leathery outside layer from the spring onions, trimming away the stalk base. The onions can now be finely shredded. Warm a frying pan with half of the butter and, once foaming, add the sliced spring onions, stirring and cooking for just a minute or two until softened. These can now be added to the mashed potato along with the steamed haddock flakes. Season well with salt and pepper, mixing the ingredients all together. Divide the fishcake mix into eight, dusting with flour and pressing each into patties.

To make the salad, peel and cut the cooked beetroots into rough 5mm (¼in) dice. Whisk together the two oils, adding a generous squeeze of lemon juice. Season with salt and pepper. Add the diced beetroot to the dressing.

To finish the fishcakes, heat the 2 tablespoons of olive oil in a frying pan, preferably non-stick. Once hot, place the cakes in the pan (making sure they are dusted with flour on both sides to prevent them from sticking). Add the remaining butter and fry over a medium heat for 3–4 minutes on each side (5–6 if they have been refrigerated), until golden brown.

With the fish cakes almost ready, warm the beetroot and dressing in a wok or frying pan. Present the fishcakes on warm plates, quickly mixing the mâche leaves with the beetroot, before dividing between the plates.

A tablespoon or two of broken walnuts can be added to the warm beetroots.

coley and cabbage

Coley is an all-year-round, cod-like fish, adapting itself to just about any cod or fresh haddock creation. The title of this recipe is as simple as the fish itself, sounding perhaps a bit uninteresting and bland, but as you read on it reveals itself as something quite different – a sort of stir-fry of goodies.

The cabbage is *cavolo nero* – black cabbage. This is an Italian cabbage that's recently found its way onto menus as a result of fashion trends. What I like about this cabbage is its delicious nutty taste, which is strong enough to take on other flavours – chillies, garlic and onions here. An extra I'm adding is a splash of rice wine (mirin). This is made from fermented rice, a sort of sweetened sake, helping to calm the chilli bite.

So, we have a basic title with an extraordinary finish.

SERVES 4
450g (1lb) black cabbage (*cavolo nero*)
salt and pepper
iced water
2 small red chillies
675g (1½lb) coley fillet, pin-boned (page 9) and skinned
4 tablespoons olive oil
flour, for dusting
1 red onion, finely chopped
2 garlic cloves, finely sliced
1–2 tablespoons rice wine (mirin)
large knob of butter

Separate and wash the cabbage leaves. Any large thick stems should be cut away. Stack the washed leaves together, cutting across into 1cm (½in) slices or rough 2.5cm (1in) squares. These can now be blanched in shallow boiling salted water, cooking for a few minutes until just approaching tender. Drain and refresh in iced water, draining again and drying on a clean tea towel. Slice the red chillies into very thin round slices (making sure you scrub your fingers afterwards, as chillies love to linger).

The coley can be cut into 2.5cm (1in) chunks, seasoning them with salt and pepper. Heat a frying pan for the coley with 2 tablespoons of the olive oil, also heating a wok with the remaining 2 tablespoons of olive oil for the cabbage. Lightly dust the coley chunks with flour and fry over a fairly high heat for just a few minutes, turning the fish carefully until golden brown. While frying the fish, add the chopped onion to the wok and pan-fry for a few minutes before adding the chillies, garlic and cabbage. Continue to fry for a couple of minutes, seasoning with salt and pepper, until the cabbage has heated through. Add a tablespoon of the rice wine, using the rest if a sweeter finish is preferred. Gently stir in the fried coley and knob of butter and serve.

When stirred into the cabbage, the coley will begin to separate into flakes, distributing the fish throughout the cabbage.

steamed turbot with tarragon and orange caramelized salsify

Turbot tends to be with us almost throughout the year, with a season that begins in mid-spring and goes right the way through to late winter. It is known as 'the king of all flat fish', and has every right to carry that title.

To accompany the turbot we have salsify, mostly an imported vegetable during mid-to-late autumn and through the months of winter. Here the salsify are lightly caramelized with fresh orange juice, creating quite a distinctive finished flavour.

OPPOSITE: STEAMED TURBOT WITH TARRAGON AND ORANGE CARAMELIZED SALSIFY

SERVES 4

4 × 175g (6oz) portions of turbot fillet, with skin on
50g (2oz) butter, plus more for greasing
salt and pepper, plus coarse sea salt
squeeze of lemon juice
10–12 tarragon leaves, torn into small pieces

FOR THE SALSIFY

8–10 salsify sticks
juice of 1 lemon
1 heaped teaspoon finely grated orange zest and juice
  of 2 oranges
1 tablespoon olive oil
1 level teaspoon caster or demerara sugar
knob of butter

First prepare the salsify. Peeling it is made cleaner and easier by wearing rubber gloves and using a swivel peeler. Place the root on a suitable chopping board and peel in long strips. Once each stick has been peeled, rinse under water and then halve it. Place in a saucepan of cold water with the lemon juice. Once all are cleaned, bring the water to a rapid simmer and cook the salsify for 10–12 minutes, until tender; 15 minutes should be the maximum time required. Remove the roots from the pan and leave to drain and cool.

While the salsify are cooling, place the grated orange zest in a small saucepan and cover it with cold water. Bring to a simmer, then drain in a sieve and refresh under cold water. Repeat the same process twice more. This softens the zest and removes the raw bitter flavour. Keep to one side.

Heat the olive oil in a frying pan. Once hot, add the drained salsify and fry until golden brown. Remove from the heat.

At this point, the turbot can be steamed. Place the fillets, flesh-side down, on buttered and seasoned greaseproof paper squares and steam over a pan of rapidly simmering water, covering them with a lid, for 6 minutes.

While the fish are cooking, return the salsify to the heat, adding the sugar. Once this begins to caramelize gently to a richer golden brown, add the orange juice and orange zest. Boil over a high heat to cook to a syrupy consistency. Season with salt and pepper, adding the knob of butter for a smoother and shinier finish.

To make an instant tarragon butter, heat 3 tablespoons of water with a good squeeze of lemon juice. Once boiling, remove the pan from the stove and whisk in the 50g (2oz) of butter, a few knobs at a time. The butter emulsifies with the flavoured water to form a silky liquor to spoon over the fish.

Once all the butter has been added, season with salt and pepper and add the tarragon leaves.

To serve, divide the orange salsify between four plates. Remove the turbot fillets from the steamer and carefully pull away the skin, sprinkling each with a little coarse sea salt. The fish can now be presented next to the orange-flavoured salsify, and the tarragon butter spooned over and around the fish.

When taking the fish from the greaseproof paper squares, strain any juices through a tea strainer into the tarragon butter sauce for maximum flavour.

pan-fried black bream with sautéed juniper and kumquat potatoes

Black bream approaches the end of its popular season during the first month of winter, so it's a question of cooking it before missing it. Red and gilthead bream hold on for an extra couple of months, and both also work well in this recipe.

I prefer to use second earlies here, which are the second run of new potatoes, available from August to March. Charlotte and Estima both have a pale-yellow skin, with quite a waxy texture, sautéeing nicely. The juniper berries are crushed and chopped very finely to resemble coarse pepper (a coffee grinder does this very well), with their distinctive flavour matching the orangey bite from thinly sliced kumquats.

SERVES 4

4 × 175–225g (6–8oz) black bream fillets, scaled and pin-boned (page 9)
flour, for dusting
2 tablespoons olive oil
knob of butter

FOR THE POTATOES

450–675g (1–1½lb) second early new potatoes (see above)
salt and pepper
2 tablespoons olive oil
8–10 kumquats
8 juniper berries, crushed and finely chopped
50g (2oz) butter
1 tablespoon chopped parsley
squeeze of lemon juice

With the point of a sharp knife, score three or four lines in the skin of the black bream fillets. These can now be chilled ready for frying.

Cook the new potatoes in boiling salted water for 20–25 minutes, until tender. Drain in a colander. While the potatoes are still warm, cut them in half lengthwise. Heat the olive oil in a large frying pan or wok and fry the warm potatoes until beginning to take on a little colour.

While the potatoes are colouring, top and tail the kumquats, then slice them into thin rounds, removing any seeds.

Add the chopped juniper berries to the potatoes and continue to sauté to a richer colour. Add the kumquat slices and the butter, allowing it to melt rather than fry. Add the chopped parsley and lemon juice just before serving.

While the potatoes are sautéeing, flour the skin side of the sea bream and season with a pinch of salt. Heat the olive oil in a large frying pan and place the fish in the oil, skin-side down. Should the fillets begin to curl, press them down with a fish slice. After a minute or two they will have relaxed and won't curl. Add the knob of butter and fry the fish for 4 minutes, seasoning the flesh side with salt and pepper, before turning the fish in the pan. Remove the pan from the stove. The residual heat in the pan will continue to cook the fish, providing enough time to finish the potatoes without overcooking the bream.

Spoon the finished sautéed potatoes onto warm plates, drizzling with any remaining butter from the pan. Place the black bream fillets just next to the potatoes and serve.

A slice of English cabbage plate (page 359) or Sesame and ham sprouts (page 317) are good accompaniments. Spinach cooked in sizzling butter is a simple alternative.

buttered salmon with a leek velouté soup and steamed potatoes

Leeks are one of our most luxurious home-grown autumn and winter green vegetables. Not only do they offer a rich depth of flavour, but they also provide us with a range of green tones to add colour to our plates. It is during the winter months that this vegetable is at its best, so with that in mind I thought I would pair this soup with softly cooked salmon, the two very natural flavours working well together, particularly as a starter on that big day in late December.

The potatoes can be omitted from the recipe, but do offer another texture, also reflecting the leek and potato soup combination, but served in a slightly different form. The potatoes can be shaped as you like, just large or small dice, or perhaps even formed into balls or small barrels. The extras are purely optional, the chives lending an additional bite and the dressing of lime juice and oil a glossy sharp finish.

SERVES 8 AS A STARTER (EASILY HALVED)

6 small–medium potatoes, peeled
1 large onion, finely chopped
25g (1oz) butter, plus an extra knob for the onion
1kg (2¼lb) leeks, thinly sliced and rinsed
salt and pepper
600–800g (1lb 6oz–1¾lb) salmon fillet, skinned and
**   cut into 8 equal portions**
1 teaspoon 1cm (½in) chive sticks (optional)
2–3 teaspoons lime juice (optional)
2 tablespoons olive, walnut or hazelnut oil (optional)

As mentioned in the introduction, the potatoes can be shaped as wished, cutting them into dice or scooping them into balls. Another method is to 'turn' them into barrel shapes. To do so, quarter the potatoes lengthwise, then cut a little away from top to bottom with a small knife to establish a curved barrel shape. The potatoes can be steamed from raw or parboiled for 5–6 minutes, until tender, then removed from the water and allowed to cool. They can now be reheated when needed, either by steaming, boiling or microwaving. The quantity of potatoes listed will provide enough for three pieces per portion as a garnish.

In a large saucepan, cook the chopped onion in the knob of butter for 6–7 minutes, until softening without colouring. Add 900ml (1½ pints) of water and bring to the boil. Once at boiling point, season with salt, then add the leeks. Cook on a high heat, bringing back to the boil for a few minutes, until the leeks are tender. Remove the pan from the heat and liquidize the soup to a purée in batches, then push through a sieve. It's important when straining the soup to push well to get all of the liquor and texture through. You will now be left with a very naturally flavoured leek soup. Season with salt and ground white pepper.

To cook the salmon, melt the measured butter in a saucepan over a low-to-medium heat. Once gently bubbling, place the salmon in, skinned-side down. Season with salt and pepper, and cook gently for just 4–5 minutes, then turn the fillets over in the pan and remove from the heat. The residual heat of the pan will finish the cooking of the fish, if you leave it to stand for just a further 2–3 minutes.

The salmon fillets can now be presented in soup plates, with the leek velouté soup ladled around. The steamed potatoes can be arranged around the salmon or presented on top of the fillets. If adding the optional garnishes, sprinkle the chive sticks on top of the potatoes, then whisk the lime juice and oil together, and season with salt and pepper. This can now be drizzled over and around the salmon.

beer-braised pheasants with leeks, potatoes, prunes and bacon

The smaller hen pheasant offers two portions per bird, perfect for this recipe. These can be prepared by your butcher, requesting that any excess backbone carcass be trimmed away. This will leave the legs attached to the breast, which is still on the bone.

Braising usually requires several hours' cooking. Here, just 15–20 minutes is needed, preserving a moist tender touch in the breasts, with the beer taking on the pheasant game flavour.

Leeks are very much an early-winter vegetable. Although they have a longer life span, they are probably at their best during December and January. Together with the potatoes, prunes and bacon, the leeks help form a bowl of mixed flavours.

SERVES 4

2 × oven-ready hen pheasants, each halved and
    trimmed (see above)
1 tablespoon groundnut oil
knob of butter
4 large shallots or 2 small onions, sliced
generous sprig of thyme
3 tablespoons calvados (brandy can also be used,
    optional)
2 teaspoons brown sugar
2 teaspoons clear honey
300ml (½ pint) beer
100–150ml (3½fl oz–¼ pint) double cream
squeeze of lemon juice

FOR THE VEGETABLES

3–4 large potatoes, suitable for mashing and boiling
    (Desirée, King Edward or Maris Piper all work well),
    peeled and quartered
salt and pepper
2 leeks
100g (4oz) piece of streaky bacon, cut into 1cm (½in)
    dice (this can be obtained pre-cut, or diced pancetta
    can also be used)
15g (½oz) butter
8–10 ready-to-eat prunes, halved

OPPOSITE: BEER-BRAISED PHEASANTS WITH LEEKS, POTATOES, PRUNES AND BACON

First prepare the vegetables. Place the potatoes in a saucepan, top with cold water and add a generous pinch of salt. Bring to the boil and cook until completely tender, approximately 20 minutes.

While the potatoes are cooking, start cooking the pheasants. Preheat the oven to 220°C/425°F/Gas 7. Season the birds with salt and pepper. Heat the groundnut oil and butter in a roasting tray. Once bubbling, place the birds in, flesh-side down, and fry over a moderate heat for a good 5–10 minutes, until golden brown. Turn the halves over in the tray and cook for a further 2 minutes. Remove the pheasants from the tray and keep to one side. Return the roasting tray to the heat, add the shallots or onions and the thyme and fry for a few minutes, until they are softening. Add the calvados, if using, and allow it to boil and reduce until almost dry. Add the sugar and honey, stir them in well, top with the beer and bring to a simmer. Return the pheasants to the tray, flesh-side up and, once simmering, place in the oven and roast for 15–20 minutes.

While the birds roast, prepare the leeks. Trim the base stalk and untidy tops from each, removing the outer layer, and wash well. Cut each across into 1cm (½in) thick slices and place to one side.

The potatoes will have reached their tender stage while the birds are roasting. Simply drain, return to the warm pan, cover with a lid and keep warm to one side.

Dry-fry the bacon pieces in a wok or frying pan over a moderate heat. This helps release their own fat, in which they will begin to fry until golden brown. For a very crunchy finish, continue to cook until dark and crispy, drain and keep warm to one side.

Remove the pheasants from the oven and their cooking liquor and leave to rest in a warm place. Return the pan to the hob, bring the liquid to the boil and allow it to reduce in volume by half. Remove the sprig of thyme from the liquor. Add 100ml (3½fl oz) of the double cream and simmer for a few minutes, until the sauce is thickening slightly. For a creamier finish add the remaining cream. Season with salt and pepper, skimming away any impurities. Finish with a squeeze of lemon juice.

While the sauce is simmering, cook the leeks. Melt the butter in a saucepan. Once bubbling, add 3 tablespoons of water and drop in the leeks. Stir, cover with a lid and cook for 1 minute. Stir again, covering once more, and repeat this process for 4–5 minutes, until the leeks are tender. At this point, add the prunes and continue to cook with a lid on for a further minute. This will create steam, helping to soften the prunes and finish the leeks. Season with salt and pepper.

Cut the potatoes roughly while still in the saucepan, using a small knife, or break them with a fork into rough chunks. Season with salt and pepper.

The pheasants can be left as halves, with the meat on the bone. If so, they can be quickly rewarmed in the preheated oven for 2 minutes before plating. To take off the bone, cut the legs away from the breasts. The breasts can now also be cut from the bone with a sharp knife, naturally following the breast bone. These can now be placed into the oven, with the legs skin-side up, and warmed for just a minute or two. In a warm serving bowl, mix the potatoes, leeks, prunes and bacon, then spoon over any buttery liquor from the leeks. Divide the pheasant halves or portions between the plates. Spoon the sauce over the pheasants and the dish is ready to serve.

crown of roast turkey served with its own bacon and sherry raisin pâté

For a 'crown' of turkey, the legs and backbone are removed, leaving only the breasts on the bone. This reduces the cooking time of the bird quite considerably. The thigh meat is used to flavour the pâté mix and the drumsticks can be chopped and added to the stock or you can roast them with the crown.

This recipe stands well as an alternative to our regular Christmas turkey meal, the pâté replacing the chestnut stuffing, with the addition of the sherry raisins for a slightly sweeter finish. The pâté mix can be made up to 48 hours in advance, giving it time to mature before cooking.

Please don't be put off by the length of the ingredients list or method. I'm sure you'll notice that many are storecupboard regulars at this time of year.

SERVES 8 GENEROUSLY
1 × 3.5–4.5kg (8–10lb) turkey
50g (2oz) butter
salt and pepper
cooking oil

FOR THE PÂTÉ
75g (3oz) raisins
100ml (3½fl oz) sweet sherry
16–18 rashers of unsmoked streaky bacon
   (20–24 if only very thin)
small knob of butter, plus more for greasing

350g (12oz) rindless pork belly, chopped into rough
   small dice
175g (6oz) streaky or back bacon, chopped into
   rough small dice
100g (4oz) pork fat, chopped into rough small dice
175g (6oz) chicken livers, chopped into rough small dice
1 onion, finely chopped
5 tablespoons whisky
1 teaspoon ground mixed spice
½ teaspoon dried herbes de Provence
2 tablespoons chopped parsley
1 egg
4 slices of thick-cut white bread, crusts removed and
   crumbed (approximately 100g/4oz)

FOR THE GRAVY
1–2 tablespoons cooking oil
1 onion, chopped
2 celery sticks, chopped
1 carrot, chopped
2 × 400g tins of consommé or 1.2 litres (2 pints)
   Instant stock (page 416)
1 tablespoon butter (optional)
1 tablespoon flour (optional)

The legs can simply be removed from the bird by cutting between the breast and leg itself. Once reaching the thigh joint connecting the leg to the carcass, pull the leg away from the bird at an angle of 180°. Continue to cut the leg away, following the meat connected to the bone. The leg will now come free. Repeat the same process with the remaining leg.

Separate the thigh from the drumstick by simply cutting between the joint. The drumsticks can now be kept for roasting or chopped for making stock (see below). Remove the skin from the thigh and cut the meat away from the bone. Chop 350g (12oz) of it into rough small dice. Any remaining trimmings can be kept for the stock.

Now cut away the backbone. Stand the bird upright with the backbone facing you. Cut either side of the bone, following it to the neck end and releasing. The breasts are now left sitting on the breastbone, still with wings attached. The wings can be left on the bird as they are, the wing tips folded beneath the bird.

To help enrich the flavour of the turkey, gently release the skin from the breasts. Beginning from the neck end, 25g (1oz) of the butter can be pushed between the skin and meat. This will melt during the roasting, enriching the finished flavour. The remaining butter can now be brushed over the breasts ready for roasting. Chill the turkey and wrap in cling film once the butter has set. Store in the fridge until needed.

Before making the pâté, place the raisins in the sherry, leaving to soak for 1–2 hours. Once soaked, drain the raisins, collecting the sherry in a small saucepan, and keep to one side. Lay four of the bacon rashers between two sheets of cling film and roll with a rolling pin. This will extend the length of the rashers and thin the texture. Repeat the same process with the remaining rashers. As the pâté is to be presented as a savoury gâteau, butter a 20 × 6cm (8 × 2½in) loose-bottomed cake tin and line it with the streaky bacon rashers, placing an end of each rasher in the central point of the tin base. These will encase the pâté and add flavour to the finished dish, as well as ensuring a moist result. Press the bacon into the tin firmly, leaving any excess hanging over the edge. Continue this process, very slightly overlapping each rasher, until the tin is completely lined. Refrigerate.

Pass the 350g (12oz) of chopped turkey thigh meat, the pork belly, chopped bacon and pork fat through the coarse blade of a mincer once. Add the chicken livers and repeat the mincing process. Place in the bowl of an electric mixer and refrigerate. Add the chopped onion to the reserved sherry and bring to a simmer. Cook over a moderate heat for 6–7 minutes, until the onion is tender, and allow the sherry to reduce to an almost-dry finish. Leave to cool. Add the sherry, onion, raisins, whisky, mixed spice, herbes de Provence, chopped parsley, egg and breadcrumbs to the minced meat, and season well with salt and ground white pepper. With a beater attachment, place the bowl on the machine and beat moderately for a few minutes (or by hand) until completely mixed in.

To check for seasoning, make a mini-burger and fry in a small knob of butter for a few minutes on each side. This can now be tasted and more salt and pepper added to the mix, if needed.

Spoon and press the pâté stuffing into the lined cake tin, then fold the overhanging bacon over the top. Cover the pâté with a disc of buttered greaseproof paper and place a suitable plate on top to press lightly. Seal the lid with foil. This can now be refrigerated for up to 48 hours (see above), maturing in flavour with time.

To make the gravy, heat the cooking oil in a large frying pan. Add the chopped turkey bones and trimmings and fry until well coloured. Transfer to a saucepan (previously draining in a colander if too fatty), then add the chopped vegetables to the frying pan. Fry over a moderate heat for 8–10 minutes, until beginning to soften and taking on a golden edge, lifting any turkey flavours left in the pan. Add the vegetables to the turkey bones, top with the consommé and

300ml (½ pint) of water, or the 1.2 litres (2 pints) stock. Bring to a gentle simmer and cook for 30 minutes.

Strain the stock through a fine sieve or muslin cloth and skim off any fat for a clean finish. This element of the complete dish can also be made up to 48 hours in advance, ready for reheating on the day. Should a thicker consistency be preferred, mix together the flour and butter and whisk a little at a time into the simmering stock. Once added, continue to simmer for a few minutes. The finished colour of the gravy, particularly if thickened, will be a pale *café au lait* colour but with a rich turkey flavour.

For the crown roast, preheat the oven to 220°C/425°F/ Gas 7. Spoon a tablespoon of cooking oil into a roasting tray and place in the buttered turkey crown and the drumsticks, if using. Put the pâté on a baking tray and place with the turkey crown in the preheated oven. The cooking time for both is the same, between 1½ hours and 1 hour 40 minutes. During this time the turkey can be basted with its melted butter and juices every 20–30 minutes. To test if the pâté is cooked, pierce it with a trussing needle, skewer or small knife and leave this in the pâté for 10–15 seconds. Carefully check the warmth of the needle against your lip – the pâté should be very hot to be cooked through. If using a temperature probe, the reading must reach that of at least 70–72°C (158–162°F; see below). The same testing process can also be used to check the turkey.

Remove the turkey, drumsticks and pâté from the oven and leave to rest for 10–15 minutes before carving. During the cooking of the pâté, some bacon and other juices will have been released into the baking tray. These can be carefully added to the loose gravy just a little at a time, taking into account the strength of the salty bacon flavour.

Turn out the pâté from the tin. To give the flat presentation side a richer golden-brown finish, preheat a hot grill. Place the pâté cake under it, cooking until well coloured.

The turkey is now ready to carve; offer the slices with a wedge of the pâté and some warmed turkey gravy. Here are a few suggestions for perfect seasonal accompaniments to be found within the book: *Cranberry sauce* (page 419), *Sweetened potatoes and chestnuts with chives* (page 279), *Sesame and ham sprouts* (page 317), *Sage roast parsnips, apples and prunes* (page 340). A generous bunch of watercress can also be used to garnish the roast.

The temperature probe instructions may suggest cooking poultry to 90°C (194°F). This can, of course, be adhered to. However, I have always found 70–72°C (158–162°F) to be more than sufficient, offering a well-cooked and moist finish.

Should potatoes or vegetables be roasted with the turkey and pâté, an extra 20–30 minutes' cooking time may be needed. When using chicken livers for any recipe, it is best to buy them 24–48 hours in advance. During this time the livers can be soaked in milk and chilled before use. This will help remove excess blood and bitterness. This is not essential, but does produce a more refined finish.

If a mincer is unavailable, a food processor can be used to bind the pâté ingredients together. It is important, however, that the various meats and chicken livers are first cut into rough small dice. This will help the processor bind and break down their texture quickly, without overworking and puréeing them.

For a deeper gravy colour, an instant gravy thickener can be used in place of the butter and flour listed in the recipe. A tablespoon of redcurrant or cranberry jelly can be whisked into the finished gravy for a sweeter flavour.

roast turkey and cranberry wellington

Turkey took over from goose as our first choice for the Christmas roast bird and, although available all year round, has become very much a seasonal favourite, hence its inclusion in this book.

The term 'Wellington' is usually associated with beef fillet baked within a pastry case, enhanced by the addition of pâté and mushrooms. Here the turkey – the breast only – is wrapped in a stuffing made from its own meat and some pork sausage, and flavoured with a chestnut purée and dried cranberries. The turkey is also encased in rashers of bacon and puff pastry.

This recipe will provide eight generous portions from just one large 2.25kg (5lb) turkey breast. A loose red wine gravy is also included to accompany the Wellington, and *Cranberry sauce* (page 419) can be offered separately.

SERVES 8 GENEROUSLY

1 × **2.25kg (5lb) turkey breast, skin removed**
cooking oil
salt and pepper
16–20 rindless rashers of streaky bacon
500g (1lb 2oz) *Quick puff pastry* **(page 426, or bought)**
flour, for dusting
1 egg, beaten
Cranberry sauce **(page 419), to serve**

FOR THE STUFFING

2 onions, finely chopped
knob of butter
225g (8oz) pork sausages, skinned
2 eggs
150g (5oz) dried cranberries, roughly chopped
150g (5oz) unsweetened chestnut purée
100g (4oz) fresh white breadcrumbs

FOR THE SAUCE

25g (1oz) butter, plus an extra knob
50g (2oz) shallots or onions, sliced
1 tablespoon clear honey
1 tablespoon red wine vinegar
400ml (14fl oz) red wine (approximately ½ bottle)
300ml (½ pint) *Instant stock* **(page 416) or tinned consommé**
1 heaped teaspoon plain flour

The natural shape of the turkey breast does not really suit the rolled and wrapped Wellington. So, first trim off the wider meat at the thicker neck end to establish a more cylindrical shape. The trimmings from a breast of this size should be about 350g (12oz), which is enough to make the stuffing. Once trimmed, tie the breast in sections, leaving a 2.5cm (1in) gap between each one, to secure its cylindrical shape. Heat 2–3 tablespoons of cooking oil in a large frying pan or roasting tray. Season the turkey with salt and pepper, then fry, turning, until golden brown all over. Remove from the pan and leave to cool. The breast can now be chilled to firm and set before the string is removed.

To make the stuffing, cook the chopped onions in a knob of butter for several minutes until softened. Remove from the heat and allow to cool. Roughly chop the turkey trimmings, then blitz in a food processor until smooth. Add the skinned sausages and continue to blitz for a further 30–40 seconds until mixed in. Season with salt and pepper and add the eggs, blitzing them into the meat for a further minute, until the texture has thickened. Remove the stuffing from the processor and put into a large bowl. Mix in the cooked onions with the remaining stuffing ingredients. The stuffing can now also be chilled while the pastry and bacon are prepared.

The streaky bacon first needs to be rolled out thinly to extend the length of the rashers and help them wrap around the turkey and stuffing. The easiest method to follow is to lay four or five rashers between two sheets of cling film and simply press with a rolling pin as if rolling pastry. Peel away the top layer of

OPPOSITE: ROAST TURKEY AND CRANBERRY WELLINGTON

cling film, remove the rashers and place them on a tray. Repeat the same process until all are rolled, then chill until needed.

Roll the puff pastry on a floured surface into a rectangle approximately 46 × 35cm (18 × 14in). Lay the bacon rashers on top of the pastry, leaving a 3–4cm (1¼–1½in) border around the edge and slightly overlapping each rasher as they are laid. Covering the pastry should use 14 or 15 of the rashers. Spread three-quarters of the stuffing over the bacon, first mixing well to loosen if chilled and set, reserving a quarter to finish the covering. Remove the string from the turkey and lay it, presentation-side down, on top of the stuffing. Spread the remaining stuffing along the top of the turkey. Lift four or five of the bacon rashers and stuffing at a time over the turkey breast and press against it. This is a simple operation and the stuffing holds well. Continue until all the rashers from both sides have been lifted. The remaining rashers can now be laid lengthwise along the top to cover the extra stuffing. Fold one long side of the puff pastry over. Brush the other with beaten egg along the edge before lifting and sealing in all of the ingredients. Now brush both ends with egg before folding both on top. Turn the Wellington over and place on a large greased baking tray (alternatively the tray can be covered with greased parchment paper or non-stick sheets) and chill until needed.

Preheat the oven to 200°C/400°F/Gas 6. Place the Wellington in the oven and bake for 1¼–1½ hours. After the first 45 minutes of baking, brush the Wellington with egg to help colour the pastry. For the most golden of finishes, brush again with egg about 15–20 minutes before it is due to come out of the oven.

Remove from the oven. Leave to rest for 15–20 minutes, then lift carefully with two large fish slices, transferring it to a carving board.

While the Wellington is baking, make the sauce. Melt the knob of butter in a saucepan and, once bubbling, add the sliced shallots or onions. Cook on a medium-to-high heat until well coloured and taking on a rich deep colour. Add the honey and continue to cook for a few minutes more, until bubbling well and approaching a caramelized stage. At this point, add the red wine vinegar and red wine, bring to the boil and reduce in volume by half. Add the stock or consommé and bring back to a simmer. While the stock is warming, mix the flour with the measured butter. Spoon and whisk well into the sauce until completely mixed in. The flour serves as the thickening agent, but this small quantity doesn't make it over-starchy or too thick. Bring the sauce back to the boil, then reduce to a gentle simmer and cook for a few minutes. Strain the sauce through a fine sieve and season, if needed, reheating before serving. The turkey Wellington is now ready to carve and serve, offering the sauce separately.

For accompanying potatoes and vegetables, I suggest *Noisette potatoes* (page 422) and *Buttered Brussels sprouts* (page 423).

Should other items such as roast potatoes or roast parsnips be cooked in the same oven with the Wellington, extra cooking time will be needed, as these items draw the heat from the Wellington. An extra 20–30 minutes will cover the lost heat. For a looser or extra sauce, simply add extra Instant stock (page 416), or consommé.

roast venison with chestnut leeks and blackcurrant grapes

The individual loin cuts of venison chosen for roasting have been taken from the saddle. These are the prime cuts from the deer. When bought particularly young, the flavour will be quite light. For this recipe, however, it's best to order the meat 7–10 days in advance, this hanging period leaving the meat with a stronger flavour. The maximum time for hanging should be two weeks. This will offer the most strength, without becoming over-sticky and with not too much of a stale and overpowering aroma.

The leek slices are softened with cooked chestnuts, their nuttiness biting into the onion edge of the tender leeks. Black grapes, preferably seedless, become blackcurrant-flavoured with the influence of crème de cassis (blackcurrant liqueur). The juiciness of the grapes provides enough moisture, so a sauce is not really essential. Included, however, is an optional red wine cream sauce to offer separately or to trickle around the finished plate.

SERVES 4

2–3 leeks
10–12 chestnuts, cooked and peeled (see page 424)
1 tablespoon groundnut oil
4 × 175–225g (6–8oz) cuts of venison loin (taken from the fallow deer), trimmed of all sinew
salt and pepper
15g (½oz) butter, plus a knob for the venison and a small knob for the grapes
100ml (3½fl oz) full-bodied red wine
24–28 seedless black grapes, halved
generous pinch of demerara sugar
2 tablespoons crème de cassis

1 shallot, finely chopped
200ml (7fl oz) full-bodied red wine
1 × 400g tin of game or beef consommé
100ml (3½fl oz) double cream

Preheat the oven to 220°C/425°F/Gas 7. Peel away and discard the outside layer of the leeks and wash them well. Cut the leeks into 1cm (½in) thick round slices and keep to one side. Chop the chestnuts into small rough pieces.

To cook the venison, heat the groundnut oil in a roasting tray. Season the loins with salt and pepper and place them in the hot pan. Add a knob of butter and fry for a few minutes, until well coloured on all sides. Place the roasting tray into the preheated oven and cook the venison for 4 minutes; turn the pieces over and continue to roast for a further 4 minutes. This will leave the meat with a medium-rare finish. If medium is preferred, add a further few minutes to the total cooking time; well done will need between 15 and 20 minutes, depending on the thickness of the meat. Remove the venison from the oven and tray and leave to rest for 6–8 minutes.

While the venison is roasting, cook the leeks. Melt the measured butter in a large saucepan with a few tablespoons of water. Once bubbling, add the sliced leeks and turn them once or twice in the pan. Season with salt and pepper, and cover with a lid. Cook over a moderate heat, stirring the leeks around from time to time, for 8–10 minutes, until very tender. When they are approaching the tender stage, add the chopped chestnuts. Keep warm to one side and drain off any excess water before serving.

While the venison is resting, make the sauce, if using. Pour away excess fat from the roasting tray, placing it on top of the stove and heating through. Add the chopped shallot and stir to help release all of the residue. Pour 200ml (7fl oz) wine into the pan, bringing it to the boil and allowing to reduce in volume by three-quarters. Add the consommé, return to the boil and reduce in volume by half. Add the double cream and simmer to a sauce-like consistency. Season with salt and pepper, then strain through a fine sieve into a clean pan or sauceboat.

Meanwhile, melt the small knob of butter for the grapes in a non-stick frying pan. Once sizzling, add the grapes and cook over a fairly high heat for just 30 seconds. Add 100ml (3½fl oz) red wine, along with the pinch of sugar, increasing the heat and reducing in volume until dry. Add the crème de cassis, rolling the grapes gently in the pan as it simmers around them. While still moist, remove the grapes from the heat.

To serve, carve the venison into thin round slices, or cut each piece more thickly into three medallions. All the items – venison, chestnut leeks, grapes – can be placed separately on each plate, or place the leeks in the centre, topping with the venison and spooning the grapes around. If serving the cream sauce, it can either be poured around or served separately.

seared escalopes of lamb with tangerines and greens

Escalope is a French culinary term meaning a thin slice. These escalopes are to be taken from lamb leg steaks. The steaks, each 175–200g (6–7oz), need to be without bone. This can quite easily be cut away, before batting the steak to a thinned-out slice with a meat tenderizer. If a tenderizer hammer is unavailable, simply place the meat between two sheets of cling film and beat it flat with a rolling pin. This will spread and tenderize the meat. To guarantee the escalope does not curl during its cooking, snip with scissors around the border of fine sinew, making four or five cuts.

The tangerines and greens make a lovely winter combination, the fruits imported and plentiful, and many different home-grown greens to choose from. Curly kale, spinach, cabbage or Brussels sprouts can all be used, each just gently softened before they are rolled in a knob of butter and seasoned.

The sauce to accompany the lamb is flavoured with green peppercorns, tangerines, brandy or Grand Marnier, and cream.

SERVES 4
6–8 tangerines
450–675g (1–1½lb) greens (curly kale, spinach, cabbage
**   or Brussels sprouts)**
salt and pepper
iced water (optional)
15g (½oz) butter, plus a large knob for the greens
4 × 175–200g (6–7oz) lamb steak escalopes, prepared
**   (see above)**
1 tablespoon groundnut oil
1 shallot, finely chopped
2 teaspoons green peppercorns, lightly crushed
4 tablespoons brandy or Grand Marnier
200ml (7fl oz) whipping cream
1 tablespoon picked and torn flatleaf parsley (optional)

Halve and juice four of the tangerines, peeling and segmenting the remainder. Each segment can now be carefully peeled of its fine skin to reveal the fruit itself. The peeled segments can be left whole or halved and kept to one side.

To prepare the greens, if using curly kale or spinach, tear away the tough stalks, breaking the leaves into bite-sized pieces. Cabbage can be quartered, removing any damaged and tough outside leaves, along with the central core. It can then be finely shredded or torn into bite-sized pieces. Brussels sprouts are best peeled of their outer leaves and halved, with the base cut away, then finely shredded.

Any of these greens can be cooked in advance by blanching in boiling salted water until tender. Kale and cabbage will take 4–5 minutes, the spinach and shredded sprouts needing just half that time. Once cooked, refresh in iced water and drain, squeezing out excess water. Melt the large knob of butter, mixing it with the greens, and season with salt and pepper. Place in a vegetable dish and cover with cling film, ready to microwave just before serving.

Alternatively, to cook the greens while frying the lamb, melt the butter in a large saucepan with 4–5 tablespoons of water. Once bubbling, add the greens, cover with a lid and cook, stirring from time to time, for more or less the same time as above. Season and drain once tender and ready to serve.

To cook the lamb, first season the escalopes with salt and pepper. Heat two large frying pans (once beaten, the lamb steaks become quite large) and add the groundnut oil and measured butter. Once hot and sizzling, place the lamb in the pans and sear for just 2 minutes, then turn over and continue to fry for a further 2 minutes. At this point the lamb will still be pink to serve. For well done, at least double the cooking time. Remove the lamb from the pans and keep warm to one side.

Pour away excess fat from the pans and divide the shallot and green peppercorns between them. Add 2 tablespoons of brandy or Grand Marnier to each. Over a fairly high heat this will flambé very quickly and reduce until almost dry. Divide the tangerine juice between the two pans. Once simmering, one pan can be poured into the other. Allow the juice to reduce in volume by two-thirds, then add the cream. Simmer to a loose coating consistency and season with salt and pepper. The peeled tangerine segments can now be quickly warmed in the sauce. Finish the sauce with the torn parsley leaves, if using. The making of the sauce takes literally minutes, with all reducing very quickly. There may be impurities from the pan in the sauce, which are not so good to look at but full of lamb flavour. If you prefer a cleaner finish, the sauce can be made in a small saucepan totally separate from the lamb pans.

To present, divide the greens between four plates with the lamb escalopes (any juices from the meat can be added to the sauce), spooning the *au poivre* sauce over.

roast leg of pork with sage roast parsnips, apples and prunes

Roasting a whole leg of pork tends to suit big event days. Christmas Day is the most obvious, particularly as it happens to fall during the season of home-grown parsnips and apples. Whole legs are about 3.5–4.5kg (8–10lb) in weight, so more than enough for 8–12 people. The *Classic roast potatoes* on page 422 can be doubled to serve with this dish.

An optional extra is to roast the pork on halved onions, leaving their skins on to protect them and prevent them from breaking during the long cooking process. Serve them spooned from their skins to accompany the finished pork. If roasting without them, a wire rack can be used to prevent the meat from sticking to the base of the pan.

SERVES 8–12

1 × 3.5–4.5kg (8–10lb) leg of pork
2 tablespoons lard or cooking oil
salt and pepper
4–6 onions, halved and skins left on (optional), plus
    1 extra onion, finely chopped
8 apples
600ml (1 pint) *Chicken stock* (page 416) or *Instant stock* (page 416)
20 ready-to-eat prunes, halved
300ml (½ pint) white wine
1.75kg (4lb) parsnips, peeled and quartered lengthwise
4–6 tablespoons olive oil
1 bay leaf
150ml (¼ pint) double cream (optional)
squeeze of lemon juice (optional)
50g (2oz) butter
1–2 tablespoons chopped sage leaves
1–2 tablespoons clear honey (optional)

Preheat the oven to 200°/400°F/Gas 6. To achieve a good crisp crackling, the leg must be scored in lines just deep enough to break through the skin. Brush with the lard or cooking oil and sprinkle liberally with the salt. Place the onion halves, skin-side up, if using, or a wire rack, in a large roasting tray. Place the leg of pork on top of the onions or rack and roast in the preheated oven for 30 minutes without basting. Turn the oven temperature down to 180°C/350°F/Gas 4 and continue to roast, again without basting, for a further 3½–4 hours. If becoming too deep in colour, loosely cover with foil. To check the meat is cooked, pierce the thick end of the joint with a skewer. When clear moist juices are released, the pork is ready. Remove it from the oven and keep warm to one side (along with the onions, if using), allowing it to relax for a good 20–30 minutes before serving.

While the pork is roasting, the parsnips can be cooked and the sauce prepared. For the sauce, peel and core two of the apples and roughly chop into relatively small pieces. Add these to the stock, along with seven or eight of the halved prunes. Bring to a simmer and reduce in volume by two-thirds. Remove from the heat and keep to one side to allow the flavours to infuse. Boil the white wine in a separate pan until reduced in volume by three-quarters, then add it to the apple and prune stock.

Cut the central core from the parsnips. Heat 3–4 tablespoons of the olive oil in a large roasting tray, add the parsnips and fry over a moderate heat until a rich golden brown on all sides. This can be done well in advance, ready to finish roasting in the pan for 30 minutes. The parsnips can be cooked while the pork is resting; if so, increase the oven temperature back to 200°C/400°F/Gas 6.

Prepare the remaining six apples. Peel, quarter and cut away their cores and seeds. Fry them in batches in the remaining olive oil, allowing them to colour to a golden brown, ready for adding to the parsnips when needed.

Season the parsnips with salt and pepper and place them in the oven. After the first 15 minutes, add the apples and continue to roast for a further 10 minutes before adding the remaining prune halves. These will now have just 5 minutes to soften and warm through. Should the apples feel too firm, continue to roast with the parsnips, which can now be overcooked for a further 5–10 minutes to give a soft fluffy filling.

While the parsnips are roasting, remove the pork and onions from the tray and pour away the fat. Scoop the onions from their skins and warm through in the oven. Season with salt and pepper.

Warm the tray on top of the stove and add the finely chopped onion and bay leaf. Cook for a few minutes, until beginning to soften, then add the flavoured (prune, apple and white wine) stock. Bring to a gentle simmer and cook for 5 minutes, lifting all of the flavours from the pan. Liquidize to a purée and strain through a sieve for a smooth finish. The liquor can now be checked for seasoning and served as it is or simmered for a few minutes with the addition of the double cream. Check the seasoning again. Add a squeeze of lemon juice to lift the flavour, if necessary.

To finish the parsnips, remove the tray from the oven and place it on top of the stove over a very low heat. Add the butter and chopped sage, then trickle over the clear honey, if using. Spoon the parsnips into a large hot vegetable dish, to be presented on the table.

Remove the crackling from the pork and carve the meat, presenting each portion with a piece of crackling. The dish is ready to serve.

Mashed potatoes (page 422) are also a good accompaniment for roast pork. Other vegetables that work well with the roast are English cabbage plate *(page 359),* Sesame and ham sprouts *(page 317) and* Sweetened potatoes and chestnuts with chives *(page 279).*

roasted and braised wild duck with red wine juniper onions and buttered pears

Wild duck is in season from early September to the end of January and includes the mallard, the largest of the wild duck family, as well as widgeon and teal. If wishing to use any of these, it's best to pre-order from your butcher. Here, I use mallard with the legs removed and braised, while the breasts are roasted on the bone. The legs are then completely well done, soft and succulent, while the breasts are kept pink and tender. This is not essential – you can simply roast a whole duck or even just duck breasts.

The onions – sweet white onions, if available – are softened and stewed in red wine with crushed juniper berries, leaving a spicy edge and aroma. The chosen pears are Comice, which are at their best during the winter months and suit meats, game in particular. One pear per portion may appear to be a little over-generous, but it is only a 2.5cm (1in) central slice (to include the stalk) per portion. The trimmings are then braised with the legs, giving their finished sauce a slightly fruity edge.

SERVES 4

2 mallards, legs removed
2 tablespoons groundnut oil
salt and pepper
1 tablespoon plain flour

2 shallots or 1 onion, roughly chopped
3 juniper berries, lightly crushed
1 strip of orange zest
1 bay leaf
sprig of thyme
1 bottle of red wine
4 pears, preferably Comice
squeeze of lemon juice
300ml (½ pint) Chicken Stock (page 416) or
    Game stock (page 416) or tinned game consommé
2 tablespoons cooking oil
2 knobs of butter

FOR THE ONIONS

1 tablespoon groundnut oil
large knob of butter
675g (1½lb) onions, preferably sweet white, peeled
    and sliced
1 garlic clove, crushed (optional)
10 juniper berries, very finely chopped
2 tablespoons red wine vinegar
1 level teaspoon demerara sugar

Preheat the oven to 180°C/350°F/Gas 4. With the legs removed, the duck breasts are still attached to the bone – this will help maintain their shape and prevent the breasts from shrinking during cooking. The backbone of the carcass can also be cut away, then rinsed and chopped to add to the legs while braising for extra flavour.

Heat 1 tablespoon of the groundnut oil in a suitable braising pot. Season the duck legs with salt and pepper and generously dust them with the plain flour, saving any excess. Fry the duck legs in the oil, along with the chopped backbone, until well coloured. Remove the legs, pour away most of the excess fat and return the pot to the stove. Add the chopped shallots or onion, crushed juniper berries, orange zest, bay leaf and thyme, and continue to fry over a moderate heat for a further 6–8 minutes. Add the duck legs and pour over two-thirds of the red wine. Increase the heat to a rapid simmer and allow the wine to reduce in volume by half.

While the wine is reducing, prepare the pears. You need a 2.5cm (1in) thick vertical central slice, cutting either side of the stalk with the skin left on to give a natural pear-shaped slice. Place the slices in a saucepan, cover with water and add the lemon juice to prevent them from discolouring. Bring to a simmer and cook for just 2 minutes, then leave to cool, before drying the slices on a kitchen cloth.

Cut each of the pear 'trimmings' in half and add them to the pot containing the reduced red wine and the duck legs.

Add the stock or consommé, bring back to a simmer and skim away any impurities. Cover with a lid and braise in the preheated oven for 1¼ hours.

The moment the legs are in the oven, start preparing the onions. Heat the groundnut oil and the large knob of butter in a large saucepan. Once bubbling, add the sliced onions and garlic, if using, with half of the chopped juniper berries. Cover with a lid and cook over a very low heat, stirring from time to time, for 15 minutes. It's important to cook over a low heat to prevent the onions from colouring. Remove the lid and add the red wine vinegar. Increase the heat and allow the vinegar to reduce until almost dry. Add the sugar along with the remaining red wine. Continue to braise the onions for approximately 15 minutes, stirring from time to time, until they are taking on the rich red wine flavour. At this point the wine should be almost completely reduced in volume. If not, increase the heat and reduce until dry. Season with salt and pepper and add the remaining juniper. This now offers a fresh spiciness to the onions. Cover with a lid and keep to one side.

About 10 minutes before the duck legs are due to be ready, start cooking the duck breasts. Season them with salt and pepper. Heat the cooking oil in a roasting tray. Place the birds in, breast-side down, and fry on one side for a few minutes until golden, then turn on to the other breast and repeat the frying and colouring. Turn the birds breast-side up before removing the cooked legs from the oven and increasing the oven temperature to 200°C/400°F/Gas 6. Place the breasts in the oven and roast, basting from time to time, for 15 minutes, for a good medium-rare finish; an extra 5 minutes will be needed for medium and 25–30 minutes for well done. Once cooked to your preferred taste, remove the birds from the oven and leave to rest for 10 minutes.

While the breasts are roasting, remove the duck legs from their cooking liquor and keep warm to one side. Remove and discard the carcass pieces, then place the pan on top of the stove and bring the liquor to a simmer. Skim off any impurities, then allow it to reduce in volume a little if needed to increase the flavour. It is important to taste while reducing. If the liquor is too thin, mix the reserved flour with a knob of butter, and whisk this into the sauce a bit at a time over a gentle simmer, until a sauce-like consistency is obtained. The pure cooking liquor may well provide this, offering a very rich and strong flavour. Only a few tablespoons per portion will be needed. Season with salt and pepper and strain through a sieve, squeezing all of the juices from the pear pieces. The legs can now be placed back in the sauce.

To finish the pear slices, heat the remaining groundnut

oil in a frying pan with the other knob of butter. Once the butter is foaming, place the pears in the pan and fry over a fairly low heat, until just golden brown. Turn the pears over and continue to fry for a few minutes, basting as they cook, until golden brown.

To assemble the dish, warm the legs through in the sauce. Remove the breasts from the bone and trim into a neat shape (the skin can be left on or removed, as you wish). Spoon a pile of juniper onions on each plate, then place a pear slice beside it, its stalk pointing towards the top of the plate. Place a leg on top of each pear and spoon a little of the sauce over and around the onions before topping them with the duck breasts.

A tablespoon or two of the finished sauce can be quickly boiled and reduced to a sticky, treacly consistency. When brushed over the cooked legs, this leaves a very shiny, glazed finish.

ROASTED AND BRAISED WILD DUCK WITH RED WINE JUNIPER ONIONS AND BUTTERED PEARS

sabayon-glazed grapefruit with cox's apple cream

Grapefruit are available throughout the year, hitting their peak in the winter and spring months. Generally regarded as a breakfast fruit, they have also over the years found their way into cold salads and quite a few desserts. The fruit themselves don't really benefit from cooking, with no extra flavour to be found and sometimes more lost. In this dish, they are just warmed and finished with a sabayon flavoured with grapefruit juice and Grand Marnier.

The Cox's Orange Pippin has a season between the months of September and February, offering a quite distinctive spicy, honey, nutty and almost pear-like flavour. The creamy flesh of the apple cooks to a purée very well, blending with the mascarpone cream. The *Tuile biscuits* on page 429 are very nice to serve with this dish, topped with pistachio nuts to offer a nutty crunch. The biscuits can also be shaped into small baskets, as described in the recipe, ready to hold a ball or scroll of the cream.

SERVES 4
4 grapefruit (pink grapefruit can also be used)
50g (2oz) caster sugar
icing sugar, for dusting

FOR THE SABAYON
3 egg yolks
4 tablespoons Grand Marnier or Cointreau
¼ teaspoon cornflour

FOR THE APPLE CREAM
3 Cox's Orange Pippin apples
squeeze of lemon juice
25g (1oz) caster sugar
100g (4oz) mascarpone (or full-fat soft cream cheese)
100ml (3½fl oz) double cream
icing sugar (optional)

First make the apple cream. Peel and quarter the apples, removing the cores and seeds from each. Roughly chop the apples into small dice, then squeeze lemon juice over them to prevent discoloration. Place the chopped apples in a saucepan with 2 tablespoons of water, cover and cook over a medium heat for several minutes, until the apples begin to soften. Remove the lid and add the caster sugar. Continue to simmer, slightly increasing the heat, until the apples are completely cooked through, breaking and almost dry in the pan. Once they are at this stage, remove from the heat and liquidize until smooth. Leave to cool.

Beat the mascarpone or cream cheese until smooth, then stir in the cold apple purée. Lightly whip the double cream to soft peaks, then fold it into the apple mascarpone. Check for sweetness; if a sweeter finish is preferred, add icing sugar to taste. This can now be chilled until needed.

To prepare the grapefruit, cut the tops and bottoms from each, revealing the fruit. Cut the remaining peel and pith away in strips, using a sharp knife, then segment the fruit. As the segments are being cut from the fruit, save all the juice. Also squeeze any remaining in the central membrane once all the segments have been removed and lay the segments on a clean kitchen cloth. Pour the saved grapefruit juice into a saucepan and add the caster sugar. Bring it to the boil and allow to reduce in volume by about half, to a thick syrupy consistency. This will have intensified the grapefruit flavour, also sweetening as it does so. Divide the segments between four small shallow bowls, arranging them in a circular fashion or in a simple rustic style.

To make the sabayon, place the grapefruit syrup, egg yolks, Grand Marnier or Cointreau and the cornflour in a bowl. Whisk, preferably with an electric hand whisk, over a pan of simmering water, until thick and creamy and at least trebled – if not quadrupled – in volume. This process can take 8–10 minutes.

Dust a little icing sugar through a small sieve or tea strainer over each portion of grapefruit. Spoon the sabayon on top and glaze under a preheated grill or with a gas gun (page 9). Once golden brown, the glazed fruits are ready to serve. Spoon the Cox's apple cream into scrolls or balls and sit these on top or offer it separately.

The sabayon can be made an hour or two in advance.
If you wish to do this, once it is at the thick frothy stage,
remove it from the heat and continue to whisk until cold.
This can now be quickly rewhisked before spooning over
and glazing.

OPPOSITE: SABAYON-GLAZED GRAPEFRUIT
WITH COX'S APPLE CREAM

cranberry, orange and port jelly with tangerine biscuit fingers

Christmas pudding is a great British tradition that no Christmas meal should be without. This recipe, although certainly not trying to compete with it, does offer a cold, lighter alternative. It is during this month, December, that cranberries and tangerines are in such abundance. Although today both are imported, cranberries were and still are, although not commercially, grown wild on our own soil. This fruit, supplied to us predominantly by the USA, is enhanced by cranberry and orange juice, finishing with rich ruby port. The tangerine biscuits to accompany are very simple, sweet, buttery, crumbly affairs lifted by a touch of bitter-orangey tangerine (satsumas or clementines can also be used).

SERVES 4

4 tangerines
about 300ml (½ pint) orange juice (fresh or from a carton)
150ml (¼ pint) cranberry juice
225g (8oz) fresh cranberries
100g (4oz) granulated sugar
150ml (¼ pint) ruby port
1 sachet of powdered gelatine (approx 11g)

FOR THE BISCUITS (MAKES 12–16)

100g (4oz) butter
75g (3oz) icing sugar
100g (4oz) plain flour, sifted

Finely grate the zest from the tangerines and reserve for the biscuits. Halve and juice the fruits. Pour the juice into a measuring jug and top up with orange juice to 300ml (½ pint). Strain this juice through a sieve into a saucepan and add the cranberry juice, cranberries, sugar and port. Bring to the boil, then reduce to a very gentle simmer for 12 minutes. Remove from the heat and whisk in the powdered gelatine. Leave to stand for 10 minutes, stirring occasionally, until the gelatine has completely dissolved. Strain the jelly juice through a fine sieve or muslin cloth, squeezing all the juices from the cranberries. Divide between four glasses, each approximately 125–150ml (4fl oz–¼ pint). Once they have cooled, chill for a few hours to allow the jelly to set.

While the jellies are setting, make the biscuits. Preheat the oven to 180°C/350°F/Gas 4. Place all of the ingredients, including the reserved tangerine zest, into a food processor or food mixer, using the beater attachment, and blitz to a soft

pipeable consistency. Spoon into a piping bag fitted with a 1cm (½in) plain or star nozzle.

Cover one or two baking trays with parchment paper (or use non-stick trays), then pipe 7.5cm (3in) strips, leaving a 4cm (1½in) gap between each to allow the biscuits to spread. Bake in the preheated oven for 15–20 minutes, until the biscuits are a light golden brown. Remove from the oven and leave for 5–6 minutes to cool and firm up, then transfer to a cooling rack. Once the biscuits are cold, carefully remove them with a palette knife – they will be very crumbly and tender – and place them in a suitable airtight container.

When serving, it's best to remove the jellies from the fridge 10–15 minutes in advance, to allow a slight softening. These are now ready to present with the tangerine biscuit fingers.

A little single cream can be poured on top of each jelly, offering a classic jelly and cream combination.

tangerine curd ice-cream with marshmallow meringues and grand marnier syrup

The tangerine, a member of the citrus family, joins us during our winter months and has become a standard on our Christmas shopping lists. There are so many of these small varieties of orange, which all seem to be so closely related, but with different names, and all or any of them can be used in this recipe.

This dessert is very light and refreshing, and many of its features can be made in advance. The tangerine curd and Grand Marnier syrup will keep in sterilized jars refrigerated for up to 3 weeks.

I've included candied orange peel in this recipe. This can be bought ready-made, which will work just fine. If possible, however, I suggest purchasing the whole pieces of candied orange peel, rather than ready-chopped, leaving you in complete control when dicing.

SERVES 8
FOR THE CURD

grated zest and juice of 8 tangerines (or satsumas)
150g (5oz) caster sugar
150g (5oz) butter, chopped
4 egg yolks

FOR THE ICE-CREAM
150ml (¼ pint) crème fraîche
150ml (¼ pint) natural yoghurt
2–3 tablespoons Grand Marnier

FOR THE SYRUP
grated zest and juice of 6 tangerines (or satsumas)
100g (4oz) caster sugar
2–3 tablespoons Grand Marnier
½ teaspoon arrowroot or cornflour
1 teaspoon orange juice or water
50g (2oz) candied orange peel, cut into 5mm (¼in) dice
   (pre-chopped can be used)

FOR THE MERINGUES
4 egg whites
225g (8oz) caster sugar
2 teaspoons cornflour
2 teaspoons lemon juice
oil, for greasing

TO DECORATE (OPTIONAL)
4 tangerines (or satsumas), segmented
icing sugar, for dusting

First make the curd. Place the tangerine zest and juice in a saucepan and bring to the boil. Cook until reduced in volume by half, then mix in the caster sugar and chopped butter. Once the butter has melted, whisk in the egg yolks. Cook over a low heat, stirring continuously for 3–4 minutes, until thickened. This stage can also be achieved by placing all the above ingredients in a bowl set over a saucepan of simmering water and cooking for 20–25 minutes, stirring from time to time. This will prevent the egg from possibly scrambling, leaving a safe, smooth finish. Once thickened, transfer to a clean bowl and cover with cling film or greaseproof paper, or pour into a sterilized jar (page 9). Leave to cool.

To make the ice-cream, whisk the crème fraîche and yoghurt into the curd, then flavour with the Grand Marnier. Churn the mixture in an ice-cream machine for 20 minutes and then put in the freezer. Alternatively, just freeze the mixture for several hours without churning. If this method is followed, remove the ice-cream from the freezer 20–30 minutes before serving to allow its consistency to soften.

To make the syrup, mix the tangerine zest and juice with the caster sugar in a saucepan, and simmer rapidly until reduced in volume by a third, then add the Grand Marnier. Mix the arrowroot or cornflour with the orange juice or water and whisk into the simmering syrup. Once returned to a gentle simmer, cook for just 2 minutes, then remove from the stove. While still warm, the candied orange peel can be added. Leave to cool. Alternatively, reheat the syrup just before serving, adding the peel while the syrup is warming.

To make the meringues, preheat the oven to 140°C/275°F/Gas 1. Whisk the egg whites to soft peaks, then add two-thirds of the caster sugar. Continue to whisk until approaching stiff peaks. Now add the remaining sugar, continuing to whisk. The meringue will now have reached a good thick creamy consistency. Add the cornflour and lemon juice, whisking for a further minute. Keep the meringues very naturally shaped, just spooning individual portions onto very lightly oiled parchment paper on a baking tray. Alternatively, spoon the meringue into a piping bag fitted with a 1cm (½in) plain tube and pipe large domes onto the paper. Whichever method you choose, it is important to leave ample space between the meringues to allow them to swell and rise.

Bake in the preheated oven for 45–50 minutes, 1 hour maximum. During this time they will have taken on a very light colour, forming a crisp shell around the pillow-like marshmallow centre. For a touch more colour, the meringues can be cooked at a slightly higher temperature – 150°C/300°F/Gas 2. If so, they will take just 40–45 minutes.

Assemble the dish. If dome-shaped meringues have been made, it is best to crack the tops gently, then place five or six tangerine segments on top, if using. The ice-cream can now be scooped or scrolled using a warm tablespoon, and placed on top of the meringue. The syrup with candied fruit can now be drizzled over to finish. The alternative is simply to sit the ice-cream and meringue side by side, garnishing with the segments and syrup. Whichever way you choose, the dish can be finished with a light dusting of icing sugar and, if it's for Christmas, perhaps a leaf or small sprig of holly.

The recipe for tangerine curd can be replaced with bought orange curd.
Tinned mandarin segments can be used for the garnish instead of segmenting your own.
For a cleaner finish, the fresh tangerine segments can be peeled of their outer skin, revealing the rich orange fruit.

chestnut mascarpone cheesecake with chocolate and warm syruped kumquats

The cheesecake has a long but mixed history, with very similar recipes dating back to the Romans in the second century BC. Other recipes found their way into the records during the thirteenth and seventeenth centuries, and today almost all cookbooks contain a version. This one is very much in the English mode – cold and creamy. Usually digestive biscuits are used as the base, but I'm exchanging these for chocolate chip cookies, lightly crushed and mixed with freshly cooked chopped chestnuts.

Kumquats are small, oval, orange-coloured fruits. Once thought to be part of the citrus family, in fact they stand quite proud as a species all on their own. Kumquats at their ripest can be eaten whole. Here, they are to be cooked until very tender, served just warm.

SERVES 6–10

225g (8oz) chocolate chip cookies
100g (4oz) cooked chestnuts (page 424), chopped
50g (2oz) butter, melted
200g (7oz) tin of sweetened chestnut purée
225g (8oz) mascarpone
25g (1oz) caster sugar
300ml (½ pint) double cream

FOR THE KUMQUATS

350g (12oz) kumquats
300ml (½ pint) orange juice
225g (8oz) caster sugar

FOR THE CHOCOLATE TOPPING

225g (8oz) bitter dark chocolate, chopped
250ml (8fl oz) whipping cream
50g (2oz) butter, softened

To make the base, place the cookies in a plastic bag or between sheets of cling film and crush them with a rolling pin. Mix the crumbled biscuits in a bowl with the chopped chestnuts. Add the melted butter and stir it amongst the crumbs. Spoon and press the mix into the base of a 23cm (9in) loose-bottomed cake tin and chill to set.

To make the cheesecake cream, beat the chestnut purée in a bowl until smooth. Add the mascarpone and sugar and continue to beat until totally combined. Lightly whip the double cream to soft-peak stage, then fold the cream into the chestnut mascarpone mix. Spoon the mix on top of the chestnut biscuit base and spread for a smooth finish. This will now need to be chilled for several hours to set completely.

While the cheesecake is setting, prepare and cook the kumquats. Halve each kumquat across, not lengthwise, gently removing any seeds. Place the orange juice and sugar in a saucepan with 150ml (¼ pint) of water and bring to the boil, then reduce the temperature to a simmer and cook for 5 minutes. Add the kumquats to the orange syrup, bringing the liquor back to a very gentle simmer. If very young and ripe, the fruits may only take 30 minutes to become tender. They can, however, take up to 1–1½ hours (2 hours maximum), before they are tender to the bite. Whatever the cooking time, the results will be the same – very tender and sweet with a slight bitter bite. Once cooked, leave to cool slightly to a warm serving temperature. If stored in airtight preserving jars, the syruped fruits will have a fairly long shelf-life, particularly if refrigerated.

To make the chocolate topping, melt the chocolate with the cream in a bowl over a saucepan of simmering water, making sure the bowl is not in contact with the water, as this overheats the chocolate, leaving a grainy consistency. Once the chocolate has melted, remove the bowl from the saucepan and add the softened butter.

Remove the cheesecake from the fridge and release around the edge of the cake tin with a small warmed knife. Remove the cake from the surrounding tin. To reset the edge quickly, place the cake in the freezer for 5–10 minutes.

The chocolate topping can now be poured and spread across and around the sides of the cake. This can now be left to set just at room temperature or chilled until needed. If chilling, it is best to remove the cheesecake from the fridge 20 minutes before serving, to help the chocolate return to a softer finish.

For an extra-glossy finish, a gas gun (page 9) can be quickly and lightly flashed over the chocolate. Rather than melt completely, it just softens, leaving the shiniest of finishes.

The cheesecake is now ready to serve, with spoonfuls of the warm kumquats.

OPPOSITE: CHESTNUT MASCARPONE CHEESECAKE WITH CHOCOLATE AND WARM SYRUPED KUMQUATS

quince-topped almond bake

In December there are still a few quinces around, some joining us from Greece, maybe even one or two of our own. With the *Baked cider, cinnamon and honey quinces* (page 274), the quinces are simply halved and then baked, to bring out the full depth of their flavour and fragrant scent. In this recipe they are cut into chunks and cooked in a sweet lemon-flavoured syrup, before they are spooned over a rich almond bake.

SERVES 6–8

175g (6oz) butter at room temperature, diced,
 plus more for greasing
175g (6oz) caster sugar
175g (6oz) ground almonds
2 eggs

FOR THE QUINCES
200g (7oz) caster sugar
3 strips of lemon zest
1kg (2¼lb) quinces (4 small or 2–3 medium–large)

Preheat the oven to 190°C/375°F/Gas 5. Place the butter, sugar, ground almonds and eggs in a food processor and blitz to a smooth, creamy finish. Butter a 23cm (9in) pudding dish (4–5cm/1½–2in deep), then spread in the almond mix. Bake in the preheated oven for 35–45 minutes, until firm to the touch. Remove from the oven and keep to one side.

While the sponge base is cooking, prepare the quinces. Pour the sugar into a large saucepan with 300ml (½ pint) of water and the lemon zest. Bring to the boil and simmer for 5 minutes. Peel the quinces, cut them into quarters and remove the cores. Cut the flesh into small dice and add it to the syrup. Bring to a simmer, stirring from time to time, then cover with a circle of greaseproof paper and gently cook for 25–30 minutes, until the fruit is tender. Remove from the heat and discard the lemon zest.

Spoon the warm quince on top of the almond bake, allowing just a little of the syrup to seep into the sponge. Any excess syrup can be offered separately, or chilled for later use with other fruits.

The bake is now ready to serve just warm or cold, perhaps offering whipped or pouring cream (or crème fraîche) to accompany.

A vanilla mascarpone cream is a luxury extra to offer with the bake. Split a vanilla pod and scrape the seeds into 100g (4oz) of mascarpone and beat to a smooth consistency. Whisk 150ml (¼ pint) of whipping cream with 2 heaped tablespoons of icing sugar to soft peaks, then fold it into the vanilla-flavoured mascarpone. The cream is now ready to serve; for a firmer finish chill for 30 minutes.

warm carrot cake with hazelnut marmalade syrup and nutmeg mascarpone cream

This carrot cake is quite spicy and rich, with added syrup and oil to keep it moist, also extending its shelf-life. To soften the total eating experience, I've included a recipe for a mascarpone cream and a hazelnut and orange syrup to finish.

SERVES 8
butter, for greasing
175g (6oz) self-raising flour, sifted, plus more for
 dusting
150ml (¼ pint) sunflower oil
100g (4oz) soft brown sugar
2 eggs
75g (3oz) golden syrup
1 teaspoon ground cinnamon
½ teaspoon ground cloves
½ teaspoon ground ginger
½ teaspoon bicarbonate of soda
200g (8oz) carrots, finely grated

FOR THE SYRUP
16 hazelnuts, shelled
150g (5oz) orange marmalade
3–4 tablespoons Grand Marnier

FOR THE MASCARPONE CREAM
100g (4oz) mascarpone
150ml (¼ pint) double cream
2 teaspoons icing sugar
1 teaspoon freshly grated nutmeg

Preheat the oven to 200°C/400°F/Gas 6. To prepare the hazelnuts for the syrup, place them on a baking tray and cook for 8 minutes in the preheated oven. These can now be rubbed in a cloth while still hot to remove all of the skins. If the hazelnuts are still a little opaque, return them to the oven for just a minute or two, to give them a roasted edge. Leave

Sweet
they a
colour
the va
potatc

daily c
begin
abund
vegeta
all of c
frying.

introd
on the
culina
refers
panca
potatc
be ser
course
recipe

the nuts to cool before chopping roughly. Reduce the oven temperature to 180°C/350°F/Gas 4.

Butter and flour a 15cm (6in) cake tin or eight size-1 ramekins. To make the carrot cake, whisk together the oil, sugar, eggs and golden syrup until well combined. Beat in the flour, spices and bicarbonate of soda, then add the finely grated carrots. Transfer the mix to the buttered and floured tin, and bake in the preheated oven for 50–55 minutes, or divide between the ramekins and bake for 20–25 minutes. To test if it is done, push a skewer into the centre of the cake; if it comes out clean, the cake is cooked. Leave to rest in the tin or moulds for 10 minutes before turning out.

While the cake is baking, make the syrup and mascarpone cream. Place the marmalade and 3 tablespoons of the Grand Marnier in a small saucepan with 100ml (3½fl oz) of water and bring to a simmer. Cook on a low heat until the marmalade has completely dissolved. Add the remaining Grand Marnier, if preferred. Strain through a sieve.

To make the mascarpone cream, place the mascarpone, double cream, icing sugar and nutmeg in a bowl and whisk together to a lightly-whipped-cream stage.

To serve, place wedges cut from the warm carrot cake (or whole small individual cakes) onto warmed plates. Add the chopped roast hazelnuts to the warm syrup and spoon it over and around the cake. The nutmeg mascarpone cream can be offered separately or spooned on top of each portion, beginning to melt as it warms.

The carrot cake also eats well cold, simply accompanied by the nutmeg cream. If serving cold, the roasted and chopped hazelnuts can be added to the cream along with 50–75g (2–3oz) of raisins.
The carrot cake reheats very well in the microwave.

roast fig and stilton salad with parma ham and a port vinaigrette

Peel tl
dice. I
until j

(prefe
chopp

potatc
olive c
omele
very t
minut

OPPO

Figs, generally looked upon as a dessert fruit, lend themselves equally well to savoury dishes. This autumn and winter recipe is ideal for lunch, supper, or alternative dessert, also making a perfect starter for the Christmas meal.

Whenever purchasing Parma ham, it is always best to take the cut from the middle of the ham. Here it will be at its most plump and tender, without an over-fatty edge. Also it's best to ask for the thinnest of slices. For the salad leaves, bags of pre-washed mixed leaves can be found in most supermarkets. As a starter, one bag for four people will be plenty.

SERVES 4 AS A PUDDING OR STARTER,
OR 2 AS A MAIN COURSE
6 ripe figs
knob of softened butter
sprinkling of light soft brown sugar
100ml (3½fl oz) port
3 tablespoons crème fraîche
1 tablespoon cider vinegar
3 tablespoons olive oil
salt and pepper
12–16 thin slices of Parma ham
2 handfuls of mixed salad leaves (rocket, curly endive,
**   radicchio, oak leaf, watercress, etc., see above)**
100g (4oz) Stilton cheese, crumbled and at room
**   temperature**
1 tablespoon 1cm (½in) chive sticks

Preheat the oven to 220°C/425°F/Gas 7. Trim the tips off the fig stalks, and then halve each fig. Place the figs, cut-side up, in a lightly buttered roasting tray. Brush each fig with butter and lightly sprinkle a little sugar over each.

Place in the preheated oven and roast for 10–12 minutes, until softening. Remove the figs from the tray and keep warm by turning off the oven and returning the figs to it on a separate plate.

Place the roasting tray over a medium heat on the stove and add the port. Boil to reduce in volume by three-quarters, until slightly syrupy. Remove from the heat.

In a bowl, whisk together the crème fraîche, cider vinegar and olive oil. Strain the reduced port into the dressing through a tea strainer or sieve and whisk it in well. Season with salt and pepper.

Place the slices of ham on large plates. Season the salad leaves with just a little pepper, then add the crumbled Stilton and chives. The salad and warm figs can now be arranged in a rustic fashion towards the top or centre of the plate and drizzled with the port dressing. Any juices released from the figs while keeping warm can also be spooned over the salad.

Roquefort cheese also works very well with this recipe.

walnut-crusted cod with parsnip sauce

Cod has more or less an all-year-round season, really coming to the fore and shining between the months of September and February. The parsnip also presents itself during a similar season, finding its prime between November and January.

This quite meaty, succulent fish is here enhanced with a breadcrumbed crust, with the oily nuttiness of walnuts creating an even richer overall taste.

SERVES 4

3 thick slices of white bread, crusts removed
50g (2oz) curly parsley, picked and roughly chopped
1 teaspoon picked thyme leaves (optional)
salt and pepper
8 walnut halves, chopped
2 shallots, very finely chopped
3 tablespoons walnut, olive or groundnut oil
4 × 175g (6oz) portions of cod fillet, skinned
butter, for greasing

FOR THE PARSNIP SAUCE

2 parsnips, peeled and quartered lengthwise
knob of butter
200ml (7fl oz) milk
squeeze of lemon juice

FOR THE CARROTS (OPTIONAL)

4 carrots, peeled
still mineral water
knob of butter, plus extra 15g/½oz (optional)
½ teaspoon sugar

Cut the crusted bread slices into cubes, then place in a food processor, blitzing until beginning to crumble. Alternatively you could buy fresh white breadcrumbs. Add the parsley and thyme, and continue to blitz until the crumbs are reasonably fine and a rich green colour. Season with salt and pepper, and add the chopped walnuts. To break down their texture a stage further, quickly blitz again, crushing the walnuts into the mix. Add the shallots, and pour in the oil as the crumbs turn, simply to moisten their loose texture.

Season the cod fillets with salt and pepper, then cover the flat skinned side of each fillet with the crumbs. Place the topped cod fillets on a greased baking tray. These can now be chilled until needed.

To make the sauce, cut away the central core of each of the parsnip quarters. Cut each piece of parsnip into 1cm (½in) thick pieces. Melt the knob of butter in a saucepan and, once bubbling, add the parsnip pieces. Cover and cook over a low heat for 6–8 minutes, stirring from time to time and not allowing the parsnips to colour, until just beginning to soften. At this point add the milk and bring to a simmer. Cook gently for 15 minutes, until the pieces are completely cooked through. Season with salt and pepper. Liquidize the parsnips to a silky-smooth puréed sauce. A squeeze of lemon juice can now be added to enliven the finished flavour. Keep to one side ready to reheat.

If serving the carrots, cut each into quarters lengthwise. These can now be cut into 1cm (½in) thick pieces. Place them in a saucepan, pour enough still mineral water on top just to cover and add the knob of butter and the sugar. Bring to a simmer and cook for approximately 10 minutes, until tender. Increase the heat and continue until the carrots are overcooked, allowing the water to reduce in volume by at least two-thirds to three-quarters, developing a loose syrup consistency. Just before serving, the extra 15g (½oz) butter can be added, if using, stirring it into the pan to emulsify. Season with salt and pepper.

Preheat the oven to 200°C/400°F/Gas 6 and the grill to hot. Place the cod fillets under the grill, not too close to the heat, for a few minutes, allowing the crumbed topping to reach a slightly golden edge. Transfer to the preheated oven, cooking for approximately 8–10 minutes. The cod will now be cooked through, but still maintaining a moist finish.

To serve, present the cod fillets and parsnip sauce on plates, offering the overcooked sweet carrots separately, if serving. The dish is now ready; offer any extra parsnip sauce separately.

OPPOSITE: WALNUT-CRUSTED COD WITH PARSNIP SAUCE

pan-fried sea bass with two leeks

Although an expensive fish to buy, sea bass warrants this price because of its pure quality and very distinctive flavour. Fish that can take its place are the sea bream, which comes in many varieties – gilthead, red and black – and grey mullet, both fish still very individual in their flavour, but with a more competitive price.

'Two leeks' actually refers to the two parts of the vegetable, which are separated for this dish: the whites creamed with potatoes to form a sort of vichyssoise purée; the greens shredded, softly buttered and finished with a spoonful of yoghurt.

The sea bass portions are best cut from a fish at least 1.5kg (3lb) in weight, that has been scaled, filleted and the pin bones removed (page 9). The fish meat is then thick enough not to overcook while the skin is crisping.

SERVES 4 AS A MAIN COURSE
1 tablespoon olive oil
4 × 175g (6oz) portions of sea bass fillet
flour, for dusting
knob of butter

FOR THE LEEKS
4 medium potatoes, suitable for mashing
   (Maris Piper or King Edward), peeled and quartered
salt and pepper
3 medium leeks
25g (1oz) butter, plus an extra knob
100–150ml (3½fl oz–¼ pint) milk, warmed
50–100ml (2–3½fl oz) whipping or double cream
   (optional)
freshly grated nutmeg
100–150ml (3½fl oz–¼ pint) natural yoghurt
1 teaspoon chopped dill (optional)

Place the potato quarters in a large saucepan and cover with cold water. Add a level teaspoon of salt, bring to a rapid simmer and cook for approximately 20 minutes, until tender. Drain well in a colander. Return the potatoes to the pan, stirring over a very low heat to help draw off any remaining moisture.

While the potatoes are cooking, top and tail the leeks and split them in half lengthwise. Rinse and wash well to remove any soil and grit, then cut across to separate the white and green.

There is obviously a very pale green point – this can be included with the white. Cut the white into rough 1cm (½in) dice.

Melt half of the measured butter in a saucepan and add the diced leek whites. Cook for a few minutes, adding 1–2 tablespoons of water and covering to create steam that helps to soften the leeks, stirring from time to time, until completely overcooked. This will take up to 15 minutes. Drain, saving all of the buttery leek juices. To purée, place the cooked leeks in a food processor and blitz until smooth. Add the potatoes, a few at a time, quickly blitzing so as not to be left with a starchy finish. To help soften, pour in some of the warm milk, little by little, until the right consistency is achieved. The cream can be used to replace some of the milk, or simply added to provide you with the softest of vichyssoise-like purées. Add the remaining measured butter and season with salt, pepper and nutmeg to finish. The potatoes can be mashed quite separately from the leeks, and the milk, cream, butter and seasonings added before the puréed leeks are stirred in. This can now be kept to one side ready to rewarm when needed.

Finely shred the leek greens, ready to cook while the fish is frying.

Heat the olive oil in a large frying pan. Lightly flour the skin side of the sea bass and season each side with a pinch of salt. The flesh side can also be seasoned with pepper (seasoning any fish with salt only on the presentation side is to prevent the finished appearance being speckled with black spots of pepper). Place the fish, skin-side down, in the pan, adding the knob of butter. Cook on a moderate heat for 6–7 minutes, until the skin has become richly coloured and crispy. Turn the fish over in the pan and remove the pan from the heat. The residual heat in the pan will continue to cook the fillets without leaving a leathery edge, also providing time for the garnishes to be brought together.

While the fish is frying, melt the extra knob of butter in a saucepan and add the shredded leek greens. Cook for 5–6 minutes, seasoning with salt and pepper. The leeks can now be finished with 100ml (3½fl oz) of the natural yoghurt, stirring in to achieve a softening, but not too loose, effect. The extra 50ml (2fl oz) can be added if needed. Finish with the chopped dill, if using, and check the seasoning.

Spoon the leek greens onto plates and top each with the fried sea bass portions. Spoon the creamy vichyssoise purée beside. The buttery leek juices saved from the whites can be quickly warmed and a little spooned over the purée.

fresh turbot with avocado and mango salad

For this recipe, the turbot is to be very gently pan-fried, only allowing the faintest of golden edge; this leaves the flesh with an almost steamed texture and very tender to eat.

Avocados are still plentiful, with Brazilian and Kenyan mangoes now in their prime. There are over 2500 varieties of mango, coming in different colours and weights, each holding its own texture and personality. The cultivated varieties, Kent and Tommy Atkins, both available right now, have a thinner skin than the wild, with a less fibrous flesh.

The salad takes on flavours associated with a Mexican salsa, in particular lime and chillies. This dish offers a much lighter approach than usual at this time of year.

The avocado and mango salad ingredients are listed in fairly generous quantities. If you choose this recipe as a starter, these quantities will serve six portions. The salad can be made several hours in advance – keep it covered and refrigerated.

SERVES 6 AS A STARTER OR 4 AS A MAIN COURSE

4 × 175g (6oz) portions of turbot fillet, skinned
salt and pepper, plus sea salt flakes
flour, for dusting
large knob of butter

FOR THE SALAD

2 small avocados
juice of 2 limes
2 small mangoes
2 red chillies, seeded and finely diced
1 small red onion or 2–3 spring onions, finely chopped
1 heaped tablespoon chopped coriander leaves
4 tablespoons olive oil

To make the salad, halve the avocados, removing the stone and peeling away the skin. Roughly cut the flesh into 1cm (½in) dice, placing it in a large bowl. Squeeze the juice of 1 lime over the avocados, stirring gently. This will prevent the green fruits from discolouring.

Peel the mangoes and slice the flesh off the stone, before dicing as per the avocados. Place all of the remaining salad ingredients in a bowl, stirring them together and seasoning with sea salt before adding the avocados and mangoes.

Season the fish with salt, lightly dusting the filleted side with flour. Melt the butter in a frying pan and, once bubbling, place the fillets in the pan, floured-side down, seasoning the skinned side with a twist of pepper. Fry gently for 4–5 minutes, allowing the lightest of golden touches, before turning the fish in the pan and removing it from the heat. The retained warmth in the pan will continue to cook the fish if you leave it to stand for a further 2–3 minutes.

During this time the salad can be arranged on plates, before placing on the fish. Any remaining butter in the pan can be drizzled over the turbot fillets.

A 2cm (¾in) nugget of peeled fresh root ginger can be finely grated before adding it to the salad.
A level teaspoon of brown sugar can also be stirred into the lime juice for a sweeter dressing.

braised seville orange beef with horseradish dumplings

Seville oranges have a very short season, first arriving in the UK in January and gone by mid-February. Known in France as *bigarade* (bitter orange), the Seville is not an orange to buy for general eating; instead it is one that comes into its own when cooked. To increase its already pretty intense flavour, the rind can be pared in curls from the fruit, then dried in the oven on its lowest setting for 45 minutes–1 hour (this can even sometimes take up to 2 hours). As the peel dries, its bitter flavour becomes stronger and richer. The dried peel can now be kept in an airtight jar, ready to add to stews and casseroles throughout the year.

The beef to be used here is braising or chuck steak. This has an open texture that absorbs the juices, leaving the meat moist as well as very tender after a long stewing. The beef can just be diced, but here it's kept as 100g (4oz) pieces, like mini beef joints, so that the meat is not lost amongst the carrots and onions cooking with them.

The horseradish dumplings are steamed rather than poached in the sauce. This keeps the flavours quite separate during cooking, only to meet once on the plate.

SERVES 4

8 × 100g (4oz) lean pieces of chuck or braising steak
salt and pepper
2 tablespoons plain flour
2 tablespoons groundnut oil
large knob of butter
2 large carrots, quartered
2 onions, quartered
3 tablespoons red wine vinegar
1 bottle of red wine
8 pared strips of peel from 1 Seville orange, plus finely
** grated zest of 2 more and juice of all 3**
sprigs of thyme
sprigs of rosemary
3 bay leaves
3–4 black peppercorns
2 teaspoons demerara sugar
600ml (1 pint) *Beef stock* (page 416) or tinned
** consommé or water**

OPPOSITE: BRAISED SEVILLE ORANGE BEEF
WITH HORSERADISH DUMPLINGS

FOR THE DUMPLINGS
75g (3oz) self-raising flour, plus more for dusting
75g (3oz) fresh white breadcrumbs
75g (3oz) butter, diced, plus more for greasing
2 heaped tablespoons grated fresh horseradish
** (or 50g/2oz horseradish cream or purée)**
1 tablespoon chopped parsley
pinch of chopped thyme
pinch of chopped rosemary
1 teaspoon finely grated Seville orange zest
1 egg white, or 1 whole egg (optional)
milk, to loosen (optional)

Preheat the oven to 160°C/325°F/Gas 3. Season each piece of beef with salt and pepper, then roll them in the flour, saving any excess flour. Melt the groundnut oil in a large frying pan and add the beef. Fry for 6–8 minutes, until coloured on all sides.

While the beef is frying, heat a braising pan on top of the stove and melt the large knob of butter in it. Add the carrots and onions, and cook on a gentle heat until golden brown. Remove the vegetables from the pan and add the red wine vinegar. Boil until almost dry. Add the red wine, along with four strips of the orange peel (the rest can be dried as described in the introduction for later use), the thyme, rosemary, bay leaves, peppercorns and demerara sugar, and bring to the boil. Reduce in volume by two-thirds, then add the stock, consommé or water. Add the pieces of beef along with the carrots and onions, and any remaining flour. Bring to a simmer, cover with a lid and cook in the preheated oven for 2½–3 hours, until very tender. During this cooking time, the sauce can be skimmed of impurities from time to time, to produce a cleaner finish.

To make the dumplings, place the self-raising flour, white breadcrumbs, butter, grated horseradish (or horseradish cream or purée) and salt and pepper in a food processor. Blitz to a crumbly consistency, then stir in the chopped herbs and orange zest. Add the egg white to bind; if slightly too dry, a little milk or the egg yolk can be added for a looser, richer finish. Once it is forming into a ball, dust your hands with flour, then separate the mix into eight small dumplings. These can now be cooked once the stew is almost ready, steaming them on buttered greaseproof paper for approximately 15–20 minutes over rapidly simmering water, until risen and firm.

To finish the stew, remove the meat, onions and carrots from the pan, cover and keep warm to one side. Strain the sauce through a fine sieve, then bring it to the boil, skimming off any impurities. Reduce, if necessary, to a loose sauce consistency. Boil the orange juice in a separate pan and reduce in volume by three-quarters, then add it to the sauce. Season with salt and pepper. Return the meat and vegetables to the saucepan and bring to a gentle simmer.

The stew is now ready to serve, dividing the meat, vegetables and sauce between plates and topping with the dumplings. Strips of dried zest can also be used as an optional garnish if available (see above). This dish eats very well with *Orange caramelized salsify* (page 329).

The horseradish for the dumplings can be replaced with 2–3 teaspoons of Dijon or wholegrain mustard, or omitted, leaving them just flavoured with the orange and herbs.
For a glossy finish, brush the dumplings with melted butter before serving.
For a thicker sauce, stir in a little arrowroot or cornflour loosened with red wine or water.
The more often the sauce is skimmed of any impurities during the braising of the beef, the cleaner and neater the finished result will be.

roast streaky bacon with stir-fried pak choi, water chestnuts and mushrooms

The streaky bacon is going to be cooked in one large piece as a joint of meat. This is the same cut as belly of pork, the lines of fat running through the meat melting to moisten it. When cooking a slab of 'streaky', as it's known, in one piece, approximately 30 minutes per 450g (1lb) will be plenty to leave a tender finish. I prefer a slower roast, however, allowing double the time. This leaves it not only tender, but almost melting.

Pak choi (also known as bok choi) is 'Chinese celery cabbage'; the thick-based stems of these plants are celery-like in appearance. As with most 'Chinese leaves', pak choi is becoming available all year round, now growing quite easily in Britain's climate. These green, spoon-shaped leaves ('spoon' is another title this plant carries due to the shape of its leaves) and pale stalks hold a slight pepperiness, without quite the hot bite of mustard greens. At this time of year, trying to find small pak choi may be a problem, but there are plenty of large plants happy to act as stand-ins. The leaves and stalks can be cooked separately as you would Swiss chard, the stalks needing just an extra minute or two.

Water chestnuts are mostly available between December and January, to be found in Chinese stores or supermarkets.

The nuts have a dark brown shell, easily peeled away with a small knife, to reveal a crisp white interior. I find they add a refreshing bite to the cooked greens.

The mushrooms used here are the cultivated 'wild' oyster mushrooms, now available throughout the year.

To complete the home-made Chinese feel of this dish, I like to serve it in large rice bowls.

SERVES 4

1 tablespoon vegetable oil
1.25kg (2½lb) boneless, unsmoked piece of streaky bacon, rind removed
pepper
1–2 tablespoons demerara or light soft brown sugar (optional)

FOR THE STIR-FRY
450g (1lb) pak choi (preferably small)
350g (12oz) oyster mushrooms
10–12 water chestnuts
1–2 tablespoons sesame oil
3 garlic cloves, thinly sliced
2 cm (¾in) nugget of fresh root ginger, peeled and finely grated
1 red chilli, seeded and finely chopped
1 teaspoon light soft brown sugar
1 tablespoon light soy sauce

Preheat the oven to 160°C/325°F/Gas 3. Put a large ovenproof braising pot on top of the stove, heating the vegetable oil. Season the bacon with a twist of pepper, placing it rindless-side down in the pot and frying to a golden brown. Turn the joint, adding 300ml (½ pint) of water to the pot and bringing to a gentle simmer. Cover with a lid and bake in the oven for 2½–3 hours, checking every 30 minutes. If the water has almost run dry, simply refill to the original quantity.

While roasting the bacon, cut the base from the pak choi stalks, separating the leaves before washing and drying. Any larger outside leaves can be cut lengthwise in two. Trim any thick base of stalk from the oyster mushrooms, before tearing into halves or 1cm (½in) thick strips.

The water chestnuts simply need peeling with a sharp small knife, before slicing thinly. The chestnut slices can now be quickly plunged into boiling water, stirring just once or twice before draining. This blanching will release their initial rawness, although it is not essential.

Once the bacon is roasted, remove the pot from the oven and leave to one side, allowing the joint to rest for at least 20 minutes. Reserve the cooking liquor.

With the bacon rested and ready to eat, heat a wok with a tablespoon of the sesame oil, adding the garlic and ginger and stir-frying for 30 seconds–1 minute. Add the pak choi, oyster mushrooms, water chestnuts and chopped chilli, cooking until the pak choi begins to wilt and the mushrooms are tender.

At this point, add 2–3 tablespoons of cooking liquor from the bacon pot with the teaspoon of light soft brown sugar and bring to a simmer, cooking the pak choi for a further 2 minutes until the stems are tender. Add the soy sauce, along with an extra tablespoon of the oil for a stronger sesame flavour, if preferred.

While cooking the pak choi, as an optional extra, the streaky bacon can be removed from the pot, placing it on a baking tray and sprinkling with the demerara or light soft brown sugar. This can now be placed under a preheated grill, cooking the sugar to a melting caramel finish.

To serve, spoon the pak choi, water chestnut and mushroom stir-fry into bowls, carving the streaky bacon into long 1cm (½in) thick slices and placing them on top.

If pak choi is unavailable, fresh cabbage, kale or spinach can also be used.
Tinned water chestnuts are always on offer.

slow-roast shoulder of lamb with jerusalem artichokes and a horseradish paloise sauce

The shoulder of lamb can be bought already boned and rolled for carving or left on the bone, retaining more flavour and a moist finish. The cooking process is in two stages. First there is a 30-minute roasting time, then 2½ hours of pot-roasting in water that slowly becomes a flavoursome lamb stock.

The Jerusalem artichokes act as our potato-shaped accompaniment here. Roasted in any lamb fat saved from the shoulder's first 30 minutes in the oven, they go well with the 'one-pot' cooking.

The horseradish, normally associated with beef, is usually available throughout the year. It works well here, its sharp strong oniony edge cutting through the sweet lamb and artichokes. *Sauce paloise* is a mint-flavoured béarnaise (a hollandaise-style sauce), to which the grated horseradish lends its bite.

SERVES 4

1.5kg (3lb) shoulder of lamb
salt and pepper
2 tablespoons cooking oil
600ml (1 pint) white wine
675g (1½lb) carrots, peeled and cut into 1cm (½in) slices
1 large onion, quartered
2 bay leaves
sprig of thyme
2 garlic cloves (optional)
1kg (2¼lb) Jerusalem artichokes
juice of ½ lemon
flour, for dusting (optional)
50g (2oz) butter

FOR THE SAUCE (MAKES APPROXIMATELY 200ML/7FL OZ)
2 shallots, finely chopped (optional)
½ teaspoon crushed black peppercorns (optional)
3 tablespoons white wine vinegar
2 heaped teaspoons snipped mint leaves
175g (6oz) unsalted butter
2 egg yolks
squeeze of lemon juice
2 tablespoons finely grated horseradish or horseradish relish

Preheat the oven to 220ºC/425ºF/Gas 7. Season the lamb with salt and pepper. Heat the cooking oil in a roasting tray on top of the stove. Place the lamb, fat-side down, in the tray and fry on a medium heat for 10–15 minutes until a rich golden brown. Through not frying too quickly, quite a lot of fat will be released. This process may well take up to 20 minutes to achieve the richest colour. Turn the lamb in the pan, before placing in the preheated oven and roasting for 30 minutes. At this point, remove the lamb from the oven and tray, pouring off and saving any collected lamb fat.

Place the tray back on the stove over a high heat and add the white wine. Boil until reduced in volume by three-quarters. Place the carrots, onion quarters, bay leaves, thyme and garlic, if using, in the pan and put the lamb on top, fat-side up. Pour 600ml (1 pint) boiling water into the tray and cover with a double layer of foil. Return the tray to the oven, reducing its temperature to 160ºC/325ºF/Gas 3. Bake for a further 2 hours, basting from time to time. At this point, discard the foil and continue to roast for a further 30 minutes.

At least 1 hour before the lamb's total roasting time is complete, the Jerusalem artichokes and the sauce can be prepared.

To make the sauce, combine the chopped shallots and crushed black peppercorns, if using, with the white wine vinegar and 1 teaspoon of the mint leaves. Bring to the boil and quickly reduce in volume by half. Leave to cool, then strain through a sieve. Melt the butter until its solids have separated from its rich yellow oil. Remove from the heat and leave to cool until just warm. Most solids will now have sunk to the base of the pan, and any remaining on top can be skimmed away, leaving the butter clarified. Mix together the egg yolks, 3 tablespoons of water and the reduced vinegar, whisking in a bowl over a pan of simmering water until at least doubled in volume and at a sabayon (softly whipped cream) stage. Remove from the heat and slowly add the clarified butter, whisking continuously. This will emulsify the butter into the egg yolk mixture. If the sauce seems too thick and sticky while adding the butter, loosen slightly with a squeeze of the lemon juice or a trickle of water. Season with salt and pepper, add a squeeze of lemon juice, then strain the sauce through a sieve. The finely grated horseradish or horseradish relish can now be whisked in and the sauce left in a warm place to infuse (if béarnaise or hollandaise sauce become too cold, the butter begins to set, separating the sauce). You may find more horseradish will be needed for a sharper bite.

Peel the Jerusalem artichokes and place in a saucepan of water acidulated with the juice of ½ lemon. Bring the chokes to the boil and simmer for just a few minutes to blanch, then drain in a colander and leave to cool. These can now be patted dry and lightly rolled in flour. Heat the saved lamb fat in a roasting tray and fry the artichokes to a golden brown. Sprinkle with a pinch of salt, then place in the oven for the last 30–40 minutes of the lamb's cooking time.

Once the lamb is cooked, remove it from the roasting tray and keep warm to one side. The oven can now be returned to its original temperature of 220°C/425°F/Gas 7. The artichokes will now begin to crisp; roast them for a further 15–20 minutes.

Remove the garlic, thyme and bay leaves and drain the liquor from the roasting tray, keeping the carrots and onions warm to one side. Boil and reduce the liquor to 200–300ml (7fl oz–½ pint), seasoning with salt and pepper. This will now be a thin but flavoursome lamb stock. To enhance, whisk in 25g (1oz) of the butter. The remaining 25g (1oz) can be added to the Jerusalem artichokes for a richer finish.

To serve, divide the carrots between four plates, offering an onion quarter on each. The shoulder can now be carved and shared, before spooning some of the cooking liquor over. Add the remaining mint to finish the paloise sauce, ready to offer separately.

parsnip pot-roast chicken with spicy red cabbage and bacon

Parsnips are at the height of their season during the winter, as is the red cabbage which, as with all cabbage running from autumn to summer, responds to the chill with crisper leaves and a fresher taste.

This recipe works well with all poultry and game birds. Guinea fowl is a good alternative to chicken, with pheasant – which so often needs a helping hand to maintain its moistness – following on.

An optional extra which can be added is a garlic and parsley butter left to melt into the bird itself. It's really not essential, but does give an extra edge to the overall flavour of the dish.

SERVES 4
1.75kg (4lb) free-range chicken
4 parsnips
2–3 tablespoons groundnut or cooking oil
2 knobs of butter
150–200ml (¼ pint–7fl oz) *Chicken stock* **(page 416),**
  Instant stock **(page 416), tinned chicken consommé**
  or water
4–8 rindless rashers of streaky bacon

FOR THE GARLIC AND PARSLEY BUTTER (OPTIONAL)
25–50g (1–2oz) butter
1 large garlic clove, crushed
1 tablespoon chopped parsley
salt and pepper

FOR THE RED CABBAGE
knob of butter
1 small or ½ large red cabbage, finely shredded
2 onions, sliced
peeled zest of ½ orange
1 bay leaf
6 juniper berries
⅛ teaspoon ground cinnamon
⅛ teaspoon freshly grated nutmeg
2 cloves
4 tablespoons red wine vinegar or cider vinegar
2 tablespoons demerara sugar
300ml (½ pint) apple juice

Preheat the oven to 200°C/400°F/Gas 6. To make the optional garlic and parsley butter, mix together the butter, crushed garlic and chopped parsley, seasoning with salt and pepper. This will now be placed between the chicken skin and breast, melting within the bird as it roasts. To do so, release the skin carefully from the chicken breasts, starting at the neck end. This is very easy, but it is important to do it gently so as not to split the skin. Spoon the butter mix underneath the skin and over the breast, dividing between the two sides. Pull the skin over and press gently to spread the butter across the breasts. Pull the excess skin underneath the bird and secure with one or two cocktail sticks. To maintain a good chicken shape, tie the legs together. Set to one side.

Peel each of the parsnips and quarter, cutting away the woody central core. Heat 1–2 tablespoons of the oil in a large frying pan. Place the parsnips in the pan and fry reasonably quickly until golden brown on all sides. Season with salt and pepper. The parsnips can now be transferred into a suitably sized pot in which to cook the chicken.

Season the chicken with salt and pepper. After wiping the frying pan clean, heat the remaining tablespoon of groundnut oil and fry the bird on both breasts and legs, to colour to a rich golden brown. Place the chicken on top of the parsnips and brush with a knob of butter. Cover with a lid and place in the oven for 1 hour. After 20 minutes, remove the lid and baste the chicken with the juices. Add a third of the stock, consommé or water, replace the lid and continue to pot-roast for a further 20 minutes. As the chicken is cooking, the parsnips will be softening, becoming overcooked with a creamy texture as they absorb the juices. For the final 20 minutes of cooking, remove the lid and add another third of the stock, if required, basting regularly.

While the chicken is in the oven, the red cabbage can be cooked. Melt the knob of butter in a large saucepan and add the shredded cabbage, onions, orange zest, bay leaf and spices. Cook for 6–7 minutes, until beginning to soften, then add the red wine vinegar or cider vinegar. Continue to cook until the vinegar has almost completely evaporated. Add the demerara sugar and apple juice, cover with a lid and gently simmer until completely tender. This can take up to 40 minutes or more, depending how finely the cabbage has been shredded. Once tender, remove the lid and increase the heat to allow any excess apple cooking liquor to boil and reduce, just leaving enough to maintain a moist finish. Season with salt and pepper, discarding the orange zest.

To crisp the bacon, lay the rashers on a baking tray and cover with another. Place in the preheated oven for 20 minutes while the chicken is pot-roasting. If the bacon is not yet at a crispy stage after this time, pour away excess fat from the tray and return to the oven for a further 10–15 minutes. Remove the rashers from the oven and tray and leave to cool. The bacon will now be very crispy, ready to reheat quickly in the oven when needed. It's not essential to cover the rashers with the second tray, but this does keep them completely flat and helps them crisp. They can, of course, be baked and left to curl, or grilled.

Remove the chicken from the pot and keep warm to one side, along with the soft parsnips. Boil any juices, adding the remaining stock. Cook for a minute or two, checking for seasoning. This is not a sauce, purely a cooking liquor with which to moisten the carved bird. A large knob of butter can be whisked in to emulsify the flavours and consistency slightly.

To serve, remove the chicken breasts and legs, offering either a thigh or drumstick with a half a breast per portion. Arrange the softened parsnips and cabbage on plates, along with the chicken pieces and warmed crispy bacon. Spoon the cooking liquor juices over the chicken and serve.

Extra chopped parsley can be added to the liquor before serving, along with a tablespoon or two of crème fraîche or double/whipping cream. This creates a more sauce-like consistency.

salted roast pork ribs with mustard parsnip cream

Parsnips can often be found from late summer leading through to the following spring. They are, however, a root vegetable that prefers very cold ground, even enjoying a touch of frost, so January is one of the months that finds them at their best.

The mustard flavouring of the purée should be either French Dijon or wholegrain (English mustard can be too strong for this sweet vegetable). The Dijon works as an enhancer, with little needed to lift the basic parsnip flavour. The wholegrain mustard provides more of a tartness, carrying a soft warmth behind it.

The pork ribs are roasted as a French-trimmed loin, with coarse sea salt to help flavour the crispy crackling, which will be balanced by the moist tenderness of the meat. 'French-trimmed' is purely a loin left on the bone. This basically means the number of bones, all exposed and cleaned, indicates the quantity of portions. It is important to ask your butcher to remove the chine bone. This is the central bone that runs down the back of the joint, connecting the two loins together.

Once this is removed you are able to cut cleanly between each rib, using the kept chine bone purely as a trivet on which to roast the pork.

To make a loose gravy, honey, lemon and thyme will help lift the residue from the pan, loosened with some stock or water. This is quite a simple dish that will eat well with *Classic roast potatoes* (page 422).

SERVES 6

1 × 6–8-bone French-trimmed loin of pork
salt and pepper, plus coarse sea salt for sprinkling
cooking oil, for brushing
1 tablespoon clear honey
1 teaspoon picked thyme, saving the stalks (optional)
juice of ½ lemon
300ml (½ pint) *Chicken stock* (page 416), *Instant stock* (page 416) or tinned consommé or water
25g (1oz) butter

FOR THE PARSNIP CREAM

1.5kg (3lb) parsnips
milk, to cover (approximately 450–600ml/¾–1 pint)
knob of butter
1 tablespoon Dijon or wholegrain mustard

Preheat the oven to 230°C/450°F/Gas 8. Score the skin of the pork with a sharp knife in a line between each bone. Season the underside and meat ends of the pork with salt and pepper. Brush the skin with cooking oil, then sprinkle with table and coarse sea salt. Place the joint in a roasting tray, sitting on its arched bones, skin-side up. To prevent the meat from becoming dry in contact with the roasting tray, the removed chine bone can be placed in the tray and any exposed meat sat on top of it. Place in the oven and roast for 15 minutes at this high temperature to begin the crisping of the skin. Reduce the oven temperature to 200°C/400°F/Gas 6 and continue roasting, basting from time to time, for a further 50 minutes–1 hour. During this time, the skin will have crisped to a salted crackling finish. Remove the joint from the tray and keep warm to one side, allowing to rest for a good 15 minutes.

Pour away any excess fat from the roasting tray and place it on a medium heat. As the residue begins to bubble and crackle, add the honey and thyme stalks, if using. The honey will melt instantly and begin to sizzle within a minute or two. When it begins to caramelize, add the lemon juice, which will begin to spit, lifting all of the flavours. Add the stock, consommé or water and bring to a simmer. Cook gently for a few minutes, seasoning with salt and pepper. Stir in the butter, then strain through a fine sieve. Add the fresh thyme leaves just before serving, if using.

While the pork is roasting, make the parsnip cream. Peel the parsnips, splitting each lengthwise into quarters and cutting away the core. Cut the strips into rough dice. Place the diced parsnips in a saucepan and add enough milk almost to cover. Season with salt and pepper and bring to a gentle simmer. Place a lid on top and cook for 15–20 minutes, until the parsnips are completely tender. Using a slotted spoon, place some of the cooked dice into a liquidizer and blitz to a smooth purée, adding some of the milk if needed. As the parsnips begin to cream, more parsnips can be added. This may have to be done in two batches. If slightly grainy, then push through a sieve. Once all of the purée has been made, keep to one side, ready to rewarm when needed. When reheating, the knob of butter and mustard can be added and the seasoning rechecked.

To carve the pork, simply separate the portions by carving between each rib. An alternative is first to cut away the crackling. This can now be broken into pieces ready to serve with the carved pork. Present the pork on plates with a spoonful of the parsnip cream and a drizzle or two of the thyme-flavoured gravy.

An extra 10–15 minutes can be added to the pork roasting time, ensuring completely well-done meat.
A teaspoon of flour can be added to the 25g (1oz) of butter before stirring it into the stock. This will immediately thicken the liquor; cook for a few minutes to finish the gravy.

OPPOSITE: SALTED ROAST PORK RIBS
WITH MUSTARD PARSNIP CREAM

Preheat the oven to 180°C/350°F/Gas 4. Beat together the butter and sugar to a creamy light and fluffy consistency. Sift together the flour and baking powder, adding the ground almonds and crushed digestive biscuits. Stir the dry mix into the creamy sweet butter, followed by one egg at a time until the mixture is totally combined and smooth.

Grease the moulds with butter, dusting lightly with flour. Divide the mixture between the moulds, lightly smoothing on top, before baking in the preheated oven for 18–20 minutes until the cake is just beginning to come away from the side of the moulds. (One large cake will need 22–25 minutes). Remove from the oven and leave to cool slightly.

Remove the almond cakes from the moulds, placing them on a baking tray. Arrange the orange segments on top, dusting with icing sugar through a sieve or tea strainer. Place under a preheated grill, just allowing the oranges to warm and the sugar to dissolve. The cakes are now ready to serve.

If baking one large cake you may find one or two extra oranges will be needed, providing plenty of segments with which to cover.
The Hot chocolate sauce *on page 72 eats very well with this dessert, or you could simply serve thick pouring cream.*

rum baba buns with caramelized pineapple and pineapple sauce

Pineapples are available throughout the year. When selecting ripe pineapples, use the nose rather than the fingers, as the rich fruitiness releases its scent through the skin.

Rum babas are usually cooked in dariole moulds, giving them a domed flowerpot finish. Here, the dough is rolled into balls and baked like buns. Individual tartlet cases (about 7.5cm/3in) or large Yorkshire pudding trays can be used to help maintain the base shape. It is often a good idea to make the buns 24–48 hours in advance. This is not essential, but does allow them to firm and dry, ready to absorb the warm rum syrup and resoften. If baked, cooled and soaked within just a few hours, the texture can sometimes finish a bit stodgy.

MAKES 8–10 BUNS
3 tablespoons lukewarm milk
2 teaspoons dried yeast or 1 × 7g packet of dried rapid-action yeast
225g (8oz) plain flour, sifted, plus more for dusting
1 tablespoon caster sugar
pinch of salt
3 eggs, lightly beaten
75g (3oz) butter, softened, plus more for greasing

FOR THE SYRUP
325g (10½oz) caster sugar
250ml (8fl oz) rum (or more)

FOR THE PINEAPPLE SAUCE
1 small pineapple (approximately 350–450g/12oz–1lb), peeled, cored and chopped into small pieces
200ml (7fl oz) coconut milk
2 teaspoons cornflour
icing sugar, to sweeten (if needed)

FOR THE CARAMELIZED PINEAPPLE (MAKES 8 PORTIONS)
1 small–medium pineapple
15g (½oz) butter or 2 tablespoons vegetable oil
3 tablespoons caster sugar

RUM BABA BUNS WITH
CARAMELIZED PINEAPPLE AND PINEAPPLE SAUCE

To make the babas, pour the lukewarm milk into a bowl. Sprinkle over the yeast and leave for a few minutes to dissolve. Sift the flour, sugar and salt together into a mixing bowl. Add the yeast mixture to the flour mix and stir in. Then add the eggs and work for a few minutes until a smooth dough is reached. This stage can be achieved with an electric mixer. Dot the dough with nuggets of the softened butter, cover the bowl with a damp cloth and leave to rise in a warm place for 45 minutes.

If using tartlet cases or moulds, butter them well and refrigerate to set, then repeat the process with a second coating of butter. If just using a baking tray, butter it only once.

At the end of the rising time, the butter will have started to work its way into the dough. Knead the dough back to a smooth consistency. It will now have a quite firm elastic texture. Divide it into 8–10 pieces with a spoon. With well-floured hands, roll these into 8–10 balls and place them on the prepared baking tray or in the moulds. Leave uncovered in a warm place to rise for 15–20 minutes. Preheat the oven to 200°C/400°F/Gas 6.

Bake the baba buns in the preheated oven for 10–15 minutes, until golden brown. Remove from the oven and, if moulds were used, leave to stand for 10 minutes before turning out. As mentioned in the introduction, these are best made in advance, and stored in an airtight container once cooled.

To make the syrup, boil the ingredients together with 450ml (¾ pint) of water, then simmer for a few minutes. Keep to one side and reheat when needed.

To make the pineapple sauce, place the chopped pineapple in a food processor and blitz it to a purée. Place the purée in a small saucepan with the coconut milk and cornflour. Whisk all together, bringing the sauce to the boil. Remove from the heat and strain through a fine sieve for a smooth finish. If necessary, sweeten with icing sugar to taste. This can be served just warm or cold.

Before cooking the pineapples, it is best to soak the babas in the hot syrup for at least 20–30 minutes, allowing plenty of time for the syrup to be absorbed, swelling and softening the buns. These can now be turned from time to time, ensuring an even soaking. Just before serving, the buns can be split in half horizontally to ensure the syrup has soaked to the centre.

Prepare the pineapple by topping and tailing, then cut away the skin. Split the pineapple into quarters lengthwise, then cut each in half again to provide eight shorter pieces. Heat the butter or oil in a large frying pan over a moderate heat. Once bubbling, place in the pineapple pieces and cook for 5–6 minutes on each side. Add the caster sugar, sprinkling it over the fruit. Slightly increase the heat and the sugar will begin to caramelize. As it does so, turn the pineapple to spread the flavour. Add 2 tablespoons of water to lift the caramel from the base of the pan, creating a syrup. Continue to cook for just another minute or two, basting the wedges with the caramel.

To present the dish, place the warm soaked rum babas on plates, along with a caramelized pineapple wedge. Any remaining caramel can be drizzled over the fruit, and extra rum syrup offered separately. Spoon the pineapple sauce on to the plates and the pudding is ready.

Extra-thick cream makes a lovely accompaniment.
If using fresh yeast, 15g (½oz) will be needed.

baked or steamed date pudding with toffee grand marnier sauce

Dates, the fruit of the palm tree, originate from many a hot, dry region, ranging from North Africa leading through to the Middle East and India. Today most are imported to Britain from Egypt, the Middle East and California. There are many varieties of this particular fruit, both fresh and dried. The finest, without doubt, are the Medjool from California and Egypt. These have a moist treacle texture and sticky flavour, which is perfect for this dessert. The season for Medjools is generally between September and March, the price becoming more reasonable towards Christmas and the New Year.

As the title implies, this pudding can be baked or steamed. Baking will leave a crusty-style top with a soft centre. The steaming method finishes with a soft sponge that can become richer depending on its cooking time – the minimum cooking time is 40–50 minutes. This can be continued for a further 1–2 hours; instead of overcooking, it will allow the pudding to become even more toffee-like.

The orange zest is an optional extra, but I find it blends the flavour of the Grand Marnier in the sauce with the sponge.

SERVES 4–6
FOR THE SPONGE
175g (6oz) Medjool dates, stoned and roughly chopped
1½ teaspoons bicarbonate of soda
50g (2oz) butter, plus more for greasing
100g (4oz) light or dark soft brown sugar

2 eggs, beaten
100g (4oz) self-raising flour, sifted, plus more for the tin
finely grated zest of 2 oranges (optional)

FOR THE SAUCE
300ml (½ pint) double cream
100g (4oz) light soft brown sugar
2 teaspoons black treacle
3–4 tablespoons Grand Marnier (or Cointreau)

If baking the sponge, preheat the oven to 180°C/350°F/Gas 4 and butter and flour an 18cm (7in) diameter cake tin (not loose-bottomed). Boil the chopped dates with 200ml (7fl oz) of water for a few minutes until the dates are beginning to soften. Remove the pan from the heat and stir in the bicarbonate of soda. Beat the butter and sugar together until creamy. Add and beat in the eggs a little at a time until bound with the butter. Stir in the sifted flour, dates (including all the liquor from the pan) and orange zest, if using. Pour the pudding mix into the prepared tin and bake in the preheated oven for 30–40 minutes, until just firm to the touch.

Once baked, remove the tin from the oven and leave to cool for 10 minutes before turning out the cake. For a pudding, this is best served immediately, dividing it into wedges. Or allow to cool and offer it as a cake (a cold wedge of cake microwaves perfectly to serve once more as a dessert).

To steam the sponge, cover the tin with a circle of thick buttered foil, tightening around the top rim. Steam for 50 minutes–1 hour until firm to the touch or continue as described in the introduction for a richer, toffee finish. Remember to keep the water in the steamer topped up. Once cooked, the pudding can be rested and turned out as for the baked pudding above.

To make the sauce, place the double cream, sugar and treacle in a saucepan over a low heat, stirring until well blended. At this point, bring the cream to the boil, simmering for 2–3 minutes before adding the Grand Marnier (or Cointreau) to taste.

The sauce is now ready to pour over portions of sponge.

chocolate and date tiramisù

Tiramisù has become one of Italy's most famous and popular desserts. The recipe is in fact quite young, put together some 30–35 years ago. The translation, 'pick me up', suits it well, with the strong coffee-and-rum-laced Italian savoiardi biscuits (these are lighter and less sweet than sponge fingers) forming layers in the rich mascarpone cream. It's exactly these ingredients I use here but, instead of interlayering, this recipe is just biscuit-based with a mascarpone topping.

Chopped dates, Medjools being the most obvious kind to use, perfectly in season and having such a toffee-like texture, blend well into a tiramisù.

An alternative is to omit the savoiardi biscuits and replace them with layers of *Chocolate coffee sponge* (page 428). This is baked separately and a layer is cut to fit the pudding basin, topping with one-third of the mascarpone, then another sponge layer, followed by another third of the mascarpone, the final sponge layer and the remaining mascarpone. This makes a more refined 'pick me up'.

SERVES 4–6
150ml (¼ pint) strong black espresso coffee
4 tablespoons Tia Maria, Kahlua or dark rum
15–18 savoiardi biscuits (ladies' or sponge fingers)
10 Medjool dates, stoned and chopped
100–125g (4–4½oz) bitter dark chocolate, finely grated
3 egg yolks
75g (3oz) caster sugar
250g (9oz) mascarpone
100ml (3½fl oz) double cream

Mix the coffee with your chosen liqueur. Dip a sponge finger in the flavoured coffee, turning it quickly so it does not become soggy and disintegrate. This can now be placed in the base of a 1 litre (1¾ pint) pudding dish, repeating with the remaining biscuits. Any excess coffee can be trickled over the fingers without over soaking, sprinkling the chopped dates and 50g (2oz) of the grated chocolate on top.

Whisk the egg yolks and sugar in an electric mixer for about 10 minutes on full speed until thick, pale and fluffy. The mascarpone can now be added, a quarter at a time, on a slower speed, preferably using a beater attachment. Lightly whip the cream to a soft-peak stage and fold into the mascarpone mix.

OPPOSITE: CHOCOLATE AND DATE TIRAMISÙ

Spoon and spread the mascarpone cream on top of the fingers, refrigerating for several hours, preferably 5–6 hours, to set. Before serving, sprinkle the remaining grated chocolate over.

Most tiramisù recipes use whisked egg white as a softener for the mascarpone. This has been replaced here with the double cream for a stronger finish. If you'd prefer to use egg white, omit the cream, whisking 2 egg whites with 25g (1oz) of caster sugar to a soft-peak stage, before folding into the mascarpone.
If making the chocolate coffee sponge alternative, you'll only need 100ml (3½fl oz) strong espresso coffee, mixed with 3 tablespoons Tia Maria. Sprinkle it over the sponge as the dessert is layered.

brazilian mango salad and sorbet with honey and brazil wafers

The Brazilian mango has a six-month season, ranging from September to March, with the fruits so beautiful and ripe from mid-season onwards. It's not essential to use only the Brazilian fruit, as there are plenty of others from around the world displaying themselves on our shelves. They do, however, run with the theme of this dessert, matching up with the Brazil nuts, which joined us in November lasting to this month.

When choosing your mangoes, the Kent and Tommy Atkins varieties are good to use, having less fibrous flesh.

Brazil nuts are borne on a non-cultivated tree in the Amazon jungle (they are also exported from Bolivia and Venezuela). The small, dark, segment-shaped nuts are collected almost like orange segments within a large, round, woody husk, usually about 15cm (6in) in diameter and with the appearance of a bald coconut. Once ripe, these fall from the tree, ready to be cracked open to supply the nuts. Fresh Brazil nuts can keep for up to six months, revealing a pale cream kernel once broken and peeled. Deeper yellow kernels reveal their old age and are past their best.

Here, the nuts are broken and set amongst honey wafers or biscuits, moulded as you would brandy snaps, providing a basket in which to arrange the salad and sorbet. Extra chopped nuts can be lightly toasted and sprinkled over the finished dish. A nice addition is to halve and scoop passion fruits over the finished dish.

SERVES 6

FOR THE SORBET
3 ripe mangoes
100g (4oz) caster sugar

FOR THE WAFERS
6 Brazil nuts, shelled and peeled
50g (2oz) butter
50g (2oz) icing sugar
100g (4oz) clear honey
75g (3oz) plain flour, sifted
pinch of ground cinnamon (optional)

FOR THE SALAD
3 ripe mangoes
6 Brazil nuts, shelled and peeled

To make the sorbet, peel the mangoes, cutting away the flesh from the stone. Roughly chop the flesh and place it in a food processor with the caster sugar. Blitz to a smooth purée; this will dissolve the sugar, creating its own syrup with the fruit. For the smoothest of purées, push the sweet mango through a sieve. This can now be churned in an ice-cream machine for approximately 20 minutes, until thickened and creamy. Pour into a suitable container and freeze to finish the setting. If an ice-cream machine is not available, simply freeze the purée, stirring from time to time. Once at setting point, blitz the mix in a food processor very quickly and refreeze. This can be repeated several times for a smooth sorbet finish.

Preheat the oven to 180°C/350°F/Gas 4. To make the wafers, chop the Brazil nuts into small nibbed-almond-size pieces. Beat together the butter, sugar and honey until light and creamy. Add the flour, cinnamon, if using, and chopped Brazil nuts, beating them in well.

The mix can now be spooned and spread into six large circles (possibly seven or eight) with a damp palette knife on a non-stick baking tray (two trays may be needed), leaving space between each for spreading. Bake the biscuits in the preheated oven for 7–8 minutes. Remove from the oven and leave to stand for 30–60 seconds, before lifting the biscuit discs with a thin fish slice or palette knife and pressing them into a bowl or cup to create a basket shape. If the biscuits become too firm, place the tray back in the oven for a few seconds to rewarm and soften the biscuits.

Preheat the grill. To make the salad, peel and cut the flesh from the mangoes, dicing it into 1cm (½in) chunks. The Brazil nuts can be chopped into rough chunky pieces before toasting very lightly under the preheated grill to a pale golden brown. Once coloured, leave to cool.

To present the dessert, spoon the mango between the six biscuit baskets, scooping a ball of the sorbet on top of each. Scatter the toasted Brazil nuts over and serve.

Fresh cream makes a good accompaniment.

It's not essential to serve the salad and the sorbet in the biscuit basket. The wafers can be offered separately.

baileys custard cream
with williams wedges

Irish whiskey cream is a long-standing 'home-made' that only became a commercial product, Baileys, in the 1970s. With much technical testing a formula was found for preventing the cream from curdling with the alcohol. Almost instantly it became a hit, now accounting for close to a quarter of the world's liqueur business. Apart from being a pleasurable drink, it blends well with many other flavours, here with custard creams. These are similar in texture to a *crème brûlée*, but cooked on top of the stove, with gelatine acting as a setting agent.

The Williams wedges are simply poached Williams pear slices served with the Baileys custard cream. The Williams Bon-Chrétien is a large oval pear usually taking a bulbous slant towards one side of the stalk. The speckled, golden-yellow, russet-patched skin reveals a very juicy, creamy-white flesh, which results in a sweet, slightly musky flavour. These are available at some point during all four seasons, imported from around the world. In the UK, September and October are probably the prime months for home-grown, with America and South Africa delivering to us right now.

The Williams is known in the United States as the Bartlett, after Mr Enoch Bartlett who introduced this fruit to his home soil on his return from the UK. It is perfect for cooking, hence becoming popular and successful in the tinning market in the States. Of course, other varieties of pear can also be used, though the Williams takes first place.

One large shallow dish, preferably glass, approximately 18–20cm (7–8in) in diameter, is needed to present the custard cream. Individual dishes or glasses can also be used.

SERVES 6–8

FOR THE BAILEYS CUSTARD CREAM

8 egg yolks
65g (2½oz) caster sugar
600ml (1 pint) double cream
150–200ml (5–7fl oz) Baileys Irish Cream
2 leaves of gelatine, soaked in cold water

FOR THE PEARS

50g (2oz) caster sugar
2 tablespoons honey
½ cinnamon stick (optional)
3 Williams pears
juice of 1 lemon
icing sugar and cocoa powder (optional)

To make the custard cream, whisk together the egg yolks and sugar. Bring the cream to the boil, pouring and whisking it into the egg yolk mix. Add the quantity of Baileys preferred (make it even stronger, if you wish), returning the loose custard to the saucepan. Warm and stir the custard over a low heat to 70°C (158°F) – test with a temperature probe. This provides enough warmth to thicken the custard, cooking without curdling the egg yolks. Remove the pan from the heat. Squeeze the excess water from the gelatine leaves, stirring them into the custard well, before straining through a fine sieve into a bowl or large jug. The cooked custard can now be poured into the chosen dessert dish (see above), refrigerating for several hours to allow the 'mousse' to set.

For the pear-poaching syrup, place the caster sugar, honey and cinnamon stick, if using, into a saucepan with 300ml (½ pint) of water, and bring to a simmer.

Meanwhile, peel the pears from 'top to tail' – this maintains the natural shape of the fruit. Cut each into eight wedges, trimming away the core with a small knife. As each fruit is prepared, place in a bowl with the lemon juice to prevent discoloration. Once all the pears are cut, add to the simmering syrup with their juice, covering with a disc of greaseproof paper. Poach for just 2–3 minutes before removing the pan from the heat (as the syrup cools it will continue to soften the pears).

To finish the custard cream, dust with icing sugar, followed by a light sprinkling of cocoa powder, if using. This leaves a cappuccino look, the bitter cocoa flavour blending with Baileys very well. A scoop of the custard cream and three or four warm or cold pear wedges, drizzled with syrup, creates each portion.

The honey syrup can be kept refrigerated for later use.

lychee lemon whip
with shortbreads

In December, colourfully skinned lychees are in abundance. They are very attractive in and out of their skins, the fruit releasing a very perfumed juicy fragrance. They are without doubt at their best just eaten raw, a very simple *petit four* to offer friends.

On Chinese menus, lychees are often served as an accompaniment to savoury dishes, such as duck. The lychee also works well in wintry fruit salads. Here it's topped with a lemon whip, flashed under the grill to glaze.

The shortbreads are left in a rustic form, then baked to a crispy crumbly texture to accompany the dessert.

SERVES 4
16–20 lychees (8–10 halves per portion)
2 eggs, plus 1 extra yolk
100g (4oz) caster sugar
finely grated zest and juice of 2 lemons
50g (2oz) cold butter, diced

FOR THE SHORTBREADS
75g (3oz) icing sugar, sifted
1 egg yolk
100g (4oz) butter, softened
150g (5oz) plain flour, sifted

The shortbreads can be made in advance. To do so, mix the icing sugar, egg yolk and butter together in a bowl. Add the flour and rub it into the butter to create a crumb texture. Knead the mix by hand into a dough, wrap in cling film and chill to rest for 1–2 hours. The dough can be made in a food processor or electric mixer. It is important, however, not to over-mix, as this will leave you with a tougher elastic texture.

Preheat the oven to 180°C/350°F/Gas 4. Remove the rested dough from the fridge and break and press it into 12–16 rustic shapes directly onto a non-stick baking tray, leaving a space between each to allow for spreading. Bake the biscuits in the preheated oven for 10–12 minutes (15 minutes maximum), until just a pale golden colour. Remove them from the oven and transfer to a wire rack to cool.

Peel the skin from the lychees by simply cutting around, and remove the central stone to halve each fruit. The halves can now be divided between four shallow bowls, glasses or 150ml (¼ pint) ramekins.

Place the eggs, egg yolk and sugar in a bowl. Heat 5cm (2in) of water in a small saucepan and bring to a simmer. Place the bowl on top of the pan (it is important that the water is not in contact with the base of the bowl) and whisk vigorously. An electric hand whisk is best used here; make sure the electric lead is not in contact with the heat. Once a foaming consistency is reached, add the lemon zest and juice. Continue to whisk until a very thick sabayon is achieved that leaves a thick trail when the whisk is lifted from the bowl. By hand, this will take up to 10–15 minutes, probably just 6–8 minutes if using the electric whisk.

Preheat the grill to hot. Remove the saucepan and bowl from the heat, still together, and continue to whisk while adding the diced butter. This will take some of the warmth from the sabayon, at the same time enriching its finished flavour. Spoon the lemon whip over the lychees and place them under the preheated grill until a rich golden brown. The warm lychee lemon whips are now ready to serve with the shortbreads.

The shortbread biscuits can be sprinkled with caster sugar before or after baking, leaving them with a sweeter touch.

OPPOSITE: LYCHEE LEMON WHIP
WITH SHORTBREADS

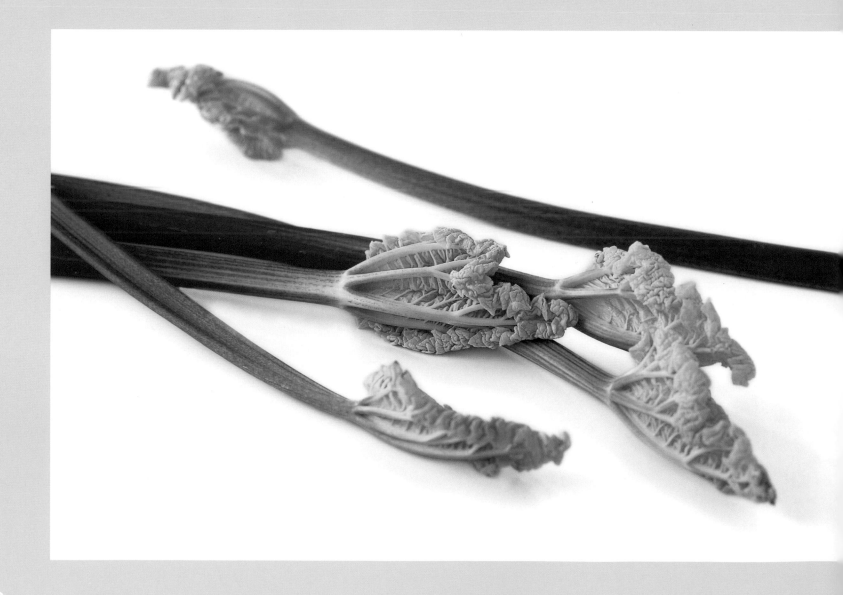

vegetables

fish

meat

fruit and puddings

chinese artichokes with lemon and parsley

Chinese artichokes are an oriental root vegetable, a native of Japan and China. Although carrying the name artichoke, they are no relation to the globe or Jerusalem, being instead part of the same family as mint, lavender and many other herbs. These small, maggot-shaped tubers do have a slight resemblance in shape to Jerusalem artichokes, which is possibly how the name derived. In flavour, again the Jerusalem has some similarity; the Chinese chokes are a bit nuttier, however, with a lingering finish somewhere between that of the globe artichoke and salsify.

Although Chinese artichokes never really hit the British commercial scene, when introduced to France in the late 1900s they became very popular, and that still holds true today. Across the Channel their title is 'Crosne', after the town in which they were first harvested. The artichokes, however, do begin to deteriorate very rapidly once picked from the soil, hence their limited commercial appeal. The plus factor is how well they store beneath the soil, lasting between October and late February/early March, though you may need to go hunting to find them from a quality greengrocer or delicatessen, usually having to pre-order.

This recipe keeps the chokes very simple, giving them a quick par-boil before tossing in butter with a squeeze of lemon juice and chopped parsley – just right for grills or roasts. Other combinations can be considered, such as adding spinach leaves for a more substantial vegetable dish, or perhaps peeled prawns before garnishing as a salad.

SERVES FOUR AS A SIDE DISH
500g (1lb 2oz) Chinese artichokes (Crosnes)
salt and pepper, plus coarse sea salt
1 tablespoon olive oil
25g (1oz) butter
1 lemon, halved
1 tablespoon chopped flatleaf parsley

Quickly rinse the artichokes. Bring a pan of well salted water to the boil, adding the cleaned chokes, simmering rapidly for 3–4 minutes before draining.

Heat the olive oil and butter in a wok or frying pan. Once bubbling, add the blanched chokes, frying them over a medium heat for 2–3 minutes, squeezing over the juice from one

OPPOSITE: CHINESE ARTICHOKES WITH LEMON AND PARSLEY

half of the lemon, seasoning with sea salt and pepper. The extra lemon juice can be added for a sharper citrus bite if preferred. Sprinkle over the chopped parsley and stir in to finish.

Chinese artichokes can also be grated raw and tossed through salads.

palestine soup with crispy jerusalem artichokes

This Palestinian soup is made purely of creamed Jerusalem artichokes. The crispy artichokes accompanying it offer another texture.

Jerusalem artichokes are available between the months of October and March, so this soupy recipe is probably best made during the last month of winter, February, to use up the remaining few. Whenever choosing Jerusalem artichokes, it is always best to try to find the smoothest and cleanest available, rather than spend hours cleaning the many over-knobbly ones on the market.

SERVES 4
450g (1lb) Jerusalem artichokes
squeeze of lemon juice
large knob of butter
1 tablespoon olive oil
1 large onion, finely chopped
300ml (½ pint) *Vegetable stock* (page 417), *Chicken stock* (page 416) or *Instant stock* (page 416)
300ml (½ pint) milk
150ml (¼ pint) single cream (optional)
salt and pepper
freshly grated nutmeg
groundnut oil, for frying

Save one large or two smaller artichokes for frying. Scrub or peel the remainder thoroughly, then slice thinly or chop into rough dice. As they are cut, place in a bowl of water acidulated with lemon juice to prevent discoloration.

Melt the knob of butter in a saucepan with the olive oil and add the onion. Cook on a low heat for several minutes, until the onions are beginning to soften without colouring. Drain the artichokes and pat them dry with kitchen paper or a cloth, then add them to the pan with the onion. Cook for 6–8 minutes, then add the stock and milk. Bring to a simmer, season with salt and pepper and cook for 20 minutes, or until the artichokes are well softened. During the simmering of the artichoke soup the milk may take on a curdled consistency; this is due to the artichokes being placed in acidulated water but, once liquidized, a totally smooth finish is regained.

Liquidize the soup in batches until smooth, straining it through a sieve, if necessary, for the creamiest of finishes. Return the soup to a saucepan and warm through, then add the single cream, if using. If the single cream is to be omitted and the soup is too thick, simply loosen with a little more milk. Adjust the seasoning with salt and pepper, and add the freshly grated nutmeg.

To make the Jerusalem artichoke crisps, scrub or peel the reserved artichokes and then slice very thinly, preferably on a mandolin slicer. Dry on a cloth or kitchen paper. Heat 1cm (½in) of groundnut oil in a saucepan or wok. Once hot, fry the slices in batches, until all are crispy and golden brown. Once fried, season with a pinch of salt.

Serve the soup in bowls, topping each with some of the crispy slices.

The crispy artichokes are by no means essential. Serving the soup with fresh crusty bread is just as good.
An extra squeeze of lemon juice can be added to the soup once finished, for a slight citrus edge.

braised stuffed cabbage with carrots and parsley

Braised stuffed cabbage is traditionally a French dish, but the two main ingredients, cabbage and sausagemeat, warrant its place among the Great British classics. The cabbage, here a typical winter Savoy, has all of its leaves blanched and is then rebuilt, formed into its original cabbage shape around a savoury stuffing. With its intense flavours, this dish will suit all the winter months.

SERVES 4–6 AS A MAIN COURSE
1 Savoy cabbage, trimmed of very large outside leaves
salt and pepper
iced water
large knob of butter
2 onions, finely chopped
2 garlic cloves, crushed (optional)
450g (1lb) sausagemeat (pork sausages can be skinned and used in place of the sausagemeat)

100g (4oz) streaky bacon or pancetta, cut into 5mm (¼in) dice
4 thick slices of white bread, crusts removed, broken into crumbs
6 sage leaves, chopped
pinch of ground mace
dash of Worcestershire sauce (optional)
2 eggs
oil, for frying (optional)
4 large carrots, peeled and cut into rough 1cm (½in) dice
1.2 litres (2 pints) *Chicken stock* (page 416) or *Instant stock* (page 416)
1 tablespoon chopped curly parsley (optional)

Using a sharp knife, cut away each cabbage leaf from the stem, until you reach the small heart. Blanch batches of the leaves in boiling salted water for a minute or two, refreshing them in iced water. Once all are blanched and refreshed, remove them from the iced water and place them on a kitchen cloth to dry.

To make the stuffing, melt the large knob of butter in a frying pan and, once bubbling, add the chopped onions and

crushed garlic, if using. Cook for 7–8 minutes, until light golden brown and softened. Leave to cool. Place the sausagemeat in a large bowl and add the diced bacon or pancetta, followed by the cooked onions, along with the breadcrumbs and chopped sage. Season with salt, pepper and a good pinch of mace, add a dash of Worcestershire sauce, if using, and mix in the eggs. To check the finished flavour, a small 'burger' of the mixture can be fried in a drop of oil for a few minutes.

To assemble the cabbage, first rinse a tea towel or muslin cloth and squeeze out all the excess water, then lay on a suitable surface. Overlap four or five of the large leaves in a circular fashion on the cloth with the stalks towards the outside and the inside of each facing up. Spread a quarter of the stuffing over and leave a 5cm (2in) border, then place one or two layers of the next-size leaves on top. Season the leaves as you build with a little salt and pepper. Spread another layer of stuffing over, then lay on more leaves. Continue this process until all of the stuffing and leaves have been used. To shape into a sphere, pull together the four corners of the muslin cloth, lift and place in a suitably sized bowl to help maintain the shape. Tie the corners of the cloth together. This can be left as it is or secured with three long pieces of string, each placed at different angles beneath the 'cabbage', pulled together and tied. This will leave an almost star-like shape, with the six wedges formed providing the six portions to be served. Now tie the cloth knot with string to help maintain the cabbage shape.

Scatter the carrots in a large saucepan and sit the cabbage on top, dome-side up. Add the chosen stock and top up with water, if needed, just to cover the cabbage. Bring to a gentle murmuring simmer, cover with a lid and cook for 1½ hours. To check, pierce with a skewer for 10 seconds, making sure it is piping hot once removed. If not, continue to cook for a further 20–30 minutes. The cabbage can now be lifted into a large colander to drain.

Check the cooking liquor for fullness of flavour. If too loose and light in depth, bring to the boil and allow to reduce in volume by a third to a half. Once at this stage, add the chopped parsley, if using, and ladle some carrots and cooking liquor into four or six large bowls. Remove the cabbage from the cloth, cutting away the strings. Cut the stuffed cabbage into six portions and place a wedge in each bowl. *Mashed potatoes* (page 422) eat very well with this dish.

celeriac, potato and apple rösti

Rösti is a Swiss potato dish, the name meaning 'crisp and golden'. This version consists of celeriac, potato and apple (all currently in abundance), pan-fried as you would the Swiss classic into a crispy cake. This makes a good side dish for roasts, with lamb or pork being first choice. A spoonful of chopped flatleaf parsley or chives can also be added to the celeriac mix.

SERVES 4–6 AS A SIDE DISH
2 small or 1 large celeriac
2 potatoes, preferably Desirée, peeled
2 apples, peeled and cored
1 dessertspoon plain flour
2 eggs
salt and pepper
2 tablespoons olive oil

Top and tail the celeriac, cutting away the coarse outer skin, before dividing into four pieces. These can now be coarsely grated, along with the peeled potatoes and apples. To remove excess water, wrap all three together in a kitchen cloth, squeezing as you twist, before placing in a large bowl. The flour and eggs can now be added, mixing all together well and seasoning with salt and pepper.

Warm the olive oil in a 25cm (10in), preferably non-stick frying pan over a medium heat. Add the seasoned mix, spreading and pressing to cover the base. A potato masher is very useful for helping to press the mix evenly. Pan-fry for 3–4 minutes, shaking the pan to prevent it from sticking, before covering with a lid. Continue to pan-fry (and shake from time to time) for a further 8–9 minutes until deep golden brown on the base. Meanwhile, preheat the grill.

To colour the top, place the pan under the preheated grill, cooking for 5–6 minutes, until golden brown and cooked through. The rösti is now ready to turn out (or cut while still in the pan) and divide into four to six portions.

OPPOSITE: BRAISED STUFFED CABBAGE
WITH CARROTS AND PARSLEY

brown shrimp soup with crisp sesame croûtons

The common brown shrimp is a very flavoursome crustacean, more or less available throughout the year, with its main season between February and October.

For this recipe, the cooked brown shrimps are left still in their shells, with only 100g (4oz) needing to be peeled. Cooking the remainder in their shells helps create the shrimp-flavoured stock, forming the base to the soup, once creamed. Should only peeled shrimps be available, however, I suggest you use *Fish stock* (page 417) or *Instant stock* (page 416) instead of water.

The croûtons are chunks of white bread, pan-fried until crispy, finished with toasted sesame seeds and the peeled shrimps.

SERVES 6 AS A STARTER OR 4 AS A MAIN COURSE
550g (1¼lb) cooked brown shrimps, washed (see below)
3 tablespoons olive oil
1 onion, finely chopped
2 carrots, cut into small rough dice
1 small–medium fennel, cut into small rough dice
1 small–medium potato, peeled and roughly chopped
2 garlic cloves, chopped
1 tablespoon tomato purée
pinch of saffron (optional)
150ml (¼ pint) white wine
juice of 2 oranges
100ml (3½fl oz) whipping cream or crème fraîche
salt and Cayenne pepper

FOR THE CROÛTONS
4 thick slices of white bread, crusts removed
1 heaped teaspoon sesame seeds
2–3 tablespoons olive or sesame oil
25g (1oz) butter

Peel 100g (4oz) of the shrimps, refrigerating until needed, keeping the shells to use in the soup. Warm the olive oil in a large saucepan, adding the chopped onion, carrots, fennel, potato and garlic. Cover and cook gently, without colouring for 15–20 minutes, stirring from time to time, until beginning to soften. Add the remaining shrimps and saved shells, tomato

OPPOSITE: BROWN SHRIMP SOUP
WITH CRISP SESAME CROÛTONS

purée and saffron, if using. Pour in the white wine and bring to the boil, cooking until reduced in volume by half. Stir in 750ml (1¼ pints) of water and the orange juice, returning to the boil and simmering for 30 minutes.

Remove the soup from the heat, leaving to stand for 10 minutes before liquidizing to a smooth finish. Push through a fine sieve, pressing every last drop of juice from the debris.

Return the soup to the heat, whisking in the chosen cream and seasoning with a pinch of Cayenne pepper. The shrimps themselves may have already provided enough salt for the soup (see below).

To make the croûtons, cut the thick white bread slices into cubes. Heat a frying pan, adding the sesame seeds and cooking and stirring until the seeds have become golden brown. Remove the seeds from the pan and keep to one side.

Reheat the pan with the oil and pan-fry the bread cubes until golden brown and crispy. Add the butter, along with the peeled shrimps and sesame seeds. Stir all together for a minute or two until the shrimps have warmed through. It is important once you have added the shrimps that they are not fried at too high a temperature, as this will toughen their succulence. Divide the soup between bowls, spooning the shrimps and sesame croûtons on top.

Cooked, unpeeled shrimps can be very salty. It's important to wash them well before making the soup, and to take great care when checking the finished soup for seasoning. A squeeze of lemon juice can be added to the finished soup, along with a sprinkling of chopped chives over the croûtons.

sprat tempura

The sprat is an attractive young herring, presenting itself to us between October and March. Today most sprats will be found smoked or cured, but a few crates of fresh can still be found. The sprat also provides us with its younger self as whitebait, the fried fishy crisps we still find featured on many a menu.

One of the reasons I love all of these small fish is how little help they need. Whether it be sprats, sardines or pilchards, quick frying or grilling and serving with a lemon wedge more than suffices. Here, the fish are left whole and gutted but, if you like, you could also take the fillets off the bone.

Tempura has become one of the most common Japanese-style dishes since it hit our culinary scene in the 1970s and 1980s. Seafood and vegetables are dipped in a light batter and deep-fried. This cooking method suits the sprats perfectly, eating very succulently beneath the crisp batter.

To round off the dish I've included a mango, yoghurt and lime dip, nothing more than the three blended together for a sweet, sharp, sour finish.

It's always best to fry just eight sprats at a time, not over-crowding the pan, and frying the rest freshly as you need them.

SERVES 6 AS A STARTER

24 sprats, gutted
salt and pepper
flour, for dusting
vegetable oil, for deep-frying

FOR THE DIP

1 ripe large mango, peeled and roughly chopped
150ml (¼ pint) Greek yoghurt
juice of 1 lime

FOR THE BATTER

2 egg yolks
400ml (14fl oz) iced carbonated water
175g (6oz) plain flour
25g (1oz) cornflour
½ teaspoon bicarbonate of soda

First make the dip. Purée the chopped mango, yoghurt and lime juice in a liquidizer or food processor. Once smooth, add a twist of pepper and the dip is ready.

Heat the vegetable oil in an electric deep-fat fryer or large, deep frying pan (filling with a minimum of 4–5cm/1½–2in vegetable oil) to 180°C (356°F).

To make the batter, beat the egg yolks with the iced carbonated water. Add the flour, cornflour, bicarbonate of soda and ½ teaspoon salt and stir in, leaving the batter with a lumpy rather than a smooth finish.

Season the sprats with salt and pepper, very lightly dusting them with flour. Dip the fish in the batter, placing them in the hot oil. Fry for 2–3 minutes, until crispy with a light golden finish.

Remove the fish from the oil, draining them on kitchen paper. Serve immediately with the mango dip.

grilled blue cheese mackerel with soft beetroot and apple

Mackerel, blue cheese, beetroot and apples are all available throughout the autumn and winter. I enjoy putting this dish together in the last of our winter months, February. It's the time when being able to find all of these ingredients from our own soils and waters is coming to an end, so this makes it quite a special occasion.

Most blue cheeses can be used in this recipe, but there are a couple that work particularly well. Beenleigh Blue, a crumbly sheep's-milk cheese, releases a slight spiciness as it melts across the mackerel. Harbourne Blue is a goat's-milk semi-soft cheese that also has an aromatic and distinctive edge.

Apples still around in February include Royal Gala, Ellison's Orange Red, Laxton's Superb, Crispin, Cox's, Red Pippin, Red Falstaff and Newton Wonder.

SERVES 4 AS A STARTER

2 medium–large raw beetroots (approximately 225g/8oz)
2 apples
knob of butter, plus more for brushing and greasing
4 mackerel fillets, preferably from 2 × 350g (12oz) fish, pin-boned (page 9)
50–75g (2–3oz) blue cheese (see above), crumbled

FOR THE DRESSING (OPTIONAL)

1 small raw beetroot
1–2 tablespoons red wine vinegar (preferably a strong Cabernet Sauvignon)
salt and pepper
4 tablespoons olive oil

In a saucepan, cover the two beetroots with cold water, bringing to the boil and cooking until tender. This can take up to 1 hour or more. To check, rather than piercing them, as this releases their juices and flavour, push the skin away from the flesh beneath with the thumb. This will tell you when they are ready. Remove from the pan and allow to cool slightly until comfortable to handle.

While the beetroots are cooking, peel the apples and cut each into eight wedges, removing the central core and pips. Roughly chop the wedges.

Melt the knob of butter in a saucepan and add the apples and 1 tablespoon of water. Cover with a lid and cook on a low heat, stirring from time to time, until completely softened, then leave to cool.

If serving the dressing, it's best made well in advance. Peel the raw beetroot and finely grate into a small bowl. Add 1 tablespoon of the vinegar and season with salt and pepper. Stir in the oil and leave to infuse until the dressing is needed.

Peel and roughly dice the cooked beetroots. Place in a food processor or liquidizer and blitz to a purée, adding the apples as the beetroot breaks down. This combines the two flavours, with the apple loosening the beetroot. Season with salt and pepper. If not silky-smooth, the purée can be pushed through a sieve. This can be served warm, but also eats very well cold.

Preheat the grill to hot. Place the mackerel fillets on a greased and seasoned baking tray, skin-side up, and brush each with butter. The fish can now be cooked under the grill for 5–6 minutes, until becoming crispy. Crumble the blue cheese over each fillet, return to the grill and warm until the cheese begins to melt.

To serve, strain the dressing, if using, through a sieve, pressing out all the juices from the beetroot. The grated waste can be discarded. Taste the dressing for piquancy. For a sharper bite, add the remaining tablespoon (or just a few drops) of the red wine vinegar.

To finish, spoon the soft beetroot and apple purée on to the plates and place the grilled mackerel fillets on top. If serving with the dressing, drizzle it over and around the fish.

baked brill wih grapes, mushrooms and purple sprouting broccoli

It is during these wintry days, particularly in February, that purple broccoli tops begin to appear (a good year will present them a month earlier). They should be treated with as much respect as English asparagus; eating the tender colourful stalks with just some *Simple hollandaise sauce* (page 418) is heavenly.

Here they are the equal main feature with the brill, the grapes and mushrooms becoming the shallow-fried meunière garnish, sizzling in frothy lemon butter.

SERVES 4 AS A MAIN COURSE
1 × 1.5kg (3¼lb) brill, head removed, fins and tail trimmed and cut into 4 portions
450–675g (1–1½lb) purple sprouting broccoli

2 tablespoons olive oil
flour, for dusting
salt and pepper
175–225g (6–8oz) button, cup or chestnut mushrooms, wiped and stalks trimmed
25g (1oz) butter
4–6 tablespoons crème fraîche
juice of ½–1 lemon
24–28 seedless white grapes, peeled

Preheat the oven to 200°C/400°F/Gas 6. The skin is being left on both sides of the brill portions. The white skin, when fried and roasted, will become crispy, with the dark skin protecting the flesh in contact with the pan as it roasts.

If small trimmed broccoli sprouts can be found, 450g (1lb) will be plenty. If they are large, simply break the spears from the thicker central stalk. If very fresh and young, the stalks need not be peeled. This is best tested by taking a raw bite: if tender to eat, then leave them unpeeled. Once prepared, the broccoli will take just a few minutes to steam over or boil in salted water.

To cook the fish, heat the olive oil in a roasting pan. Lightly flour the white-skin side of the fish and season with a pinch of salt. Season the dark skin with salt and pepper. Using salt only on the white side prevents the fish from taking on black spots of pepper during cooking, spoiling the finished presentation. Place the fish in the pan, white-side down, and fry over a moderate heat for 6–8 minutes, until a rich golden brown. Turn the fish in the pan, then roast in the preheated oven for a further 8 minutes.

If using cup or chestnut mushrooms, halve or quarter them. Button mushrooms can be left whole. Fry the mushrooms over a fairly high heat in half of the butter. Season with salt and pepper.

While the mushrooms are frying, plunge the prepared broccoli into boiling salted water. Cook for just 3–4 minutes, until tender but still with a bite. Drain in a colander and season with salt and pepper. Warm the crème fraîche (microwaving for a few seconds works well), add a squeeze of lemon juice and season. Add the grapes to the fried mushrooms and warm for just a minute or two.

Spoon the remaining butter into the pan and allow to sizzle to a nutbrown stage. When it is sizzling, present the brill and broccoli on plates and trickle the warmed crème fraîche over the broccoli. To finish, squeeze lemon juice over the mushrooms and grapes, 'souffléing' the butter, and spoon it over the roasted fish. Soft creamy *Mashed potatoes* (page 422) would be a perfect accompaniment for this dish.

Rhubarb is generally regarded as a fruit, although botanically it is a vegetable: it is the stalk which is eaten, and there is no actual fruit. The 'fruitiness' has probably become established because the acidic tartness of the vegetable needs the sweetness of sugar to balance it, and so it is popularly cooked in pies, crumbles and tarts and used to make sauces and wine.

Native to Asia, rhubarb was known in the western world as a medicine long before it was recognized that the stems were edible. (The leaves have never been considered edible, as they contain high concentrations of oxalic acid.) Although rhubarb reached British shores by the sixteenth century, it wasn't until the nineteenth that it began to appear in cookery books.

Rhubarb is a herbaceous perennial plant, which means that it dies down each autumn/winter, only to grow again vigorously in the spring and summer. The prime season for outdoor garden-grown rhubarb in Britain is the summer, but

the plants are now 'forced' to produce earlier crops of succulent, more tender stalks, often known as 'champagne rhubarb'. The main area of rhubarb forcing in England is a 'rhubarb triangle' around Leeds in Yorkshire. This forcing involves taking vigorous two-year-old plants whose roots are dormant (because of the cold) and encouraging unseasonal growth in warm, dark and moist conditions (in forcing sheds). Because the shoots are grown in the dark, they are pale in colour, with very pale leaves. The harvesting is even done in virtual darkness, the hand-pickers working by candlelight or with lamps on their hats like coal-miners.

The pale pink stalks of champagne rhubarb are tender and slim, and not in need of too much of a helping hand (unlike the later garden crops, which are sourer, fatter and slightly tougher). Cooking champagne rhubarb takes only a little time; it softens quite quickly with a finished flavour that really does warrant its champagne title.

steamed oysters with rhubarb and oyster cream

Here, we're using Pacific oysters, which are plentiful and not too expensive at this time of year. The rhubarb is the forced variety, champagne rhubarb. Both components are served warm, the rhubarb quickly softened in red wine vinegar and sugar (red wine vinegar mixed with chopped shallots is an accompaniment often offered with raw oysters), finishing with oyster juice cream. Five oysters per portion will be plenty, saving the cleaned shells to serve them in or just presenting the warm molluscs directly on plates.

SERVES 4 AS A STARTER

knob of butter, plus more for greasing
20 oysters, opened, saving their juices (page 424), and
   the bottom shells for serving (optional)
3–4 sticks of forced rhubarb
1 tablespoon caster sugar
4 tablespoons red wine vinegar
100ml (3½fl oz) double cream or crème fraîche
black pepper
squeeze of lemon juice

Lightly butter a piece of greaseproof paper (large enough to fit the 20 oysters and be folded), placing the oysters on it. Brush each with more butter, folding over the paper. Refrigerate until needed.

Top and tail the rhubarb sticks, wiping them clean before cutting into a small dice (approximately 5mm/¼in).

Put the caster sugar and red wine vinegar in a saucepan and bring to a simmer. Add the rhubarb, stirring and warming and softening for just a minute or two. Remove the pan from the heat, keeping warm to one side.

Strain the saved oyster juice into a bowl, with the cream or crème fraîche, black pepper and a squeeze of lemon juice. Lightly whip to a soft peak, spooning it into a suitable serving bowl.

Boil 5–7.5cm (2–3in) of water in a large saucepan, covering with a trivet or steamer. Place the oysters on the trivet or in the steamer, covering with a lid. Steam for 2–3 minutes before removing them from the heat.

The warm rhubarb can now be spooned into the cleaned reserved shells or arranged in five little piles on each plate, topping each with a warm oyster. Brush each with any liquor left on the greaseproof paper, serving the whipped oyster cream separately.

OPPOSITE: STEAMED OYSTERS WITH
RHUBARB AND OYSTER CREAM

fillet of john dory with raisin and thyme onions and bigarade mashed potatoes

John Dory, also known as St Pierre (because of the story that's told about the John Dory being held by St Peter himself, whose fingers gave it its characteristic black markings), is an all-year-round fish, with a quite exquisite texture and flavour. It is at its prime between January and March.

To serve with the fish I've chosen *bigarade* mashed potatoes. *Bigarade* is French for the bitter orange better known to us as the Seville orange. Arriving in January and gone by mid-February, this famous citrus fruit is the one that suits home-made marmalade better than any other. As it is too bitter to eat raw, cooking is essential to enjoy its flavours. The juices and grated zest are boiled and reduced in volume together, spooning through the soft potatoes loosened with crème fraîche. The orangey bite of the soft potatoes blends very well with the flavour of onions, thyme and raisins.

SERVES 4 AS A MAIN COURSE

3 onions, sliced
3 shallots, sliced
50g (2oz) raisins
3 tablespoons sherry vinegar
1 teaspoon demerara sugar

3 tablespoons olive oil (walnut or hazelnut oil can
   also be used)
1 scant teaspoon thyme leaves
sea salt
black pepper
flour, for dusting
4 × John Dory fillets (each approximately 175g/6oz),
   skinned
2 tablespoons groundnut oil
large knob of butter

FOR THE POTATOES
675g (1½lb) floury potatoes (Maris Piper or King
   Edward are best), peeled and quartered
salt and pepper
50g (2oz) butter
100–150ml (3½fl oz–¼ pint) crème fraîche
finely grated zest and juice of 2 Seville oranges
1 teaspoon caster sugar (optional)

Make the mashed potatoes first. Boil the potatoes in salted water until tender, approximately 20–25 minutes, before draining off the water. The potatoes can now be mashed, adding the butter a little at a time, along with the preferred quantity of crème fraîche. Season with salt and ground white pepper.

Boil together the orange zest and juice, allowing it to reduce in volume by at least three-quarters. The caster sugar, if using, can now be added to the reduction, balancing the sharp bitter-orange flavour. Stir the juice into the potatoes. These can now be rewarmed just before serving.

While the potatoes are cooking, prepare the onions and shallots. Blanch the onion and shallot slices in boiling water for just 15 seconds, then drain in a colander. This softens both, allowing them to be stewed with the olive oil and thyme, rather than fried.

Place the raisins, sherry vinegar and demerara sugar in a small saucepan and bring to a simmer, then remove from the heat, cover and leave to one side. This opens up the raisins, releasing their quite strong flavour.

Pour the olive oil into a saucepan and add the blanched onions and shallots and the thyme leaves. Cook over a low heat for at least 15–20 minutes, until completely softened. Add the sherry vinegar and raisins and season with sea salt and a good twist of black pepper. Continue to cook for a further 5–10 minutes, until all the flavours have combined.

Lightly flour the filleted presentation side of the John Dory and season with a pinch of salt. Heat the groundnut oil in a large frying pan (two pans may be needed). Once hot, place the fish in the pans, floured-side down. Season the fish again with salt and pepper. Fry for 3 minutes, until golden brown. Add the knob of butter and continue to fry for a further minute, then turn the fish over. Cook for just 1 more minute and turn off the heat. The residual heat of the pan will continue to fry the fish for at least 2–3 more minutes, providing enough time to plate the garnishes.

Present the raisin onions and *bigarade* mashed potatoes side by side on the plates, then place the John Dory fillets on top of the onions. Any remaining butter in the pan can, if wished, be spooned over the fish.

OPPOSITE: FILLET OF JOHN DORY WITH RAISIN AND THYME
ONIONS AND BIGARADE MASHED POTATOES

roast blade of pork with honey spiced gravy and pear pak choi

Blade of pork is taken from the forequarter, a shoulder cut usually weighing in at around 1.5–2kg (3¼–4½lb). For four portions it is best to ask your butcher for a 1.5kg (3¼lb) piece. It can be roasted on or off the bone – here I am cooking it on the bone (hence the weight), so slowly that it will almost melt rather than need to be carved.

The natural flavour of the pork contrasts with the gravy – a loose mixture of honey with hoisin and soy sauces working alongside shredded pak choi (Chinese celery cabbage), butter-fried with diced pears.

SERVES 4

1 × **blade of pork, approximately 1.5kg (3¼lb) on the bone**
1 tablespoon vegetable oil
salt and pepper, plus sea salt flakes
2 large tablespoons clear honey
2 tablespoons hoisin sauce
1 tablespoon soy sauce
450g (1lb) pak choi
2 pears, Comice or Conference
squeeze of lemon juice
25g (1oz) butter
1 heaped tablespoon finely chopped shallot or onion

Preheat the oven to 160°C/325°F/Gas 3. Score the rind of the pork with the point of a sharp knife. Brush with the vegetable oil, sprinkling with the salt and a teaspoon or two of sea salt flakes. Put the meat, rind-side up, on a wire rack, placing it over a roasting tray. This will prevent the pork from sticking. Pour water into the tray, measuring approximately 1cm (½in) deep. Any juices drizzling from the pork will now not burn in the pan but instead form a stock from which to make the gravy. Place in the preheated oven and roast for 3½–4 hours until tender and melting with a crispy crackling top. Every 1½ hours the tray may need to be topped up with water. During this cooking time the meat will be self-basting, the fat content beneath the rind melting as it cooks. Once roasted, remove from the oven and keep warm to one side, allowing the meat to rest for 15–20 minutes.

OPPOSITE: ROAST BLADE OF PORK WITH HONEY SPICED GRAVY AND PEAR PAK CHOI

Pour the pork water from the roasting tray into a suitable bowl or jug, skimming away the floating fat, but keeping a little for flavour.

Heat the roasting tray on top of the stove, adding the honey. This will quickly begin to bubble, soon turning to a caramel stage. At this point, add the hoisin and soy sauces, stirring in while adding the saved pork water – be careful as it has a habit of spitting as it hits the pan. Bring to a simmer, tasting for strength. For a stronger finish, allow to carry on reducing in volume to your preferred stage. Strain through a sieve, ready to serve.

While the pork is roasting, rinse the pak choi, before shredding across the leaves and stalks.

Peel and quarter the pears, removing the core with the point of a sharp knife. The pears can now be cut into a small rough dice, stirring in a squeeze of lemon juice to prevent them from discolouring.

Boil a large saucepan of salted water, quickly plunging in the shredded pak choi. Stir once or twice, then drain into a colander.

When ready to serve, melt the butter in a wok or frying pan. Once foaming, add the chopped shallot or onion, frying for a few minutes until tender. Add the pears and, after just a minute or two, the blanched shredded leaves. Stir together, seasoning with salt and pepper. The pork is now ready to 'carve', cracking into the rind and serving with the pear pak choi and warm honey spiced gravy.

Finely shredded cabbage can be used in place of the pak choi.

simmered lamb neck fillet with double potato savoy soup

This cut of meat is found between the scrag end (next to the head) and the best end, from where the cutlets and rack are taken. It is quite a fatty and bendy joint, usually cubed for stews and casseroles. The middle neck fillet to be used here, however, can be boned and sold separately as individual joints.

The double potato Savoy soup is a combination of sweet and ordinary potatoes and wedges of Savoy cabbage. These are all stewed with the lamb, creating a complete one-pot meal.

Sweet potatoes have a long autumn and winter season, coming in different skin shades of reds and browns and in many sizes, ranging from that of a baked potato upwards.

**4 × 275g (10oz) middle neck lamb fillets, trimmed
  of sinew**
salt and pepper
1 tablespoon olive oil
50g (2oz) butter
4 large shallots, preferably the long banana variety
large sprig of rosemary
2 garlic cloves, sliced
3–4 potatoes, preferably Desirée, peeled
2 small–medium sweet potatoes, peeled
1 small Savoy cabbage

Preheat the oven to 150°C/300°F/Gas 2. Season the neck fillets with salt and pepper. Heat the olive oil and a knob of the butter in a frying pan. Once foaming, fry the fillets for a few minutes on each side until totally sealed and well coloured, then place them in a large braising pot.

Pour away the butter from the frying pan, reheating the pan with 150ml (¼ pint) of water. Stir, lifting any residue before straining it over the lamb. Add a further 750ml (1¼ pints) of water (half a lamb stock cube can also be added for a fuller flavour), along with the shallots, rosemary and garlic. Bring to a simmer, cover with a lid and place in the preheated oven, braising for 1½ hours.

With the lamb in the oven, cut the sweet potatoes and ordinary potatoes into large (about 4cm/1½in) rustic chunks. Remove the coarse outside leaves from the cabbage and discard, cutting the Savoy into quarters, leaving the core intact and so keeping the wedges together.

After the 1½ hours of braising, the prepared vegetables can be added, returning the pot to the oven for a further hour. The two potato varieties will absorb the stock, with the cabbage losing its rich green colour but gaining a new strength of taste.

Spoon the casseroled lamb into large bowls with the vegetables, stirring the remaining butter into the stock and seasoning with salt and pepper, if needed, before ladling over the finished dish.

Chopped parsley can be added to the finished stock.

fried skirt steak with sautéed salsify potatoes

Beef skirt is a cut of meat that's normally confined to stews and casseroles, needing long slow cooking due to its quite tough texture. However, there's a butchers' secret that this quite cheap cut can became one of the tastiest steaks you can imagine. It's not a particularly big joint of meat – in French it's called *la pièce du boucher*, 'the butcher's piece' – with there being just enough to take home to feed the family. Other names for it include thin flank, hanger steak and *onglet* (as it is also known in France). I find it's always best to ask for thick skirt from the butcher, also requesting it be cleaned of any membranes and sinew, and 'butterflied'. This means the joint is cut horizontally through the middle, creating a large, thinner piece, ready for cutting into the four steaks required, and ideal for quick, hot pan-frying, keeping it from rare to medium-rare or medium (cooking it any further will return it to being tough). A 675–900g (1½–2lb) piece will feed four people.

Salsify usually appears around September/October, staying with us through autumn and winter, sometimes lasting through to April/May. This long dark root is often thought to resemble a black carrot, only to reveal an off-white stalk once peeled. There's also the scorzonera – this is a black-skinned variety of salsify, whereas salsify has more of a brownish, muddy finish. The two are members of the same family, with dandelion and lettuces as other relatives. The flavour they offer is likened to artichokes and asparagus, with salsify also being credited with a resemblance to oysters. Whenever preparing, it's best to peel with a swivel peeler or small sharp knife, keeping the peeled stalks in lemon-acidulated water to prevent discoloration before cooking.

8 sticks of salsify or scorzonera
juice of 1 lemon
4 large (jacket-sized) potatoes, peeled
4 tablespoons olive oil
salt and pepper
75g (3oz) butter
**1 × 675–900g (1½–2lb) piece of thick beef skirt,
  butterflied (see above) and cut into four**
1 tablespoon chopped flatleaf parsley (optional)

Peel the salsify or scorzonera, rinsing each stick under cold water before placing in a saucepan of water acidulated with half the lemon juice. Once all are cleaned, bring the water to a fast simmer, cooking for 15 minutes until tender. Remove the roots from the pan and leave to drain and cool. Once cold, these can be cut into 2cm (¾in) sticks, keeping to one side.

Cut the potatoes into rough 1cm (½in) dice, rinsing under cold water, before drying with a clean kitchen cloth. Heat a large frying pan (two pans may be needed) with 2 tablespoons of the olive oil. Add the potatoes to the pan and shallow-fry over a medium heat for 12–15 minutes, turning them from time to time until golden brown and tender. While sautéeing the potatoes, heat another large frying pan with the remaining 2 tablespoons of olive oil for the beef.

Season the skirt steaks with salt and pepper. Once the pan is hot, almost at smoking point, add 25g (1oz) of the butter, allowing it to foam until it reaches a nutbrown stage. At this point, put the steaks in the pan, frying over a fast heat for 2–3 minutes before turning and cooking for a further 2–3 minutes. This will leave you with a medium-rare stage (one large skirt – not 'butterflied' – will need at least 5–6 minutes on each side). Remove the steaks from the pan and leave to rest for 5 minutes, saving the pan with its juices.

During the pan-frying of the beef, the blanched salsify pieces can be added to the potatoes with another 25g (1oz) of the butter, seasoning them with salt and pepper. These will need just 5–6 minutes to warm through in the pan.

Once the beef has rested, return the saved pan to the heat. Once hot, add the remaining lemon juice and 100ml (3½fl oz) of water, stirring to lift all the beef residue left in the pan. Stir in the remaining butter and parsley, if using.

Carve the skirt steaks, cutting across the grain, serving immediately with spoonfuls of the sautéed salsify potatoes, pouring the lemon-flavoured liquor over the steaks.

An extra wedge of lemon can be offered with the steaks.

pippin's pigeon red cabbage salad

The pigeons here are wood pigeons, which are available throughout the year. In this recipe, the breasts are to be cooked on the bone, with the legs and central backbone cut away: these are not used in this recipe, but can be frozen, ready to turn into a game stock or sauce at a later date. The quantities listed provide four small starters, offering just one breast a portion. The recipe will, however, double very comfortably.

The 'Pippin' in the title represents the Cox's Orange Pippin apple, which is with us throughout the autumn and winter. Red cabbage is usually braised, with the addition of apple, onion and red wine. The apple this time is with the pigeon, while red wine and shallots become the dressing, bound with the raw cabbage itself.

SERVES 4 AS A STARTER
2 large wood pigeons, legs and backbone removed
2 Cox's Orange Pippin apples
knob of butter, plus more for greasing
juice of 1 lime
caster sugar, for sprinkling
½ small or ¼ medium red cabbage (approximately 175g/6oz)
1 tablespoon groundnut oil
2 shallots, very thinly sliced

FOR THE DRESSING
2 tablespoons red wine
½ teaspoon caster sugar
1 teaspoon Dijon mustard
2 tablespoons red wine vinegar
1 tablespoon ready-made mayonnaise
4 tablespoons groundnut oil
4 tablespoons walnut oil (or groundnut or olive oil)
salt and pepper

Remove the wishbone from the pigeons by scraping with a small knife to reveal the bone. Cut either side against the wishbone, then twist to release. Chill the birds until ready to cook.

Preheat the grill to hot. Peel the apples, quarter each and cut away the core from the pieces. Cut each quarter into five or six slices and place them on a greased baking tray. Brush the apple slices with the lime juice (any leftover juice can be added to the dressing), then sprinkle very lightly with the caster sugar. Place the apples under the preheated grill and cook until approaching golden brown and tender. Remove and leave to cool.

Cut the red cabbage into quarters. Turn each piece on its side and cut away the core, then finely shred the cabbage, preferably with a mandolin slicer for the finest of results.

To make the dressing, warm the red wine with the caster sugar. Once the sugar has dissolved, remove from the heat and pour the wine into a bowl. Add the Dijon mustard, red wine vinegar and mayonnaise, and mix all together. Slowly whisk the oils into the mix, as you would when making mayonnaise. This will help emulsify all of the ingredients. Season with salt and pepper, and the dressing is ready.

Preheat the oven to 220°C/425°F/Gas 7. To cook the pigeons, heat the groundnut oil in a small roasting tray. Season the birds with salt and pepper, then place them on one side in the tray. Fry for a minute or two until golden brown, turn and continue to fry until the other sides are also golden brown. Arrange the pigeons breast-side up, and roast in the preheated oven for 6–8 minutes. At this stage, the pigeons will be very moist and pink. Leave to rest for 8 minutes, then remove the skin from the breasts and release the breasts from the bone.

Preheat the grill to hot. Lay the four breasts on a baking tray, skinned-side up. Cover them from top to bottom with apple slices, overlapping the slices. The softened apples will follow the natural curve of the breasts, giving a neat, natural finish. Quickly warm under the grill.

Mix the sliced red cabbage and shallots with the red wine dressing, spooning over just enough to bind. Any remaining apple slices can also be added to the salad. Divide the red cabbage between the plates and top each with a Pippin's pigeon. Extra dressing can be drizzled around each portion.

steamed chicken leg jardinière

Jardinière is a French culinary term for a dish garnished with a selection of vegetables. The other feature with a *jardinière* dish is the way the vegetables are cut. This doesn't have to be followed, but it does help with the presentation. Each item is cut into batons approximately 5cm × 5mm × 5mm (2 × ¼ × ¼in). These are scattered around the plate, surrounding the steamed legs. There is no chicken stock used in this recipe, as the steaming water from cooking the chicken and vegetables is used to finish the dish, giving a very natural flavour.

One of the advantages of this dish is that it will hold its own through both the autumn and winter seasons. The vegetables can be as varied as you wish, but I prefer to use the root vegetables – carrots, turnips, swedes, parsnips and celery. Most of these, bar the celery, are still in season until the end of winter – you could always use imported celery instead.

SERVES 4

2 medium carrots
1 medium swede
2 large turnips
2–3 celery sticks
2 parsnips
4 chicken legs
½ small onion, very finely chopped

1 bay leaf
salt and pepper
25–50g (1–2oz) butter (optional)
squeeze of lemon juice (optional)
1 tablespoon picked and torn flatleaf parsley

Cut the carrots, swede, turnips and celery into batons as described above. Cut the parsnips into 5cm (2in) pieces. These can now also be cut into rough batons, discarding the woody central core of each parsnip.

It is best to remove any backbone that may still be attached to the base of the chicken thighs. The thighbone itself can also be removed, if you wish. To do so, cut along the thighbone on the opposite side to the skin. Once revealed, gently cut either side of the bone, then scrape the meat away towards the drumstick. At this point, the drumstick and exposed thighbone can be folded against themselves to break the connection. The only remaining bone is that within the drumstick. The boning of the thigh is not essential, but can make eating a little easier.

Sprinkle the chopped onion and bay leaf in a saucepan large enough to accommodate a suitable steamer to hold the four chicken legs. Cover with 1.2 litres (2 pints) of water and bring to a rapid simmer. Season the legs with salt and pepper and sit them in the steamer, skin-side up. Place over the simmering water and cover with a lid. The total cooking time needed for the chicken legs is 25 minutes. After 15 minutes, add the carrots, swede and celery to the steaming water. Bring to a simmer again before returning the chicken legs to steam. Continue to steam for a further 5 minutes, then add the turnips and parsnips to the steaming water. Once simmering again, the legs can be replaced to finish their cooking time with a further 5 minutes.

At this point the vegetables will also be tender. Remove the chicken legs and keep them warm within the steamer. Strain the vegetables from the pan, discarding the bay leaf and saving the liquor in a saucepan. Arrange the vegetables on warm large plates or bowls. Remove the skin from the chicken and place the legs on top of the vegetables.

Whisk the butter into the simmering cooking liquor and add a squeeze of lemon juice, if using. The liquor can be left absolutely natural, if preferred. Finish the liquor with the torn parsley, then pour it over the chicken and vegetables. The dish is ready to serve.

OPPOSITE: STEAMED CHICKEN LEG JARDINIÈRE

Preheat the oven to its lowest possible temperature. To make the crisps, cut the extra rhubarb sticks (choosing the pinkest) into 10cm (4in) pieces, then slice them lengthwise into very thin strips. For consistency, it is best to use a mandolin slicer. Lay the strips on a baking tray lined with greaseproof paper and sprinkle each lightly with caster sugar. Place the tray in the warm oven and leave for up to 12 hours, possibly longer. During this time the moisture will be dried from the rhubarb strips, leaving them crisp. If the heat is increased, the rhubarb begins to bake rather than dry, becoming discoloured and spoilt. Once the strips are crisp, leave to cool.

To make the fool, first top and tail the rhubarb, peeling any that appears to be stringy. Chop it into 1cm (½in) pieces and place in a large saucepan with the caster sugar and the tangerine juice. Cover with a lid and cook over a low heat on top of the stove for 15–20 minutes, stirring from time to time. The pieces will now be at a pulp stage, softened through and tender. Strain through a sieve, collecting the syrup. Once drained and cooled, the pulp can be used as it is, producing a chunkier and more rustic finish to the fool. For a smoother touch, blitz the purée in a food processor.

Boil the reserved syrup, allowing it to reduce in volume by two-thirds, then leave it to cool.

Whip the double cream to a loose soft-peak stage. If using, split the vanilla pod lengthwise, scraping out the seeds with the point of a small knife. Add the seeds to the whipped cream, along with the rhubarb purée and half of the syrup. Spoon everything together and the fool is ready to be served in glass bowls or dishes, topped with a drizzling of the remaining syrup and the rhubarb crisps.

For an extra-orangey edge, the zest from the tangerines can be finely grated and added to the rhubarb while it is cooking.
For a thicker fool, half of the cream can be replaced with 'fresh' bought (or tinned) custard.

champagne rhubarb clafoutis

The word 'champagne' in the recipe title merely refers to the actual variety of rhubarb to be used. During the late autumn and winter months, it's forced rhubarb (its quality has inspired its champagne title) that is available to us.

Clafoutis is a French speciality, originating in the Limousin region of central France. Classically it consists of cherries embedded in a soft creamy batter, but plenty of other fruits, such as peaches, plums and apricots, have all been introduced at some stage. Here the sweet rhubarb works very well. This style of pudding is normally served in individual *sur le plat* dishes. Here I'm simply using one large 20–23cm (8–9in) flan or earthenware dish.

SERVES 6
8 sticks of forced rhubarb
50g (2oz) caster sugar
butter, for greasing
icing sugar, for dusting

FOR THE BATTER
100ml (3½fl oz) milk
150ml (¼ pint) whipping cream
100g (4oz) caster sugar
3 eggs
25g (1oz) plain flour
pinch of salt
2–3 tablespoons amaretto or kirsch (optional)

Preheat the oven to 190ºC/375ºF/Gas 5. To make the batter, blitz all of the ingredients in a food processor, adding the amaretto or kirsch, if using (or whisk them to a smooth consistency). Leave the batter to relax while cooking the rhubarb.

Top and tail the rhubarb sticks, then cut each into 2cm (¾in) pieces. Scatter these on a baking tray and sprinkle with the caster sugar and 4 tablespoons of water. Place the tray in the oven and bake for 6–8 minutes, until the rhubarb is just becoming tender. If too firm, continue for a further few minutes. Once the rhubarb is just approaching tender, remove it from the oven and carefully spoon it into a large colander. Leave to drain and cool, saving all of the juices.

Butter the flan dish and spoon in the rhubarb pieces. It is not essential to use all of the fruit; any excess can be made into a syrup to serve with the finished dessert. Stir the batter, then pour it over the rhubarb sticks.

Bake the pudding in the preheated oven for approximately 25–30 minutes. The pudding will have risen more predominantly around the edges than in the centre, which will have just set. If the batter still appears to be too soft, simply continue to bake for a few extra minutes. About 40 minutes should really be the maximum.

Remove from the oven and leave to rest for 10 minutes, before serving very warm. During this time the batter will have collapsed from its soufflé look; this is exactly how this dessert is served, with the main concentration on the flavour. Dust lightly with icing sugar just before serving.

During the cooking of the pudding, any remaining pieces of rhubarb can be placed in a small saucepan with all of the saved juices and a few more tablespoons of water. Bring to a gentle simmer and cook for a few minutes until the rhubarb is very tender. This can now be squeezed through a sieve for a loose syrup, or just liquidized to a thicker sauce consistency. Should either need to be slightly sweeter, just add icing sugar to taste.

When serving the clafoutis, you can brush it with the syrup before dusting with icing sugar or offer the syrup separately.

CHAMPAGNE RHUBARB CLAFOUTIS

413

and close with a cork or screw top. For the best results, leave to marinate for a week, which will allow all the flavours to enhance the oil. To help the dressing along, shake the bottle once a day. Taste for seasoning before using. Once marinated, this keeps for several months if refrigerated.

This recipe can have its acidity level increased with the addition of extra balsamic vinegar. When doing so, it's best to add a tablespoon at a time, until the required strength of flavour has been obtained. Red wine vinegar can be used in place of balsamic vinegar.

quick basic vinaigrette dressing

For a quick basic dressing, mix 1 teaspoon of balsamic vinegar with 2 tablespoons of olive oil. Season with salt and pepper, and the dressing is ready. This recipe can be increased accordingly to the quantity required.

vegetable vinaigrette

The vinaigrette dressing here can be used for most salads. Once all of the vegetables have been added it does take on a completely new character with their freshness and different strength of flavours. An alternative to this chunky oil is to cook everything together, before straining and discarding the vegetables. This provides you with a very full-flavoured vegetable oil, again lending itself to potato, leaf and other salads.

MAKES 300ML (½ PINT)

1 tablespoon neat finely diced carrots
1 tablespoon neat finely diced celery
1 tablespoon neat finely diced onion
1 tablespoon neat finely diced fennel
1 tablespoon neat finely diced leek
1 tablespoon neat finely diced red pepper
1–2 small knobs of butter
2 tablespoons olive oil (optional)
salt and pepper

FOR THE VINAIGRETTE DRESSING

300ml (½ pint) olive oil (if too strong, use equal parts olive oil and groundnut or grapeseed oil)
4 tablespoons white wine
4 tablespoons white wine vinegar
sliver of orange zest (without pith)

1 bay leaf
sprig of rosemary
sprig of thyme
sprig of tarragon
sprig of parsley
1 teaspoon caster sugar
1 garlic clove, halved
6 black peppercorns
pinch of salt

To make the vinaigrette dressing, mix all of the ingredients together and bring to a gentle simmer. Cook for 10–15 minutes, then remove from the heat and leave to cool. This dressing can now be refrigerated and left to infuse for several hours, even days, before straining or passing through a fine sieve.

Blanch all of the vegetables, bar the red pepper, individually in boiling water for a minute or two until tender. Leave them to cool naturally once drained. Cook the red pepper in a small knob of butter until softened to help maintain its sweet pepper juices.

Alternatively, you can sauté the vegetables. To do so, warm the olive oil and a knob of butter together over a fairly gentle heat. Add the carrots, celery, onion and fennel, stirring, for a few minutes, until approaching tenderness. This can be helped by placing a lid on the pan to create a steamed rather than fried finish. Add the leek and continue to cook for a minute. Cook the red pepper separately in a small knob of butter. Remove the pans from the stove and leave to cool.

The vegetables and peppers can now be added to as much of the vinaigrette as you require. Check for seasoning and it is ready to use.

A squeeze of lemon juice can be added or a drop of balsamic vinegar for a more acidic finish. Fresh herbs can also become part of the finished vinaigrette.

red wine dressing

This dressing is sharper and creamier than the *Sweet port red wine dressing* (see right). Here, a Cabernet Sauvignon red wine vinegar is best as it has a rich, mature flavour. Consequently, less is needed to enhance the dressing. If using a basic red wine vinegar instead, it can be strengthened by adding a few tablespoons of boiled and reduced red wine, cooled and added as the last ingredient. White wine vinegar can also be used. Adding

the egg yolk gives a creamy emulsion to the finished dressing, but be sure to refrigerate if using this. The egg yolk can be replaced by bought mayonnaise.

MAKES ABOUT 150ML (¼ PINT)

2 teaspoons Dijon mustard
2 tablespoons red wine vinegar (if using Cabernet Sauvignon, add 1½ teaspoons, adding more once finished if preferred)
1 egg yolk or 1 tablespoon bought mayonnaise
4 tablespoons walnut oil
4 tablespoons groundnut oil
salt and pepper

Whisk together the mustard, vinegar and egg yolk or mayonnaise. Mix together the two oils and slowly and gradually whisk them into the mustard and vinegar. The oil will emulsify with the base ingredients. Season with salt and pepper and the dressing is ready to use.

A simple version, mixing just the vinegar with the oils (pure groundnut or olive oil can be used instead of the walnut and groundnut oil combination), can be made, omitting the mustard and egg yolk/mayonnaise.

sweet port red wine dressing

This dressing is featured in one or two recipes within this book, but I do hope you find other flavours for it to help and lift. Although a vegetarian dressing, it does hold quite a meaty full finish, the depth of the red wine vinegar marrying well with the sweet reduced port.

Finely chopped shallots can also be added to this recipe. If so, it's best first to cook them lightly in a drop of the measured oil until tender. This prevents a raw oniony taste overwhelming the finished flavour.

MAKES ABOUT 200ML (7FL OZ)

150ml (¼ pint) ruby port
2 tablespoons red wine vinegar
pinch of icing sugar
5 tablespoons olive oil
5 tablespoons groundnut or grapeseed oil
salt and pepper

Boil the port to reduce in volume by two-thirds. Remove from the heat and add the red wine vinegar and icing sugar. Stir in the oils and season with salt and pepper. This can now be stored in an airtight jar and kept refrigerated until needed. To appreciate its full flavour, serve at room temperature.

citrus dressing

This dressing eats well with almost all salad combinations.

SERVES 4–6
juice of 1 orange and finely grated zest of ½ orange
juice of 1 lemon and finely grated zest of ½ lemon
1 tablespoon caster sugar
1 teaspoon Dijon mustard (optional)
6 tablespoons olive oil
salt and pepper

Place the orange and lemon zest in a small saucepan with the orange juice. Bring to a simmer and allow to reduce by two-thirds. Remove from the heat and allow to cool. Whisk together the lemon juice, sugar and mustard, if using. Whisk the olive oil into the mixture and add the reduced orange juice and zests. Season with salt and pepper and the dressing is ready.

If stored in an airtight jar and refrigerated, this dressing will keep well for 2–3 days. This recipe can easily be doubled in volume. If trebling or quadrupling the recipe, only double the grated zests as any more will make it too bitter.

tarragon oil

This oil works well with many fish and chicken dishes, as well as being a good base for salad dressings. Once made, it will keep almost indefinitely if refrigerated. Bunches of tarragon, like most herbs, come in many different sizes. Obviously, a generous bunch (50g/2oz), will give you a strong-flavoured oil.

MAKES 150ML (¼ PINT)
bunch of tarragon
150ml (¼ pint) olive oil (one-third to a half can be replaced with groundnut oil for a softer flavour)

Tear the tarragon leaves and stalks and place in a small saucepan with the oil. Bring slowly to a simmer and cook for 1–2 minutes without allowing the tarragon to colour. Remove from the heat, place a lid on the pan and leave for several hours to cool and infuse. When ready, push through a sieve, squeezing every bit of flavour from the tarragon. The oil will have taken on a pale green colour with a rich tarragon flavour.

chive and tarragon oil

This flavoured oil takes on not just the flavours of each herb, but also their rich green colour. For a more piquant finish add a squeeze of lime or lemon juice, just before serving.

MAKES 150ML (¼ PINT)
bunch of tarragon
bunch of chives, roughly chopped
100ml (3½fl oz) olive oil
3 tablespoons groundnut oil
salt and pepper

Place the tarragon leaves and chopped chives in a liquidizer. Warm the two oils together to just above room temperature, then pour over the herbs. Liquidize, then strain through a fine sieve or preferably a muslin cloth. The oil can now be kept in a screw-top jar in the refrigerator until needed. To enjoy the maximum flavour, season with salt and pepper, and serve at room temperature.

red pepper oil

Red peppers hold a natural sweet edge that is so pleasant as a main feature in a dish, or assisting other flavours.

This recipe provides the latter, a flavoured oil that can be used alone or quickly turned into a vinaigrette with a splash or two of balsamic, white wine or red wine vinegar.

British peppers, with their real sweet edge, are available during late summer and early autumn. This recipe can be followed all year round, however, with so many other countries presenting peppers to us.

MAKES ABOUT 175ML (6FL OZ)
200ml (7fl oz) olive oil
2 shallots, finely chopped
1 garlic clove, chopped
2 red peppers
1 dessertspoon tomato purée
1 teaspoon caster sugar
salt and pepper
sprig of thyme
sprig of rosemary

Warm 3 tablespoons of the olive oil and add the chopped shallots and garlic. Cook for 5–6 minutes, allowing them to begin to soften without colouring.

While these are cooking, split the red peppers lengthwise and remove the stalks and seeds. Cut the flesh into rough 1cm (½in) dice and add to the shallots and garlic. Continue to cook for 8–10 minutes until tender.

Add the tomato purée, sugar, salt and pepper, and continue to cook for 5 minutes. Add the herbs and remaining oil, and allow simply to warm in the pan over a low heat for a further 5–6 minutes. Remove from the stove and leave to stand and cool.

Transfer to a clean bowl, cover and leave to infuse in a cool place (the refrigerator if necessary) for 24 hours. The oil can now be strained to release all the flavours from the peppers. It is important not to overpress or you will create a purée. The red pepper oil is ready, seasoning again when needed. If refrigerated, this oil can last for several months.

The oil and peppers can be liquidized before straining. This will create a puréed oil, holding a thicker consistency, but with a much shorter shelf life (of several days rather than months) and needing to be refrigerated.

lemon oil

Lemon juice and olive oil together can be the best basic dressing, with the citric acidity blending well and not masking other flavours. These quantities can be increased to almost any volume to suit your requirements.

2 tablespoons olive oil
2 teaspoons lemon juice
salt and pepper

Mix the oil with the lemon juice and season to taste with salt and pepper.

extras

mashed potatoes

These potatoes eat beautifully with almost any dish.

SERVES 4–6

900g (2lb) large floury potatoes (preferably Maris Piper), peeled and quartered
salt and pepper
75–100g (3–4oz) butter
100ml (3½fl oz) milk, or single cream for a richer finish
freshly grated nutmeg

Boil the potatoes in salted water until tender, approximately 20–25 minutes, depending on size. Drain off all the water and replace the lid. Shake the pan vigorously, which will start to break up the boiled potatoes. While mashing the potatoes, add the butter and milk or cream, a little at a time. Season with salt and pepper and freshly grated nutmeg, according to taste. The mashed potatoes are now ready to serve.

For an even softer creamier finish, the milk or cream quantity can be increased to 150ml (¼ pint). Pushing the boiled potatoes through a drum sieve or potato ricer will also create a smooth finish. If using one of these utensils, it is important that the potatoes are sieved while still hot, and mashed while still warm. If left to cool before being mashed, they can become granular in texture.

classic roast potatoes

For the very best roasts, using the right potato is crucial. Almost any potato will roast, but if you prefer a crispy edge with a light, fluffy and creamy centre, then floury potatoes are needed. I choose between the following four varieties that will always give you this result – Maris Piper, Cara, King Edward or Desirée. To achieve the right finish, these potatoes will take at least 1 hour to cook; for ultimate crispiness, 1½ hours.

SERVES 4–6

6–9 medium potatoes (allowing 3 halves per portion)
salt
cooking oil or lard
plain flour

Preheat the oven to 200°C/400°F/Gas 6. Peel the potatoes and halve them lengthwise. The peeled side of the potatoes can now be scraped with a knife to give a smooth domed shape to all the halves. Place in a saucepan and cover with cold salted water. Bring to the boil and simmer for 5–6 minutes. Drain in a colander, leave to stand for 2–3 minutes, then shake the colander gently. This will begin to break down the edge of the potatoes. These slightly rough edges will become crisp and crunchy during the roasting.

Heat 5mm (¼in) of oil or lard in a frying pan. Roll the potatoes lightly in flour, shaking off any excess. Fry them in the hot oil or lard, turning them occasionally, until golden brown all over.

Now transfer the potatoes to a roasting tin. Pour some of the cooking oil or lard into the tin (approximately 3mm/⅛in deep), sprinkle the potatoes with salt and roast in the oven for 30 minutes before turning in the tin. Roast for another 30 minutes. Remove the crispy roast potatoes and serve.

A knob of butter can be melted over the potatoes to enrich the crispy roast taste.

noisette potatoes

Noisette potatoes are balls scooped from the potato, using a noisette spoon cutter. These are approximately 2.5cm (1in) in diameter and, once fried and baked, offer a sautéed roast flavour. The potatoes can take on many other flavourings if wished; add fried bacon, onions and herbs, to suggest just a few. For fairly generous servings, I suggest two large potatoes (approximately 225g/8oz) per portion. The potato trimmings need not be wasted – simply boil them and mash on another day.

SERVES 8

16 large potatoes, peeled
cooking oil
knob of butter
salt and pepper

Preheat the oven to 200°C/400°F/Gas 6. Scoop the potatoes into balls as above, rinsing well once all are shaped. Dry the potatoes on a clean tea towel, ready for frying.

Heat 2 tablespoons of cooking oil in a large frying pan and fry two or three handfuls of the potato balls on a medium-to-hot heat until golden brown, then transfer them to a roasting tray. Repeat the process until all are coloured. The potatoes can now be finished in the preheated oven for 15–20 minutes, until tender.

Once they are cooked, remove the tray from the oven, then add the butter and season with salt and pepper. The noisette potatoes are now ready to serve.

focaccia

Focaccia is made from Italian pizza dough, baked thicker than the pizza, leaving a bread texture. They say its name is a descendant of late-Latin *focacia*, which apparently derived from Latin *focus*, meaning 'fireplace', where bread was baked on stone.

SERVES 6

500g (1¼lb) strong white plain flour, plus more for dusting
1½ teaspoons easy-blend dried yeast
1 teaspoon salt
250–275ml (8–9fl oz) lukewarm water (blood temperature)
4 tablespoons extra virgin olive oil, plus more for greasing

FOR THE TOPPING

4 tablespoons olive oil
1–2 teaspoons coarse sea salt
1 teaspoon roughly chopped rosemary (optional)

Sift the flour into a bowl, sprinkling with the dried yeast and salt, leaving a well in the centre. Pour the oil and 250ml (8fl oz) water into the centre, mixing until a soft dough is formed, adding the remaining water if needed.

Transfer the dough onto a floured surface, kneading it for 5–10 minutes until springy to the touch. Place into an oiled bowl, covering with a damp tea towel. Leave in a warm, draught-free place for 1–1½hours until doubled in volume.

Knead the dough once more to remove any air bubbles, shaping with a rolling pin to a large circle 25–30cm (10–12in) in diameter and 2cm (¾in) thick. Place the rolled disc on an oiled baking tray, covering with the tea towel once more, and leave to rise for 25–30 minutes, until close to doubling in volume again. Preheat the oven to 240°C/475°F/Gas 9.

Before baking, indentations can be made across the top of the dough with your fingers, brushing over with 2 tablespoons of the oil, sprinkling with the sea salt and chopped rosemary, if using. Reduce the oven temperature to 200°C/400°F/Gas 6 as you put the tray in (this gives a good hot start to the baking, calming slightly as it cooks), baking for 15–20 minutes until golden brown. Transfer the focaccia to a wire rack, drizzling with the remaining oil. This eats best warm, reheating well in the oven.

poached eggs

For the 'perfect' poached egg, the secret is to use only the freshest of eggs. These will then need little help, poaching simply in simmering water. Should the eggs need a helping hand, a fairly generous quantity of vinegar, up to one-third of the water content, can be added. This helps set the protein of the whites almost instantly around the yolks, without tainting their fresh flavour. It's very important that the water is always deep. This means that the egg will start poaching before reaching the base of the pan and spreading.

SERVES 4

4 eggs
malt or white wine vinegar (optional)

Fill a large, deep saucepan with water (replace up to one-third with vinegar should it be required). Bring to a rapid simmer and whisk vigorously in a circular motion. Crack an egg into the centre. As the liquid spins, it pulls and sets the white around the yolk, before the egg reaches the base of the pan. Poach the egg for 3–3½ minutes, before serving.

If wishing to poach the eggs in advance, once cooked plunge them into iced water to stop the cooking process. These can now be trimmed of any excess whites to leave perfectly shaped eggs. To reheat, plunge into rapidly simmering water for 1 minute.

All four eggs can be poached together, placing one after the other in the centre of the rotating liquid. However, if cooking beforehand and keeping refrigerated in iced water until needed, poach each separately for perfect results.

buttered brussels sprouts

This is one of our most classic of winter vegetables. There are a few golden rules to choosing and buying sprouts. To appreciate the great flavour – quite different from cabbage – and their slightly nutty crunch, it's important to buy them as small and tight-leaved as possible. Never buy yellowing sprouts, those whose colour is fading, or those with too many loose leaves. All these signs will tell you they are old and they'll taste pretty old too. Another important point to remember is that, once they are cooked and unless you are refreshing them in iced water, you should always serve them immediately. Holding sprouts at high temperatures for too long – for example, keeping them warm in the oven – leads to a bitter finished flavour.

SERVES 8

900g (2lb) small Brussels sprouts
salt and pepper
25g (1oz) butter

First bring a large pan three-quarters full of salted water to the boil. While waiting for the water to boil, remove any damaged or loose outside leaves from the sprouts to reveal the rich green nugget. When the water is boiling, remove the lid and add the sprouts. It is important not to replace the lid, as this usually leads to the vegetables losing their rich colour. This is a rule that holds true for all green vegetables.

Return to the boil; the sprouts will need just a few minutes for that nutty bite, up to 6 minutes for a softer touch. Larger sprouts may well need up to 10 minutes. If not serving immediately, refresh them in iced water to cool, then drain and chill until needed. These will then take just a minute or two to reheat in boiling water or in the microwave.

To finish, drain the sprouts well, then roll in the butter and season with salt and pepper.

It is important, whenever cooking green vegetables, in particular Brussels sprouts, not to overfill the pan with too many at once. This will result in the water taking too long to return to the boil, consequently stewing the vegetable. For large quantities as above, it is best to cook small batches in advance, refreshing in iced water as mentioned in the method, repeating the process until all are cooked.

wild mushrooms

Wild mushrooms come in so many shapes, sizes and colours, all offering their own distinctive texture and flavour. Most begin to come into season during the last months of summer, becoming plentiful throughout the autumn. It is best to purchase young mushrooms, which are much firmer to the touch, without bruising or discoloration. It is also important not to store mushrooms of any variety in plastic bags. This will steam and sweat the fungi, causing them to deteriorate quite rapidly.

There is a selection of recipes throughout the book featuring wild mushrooms (all can be replaced with button, cup and chestnut, should wild be unavailable). Some varieties need very little cleaning, just trimming and wiping clean with a damp cloth or brushing to remove any grit. This avoids increasing their natural water content. There's also no need to peel most types: just trim any stalk or stem bases. Ceps, chanterelles and our everyday mushrooms all have a stem that is as good to eat as the caps themselves. Here is a list of wild mushrooms featured, and how to clean and trim each.

Cep Known in France as *cèpe* and in Italy as *porcini*, these mushrooms need only trimming at the base of the stem, then wiping well with a damp cloth. They are now ready for slicing. Dried ceps can also be purchased and these need soaking in water to soften them before use. The soaking water makes a good wild mushroom stock. (This also applies to dried morels and mixed dried wild mushrooms.)

Chanterelle and girolle These range in colour from a pale cream to a deep orange-yellow. On the outside of the cap leading into the stalk, the chanterelle has a wrinkly ribbed finish, quite distinctive in its appearance. The girolle is often looked upon as the firmer, smaller variety with a smoother finish. As with the cep, these mushrooms are totally edible, needing just the base of the stalk trimmed. They can now also just be wiped clean and the stalk scraped with the point of a small knife if it is damaged or particularly dirty. They can also be washed in cold water (treat them with care), then lift from the water and dry over an hour or two on a kitchen cloth. Particularly large chanterelles can be cut or torn in half.

Black trumpet mushrooms Known as *trompettes-de-la-mort* ('trumpets of death') in France, these are jet-black in colour, and feel quite dry if in good condition. They must, however, be split and washed to ensure all impurities are removed. Cut away the base of the stalk, and split each mushroom into two or

432